Exits and Entrances

Other Books by Frank Manchel

Every Step a Struggle: Interviews with Seven Who Shaped the African-American Image in Movies
Film Study: An Analytical Bibliography. 4 Vols.
An Album of Modern Horror Films
Great Science Fiction Films: Revised Edition
Great Sports Movies
The Box Office Clowns: From Bob Hope to Woody Allen
Gangsters on the Screen
Women on the Hollywood Screen
An Album of Great Science Fiction Films
The Talking Clowns: From Laurel and Hardy to the Marx Brothers
Yesterday's Clowns: The Rise of Film Comedy
Film Study: A Resource Guide
Cameras West
Terrors of the Screen
When Movies Began to Speak
When Pictures Began to Move
Movies and How They are Made

Exits and Entrances

Interviews with Seven Who Reshaped African-American Images in Movies

FRANK MANCHEL

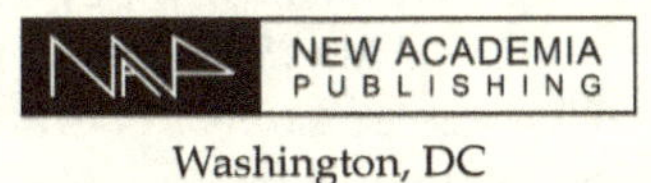

Washington, DC

New Academia Publishing 2013

Printed in the United States of America

Library of Congress Control Number: 2013940394
ISBN 978-0-9886376-3-4 paperback (alk. paper)
ISBN 978-0-9886376-4-1 hardcover (alk. paper)

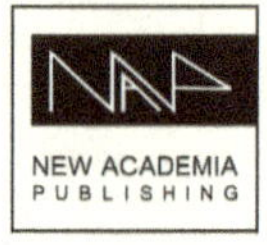

New Academia Publishing
PO Box 27420, Washington, DC 20038-7420
info@newacademia.com - www.newacademia.com

Unless otherwise noted, all visuals are from the Frank Manchel Cinema Collection at the University of Vermont or at Burlington College.

Cover Illustration: Ivan Dixon (Duff) and Abbey Lincoln (Josie) starred in Michael Roemer's *Nothing But a Man* (1964). In this extremely significant sixties movie, we witness the rise of a new generation of actors and a shift in themes about black film heritage.

Three people proved indispensible to this book: the person who encouraged me never to give up, the individual who changed her life to make this project possible, and the friend who loved me blindly throughout my journey. Her name is Sheila Manchel. As I have dedicated my life to her, so I dedicate this book

To my bride and best friend, Sheila

One Rose
One Life
One Love

Now and Always

Lest We Forget

Olga and Lee Manchel, Pearl and Harry Wachtel, Barton Bereck, Arnold Gunar, Lucille Jarvis, Professor Littleton "Tiny" Long, Professor Errol Hill, Dr. Lawrence McCrorey, Prof. Albert Johnson, Jack Barry, Jason Robards Jr., Sylvia Silvano, Sy Gomberg, Dugan Foley, Maggie Mae Hathaway, Leroy Bowser, Albert Murray, Dr. Alfred Rollins, and Lester Glassner.

"Clearly, the cultural debate continues, and it continues in spite of what professional historians may write or say. For the vision of the past and its interpretation do not belong to the historian alone, nor are they simple issues for classroom discussion. It makes little difference if we tell ourselves that our vision is simply a rationale for what we want in the present or the future. The point is that in Western society history is culturally important. It will continue to be used, mythically or ideologically, whether we like it or not. Man will insist on an historical view and he will use it, come what may, to help him determine his present and his future. What the role of the professional historian ought to be in all of this is too big a question for this occasion. But it is important that we know that what is said about the past is important, is culturally significant. Too easily intimidated by what appears to us to be the significance of science in our cultural life (and worried because scientists themselves fail to realize this fact), we historians have often forgotten that what we deal with is of enormous cultural consequence, too."[1]

Warren Susman

"There are still a few of us who trudge alone along a lonely, rocky road.... This [is what makes us who and what we are]. We don't move as fast as our cousins on the highways; we don't get as much accomplished as the wealthy and the powerful. What we come up with is not necessarily better. It is just different. If there is any excuse for us, it is that we are following the old American tradition of the maverick—a vanishing breed...."[2]

Orson Welles

"Any discussion that involves terms like 'the black community' or 'black people' is an exercise, however harmless, in defining African Americans as a homogenous cluster with an unchanging set of characteristics—characteristics that are necessarily indistinguishable from other racial groups. In some respects, it is impossible to talk about racial sameness—to assert that black and white people are fundamentally alike—without talking about racial difference—to imply that, in their very state of being black or white, the two groups are fundamentally different. This is the riddle of race...."[3]

Emily Bernard

"It is the consistency of the pursuit of the highest possible vision that you can find in front of you that gives you the constancy, that gives you the encouragement, that gives you the way to understand where you are and why it's important for you to do what you can do."[4]

Ossie Davis

"May fortune favor the foolish."[5]

Captain James T. Kirk

Contents

Illustrations

Acknowledgments

It is with considerable joy and appreciation and respect that I recognize the thoughtful and generous individuals who transmitted their knowledge, gave their support, and provided their friendship throughout the writing of this book.

I thank first the artists who more than forty years ago graciously took the time to share their thoughts and dreams. Without their gifts, *The Interviews* would not have been possible. My very special thanks go to Ruby Dee and Berlie Dixon.

To my students in the courses on Blacks in American Films who initiated the first steps towards the writing of *The Interviews*.

Unless otherwise noted, all visuals are from the Frank Manchel Cinema Collection at the University of Vermont or at Burlington College.

I wish to thank The Wisconsin Historical Society for permission to use number 99306 (*Nothing But a Man* scene) for the cover; and number 99289 (*Black Like Me* pressbook shot) in the James Whitmore chapter.

I wish to thank the wonderful Susan Green for permission to use her picture of the author printed in the *Burlington Free Press.*

I am grateful to an old friend, Julien Yoseloff, for permission to use my material from *Film Study: An Annotated Bibliography* in this book.

My thanks as well to the colleagues who took the time to read portions of the manuscript and to offer valuable comments and suggestions: Professors John Gennari, Ted Perry, Peter A. Rollins, and Howard Suber.

For teaching me to love jazz as they did, I am forever in debt to my Canadian network: Graeme Humphrey, Peter Marko, Benjamin

Scarelli, Curtis "Jazzman" Wright, Daniel Moisan, Gilles Boisclair, Art Brooks, and Nathan Caskey.

For those helpful strangers who became friends in moments of need: Nora Davis Day, Dr. Leslie Fife, Rick Rayfield, Peggy Powell, Sylvia Jeanne Bugbee, and Emil A. Hoeiter.

A special thanks to two men and one woman whose knowledge, compassion, and friendship over the past nineteen years kept me alive to complete this journey: Drs. Paul S. Unger, Jonathan Hayden and Ms. Michelle Paschelle.

Then we move to another level, to the extraordinary coworkers and librarians whose unique abilities and companionship never failed me for all these years: Peter H. Spitzform and Hope Greenberg at the University of Vermont Library, and Jessica Allard at Burlington College.

At an even higher level are two individuals who read every word of the manuscript and then proceeded with kindness and generosity to shape my thoughts and enthusiastically support my journey: Professor Denise Youngblood and Dean John G. Jewett. No words can adequately convey my appreciation.

Also deserving of a place in this treasured circle is Anna Lawton, who sets the standard for what a publisher should be. Her wisdom and compassion defy description.

Next, my family without whom the author could neither write or think or survive: Steven, Sharon, Gary, Harrison, Benjamin, Rose, Louis, and Barbara.

Finally, my wife whose patience, understanding, encouragement, and love not only made this project possible but also made it worth undertaking. I also ask for her forgiveness for my countless and thoughtless acts. She remains proof that miracles are possible and that love never dies.

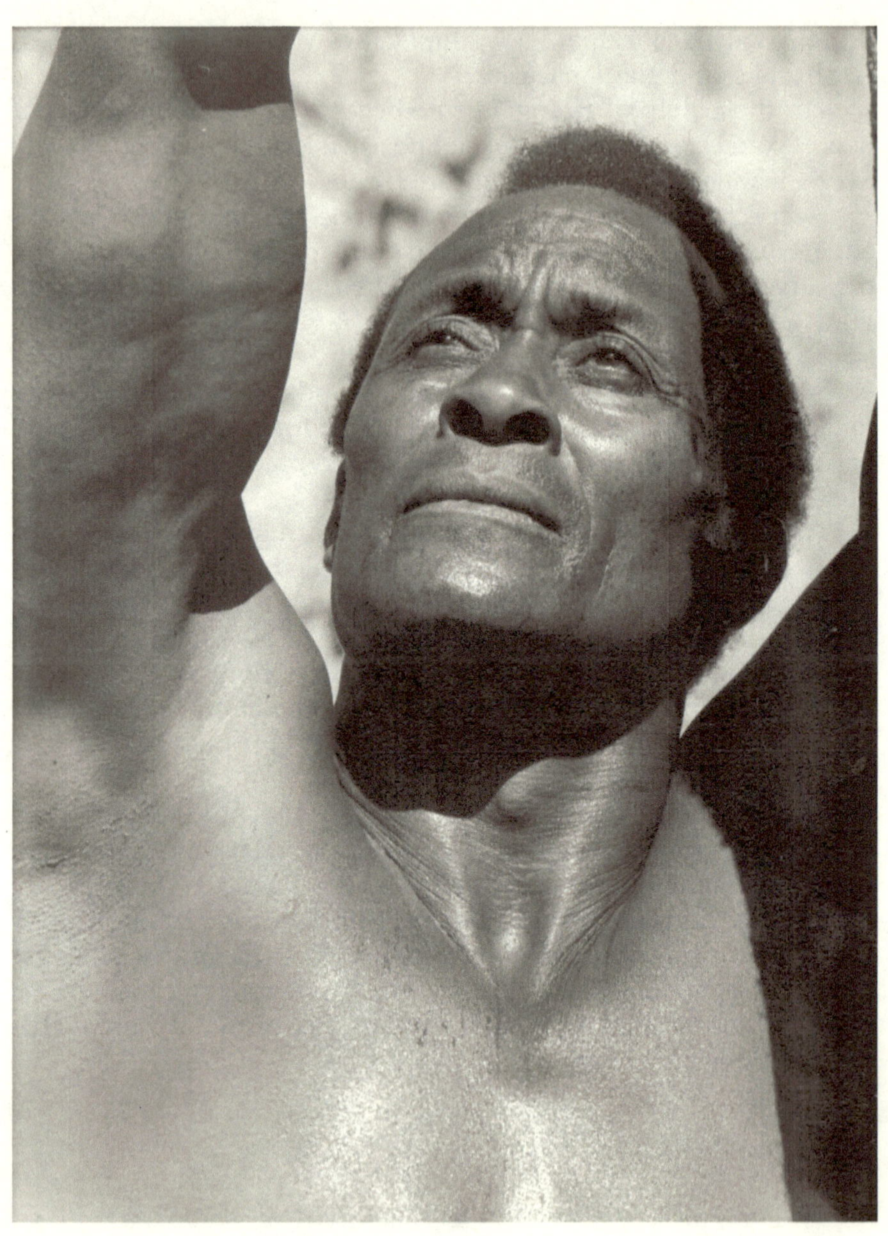

1. Woody Strode, one of the most popular action heroes of the fifties and sixties, has a chapter devoted to him in *Every Step a Struggle*.

Preface

> "Film is the only art in which the United States made a real difference. Strike the American contribution from drama, painting, music, sculpture, dance, and even possibly from poetry and the novel, and the world's achievement is only marginally diminished. But film without the American contribution is unimaginable. The fact that film has been the most potent vehicle of the American imagination suggests all the more strongly that movies have something to tell us not just about the surfaces but about the mysteries of American life."[6]
>
> *Arthur Schlesinger, Jr.*

> "Black movies are like black power: we may not know exactly what they are, but we know they are worth fighting over. Any form of Art is a form of power; it has impact; it can effect change—it not only moves us, it makes us move. And therein lies the danger. And the opportunity."[7]
>
> *Ossie Davis*

The cultural historian Warren I. Susman concludes "The American is most characteristically a reformer and his history a series of reforms."[8] Looking back on motion picture history, a similar case could be made for the academic who studies the African-American film experience. Identifying landmark changes, he offers his explanations of cinematic shifts from the birth of movies to the present. His concern is with finding specific racial problems, probing how these difficulties affected black performers, and what if anything has changed over the years. In the process, the scholar singles out trailblazers whose inspirational battles against ethnic barriers in the film industry bettered both the business and society. Such choices draw attention to how history contributes to our lives, our art, and our national interests. Thus, the reformer reminds us of the debt we owe these artists who made the road easier for future film communities.

Such histories, while documenting the industry's perversions, also identify paradoxically certain movies as being traces of how blacks behaved, felt, looked, and lived during the twentieth century. Such a leap is possible because, as the judicious Marc Ferro pointed out decades ago, films contain within them clues to the relationship between the medium and society, how screen images related to the age and circumstances of the world in which they were recorded.[9] And that insight provides a timely rationale to reconsider periodically our views of the transitional years from 1945 to the mid-1970s when racial and industrial changes dramatically altered the status and perceptions of black artists in motion pictures.

This perception of the ties between movies and society did not originate in the early seventies. However, the concept remains an integral part of film analysis. Consider, for example, the use of clips shown from early independent black films featuring African-American performers. "Bessie Smith sang for these cameras, and Josephine Baker danced for them," critic Richard Schickel reminds us. "Dizzy Gillespie bopped there, and the novelist Richard Wright played his own creation, Bigger Thomas, in the film version of *Native Son*. Taken together, this body of film is a priceless record of the styles and manners, aspirations and attitudes of black America between 1920 and 1950, when these little pictures (they usually were about $20,000) made their way along the circuit of more than 600 theaters segregated formally or de facto that served the black community."[10] Such cinematic illustrations from our past furthermore represent the trials America faced in reforming its bigoted culture. They light the steps taken to prevent people of color from becoming major players in the studio system. Still further, these same filmic texts offer evidence of evils that continue to resist resolution: e.g., racism, sexism, social injustice, class warfare, and poverty.

Accordingly, I see movies as a vital historical repository. So too are the recent books about African-American film history. These new publications reflect modern accounts of leading actions and inspiring performers who deserve both our attention and gratitude. Such efforts also suggest, as Marvin Gelfand observes, the necessity of making "white Americans more aware of the black dimension of their experience."[11]

By reconsidering African-American film heritage, I sense how imaginary screen depictions not only provide uncritical audiences with alleged images of authenticity, but also generate in the audience's mind standards of taste, agreement, and support for people and cultures alien to the viewers themselves.[12] Unless critically examined, I submit, these problematic perceptions get passed on from one generation to another, not just by racists but also by the people society trusts most: parents, relatives, political leaders, teachers, friends, and clerics. We are inundated with absurd ideas not out of hatred or anger or fear, but as a result of widespread ignorance grounded in a society unaware or uninterested in how our culture works or grows. And no matter how such distortions get repackaged by present-day devotees, the problems persist. That is, racism moves from distortions of Jews and Blacks to misrepresentations of Latinos and Muslims. Hence, every vigilant generation uses the past as a reminder to remain heedful and prepared to take up arms against such a sea of troubles.[13]

To recognize an academic's obligation in such matters, one needs to appreciate how film historians operate as well as why the nature of their work forces them to be schizophrenic. As my friend, historian Mark A. Stoler, points out, "[They have to be] able to sit in the past and the present simultaneously. In the present we sit in judgment because we know what happened. But by itself that is unfair to the people and the events of the past we study. We need to sit in their shoes in the past. And such sitting in the past requires not only knowledge of the past but also suspension of our knowledge about what happened after the event being studied in order to understand properly how and why people behaved in certain ways within the context of their times and values. Yet we do have that knowledge of what happened, and with it the ability/need to judge."[14] In other words, schizophrenia becomes a historian's worthy ally. Society then considers how well we did our jobs.

To weigh the black film experience, what happened and why,

we best begin with the conditions African-American entertainers encountered from before the origins of film to the early 1970s when my research for this project formally started. In that regard, we remain sensitive to the challenges faced by torchbearers in taking on not only the motion picture industry, but also America itself. We see, as Professor Cornell West describes, the generation after generation of blacks for over 244 years who courageously fought for freedom and self-determination mainly "through their voices and their bodies."[15] As well, we consider the sacrifices and consequences of their heroic efforts.

Every Step a Struggle: Interviews with Seven Who Shaped the African-American Image in Movies[16] and *Exits and Entrances: Interviews with Seven Who Reshaped African-American Images in Movies,* collectively entitled *The Interviews,* represent my guarded thoughts about the African-American experience during the first seventy years of the twentieth century. In vastly oversimplified words, the fourteen representative celebrities interviewed for this project worked during different historical periods and in dissimilar circumstances to create, to maintain, and to transform a penny arcade novelty into an influential art and industry. These performers witnessed the rise of studios, production centers, where business people distributed incredibly convincing films to powerful theater chains strategically located throughout the country. Casts and crews of these emerging, extremely popular industrial products were put under long-term contracts; a dazzling star system turned celebrities into demi-gods who embodied our nation's new folklore; and production formulas were developed not only to maximize profits, but also to shape the vulnerable audiences' reception to the Machiavellian film narratives. Owned and operated by profit-motivated moguls, these studios saw their cultural mission mainly as supporting the status quo and encouraging a growing industrial society to become "a melting pot," which catered to the existing state of affairs as well as molded America's dreams and fantasies. Strangers to our republic learned about their new country primarily through what they saw on the silver screen. This "social contract" was closely monitored not only by wary government agencies, but also by alarmed social and religious institutions. Were these the right "messages," these organizations worried, for audiences at home and abroad about the American Dream? To insure the "appropriateness" of the industry's dream factory, a production code came into being, stating what was and was not suitable for Americans to watch. Those not-so subtle methods remained firmly fixed in the nation's cultural life until the end of the sixties.

What constantly changed, however, from the start to the present, is the way in which audiences received and reacted to the film experience. Were they complacent and passive, or were they provoked and inspired? No one could ever be certain of just who the onlookers were and how they would respond to the pictures on screen. Nor could anyone predict the lengths the dominant culture would go to suppress interference with the Establishment's priorities and behavior.

At the heart of America's predictable film industry stood two crucial influences. The first spur concerned the industry's prototypes—e.g., the Minstrel shows, Burlesque, and Vaudeville—and how the filmmakers used these models to create the business structure of moviemaking. Each historical show business group used stereotypes to attract as well as to entertain its massive audiences. No ethnic group was spared from scorn and ridicule. What made the racism acceptable was the belief that such antics were innocent amusements, all done in fun. These accepted practices became central to the workings of the film factories. The second stimulus derived from the recognition Hollywood was dominated by founding Jewish immigrants who themselves were ostracized in American life. They had gone into the film business because they were prevented from going into almost any other occupation. Especially important, these crafty émigrés used the lessons learned from popular entertainment to ingratiate them to a native-born, white, Protestant Anglo-Saxon establishment. Assimilation became the task, acculturation the endgame.

It should come as no surprise that those who acted, spoke, or looked different from the white establishment were systematically excluded from any meaningful voice in the motion picture process. For instance, black people had little or no say in telling their story on screen. In other words, as Professor William Grant stated, "Film taught immigrants how to be American, it taught the world what it meant to be American, and unfortunately it made the masses believe that African-Americans were repulsive and vile caricatures found at the theater near you."[17] Just as bad, explained writer/director Robert Benton: "It [Hollywood] invented a kind of America we all believed in, whether it was true or not."[18] For reasons like these, I decided to revisit the place of the movies in our lives and their effect on our nation.

In retracing the black film legacy, this book works as a companion to *Every Step a Struggle*. Published in 2007, the first volume explores the American film industry's pivotal years as experienced by insiders who participated in the rise and distribution of longstanding, disturbing black screen images. Even when forced to play roles antithetical to their very being, these audacious actors gave those characters distinction and appeal. Not every historian shares my judgment. When Hollywood underwent a tumultuous transition during the fifties and sixties, these same screen veterans came under attack from progressives and black nationalists who labeled them racists, accommodationists, and obstructionists. *Every Step a Struggle* tells their side of the story.

Another part of the story starts with *Exits and Entrances*. This current chronicle centers on representative actors who replaced the film pioneers. Refusing to accept Jim Crow traditions and risking their careers in their rebellion, they worked fearlessly to break down the racial barriers in every aspect of the film, the stage, and the television world. While building on the observations obtained from Volume 1, this study searches the post-World War II changes that took place in Hollywood, the nation, and in black Americans. What happened and what was the fallout that followed? What significant trials and errors did these latter-day innovators face? How did their work reshape the past? Or did it? And what were the consequences?

The tapings for *The Interviews* took place between November 1971 and March 1974. It was a time when President Richard M. Nixon was running for re-election; when democratic presidential nominee George McGovern based his failed campaign on stopping the Vietnam War; and when *Washington Pos*t reporters Bob Woodward and Carl Bernstein made newspaper history tracing the Watergate break-in to the White House and to Nixon's eventual resignation as President.

The early seventies were also a time when African-American artists momentarily solidified their mutiny against film traditions. Due to dramatic changes taking place in mainstream movies, multi-racial audiences found themselves with a range of cultural choices rarely seen before in Hollywood history. Popular consensus has "blaxploitation" films at center stage. These low-budgeted action movies with black stars battling social injustice and economic inequality in white-controlled urban communities personify the period. Not everyone, however, viewed these unapologetic, angry moving pictures as progress. "Where white suburban America saw violence and destruction," Professor Paula J. Massood wrote, "black audiences saw resistance to specific wrongs of the inner city—disenfranchisement, poverty, decay, and unchecked police brutality."[19] Clearly the long-awaited African-American "reformation" in the motion picture industry did not by itself guarantee support or reform. While one group attacked the senseless violence, another railed against manipulation by the white-power structure. The blaxploitation films proved so polemical that pundits still debate their worth today.

Traveling between New York and California in these chaotic times, I set out to explore the movie making mayhem from the perspective of the film personalities themselves. How did they see the reform movement in the motion picture industry? What was their role and responsibility in the struggle? Could I help? To that end, fourteen celebrities were selected for the interviews. Most of the choices resulted from industry insiders identifying appropriate and willing candidates. That is, chance rather than design set the talks in motion. Like Blanche DuBois, "I depended upon the kindness of strangers." In chronological order, my obliging subjects were Lorenzo Tucker, Lillian Gish, Clarence Muse, King Vidor, Mae Mercer, Brock Peters, Charles Edward Gordone, Woody Strode, Jim Brown, Ivan Dixon, James Whitmore, Frederick Douglass O'Neal, William Marshall, and Ruby Dee.

One major regret is that this original account omits my valued interaction with the memorable Roscoe Lee Browne. As noted earlier, these historical conversations were recorded with cheap cassettes on an inexpensive tape recorder between 1971 and 1974. After arriving home, I found Roscoe's interview totally chewed up by the mechanical device and with no possibility of salvage. I consider Roscoe's absence here a major loss.

Without the audio material, my memories of him are even more suspect than elsewhere. But this much I recall clearly. In the five hours we spent together, first at a local Chinese restaurant and then later at his apartment, Roscoe, with his rich voice and dignified disposition, spoke to me about his pride in African-American history. Owing to his background as an ex-English teacher, poet, as well as a stage, film, and TV actor, he possessed a marvelous grasp of black literature, drama, and history, and was truly proud of what his brothers and sisters had achieved over the past four hundred years. He performed extemporaneous soliloquies, commented on the films he had made, and told me about his plans for the future. His death at 81 took from us the son of a Baptist minister who rose to the heights of the acting profession. While we do not have any visual records of his notable stage performances and rely heavily on hearsay, we can see his urbane artistry in motion pictures like Carl Lerner's *Black Like Me* (1964), Peter Glenville's *The Comedians* (1967), Jules Dassin's *Up Tight* (1968), Alfred Hitchcock's *Topaz* (1969), William Wyler's *The Liberation of L.B. Jones* (1970), Mark Rydell's *The Cowboys* (1972), Sidney Poitier's *Uptown Saturday Night* (1974), and Robert Aldrich's *Twilight's Last Gleaming* (1977). I hold Roscoe in the highest esteem and feel forever grateful for the brief moments we shared together.

These previously unpublished talks form the soul of *The Interviews*. They are annotated transcriptions, discussions with film professionals taped over forty years ago. The term "interview" is somewhat misleading. More like encounters between outsiders trying to communicate clearly with strangers, these exchanges sample unstated assumptions about such things as aesthetics, education, ambition, social injustice, industrial patterns, race, class, identity, and gender. At their core, they illustrate the puzzling times in which these meetings occurred. In that sense, they add to the growing literature on the human condition. Because pursuing the complexity of such representational issues goes beyond the scope of this project, I use the term "interview" for convenience rather than precision.

Essentially, *The Interviews* rely on personal observations arising from distinct careers that achieved varying degrees of success. While I draw on data from the social sciences and black film scholarship, I primarily use individual interviews in a novel way to evoke our nation's film history. This debatable strategy—e.g., introductions, interviews, endnotes, and annotations—permits me to give my audience a flexible segue to historical impressions about the changes I witnessed. By showcasing the African-American experience in a firsthand light and from different outlooks, the methodology proposes innovative ideas about the black film experience.

What follows from these collected meetings is our shared memory of what "occurred" back in the post-World War II years up to the mid-seventies. Preparation for the talks remained minimal. There were no set questions. Appointments were hastily arranged and conversations matter-of-factly recorded. No one regrets more than I do the inability for follow-up visits. Accordingly, how you receive the conversations depends on how you feel about academic rigor versus open-ended discussions. If the latter unsettles you, then my method proves unsettling. On the other hand, if you are mindful of the freedom such directness provides, you discover the benefits of my experiences.

In *The Interviews,* I am more interested in gathering information than in attaining thoroughness. I wanted to grow not only as an academician but also as a person. It should surprise no one that our reflections proved selective and self-serving. Like the revelations in Robert Browning's *My Last Duchess,* our personal feelings predictably exposed our self-absorbed biases. We never came to any conclusions. That outcome was hardly startling. These informal interviews were never designed to resolve complex issues. No one expected a consensus. We traded insights so that we might better identify a greater whole. To paraphrase Art Pepper, "That's what took place then. That's the way [I believe] it was...."[20]

So just what is claimed for these historically flawed and roughly transcribed interviews? First, they add to a database that considers black people as part of, not excluded from, American culture and society. The personalities' testimony made during a predominantly Jim Crow century illuminate many key events that contain worthwhile information not only about the actors' lives and careers, but also about a bygone America and us. Primarily, the interviews attest to what these artists did, and why, and how they did it. Equally important, the books testify to why these fourteen performers should not be ignored or dismissed, but instead be re-experienced, reconsidered, and remembered. If *The Interviews* are read patiently and judiciously, I believe it will underscore what Albert Murray states is the function of education: "it will "develop citizens who are fully oriented to cultural diversity—and are not hung up on race." [21]

Let me be very clear about my goals. In sharing these reflections with you, I am not acting as an apologist for a colonial and imperialist ideology. Nor am I interested in jumping on any academic bandwagon that singularly blames Hollywood for its deplorable screen abuses distributed around the world over the past hundred years. Moreover, no claim is made you are about to discover the definitive account of movie history, the accurate meaning of the black film experience, the nature of the celebrities themselves, or what I truly feel about the human race. Under no circumstances, therefore, should *The Interviews* be construed as a replacement to present approaches to black film studies. I only want to add to the discussion.

Hence, *The Interviews* shy away from finger pointing or pigeonholing. In a straightforward manner, the celebrities discuss their personal experiences, speculate on possible reasons for the then current conditions, and consider probable outcomes. No one account satisfactorily clarifies why films operated in the manner they did or how they can effectively be reformed. Together, however, the talks enlarge our understanding of what has happened, when, where, and how; as well as show the part individuals did perform in bringing us closer as Americans.

I also want to be clear that despite the movies' scandalous reputation, often justified, for as long as I can remember, films have been dear to my heart. In their historical record, I view, as critic historian Leonard Maltin aptly states, is "the history of America."[22] That does not mean I am naïve about the filmmakers' faults, nor oblivious to their intellectual inadequacies. My previous writings testify to that truth.

The journey explored by *The Interviews* begins as familiar territory to serious film students. It circuitously traces western civilization's artistic legacy up to the origins of the motion picture business, how the new medium copied distorted black imagery initiated by popular stage and literary traditions, how those tainted likenesses took shape on screen, the barriers that existed, the abuses that ensued, and how the subsequent humanistic quest for an "authentic" black image progressed. Then the road diverges. In the popular narrative, scholars routinely assess how powerful, conservative forces fought insistently to retain outmoded values based on an "ideal" nation that barred outsiders like African-Americans from full participation in the American Dream. *The Interviews* provide new documents that shed light on the reforms film activists achieved as well as the sacrifices made by the pioneers themselves. By doing such, the two books put a human face on the passage. They educate by example not by proselytizing.

Such human inquiries about who we are and what we are and what needs to be done remain commonplace in academic circles. Often, process proves more valuable than assertions, awareness more crucial than conclusions. As a result, studies like *The Interviews* assume that if we are to fix our world, we should begin at home, with ourselves first. But self-improvement does not come to the Comfortable, the Convinced, the Cowardly, and the Complacent. Rather, as Professor Donald Murray once said, "For those of us who are introspective, life is a continuous exploration into the self, where we hope to find the person we are and the person we may become."[23] Changing oneself, however, frequently proves difficult. That is no excuse for not trying. "Remember," wrote former Princeton University president Harold T. Shapiro," it is difficult to understand who we humans really are, even harder to know what we should be, and most daunting of all to perceive who we might, or should, become."[24]

Changing America's perception about the African-American movie experience remains a case in point. Those of us fortunate enough to have helped initiate the inquiries concerning a black film heritage marvel at the growth in film scholarship since the days when the popular arts themselves remained *persona non grata* in educational circles. The lonely, solitary scholars who broke through the scholastic barriers more often than not came from English and Foreign Language departments rather than non-existent cinema programs. They faced considerable, often unreasonable trials from their print-oriented, classically trained, and entrenched peers in getting media literacy into the classroom, let alone accepted in the standard curriculum. To me, my adversaries' greatest confusion lay in thinking the "Young Turks" were out to replace the Old Guards' respected traditions with artistic vulgarity. That barbarism rarely crossed our minds. Our errand dealt with academic equality, not institutional superiority. We saw film as the great art form of the twentieth century. Victories did not come early or easily. But with time, the Turks became the Establishment and their groundbreaking goals now flourish as respected and indispensible areas of higher learning.

Once such scholarly activity is the ever-changing research concerning the black film experience. Currently, and again in simplistic terms, what once started as groundbreaking but imperfect film histories reporting anecdotal tales of landmark events evolved in contemporary times as chronicles carefully rooted in techniques used in subjects that incorporated psychoanalysis, feminism, linguistics, anthropology, and Marxist economics. Relying more on once inaccessible studio records instead of aging eyewitness accounts, the new breed of film historians found a valuable niche in higher education.[25] The indictments prepared by these stalwart, demanding academics is lengthy, almost always accurate, and based upon impressive, imaginative, and powerful evidence. Their names and accomplishments appear throughout the scholarly literature. Not only does this gifted cadre deserve our respect; they also merit our gratitude.

There are a few of us old-timers, however, who echo Orson Welles' cinematic principles. We admire our peers and applaud their achievements. Nonetheless, we choose to remain distinct from the academic mainstream. We do not argue either our views or we are better than those of our colleagues. If our voices have any virtue, it is because, as Welles said, we follow "the old American tradition of the maverick—a vanishing breed...."[26]

I feel no shame in claiming membership in this small, elitist society. But such associations inevitably evoke a basic question: why should anyone pay attention to eccentrics who present imprecise ideas on this problematic, persistent, and perennial topic? Daniel J. Wakin raises yet another question, albeit in a different context. In what he aptly describes as "a digitized, electronic and screen-laden world," why would you, the reader, be interested in a set of interviews about African-American film from the mid-fifties to the present?"[27]

First things first. While I understand the persistent, historical outcry for a clear definition either of black-themed films or black films per se, I do not consider either of those options intellectually or emotionally useful either in *The Interviews* or in this approach to black film history. I do, however, recognize the usefulness of those definitions for other projects. For example, scholars find many good reasons to dismiss American film productions produced by white filmmakers, which falsely claim to be authentic representations of "blackness" but are marketed mainly at Caucasians not African-Americans. Here we have no disagreement. In addition, I am not insensitive to the daunting debate. When civil, such conversations help clarify the crude, biased, and disgraceful manner in which white Hollywood maligned blacks throughout much of the twentieth century. For me, however, the outcome of complex questioning sometimes redounds to the disadvantage of films and actors that validated the black artists' considerable contributions to motion picture history.

Thus for our purposes, I examine not black films, but the black film experience primarily through the lives and careers of African-American artists. How truthful or precise these film representations are about black America remain above my grade level. Highlighting some of the historic movies and vibrant performers in the twentieth century seems more manageable. Using ethnic film categories like black films or black-themed movies omits from consideration some of the most innovative, significant, and popular movies featuring black artists in the past hundred years: e.g. *The Birth of a Nation, Hallelujah, The Green Pastures, Judge Priest, Steamboat Round the Bend, Imitation of Life* (1934, 1959), *Show Boat* (1936, 1951), *Gone with the Wind, The Ox-Bow Incident, Cabin in the Sky, Stormy Weather, Lifeboat, Body and Soul, Song of the South, Intruder in the Dust, Pinky, Carmen Jones, Spartacus, Odds Against Tomorrow, A Raisin in the Sun, High Society, Sergeant Rutledge, The Man Who Shot Liberty Valance, To Kill a Mockingbird, The Pawnbroker, The Liberation of L. B. Jones, Nothing But a Man, The Cotton Club, Lilies of the Field, In the Heat of the Night, Dr. Strangelove or: How I Learned to Stop Worrying and Love the*

Bomb, The Great White Hope, Sounder, Lady Sings the Blues, The Dirty Dozen, Star Wars, Claudine, The Color Purple, The Blues Brothers, Field of Dreams, An Officer and a Gentleman, Tap, Bird, Driving Miss Daisy, Kansas City, The Pursuit of Happyness, Unforgiven, Monster's Ball, The Soloist, Ray, Dreamgirls, Collateral, Lincoln, and *Django Unchained.*

I find it counterproductive to study the motion picture legacy of African-Americans and omit the aforementioned films from consideration. When talking about our national film history and its relationship to black artists, the narrative should not operate in a cultural vacuum and ignore the contributions of white actors, directors, screenwriters, studio heads, and distributors. I find such chronicles just as unproductive if they ignore the mainstream work of artists like Paul Robeson, Nina Mae McKinney, Daniel Haynes, Josephine Baker, Fredi Washington, Hattie McDaniel, Leigh Whipper, Louis Armstrong, Clarence Muse, Woody Strode, Dorothy Dandridge, Billie Holiday, Whoopi Goldberg, Sammy Davis Jr., Lena Horne, and Ethel Waters.

The only caveats with all or any of these films is that audiences should understand the context in which these films were made, as well as be aware of the issues that many socially conscious protesters raise about the intentions and construction of the films themselves! Tolerant of that perspective, this investigation of black film history hopefully allows my "autobiographical journey" to become a learning experience for others.[28]

Obviously, it is not enough to be a maverick. The selections you make and the judgments you reach remain the critical tests. My distinguished colleagues throughout the past half-century already provide valuable insights on the subject. In fact, much of what *The Interviews* dispute benefits considerably from the investigations of other younger and more talented researchers. With so many respected, absorbing, and handy versions already available, why these books?

Let me advance a few rejoinders. One comeback is that even leading authorities readily admit they do not know the whole story. Too many questions remain unanswered, unexplored, and misinterpreted. Certainly, the debate is far from concluded. A second answer comes from a cultural critic like Stanley Crouch who acknowledged, "At large in America, much of what people think they know about the identity of any other people arrives not from reading about them but by absorbing true, false, half-true, and fantasy images delivered through television and film."[29] Since none of us sees the world in the same way, why not entertain different viewpoints? A third response entails Time itself. To reword Louis Armstrong biographer Terry Teachout, we live in a world distant from twentieth century film history; and it becomes harder each day "to bridge the gap" and see the struggle clearly. Yesterday's film personalities are too often tried by today's detractors "whose standards they did not know or even thought possible and are found wanting."[30] In a sense, it is similar to the argument Professor Stoler made earlier. Having lived through the period under discussion, I believe fair-mindedness calls out for reconsideration. A fourth rejoinder, suggested indirectly by *New Amsterdam News* reporter Herb Boyd, is the advantage of viewing black screen history with "the naiveté of a child; to revisit and not just retread the rails."[31] Far too often, grown-ups confuse opinions with facts, experience with wisdom, passion with substance, and change with progress. Taking a fresh, novel look at a difficult topic often helps in clarifying many uncertainties. Fifth, let me unashamedly share with you my reason given when this project originated decades ago: "[We] the public influence the kinds of film images that movies project. The Afro-American has been and continues to be distorted on the screen because an ignorant and prejudiced audience remains visually illiterate about the types presented and the effects such stereotypes have on our imagination."[32] Thus we need to be better educated to appreciate the experiences we share together. Movies are not now, nor have they ever been, merely escapist entertainment. *The Interviews* demonstrate why. Finally, as I hope to demonstrate, there are numerous unforeseen benefits in going where one has not gone before.

Granting these arguments, the ultimate issue still remains: How valid are your ideas? That is what I expect you the reader to decide.

There is, however, another pricklier matter needing comment. During the time of these interviews and since, various people felt they had nothing to learn from whites about African-American history in general and black film history in particular. That feeling permeated our society. It was not unusual in academic settings for militant colleagues to use daunting tactics against dissenting equals, "Do it my way or be dismissed from the table." In fact, the effects of that aggressive attitude remain with us today. For instance, in 2011, when David Margolick, a longtime contributing editor at *Vanity Fair*, did a *New York Times Book Review* critique of Harvard scholar Henry Louis Gates Jr.'s new non-fiction work *Life Upon These Shores*, he began, "Who was I, a white man, to write on such a topic?"[33] The problem will not go away, although the recognition bestowed on George Lucas' production of *Red Tails* (2012) is heartwarming.[34]

No easy retort occurs for resolving this highly sensitive quarrel. In fact, younger academicians assure me, the problem no longer exists. Unfortunately, that is still not my experience. But clouding the debate is that some factions consider such an alternative outlook to be "politically incorrect." That troubles me. Like the distinguished film scholar Robin Wood, I bought into the basic principles of political correctness long before it became fashionable: "antisexism, antiracism, antihomophobia, support of environmentalism..." as well as a loyalty to liberal values. But again like Wood, I break with political correctness when its excesses become silly and foolish, and especially when its attitudes toward the past become dangerous.[35] I refuse to be intimidated by analysts who dismiss films like *The Color Purple, Bird,* and *Amistad* because white men made them; or by colleagues who want me to discard interviews with those filmmakers who happen to be white. As the reader quickly discovers in *The Interviews,* I remain politically correct only as long as it meaningfully adds to the dialogue. Once it shuts down the discussion, political correctness and I part company.

Thanks to the wisdom of intellectuals like Murray, serious students like me are unapologetic about our modern-day incursions into African-American film study. "Being black," he made clear, "is not enough to make anybody an authority on U.S. Negroes, any more than being white has ever qualified anybody as an expert on the ways of U.S. white people."[36] Murray argued no differently from his friend Ralph Ellison, who believed that black and white Americans are part of each other."[37] That message was reinforced by Crouch, who stated categorically, "Race, class, and sex can never be ignored when analyzing the story and the meaning of American life, but categories that deny the imperturbable mixtures we should by now know make us all who we are...."[38] In a sense, speaking freely about what you believe is what it means to be an American.

For those still seeking more reasons for justifying my views, let me cite common sense. "Movies don't exist in a vacuum," stated noted film producer Walter Mirisch. "Movies exist in conjunction with their audiences."[39] Just as it is vital for successful actors to listen and to learn from each other as they play their roles upon the stage, so we as multi-racial Americans benefit from questioning each other's private perceptions. More to the point are the words the late Una Mulzac had on the door of her famous Harlem Liberation Bookstore. On one side, there was "If you don't know, learn." On the other side, "If you know, teach."[40]

I deliberately belabor this delicate problem because of its relevance to *The Interviews*. For more than four decades, it has dogged my research. Now the issue appears full-blown when I include interviews with white celebrities in texts on the black film experience. For example, several reviewers of *Every Step a Struggle* suggested I either eliminate Lillian Gish and King Vidor from the anthology altogether, or at the very least move them to the back of the bus, I mean the back of the book. Another colleague dismissed the publication because he felt he had nothing to learn from Gish about African-American film history. Understand that these comments were being leveled by well-liked, respected peers at two of the most honored artists in motion picture history, superstars whose films were vital to describing, understanding, and criticizing Hollywood's mistreatment of its black legacy. Plainly, I rejected such well-intentioned but misguided opinions. I take the same stance as regards James Whitmore's thoughts in *Exits and Entrances*.

Let's be even clearer on this touchy issue. By including either the aforementioned white-produced films or these film giants in *The Interviews* I am not endorsing their politics or all of their films. Much like Meryl Streep's response to critics regarding her Oscar-winning portrayal of Margaret Thatcher in Phyllida Lloyd's *The Iron Lady* (2011), what interested me about Gish, for example, was the role of someone who not only could make a racist film like D. W. Griffith's *The Birth of a Nation* (1915), but also defend the film for the rest of her life. As Streep cleverly asks in a similar context, " Where did her views come from? How did these formulations begin, how do they solidify, calcify, become deficits? How does a person's strengths become weaknesses?"[41]

As to why I, a white man, chose to study African-American films for so long, my answer remains clear-cut. On the simplest level, I love the subject matter and the extraordinary rewards it continually provides. No matter how many films I watch, no matter how many books I read, and no matter how much music I absorb, I find something new, and exciting, and stimulating. On another level, for me, how we treat the "Other" acts as the measuring rod of what we stand for as a people; what is working or not working in our society. The distinguished historian Manning Marble said it even better: "African-Americans have always been the litmus test on the viability of American democracy, what America says about itself and what it actually is."[42] That notion underscores much that follows. Studying black film history makes me feel my work has purpose, and that *The Interviews* have relevance for all of us.

It also is not just because *The Interviews* represent a maverick's slant on African-American film history that they deserve a place at the table. And it is not just because this skeptical writer offers alternative observations based on his age, experience, and education. My view stems from what Murray calls "The Omni-Americans" dichotomy between "victimization and celebration." That is, should the history of black pride, black identity, and black power be told in what has been achieved or what has been the obstacle and results of racism? In brief, "black pathology or black achievement."[43] I come down on the side that argues there is as much to praise about the past as to condemn. To me, *The Interviews* are not mainly a history of victims and perpetrators; they are also a history of heroes and achievements. In essence, these two books collectively present my reasons why. They explore subjects and ideas ignored, overlooked, or rejected by conventional wisdom. Intentionally or not, these fourteen artists, through their lives and careers, produced memorable entertainment and important artifacts. Their callings made it possible to change American film history. In examining their gifts and limitations, we get not only an important account of the past, but also a view of the popular arts as they progressed through the twentieth century.

Consequently, in making a decision to go forward, do not be

fooled by my emphasis on bygone theories or my refusal to conform to conventional wisdom. *The Interviews* are as relevant to the public today as their personalities were then. And do not mistakenly assume these accounts are intended exclusively for academics and students. At one level, each book *does* focus on African-American movie history, as revealed in the words, thoughts, and actions of specific film celebrities whose passions affected art, race, and civilization. But at another level, these same accounts explore how popular culture generally and movies specifically reflect and influence our lives and our times. In addition, my failure to designate a specific audience for *The Interviews* is not unique when dealing with white-black issues. Even the great poet James Wendell Johnson once wrote about his own work: "To whom should he address himself, to his own black group or white America?"[44]

Although rooted in the divisive days of the late sixties and early seventies, the fourteen conversations remind us of a time before our nation was born. It searches our past as well as our present. Projects like *The Interviews* remain relevant because those industry insiders who worked in a particular time and place reflected and affected the era in which they acted. That understanding moves us forward. And if there is any lasting value to be found in this unconventional project, it is that the discussions published here are found nowhere else. Thus, *The Interviews* serve as a rare reminder of who we were, where we came from, and where we yet need to travel.

One last piece of business remains. Those familiar with *Every Step a Struggle* know the territory already covered prior to this new book. So there is no need for them to continue in the Preface and they should feel comfortable moving on to the Introduction in *Exits and Entrances*. But for first-time readers, I want to assure you that it is not necessary the texts be read sequentially. To facilitate your understanding of *Exits and Entrances*, let me explain briefly what the initial volume contains.

Throughout the first sixty years of American film history, black trailblazers, the focus of *Every Step a Struggle*, fought back. Both in independent films and in Hollywood itself, they sought to influence alternative screen images that appropriately addressed their heritage. Just as importantly, these scorned black entertainers risked their careers to gain equal employment and artistic freedom.

Proud, determined, and talented, but straddled by poor working conditions, miniscule budgets, and institutional racism, these actors often found themselves isolated and ignored by mainstream audiences. What few independent films they made were shown in mostly white theaters where blacks had to sit in the balconies. There they often experienced inhuman conditions just to see "their" demeaning images on screen. Often overlooked is the fact they did not consider the film depictions as did their oppressors. Nor was everyone in agreement as to what mainstream Hollywood's black experience truly signified. Even the black press remained confused on whether to champion or to condemn the problematic film industry. Thus the insiders' take on the first sixty years of film history does not seamlessly square with what has been written and said about the times, the events, and them. Not only did the celebrities see the same film from different perspectives, but also for different reasons.

What these dreamers did in their profession, how they did it, and why it opened doors for many black actors from the post-World War II period to today is the stuff of the Introduction to *Every Step a Struggle*. The overview outlines the scope, purpose and intent of the book. It also includes a bibliography on the history of black film criticism, along with perceptions concerning the tumultuous 1960s and the rise of the blaxploitation cycle in the early 1970s. In addition, biographical information on the author, included with the social data, prepares the reader for the interviews that follow. It sheds light on why these conversations took decades to appear.

In Chapter 1, "Heroes and Villains: Lorenzo Tucker," I examine not only the influence of Oscar Micheaux, the "Dean of Black films," but also the part played by his leading African-American star from the early days of sound up to the 1940s. Moreover, several other contributors emphasize how a black person's skin color played a major role both in mainstream Hollywood movies and race films throughout the first seventy years of movie history. The parties similarly discuss the links between Lorenzo Tucker, Oscar Micheaux, and the rise of what is sometimes loosely referred to as "Black Cinema," or "Independent Black films." Among the surprises are the inclusion of comments by Pearl and Leroy Bowser, two black advocates of an emerging new era in Negro film history. Their encounters with the Tuckers reveal the tensions between different African-American generations. My views on the minstrel tradition and Jack Johnson signal issues that appear repeatedly throughout the interviews to follow.

In Chapter 2, "The Movies, Mr. Griffith, and Miss Gish: Lillian Gish," the conversation turns to the legendary actress and her life and film career. Among many biographical issues discussed, we reflect on the making of D.W. Griffith's *The Birth of a Nation* (1915), the central historical film in establishing Hollywood's outrageous, insulting black screen images, as well as the nation's unwavering attitudes prevalent during the Jim Crow period. In addition, we touch on the growth of film aesthetics in the silent era. Readers also discover, through Gish's own words, her personal and professional relationship with Griffith.

In Chapter 3, "Scarred by History: Clarence Muse" my attention remains on the "Dean of Black film character actors" from the early silent days until the end of the 1960s. Attacked by black film purists as an "Uncle Tom," Muse was anything but complacent, politically indifferent, and unattractive. The talks explore not only Muse's fellow actors and how together they influenced black screen history during Hollywood's first half century but also the role music and the stage continuously plays in an African-American film experience. Throughout, the defiant Muse remains insistent in turning the conversation into a history lesson about black entertainment.

Chapter 4, "The Well-Intentioned Poet: King Vidor," not only provides a snapshot of nineteenth century Southern myths about blacks and whites living together in the first thirty years of the twentieth century, but also gives helpful insights into the problems liberal white filmmakers faced trying to make and to exhibit black-themed movies through intransigent Hollywood distribution channels. In discussing the economic and social issues associated with creating *Hallelujah* (1929), the famous director illustrates what type of roles black actors took, and he gives his reactions to their marginalized situations. Because his revolutionary film added a problematic aspect to black screen imagery absent in silent films, one could argue, as it often is, that if Griffith molded America's racist cultural image of blacks prior to the 1930s, Vidor not only offered an alternative to past African-American symbolism, but also, with revolutionary technological techniques, added a timeless look at a black Southern spiritual legacy. Accordingly, *Hallelujah*'s values remain a source of debate to the present time.

Chapter 5, "The Man Who Made the Stars Shine Brighter: Woody Strode," presents his perspective on the predicaments faced by the actor *Jet* magazine called "the Jackie Robinson of Cinema." His candid remarks detail a conservative artist's challenges during the unbridled fifties and sixties and describe why he had to settle for a career as a character actor. Strode also movingly reviews what effect the Black Nationalist Movement had on his life and work. Particularly noteworthy is his explanation of what the legendary John Ford meant to the actor's film legacy.

Chapter 6, "Somebody Who Refused to be Nobody: Charles Edward Gordone," looks at the life and career of the first black dramatist to win the Pulitzer Prize for Drama. At the same time, Gordone discusses his perceptions about the political and aesthetic issues facing African-American artists in the sixties and early seventies. His outspoken and articulate observations shed light on the feelings, storms, and difficulties independent, creative people faced during the black separatist crusade.

In Chapter 7, "From Actor to Activist: Frederick Douglass O'Neal," the interview operates as a summary of the period starting in the late 1940s when post-World War II America underwent important changes not only for black people in the theatre but also in mainstream Hollywood. Readers review many of the renowned actor/director's accomplishments, including his creation, along with Abram Hill, of the American Negro Theatre. It was a drama group that gave rise among many others to Sidney Poitier, Earle Hyman, Harry Belafonte, Ruby Dee, Brock Peters, and Ossie Davis.

Taken collectively, these seven distinctive chapters create a framework for examining the racial challenges that confronted black artists, mainstream American filmmakers, and the general public during the transition from the birth of film, the rise of African-American alternatives to Hollywood, the routes black entertainers followed from the stage and nightclubs to film, and what is was like for black pioneers trying to establish a motion picture career. At the same time, the reader grasps the problems African-Americans encountered throughout the entertainment world, as well as their demands for change. In short, the stories told by these artists allow us to celebrate the history and contributions of courageous performers whose gifts to music, film, theater, and radio were considerable. Their cultural influences may not be fully appreciated by many people in our society, but they proved inspirational to me.

And now for *Exits and Entrances*!

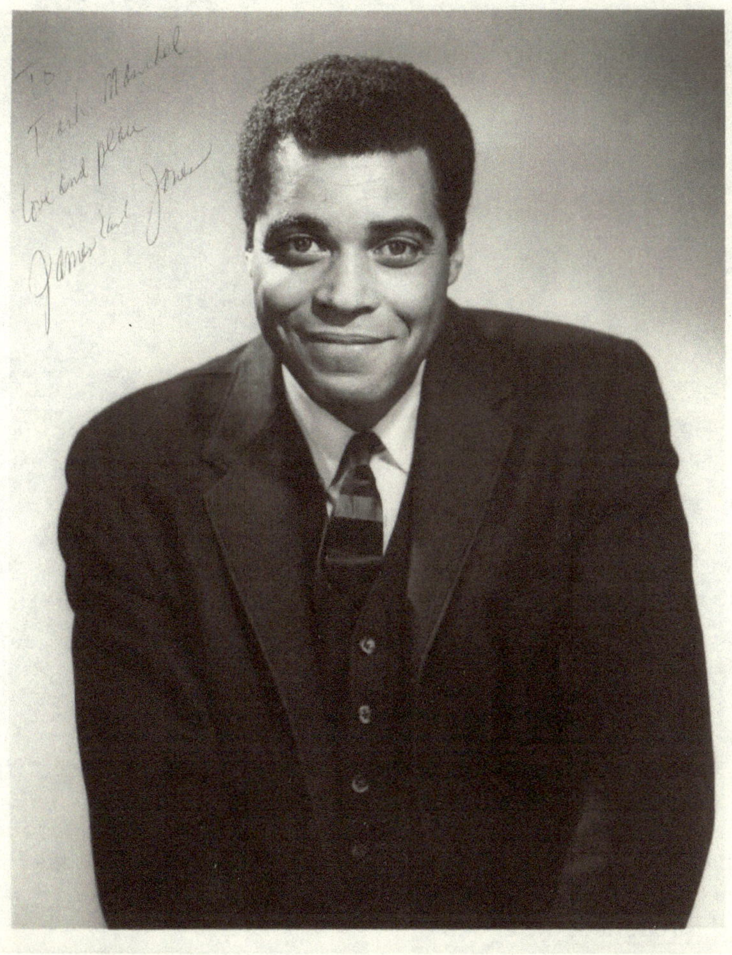

2. The caption reads, "To Frank Manchel, Love and peace, James Earl Jones."

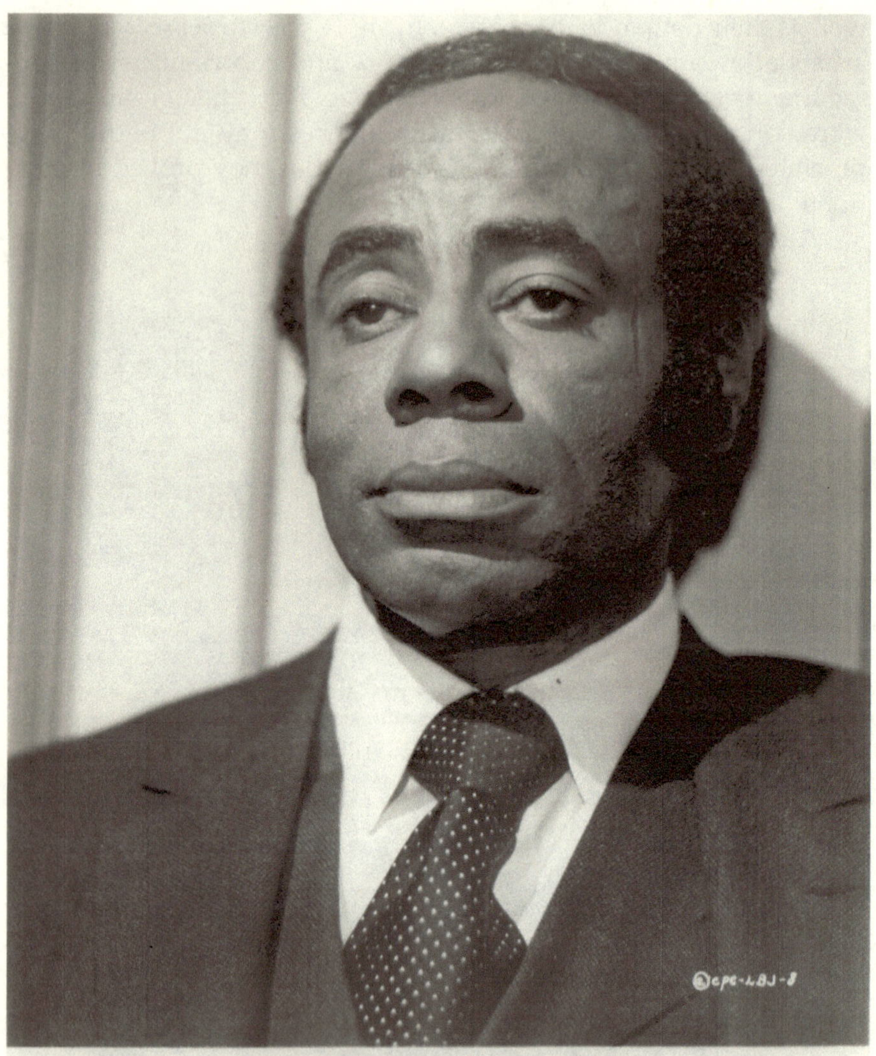

3. Although Roscoe Lee Browne's interview was unable to make *Exits and Entrances*, the gifted actor's contributions influence much of what is discussed throughout the book.

Notes

[1] Warren I. Susman, *Culture as History: The Transformation of American Society in the 20th Century. 1 Ed.* (Washington, D.C.: Smithsonian Institution Press, 2003), 49.

[2] Orson Welles, "American Film Institute Lifetime Award Acceptance Speech," (USA, 1975).

[3] Emily Bernard, *Carl Van Vechten & the Harlem Renaissance: A Portrait in Black & White* (New Haven and London: Yale University Press, 2012), 3.

[4] Ossie Davis, *Life Lit by Some Large Vision: Selected Speeches*, ed. Ruby Dee (New York: Atira Books, 2006), 251.

[5] Leonard Nimoy, "Star Trek IV: The Voyage Home," in *Star Trek*, ed. Harve Bennett (USA: Paramount Pictures, 1986).

[6] John O'Connor and Martin Jackson, *American History/American Film: Interpreting the Hollywood Image*, Expanded ed. (Frederick Ungar, 1988), xvii.

[7] Christopher Sieving, *Soul Searching: Black-Themed Cinema from the March on Washington to the Rise of Blaxploitation* (Middleton, Connecticut: Wesleyan University Press, 2011), 1.

[8] Susman, *Culture as History: The Transformation of American Society in the 20th Century. 1 Ed.*, 86.

[9] Marc Ferro, "Film as an Agent, Product and Source of History," *Journal of Contemporary History* 18, no. 3 (1983): 318.

[10] Richard Schickel, "Artifacts of a Lost Culture," *Time* 123, no. 9 (2009): 1.

[11] Marvin Gelfand, "Taking a Leaf: A Talk with Albert Murray," in *Conversations with Albert Murray*, ed. Roberta S. Maguire, *Literary Conversation Series* (Jackson: University of Mississippi, 1977), 11.

[12] William R. Grant IV, *Post-Soul Black Cinema: Discontinuities, Innovations, and Breakpoints, 1970-1995*, ed. Graham Russell Hodges, Studies in African American History and Culture (New York & London: Routledge, 2004), xi.

[13] Susman, *Culture as History: The Transformation of American Society in the 20th Century. 1 Ed.*, 87.

[14] Mark Stoler, Nov. 3, 2009.

[15] Deborah Morales, "On the Shoulders of Giants," (USA: Union Productions, 2011).

[16] Frank Manchel, *Every Step a Struggle: Interviews with Seven Who Shaped the African-American Image in Movies* (Washington, D.C.: New Academia Publishing, 2007).

[17] Grant IV, *Post-Soul Black Cinema: Discontinuities, Innovations, and Breakpoints, 1970-1995*, xiii.

[18] Jon Wilkman, "Fade out, Fade In: 1960-1969," in *Moguls and Movie Stars: A History of Hollywood* (USA, 2011).

[19] Paula J. Massood, *Black City Cinema: African American Urban Experiences in Film*, ed. Robert Sklar, Paperback ed., Culture and the Moving Image (Philadelphia: Temple University Press, 2003), 83-4.

[20] Pepper, Art, as told to Laurie Miller. "Linear Notes for "The Way It was." In The Way It Was. Chicago: Mobility Fidelity Sound Lab, Inc., 2008.

[21] Albert Murray, *The Omni-Americans: Some Alternatives to the Folklore of White Supremacy* (New York: De Capo Press, 1970), 8.

[22] Wilkman, "Fade out, Fade In: 1960-1969."

[23] Donald M. Murray, "Now and Then: Friends Caring and Sharing Shows the Way," *The Boston Globe*, January 2, 2007.

[24] Harold T. Shapiro, *A Larger Sense of Purpose: Higher Education and Society* (Princeton, N.J.: Princeton University Press, 2005), 161.

[25] Thomas Cripps, *Making Movies Black: The Hollywood Message Movies from World War II to the Civil Rights Era* (New York: Oxford University Press, 1993).

[26] Welles, "American Film Institute Lifetime Award Acceptance Speech."

[27] Daniel J. Wakin, "Orchestras on Big Screens: Chase Scene Needed?," *New York Times*, Nov. 8, 2010, 1.

[28] Susman, *Culture as History: The Transformation of American Society in the 20th Century. 1 Ed.*, xii-xiii.

[29] Stanley Crouch, *The Artificial White Man: Essays on Authenticity*, Paperback ed., Central Studies/African American Studies (New York: Basic Civitas, 2005), 141.

[30] Terry Teachout, *Pops: A Life of Louis Armstrong* (Boston: Houghton Mifflin Harcourt, 2009), 378-79.

[31] Joe Nocerito, "Charlie Rose: Michael Boyd, Artistic Director, Royal Shakespeare Company," (USA: Charlie Rose, Inc., 2011).

[32] Frank Manchel, *Film Study: A Resource Guide* (Rutherford: Fairleigh Dickinson University Press, 1973), 108.

[33]David Margolick, "Heroes and Victim: A Visual Summary of the American Black Experience," *New York Times* December 11, 2011, 22.

[34] Bryan Curtis, "George Lucas Is Ready to Roll the Credits," *The New York Times Magazine*, January 22, 2012, 42-6, 54-5.

[35] Robin Wood, *Sexual Politics and Narrative Film: Hollywood and Beyond*, ed. John Belton, Film and Culture (New York: Columbia University Press, 1998), xi.

[36] Murray, *The Omni-Americans*, 97.

[37] Crouch, *The Artificial White Man*, 140-41.

[38] Stanley Crouch, *The All-American Skin Game, or the Decoy of Race* (New York: Vintage Books, 1995), xiv.

[39] Wilkman, "Fade out, Fade In: 1960-1969."

[40] Douglas Martin, "Una Mulzac, 88, Bookseller with Passion for Black Politics," *New York Times*, Feb. 5, 2012, 26.

[41] Charles McGrath, "Streep Dons Thatcher's Armor," ibid., December 25, 2011, 16.

[42] Joe Nocerito, "We Remember the People We Lost in 2011," in *Charlie Rose* (USA: Charlie Rose, Inc., 2011).

[43] Murray, *The Omni-Americans*, 129.

[44] Joe Wood, "The Soloist: Albert Murray's Blues People," in *Conversations with Albert Murray*, ed. Roberta S. Maguire, *Literary Conversation Series* (Jackson: University Press of Mississippi, 1997), 99.

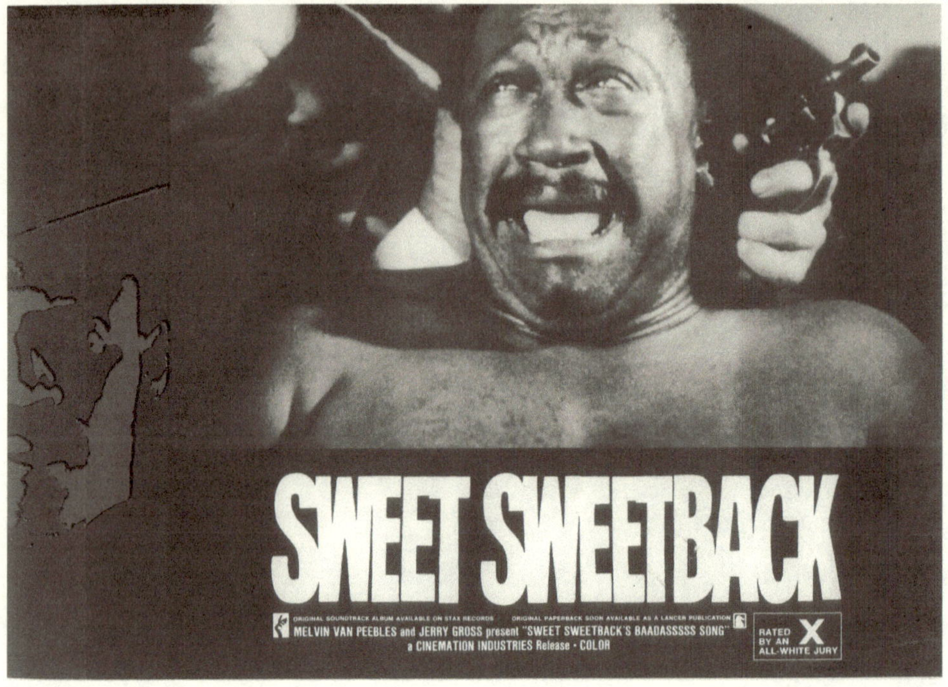

4. In 1971, Melvin Van Peebles' confrontational *Sweet Sweetback's Baadasssss Song* became the first African-American film created exclusively outside the dominant culture's control and trumpeted the end of the once powerful Motion Picture Production Code.

Introduction

> "All the world's a stage, /And all the men and women merely players;/They have their exits and their entrances;/And one man in his time plays many parts, /His acts being seven ages."[1]
>
> *As You Like It,* Act II, Scene 7
>
> *William Shakespeare*

> "The power of black movies to affect our lives...[is] beyond dispute. Whether that power brings life into our communities—'life lit by some large vision,' as Du Bois dreamed—or whether it brings death is not up to Hollywood—it's up to us."[2]
>
> *Ossie Davis*

Reassessing the nation's traditional values proved essential as my generation entered the disillusioned seventies. Moreover, an aroused electorate knew that the unrest enveloping us in the sixties and seventies went further back than the times signified. Nowhere was this fact clearer than in studying American film history. Many academics realized the need for changing a racist Hollywood was not only long overdue, but also had begun centuries before the rise of the civil rights movement confronted a racist society. So in preparing for what eventually became *The Interviews,* I kept reminding myself African-American film history did not emerge out of nothingness. Stanley Crouch spoke indirectly to the point, saying anyone seriously interested in black history could not "escape the past."[3]

What does "looking at the past," mean and how does it apply to this project? In oversimplified terms, examining *yesterday* involves seeing film and its mores emerging, as Professor John Gennari reminded me, "within the context of larger historical narratives: migration, modernization, industrialization, and urbanization."[4] That is, the black film experience rises early in the twentieth century just as overconfident movie pioneers react to the industrial revolution's developing technology.

But it is much more than that. Its story starts well before pictures began to move. Thus, if we are to understand the African-American film legacy, we should begin by considering the cultural effects of the U.S. slave trade, plantation life and culture, the Civil War, Reconstruction, and the Jim Crow system.[5] Only then, I suggest, and following Gennari's lead, should we start examining an era "when [film], jazz and American culture itself were changing in response to World War II and the cold war, suburbanization, the democratization of U.S. higher education, and the first stirrings of the modern civil rights movement." Accordingly, *Exits and Entrances* seeks not only to discover through the book's seven interviews meaningful changes taking place in the black film experience, but also to use motion pictures "as a means of better understanding American history and culture as a whole."[6]

In setting up such daunting goals, I, like many pilgrims before me, acknowledge a debt to the journey previously taken by Professor Constance Rourke. Her pivotal scholarly research established that the antebellum Yankee, the frontiersman, and the Negro functioned as prototypes of our national character. Years later, Albert Murray adopted Rourke's work as a "bible" for his views throughout his life.[7] He built his perceptions in part standing on her shoulders. Drawing upon her distinguished books such as *American Humor: A Study of the National Character* (1931)[8] and *The Roots of American Culture* (1942),[9] the "Dean of Black Fiction" concluded that American culture was "incontestably mulatto."[10] He believed Rourke's deductions about a composite national image confirmed his belief that we as a nation are "Omni-Americans."[11] That is, in interpreting Rourke's conclusions, Murray latched on to the notion that "each had been a wanderer over the lands, the Negro a forced and unwilling wanderer. Each in a fashion of his own had broken bonds, the Yankee in the initial revolt against the parent civilization, the backwoodsman in revolt against all civilization, the Negro in a revolt which was cryptic and submerged but which nonetheless made a perceptible outline.'"[12]

I do no less by following Murray's wisdom in *The Interviews.* Like Rourke and Murray before me, I see what Ossie Davis labeled "The Struggle" as a movement by African-Americans for equal status and dignity in our country's life. *Exits and Entrances* reminds us of the powerful role played by individuals on the silver screen moving us toward those utopian goals.

But where to begin? By 1972, when the first interview in *Exits and Entrances* occurs, political and social revolutions were changing our cultural map. Since the end of World War II, we found ourselves fearing a nuclear holocaust, fighting two conflicts—one in Korea; the other, Vietnam—and being caught up in the Cold War. The fifties' witch-hunts made Americans paranoid, and the entertainment industry either out of fear or expediency caved in to McCarthyism. Broad-based blacklists targeted progressives, and, as a result, many promising careers came to a halt. Then came the even more divisive sixties. Adding to the national disorder were the civil rights movement, the women's liberation struggle, a passionate anti-war crusade, the black power crusade, and the stirrings of the Gay freedom drive. And throughout the disturbing decade, came riots, marches, sit-ins, boycotts, demonstrations, shootings, bombings, police brutality, and assassinations that shocked the nation as never before in the twentieth century. Not unexpectedly, a disillusioned America railed against its disgraced establishments and cries for reform echoed throughout the country. Yet for all that turmoil, America became stronger and her citizens more courageous.

For a young, white Jewish-American professor teaching at the University of Vermont in 1972, Hollywood's attitudes toward race relations seemed more confusing and irrational than usual. On one hand, a fragmented movie industry anxiously turned out quickly made, poor quality blaxploitation films, which, according to cultural commentators like Crouch, "were obnoxious, vulgar and crude."[13] Although the critic cited no specific films, the following movies were playing in theaters at the time: *Shaft, Superfly, Slaughter, The Legend of Nigger Charley* (all in 1972), and *Shaft in Africa, Superfly T.N.T, Cleopatra Jones, Coffy, Trick Baby,* and *The Mack* (all in 1973). *New York Times* commentator Clayton Riley seconded his colleague's opinions, noting that the characters in these films "'the cowboys and the sleuths, the dope traffic aristocrats and empty-headed women, the colored Keystone Cops' are products of the same Hollywood minds that made millions of dollars while excluding Blacks from the industry. Now they've discovered a latter-day vein of gold to rip off. That's not surprising. The help they are getting from Black film artists is."[14] On the other hand, as *Encore* pointed out, the Academy of Motion Picture Arts and Sciences looked at black-themed films from a wider perspective by championing three notable movies that collectively garnered eleven Oscar nominations. *Sounder* was considered for the Best Picture and Best Adapted Screenplay; its stars Paul Winfield and Cicely Tyson, along with Diana Ross (*Lady Sings the Blues),* for Best Acting. The Billie Holiday biopic also received nominations for Best Original Screenplay, Best Art-Set Decoration; Best Costume Design; and Best Scoring. Still further, there was a Best Documentary nomination for Warner Brothers' *Malcolm X.* Clearly, African-Americans had begun making breakthroughs in a range of new cinematic areas. Not surprisingly, however, given the times, black artists lost out in every category, and as *Encore* reminded us, "everyone in and outside the industry settled back to see what would happen next."[15]

This much we did know. A badly shaken Hollywood still dominated the movie business. But radical changes had occurred. For example, the late 1960s witnessed The Motion Picture Production Code being replaced by a ratings system. The new censorship policies resulted in such independent movies as Melvin Van Peebles' provocative *Sweet Sweetback's Baadasssss Song* (1971), "the first American film in the black idiom made entirely outside the white power structure's control";[16] and Gerard Damiano's sexually explicit hit, *Deep Throat* (1972). In the minds of many Americans, not only did no one know which movie was truly a "pornographic film," but also the public worried aloud about what was happening to the nation's values. In addition, and against the backdrop of an anti-colonial uprising worldwide, popular ethnic films showcased liberal views both on slavery and the Reconstruction era, as well as underscoring racial injustice in American cities North and South. These same films also emphasized black rage, provided racial exposés, created unfamiliar characters, added explosive idiomatic language, and inspired us with new musical soundtracks. Understandably, artists like Van Peebles's son Mario who embraced these positions but disagreed with his more conservative colleagues, called these productions "Black Soul films," not blaxploitation movies.

Meanwhile, a nostalgia craze had swept the nation. A television channel like Turner Classic Movies promised Americans that the past would never become the past. The general population delighted in the fact it could forever watch their favorite films on the small screen in their living rooms, no matter how racially inappropriate such movies might be. All that was needed, optimistic viewers believed, was a well-meaning host suitably contextualizing the films.

Many academics also remained unconcerned. Not for one moment did they think that those who sought pleasure, information, and inspiration from traditional movies were fools, victims, or automatons "mechanically delivered into passivity and conformity by the monolithic channels of the mass media and the culture industries."[17] Rather there were many contributing variables—e.g., sex, age, class, education, and status—that mediated between the films and us in what Marshall McCluhan described as "the medium is the message."

As for black audiences, while they certainly despised the by-now familiar film perversions, they almost from Hollywood's beginnings, so went the argument, had substituted their own "readings" to come up with alternative analyses that gave more satisfying connotations.[18] So let the films live long and prosper!

However, an increasingly vocal community grew outraged by the nostalgia craze. They felt the civil rights movement had been betrayed. After all, as B. J. Mason explained, the movies of the civil rights era built their myths and stereotypes from rebellious attacks on the first sixty years of motion picture history. In the film critic's words', "...the past is not quite dead;...it is alive and grinning at us from the dark balconies of our modern movie houses."[19] Professor William R. Grant went further, asserting, "The pervasive presence of stereotypes of Blacks in the culture industry at large and particularly in commercial film [and television] indicates that folk fallacies are not confined to bygone forms of entertainment [e.g., television; Turner Classic Movies]." He took aim at "The racist roots that influenced the popular imagination that created and supported vaudeville, burlesque, and the minstrel show" and argued these origins "have appeared, often thinly disguised, in the works of sociologist[s], historians, and folklorists. The fallacies embraced by the popular imagination about Blacks," he reasoned forcefully, "can be found in nearly every area of the culture industry."[20] The status quo had become Alice through the Looking Glass.

Thousands of miles away in Vermont, known in those days as the "whitest state in the union," a totally different world survived. For example, in 1969, when John Schlesinger's Oscar-winning, X-rated film *Midnight Cowboy* played at a local Burlington theater, *The Burlington Free Press* refused to say anything except that there was an X-rated movie in town. Rarely did a black film, let alone a blaxploitation movie, appear anywhere in the state, mainly I suspect because none of the exhibitors wanted to attract the "wrong type" of people into their theaters. And if you wanted to keep abreast of the radical black film experience, you often had to go outside of Vermont's borders.

As for the open-minded UVM English Department that had recently hired me, the only departmental major a student could have was in English literature. American literature proved to be a second-class citizen for the moment. Writing was considered our sole responsibility college-wide, and those required courses were taught almost exclusively by marginalized part-timers, appointed without benefits on an annual basis. Except for audio-visual films, the only mainstream movies on campus appeared in a single course once taught in the controversial Department of Communication. Regarding the English Department's two major rebels—a wonderful white Southern instructor named Mary Jane Dickerson who was leading an effort to introduce black literature into the college, and yours truly who was lobbying for mass media literacy and film courses—neither one met with much success at first. Vermont schools remained adamant that movies and black literature were not only trivial disciplines, but also their language and narratives and formats were inappropriate for decent educational programs.

My favorite anecdote for the times relates to Van Peebles' *Sweet Sweetback's Baadasssss Song*. Considered a milestone in black film history, the narrative tells of a young boy, nicknamed Sweetback, who grows up in a Los Angeles brothel. One evening, the now mature and widely admired "stud" sees a black man unmercifully beaten by two white cops. Unable to control his outrage, Sweetback brutally murders the policemen. The remainder of the movie follows the police as they attempt to capture the fugitive, who eventually escapes over the Mexican border. As the film ends, the following words appear on the screen: "Watch out. Watch out. A Baadasssss Nigger is coming back to collect some dues." According to the distinguished black scholar Lerone Bennett, "*Sweet Sweetback* is the story of the radicalization of a pimp."[21]

For me, this movie was one my students and I needed to see. I was teaching an "experimental' course entitled "The Black Man in Film." Keep in mind there were no DVDs, DVRs, or streaming, that not only was this a time when the only media possible for classroom use were badly mutilated film prints, but also our film budgets never exceeded $250 per course. One good 16mm print, even if such a print existed, wiped out the entire semester's funds. Thus we depended mainly on the local theaters for our seeing any contemporary film about the black experience.

The problem was how to get *Sweet Sweetback* to the Burlington area. As fortune allowed, near my home in South Burlington was Cinema 1 & 2, a now-defunct movie theater managed by Merrill Jarvis,[22] who along with his late wife Lucille and family eventually became my lifelong friends. One day, Merrill mentioned that the Van Peebles movie would be coming to the theater. For several weeks I waited, but no *Sweet Sweetback* appeared. Finally, I went to Merrill and asked what was going on. He told me that the distributors nationwide had bought the film, but had no intention of allocating it. They would just put it on the shelf and hope that the movie vanished from the public imagination.

Refusing to accept that policy, I rallied my students and their friends, hundreds in numbers, and we organized a phone campaign. For every minute Cinema 1 & 2 was open, we dialed in asking for information about when *Sweet Sweetback* would arrive at the theater. This campaign went on for roughly two weeks, and Merrill and his bosses found it almost impossible to run Cinema 1 & 2 effectively. Finally, a settlement was reached. If we stopped calling, the Boston distributors would release the film for circulation, but they made clear they had no intention of bringing it to any of their theaters.

The next challenge was to find a theater to screen the film. In downtown Burlington, on Bank Street, there existed a small mom and pop movie house called the *State Theatre*. By promising the owners that the University would guarantee them a sell-out audience for one showing of *Sweet Sweetback,* I succeeded in getting the exhibitors to rent the film. For several weeks prior to the special screening, posters appeared all over the campus explaining the situation and asking people to turn up at the *State Theatre*.

Finally, the big event arrived, and more that 600 ticket holders appeared at the movie house that had a seating capacity for about 400 patrons. Consequently, there were people sitting in the aisles, standing in the back and on the sides, all eagerly anticipating the showing of the film. To our utter amazement, the lights dim and we see flickering on the screen a "Slam-bang-thank you ma'am" porno film that ran for over fifteen minutes. It seems as if the owners were so grateful for the UVM turnout that they decided to reward us, free of charge, with another "porno" film they had in their possession. In other words, we got two "pornographic" movies for the price of one.

Once the "quickie" film finished, the Burlington Fire Department raided the Bank Street movie house, demanding that we strictly follow the *State Theatre*'s mandated seating capacity. It fell to me to decide who should stay and who should leave. [For the record, *Sweet Sweetback* became the most successful independent film of the day.] And to paraphrase the late, great Walter Cronkite, "That's the way it was when you wanted to see a black film in Burlington in 1971."

It is against the backdrop of this disaffection in the early seventies that *Exits and Entrances* emerges. In hindsight, the task remained clear-cut from the start. A white regulated American film industry, described briefly in the Preface, had established a commercial system that proved damaging politically, socially, economically, and culturally to its naïve constituency and was seriously in need of reform. But despite the revolutionary changes that had occurred since World War II, no meaningful industrial restructuring could take place unless America itself changed. And few critics were certain that such a change would sustain itself. No one doubted, however, that those who had the courage and talent to mutiny against Hollywood faced great risks and could jeopardize their careers. *Exits and Entrances* offers one version of that story.

These seven interviews reveal the trials facing innovators who took up the torch of rebellion in their struggle to free multi-cultured Americans from the misrepresentations of a prejudiced culture. Denied an adequate outlet for their stories, the actors fought back and found their voices. They won some battles; they lost some battles! The performers' memories suggest the difficulties faced, but credit no one strategy for working best in reforming the prejudices of the nation and the film industry. Moreover, the artists' careers dramatically remind us how risky it was to endorse alternative ideas occurring from within the black community itself. No monolithic black consensus existed then or ever. And, as we discover, the seven performers faced many unnerving disputes from within and without the black community.

Among the many questions interesting me in approaching these representative entertainers included the following: during the film revolt that occurred, what special role did these individuals perform in the revolutionary process? What had their experiences been so far? What assets did they have that the earlier film pioneers lacked? What set of problems did they face as they forged forward? What dangers did they encounter if they dared defy the system? Should they dwell on black pride, black achievements, and a black aesthetic; or on industrial barriers, racism, oppression, and persecution? How practical was it to rock the boat? What responsibility, if any, did they have to African-Americans other than to do their best work in their chosen profession?

The last question is particularly relevant but seldom asked. No one addressed it better than one of Hollywood's legendary stars, Bette Davis. "What do we owe anybody?" she asked. "Just what is our responsibility to the rest of the world?" Then responding to her rhetorical query, she snapped, "If our primary concern becomes the protection of every race, every creed instead of producing entertainment—there won't be any time to even make pictures."[23] In the end, Davis decided, "We always get it in the neck. We're treated like criminals no matter what. Nobody seems to realize we're not a philanthropic industry. Nobody ever thinks of us as people who have to earn a living."[24]

Taken collectively, the interviews in *Exits and Entrances* offer an alternative reading to popular historical accounts describing an appalling African-African film experience. Mae Mercer, Brock Peters, Jim Brown, Ivan Dixon, James Whitmore, William Marshall, and Ruby Dee never discount the disgust they felt working in a prejudiced film industry. Nor do they ignore the stained national history of lynchings, church burnings, police brutality, and official racism as it related to their work. Instead, the artists stress the tests faced and the defeats experienced, as well as the victories won on their watch. And they are not naïve. In interview after interview, they explain what yet remains to be done and the barriers still to be removed. If nothing else, therefore, *Exits and Entrances* hopefully proposes a balanced look at the black film experience, of triumphs as well as failures.

What connects these celebrities to each other? Just as in *Every Step a Struggle,* the personalities chosen for *Exits and Entrances* seem dissimilar. Except for the fact that all the interviewees were actors, little uniformity appeared in their make-up and their social backgrounds. Three of the seven individuals came from the New York City area. Brock Peters and Ivan Dixon were born in or near Harlem; James Whitmore was born in White Plains. The other personalities were far more distant from each other. Mae Mercer was born in Brattleboro, North Carolina; Jim Brown, St. Simons, Mississippi; William Marshall, Gary, Indiana; and Ruby Dee, Cleveland, Ohio. Yet the influences these players had on the black film experience range from performing and directing to writing and producing, not just with film, but also in television, stage and musical theater. Equally significant, as you will discover, they personify a particularly relevant moment in history, the history I experienced.

As the reader also will discover in these interviews, the performers each answered Bette Davis' doubts differently. They advocated no one-way to get the job done. They all made daunting choices, and these selections did not always turn out successfully. You may judge their decisions; I do not. These artists followed their moral consciousness; they reacted intellectually to the civil rights movement arising from their personal history. Once committed, they refused to be distracted from their goals. From their experiences, the actors realized change would be hard and long in coming. What mattered was that it would come, and they would be part of the process.

Once again, I remind my audience that *Exits and Entrances* acts as a recap of a bygone age. Times, circumstances, and settings were significantly different from the present. It was a racist era when strong-willed reformers faced intimidation, oppression, and isolation. Remember too that black employment in the film industry since the start had been minimal compared to the number of people seeking access. These actors lived in difficult economic, political, and cultural times. Thus these intrepid performers who spoke honestly to me in many cases braved the possibility of reprisals and unemployment.[25]

In looking back at the early 1970s, as the interviews unfolded, I was not alone in seeing movies as mystifying. Particularly alarming was the belief that the black film legacy remained largely an account of stereotypes and distortions. Americans knew Hollywood had grown popular portraying "blacks as lazy darkies, happy slaves, cannibals and brainless phalli-negative images."[26] The shame was that these spectators saw such viewpoints, according to one scholar, as "harmless entertainment."[27] And because "yesterday's movies" proved so pleasurable for millions of viewers, many careless viewers left their local movie theaters convinced that to be white was to be unquestionably good, but to be black was utterly evil."[28]

Such "harmless entertainment" corrupted the American imagination, primarily because the stereotypes appeared to be a national consensus. Before moving forward, therefore, we should define what we mean by "stereotyping." The gifted Richard Dyer speaks for many scholars: "The stereotype is taken to express a general agreement about a social group, as if the agreement arose before, and independently of, the stereotype. Yet for the most part it is *from* the stereotype that we get our ideas about social groups."[29] By failing to examine critically these typecasts, Professor Ellen Seiter cautions, "there is a danger of mistaking the PRESENCE of white, bourgeois values for the ABSENCE of stereotypes and, therefore, for mere truth and realistic representations."[30]

There is also the same danger of mistaking today's new minstrelsy for "truth and realistic representations." Skeptical readers who doubt the dangers of such stereotyping need only consult Harvard psychologist Alvin F. Poussaint's findings, which for close to four decades have deconstructed the harmful effects of media imagery and misrepresentation "on the young, disadvantaged and impressionable."[31] In his words, "Outside a few black sports heroes, movie characters and movie actors become the prime models for black youth to emulate." Furthermore, he insists, "There is a high correlation between concept of self and fantasy among black youth."[32]

One more observation on stereotyping merits attention before leaving the topic. Central to the research in *Exits and Entrances,* as well as to the manner in which intellectuals see film as art, is the way in which both humanists and social critics traditionally perceive the concept of stereotyping. That is, humanists use the term disapprovingly to distinguish one-dimensional, flat, and false characterizations from, as Seiter points out, "well-rounded, individual ones."[33] That mistake results in the false assumption that art and stereotypes are incompatible. Actually, they are not. Great novelists like Jonathan Swift, Charles Dickens, Mark Twain, and George Orwell often used stereotypes in their characterizations. The same is true of notable filmmakers like King Vidor, John Ford, Alfred Hitchcock, and Spike Lee. Social critics go even further in rejecting such elitist notions and argue instead that stereotyping is part of ALL forms of fiction. In essence, as Seiter maintains, the humanistic perspective is too naive: it oversimplifies "the relationship between culture and society by treating it as direct and unmediated."[34] Moreover, the humanistic approach frequently fails to gauge the relationship between the works produced and the society that produced them. Even so, as Ossie Davis once explained to me, the problem is not so much the stereotype but who uses it and how and why.

Changing misperceptions and their consequences resulting from such efforts proved vital to the celebrities in *Exits and Entrances.* They evidenced extensive knowledge about screen distortions and thus tried throughout their careers to counteract the repugnant results of such mockeries. As the reader soon realizes, many of the interviewees, like blacks elsewhere, approached reforms in ways that, as Bennett insists, were appropriate for post-Watts era

African-Americans. In his words, blacks needed "to redefine themselves not just in relation to white racial history, or black history reacting to white influence, but in ways that focus not on attacking whites or evolving new black stereotypes, but in positive images of black people independent of white influence."[35] Not everyone interviewed or people throughout the nation agreed with the noted commentator. As becomes evident midway through the discussions, different interviewees saw film reform differently. Even so, Bennett's argument shows up surprisingly in Ivan Dixon's progressive cult film *The Spook Who Sat by The Door* (1973).[36]

Exposing why insufferable stereotypes made it impossible for Americans to reach the American Dream[37] turned out to be only one of our celebrities' priorities. Artists like Mercer, Peters, Brown, Dixon, Whitmore, Jones, Marshall, and Dee did not preoccupy themselves just with revisiting and revising Hollywood's racist film traditions; rather, they saw the times as an opportunity not only to tell their own black film narratives, but also to discuss the intellectual challenges of their profession. Thus in the works in which these artists appear and produce, audiences see stories about both black history and America itself.

That universal emphasis gave birth to a new perspective for African-American entertainers. From the post-World War II era forward, black performers fought for the freedom to be actors, not just black entertainers, and to access all their profession's benefits and challenges. They fought for a voice, an outlet to express their ideas and experiences in a post-colonial world. Not all their dreams may have been realized, but at the very least, they put the industry on notice that times were a changing. Particularly important and frequently overlooked are the outlooks they provided for black America emotionally. By opening doors, they taught their audiences anything was possible for African-Americans. With each breakthrough, the artists encouraged their viewers not to quit. As described in *Exits and Entrances*, therefore, these seven performers played a significant role in leading the march to today's multi-talented American film community.

To appreciate the steps they took and realize the risks they faced, let us briefly revisit the crucial post-World War II period and recall what hopes it presented minorities for reshaping the American film industry, when and why these possibilities materialized, what drawbacks limited change, and the era's relevance not only to black artists but also to me. The world was so much different fifty years ago than it is now. I especially want you to see how dissimilar I was from the performers I met. To paraphrase our sixteenth president, "If we know where we came from, we could tell how far we have come."

We begin by glimpsing back at our culture during the mid-1940s. Next, the narrative explores how those post-war times presented problems not only in studying black film history, but also in studying film in higher education. The text then introduces several influences on *Exits and Entrances* downplayed in *Every Step a Struggle*: the emergence of Television, the effects of a black pride movement on industrial reforms, and the ties between black music and African-American film history.

Once more I remind the reader, this book does not seek to replace other, more informed studies. I have neither the time, nor the space, nor the expertise to do more than rapidly reconsider the post-World War II era and its consequences for the black film experience. Any other ambitions go beyond the range of this undertaking.

I

The myth is that revolution in the black film experience took hold during the mid-sixties. It is a view I understand but do not share. My reservation is not so much about who is right, but which approach works best for the project at hand. Different contexts produce different priorities. For my purposes, the practical starting point for *Exits and Entrances* is in the days leading up to the end of World War II. It was a time when conflicts and pressures produced remarkable opportunities for breaking down racial barriers as well as offering new hope to marginalized artists. As a result, the mid-forties seemed ripe not only for democratic reform, but also to begin dreaming of things that never were.

America was changing. It had been decades since Southern blacks had left the rural South for industrial cities throughout the country. "From the moment the first migrants set foot in the North during World War I," Pulitzer-Prize winning author Isabel Wilkerson writes, "scholars began weighing in on the motivations of people...[as to] whether it was the pull of the North or the push of the South, whether they were driven by economics or by injustice and persecution, whether changes in cotton production started the Migration or merely hastened what was already under way, and whether the Migration would end, as some wrongly anticipated, with World War I."[38] Many black migrants never found what they were searching for, and by the publication of *Exits and Entrances* were moving back South. But in 1945, these same migrants had brought about many changes in urban America, changes that would have widespread importance for the black film experience. "So, too," Wilkerson continues, "came the people who might not have existed, or become who they did, had there been no Great Migration. People as diverse as James Baldwin and Michelle Obama, Miles Davis and Toni Morrison, Spike Lee and Denzel Washington, and anonymous teachers, store clerks, steelworkers, and physicians, were all products of the Great Migration. They were all children whose life chances were altered because a parent or grandparent had made the hard decision to leave."[39]That tribute is reinforced repeatedly in *Exits and Entrances*.

In the latter half of the 1940s, President Harry S. Truman took important first steps toward addressing America's ongoing racial struggle. Starting in 1945 with his special Committee on Civil Rights, the President seemed determined to eliminate "segregation, based on race, color, creed, or national origin, from American life." Three years later he proposed legislation aimed at ending lynching, discrimination in interstate transportation, and insuring voting rights for all Americans. That same year, by executive order, he established fair-employment practices throughout the various branches of government, making merit and fitness the only qualifications for employment or advancement.[40] In another decision on July 26th, Truman signed Executive Order 9981, which ended segregation in the United States armed forces.[41] America appeared different. Hollywood appeared ready to follow.

It may be worth pausing for a moment to reflect on the importance of dates and to understand the complexity of individuals, on what some intellectuals label "context dependent" moments in history. Why did someone like Truman, from the southern border state of Missouri and known for countless ethnic blunders and bigoted behavior, reverse himself and make two of the most positive racial decisions in the second part of the twentieth century—declaring for the State of Israel and desegregating the armed forces—at precisely the same time? Historians provide no definitive answer, but many scholars speculate the President's actions were linked to his 1948 re-election campaign. He needed both the Jewish and the African-American vote to stay in the White House. I mention this issue only to remind my readers how little we really know about the whys and wherefores of the world we inhabit. Reform comes in mysterious ways, nowhere more clearly than in the black film revolution.[42]

Complementing Truman's historic actions was the unexpected revolution surfacing in Hollywood. A white America, presumably ignorant and indifferent as to the ways its laws and traditions had oppressed blacks, was being transformed by mainstream movies. The change occurred because the war years had raised the nation's consciousness about social injustice and inequality. Now something had to be done about the social injustice. This dramatic mission infused not only the lives and careers of the artists interviewed in *Exits and Entrances*, but also my journey. Here, I only summarize what has been discussed in greater detail elsewhere.[43]

For over sixty-five years, intellectuals have debated whether what happened to mainstream movies from 1945 to the mid-seventies advanced our screen images of blacks or merely gave us a new minstrelsy. But African-Americans in the aftermath of World War II harbored no doubts. They were euphoric. A sense of brotherhood and common objectives permeated the land. People seemed organized to fight social inequality and intolerance. Long before the outcry for "Black power" in the mid-sixties, as historian Peniel E. Joseph insists, "there was a group of self-identified 'Black Power activists,' African American radicals [who came of age before and during the post-war years] such as Paul Robeson, Lorraine Hansberry, Malcolm X, Robert Williams, Gloria Richardson, and William Worthy...."[44] Returning servicemen like Ossie Davis and Harry Belafonte recall vividly how elated they felt having just defeated fascism abroad, particularly because of the Axis powers' links to white supremacy. These black romantics anticipated a new nation awaiting them, one "open, generous, and rewarding."[45]

Davis and Belafonte symbolized not only the African-American population in 1945, but also many aspects of the entertainment industry, including the Off-Broadway community. World War II had ignited what J. Fred MacDonald labeled "a new militancy and self-awareness among blacks...."[46] Where once fear and the threat of Jim Crow violence intimidated Negroes, now there was a new colored man. But the roots of the rebellious theatrical movement, James Earl Jones suggested, "were probably planted...in ground prepared in the thirties by such groups as the Federal Theatre Project and the Group Theatre to protest Broadway's commercialism and conventionality."[47] It was also a movement tied to the manipulation of socially conscious Americans by the American Communist Party. The connection is too complex to discuss here. Suffice to say, that there is considerable disagreement about whether the connection was one of practicality or purpose.

At the forefront of the post-World War II era stood many iconic African-American celebrities: e.g., Frederick Douglass O'Neal, Paul Robeson, Canada Lee, Katherine Dunham, Hazel Scott, and Lena Horne. Now, more than ever before, they fearlessly protested the racial barriers faced in their careers and everyday lives.[48] Here was a new Negro, brave, bold, and fearless. Years later, In *Guess Who's Coming to Dinner* (1967) Sidney Poitier (Dr. John Prentice) captured the dramatic transformation when he told his father (Roy Glenn, Jr.): "The difference between you and me is that you think of yourself as a colored man, and I think of myself as a man."[49]

From these ranks emerged most of the artists interviewed in *Exits and Entrances*. Ossie Davis, Ruby Dee, Ivan Dixon, Brock Peters, and William Marshall became familiar faces over the next two decades, and from their efforts on stage, screen and television came a more supportive crossover audience and a greater industry appreciation of their talents. Jim Brown and Mae Mercer would take a different route. But collectively, these performers, admittedly with acknowledged differences, did for their times what Nelson George explains artists like Halle Berry, Cuba Gooding Jr., Samuel L. Jackson, Wesley Snipes, Queen Latifah, Ice Cube, Regina King, and Nia Long are doing for today's generations.[50] The era became, as Gerald Early stated, "the age of the cultural crossover, a time when African American writers, performing artists, and athletes cut high profiles in mainstream public life."[51]

But as life teaches, perception and reality are not the same. While Hollywood proved to be a prime target for reform, the freedom road took many ironic twists and turns.[52]

In the early days of 1947, no one in the film capital sensed that the revival of Europe's domestic movie industries, the labor strikes in the motion picture business, the resurrected pre-World War II Congressional witch-hunts, the move to the suburbs, and America's shifting approaches toward relaxation would have so many momentous outcomes for either the world's wealthiest and most powerful movie industry, or for the black film experience. Hollywood's facility to "rise again" despite the fiscal difficulties triggered by the Depression and World War II made its filmmakers overconfident about their triumphs and naive about their future. After all, Hollywood films had recorded their biggest grosses in 1946, and the industry was doing "socko" business delivering its film libraries to the newly reopened European and Asian markets.

Then disaster struck the presumed indestructible Hollywood system. During the summer of 1948, after decades of unsuccessful legal battles, the government finally drove a dagger into the heart of the film industry's oligopolistic heart. The eight chief corporations were ordered by the federal courts to stop specific unlawful practices in nine commercial areas. Known as the "Paramount Decree," this antitrust decision wrecked the industry's vertical system and forced the film business to become more egalitarian in production, distribution, and exhibition.

The immediate impact of the Paramount antitrust case struck every level of the industry. Not only were there sharp declines in employment and a precipitous drop in production, but also expensive film formulas got shelved and low-budget dramas became fashionable. In addition, many people in the industry took significant pay cuts, and studios began shedding their stable of stars, producers, directors, and screenwriters. This downsizing immediately put a number of the "B"-production companies out of business, with more to follow in the 1950s. These steps ironically provided a more level working field for black entertainers previously marginalized in the once exclusive white film factories.

Hollywood's woes mounted further in 1948. The United States Supreme Court felt that the lower courts had not gone far enough in breaking up the oligopolistic Hollywood structure. Now, the Court demanded that ownership of theaters be taken out of the hands of the studios. The "Separation Decree" resulted in the rise of new theater chains, stars making deals with independent producers and the revamped production companies. Within a decade, all of the defendants of the Paramount antitrust case (with the exception of Warner Brothers) had undergone major changes in management. The key to the future success of the big film companies was now in distribution rather than in production. Every American film faced stiff competition with every other movie released for screen time. That dramatic change resulted in the movies becoming even more central in reshaping America's changing consciousness of black life and history.

United Artists became the role model for the new era. It alone of the eight important firms proved immune to the legal attacks on Hollywood. Why? Because the studio lacked it's competitors' draining organizational structure. While other companies tried to cut their huge overheads, the independent company continued its film-by-film operations. It warmed quickly to the modern "package deals," and by the 1950s became the prototype of the new Hollywood.

True to the cliché that one person's loss is another person's gain, the economic benefits for the still marginalized black artists proved considerable, and these openings did not stop just with fresh employment prospects. The area of film content also proved ripe for giving blacks a fresh voice. Post-World War II audiences wanted more complex and topical movie formulas than in the past. Hollywood proved responsive, particularly when it came to portraying racial issues. For example, westerns like *Duel in the Sun, My Darling Clementine* (both In 1946), *Fort Apache, Red River* (both in 1948), *She Wore a Yellow Ribbon* (1949), *The Gunfighter*, and *Broken Arrow*, (both in 1950), and *Shane* (1953) took on "Adult" themes of racism, moral ambiguity, and the questioning of authority. Other film formulas followed suit. And in the changeover, as is shown in the interviews, emerged not only a new interpretation of black history but also of the black contribution to the building of America.

The comeback of foreign films in America also opened doors for black filmmakers. Over the next decade, movies from Sweden,

France, England, Japan, and India proved more thoughtful and enjoyable than many standard Hollywood productions. But nowhere was the overseas influence greater than in the films from Italy. As a result of the nation's tragic experiences in World War II, Italian filmmakers had dumped their once popular escapist movies and substituted them with "humanistic films that examined the despair and suffering of ordinary individuals." Labeling their post-war movies "Neo-realism," the Italian filmmakers focused on real events and used documentary techniques.[53]

Prompted by economic, social, and political matters, as well as from the growing influx of foreign films on American screens, Hollywood in the mid-to-late-1940s favored directors who used documentary film techniques in their cost-effective moving pictures. A new film protocol emerged: e.g., smaller casts, location shooting, and socially conscious themes. In addition, a number of "new" directors—e.g., Jules Dassin, Edward Dmytryk, Elia Kazan, Joseph Losey, Robert Rossen, Don Siegel, and Fred Zinnemann infused their "problem" films with a psychological twist that altered the traditional acting styles of Hollywood performers. Two of the most prominent "problem" film topics of the post-war period were anti-Semitism—e.g. *Till the End of Time* (1946), *Crossfire, Gentleman's Agreement* (both in 1947)—and race relations—*Pinky, Home of the Brave, Lost Boundaries, Intruder in the Dust* (all in 1949), and *No Way Out* (1950).

Today, these consciousness-raising "problem" films appear to many viewers passé and unacceptable, mainly because they put the focus on well-intentioned whites and minimize the role of alienated blacks. Dr. Poussaint, for example, felt such films "purported to show the black man's plight; but they had a white-man's burden tone that stopped far short of advocating integration and equality between the races."[54] Film critic Richard Schickel even raises the possibility that these 1949 socially conscious movies destroyed what remained of the black independent film movement."[55] That certainly was not the verdict in the late forties. These notable narratives, as *New York Times* critic Vincent Canby explained, "served notice that blacks existed as something more than happy cotton pickers...maids, chauffeurs and handymen."[56] J. Fred MacDonald concurred: "After decades of negative stereotyping of minorities, Hollywood motion pictures became persuasive vehicles for disseminating ideas of racial equality and the end of discrimination."[57] Just as mystifying to the nation's consciousness was a growing awareness that everything we had been taught about American core values now seemed questionable.[58]

Perceptions about American culture changed in other ways as well. "The difference between the Thirties and the post-war period in respect of films about American social problems," as film historian Basil Wright observes, "was, in broad terms, the difference between concentration and diffusion."[59] Motion pictures reconsidered their narrow filmic focus of a particular place or a specific era. The post-war films expanded their criticisms to American culture and to institutional flaws. These revolutionary on-location dramas, with their pointed criticisms, also transformed film technology: e.g., new and lighter camera and sound equipment, novel recording techniques, and new panchromatic film stock that produced more dramatic black-and -white contrasts. Noted film scholars see these reforms as crucial to the rise of black-themed movies and a black film genre. But these attacks on American values and institutions did not go unnoticed by authority figures, and before long it produced unexpected consequences.

Center stage in these existential dramas was a film style known as "film noir." While controversy remains over what the concept actually means, Jon Tuska's description of its aims is helpful: "*Film Noir* is a darkling vision of the world, a view from the underside, born of fundamental disillusionment perhaps, but also invariably the result, no matter how timid, of a confrontation with nihilism."[60] However one defines film noir, the style itself flourished during the post-WWII period. In crime melodramas of the era, ordinary people, living in a moral vacuum and moving about in a hostile world symbolized by dark and lonely streets, cheated, lied, lusted after and murdered family and friends.

Many of these monuments to human corruption were directed by European exiles—e. g., William Dieterle, Fritz Lang, Otto Preminger, Robert Siodmak, and Billy Wilder—who entered movies during the German expressionist era and then abandoned their homelands when Hitler rose to power. The mixture of their own distrust and the low-key lighting used on location shooting intensified the impression that film noir captured the mood of city life in the postwar period. As the reader discovers these artists and their techniques in the interviews, one begins to gain a greater appreciations of the role played by the interviewees in revising the black film experience.

The destabilization of the film industry, the reshuffling of the filmmaking process, the widespread cynicism evident in film noir, the fear of an atomic apocalypse, the industry paranoia that the government would regulate American films, and the cold war, all contributed to renewed interest in film censorship. In 1945, the fervent anti-Communist Eric Johnson became head of the industry's self-censorship office and renamed it the Motion Picture Association of America (MPAA). Over the next two decades, the MPAA's code faced challenges from liberals and independent producers who felt that many of its religious, political, and sexual taboos were outdated. What made these challenges so menacing was that the Paramount Case had undermined the authority of the MPAA. So long as the studios owned the theater circuits, they not only made films that kept the theater owners happy, but also controlled, through the MPPA, what the theaters exhibited. The breakup of the vertical system, therefore, altered production policies and undermined the MPAA's authority over theaters.

This dramatic change provided exciting consequences for black filmmakers. As Americans fled their urban communities for rural happiness, thousands of city movie houses turned their attention to the current urban dwellers that crowded into the now abandoned districts. With each newly released film now competing with every other film for showing, urban exhibitors took a more favorable approach to the controversial adult movies attacking American society. Many of the most popular movies showing in urban local theaters took on unpopular causes and social injustice. The problems of ostracized people were one such cause.

At first, however, it looked as if economic problems and political threats would keep the status quo functioning throughout the late 1940s and 1950s. A major contributing factor was the blacklisting that resurfaced in the industry, beginning in the late 1940s and carrying through into the 1960s and beyond. Many screen personalities—e.g. Charles Chaplin, Jules Dassin, Paul Robeson, John Garfield, Lillian Hellman, Canada Lee, Larry Parks, Arthur Miller, and

Michael Wilson—either were forced out of the Hollywood system or, in the case of the screenwriters, used a "front" to get their work produced. Capitalizing on its power to harass, studio heads found it easier to intimidate disaffected people into following the "rules."

Let me focus on *The Jolson Story* and its star, Larry Parks, as a means of linking together the post-World War II period, the black film experience, America's changing racial consciousness, the national Inquisition, and my attitudes throughout *The Interviews*. In director/producer/writer Judy Chaikin's much-underrated documentary *Legacy of the Hollywood Blacklist*,[61] the filmmaker, through her interviews with the victims' wives and children, sets the stage for us. America found itself torn apart in the late 1940s. Progressives who had mobilized in the thirties especially found themselves under attack during the late forties. Shaped by the ethics recounted in John Steinbeck's *The Grapes of Wrath*, these idealists had tried to make the world better for the less privileged. But in 1947, the Federal inquisitors saw the progressive movement as a threat to America. Author James Gavin gives us the flavor of the times: "The Red Scare was on, fueled by fear of a superpower that seemed poised for world dominance. With a push of a button, the Soviets might unleash a nuclear catastrophe, destroying America and possibly the earth. Tension invaded almost every crevice of society, in what seemed like a black-and-white case of the bad guys out to get the good guys. Throughout America, the words "Commie," "pinko," and "Red" would become almost as widespread as "nigger.""[62]

The first post-war hearings took place in 1947, when specific Hollywood celebrities described as "unfriendly witnesses" refused to buckle under to Congressman Parnell Thomas' House Un-American Activities Committee. After the hearings proved too troubling, HUAC abruptly recessed to see just how much power the Committee had. Three years later, against the background of the Korean War, a paranoid America discovered Congress' frightening powers when the dissenters now called "The Hollywood Ten" began serving prison terms.[63]

One more piece of film history influences my upcoming anecdote: the status of jazz musicians now and then. Today, African Americans reign as preeminent jazz artists. But in the forties Hollywood saw things differently. As film historian Krin Gabbard recalls, black jazzmen remained ignored and at the mercy of the industry's discriminatory practices. While recognizing the vital role blacks played in the lives of white musicians, mainstream filmmakers remained puzzled about how to acknowledge the facts "without departing from the entrenched practice of denying black subjectivity."[64] Moreover, the scholar argues, "Blacks in jazz were not only excluded from Hollywood's highly optimistic stories of assimilation; they were invariably confined to stories of alcoholism, drug abuse, and self-destructive behavior."[65]

An alternative image appeared in 1946, when Columbia Pictures released director Alfred E. Green's enormously appealing motion picture *The Jolson Story*.[66] An idealized film biography based upon the fabled life and career of Al Jolson, the narrative showed the performer's rise from poverty to show business fame. Basic to Jolson's success, so the story suggests, was the influence both black jazz singers and the minstrel tradition had on Jolson's famous stage persona as a blackface legend. The Academy nominated the film's star Larry Parks for Best Actor, and William Demarest for Best Supporting Actor. The film also garnered nominations for Best Color Cinematography and for Best Film Editing, while winning the picture Oscars for Best Sound Recording and Best Musical Scoring. And recently, the Internet database *Allmovie* announced that it considered the feature film as "one of the finest biopics ever."[67]

Prominent film scholars also weigh in on the reputation of *The Jolson Story*. For example, George F. Custen stresses the importance of the 1946 production to the Biopic movie formula, which as a genre becomes, the reader will discover, essential to revising the black film experience. Here he explains that upon "the release of *The Jolson Story,* Al Jolson, unhappy in a bitter semi-retirement, experienced one last burst of fame as a result of renewed public interest in his performance: his record sales increased, his radio show received high ratings, and he headlined one last time, entertaining American troops in Korea before his death, from a heart attack, in 1950."[68] Both my wife and I recall vividly how often as teenagers our friends and we went to see this very popular movie.

The resourceful Gabbard adds another dimension to the film's importance. He reminds us this 1946 "white jazz biopic" was a pre-war formula that did not become popular until after *The Jolson*

Story "scored a sizable hit." The film inspired a sequel, *Jolson Sings Again* (1949), and may also have been responsible for the decision to film the lives of Tommy and Jimmy Dorsey in *The Fabulous Dorseys* (1947), also directed by Green.

After the abrupt demise of many big bands and the rise of the pop vocalists at the end of the 1940s, the cycle of white jazz biopics took an elegiac turn with most of the subsequent films building their appeal primarily on nostalgia."[69] But by the end of the fifties, explains the noted scholar, "when jazz had ceased to be a popular music and the nostalgia for swing had played itself out, Hollywood had no real use for white jazz biopics, especially as jazz became reconfigured as an art music practiced most expertly by African Americans." "Black biopics" replaced the white biopic: e.g., Billie Holiday (*Lady Sings the Blues,* 1972) and Charlie Parker (*Bird,* 1988). "In France, Bertrand Tavernier contributed to the cycle with *Round Midnight* (1986), in which a figure based on Bud Powell and Lester Young is assisted by a French admirer."[70]

That being true, today's authorities like Gabbard still take aim at the stereotypes found in *The Jolson Story*. He describes how the biopic distorted actual jazz history. In some cases, scenes including black performers were so situated that they could be edited, thereby allowing the censor to "protect" his audience from being offended by seeing white and black entertainers comingling on screen. Distinguished black jazzmen even found themselves reduced to eye-rolling stereotypes in menial jobs. This disgrace continued for decades. And as Gabbard points out in *The Jolson Story,* the stereotyping is particularly insulting because "whites are more accomplished than blacks in the performance of jazz.'" Even worse, Jolson is portrayed as a visionary who understood the appeal that 'jazz' could have for a large white audience."[71]

While I understand and appreciate these valid attacks on the 1946 production, I do not feel they reflect the film's total value. In 1946, this eleven year old and his younger sister Rose remained smitten with the movie. We were inspired by the music, admired the black musicians, and became familiar for the first time with jazz as an art form. When the sequel appeared three years later, our sainted mother allowed us to cut school, prepared sandwiches for us, and sent us off to see Jolson make a live appearance on stage to promote his new film. To this day, we delight in hearing Jolson's recordings of songs like *April Showers, Anniversary Song, Swanee, California, Here I Come,* and *Mammy.*

But *The Jolson Story* provides a much greater value for our narrative. It forever defines for me the grief and humiliations experienced generally by the victims of the blacklist, but felt personally by Larry Parks. He may well have been one of the most misunderstood and mistreated actors of his day.

In oversimplified terms, the story begins in 1941, when Columbia Pictures made Parks one of their run-of-the mill contract players. During the next five years, his career went nowhere, and he failed to impress anyone, appearing in undistinguished roles. But his breakthrough performance as Jolson finally turned the thirty-two year old actor into an overnight sensation. He seemed headed toward stardom until he and his liberal causes caught the attention of the House Un-American Activities Committee.

HUAC's earlier hearings had not gone well with the public, and the inquisitors needed to do better with their second attempt two years later. Enter California State Senator Jack B. Tenney, who chaired a local anti-Communist committee. He suggested Parks as an attention-grabbing HUAC witness. The naïve actor was summoned to appear before the Committee in 1951. Conflicted over what to do, Parks agreed to cooperate with HUAC on the promise he would not be forced to "name names." HUAC agreed, even telling the actor his testimony would be given in secret. Once before the microphone, however, Parks was told unless he became an informer, his career was over and he could face imprisonment. Frightened and helpless, begging for clemency, a sobbing Parks exclaimed, "Don't present me with a choice of either being in contempt of this Committee and going to jail, or forcing me to crawl through the mud and be an informer. I beg you not to force me to do this."[72] But the Committee was unrelenting. For Parks, his giving names provided no help to the actor. Both the Right and the Left turned on him. Liberals spurned him for cooperating with HUAC; Conservatives abandoned him because he was an unwilling witness.

Parks' starry-eyed adolescent admirers like me did not know what to make of the situation. Nevertheless, the Hollywood exile and *The Jolson Story* reappeared periodically in my life. For many white Americans, he had become the face of the Blacklisting era. For African-Americans it would be Paul Robeson.

Jump to 1970. Among my interests at UVM was being part of a group that entertained visiting celebrities who performed for The Lane Series, the University's outstanding cultural program. Word came that Larry Parks and his wife Betty Garrett would be coming to town in a road company production of Neil Simon's *Plaza Suite* on October 16th. Knowing of my feelings for the once-blacklisted actor, the Lane Series director asked my wife Sheila and myself if we would host a late night dinner for the cast and crew.

You can imagine how excited I was. We left the performance after the second act and hurried home to finalize the preparations. Soon our company arrived. But having limited resources, we hired no caterers to run the affair. So I spent all my time bartending and rarely spoke to anyone. My bride saw all this, and talked to Parks. Suddenly, I felt a tap on my shoulder, and heard Larry say to me, "Let's go for a walk, Frank." We stayed away from the house for almost two hours.

If you read Parks' life story, you'll hear details about how successful his California real estate deals were, how he managed to stake out a career in other aspects of show business, and even make an occasional film before he died in 1975. But I know differently. [Betty Garrett seventeen years later recalled the times much the same way.[73]] That memorable night in 1970, he appeared to me a beaten man, who had been ignored and insulted by friends and neighbors. He told me about the humiliations he had faced, and the suffering he had experienced, when he became a show business outcast nineteen years earlier. Those two hours remain with me when remembering the fifties and the lives of the celebrities interviewed in *Exits and Entrances*.

As for the fate of black entertainers, the story is well summarized in a 1998 documentary, *Scandalize My Name: Stories from the Blacklist*.[74] Host Morgan Freeman recollects the Red Scare during the Cold War and its shattering effects. Black entertainers had just begun to be taken seriously, he tells us, "and any outspokenness during the period was seen as the work of communist agitators." Among the African-American performers protesting against social injustice and fighting for Negro rights but seen as "red devils" by a fearful nation, were Paul Robeson, Frederick Douglass O'Neal, Ossie Davis, Robert Earl Jones, Brock Peters, and Canada Lee.[75] They lost jobs, friends rejected them, and the causes they believed in were slandered. But as you read throughout *Exits and Entrances*, you see how these horrible, unforgettable experiences in the fifties produced in the artists courage, built strong loyalties, and gave them the tools and techniques to make differences in the black film revolution.

In essence, the post-World War II era was a time when Americans remained divided over what to do about its controversial film industry. That discontent also existed in Hollywood itself. Uncertainty, self-doubt, and risk-taking engulfed the studios, the actors, and the audience. It was an historical moment, which we may or may not yet have figured out. But this much should be obvious. The times affected not only those who lived through them, but also many generations afterwards. It was the nation's perception of the past that shaped history and broke down racial obstacles. The revolutionary social, cultural, and political forces that arose during the post-WWII era to the early seventies provided countless opportunities not only for change, but also for economic and artistic mobility. The personalities represented in *Exits and Entrances* saw their chances and made the most of them.

II

Racial reform in Postwar Hollywood benefitted from another unexpected body blow to the movie industry by the end of the forties. A new medium toppled film's dominance in the entertainment world. The first coast-to-coast television broadcasts quickly turned many people away from the movie theaters and kept them in their living rooms. Why pay for entertainment when you could get it free? As the number of TV sets increased, the number of purchased movie tickets decreased.

And as more and more eyes focused on the exciting invention, the toy's content embraced what appeared to be an implicit civil rights agenda. American families witnessed a different image of black America than in the past. Unlike the movies, TV's need for immediacy and its role in shaping public opinion suggested a shift from Jim Crow ideas to positive black images that resulted in selling commercial products. Sponsors, the lifeblood of the new medium, put profit not propaganda as their goal. As long as TV producers made their entertainment lucrative to the advertisers' sales, opposition to breaking down herefore racial taboos remained muted. As *New York Times* reporter Brent Staples explained, "Advertisers, who must create the world anew every day, have to keep close tabs on changing social and cultural realities." The bottom line, he pointed out, was, "The industry began to normalize images of black affluence in response to the civil rights revolution, and embraced those images as it became clear that they were good for selling breakfast cereal and mutual funds, too."[76]

Television's early decades proved both inspiring and upsetting for many African-Americans, mainly because of the programs and commercials delivering a new sense of pride and inspiration while at the same time reminding its diverse audiences how difficult change was for the nation. As MacDonald summarized the era, it proved to be "a history of great talents, achievements, and anticipations. It is also a history of disappointments, prejudices, and failures within the video industry and American society. Ultimately, however, it is the story of a promise never fully kept—a promise whose fullest dimensions perhaps were never totally realizable."[77] The final chapter, however, has not been written on those bygone times.

The details of these revolutionary and complex events go beyond the focus of this study, and are far better covered by media scholars alluded to in the pages that follow. Here we need only glimpse at general impressions about television during the its first two decades as they impacted on the conversations in *Exits and Entrances*. These were the days that provided the road map to the revolutionary changes to come.

In oversimplified terms, the new medium proved helpful in contrasting the past with the present. Television's first contact with the public gave notice that while the up-and-coming novelty was not only birthed from the same roots as film, it also took its content and entertainers from the similar sources: e.g., vaudeville, burlesque, the stage, and radio. Now, however, the source material appeared transformed. Instead of being targeted at traditional, segregated groups, the producers aimed their material at "cross-over" audiences. The more people who watched the program, the more potential benefits for the show's sponsors. Intentionally or not, the new medium presented itself as "color-blind." MacDonald effectively summarized the moment, describing how in the late 1940s and early 1950s, the toy turned ravenous in its quest for talent, and thus discounted many Jim Crow practices. To a white-conditioned society accustomed to see, to think, and to behave white, the number of black performers in a variety of roles influencing public opinion on local and network programs proved both striking and startling. Even the usually vigilant *Ebony* magazine told its readers in 1950 "that television offered better roles for blacks than any other medium.... the appearance of numerous Afro-Americans on TV was a "sure sign that television is free of racial barriers."[78] Fresh images of African-Americans appeared periodically in heretofore-different occupations than in the past: doctors, lawyers, judges, nurses, and teachers. Equally important, popular variety talk show hosts like Steve Allen, Jackie Gleason, and Ed Sullivan campaigned for blacks appearing regularly on the new medium.[79]

Center stage in the early TV shows of the post-World War II era was comedy. For many black entertainers, the TV work proved useful and welcome. Limited in comparison to the employment given white actors and set in stories not addressing exclusively black issues, the opportunities nonetheless were a step up from opportunities in the movie business.

Early TV audiences came to expect African-Americans artists performing alongside white actors in everyday situations and comedy sketches. On one hand, the changes motivated black audiences. The more they saw continuous images of themselves, the more they believed a new era was dawning. The changes in roles and storylines gave many black artists hope. On the other hand, a culturally diverse nation, slow to embrace change, did not take positively to the shifting screen content or the frequent upbeat black images so different from the Jim Crow customs rooted in America's collective memories and reinforced for a half century by traditional entertainment.

More to the point, no evidence existed that the innovative

changes were always good for business. Nor did any consensus emerge on what for black America constituted positive images or trends. For example, distinguished film and TV historian Donald Bogle wondered what was so positive about "watching black female mammies fuss over their white employers on television (e.g., *Beulah)* or consuming television reruns of 1930s' Shirley Temple films (e.g., *The Littlest Rebel)* in which Bill "Bojangles" Robinson played an Uncle Tom character happily tap dancing his way through slavery alongside the young white moppet (Temple), who owned him."[80] Bogle was not alone in his reservations.

As always, the problem centered on raising audience awareness about the impact of racial images on naïve, vulnerable, and impressionable viewers, while not at the same time hurting black performers' jobs. Thus if one group attacked specific ethnic routines on a comedy show as demeaning and harmful, another group dismissed the criticism on the grounds that canceling the show drove down black employment and missed the point of comedy in general.[81]

Exits and Entrances offers recollections of what those times were like. And as actor Dorien Wilson testifies, "incredible people" like Ruby Dee, Ossie Davis, Sidney Poitier, and Harry Belafonte in their TV careers during the fifties and sixties paved the way for the generations that followed. Other celebrities credit black performers like William Marshall, Lena Horne, Ethel Waters, Nat King Cole, Louise Beavers, Hattie McDaniel, and Paul Robeson for instilling a sense of pride in the fact that African-Americans were represented in the birth and evolution of Television. "Without them," actor Dorien Wilson affirms, "we would not be here. Their ability to endure the hard knocks and the countless struggles made it possible for me to be where I am.[82]

Anyone who believes that America's racist institutions stood idly by as the liberals stormed the airways with their bleeding heart views should seek immediate medical assistance. The Establishment resorted to blacklists, program cancelations, boycotts, bigoted phone and mail campaigns, and numerous dismissals. Particularly damaging, and to be discussed later, the intellectual establishment denigrated Television as an art form, academics foolishly overlooked opportunities to influence the fledgling medium, and

Americans rashly believed "the boob tube" posed a great danger to the nation's mental stability. True, there was a new deal but the deck was still stacked.

Revisionist images and new sources of employment, however, were not the only or the main benefits Television offered the African-American community. The most important strides moving reform forward may well have come from TV's distinctive characteristics and the perceived danger the invention posed to the film business. In almost every instance, blacks participated in the process and evolution of the new medium. Simply stated, the small box provided a training ground for new writers, directors, musicians, and performers. Alternative methods of storytelling emerged, requiring different aesthetic techniques. These methods proved less costly than the production expenses facing filmmakers. As the novelty of these changes won broad audience support, the small screen put considerable economic pressure on the movie industry.

Declining audiences, the re-emergence of national cinemas, overseas tariffs and quotas, government anti-Communist investigations, antitrust litigation, increasing production costs, and shrinking profits had the once mighty Hollywood on the verge of a complete breakdown. Added to all these problems was the rapidly increasing number of TV sets in American homes. Within two years [1953], the new medium would become the number one form of popular entertainment in America.[83]

As the battle of the small screen versus the big screen grew, cultural observers debated the benefits to black entertainers. B.J. Mason felt "Sagging budgets and high production costs shook the old film colony to its roots and kept it from competing against new, independent filmmakers. Those who survived the widespread unemployment crisis were saved by television, occasional musicals and grade-B westerns, but almost all the beneficiaries were white. Black actors, directors, producers and writers had to make do, or do without; industry racism and skepticism permitted only one Sidney Poitier or one Harry Belafonte, or one Sammy Davis Jr. to make it—until 1970 when the experimental *Cotton Comes to Harlem* was released."[84] But other critics noted that the film industry fought back creatively; it had its own popular novelties—e.g., widescreens featuring blockbuster productions in glowing color, with hi-fidelity sound and a greater sense of visual depth. While each of these technological innovations had its own strengths and weaknesses, the strategy of making big films with stunning color, hi-fidelity sound, and greater depth illusion paid off at the box office. What made these expensive "runaway" films (co-national movies produced with multinational personnel outside the United States) especially attractive to American filmmakers is that they not only did well (commercially and aesthetically) at home, but also helped solve the problem of how to spend foreign revenues derived from overseas distribution but "frozen" in the European countries. In fact, the success of these productions led to an American "invasion" of overseas cinemas, resulting in the establishment of multinational film corporations, and a Hollywood stranglehold on the international financing of films.

As the reader finds in *Exits and Entrances*, the storytelling changes, the new roles emerging, the necessity for ongoing novelties, the use of big budgeted musicals, the emphasis on exotic locales, the interest in social problems, the emergence of new directors, writers, and actors, and the politics of the times intimately affected the seven performers interviewed.

By the mid-1960s, when television functioned as a major witness to the ongoing civil rights movement, the nation, the media, and black performers were aligned for dramatic shifts in the image of African-Americans both on small and large screens. In the South, for example, the depictions of racial battles between southern whites and blacks, the bombings of Negro churches, Freedom Riders being beaten, civil rights activists being murdered, and black students being denied entrance to schools and universities added to a growing nationwide recognition that the country could not conduct its affairs as usual. But the growing sympathy for blacks did not emerge from the racial injustice housed alone in the South. Northerners contributed mightily to the national disgrace. Housing discrimination, defacto segregation in the schools, crime and brutality in urban ghettoes, and inner-city race riots proved equally alarming as the media forced these disturbing images and events into American living rooms around dinner hour.

In essence, the revolutionary black film experience that gained national awareness by the end of the decade emerged from the experiences of a liberal America forged by the changes increasingly projected by movie and television screens that began appearing at the end of World War II. As readers search through the testimony of seven actors who made a difference during those transitional years from 1945 to 1974, they need to be aware of the challenges these artists faced and overcame. Ruby Dee speaks for many artists of her generation, when she explains that she and Ossie Davis, her husband, "were formed by that kind of immature behavior. I call it a country struggling to be intelligent, compassionate, sharing, and struggling for identity, struggling for what it was to become. That became the task. We recognized the task of helping America become what it should become."[85]

III

This Introduction thus far has troubled itself with preparing the reader to interpret and to "experience" the conversations as they occurred over forty years ago. Like diaries and journals frequently used by historians, these interviews supply a snapshot on the past. But to better grasp the benefits from the seven discussions, the reader gains from being aware of the different critical standards used then and now, the advantages of hindsight, and the alternative approaches to material discussed elsewhere. Acknowledging that *The Interviews* shun a targeted audience and recognizing the challenge distance places on the general reader, I feel it defensible to review the years from the mid-forties to early 1970s. In part, this analysis reflects my feelings that the events, the issues, the personalities, and the results remain a genuine, unending mystery.

We began the chapter by establishing the mood of the day when the interviews started, trying to recall not only clearly recognizable events, but also attempting to personalize the stark gap between my world and that of the people I was about to question. From there we moved to explaining how both the nation and African-Americans noticeably approached the post-WWII years differently from earlier times. The fall-off at the box-office resulted in socially conscious films, which began addressing the nation's racial problems and ideological flaws. These progressive attacks led to a political and industry-wide backlash that restructured the fifties and the sixties. The cerebral battles over who affected what, or what came first, or how accurate the reflections were, I gladly left to the passions of others.

Efforts were made to remind the reader of crucial events influencing black film history: e.g., the black migration from the south to the northern cities starting before and increasing after WWII, the psychological impact of the Allied victory over racism abroad and its consequences for American blacks during the cold war, as well as the postwar decline of the American film industry and its political, aesthetic, and cultural effects on the nation. These trials during the Truman and Eisenhower presidencies, as noted by critic Frank Kofsky, produced specific results: disaffiliation leads to confrontation, alienation leads to an attack on cold war society to the Civil Rights movement.[86]

The unnerving questions looming on the horizon related to just how long it would it take for African-Americans to be free, how long did the nation think this new generation of black citizens would sit patiently by, and if their patience wore thin, what were they going to do about it. Americans now began taking note of civil rights activists like Dr. Martin Luther King, Jr., Fannie Lou Hammer, and the Mississippi Freedom volunteers; and Americans worried non-violent protests might be replaced with militant positions advocated by Huey P. Newton, Malcolm X, H. Rap Brown, and Stokely Carmichael. "The daring and provocative rhetoric of activists like Malcolm X and Stokely Carmichael," explains Professor Peniel E. Joseph, "unleashed passionate debates and sparked enduring controversy over the very meaning of black identity, American citizenship, and the prospect of a social, political, and cultural revolution. Malcolm and Carmichael questioned the legitimacy of democratic institutions whose doors were closed off to African Americans." Pointing out these revolutionary voices began in the fifties," the scholar explained, "As their notoriety grew, both men publicly criticized presidential leadership in regard to domestic race relations, blasted America's participation in Vietnam, and linked struggles against Jim Crow in the United States with anticolonial movements that were raging throughout the world. In doing so, both of these Black Power icons helped to expand the boundaries of American democracy. Black Power activists, no less than their more celebrated civil rights counterparts, contributed to postwar America's transformed landscape."[87] Such actions further divided the country, while at the same time enflaming black anger and frightening the white population.

Experiencing these sweeping events tested people like Mae Mercer, Brock Peters, Jim Brown, Ivan Dixon, James Whitmore, William Marshall, and Ruby Dee. They needed to reconsider not only their identities as Americans, but also their obligations as artists. In the case of all but Whitmore, the African-American performer asked, "Am I a black actor first, and then an actor; or am I an actor first and foremost?"

Thus far, the narrative has focused more on the personalities interviewed than on me. Now, in the final section of the Introduction, we reflect on what I brought to the meetings. This emphasis allows me to highlight three historical matters not only useful to probing the conversations, but also for suggesting ongoing concerns associated with *The Interviews*. The three obligatory areas still to be addressed are the role African-American music plays both in the writing and reading of *Exits and Entrances*, the troubling negative attitudes toward popular culture in general, and black films in particular, and how being a white, Jewish educator affected my approach to the interviews. Each subject sheds light on the questions asked or omitted, the direction the interviews took or ignored, and the celebratory spirit of *Exits and Entrances* itself.

IV

Incredible as it may sound, I first came to see the relevance of black music to writing *Exits and Entrances* twenty years after the meetings had been completed. Prior to the early seventies, jazz and the blues appeared low down on my musical ladder. Except for watching occasional Biopics of Caucasian entertainers and big band musicals—e.g., Irving Rapper's *Rhapsody in Blue* (1945), Michael Curtis' *Night and Day* (1946), Alfred E. Green's three hits *The Jolson Story* (1946), *The Fabulous Dorseys* (1947), and *Jolson Sings Again* (1949), Anthony Mann's *The Glenn Miller Story* (1954), Valentine Davies' *The Benny Goodman Story* (1955), Charles Walters '*High Society* (1956), Don Weis' *The Gene Krupa Story*, and Melville Shavelson's *The Five Pen-*

nies (both in 1959)—I found nothing earth-shattering about black musical culture. I had no idea just how closely attached jazz was to the movies or how meaningful the music was to film artists around the world, not just in the civil rights era, but since the birth of the movies itself.

Why should I? Oblivious to Hollywood's racial discrimination against black musicians, growing up in a mainly white world, and persuaded by the mass media of the white jazzman's dominant position in the field, I remained content with the status quo. Only occasionally did I watch jam sessions in films like Harry King's *The Snows of Kilimanjaro* (1952), George Cukor's *A Star is Born* (1954), Alexander Mackendrick's *Sweet Smell of Success* (1957), and even Martin Ritt's *Paris Blues* (1961). Entertaining but hardly enlightening!

Also fueling my neglect was jazz's negative image. While knowledgeable listeners like Ralph Ellison identified black music with cabarets and dance halls,[88] people like me, as mentioned earlier, associated jazz and the blues with brothels, viciousness, illegal drugs, executions, and murder.[89] Not even the glaring links between celebrities like Cicely Tyson and Miles Davis, or Abbey Lincoln, Max Roach, and Ivan Dixon triggered any interest in discovering black music's importance or contribution to the African-American film experience.

In fairness, the reader needs to remember that although much has changed, much more needs to be done. Moreover, the interviews were arranged quickly and with no opportunities to study individual biographies. What follows, therefore, is a partial attempt to correct my major oversight for the reader and future generations.

Not everything in my careless parochialism proved trivial to *Exits and Entrances*. Similar to many white people growing up in Flatbush during the middle of the twentieth century, I gained a splendid but selective exposure to the nation's "major" songwriters, singers, and musicians. That introduction resulted chiefly from having spent much of my young life in the movie theaters from Broadway to Brooklyn, By the end of the fifties, when I married, left the borough, and moved to New Rochelle, I had seen almost every screen musical featuring the melodies of such virtuosos as Harold Arlen, the Gershwins, Cole Porter, Irving Berlin, Rodgers and Hammerstein, Rodgers and Hart, Jerome Kern, Benny Goodman, Glenn Miller, The Dorsey Brothers, Yip Harburg, Kay Kyser, Paul Whiteman and countless others too numerous to mention. No doubt I had also enjoyed the music of Duke Ellington, Cab Calloway, Louis Armstrong, Count Basie, and Fletcher Henderson, but such experiences hardly registered in my consciousness. Keep in mind these were also the days of Fred Astaire, Ginger Rogers, Gene Kelly, and Arthur Freed's immortal MGM musicals, featuring performers like Frank Sinatra, Judy Garland, Howard Keel, and Lena Horne. Not until the late sixties did it dawn on me the racial damage done to my psyche by radio, movies, and television. That is not to say I remained ignorant of black entertainers. It is to say I remained oblivious to their contributions.

Black musicians, however, never remained indifferent to the American songbook or to the movies' most popular music. Throughout the history of the twentieth century, the tunes of Tin Pan Alley became a mainstay with African-American musicians. This fact became clear to me as I collected hundreds and hundreds of their recordings. But I mistakenly assumed the uniqueness of African-American musicians resided in their interpretations of the nation's standards, not in the original songs and compositions imbedded in their history. That absurd misperception carried with me when the interviews took place.

Secondly, again indicative of my generation, I became a collector of vinyl recordings by my favorite artists, but those musicians appeared on records made by companies like Capitol, RCA, Verve, and Columbia; not Atlantic, Blue Note, Chess, Okeh, Perfect, Cadillac, Prestige, Elektox, Stinson, A&M, Harmony, and Vanguard. Occasionally, my sources exposed me to white jazz musicians and even a few black entertainers, but in those formative years my tastes ran to Broadway tunes, opera, and Irish music. (The latter interest resulted from the soundtracks in my favorite John Ford movies.) Not surprisingly, my college years began my love for folk singers such as Peter, Paul, and Mary, The Weavers, The Kingston Trio, Buffy St. Marie, Joan Baez, Bob Dylan, Woody Guthrie. Josh White, and Pete Seeger. Only in the nineties did I discover Nina Simone, Abbey Lincoln, Odetta, and Phil Ochs.

As I moved into the sixties and graduate school, the music of the civil rights movement and the anti-war songs took on great significance, with songs like "Blowin' in the Wind," "If I Had a Hammer," "I Wish I Knew How It Would Feel to Be Free," "The Times They are a Changing'," "This Land is Your Land," "Strange Fruit," and "We Shall Overcome." These freedom songs about social injustice blended seamlessly with my academic pursuits. By the time *The Interviews* got started, I was collecting Billie Holiday, Paul Robeson, and Ella Fitzgerald albums. Despite this progression and the way it enhanced my scholarly analyses, I did not transfer the relevance of the music either to the research or to the writing.

My epiphany occurred during the early nineties when I began writing *Every Step a Struggle*. Well, maybe it began a decade earlier while working with my friend Dr. John G. Jewett. As Dean and Associate Dean of UVM's College of Arts and Sciences, we discovered a mutual diversion cementing the bonds that have lasted over forty years. That pastime became music. John's passion for classical composers, along with his genius for musical hardware, led me to what would become a lifelong obsession both emotionally and therapeutically. Although I had always been a record collector, now I became obsessive in adding to my slender musical libraries. Increasing my hunger was the late and eccentric Lester Glassner, who supplied the stills for my young adult books. One of Lester's other jobs was working at Columbia Records. And for many years, he would send me each month the company's promotional records, many of which directed me to black music as well as to big band orchestras. In the decades that followed, my musical tastes broadened and lead me to an insatiable love for black music, jazz, and the blues.

Before describing how essential African-American music became to *The Interviews,* I offer several more of my failings, not the least of which is that on a scale of 1-10 my musical skills, knowledge, and judgment are a minus one. This is not false humility. Never having played an instrument, unable to carry a tune, ignorant when it comes to reading music, and hopeless when distinguishing a chord from a melody, I am the last person you want to consult on either black music or outstanding entertainers. What I am about to share with the reader, therefore, in no way should be construed as either informed criticism of black music or the artists themselves. If I once harbored such absurd intentions, John Gennari's *Blowin' Hot and Cold* disabused me of such ridiculous aims.

What I do suggest about the value of jazz and the blues to *Exits and Entrances* emerges from ongoing sentiments resulting from years of collecting black music recordings, reading critical writings, watching TV and film programs, going to live performances, and listening to the celebrated artists themselves. Each contact, in its own unique way, contributed strongly to the finished product. In fact, I would suggest that next to the desired intellectual stimulus provided by the interviews themselves, my untrained suggestions about black music might prove the book's extra prize.

Once aware of black music's place in the lives and history of African-Americans, I decided to complement this writing of *Exits and Entrances* with repeated listening sessions related to the topics being described. Why? First, as Murray made clear, of all the settings available to African-Americans in recounting their story—e.g., myths, comedy, history, and literature—"music does contain the most comprehensive rendering of the complexities of the American Negro experience. Whatever the reason, very few Negro writers (or painters, for example) rank in range and achievement beside musicians like Louis Armstrong, Scott Joplin, or even Charlie Parker, not to mention the great Kansas City stylists, and Duke Ellington."[90] Secondly, Wynton Marsalis justifies the jazz tradition's virtues this way: "Blues is the human element, tragic element that helps us overcome tragedy. Improvisation is the ego element. You get to play what you want to play. But Swing is about sacrifice. It's the most democratic of the elements. It forces you to consider that there are other things people want to say. It's about manners. Swing is about maintaining equilibrium and being in balance.... And maintaining balance no matter what happens."[91] Third, Gabbard points out, Jazz places a great premium on exhibition. In his words, "Especially for male jazz artists, the music provides a unique opportunity for sex and gender display. Part of what has made jazz so intriguing is the number of alternatives it has offered to conventional notions of masculinity and male sexuality."[92] Fourth, there are famed filmmaker Martin Scorsese's important observations. In his rich TV series *The Blues*, the director/producer insists that indispensible to studying black film history is an awareness of music. Exploring the subject with famed musicologist Alan Lomax, Scorsese observed, "Music was as essential to human speech and just as precious."[93]

And finally, President Obama reminds us, "Music is at the forefront of our social consciousness, challenging stereotypes, shaping our opinions about race and religion, death and disease, power and politics."[94] Why it took so long for me to figure this out is offset by the fact that so many people I know still don't get it, or even care about getting it.

Second, this musical legacy, widely and inexpensively available in the public arena, proves ideal for getting at the soul of the subject matter in *The Interviews*. The music adds to the words' emotional impact. It is what music does. It is particularly true of black music since the days of slavery. Unlike the American songbook, black music from spirituals to protest songs transmits an oral history of African-Americans. Moreover, as Murray counsels, Jazz is mainly "a blues tradition, a tradition of confrontation and improvisation—that is, to use [Constance] Rourke's word, of "resilience"—and is indigenous to the United States, along with the Yankee tradition and that of the backwoodsman."[95] I wish I had known this during the conversations in the 1970s. So much more could have been learned and so much precious time put to better use in my journey.

Sidestepping the ongoing linguistic debates about what is meant by terms like "jazz" and "blues," or the arguments over what role whites play in the history of black music, I rely on common parlance when discussing African-American composers and musicians. No one seems to have an answer to the problematic definitions, and *The Interviews* is hardly the venue for resolving the dispute. For my purposes, black music, magnificent as it is, functions in *Exits and Entrances* as one additional inroad in revealing the racial perversions and duplicities in the American Dream. By expressing the deepest emotions of African-Americans, the musicians provide the nation with courage and encouragement to end hundreds of years of segregation. The black entertainers voiced vocally what the book's celebrities expressed verbally.

Nowhere is this more clearly revealed than in Bill Guttentag and Dan Sturman's *Soundtrack for a Revolution,* a powerful TV documentary showing how the civil rights movement sustained itself through music.[96] While detailed information remains sparse in describing the ties between black music and performers like Jim Brown, James Whitmore, and William Marshall, almost everyone in post-war America watched the civil rights movement unfold on nightly television news programs. The newscasts made clear to blacks they were not alone in their struggles, and the reader should not ignore the inspiration and motivation that the images and marches and music had on the seven celebrities struggling in the motion picture industry. *Soundtrack for a Revolution* offers the opportunity to experience once more protest songs like "Wade in the Water," "Everybody Loves Freedom," "What Side are You On, Boy," "Reign Freedom," and "We Shall Overcome." Doing so contributes to a central theme in *Exits and Entrances,* a theme indebted to Rourke and Murray, that we are a multi-racial nation in search of freedom and dignity for all.

While tempted to display how much I have learned recently about the history of jazz in America, who are the legendary artists, and the rich material collected over the past two decades, all in the rationalization that it would be useful for the reader in going through *Exits and Entrances,* common sense trumps vanity. The narrative remains focused on placing the music with the words as they apply to the trailblazers' reflections on a bygone era. To that end and like my predecessors, I share my ideas gotten from critics, especially those who wrote about jazz and the blues. Thus, one finds throughout these pages references to Leonard Feather, Albert Murray, Marshall Stearns, Stanley Crouch, Gerald Early, John Gennari, Eric Porter, John Hammond, Nat Hentoff, Frank Kofsky, Krin Gabbard, Gary Giddins, Alyn Shipton, John F. Szwed, Ralph Ellison, Michael Ullman, and others.[97] In essence, my interest remains hooked on black music and thereby hopefully enhances the reader's experience with the seven interviewees, the sole heroes in the book.

To that end, and to illustrate my strategy, I suggest before leaving the Introduction readers familiarize themselves with black musical history between the mid-thirties and the late 1940s. Over this memorable fifteen-year period, one discovers not only the ties between music and ethnic politics, movies, and key themes in *Exits and Entrances,* but also the names of brilliant musicians who inspired a new generation of African-Americans to change black history. That is, during the Swing era of big band orchestras, record collecting became epidemic; the thirties also gave birth to jazz magazines, fan culture, and the development of jazz criticism.

These significant events, however, were overshadowed, as Professor Susman reminds us, "by the politics of race, and the politics of race were overshadowed by the rise of fascism and the onset of world war...." People got caught up in what the distinguished historian named the "culture of commitment."[98] By the end of World War II, great jazz musicians began addressing the issue of what it meant to be black. That investigation created problems for the public. *Time* reported, "Jazz has unhappily splintered into hostile camps, musically and racially. Lyrical and polished players are accused of 'playing white,' which means to pursue beauty before truth."[99] Almost vanished were the big band names like Woody Herman, Benny Goodman, Harry James and Benny Carter.[100] Among the last standing were Count Basie and Duke Ellington.

Replacing Swing was a new musical revolution called BeBop that emerged from after hour jam sessions spearheaded by Thelonious Monk, Dizzy Gillespie, and Kenny Clarke at Harlem's famed Minton's Playhouse.[101] The revolutionary music attempted, Frank Kofsky reminds us, "to liberate the black...[film] artist from the burdens of exploitation by white business [studios], nor could it for long prevent the inevitable copying of the style by those white [musicians], [filmmakers] for whom imitation was indeed the highest form of flattery."[102] This new music placed the individual rather than band center stage and cared more about performance than it did audience appreciation. Among the fresh names attracting attention during the early days of the post-war era were performers like Charlie Parker, Miles Davis, Bud Powell, Curly Russell and Max Roach. In the years to follow came the likes of Sonny Rollins, John Coltrane, Johnny Griffin, Charlie Rouse and Harold Land. They not only showcased their talent in an array of nightspots on New York's 52nd Street, but also provided fresh evidence of why black artists personified America's drug culture.[103]

Understanding that part of black history helps considerably in appreciating the tales recorded in *Exits and Entrances*. These musicians, with their revolutionary ideas, helped inspire not only the black community but also our fourteen celebrities. Together, the post-war African-Americans, consumed by an intense social purpose, lined the way in reforming the nation's stereotyped perceptions of black people.[104] They did not act monolithically, nor did they sit passively by and allow themselves to be controlled by powerful, conservative industry forces. Instead, the mass media proved to be a valuable psychological and inspirational source encouraging them to pursue their dreams.

V

Appreciating the nature of the black film revolution remained my primary purpose in reaching out to Mae Mercer, Brock Peters, Jim Brown, Ivan Dixon, James Whitmore, William Marshall, and Ruby Dee; but I also had a secondary purpose: defending the art of the film against its academic critics. That concealed agenda drives the questioning strategy used during the interviews. I not only desired to learn about the African-American film experience, but also I wanted to show how important black films were to us emotionally, intellectually, and culturally. Explaining why movies needed to be defended, and why I felt it my responsibility goes far beyond the scope of this project and is covered in greater detail elsewhere.[105] Here I intend only to suggest what teaching at a conservative New England university was like for a Young Turk a half century ago, and what baggage he carried with him throughout his long journey to publishing *The Interviews*.

In vastly oversimplified terms, even in mid-century America the argument between high and low culture was not novel. Thanks to historian Warren I. Susman, we realized that by the 1940s, nearly a century of distrust and disdain for mass communication, mass media, and the masses in general was prevalent. This attitude, despite the fact that our everyday personal experiences were shaping our perceptions of reality, was constant.[106]

Describe it as a fight between conservatives and progressives, or a debate between the old versus the new, the intellectual war against mass culture proved similar to many of the positions taken in Jonathan Swift's *The Battle of the Books*. Classically trained guardians of our cultural values dismissed out-of-hand the new technological products with their materialistic pleasures as a threat to society and its collective psyche. Such well-intentioned humanists indicted the mass media as a profit-motivated arrangement between administration and industry that not only preserved the status quo, but also deadened our emotions, debased our tastes, and programed us with dangerous misperceptions about our society. By encouraging a consumer-driven mentality, regimes presumably controlled nations and preserved power.

Such attitudes had gained widespread currency since the 1930s as a result of theories promulgated by European émigrés known as the Frankfurt School. Fleeing from fascism and passionately anti-Communist, critics like Theodor Adorno and Max Horkheimer based their social criticism of mass culture on their terrifying experiences with Hitler's Germany and Stalin's Russia. From their perspective, totalitarian states used popular culture to enslave the people. Later, these same intellectuals argued that McCarthyism also provided further evidence of the social control used by the American government and the mass media to corrupt democracy.

By the time I entered academia, these notions permeated higher education. Here is not the place to debate whether academics like Prof. David Jenemann are right when he argues that the members of the Frankfurt School are misunderstood,[107] or support Stanley Crouch's claims that the theories of the German émigrés are not only bogged down with "repulsive limitations," but also demonstrate the Europeans found America's values contemptible.[108] I certainly do not want to claim the assault against the mass culture had more to do with an older generation's academic insecurity than with the profession's intellectual arguments.

These assertions of vulgarity, force, and fanaticism served traditionalists well. Prior to modern times, high art epitomized the exact opposite of what the popular arts allegedly personified. The older order argued for standards, taste, judgment, and behavior determined by a cultural elite. The perception that everyday people passively massed together could credibly choose alternative and excellent social values manufactured by profit-minded cultural industries was seen by the Establishment as an abomination. Anyone extolling such heretical views was no less than a barbarian and a danger to society.

The irony of thinking that such consumer culture ideas represented my position continued throughout my career and up to the present time. Contrary to what my readers may believe, I never, as mentioned earlier, intended black studies to replace my traditional values or lifelong interests. Jazz and the blues, for example, did not remove classical music and opera and the American songbook from the world of music so dear to me. Black music added to, expanded my musical options. The same holds true for African-American film. As stated elsewhere, it has never been my intention to argue for a separatist culture, but rather to encourage through my work a multi-cultural world, a pluralistic society where *everyone* benefits and enjoys the best that civilization offers regardless of race. If the popular arts truly did what its classically trained detractors said it did, I would be just as contemptuous and outraged as its critics, and would willingly lead the fight against such a controlling and anarchistic "consumer culture."

Instead, from the fifties on, I maintained qualified respect and guarded admiration for a mass culture that enjoyed material possessions, devoted considerable time to popular entertainment, and found intellectual stimulation from the art of the film and television. Explaining my complex reasons now in this book goes beyond my obligation. Suffice to say, that throughout my journey I did not find the popular arts any more devious, tasteless, and painful than what I experienced in my formal education when foolish teachers misused, misinterpreted and misrepresented the lessons arising from classical learning. Not only is the justification in the eyes of the beholder, but also in the uses the individual makes of the arts.

Thanks to the scholarship of intellectuals like David Riesman, Dwight MacDonald, Arthur Schlesinger, and Harold Ross, I rarely dismiss moviegoers as "mass audiences." Rather, I agree with Ross who sees them as a "number of smaller, more specialized audiences.... [who instead of being] manipulated fight back, by refusing to 'understand,' by selective interpretation, by apathy."[109] Unless readers gain some familiarity with how my background influenced my purposes in this project, I fear my audience may misjudge my intentions in *Exits and Entrances*.

Imagine for the moment what my imprudent detractors back then assumed about a young Turk interested in black film history. What it was like for me at UVM in those early years I leave to the reader's imagination. Here let me reiterate briefly how I linked mass culture to African-American films.

These beliefs grew directly from my personal history, not from reading abstract theories or social science data. Differing with my more traditional elders, I believed the mass media to be a positive social force in my life. Everything my critics attributed to high art, I also ascribed to the movies. They distrusted the media. I embraced it. Clearly, the films and television programs I watched, especially after WWII, did not routinely defend the status quo, and in no way did they debase my intellectual skills or tools. Or so I believe! For example, my experiences with social problem films, film noir, and foreign movies informed and shaped my understandings of America's flaws and achievements. Films, radio, and television introduced me to a black history distorted, stolen, or lost in the public schools. More than mere escapism or harmless entertainment, the movies and television stimulated my interests, heightened my social conscious, and on rare occasions inspired me to be better than I imagined I could be.

Considering the black film experience as a prime example of the medium's powerful social influence, I turned to the fourteen celebrities as valuable resources for illustrating how black film history helped America mediate its social, economic, political, and personal problems throughout the twentieth century. At the same time, I trusted the research to champion the power of film as a major force in our lives. *The Interviews* remain a small reminder of my academic biases.

VI

In preparing the reader for the seven interviews to follow, this chapter began by identifying a larger black historical narrative as well as recalling an African-American history associated with slavery, the Civil War, Reconstruction, and a Jim Crow society. Then we turned to the post-war era and to the changes resulting from World War II, the cold war, suburbanization, and the rise of a new civil rights movement in America. My intention was to create an audience awareness that long before the birth of the movies, as historian Manning Mable made clear, "Western civilization had established a racist structure that could be described with the three Ps: Prejudice: the stigmatizing of people because of their skin color; Power: the use of institutional resources to carry out the prejudices of the powerful; and Privilege: the structure of benefits by being white.[110] By associating the "three Ps" to the ups and downs affecting both the entertainment industry and me, I next reviewed my intentions in writing *Exits and Entrances*.

One final reminder seems in order: what was I thinking as the shapeless journey began? Heading to California, I had only one definite appointment: a pre-arranged meeting with Clarence Muse. Everyone else would be identified once I touched base with Jason Robards upon arriving in Hollywood. Excited and intellectually curious but burdened with normal self-doubts and limited by time and resources, I went west with conflicted emotions.

I did, however, have one great fear: How would the celebrities themselves receive me? What made me so apprehensive? Again, space and complexity allow for only an overly modest explanation. To that end, let us go back one last time to the years from the late forties to the early seventies.

What had initially begun after World War II as a liberal White and Negro upper class crusade against a Jim Crow society changed significantly by the mid-sixties into a splintered Black, mostly working-class rebellion labeled the civil rights movement.[111] The rupture resulted from major disagreements between those who argued for civil disobedience like Dr. Martin Luther King, Jr. and those who insisted on gaining their freedom by any means possible like Malcolm X. As African-Americans mobilized during the sixties, their strategies shifted from an emphasis on non-violent marches, boycotts, freedom rides, and sit-ins to one of anger and frustration resulting from beatings, bombings, riots, and murders. By the end of the decade, with the deaths of individuals like Dr. King, Malcolm X, the Kennedy brothers, Emmett Till, Medgar Evers, four black children in a southern church, and three civil rights workers in Mississippi, militants like Charles V. Hamilton, Stokely Carmichael, Huey Newton, and members of the Black Panthers became for white America the face of the African-American revolt. "Blackness as a cultural identity," Murray reminded us, "was all but replaced by blackness as an economic and political identity."[112]

These charismatic African-American nationalists chanted slogans like "Black was Beautiful" and demanded "more power to the people." Unless they got their civil liberties now, America better beware! The Black Power forces also aligned themselves, Kofsky explains, with "anti-colonial liberation struggles, such as those in Vietnam or Central America and the Caribbean...."[113] Traditional goals of integration/assimilation got undercut by cries for Separatism. Sociologist Laura Fishman maintains, "This new militant spirit encouraged a racial ideology and a new set of political and cultural heroes, emphasizing a fresh agenda for black participation in American life." To achieve their ends, the scholar reminds us, blacks fought to free themselves "from the economic and cultural domination of white American values and institutions."[114] In essence, blacks wanted a more authentic representation of themselves and their heritage. These calls for African-American self-determination affected every personality in *The Interviews*.

At the same time, Carmichael's rallying cry of "Black Power" intensified America's feelings of discontent and dissent, and spawned a separatist ideology that alienated black militants from heretofore-white allies, many of whom came from the Jewish community. Consequently, as Joseph speculates, the rhetoric of Black Power activists and organizations, "among other things, fuel[ed] a white backlash, aiding and abetting an electoral realignment built on Middle American resentment, and inspiring violent self-destruction of the New Left in the late 1960s and early 1970s.[115] As blacks and whites wrestled with the impasse, artists and intellectuals weighed in on the issues.

Even though I recognized the justification for much of the anger and protests, I was not prepared to dismiss the way the militants behaved and spoke. Nor was I able to explain to my colleagues and friends why this project was necessary or relevant to my job or lifestyle. If blacks cared about their heritage and identity, why didn't I feel the same about my Jewish background and singularity? The misperception at the time was that they were mutually incompatible. If black people truly mistrusted whites, why would the performers selected for the interviews be truthful with me? And how could I convince them my intentions were honorable? Even more, they did not ask for my help and could care less about my sincerity. It was not unreasonable to suspect that the yet unidentified celebrities might be caught up in the heat of the day. Would they prove bigoted, anti-Semitic, and patronizing? Then what? How would I react? How would my beliefs and loyalties withstand the tests that I suspected awaited me?

VII

Exits and Entrances thus becomes a multi-faceted book about a time radically different from today. In the pages that follow are, I hope, many useful observations about black film history that remain relevant to our society but yet defy perfect description. For the most part, the conversations turned out much better than I could have imagined. That is not the same as saying given the chance, I might have done things differently.

In hindsight, these interviews set me on a memorable journey that has continued until now. So too did the cultural wars alter the course of American movies, jazz, black film history, and our national consciousness. Maybe the late Christopher Hitchens inadvertently described our passage best: "It is not so much that there are ironies of history, it is that history itself is ironic. It is not that there are no certainties, it is that it is an absolute certainty that there are no certainties."[116] From the likes of Mae Mercer to Ruby Dee, you will discover individuals who reflect the age in which they lived. They saw the world differently from the conventional wisdom of their times. They ignored the shibboleths of what it took to succeed in show business and blazed new trails regardless of the obstacles. And they not only survived; they raised the bar for others. They graciously and willingly shared their stories with me, during a difficult and divisive period in American history.

In sum, I harbor no illusions about how successfully I have conveyed my encounters with seven representative film veterans. My alternative version of the black film experience includes personal feelings alongside detached research, experience with social data, and memory as well as studio records. While my grasp of the past may be declining, my recollection of the price the book exacted remains strong. Guiding my efforts is the faith that vicarious attachments allow us, as one observer noted, to meaningfully revisit the past.[117] Yet no one knows better than I do the flaws in the book's imperfect methodology or the limitations of my prosaic writing style. But this much remains undeniable: *The Interviews* in general and *Exits and Entrances* in particular serve as unflinching reminders of why today's actors and academicians stand on the shoulders of their elders.

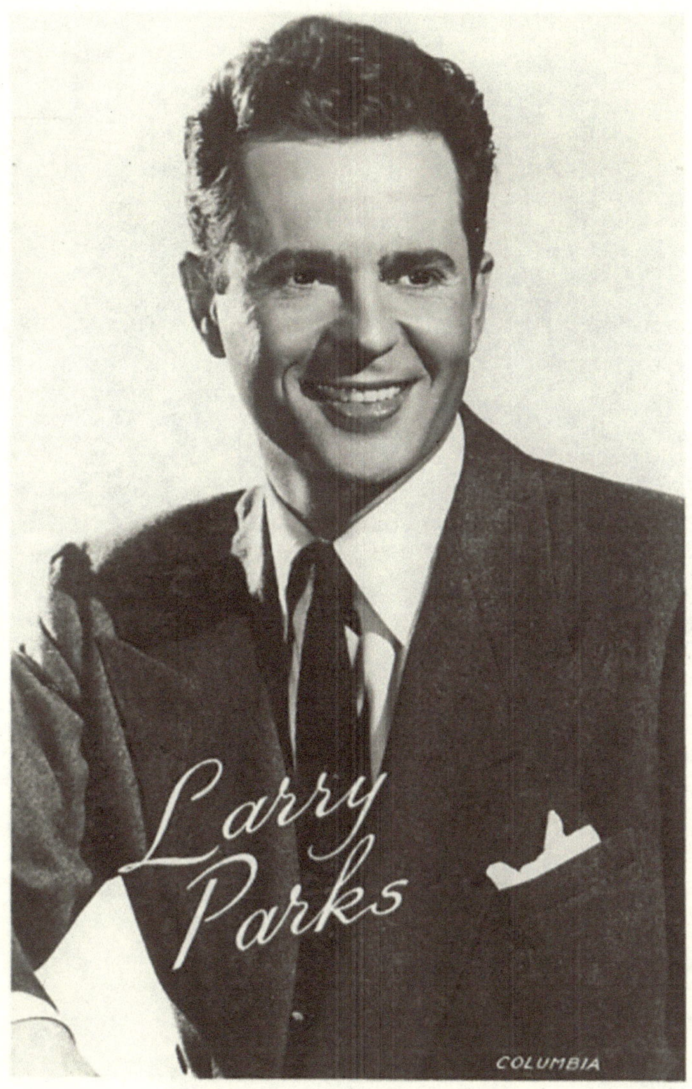

5. For many Americans, Larry Parks became the personification of blacklisted actors during the McCarthy Era.

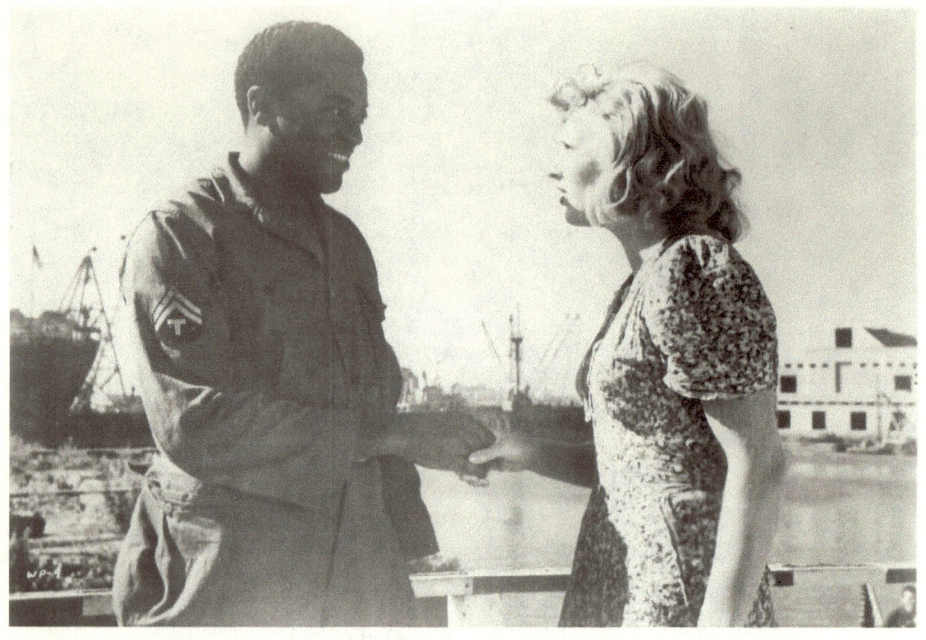

6. Melvin Van Peebles' *The Story of a Three Day Pass* (1968) became one of the first mainstream movies made by an African-American who helped revolutionize American film. Harry Baird and Nicole Berger star in the film.

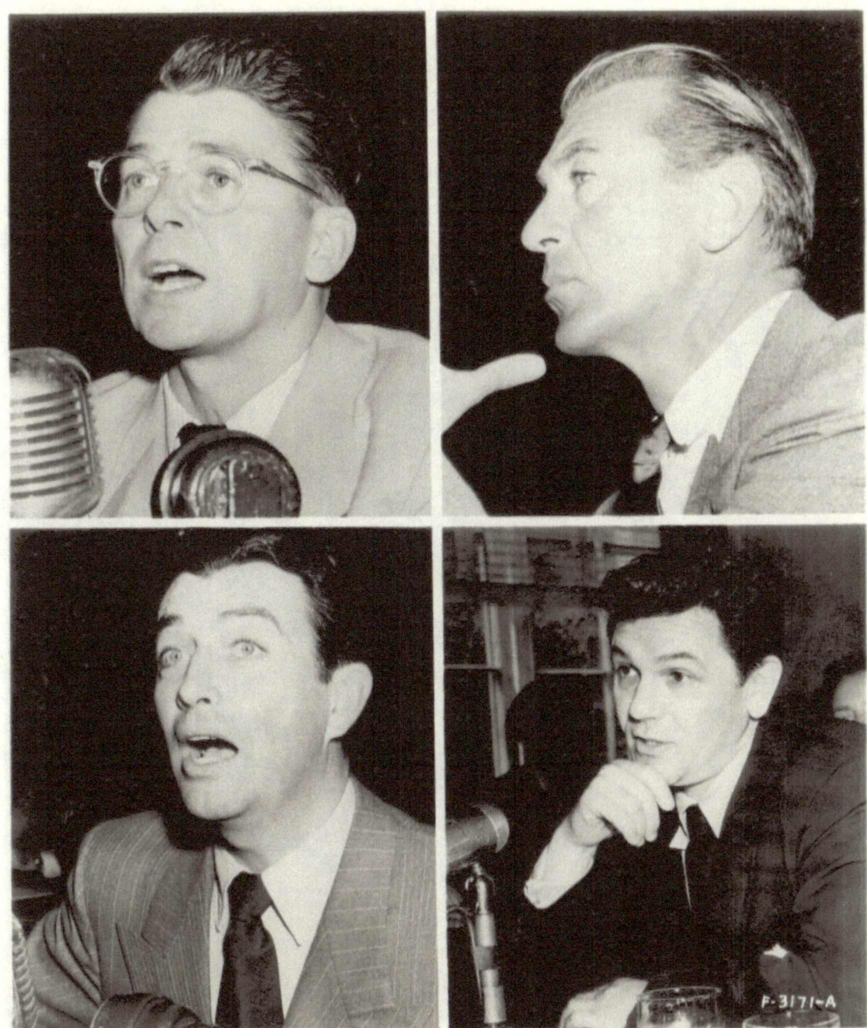

7. The House Un-American Activities Committee hearings benefitted from the testimony of "friendly" witnesses. From top left to right, Ronald Reagan, long-term head of the Screen Actors Guild; Gary Cooper, who later regretted his support and made Stanley Kramer's *High Noon* attacking HUAC; Lower right, John Garfield who testified before HUAC and then a year after (1952) died from a heart attack; and Lower Left, Robert Taylor who fully supported HUAC.

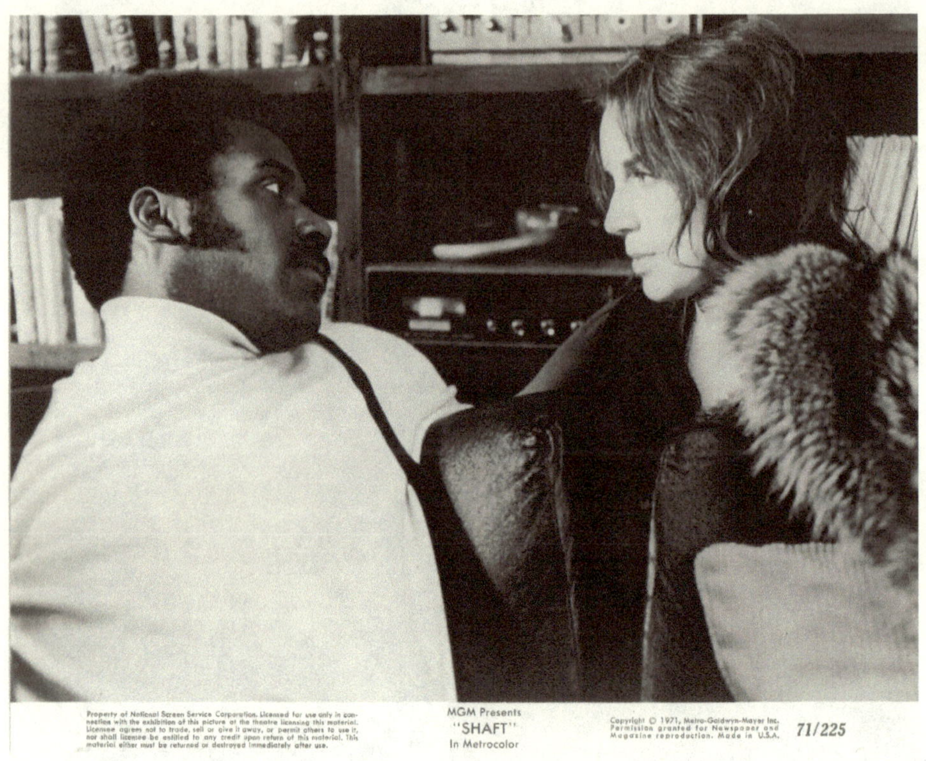

8. Richard Roundtree as Detective John Shaft in Gordon Parks' *Shaft* (1971).

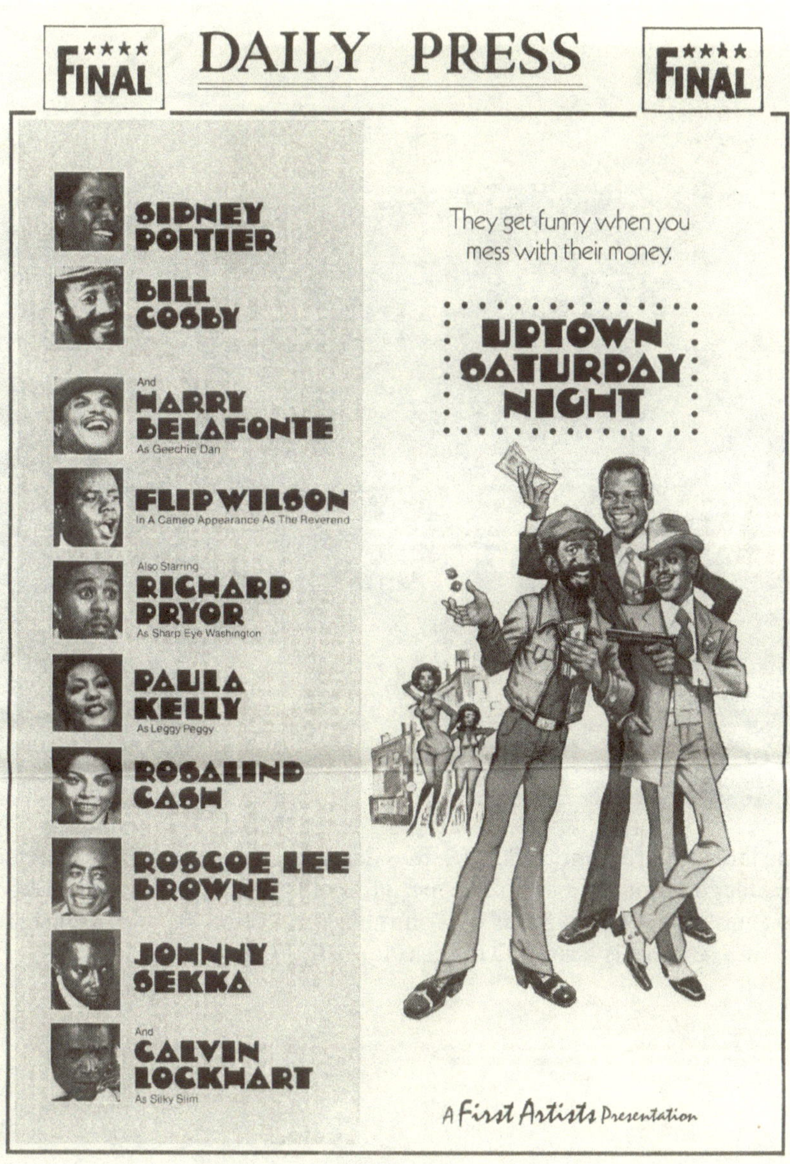

9. Despite being under attack from a new generation of young black filmgoers, Sidney Poitier and Harry Belafonte made a number of popular comedies in the early-to-mid seventies that appealed to cross-over audiences. Among them was Poitier's 1974 *Uptown Saturday Night*, featuring an all-star cast.

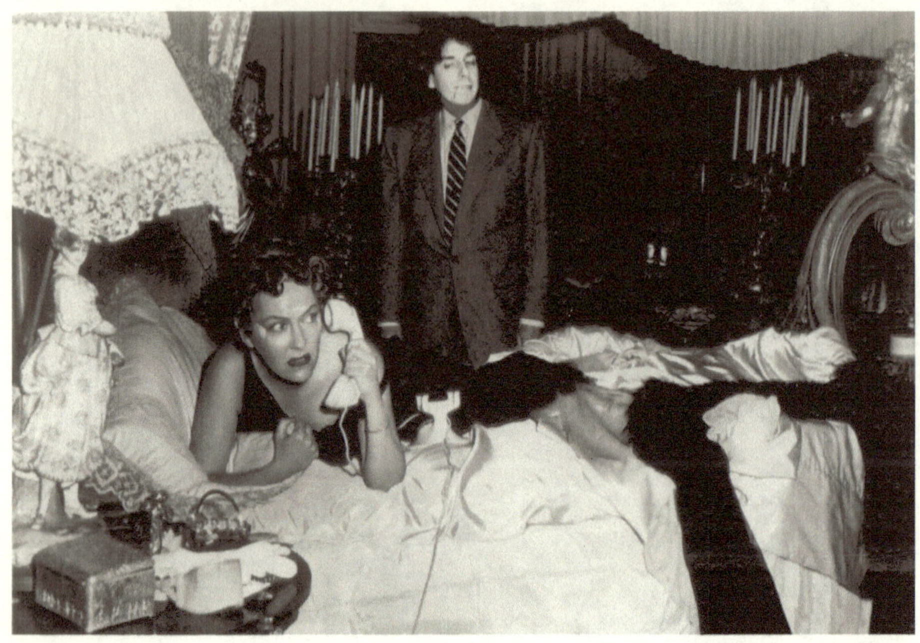

10. In the late seventies and 1980s, Lester Glassner, a highly unusual and wonderful colleague, not only supplied me with stills for my young adult books but also regularly sent me loads of Columbia promotion records on jazz and classical music. Here is a sample of his unique humor.

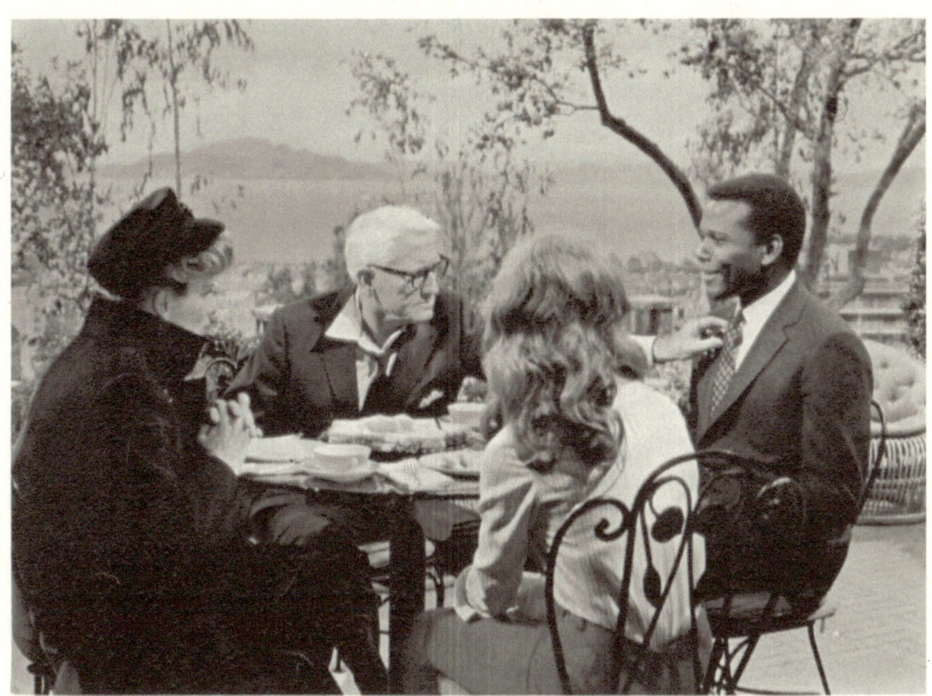

11. No moment in movie history captured the changing values among African-Americans following the post-WWII era more than the exchange between Dr. John Prentice (Sidney Poitier) and his father (Roy Glenn, Jr.) concerning the son's engagement to Joey Drayton (Katherine Houghton). Finally, Dr. Prentice explains, "The difference between us is that you think as a colored man, and I think as a man." The film is Stanley Kramer's *Guess Who's Coming to Dinner* (1967). From left to right, Katharine Hepburn, Spencer Tracy, Katherine Houghton (back to us), and Sidney Poitier.

Notes

[1] William Shakespeare, edited by G.B. Harrison, *Shakespeare: Major Plays and the Sonnets* (New York: Harcourt, Brace and Company, 1948), From *As You Like It*, Act II, Scene 7, p.509.

[2] Ossie Davis, "The Power of Black Movies," *Freedomways* 14, no. 3 (1974): 232.

[3] Crouch, *The Artificial White Man*, 9.

[4] John Gennari, *Blowin' Hot and Cool: Jazz and Its Critics* (Chicago and London: The University of Chicago Press, 2006), 121.

[5] *Blowin' Hot and Cool: Jazz and Its Critics* (Chicago and London: The University of Chicago Press, 2006), 122.

[6] *Blowin' Hot and Cool: Jazz and Its Critics*, 121-2.

[7] Tony Scherman, "The Omni-American," in *Conversations with Albert Murray*, ed. Roberta S. Maguire, *Literary Conversations Series* (Jackson: University Press of Mississippi, 1997), 128.

[8] Constance Rourke, *American Humor: A Study of the National Character*, 2nd ed. (New York: The New York Review of Books, 2004).

[9] *The Roots of American Culture and Other Essays*, ed. Van Wyck Brooks, Harvest (New York: Harcourt Brace, 1942).

[10] Paul Devlin, "Albert Murray at Ninety," *Antioch Review* 65, no. 2 (2009): 256.

[11] Murray, *The Omni-Americans*, 16.

[12] *The Omni-Americans*.

[13] Crouch, *The All-American Skin Game, or the Decoy of Race*, 190.

[14] Clayton Riley, "Shaft Can Do Everything—I Can Do Nothing," *NY Times*, August 13 1972, D9. For an excellent survey of the reactions to *Sweetback*, see Bennett, Jr., *The Challenge of Blackness*. 274-75pp.

[15] Staff, "Entertainment," *Encore* 3, no. 1 (1974): 92-3.

[16] Lerone Bennett Jr., *The Challenge of Blackness* (Chicago: Johnson Publishing Company, 1972), 273.

[17] Andrew Ross, *No Respect: Intellectuals and Popular Culture* (New York: Routledge, 1989), 52.

[18] Grant IV, *Post-Soul Black Cinema: Discontinuities, Innovations, and Breakpoints, 1970-1995*, 25-6.

[19] B.J. Mason, "The New Films: Culture or Con Game?," *Ebony* 28, no. 2 (1972): 60-1.

[20] Grant IV, *Post-Soul Black Cinema: Discontinuities, Innovations, and Breakpoints, 1970-1995*, 66-7.

[21] Bennett Jr., *The Challenge of Blackness*, 273.

[22] Merrill Jarvis, "E-Mail," (St. George, Vermont 2012), Merrill Jarvis worked as manager between May 1970 to August 1972 at Cinema 1 & 2.

[23] Staff, "Too Much of 'Negro Problem' Put at Films' Doorstep? Wonders Bette Davis," *Variety*, July 31, 1963, 2.

[24] "Too Much of 'Negro Problem' Put at Films' Doorstep? Wonders Bette Davis,"*Variety*, July 31, 1963, 21.

[25] Frank Kofsky, *John Coltrane and the Jazz Revolution of the 1960s*, The expanded and revised second edition of Black Nationalism and the Revolution in Music ed. (New York: Pathfinder, 1998), 91.

[26] Mason, "The New Films: Culture or Con Game?," 60.

[27] Richard Maltby, *Harmless Entertainment: Hollywood and the Ideology of Consensus* (Metuchen, N.J.: The Scarecrow Press, 1983).

[28] Mason, "The New Films: Culture or Con Game?," 60.

[29] Grant IV, *Post-Soul Black Cinema: Discontinuities, Innovations, and Breakpoints, 1970-1995*.

[30] Ellen Seiter, "Stereotypes and the Media: A Re-Evaluation," *Journal of Communication* 36, no. 2 (1986): 20.

[31] Bill Cosby and Alvin F Poussaint MD, *Come on, People: On the Path from Victims to Victors* (Nashville: Thomas Nelson, 2007), 142.

[32] Alvin F. Poussaint, "Blaxploitation Movies: Cheap Thrills That Degrade Blacks," *Psychology Today* 7, no. 9 (1974): 30.

[33] Seiter, "Stereotypes and the Media: A Re-Evaluation," 21.

[34] "Stereotypes and the Media: A Re-Evaluation," 22.

[35] Lerone Bennett Jr., "The Emancipation Orgasm: Sweetback in Wonderland," *Ebony* 26 (1971): 108.

[36] Ivan Dixon, "The Spook Who Sat by the Door," (USA: United Artists, 1973; reprint, 2004).

[37] John Alan Spoler, "Black Men: Uncertain Futures," (USA: Maryland Public Television, 1991).

[38] Isabel Wilkerson, *The Warmth of Other Suns: The Epic Story of America's Great Migration* (New York: Random House, 2010), 532-33.

[39] *The Warmth of Other Suns: The Epic Story of America's Great Migration* (New York: Random House, 2010), 10.

[40] J. Fred MacDonald, *Blacks and White TV: Afro-Americans in Television since 1948* (Chicago: Nelson-Hall Publishers, 1983), 4-5.

[41] Gerald L. Early, *This Is Where I Came In: Black America in the 1960s*, Abraham Lincoln Lecture Series (Lincoln: University of Nebraska Press, 2003), 103.

[42] Mark Stoler, 2012.

[43] Frank Manchel, *Film Study: An Analytical Bibliography*, 4 vols. (Rutherford, N.J.: Fairleigh Dickinson University Press, 1990), Vol.3, 1944-52.

[44] Peniel E. Joseph, *Dark Days, Bright Nights: From Black Power to Barack Obama* (New York: Basic Civitas Group, 2010), 16.

[45] Alexandra Isles, "Scandalize My Name: Stories from the Blacklist," (USA: Unapix Home Entertainment, 1998).

[46] MacDonald, *Blacks and White TV: Afro-Americans in Television since 1948*, 4.

[47] James Earl Jones and Penelope Niven, *James Earl Jones: Voices and Silences*, 1st ed. (New York: Charles Scribner's Sons, 1993; repr., 2002), 127.

[48] MacDonald, *Blacks and White TV: Afro-Americans in Television since 1948*, 4-5.

[49] Stanley Kramer, "Guess Who's Coming to Dinner," (USA: Columbia Pictures, 1967).

[50] Nelson George, "New Directors Flesh out Black America, All of It," *New York Times*, December 25, 2011, 10.

[51] Gerald Early, *One Nation under a Groove: Motown and American Culture* (Hopewell, N.J.: Ecco Press, 1995), 95. Cf. Gennari, 215.

[52] Manchel, *Film Study*, Vol. 1, 851-953.

[53] *Film Study*, Vol. III, 1944-49.

[54] Poussaint, "Blaxploitation Movies: Cheap Thrills That Degrade Blacks," 26.

[55] Schickel, "Artifacts of a Lost Culture," 2.

[56] Vincent Canby, "Critic's Notebook: Black Films: Imitation of Life?," *New York Times*, Feb. 8, 1991, C28.

[57] MacDonald, *Blacks and White TV: Afro-Americans in Television since 1948*, 6.

[58] Jon Wilkman, "The Attack of the Small Screens: 1950-1960," in *Moguls and Movie Stars: A History of Hollywood* (USA: Ostar Productions, 2011).

[59] Basil Wright, *The Long View* (New York: Alfred A. Knopf, 1974), 364.

[60] Jon Tuska, *Dark Cinema: American Film Noir in Cultural Perspective* (Westport: Greenwood Press, 1984).

[61] Judy Chaikin, "Legacy of the Hollywood Blacklist," (USA: One Step Productions, 1987).

[62] James Gavin, *Stormy Weather: The Life of Lena Horne* (New York: Atria Books, 2009), 216.

[63] Manchel, *Film Study*, Vol. II, 1067-108.

[64] Krin Gabbard, *Jammin' at the Margins: Jazz and the American Cinema* (Chicago: The University of Chicago Press, 1996), 76-7.

[65] *Jammin' at the Margins: Jazz and the American Cinema* (Chicago: The University of Chicago Press, 1996), 42.

[66] Alfred E. Green, "The Jolson Story," (USA: Columbia Pictures, 1946).

[67] Ibid.

[68] George F. Custen, *Bio/Pics: How Hollywood Constructed Public History* (New Brunswick, N.J.: Rutgers University Press, 1992), 75.

[69] Gabbard, *Jammin' at the Margins: Jazz and the American Cinema*, 76.

[70] *Jammin' at the Margins: Jazz and the American Cinema*, 77.

[71] *Jammin' at the Margins: Jazz and the American Cinema*, 28.

[72] Chaikin, "Legacy of the Hollywood Blacklist."

[73] Ibid.

[74] Isles, "Scandalize My Name: Stories from the Blacklist."

[75] Ibid.

[76] Brent Staples, "Black Characters in Search of Reality," *New York Times*, February 12, 2012, 10.

[77] MacDonald, *Blacks and White TV: Afro-Americans in Television since 1948*, ix-x.

[78] *Blacks and White TV: Afro-Americans in Television since 1948*, 2-3.

[79] Steven J. Boettcher, "Pioneers of Television: Variety," (USA: Public Broadcasting Corporation, 2007).

[80] Jeanette Covington, *Crime and Racial Constructions: Cultural Misinformation About African Americans in Media and Academia* (Lanham, Maryland: Lexington Books, 2010), 7.

[81] Ruth Adkins Robinson, "Television in Black: The First Fifty Years," (USA: Passport International Productions, 2004).

[82] Ibid.

[83] Manchel, *Film Study*, 1949-50.

[84] Mason, "The New Films: Culture or Con Game?," 61.

[85] John Lewis, "Unstoppable: A Conversation with Melvin Van Peebles, Gordon Parks & Ossie Davis," (USA: Starz Entertainment, LLC, 2005).

[86] Kofsky, *John Coltrane and the Jazz Revolution of the 1960s*, 52-6.

[87] Joseph, *Dark Days, Bright Nights: From Black Power to Barack Obama*, Location 207-20.

[88] Ralph Ellison, "The Golden Age, Time Past," (1959): 206.

[89] Gennari, *Blowin' Hot and Cool: Jazz and Its Critics*, 234-36.

[90] Murray, *The Omni-Americans*, 146.

[91] Alan Gilbert, "New York Philharmonic Opening Night Concert 2010: U.S. Premiere 'Jazz Symphony,'" in *Live from Lincoln Center* (USA: PBS, 2010).

[92] Gabbard, *Jammin' at the Margins: Jazz and the American Cinema*, 7-8.

[93] Martin Scorsese, "Feel Like Going Home," in *Martin Scorsese Presents The Blues*, ed. Jeffrey Peisch, The Blues (USA: Vulcan Productions, 2003).

[94] Joseph Camp, "In Performance at the White House: A Broadway Celebration," in *In Performance at the White House*, ed. George C. Wolfe (USA: PBS, 2010).

[95] Murray, *The Omni-Americans*, 17.

[96] Bill Guttentage and Dan Sturman, "Soundtrack for a Revolution," in *American Experience*, ed. Sharon Grimberg (USA: PBS, 2009).

[97] Gabbard, *Jammin' at the Margins: Jazz and the American Cinema*, 103-07.

[98] Susman, *Culture as History: The Transformation of American Society in the 20th Century. 1 Ed.*

[99] Staff, "Jazz: The Loneliest Monk," *Time*, February 28, 1964, 87.

[100] Michael Ullman, "The Jazz Column," *Fanfare* 32, no. 4 (2009): 367.

[101] Morgan Neville, "Troubadours: Carole King, James Taylor, and the Rise of the Song-Songwriter," in *American Masters*, ed. Susan Lacy (USA: PBS, 2011).

[102] Kofsky, *John Coltrane and the Jazz Revolution of the 1960s*, 87.

[103] Neville, "Troubadours: Carole King, James Taylor, and the Rise of the Song-Songwriter."

[104] Gennari, *Blowin' Hot and Cool: Jazz and Its Critics*, 8.

[105] Manchel, *Film Study*.

[106] Susman, *Culture as History: The Transformation of American Society in the 20th Century. 1 Ed.*, 89.

[107] David Jenemann, *Adorno in America* (Minneapolis: University of Minneapolis, 2007).

[108] Crouch, *The Artificial White Man*, 130-33.

[109] Ross, *No Respect: Intellectuals and Popular Culture*, 52-3.

[110] Nocerito, "We Remember the People We Lost in 2011."

[111] August Meier and Elliott Rudwick, *From Plantation to Ghetto* (New York: Hill and Wang, 1976), 272.

[112] Murray, *The Omni-Americans*, 172-73.

[113] Kofsky, *John Coltrane and the Jazz Revolution of the 1960s*, 225.

[114] Cited in Manchel, *Film Study*, 891-92, fn1406.

[115] Joseph, *Dark Days, Bright Nights: From Black Power to Barack Obama*, 283-306.

[116] Christopher Hitchens, *Hitch-22: A Memoir* (New York: Twelve, 2010), 420.

[117] Roberta S. Maguire, "Albert Murray: Extensions and Elaborations," in *Conversations with Albert Murray*, ed. Roberta S. Maguire, *Literary Conversations Series* (Jackson: University Press of Mississippi, 1997), 141.

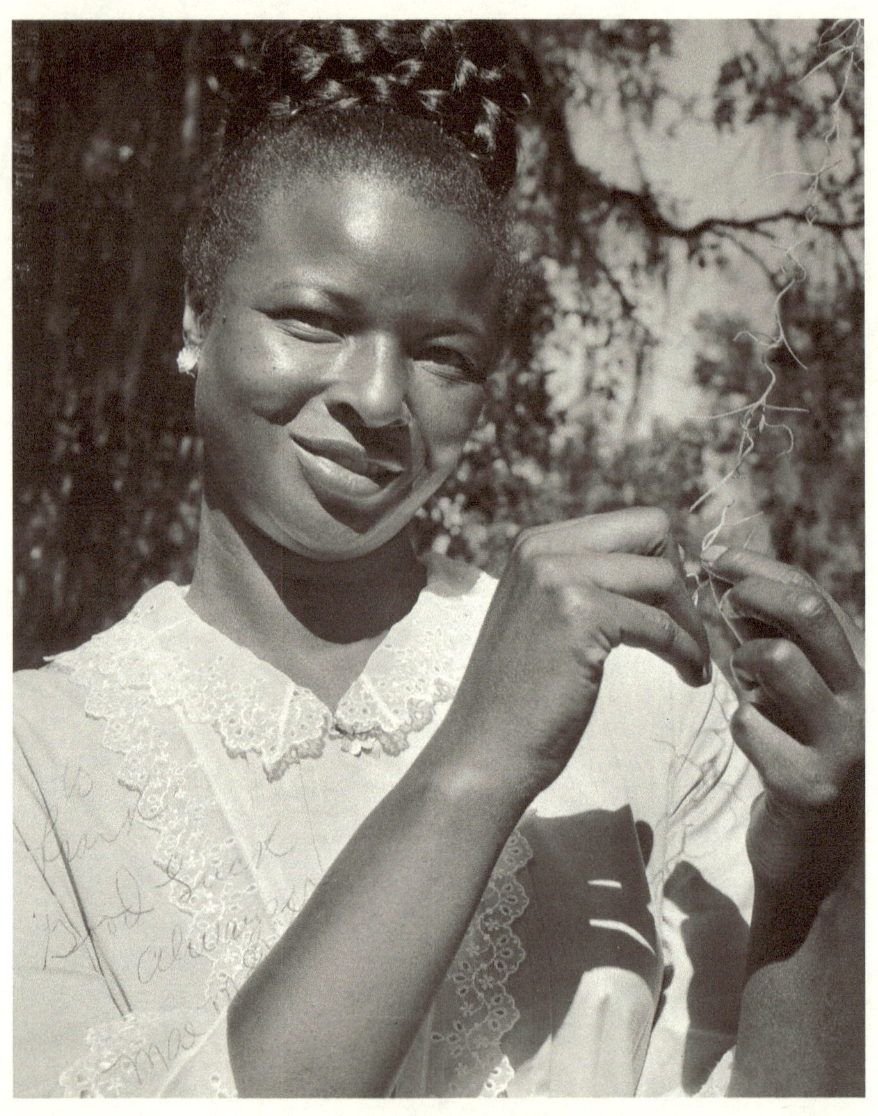

12. The caption reads, "To Frank, Good luck always, Mae Mercer."

1

Curtain Call: Mae Mercer

"American Culture, even in its most rigidly segregated precincts, is patently and irrevocably composite. It is, regardless of all the hysterical protestations of those who would have it otherwise, incontestably mulatto. Indeed for all their traditional antagonisms and obvious differences, the so-called black and so-called white people of the United States resemble nobody else in the world so much as they resemble each other. And what is more, even their most extreme and violent polarities represent nothing so much as the natural history of pluralism in an open society."[1]

Albert Murray

"...The consumption of images is basic to an understanding of our culture."[2]

Warren I. Susman

Although Mae Mercer initiates our anthology, the gifted blues singer, actress and women's rights advocate remains the least known of the celebrities in *Exits and Entrances*. She rarely received the acclaim or the wealth accorded her peers. And search as you might, you will not find her name easily accessible in the histories of either black film history or jazz encyclopedias. But for those of us who studied the performer's career and appreciate the obstacles she faced, as well as the courage she exhibited during her travels, the lanky, beautiful North Carolina-born artist deserves a respected place in the black film experience. Growing up uneducated, black and poor in a racist society, Mercer pursed her childhood dreams both in America and in Europe. She was self-taught, adventurous, independent, remarkable, and self-possessed. By the end of her journey, she had made her presence felt in show business circles, defied the skeptics, and left her footprint behind. Other entertainers may have done as much, but few did it with such grace and offered such an inspirational story, one surprisingly devoid of acrimony or recriminations in an age so deserving of reproach.

Born Mary Ruth Mercer on June 12, 1932 to tobacco sharecroppers, she was the oldest of nine children growing up in Brattleboro, North Carolina during the Great Depression. Her mother, a Cherokee Indian, married to a Negro farmer, taught her family how to make the best of difficult times. What the children learned most from this brave woman was the ability to suffer but not to hate.[3]

Mae differed from her siblings most notably in her love of music. She especially enjoyed the jazz melodies heard from listening to the radio and occasional Negro recordings. It is not difficult to understand why the child picked up more from the music than she did from her infrequent visits to the local school. The tunes spoke directly to her soul. She favored the popular sounds coming from Swing musicians like big bandleaders Duke Ellington, Paul Whiteman, Benny Goodman, Glenn Miller, and Count Basie, as well as their famed soloists such as Coleman Hawkins, Lester Young, Louis Armstrong, Teddy Wilson, and Ben Webster.

But Mercer remained mesmerized by the blues and the early fabled female singers such as Gertrude "Ma" Rainey, Sippie Wallace, Ida Cox, Victoria Spivey, and Bertha Hill.[4] It was from their songs of bygone plantation days, minstrel shows, vaudeville, and traveling black singers that the impressionable child learned her heritage in what was considered, until the advent of World War II, a rural brand of regional music that thrived on a mixture of the religious and the popular.[5] In this respect, Mae was not unique. "The music of King Oliver, Bessie Smith, W.C. Handy, Louis Armstrong, Jelly Roll Morton, James P. Johnson, and hundreds of singers," Isabel Wilkerson explains, "were impressing an affirmative consciousness of blackness not only upon other Negroes and white Americans, but upon the world at large as never before."[6]

So inspired was Mercer by the melodies, the youngster developed her singing skills almost before she finished the first grade.

It was in the church choir that Mae found her calling. By the time she became eight, she was adding to the family coffers as a paid "spiritual singer," making appearances first at local churches and then on area radio shows.[7] Meanwhile, Mercer also found the time to duplicate the strains and style of her idol, Bessie Smith, known to many as "The Empress of the Blues."

Considered by experts as the world's greatest promoter of the early blues, Smith like most of the "classic" celebrities probably appealed to Mercer because they shared many childhood similarities: e.g. poverty, suffering, loneliness, and disappointments. In her music, Bessie told of her experiences, her hopes and setbacks, and described the harsh world in which she lived. It seems reasonable to speculate that during her emerging years Mae identified with this gifted soloist, not only sharing a difficult childhood, but also offering Mercer a role model for success.

When Mae's mother died, the daring youngster left her father and siblings to strike out on her own. First, the lanky, good-looking adolescent went to Florida for singing opportunities, but by the time she reached her sixteenth birthday, the star-struck singer headed to the Black Mecca of the music world, New York City.[8] Broke, lacking a formal education, and without any professional contacts, the impressionable teenager somehow made a go of it. In many respects, Mercer signified many black teenagers, most notably Sidney Poitier, who also fled the South to gain fame in Harlem. While there are not many details about how Mae got on, Poitier, who arrived in Harlem at almost the same time she did, provides in his numerous books and interviews vivid tales of what it was like finding a job, a place to sleep, and opportunities to better himself in a strange, competitive town. What we do know about Mercer is that the resolute vocalist stayed in contact with her family and managed to earn a living for close to eleven years in New York.

What proved fascinating in hindsight was that it was not the famed jazz modernists such as Max Roach, Bud Powell, Dizzy Gillespie, Miles Davis, Thelonious Monk, and Charlie Parker that attracted Mercer in the late forties, but the chance to strut her vocal skills in the big time and maybe attract some movie producer. And there was no doubt she had talent. According to bluesman Willie Dixon, Mae embodied "the real low-down blues." Reginald D.

Brown, a friend, said, " I would classify her as a classic blues singer.... She had a deep, powerful voice. Her idol was Bessie Smith, so she sang in that idiom."[9] Not even the likes of popular vocalists like Sarah Vaughan, Dinah Washington, Ella Fitzgerald, Shirley Horne, and the legendary Billie Holiday discouraged the determined Mercer from pursuing a singing career. Her life during those years might best be described in the lyrics of the famous jazz vocalist Abbey Lincoln: "Trial and error, loss and gain. It takes a lot of doing."

Throughout the fifties Mercer worked regularly, acquired street smarts, and honed her business techniques. She also matured as a singer, even landing a recording contract at the end of the decade with a minor Harlem record company called Atlas. But when the record bombed and the general public ignored her, Mae reassessed her options in America. The nightclub owner for whom she worked promised Mae, if she wanted to try her luck abroad, he had some contacts in France who could help her.

A major concern for the budding blues singer was the growing popularity of Rhythm and Blues (R&B) recordings by the likes of Etta James, Little Esther, James Brown, and Ray Charles.[10] Targeted at urban black audiences, this heavy, beat music played a significant role in the emergence of rock and roll. Nevertheless, the raucous R & B sound did not appeal to the church-trained southerner, and it helped convince Mercer now might be the ideal time to go overseas.[11]

So the stressed vocalist turned to where many of her predecessors had gone before her, to Europe where African-Americans generally found adoring fans and the respect usually reserved for white celebrities at home. Mercer landed in Paris in 1960.[12] Through the years, I came to imagine what Mae might have found upon her first foreign trip in scenes from movies like Martin Ritt's *Paris Blues* (1961),[13] Bertrand Tavernier's *'Round Midnight* (1986),[14] and Clint Eastwood's *Bird* (1988).[15]

But nothing in those movies captured what the audacious North Carolinian singer accomplished within three years. "Her deep and powerful voice and regal stage presence," as one commentator described it, "made her a European hit, got her a nightclub job, and earned the chanteuse a recording contract."[16] Not surprisingly given her arresting appearance and powerful voice, she grew into an imposing stage personality. And few who saw her perform during the sixties ignored the passion of her singing.[17]

In addition to becoming a regular at The Blues Bar by 1962, (one source calls the Paris night club The Blue Spot),[18] Mercer "became the first blues artist to appear on French TV in a programme entitled *Singing The Blues: Mae Mercer Blues*, directed by Jean-Christophe Averty."[19] This TV show played a key role in changing Mae's fortunes. As French critic Pierre Perrone points out, "The programme-maker had already profiled artists like the New Orleans cornet-player Joe 'King' Oliver and Bessie Smith...but this was groundbreaking. Since France only had one television channel at the time, Mercer's appearance in May 1962—three months before another landmark programme featuring the pianist and vocalist Memphis Slim—had a huge impact on her career."[20] From that moment on and for the remainder of the decade Mae's career skyrocketed.

Also noteworthy during those crucial early years was the association that Mercer formed with Maurice Girodias, the owner of The Blues Bar. Born Maurice Kahanea in Paris, he survived in Occupied France during World War II by taking his mother's maiden name and hiding his Judaism from the Nazis. Girodias later became the owner of The Olympic Press, an important publishing firm known for printing sexually explicit novels by such authors as Vladimir Nabokov, J. P. Donleavy, and William Burroughs among others. He also owned several nightclubs adjoining his publishing house.

Mae began their friendship by working in The Blues Bar, proved herself to be an "intense performer,[21] and eventually wound up managing Girodias' jazz club for eight years.[22] Particularly fascinating is the fact that the once impoverished, self-educated Mercer now had become the friend of a French highbrow, suggesting how much the blues singer had grown intellectually over the years.

One can only imagine what Mercer felt about her success during the sixties. Using Paris as her base, the impressive jazz vocalist played numerous nightclubs, concert halls, and cabarets, while performing throughout Europe and the Middle East. Moreover, she kept flying back to America several times in the sixties to keep in touch with her family.[23]

Interestingly, Mercer never considered herself living abroad.

She always felt she was an American, an African-American, just working in Europe. When queried about what kept her coming back to the continent, Mae frequently talked about the freedom she found in Europe as compared to the racist climate in her native country.[24] At one point, Mercer even consulted a French physician about her nervous demeanor, asking him why she never felt at ease. According to Mae, the doctor told her she was born into that nervous condition. "Why is that?" she asked. "Because you were born a Negro in America," he replied.[25]

To add to Mercer's surprising success in Europe, she suddenly began attracting the attention of filmmakers working in Paris. First came a part in Mino Loy's *Mondo Sexy Di Notte* (*Paris by Night*), a 1962 Italian documentary, and then a year later Andre Cayatte's *Le Glaive Et La Balance* (*The Sword And The Balance/Two are Guilty*). The latter film, an ill-fated kidnapping caper starring Anthony Perkins and Jean Claude Brialy, renewed Mercer's interest in pursuing a movie career. When the thriller opened in New York in 1964, she began to gain some attention.

Over the next four years, America's involvement in the Vietnam War changed the atmosphere for expatriates living in France. A great deal of the camaraderie and good will that characterized the earlier part of the decade began to disappear as the French became more and more critical of the unpopular war. Finally, in 1968, Mercer decided to return to the United States to pursue a career in films and television.[26] That year, the popular performer landed a job at Universal Pictures in director Joseph Sargent's *The Hell With Heroes*,[27] a post-Second World War drama about smugglers in North Africa. Mercer played a chanteuse in the movie and garnered further attention at the studio.

The now-experienced entertainer found a much different racial atmosphere than the one she left nearly a decade earlier. In the fifties, the African-American struggle seemed focused most notably on the problems of the Southern black. In those days, the region's Jim Crow laws came under attack from the U.S. Supreme Court and a young Baptist minister named Dr. Martin Luther King, Jr. Starting with his 1957 Montgomery bus boycott, the famous preacher's non-violent approach to reforming the racist nation had given the country hope for a peaceful change.

But by 1968, when Mae arrived home to stay, optimism had turned to pessimism, with a splintered civil rights movement now linked to the anti-Vietnam War crusade. Black power chants overshadowed "We Shall Overcome" slogans. Among the reasons for the change, explains Christopher Lasch, was that the 1964 Civil Rights Act did not result in significantly changing the lives of most black people. Moreover, the struggle extended to the disturbing problems in the North with issues like open housing, de facto segregation, and equal employment.[28] Among the names now attracting widespread appeal among many young African-Americans as alternatives to Dr. King and his followers were Stokely Carmichael, Eldridge Cleaver, Bobby Seale, Huey Newton, H. Rap Brown, Angela Davis, and Charles V. Hamilton. And capping Mercer's shock that year were the assassinations of Dr. King and Robert Kennedy coupled with the fallout from the dreadful Chicago Democratic National Convention. No wonder so many young black people like future film star Samuel L. Jackson were running around yelling "Kill Whitey."[29]

Even further, by the end of the sixties the music America embraced struck a dramatically different chord. What captured not only our hearts but also our emotions were the protest songs sung by folk singers like Bob Dylan, Buffy St. Marie, Joan Baez, Odetta, Phil Ochs, The Weavers, and Pete Seeger. But no one epitomized the black movement more than the civil rights activist and revolutionary artist Nina Simone. Known as "The High Priestess of Soul," this remarkable "Girot," (storyteller) wrote and sang caustic tales about the years between 1963 and 1970: e.g., *Brown Baby, Four Women, Mississippi Goddam, Backlash Blues, Why? /(The King of Love is Dead)*, and *Ain't Got No/ I Got Life*.[30]

Clearly Mae's re-entrance into American society was affected by other factors than mainly the appalling black issues of the day. As she entered the seventies, she, like the rest of us, had to deal with Watergate, the Vietnam War, Gay rights, anti-colonialism, and the Equal Rights Amendment. But what might have influenced her the most appeared to be a coalition known as the Third World Women's Alliance. In 1970, the group issued a declaration called the "Black Women's Manifesto." It was aimed at reforming the notion of black feminism to better combat oppression, fight racism, and restructure capitalism.[31] For Mae and other actors in *Exits and Entrances,* the idea of empowering and portraying strong women became of paramount importance in their careers.

Mae's approach proved different from other African-American artists in Hollywood. For example, a frustrated activist like the fiery writer James Baldwin, fed-up with Hollywood's foot-dragging reforms at including blacks in mainstream movies, declared that white filmmakers were demanding too high a price for inclusion. Consequently, he urged African-American performers to refuse working with white producers until the industry leaders changed their behavior.[32] While Mercer felt sympathetic to Baldwin's arguments, she disagreed with his approach.

Getting herself grounded, the thirty-nine year old actress for the first time in her career hired an agent, who incidentally had ties to Clint Eastwood's Malpaso Productions. This agent got Mercer her second and most memorable American role in Don Siegel's Civil War drama *The Beguiled* (1971).[33] Based on Thomas Cullinan's novel *The Painted Devil,* the quirky, low-budget, disturbing film told the story of a badly wounded Union soldier, John McBurney (Eastwood), who is helped by Amy (Pamelyn Ferdin), a ten-year old student boarded at a nearby dilapidated girl's school at the end of the Civil War. The principal (Geraldine Page) and her students nurse Eastwood back to health, while at the same time scheming to make him their hostage. What follows is a Gothic horror tale dwelling on sexual passions and ethical alternatives that challenged many viewers' sensibilities in 1971.

At the core of the film is the duplicitous McBurney, a man who definitely is not what he represents himself to be. And crucial to discovering the Union soldier's real and dangerous identity is the black servant Hallie (Mercer). In fact, Richard Schickel credits the actress with the story's pivotal role in revealing the wounded veteran's ulterior motives. That is, when tending to the injured soldier's wounds, according to the critic, "McBurney comes on to the black maid: 'He stresses that they are both, in effect, prisoners and proposes an alliance that is implicitly sexual, overly practical—a joint escape.'"[34]

Not only is the character central to the film's plot, but also the movie identifies Mercer's emerging association both with black women's screen images and with women's movies overall. For example, director Siegel labeled *The Beguiled* a "woman's picture, not a picture for women, but about them. Women are capable of deceit, larceny, murder, anything. Behind that mask of innocents lurks as much evil as you'll find in members of the Mafia. Any young girl who looks perfectly harmless is capable of murder."[35] I have no idea how Mercer reacted to the director's judgment, but from the late sixties on, strong black women's roles became a hallmark of the actress' future career.

Mismarketed by Universal, *The Beguiled* was foolishly released by the studio as a typical Eastwood movie. It was anything but that. The fabled actor's film intentionally served as a bridge between his westerns of the 1960s and the start of his cops-and-robbers phase, beginning with Siegel and Eastwood's fourth collaboration, *Dirty Harry* later that same year.[36] The movie also proved to be a high-point in Mercer's film career.

Considered a box-office disaster when it was released,[37] *The Beguiled* remains today one of the rare Eastwood movies that failed to make "*Variety*'s list of all-time box-office winners."[38] Yet many viewers consider the same movie as an unusual and absorbing film. Schickel insists, "It is a terrific motion picture, one of the most powerful and interesting films he [Eastwood] ever made, and it was, indeed, a picture for which there was no appreciable audience."[39] And Eastwood biographer Patrick McGilligan concurs, saying "To this day, the unusual production…is ranked by many French critics, in particular, as a veritable masterpiece."[40]

On the surface, Mercer's next film, *Dirty Harry* (1971),[41] again directed by Siegel and starring Eastwood, should never have become noteworthy in her filmography. The narrative concerns a rogue cop, Detective Harry Callahan (Eastwood), who breaks the rules to kill a sadistic serial killer terrorizing San Francisco. Mercer has a momentary appearance as Mrs. Russell, the single, poor black mother of a murdered child. She appears on the screen for less than a minute and utters one line, telling the detective her dead son was only ten years old.

The film attracts my interest for many reasons. First, because the mislabeled right-wing screenplay unexpectedly contrasts the image of police brutality with similar behavior in the then popular blaxploitation films. The significance increases when one remembers how prominent police brutality was as an issue in black history. For those readers who may have forgotten those lawless times, viewing Roz Payne's impressive Newsreel Films collection documenting the struggles of the Black Panther Party during the late sixties and early seventies should prove very rewarding.[42] Second, Callahan's vicious conduct as a policeman is highlighted by his rationale for torturing prisoners. The characterization not only has relevance for its time but also for such current movies like *Rendition* (2007), *Unthinkable* (2010), and *Zero Dark Thirty* (2012) most notably for their alleged controversial recreations of CIA tactics used to fight terrorism worldwide since 2001. Third, *Dirty Harry* dramatically illustrates how mainstream movies were increasing the role of black extras in 1971. For example, *The Beguiled* had only one black image, Mercer, on screen during the entire film. That same year, *Dirty Harry* had dozens of African-Americans not only populating the movie during the first thirty minutes, but also presenting black actors in a variety of roles.

But, for me, the brilliance of this tiny part, dealt with what I would describe as "the Eastwood touch," an important statement made in an unannounced, matter of fact manner. In this instance, we have a presumably pitiless and obsessive cop who arrives at the murder scene of a young, black child. Ordinarily, you would not see anything revolutionary in so tragic yet so small a moment. But when you remember, as Jeanette Covington reminds us, that for decades white America dwelt on images of poverty depicting urban ghettos riddled with "drug dealers, pimps, and violent criminals"; and that such stereotypes depicted impoverished blacks, with their "self-defeating values systems" as "responsible for their own poverty and violence,"[43] Mercer's small part becomes huge. Here is a single black woman, without a positive male role model to help the struggling family. And Mrs. Russell comes off as responsible, strong and proud, doing her best to raise her son alone; it is a sick white man that kills her dreams. In other words, with a brief set of shots, *Dirty Harry* challenges an ongoing racist myth far too popular with many white Americans even today.

The film was released in December 1971 and proved to be a smash hit. It also made Eastwood the number one box-office star in the country. Nevertheless, he drew fire for shooting a black bank robber in the movie. Labeled a right-winger, a fascist, a racist, and a male chauvinist because of his controversial actions, the actor responded by claiming first that Callahan was following "a higher moral law"; and then by pointing out that the movie featured four black stunt men whose contributions were ignored by political activists.[44] Also, in hindsight, Roger Greenspun's *New York Times'* review brings a touch of the times: "*Dirty Harry* fails in simple credibility so often and on so many levels that it cannot succeed (as I think it wants to succeed) as a study in perversely complimentary psychoses."[45]

Mae's next film was George McCowan's *Frogs* (1972).[46] Directed by a Canadian filmmaker known best for his TV work, the science-fiction thriller takes place on an isolated island in the Deep South where Jason Crockett (Ray Milland), an aging, domineering, and racist patriarch has summoned his family once again to his mansion to celebrate his birthday and American independence. But there is nothing celebratory about the Fourth of July reunion. In scenes reminiscent of Alfred Hitchcock's *The Birds* (1963), we witness the island's animals kill almost every person during the preparations for the birthday party. Mercer plays Maybelle, the mansion's resident housekeeper and cook, who meets the same deadly fate as many of Jason's family members.

Although the film received mixed reviews, it did fairly well at the box-office. According to *Variety*'s Whit, "*Frogs* is slickly produced throughout with a novel premise that may be ballyed to good b.o. reception." The reviewer goes on to write, "In a sense, it is a story of Nature striking back at Man. Snakes, giant lizards, alligators, quicksand, frogs and toads, savage fish, granddad turtles… these are the heavies in a tale of mounting danger and suspense which has every element to keep audiences on the edge of their seats. Had the Alfred Hitchcock name been attached, pic might have been hailed as one of his typical thrillers; without, it's a thriller on its own."[47] On the other hand, *Moria*, a science fiction/horror/fantasy website, found the movie silly: "The film seems to have no purpose other than to set up…[victims] and the animals up to kill them off. Ray Milland's patriarch starts out interestingly as the only one who seems to have any control of the situation but degenerates into a stubborn old idiot…."[48]

What is particularly noteworthy for me about the film is not so much the narrative but the movie's revolutionary bits of business in 1972: e.g., an interracial romance between Bella Garrington, a black model (Judy Pace) and Stuart (George Skarr), a grandson of the rich racist Southern landowner. In addition, an "aging" Mercer is upstaged by a young, beautiful Pace dressed in traditional African clothes who behaves more strongly and independently than any white person at the family celebration. Moreover, the emphasis on the environment, the ironic, witty dialogue, and the three black speaking roles (the other being a black butler) all indicate notable changes in casting, writing, and dialogue in mainstream American movies featuring black performers.

Shortly after finishing *Frogs*, the imaginative and socially conscious Mercer decided to co-produce with Yolande DuLuart a documentary reflecting the increasing number of political trials dealing with blacks in America. Not surprisingly, Mae chose as her subject the remarkable and brilliant scholar/activist Angela Davis. Identified both with the Communist and Black Panther parties, Davis, who had been fired from her teaching position at UCLA Berkeley by Gov. Ronald Reagan in 1969, was currently in jail for allegedly supplying the weapons used in a failed courtroom escape by three black radicals. The trio and the Judge died in the shootout in the Martin County Courthouse parking lot. After spending eighteen months in jail, Davis was retried and acquitted.

While incarcerated, however, she gave, for me, one of the most vivid accounts of how ironic it was that white people lived in fear of blacks. Speaking to Swedish TV journalists, Davis talked about what her childhood was like growing up in Birmingham, Alabama. Routinely, she and her friends heard bombs exploding around them, and the neighbors had to arm themselves and band together to protect their community because the police had no intention of protecting them. In fact, the notorious Sheriff "Bull" Connor periodically went on the radio working up the white population against African-Americans. Because of situations like that, her father always made sure he had firearms close at hand. Especially tragic was Davis' personal relationship with the four small girls killed in the bombing of the 16th Street Baptist Church on September 15th, 1963 in Birmingham.[49] Now try explaining to blacks why whites have so much to fear from African-Americans!

Angela Davis: Portrait of a Revolutionary (1972)[50] originated as DuLuart's college project to fulfill one of her requirements for the UCLA Film Department. Having been a member of Davis' philosophy course, the young filmmaker wanted to use her teacher as an inspiration for her film. But UCLA rejected the idea, and the budding artist had to go the independent route off school grounds.[51]

Mercer, now DuLuart's friend and roommate, decided to cover the period dealing with Davis' UCLA teaching job and the two years before she entered jail. They did this in part because Davis gave few interviews. The film itself offers ample proof of the scholar's eloquence, views, and speaking prowess. Particularly effective are the scenes showing Davis' impassioned comments during a 1970 student strike protesting the murder of the four Kent State students, the arrest of the Soledad Brothers, and the murders of Michael Schwerner, James Cheney and Andrew Goodman in Jackson, Mississippi. As scholar Jeanne Betancourt observes, "Angela Davis's single-mindedness cannot be mistaken."[52]

Next on Mae's filmography was cult director Jack Hill's *The Swinging Cheerleaders* (1974).[53] If you wondered why the talented actress rarely did sexploitation movies, this mindless genre picture may provide the answer. Written and directed by the man who helmed two of the most popular blaxploitation films of the seventies—*Coffy* (1973) and *Foxy Brown* (1974)—this flippant narrative deals with Kate (Jo Johnston), an investigative college reporter who secretly joins her school's cheerleading team as a means to uncover the abuse of women. But the term "uncover" does not do justice to what is basically a smug "T&A" soft-core movie, described by Hill as a "Disney sex-comedy."[54] In addition to featuring bare breasts and heavy breathing, Kate's romps also expose a football point-shaving scheme involving the star quarterback's intended father-in-law (who also happens to be a big-time alumnus), the head coach, and an adulterous college professor who used to run numbers as a kid. As if that is not enough for a movie made in twelve days, the plot includes a villainous school radical who orchestrates a gang rape of a blonde cheerleader naively trying to lose her virginity. In the end, the football jocks prove to be high-minded and foil the villains, while at the same time proving to be sensitive, caring lovers and friends to the liberated cheerleaders.

Normally, not even the enduring popularity of *The Swinging Cheerleaders* or the fact that it exemplified a major exploitation genre during the seventies would warrant this much attention. But the 1999 reissue of the movie on DVD contains an interview, which might aptly be called "the Planet of the Apes," between film historian Johnny Legend and the fabled Jack Hill that offers unusual insights as to how exploitation movies were made and the thinking behind them. In one exaggerated explanation after another, Hill tells us how this "Disney-clone" was inspired by Watergate, thrived on reversing stereotypes of athletes and college radicals, dwelt on eroticism rather than on lewdness, and revealed the misunderstood nature of corrupt men who let their greed get out of hand. Amazingly, the commentators even confess that they know that many women truly love being gang-banged! In between these mind-boggling bombshells, we learn useful information about the era's exhibition practices regarding offensive scenes and dialogue, the distribution troubles of sexploitation films worldwide, the valuable training grounds the genre provided for actors and stunt men, and the importance of drive-ins to exploitation movies.

Okay, but what's the relevance to Mercer? Surprisingly, Mae's cameo role as Jessica Thorpe, the no-nonsense wife of the philandering Prof. Frank Thorpe, may be her most endearing role in the seventies. Stunning, powerful, and dramatic, she appears suddenly in the movie and delivers her lines so memorably that we forget what we have been watching and sit-up and pay attention. Hill may have described the moment best, when he states in his interview, "Mercer appears out of nowhere and raises the film to a higher level."[55]

In fairness to this paean to trash, I offer two quotes from reviews that provide an alternative perspective. Graeme Clark credits *The Swinging Cheerleaders* with having "an added depth…that you might not expect."[56] And Rick McGrath touts the film as "representing outside director Jack Hill at the market top of his powers."[57]

To help pay her bills in the years that followed, Mercer constantly took bit parts on various television series, including *Ironside, Mannix* and *Kung Fu*.

The actress's last major burst of work appeared in 1978 and reinforced her image as an artist interested in films with strong

African-American women. While doing such notable TV projects as the wicked stepmother in *Cindy*,[58] an all-black adaptation of the Cinderella story; and Aunt Juba in *A Woman Called Moses*,[59] the biopic of the legendary abolitionist and slave-escape leader Harriet Ross Tubman, Mae also agreed to play Mama Moseberry in Louis Malle's *Pretty Baby* (1978).[60]

For one of the few times in her career, a Mercer screen appearance drew attention to American culture, but not to her unusual female characterizations or to black history. Based on Al Rose's *Storyville: New Orleans*, a true story about the infamous Louisiana red-light district, *Pretty Baby* struck a chord with the director.[61] It became the notable Malle's first American movie venture. The Polly Platt screenplay, set in 1917, explores cautiously life in a New Orleans brothel months before the notorious jazz district is shut down. Central to the plot are the fortunes of a twelve-year old girl (Brooke Shields) who in becoming a "trick baby," first goes through a "deflowering ceremony," then becomes a prostitute, next marries a middle-aged photographer (Keith Carradine), and winds up a respectable parent years later.[62]

Mercer is cast as a fortuneteller who often gives superstitious advice to the stay-at-home residents at the brothel. Regrettably, Mercer's rantings do little for the lusty women or the bewildered audience. On the more positive side, a number of the performances in the film are haunting: e.g. Brooke Shields, Susan Sarandon, and Antonio Fargas. Also, Sven Nykvist's lush camerawork is eclipsed only by Ferdinand Morton's marvelous musical homage to the Ragtime legend Jelly Roll Morton. (A film closer to black musical history probably is Arthur Lubin's *New Orleans* (1947),[63] with featured performances by Louis Armstrong and Billie Holiday).

Despite Malle's daring depiction of the controversial subject matter—child abuse, pornography, and prostitution—and ongoing, serious problems with his American crew,[64] the now-overlooked film drew an even-handed reaction throughout the critical film community. For example, *New York Times* reviewer Vincent Canby found *Pretty Baby* "the most imaginative, most intelligent, and most original film of the year to date."[65] The only major objections came from a handful of critics who saw the director's work as thinly disguised child pornography sluggishly presented and containing uneven performances, especially the one by Carradine as the unusual historical photographer Ernest J. Bellocq.

Mercer's remaining professional years were mostly uneventful. By the eighties, she had turned her back on performing and spent most of her time with family, relatives, and private pleasures. Then, for a brief moment in the nineties, she considered a comeback, recorded an album entitled *When He Called It Quits* for Blackhawk Records,[66] and did a number of roles in TV series like *ER* and *The Shield*.

Like many of the people met in *Exits and Entrances*, Jason Robards' assistant Sylvia Silvano arranged Mae's interview. Our meeting took place at the actress' residence, where she was recovering from an accident that occurred during the filming of *Frogs*. Any doubts or fears I had about meeting black personalities so foreign to myself immediately disappeared when Mae and her roommate Yolande DuLuart took me into their home.

Understandably there are occasional problems with mechanics and diction during the following transcript. Only rarely have I made corrections. It is my intention here and throughout *The Interviews* to keep both the sense of the conversation and the subject's personality vivid to the reader.

Interview with Mae Mercer
January 2, 1972

FM: What it was like coming up in the movies?

MM: Well, I was born in the Carolina, Rocky Mountains, about 12 miles from the backwoods. I was a sharecropper's daughter.

And I always wanted to be a movie star. I always, you know, had created ideas in my head, which my family used to say I dreamed a lot, that it never could happen. And I started out first singing in church, the background for all black people.

Then I came into New York *[1947]*, because my mother died when I was quite young, and I had to take over the family, which were nine of us. So I decided at the age of sixteen that I could not survive any longer that way, you know, of not being able to go to school or do this, because I am a self-taught person; and so I came up to New York and got this job singing.

And...I worked and the man fired me; and so I went to the man and said, "Well, you fired me," and I said, "but I will work for you for a week free and show you what I can do; and that I can do better." So he did. And at the end of the week, I had become the star of the show, and the place was packed every night, and this is the same man that also got me the contract in Europe, which led to movies.

FM: Was this a white guy, or a black guy?

The man may have been Maurice Girodias, the French publisher of avant-garde novels like Vladimir Nabokov's Lolita, *J.P. Donleavy's* The Ginger Man, *and William S. Burroughs'* The Naked Lunch.

MM: White.

FM: Was there any problem in those days? I remember reading Dorothy Dandridge's autobiography;[67] it was difficult for a black girl to work in a.... Or the only place she could work was in a white nightclub.

MM: It was a white nightclub in Greenwich Village.

FM: And was it difficult to get a job? Did you just come from the backwoods and get a job in the city at that time?

MM: I had given myself like two weeks, and I said that if I didn't have a recording contract or some work, then I would go back. But I was there for a week and I had a recording contract also.

FM: How did you get it? Did you just walk in off the street?

MM: This man had heard me, I had stopped over in Baltimore where my brothers lived, and...this man had heard me singing with a group, and he had a record company, and he asked me if I would, you know, come to New York, to contact him. And I did and he gave me a recording contract. And that led from there to Europe as I played in the Modern Museum of Art with Buck Clayton and the All Stars, and all the good old timers.

Presumably, Mercer is talking about black entrepreneur Tommy Robinson and Atlas Records, started in 1951 and located in Harlem on 125th Street.

MM: And...I went to Europe, and my first film was with Tony Perkins. The man [*producer Alain Poire*] just walked in and asked me to do the film.

FM: Just like that?

MM: Just like that. And I said, "I'm no actress." And he said, "You can be." He said, "Come down tomorrow, and we'll discuss the money and sign the contract and pick up your script."

FM: You had no idea what the film was going to be about or anything?

MM: No.

FM: Do you remember how old you were at that time?

MM: No, I don't really.

FM: What was your feeling?

MM: I had just arrived in Europe, and I lived in Europe for seven years and have been back five times. So we'll have to calculate from there.

Mae was twenty-eight years old.

FM: Okay. I'll figure it out. [Laughter].... What was the film?

MM: The film was a kidnapping film, with Tony Perkins and with a French director by the name of Andre Cayatte.... I was a singer which had a flirtation going on with Perkins.

FM: Do you remember the name of the film?

MM: *Le Glaive et La Balance* [1963].[68]

FM: *Le Glaive et La Balance.*

MM: In French..... *Le Glaive et La Balance;* in English, it was *Two are Guilty/The Sword and the Balance,* which was showing in New York on Broadway for quite some time.

FM: What was the story about?

MM: A kidnapping type of thing, this director was originally a lawyer before he went into filming, you know. He liked justice types of films.

Written and directed by Cayatte, Le Glaive et La Balance *features Perkins as a struggling painter who along with two cronies abducts a rich man's son and later murders him. Brought to trial, the three men are acquitted because no one was able to determine which one of the three did commit the murder. Justice occurs, however, outside the courtroom.*

FM: What was it like on the set? You had never acted before?

MM: Well, when it was time for me to fly to Nice, I'd gotten on the plane; and I went down; and I walked on the set and we started to work. And then it was time for lunch, and I was quite shaken and nervous, so they said it was lunchtime. So I went over to the place that they had for lunch, got my lunch, and sat down, and I was completely panicked you know. And I mean, here I am going to make a movie; and this fellow walks over to me and said "Hello" and said, "My name is Tony," and I said, "My name is Mae Mercer." And he said, "Yes, I know your name." And it was Tony Perkins. He said, "May I join you for lunch?" and I said, "Yes." And he sat, and we became very good friends, and I became very calm, and everything worked out great.

FM: How about the filming itself, were there any interesting stories that happened on the set or any interesting experiences you had?

MM: No, not really. I just became great friends with Tony Perkins, which I...and I still think today that I was a lucky person because I did my work and went back to Paris and started to sing again.

FM: How long did you work on the film, a week, two weeks?

MM: I was on the set in the south of France for two weeks and then we shot again in Paris for a week.

FM: Did you get any special tips on acting or anything?

MM: No, not really, but the funniest thing was when they had said that I had this bedroom scene where I would come in, and Tony had another girl in his bedroom. And I would come in as if I was just always floating through his room you know and uh. So, being a Puritan and especially an American Puritan woman, I, uh.... He asked me to buy my own wardrobe, so I bought a pair of baby doll pajamas and put a robe on top.

And so the director looked at me and said, "Yeah, yeah, you look good, uh huh." And then it was time to roll. He said," It's time to go on," and he reached and snatched and took the robe off. And I almost died. [Laughter] Here I am standing in baby doll pajamas. I couldn't believe it. I thought it was the most awful thing that I had ever encountered that a person would do this, and they all started to laugh, and knowing the French.... And they all started to laugh and look, and I was so shook up [laughter] that I had to take five takes before I was comfortable enough to do it correctly. So that was a big thing on that one.

FM: After that, you went back to what, to Paris?

MM: Yes, and then I did a thing, an Italian film, which was called *Paris by Night*.

Records indicate the film was Mino Loy's Mondo Sexy Di Notte.

FM: That was the second one. Who was in that one?

MM: Uh, mostly Americans who were living in Europe.

FM: How did you get that contract?

MM: Well, they just came up to me and asked.

FM: Just again, you had no agent going out to locate...

MM: No, No. I never had an agent in Paris.

FM: Any stories on that set?

MM: Well, not really because I was doing nightclubs scenes there too. So I did all the hiring of the musicians and the fellow that played my boyfriend, I did the hiring of him who I wanted.

FM: What's the story about *Paris by Night*?

MM: *Paris by Night*, the glamours of Paris really, sexy girls, Paris by night you know.

FM: Who directed that?

MM: And I was chosen, I can't remember. I was chosen as one of the sexy girls, I don't why.

FM: I do.

MM: And uh.... Then I continued singing, and I came to Hollywood. I decided that I was coming back home. And one day I was out, and I came in, and there was a message on my service to call Universal Studios. So I called Universal Studios, and they said, "We are doing a movie, and it's about Paris with Claudia Cardinale and Rod Taylor, and this old boy that killed himself the other day, Peter Deuel, and uh, I went out, and they gave me the script.

FM: That's the third film you made and still didn't have an agent.

MM: No agent. This was the first Hollywood film in Hollywood.

FM: Un huh.

MM: And uh, I couldn't believe it that I had succeeded in making a Hollywood film.

FM: They were looking for you, you weren't looking for them? Amazing!

MM: Yes.

FM: What was the name of the film with [Rod] Taylor and Claudia Cardinale?

MM: *No Time for Heroes.*

The actual name of the film is The Hell with Heroes *(1968), directed by Joseph Sargent. Set in Africa after World War II, the narrative concerns a former air force hero turned mercenary running an airfreight company during the final days of colonialism in North Africa.*

FM: *No Time for Heroes,* how long did you work on that film?

MM: Uh, I think I was there about three weeks.

FM: And any stories on that particular film?

MM: No, not really, because Joe Sargent directed, and he was a fantastic man, and he could tell if I was a bit nervous or uptight. And he had a way of always calming me down. And uh, I was very friendly, and everyone got along well. That helps a lot when you are making a film.

FM: I gather that's true here out in Hollywood because of the kind of camaraderie among the performers on the set itself.

MM: Yes, you have to have that in order to make a good film.

FM: I think so.

MM: I think so too.

FM: Was there the same role again as the singer, the sexy singer in this one again?

MM: Yes, the same role as the singer.

FM: Were you getting stereotyped in this kind of role?

MM: I think so. Well, it looked that way at the time, and then my big chance came when I had gotten an agent, and they said that Clint Eastwood was making a film with Don Siegel. Yes, and they had tested every girl, black girl in America.

FM: *The Beguiled?*

MM: Yes. And I went out, and I have a habit of laughing a lot, you know, when I'm nervous, I laugh a lot. And so I just looked at Don Siegel, and I just started to laugh. I said, "Here I am. I don't want to take up your time," I said, "because I haven't done a lot of speaking roles, especially as huge as this, and so if you are looking for the sophisticated type of actress, of which I won't call any names, uh. [Laughter]

FM: Of course.

MM: Or if you are looking for a black woman to portray the way she feels about this character, well then okay, we'll talk about it." So he said, "Okay, okay, okay." He said, "You look the part." So, he gave me the script. He said take it home and study and come back in a week and read. I did, and I became awfully nervous because this was.... I don't know if you saw the film or not.

FM: That was the one film I stayed away from because of the coming attractions. It looked to me like a sex orgy about a Confederate [sic] soldier who was taken to this house and so on.

In hindsight, my observation refers to Universal's mishandling of the film, a marketing mistake that drove Eastwood to terminate Malpaso's production arrangements with Universal when the original contract ran out in 1975. You, of course, note that I had Eastwood fighting on the wrong side in the Civil War.

MM: But it's very good artistically

FM: I gather that the people that I have spoken to claim that the reviews and the coming attractions misread or misadvertised [sic] the film itself. So I am going to see it.

MM: And so as I was saying I went back, and I read for them: and he said, "Good, take the script and go back and we are going to give you a screen test." Well, when I arrived for the test, in a week, they were testing another girl. I became awfully nervous about that. So they tested me, and I shook his hand and said, "Thank you very much," and I walked out. And I came home, and I was so nervous I had taken a plane to Arizona to Carefree, and I rested there for a week. And when I came back, it was on my service: "Well, you have the role. And you need to start work." [Laughter]

FM: They didn't try to contact you at all!

MM: So uh, I went to work on that film, and I was there for three months on that film:

FM: What was that like?

MM: Fantastic, it was all in Louisiana, and if I'm not mistaken it was the same house where they shot *Gone with the Wind*. I played a slave. Uh, which all the women were left alone, you know, and the men was off to war. And I played a slave, and Clint was the Yankee soldier, who had staggered in, and one of the kids found him [because she] went off the [school] grounds.

It was just fantastic, but very hard to do because I had to pass back to history in my mind in order to portray that woman, right, because so many years ago they always, you know, would play a slave or a maid. They'd never had any characters at all. It was "Yes ma'am" or "No ma'am," or "Yes this." They never had anything to say. But the black women were running the house, but that never did come out in the films really except in *Gone with the Wind*.

FM: Hattie McDaniel.

MM: Yes, and I knew that there were different types of slaves, you know; and I wanted to portray a completely different type that I knew that did exist, like Sojourner Truth, you know, and so I had to think a lot about this.

Sojourner Truth, born Isabella Baumfree, worked as a house slave before becoming a famous abolitionist and women's right activist during the mid-nineteenth century until her death in 1883.

FM: How did you work it out in your mind? Did you do research on it and or what?

MM: Well, I am very fond of Sojourner Truth and Harriet Tubman; I'm very fond of them. So I read a lot on them and read a lot on the black women in history many years ago. Pieces that you can find, which we don't have too much. And now I'd sit, and I used to go down by the Mississippi River when I wasn't shooting and sit there and think and completely put myself into this character. And I would to go to bed at night, and I would go back through Ku Klux Klan's time and uh, I would go all and that would travel back in my mind and into slavery time and what it was like and so forth. And that is why I think that the reviews said that I carried the whole film because I threw my whole self in it.

Harriet Ross Tubman, born Araminta Harriet Ross, grew to prominence as a Civil War nurse and abolitionist, along with fighting for Women's rights. She died in 1913 at the age of 93.

FM: Tell me about the film, a little more about the experience itself as you... Did you have a chance then to influence the script, did they change the script because of your feelings or experiences that you were going through as you were trying to study for the part? Or did you have to fit [into] what you felt [was] the part they had created?

MM: The writer was a very good writer, and, uh, the way that he had written the script I would project the way that I felt that the black woman would have felt in that situation, you know, and uh, Mr. Siegel, he didn't disagree.

The reference to the writer probably refers to associate producer Claude Traverse. Originally, former blacklisted writer Albert Maltz wrote the first draft of the film, but ran afoul of both Siegel and Eastwood. Screenwriter Irene Kamp, who also proved unsatisfactory to the director and the star, replaced Maltz. Finally, Traverse came in and used material both from Maltz's script and author Thomas P. Cullinan's novel.

FM: He just let you go.

MM: Yes, Eastwood, he did not disagree; and we all got along fine.

Worthwhile noting here is Gabbard's suggestion about the star: "Like the vast majority of white men growing up in America, Clint Eastwood undoubtedly found some part of his identity in the conduct of African American men. A large portion of that identity was surely related to their displays of masculinity through music, along with sports the most important arena in which whites have partaken of a black male mystique. Throughout his career, Eastwood has carefully maintained the image of an impenetrable, autonomous male at the same time that he has cultivated a passion for jazz and black music. For Eastwood, the two are surely related, as they have been for the last two centuries in the white American imagination, We can celebrate Eastwood for expanding public awareness of black artists such as Charlie Parker, Thelonious Monk, and Johnny Hartman, but we can only speculate on the extent to which his understandings and misunderstandings of black masculinity are responsible for his cinematic image."[69]

FM: Can you tell me just a little bit because I won't have a chance to talk to you again before I get this onto paper, about the role that you had. You were a slave and what kind of person were you in the film as you saw it?

MM: I was a most human type of person. It showed that I was human, and that I cared about people, and I did not want to be there. She had a sense of humor. She did not want to be there, but she had to be there, so she was there.

FM: What kind of house was this?

MM: A huge mansion.

FM: And all the women had gotten together there?

MM: It was a school for all the little rich southern girls while the men were off fighting in the war.

FM: The impression I got from the coming attractions was that there were sex orgies all through, and he [Eastwood] goes and sleeps with each one of them hiding from the head mistress.

MM: Yes, Yes.

FM: Was that any problem on the set at all?

MM: No, not really, because it was a closed set. We had a closed set for that. I had one scene where the master, Geraldine Page's brother, when he was there, where he tried to rape me, but I defended myself. This is the first time in history that that has ever happened; that a writer has ever did this.

This flashback scene featured Mercer (Hallie) being thrown on a haystack by Patrick Culliton (Miles Farnsworth, Page's brother in the film). She defends herself with a pitchfork and prevents being raped.

FM: Prevented a black girl from being raped by a white man?

MM: Yes, especially during those times.

FM: Most of the time you see them getting away with it very successfully. And Jim Brown did a great bit on that once in a film I think called *The Split,* in which a white man rapes a black girl, where it was always the black man who had always tried to rape the white girl. That was created in the South, you know the great myth that the white men were always frightened that the black men were going to get their women. So they used to pass these laws, but Jim Brown did that; and James Whitmore was the guy who played the part, and he got killed at the end of it.

MM: Yes.

FM: Was there ever any trouble...these are the four movies you've made now? Was there ever any trouble as far as people picketing your films, or giving you a hard time about the kind of roles you were creating as opposed to being more militant roles or...?

MM: My...all of the black people that saw what I had done, they couldn't believe it, and I still to this day receive letters from all over the world from that film, you know the black people. They thought it was just fantastic what I had done with this black woman. That I had showed her human side, and with a sense of humor at the same time, and she was a very kind person.

FM: And the director, he was fine, it went well?

MM: Everything went well. Everything just went great.

FM: How did do you get your next script?

MM: My next script, what did I do next? The thing that's playing now with Clint Eastwood, which he only had....

Clint was getting ready to do *Dirty Harry*,[70] and they came to me and said that there were no roles in that one for a black woman. You know, and they were ashamed to ask me to do a cameo for them. And I said, "Why, you know? Why not? I like working with you, I like working with Don, and I like working with the cameramen, I like working with the grips, we all get along in that particular family. And he's a hell of a nice person, and Mr. Siegel too." I said, "Why? Of course, I'd do it; why not do a cameo." So I did the cameo in *Dirty Harry* with them: I had just returned from Florida doing *The Frogs*.

FM: It hasn't been released yet.

MM: No, we just finished it. I had an accident on December 3. And I arrived back here November 16 from Florida doing the film.

FM: What's *The Frogs*[71] about?

MM: It's a science fiction film with Ray Milland. He's a rich man who has made all his wealth off the woods and lumber and uh, he's very rich, rich and his family is all looking to take the money, very evil family looking to take the money away from the old man. I like grew up on the place, you know, and am there with my father, and the frogs and the animals rebel and take over.

FM: Do you think it's going to be a good film?

MM: I think so.

FM: He's making a comeback, isn't he, Ray Milland?

MM: Yes, he is. Since *Love Story*.

FM: Can you tell me about the kinds of roles you want to play?

MM: The kind of roles I want to play now which I just missed out which I had...I was supposed to start to shoot two weeks ago, but due to my illness, you know, I can't. The role that I had in that one I really wanted to play it because it was love scenes.

FM: What film?

MM: Uh, the fellow who came to visit me, and I can't even think of his name. It was a New World picture and it was called *Cool Breeze*, and I missed out on that, which I had already signed and everything, but you know love type of thing....

Now, I'm getting ready...I received a card the other day during the summer. I was in Europe, and they have started to shoot a film in Yugoslavia, which is on drugs, and they had to fire the director. He wasn't too good, so I received a letter from them from Paris two days ago that we will be shooting, and we will start it sometime in April which I have a lead role in that.

FM: Will that be your first lead role?

MM: It will be my first lead role, which I will be, a...this is a very important film I think because I watch my son die from an overdose of drugs. And no one seemed to be doing anything about to stop this drug community, and so I take it on my own to go all over the country searching for these top people that deliver the drugs and get it into our country. Another fellow, which is a white fellow, he also has something happen to his family, and he's out looking for it. He doesn't know that I am doing the same thing that he's doing until later in the story.

FM: It's a mystery then.

MM: It's a type of thriller, a James Bond type of thriller.

FM: *Dirty Harry* a little bit?

MM: Yeah,

FM: Who's going to take the other roles?

MM: Bert Convy, he worked a lot I think on Broadway. I get to shoot my machine gun, which I love to do. [Laughter] I get to blow up boats, I get to blow up warehouses, and finally find this man. And the top man I finally find, and I give him a dose of the same drug that my son had.

FM: Who is the director?

MM: They didn't mention who would direct.

I find no evidence that the film was ever made.

FM: What do you think now about acting? This will be your fifth or sixth picture. You started with no experience at all, you were a singer, and all of a sudden now you have turned into a full-fledged actress. And you have a lead in the film. And what kind of actress do you think you have to be? How does one develop into an actress of such quality?

MM: You have to study, you know. I'm a member of an actor's studio, and you have to study quite a bit, and really, really research characters and characterization and different things.

FM: Has anyone helped you in particular?

MM: Well, Sam Fuller. Each script that I have he always, he's a neighbor, he lives up the street, and he always helps me out a lot.

A controversial, prolific, and action-oriented filmmaker, Samuel Fuller (1911-1997) was a tough-minded director and screenwriter who specialized in low-budget genre movies. Among his best-known works are The Steel Helmet *(1951),* Pickup on South Street *(1953),* Underworld USA *(1961), and* The Big Red One *(1980).*

FM: Has he been coaching you?

MM: Yes,

FM: I just, you often hear these stories that you just can't come to Hollywood, and those days are over, you've gotta learn your trade and practice and get experience. Here you are getting better and better, and from what you tell me the critics just raved about this performance in *The Beguiled.* And you had no experience!

MM: Well, maybe I was a born actress, a natural one, because sometimes a person can't do certain things you know, uh. I believe that the creator or someone who's watching over you always give a person something that they can do. As I said, I couldn't finish school or go through all these things, college and all this. But I probably a much better actress than I am a singer. I think that I was meant to be an actress.

FM: And you think it's a kind of fate?

MM: I think it's fate.

FM: Who are some of your favorite actors and actress today? Do you have any?

MM: Today?

FM: Yes.

MM: Today, I don't know about today, but I like Vanessa Redgrave a lot, and you know I like Katharine Hepburn, and I like Spencer Tracy, I loved him.

FM: I do too.

MM: He was fantastic. I watched him last night as a matter of fact and uh. I don't know.... Roscoe Lee Browne is my favorite black actor, and I don't think he can do any wrong on the screen. Maybe I'm wrong to say this.

FM: I'll tell him you said that later on.

MM: But this man, he, accidentally, he coached me for *The Beguiled*. This man is one of the most fantastic black actors that we have today.

FM: I've heard that from two other people. They claim he is one of the most intelligent men to talk to and to get understand what it's all about, the acting business.

MM: He is.

FM: Let me ask you a question now. One of the problems that I've had along with the controversies that I've had as I've gone talking to people is the question particularly about black films. One group of people looks at the films by and large as a work of art. You've got to be good, and the film has to be good in order for it to be a good film. Another group of people claim that so long as the figure in the film is a positive image of a black person, that makes it a good film even though the film itself may be amateurish; that there's such a need to change the kind of images and stereotypes that have come over the years. Do you have a feeling on that, on what makes a good film, or what makes a good black film, or is there such a thing?

MM: I think that any film that one does has to be done correctly you know, not just stick it out there because it's a black person doing it. It has to show something, you know. You just can't just stick something together because you want a new image. The film has to have something going.

FM: Well, Shirley Chisholm, for example, praised as one of the ten best films, *The Bus is Coming*. I don't know whether you've seen that or not.

MM: No, I haven't.

FM: But *The Bus is Coming*[72] was a very amateurish film

MM: I understand that it was awful. And that's why I haven't been to see it.

FM: But the image of the black people was terrific. There was an idea that they were not going to be shoved around. They were going to build a better life for themselves. They were going to fight. And because of that, they claimed it was a good black film. And I was wondering what your feeling was on that?

MM: I haven't seen the film, so maybe I shouldn't even speak about it. I haven't seen it, but I think that I will go and see it, but I understand that it was horrible, amateurish and that you know it could be much better. I don't believe, I think you have to really capture something with the film. You know like the film that I just produced, co-produced, a film, which is coming out, but it's a controversial subject.

FM: Tell me about that.

MM: It's a portrait of a revolutionary, *Angela* [*(1971)*], Angela Davis.

FM: Oh, I remember reading about that. Is that a full-length feature film?

MM: It's a documentary, and it's an hour long. I co-produced it.

FM: What is that about?

MM: It's a documentary on Angela when she was at the university.

Directed by DuLuart, the documentary begins by telling viewers of former UCLA Professor Angela Davis having been arrested for alleged murder, kidnapping, and conspiracy associated with the attempted August 1970 San Rafael courtroom escape of three black defendants. In the failed getaway that followed, six people were killed: the judge, the prosecutor, a female jurist, and the three escapees. The documentary then proceeds to cover Davis' years as a teacher and political activist at UCLA in the late 1960s, before the California State Board of Regents fired her in 1969.

FM: Can you tell me a little about it so I can do some work on it? How did you come to co-produce it?

MM: Because my roommate, she [*Yolande DuLuart*] is French, and she's a director.

FM: So she directed the film. Oh, marvelous. And what was the research like? Did you go to visit Angela in jail?

MM: We couldn't get in jail, naturally. We started the film before all this. We didn't even know that all of this was going to happen, but I knew that something would happen and had to happen, you know, behind that. So, uh, my roommate asked her if she could shoot her, if she could film her, and she was very difficult about it. So I called her and asked her and said, "Look, why don't you just let us make the film on you because…."

Postscript

No doubt there may be readers who wonder why a performer with such limited screen credits is not only included in an anthology about reforming black film images, but also opens the collection itself. The most obvious answer might be because she represents the thousands of black performers who now for the first time in the second half of the twentieth century discovered it was possible to have a career in movies and television.

For me, however, the blues singer's story offers a valuable entrée into the post-World War II period up to 1972. Our recollections pick up on the optimism and determination that came with the Great Migration, as well as the challenges facing reformers in the entertainment world both at home and abroad. The discussion also introduces an alternative story to the blaxploitation narrative and the notion of black film history as victimization. For a brief time, we explore politics, film history, civil rights issues, personal identities, as well as the important part that jazz and the blues played in the African-American film experience.

Mae Mercer, vocalist, actress, and champion of women's rights suffered two mini-strokes in 2007, and she died in Northridge, California on October 29th, 2008. She was 76 years old.[73] I remember her best through the words of an old Bessie Smith song, "She was a travelling woman with a rambling mind."

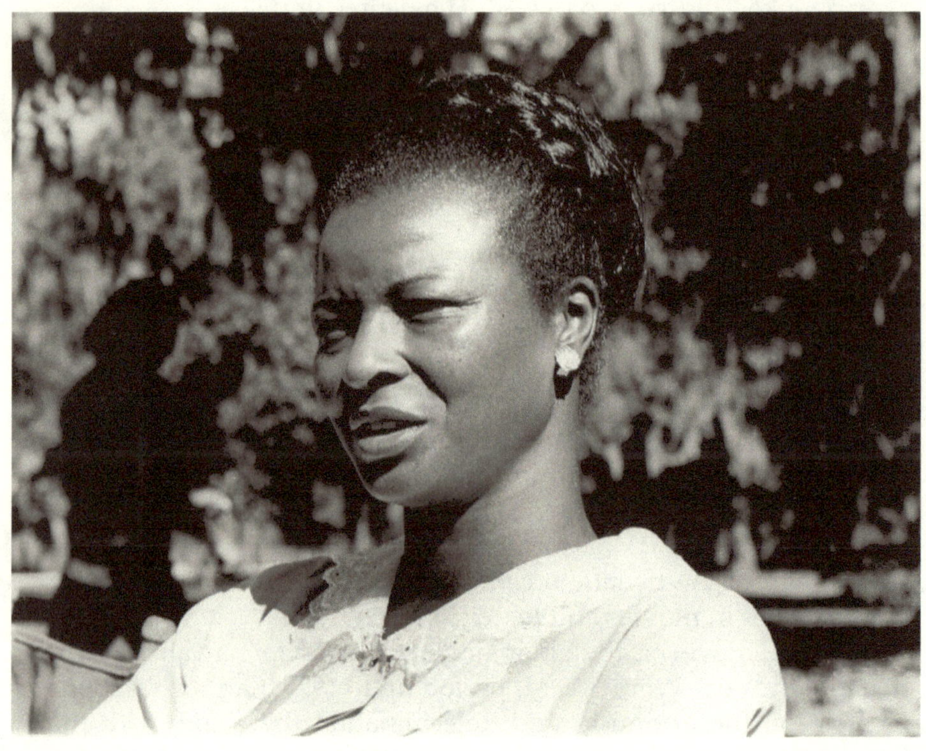

13. Mae Mercer, a courageous and talented actress who personified thousands of African-American women helping change the American film system.

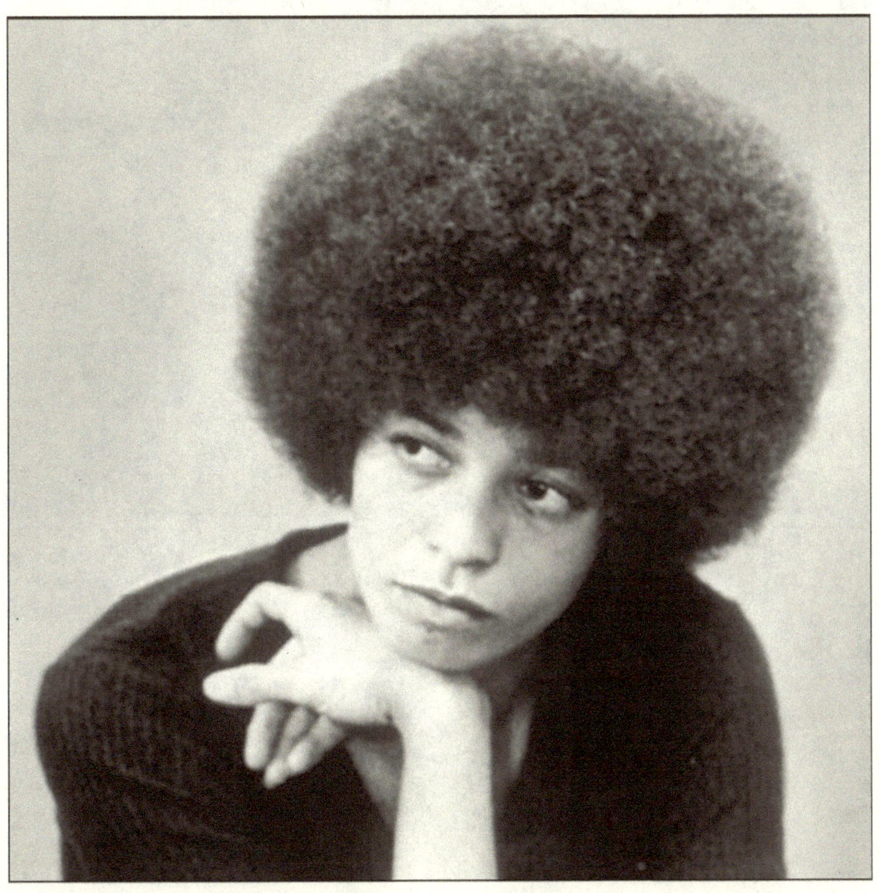

14. Angela Davis, one of the many brilliant and articulate black progressives who risked everything to see a better America.

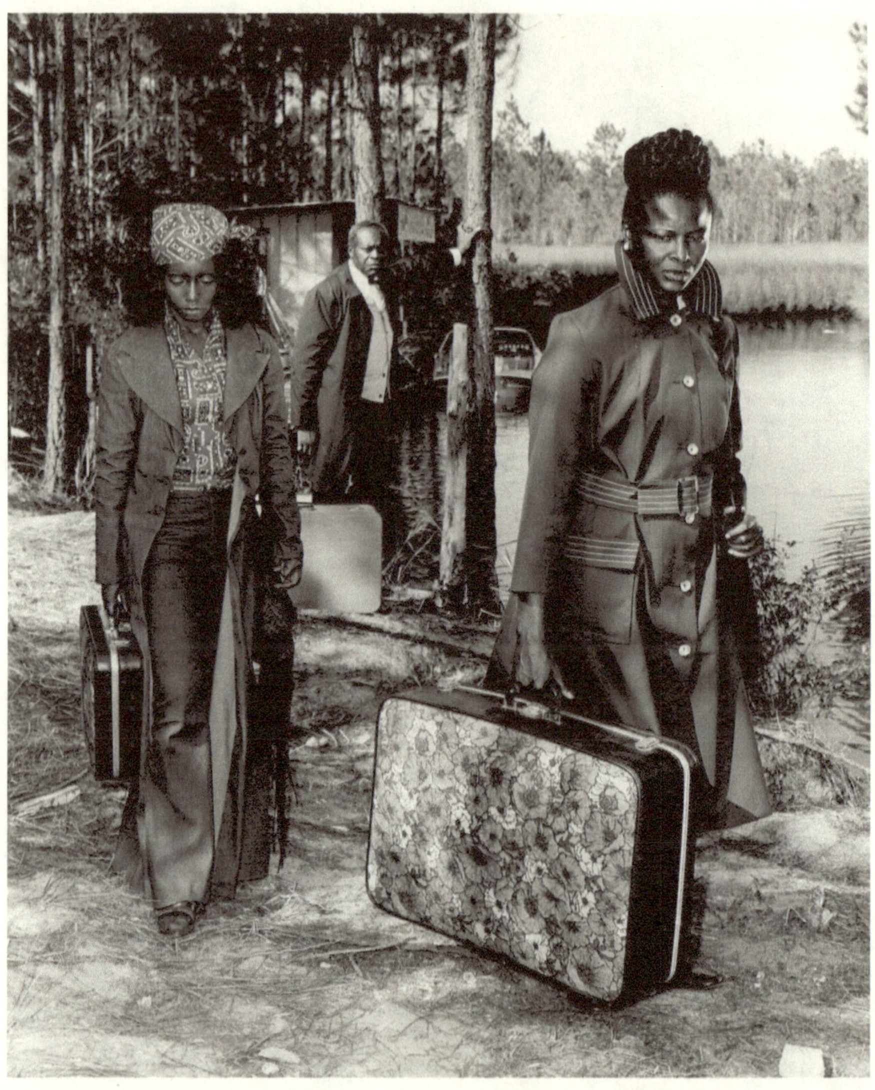

15. At the start of the seventies, black horror movies proved popular with audiences. Judy Pace and Mae Mercer in a scene from George McCowan's *Frogs* (1972).

Notes

[1]Murray, *The Omni-Americans*, 22.

[2] Susman, *Culture as History: The Transformation of American Society in the 20th Century. 1 Ed.*, xvii.

[3] John Bainbridge, *Another Way of Living: A Gallery of Americans Who Choose to Live in Europe* (New York: Holt, Rinehart and Winston, 1968), 296.

[4] Joop Visser, "Bessie Smith: Chattanooga Gal," *Illustrated Booklet* 2004, 8.

[5] "Bessie Smith: Chattanooga Gal," *Illustrated Booklet* 2004, 7.

[6] Wilkerson, *The Warmth of Other Suns: The Epic Story of America's Great Migration*, 251.

[7] Bainbridge, *Another Way of Living: A Gallery of Americans Who Chose to Live in Europe, 293.*

[8] Pierre Perrone, "Mae Mercer: Blues Singer and Actress Who Made Her Name in Europe and Worked with Clint Eastwood," *The Independent*, November 26, 2008, 2.

[9] Dennis McLellan, "Mae Mercer: Blues Singer and Actress," *Los Angeles Times*, November 16, 2008, 2-3.

[10] Staff, "Mae Mercer; Obituary," *The Times*, Dec. 4, 2008, 1.

[11] "Mae Mercer: Blues Singer with a Deep, Powerful Voice Who Ran a Paris Bar and Acted with Clint Eastwood," *The Times*, December 4, 2008, 91.

[12] "Mae Mercer; Obituary," 1.

[13] Martin Ritt, "Paris Blues," (USA: United Artists, 1961).

[14] Bertrand Tavernier, "Round Midnight," (USA/France: Warner Brothers et. al., 1986).

[15] Clint Eastwood, "Bird," (USA: Warner Brothers, 1988).

[16] Staff, "Mae Mercer; Obituary," 1.

[17] Perrone, "Mae Mercer: Blues Singer and Actress Who Made Her Name in Europe and Worked with Clint Eastwood," 2.

[18] Bainbridge, *Another Way of Living: A Gallery of Americans Who Choose to Live in Europe*, 293.

[19] Perrone, "Mae Mercer: Blues Singer and Actress Who Made Her Name in Europe and Worked with Clint Eastwood," 2-3.

[20] "Mae Mercer: Blues Singer and Actress Who Made Her Name in Europe and Worked with Clint Eastwood," 3.

[21] "Mae Mercer: Blues Singer and Actress Who Made Her Name in Europe and Worked with Clint Eastwood," 2.

[22] McLellan, "Mae Mercer: Blues Singer and Actress," 1.

[23] Bainbridge, *Another Way of Living: A Gallery of Americans Who Choose to Live in Europe*, 293.

[24] *Another Way of Living: A Gallery of Americans Who Choose to Live in Europe*, 294.

[25] *Another Way of Living: A Gallery of Americans Who Choose to Live in Europe*, 296.

[26] McLellan, "Mae Mercer: Blues Singer and Actress," 2.

[27] Joseph Sargent, "The Hell with Heroes," (USA: Universal Pictures, 1968).

[28] Christopher Lasch, "Black Power: Cultural Nationalism as Politics," in *The Agony of the American Left* (New York: Alfred A. Knopf, 1969), 115-20.

[29] Paul Jordan, "How Samuel L. Jackson Became His Own Genre," *The New York Times Magazine*, April 29, 2012, 28.

[30] Rob Bowman, "Linear Notes for Nina Simone: Live in '65 & '68," *Nina Simone*, May 2008, 5.

[31] Pam Grier and with Andrea Cagan, *Foxy: My Life in Three Acts* (New York: Springboard Press, 2010), 86-7.

[32] Sieving, *Soul Searching: Black-Themed Cinema from the March on Washington to the Rise of Blaxploitation*, 162-63.

[33] Don Siegel, "The Beguiled," (USA: Universal Pictures, 1971).

[34] Richard Schickel, *Clint Eastwood: A Biography* (New York: Alfred A. Knopf, 1996), 241.

[35] Siegel, "The Beguiled."

[36] "Dirty Harry," (USA: Warner Brothers, 1971).

[37] Marc Elliot, *American Rebel: The Life of Clint Eastwood* (New York: Harmony Books, 2009), 122.

[38] Paul Smith, *Clint Eastwood: A Cultural Production*, ed. Stanley Arnovitc et. al., American Culture (Minneapolis: University of Minnesota Press, 1993), 78.

[39] Schickel, *Clint Eastwood: A Biography*, 243.

[40] Patrick McGilligan, *Clint: The Life and the Legend* (New York: St. Martin's Press, 1999).

[41] Siegel, "Dirty Harry."

[42] Roz Payne, "What We Want, What We Believe: The Black Panther Library," (USA: AK Press, 2006).

[43] Covington, *Crime and Racial Constructions: Cultural Misinformation About African Americans in Media and Academia*, 25-6.

[44] McGilligan, *Clint: The Life and the Legend*, 212.

[45] Roger Greenspun, "Dirty Harry," *New York Times*, December 23, 1971, 1.

[46] George McCowan, "Frogs," (USA: American-International, 1972).

[47] Whit, "Frogs: Shocker, with High Exploitation Quotient," *Variety*, March 29, 1972, 30.

[48] Richard Scheib, "Frogs," in *Moria* (2012), 1.

[49] Goren Hugo Olsson, "The Black Power Mixtape 1967-1975: A Documentary in 9 Chapters," (Sweden: Sundance Selects, 2011).

[50] Yolande DuLuart, "Angela: Portrait of a Revolutionary," (USA: New Yorker Films, 1972).

[51] Jeanne Betancourt, *Women in Focus* (Dayton: Pflaum Publishing, 1974), 6.

[52] *Women in Focus* (Dayton: Pflaum Publishing, 1974), 6-7.

[53] Jack Hill, "The Swinging Cheerleaders (Aka Locker Room Girls and H.O.T.S. II)," (Centaur, 1974).

[54] "The Swinging Cheerleaders (Aka Locker Room Girls and H.O.T.S. II)," (Centaur, 1974), Supplementary Material on DVD.

[55] "The Swinging Cheerleaders (Aka Locker Room Girls and H.O.T.S. II)."

[56] Graeme Clark, "The Swinging Cheerleaders," in *The Spinning Image* (1974), 1.

[57] Rick McGrath, "An Underground Cheerleader for the Underground Press," in *Culture Court* (1974), 1.

[58] William A. Graham, "Cindy," (USA: John Charles Walters Productions, 1978).

[59] Paul Wendkos, "A Woman Called Moses," (USA: NBC, 1978).

[60] Louis Malle, "Pretty Baby," (USA: Paramount Pictures, 1978).

[61] Philip French, ed. *Malle on Malle* (London: Faber and Faber, 1993), 117-18.

[62] Nathan C. Southern and with Jacques Weissgerber, *The Films of Louis Malle: A Critical Analysis* (Jefferson, North Carolina: McFarland & Company, Inc., 1978).

[63] Arthur Lubin, "New Orleans," (USA: United Artists, 1947).

[64] French, *Malle on Malle*, 120.

[65] Vincent Canby, "Pretty Baby," *New York Times*, April 5, 1978, 2.

[66] Perrone, "Mae Mercer: Blues Singer and Actress Who Made Her Name in Europe and Worked with Clint Eastwood," 8.

[67] Dorothy Dandridge and Earl Conrad, *Everything and Nothing: The Dorothy Dandridge Tragedy* (New York: Abelard-Schuman, 1970).

[68] Andre Cayatte, "Two Are Guilty (Le Glaive Et La Balance; the Sword and the Balance)," (France, Italy: Gaumont, 1963).

[69] Krin Gabbard, *Black Magic: White Hollywood and African American Culture* (New Brunswick, New Jersey: Rutgers University Press, 2004), 71.

[70] Siegel, "Dirty Harry."

[71] McCowan, "Frogs."

[72] Wendell Franklin, "The Bus Is Coming," (USA: William Thomson Productions, Inc., 1971).

[73] Perrone, "Mae Mercer: Blues Singer and Actress Who Made Her Name in Europe and Worked with Clint Eastwood," 2.

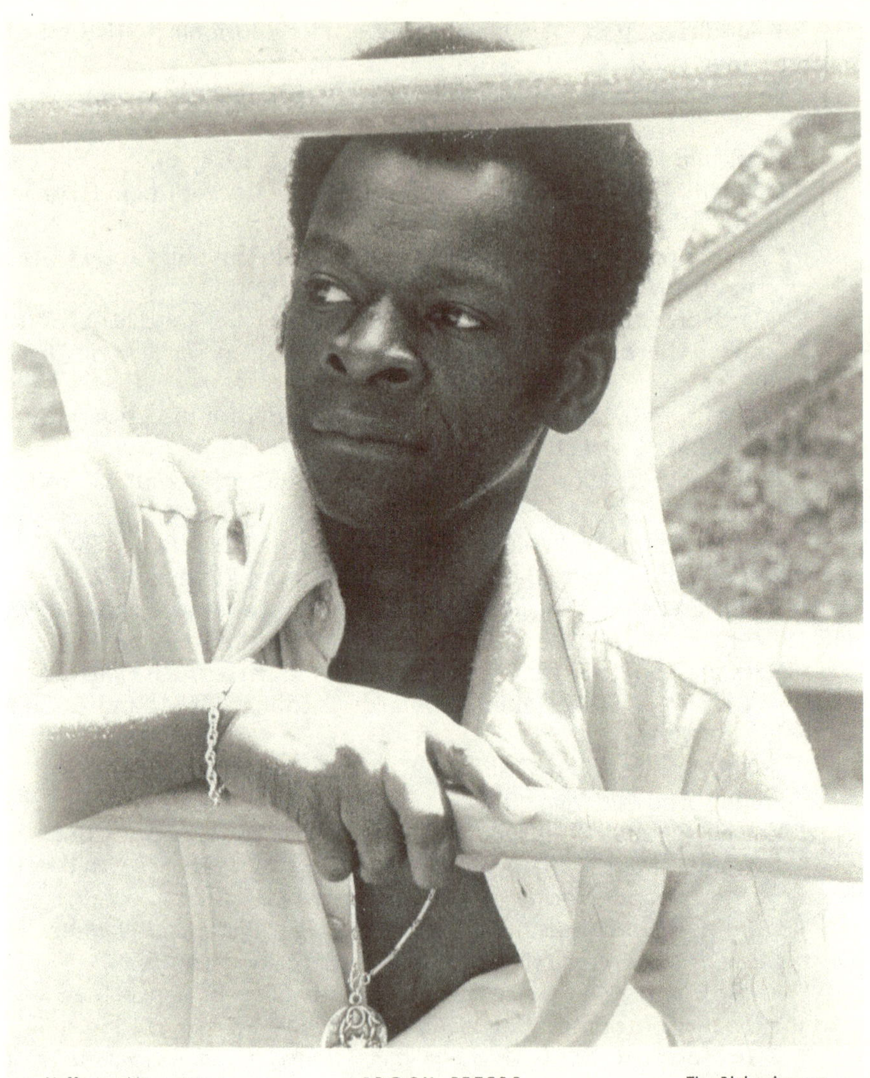

16. Signed photo from Brock Peters, with regards.

2

The Lamplighter: Brock Peters

"...there is no greater communicator than the feature film, no entity capable of pulling together so many people from so many backgrounds."[1]

Stanley Crouch

"Far too often, the movies are cited by academicians in many fields as mere 'reflections' of social trends rather than as active participants in the political arena. The interplay of culture, industry, and conflicting ideological impulses at work in the production of a film—not to mention the divergent ways in which individuals interpret mainstream narratives—can easily frustrate any monolithic reading of its 'intentions' and 'effects'."[2]

Allison Graham

In 2010, to coincide with the celebration observing the 50th anniversary of Harper Lee's only book *To Kill a Mockingbird,*[3] filmmaker Mary McDonagh Murphy neared completion on her documentary, *Hey Boo: Harper Lee and To Kill a Mockingbird* (2011).[4] She focused on the origins not only of the work's main characters but also on the sources for the best-selling, Pulitzer-Prize winning narrative that the 1999 *Library Journal* poll named "the Best novel of the Century," and Oprah Winfrey judged to be "our national novel."[5] Murphy's outstanding examination also included information on the 1962 screen adaptation released less than twenty-four months after the book's publication: Robert Mulligan's timeless film of the same name starring Gregory Peck as Atticus Finch in his only

Oscar-winning performance. [It was his fifth nomination.] And as *USA Today*'s Maria Puente reported, the story proved "just as beloved in film as the book is in literature, being voted number 1 in the American Film Institute's poll of the Best Courtroom Films ever made, while Atticus Finch received the nod as the number one hero in the AFI's Heroes and Villains poll in 2003."[6]

Horton Foote's Oscar-winning screenplay follows closely Lee's strategy of having Scout, Finch's six-year old daughter, tell us what it was like growing up with her widowed father, her older brother Jem, and their friend Dill Harris in the Deep South during the Great Depression. A critical section deals with Atticus' courage, humanity, and prudence while he tries in vain to save the life of Tom Robinson, a black man falsely accused of raping a white woman. The fact that Bob E. Lee Ewell, a white-trash troublemaker, and his ignorant, slutty daughter Mayella are obviously lying about what happened only makes Scout's memories more poignant when referring to the dangers a white lawyer encountered when going against Jim Crow mores in Maycomb, Alabama (a stand-in for Monroeville)[7] during the early 1930s.

Throughout *Hey Boo,* Murphy honors many people associated both with the book and the film. For example, various associates of the novelist, including Lee's older sister, explain that Atticus represents the author's father, that the character of Dill is based on the real-life Truman Capote, that the novel underwent extensive editing over a two-year period before being published, and even the fact that Robert Duvall makes his screen debut in the role of "Boo "Radley. To add stature to the novel and the film as well as to explain their appeal to American audiences, noted black personalities like Andrew Young, Oprah Winfrey, and James McBride testified to the book's universal qualities. Again and again throughout the documentary, as the authorities disclose minute details about the narrative and its characters, clips showing Tom Robinson are used repeatedly as background material to add depth to the commentary. Yet not once does anyone think to mention the origins of Robinson's character, nor even acknowledge the performer who played the film's pivotal screen role, this despite the fact that almost no one over forty years of age would fail to recognize the distinguished actor even if they didn't know his name. As for the performer himself, he considered the role both his favorite and the one most responsible for changing the direction of his career.

Regrettably, such slights appear far too often in Brock Peters' artistic journey. This gifted, versatile, and beloved American performer touched almost every aspect of show business both at home and overseas: the stage, television, movies, concert halls, night clubs, recordings, writing, and producing. Among the many film stars he worked with were Harry Belafonte, Dorothy Dandridge, Sidney Poitier, Leslie Caron, Charlton Heston, Rod Steiger, Ruby Dee, James Woods, Richard Harris, Peter Sellers, John Cassavetes, Claudia McNeil, Whoopi Goldberg, Jim Brown, and Edward G. Robinson. Among the famous men who directed him were Otto Preminger, Sam Peckinpah, Bryan Forbes, Sidney Lumet, Ossie Davis, John Guillermin, Robert Mulligan, Leonard Nimoy, Nicholas Meyer, and Richard Fleischer. And for good measure, he even co-produced with Michael Tolan the film, *Five on the Black Hand Side*.

Surely with such credentials, ties, and talent, Brock should have become a major leading man. However, it never happened. The conventional wisdom seemed to be when you couldn't get Belafonte, Poitier, or Jones, you turned to Peters. He was mostly the supporting actor or the brand name that starred in national road companies like *The Great White Hope* or *Driving Miss Daisy*. Nonetheless, when the famous actor-singer died, the Hon. Diane E. Watson of California entered into the Congressional Record that he was "one of America's most distinguished actors of stage and screen, whose deeds in life merit the respectful acknowledgement of his community and nation...."[8]

Brock's career probably only could have occurred during the transition years from the fifties to the late seventies. He possessed a beautiful bass-baritone voice, a handsome physique, considerable intelligence, and always delivered a passionate, effective piece of acting. When provided with inspiring material and direction, he created several unforgettable characters, including Crown (*Porgy and Bess*), Tom Robinson (*To Kill a Mockingbird*), Johnny (*The L-Shaped Room*), and Rodriquez (*The Pawnbroker*). Nevertheless, the renowned actor faced an uphill battle to escape being stereotyped as someone best suited to play dangerous villains. In large part, the problem had to do with his being an African-American who couldn't pass the "paper bag" test.

Theorists differ over why this racist idea persisted in our society, that in order for black performers to be considered star quality their skin tone could not be "darker" than a "paper bag." For example, in 1973, Stanley Crouch asserted, "Except for [Louis] Armstrong, there are no Negro-American performers who actually got to that level of popularity in performance, in film, in other media except light-skin guys. That's how it was, that's how it is."[9] Donald Bogle felt this racial bias began in the late twenties, when black performers moved out of their isolated race productions and into mainstream culture. Once they opted to seek success in mostly white venues, blacks approved whites setting the show business standards for beauty. That is, Bogle opined, "Café-O-Lay cuties, light-skinned black women, or as a popular saying went, 'Light, bright, damned near white' beauties who were thought of by white onlookers to be white" were considered "more acceptable to mainstream audiences than dark-skinned black women."[10] George Shirley described the prejudice differently: "If you are light, you are alright; if you are brown, stick around; and if you are black, get back." Shirley then added, "It is somewhat the same today [in the 1990s]."[11] Thus artists like Nina Mae McKinney, Fredi Washington, Billie Holiday, Lena Horne, and Dorothy Dandridge gained the spotlight in large measure because of their light skins.[12] Dark skinned actors like Paul Robeson, Frederick Douglass O'Neal, Stepin' Fetchit, Canada Lee, and Clarence Muse played heavies, servants, or comedians. While Crouch, Bogle, and Shirley make credible arguments, I've always felt the "bag test" in various forms went back in history to the Renaissance and Shakespearian times, where people proved just as bigoted and narrow-minded as they are today.

But let us not forget that both black and white filmmakers did this stereotyping! According to Richard Schickel, "Black movies tended to imitate the white genres.... [They almost always] endorsed the go-along-to get-ahead values of the black bourgeoisie of that time, including a color caste system. The hero and the heroine tended to be lightskinned [sic], the villain and the comic relief darker." Singling out William Greaves, a filmmaker and former stage actor who worked in black films, the critic quotes him as saying, "The Hollywood films were an environmental factor; they created certain expectations in the audience that black film makers felt they had to fulfill."[13] James Gavin concurred: "Many in the black bourgeoisie wound up emulating the values and even the looks of middle-class whites. From the 1920s through the 1960s, magazines for black readers advertised lye-based skin-lightening creams and hair-straightening treatments." Citing documentary filmmaker Gene Davis, the biographer argues, "The social structure in the black community until recently was based on how light you were. And the lighter you were, the more acceptable you were."[14]

For almost a decade, Peters' dark skin worked against him, requiring the actor, if he wanted to work in mainstream films, to accept parts as a merciless black buck. Then the situation changed for him in 1962. What happened is in part what this chapter is about. But initially it helps to recall that the "brown bag" test became unacceptable because a new generation of performers like Sidney Poitier, Miles Davis, Jim Brown, Yaphet Kotto, Ivan Dixon, Nat King Cole, and Brock Peters made it their business to broaden America's notion of what was tolerable for "dark-hued Negroes" to practice "when it came to romance and elegance, areas that had previously been reserved as almost the exclusive province of light-skinned Afro-Americans like Billy Eckstein [and Harry Belafonte]."[15]

I cannot stress strongly enough the part these artists' personal initiative played when considering their breakthroughs in black film history, because much of motion picture scholarship stresses the victimization approach when studying the black film experience. The performers listed above and hundreds more noted elsewhere clearly faced white racism and exploitation along with a rigid black caste system that impacted on their careers. But they also made it their business to resist using victimization as an excuse for failure. They rebelled against both conventional wisdom and influential spokespeople, black and white, that routinely offered pessimistic predictions on an African-American's limited opportunities in a white-dominated culture. If these visionaries intended to break through the racial ceilings, they recognized the need to ignore the "experts," and instead depend in large measure on their courage, their determination, and their talent. Self-responsibility and self-confidence became the secret to their achievements. As we proceed through these interviews and peruse the actors' lives and careers, we should look closely at where the applause rightly belongs. For me, the site is clear. No one made it alone. And no one made it by waiting around until things changed as change they would. The victories described in *The Interviews,* including the actors falsely labeled "Uncle Toms" in *Every Step a Struggle,* exuded self-reliance and self-confidence.

In 1967, when a reporter from *The New Courier* asked how Brock felt about the racial situation, he answered by saying, "It was advantageous for a Negro actor to be dark-skinned when seeking a film role." Why? "Right now," he explained, "the Negro image on television and movies screens is in the midst of the second stage of what I think will wind up being a three-part metamorphosis. First we had the Stepin' Fetchit and Mantan Moreland type of image. Now we have the all-good, intellectual portrayal as personified in the career of Poitier." Eventually, Peters hoped, the nation would reach "the honest and logical third stage—the one which shows the Negro as he really is...."[16] As the reader realizes, African-Americans are still striving for the impossible dream.

Born George Fisher to a Senegal immigrant sailor named Sonny Fisher and his West Indian wife Alma on July 2nd, 1927 in Harlem, the couple's only child soon demonstrated his artistic talents. [He changed his name to Brock Peters in 1953 for a recording contract.][17] By the time he was five, and following his father's death that year, the boy's mother encouraged him to play the violin. Eventually, he discarded that instrument and concentrated instead on singing while also demonstrating a great love for playing jazz. In the meantime, George spent considerable time trying to convince Alma that he should be an actor and not the engineer she wanted him to be.[18]

But the most influential part of Brock's Depression-era youth was spent in New York City's distinctive public schools. What made the schools so special was that many of his teachers were themselves the "New Negroes" championed by the designers of a black movement that insisted that the purpose of art by African-Americans should be to both uplift the race and provide evidence of the Negro people's creative talents. As one historian aptly wrote, the era was "the flowering of black literature, culture, and intellectual self-examination...."[19]

For Peters, first came the local elementary school, where he began his studies in black culture, and next the Frederick Douglass Junior High School, where he came under the sway of artist-teachers the likes of Langston Hughes, William E. B. Du Bois, and Countee Cullen. Now fixated on a life in show business, he entered New York's famed Music and Art High School for remarkable children where he pursued his study of singing. Thus one might easily characterize George Fisher's childhood by quoting the words of the lovely Irish ballad *Dublin in the Rare Old Times*: "Raised on songs and stories, heroes all of renown, the passing tales and glories that once were…[Harlem]."

Throughout his career, Peters never faltered in how he saw himself or his black heritage. While contemporary American culture routinely described the Harlem of those times as the exotic playground for white pleasure seekers and as a jungle of crime and violence for the Negro residents, Brock remained steadfast in his view of a place where blacks aspired to be better than they ever thought they could be. His vision was reinforced by Wilkerson, who recalls, "By the 1940s,…Harlem was a mature and well-established capital of black cultural life. It was a Harlem where nearly 'every black luminary was living within blocks of the others in the elevator buildings and lace-curtained brownstones up on Sugar Hill, from Langston Hughes to Thurgood Marshall to Paul Robeson, Duke Ellington, and W. E. B. Du Bois, on and off, to Richard Wright… and his friend and protégé Ralph Ellison….'"[20] Ruby Dee called The Apollo Theatre "Harlem's Music Mecca [sic]."[21] Murray also talks about the Harlem traditions that Peters probably experienced growing up in a place that had a "hard headed faith in Christianity, [and an area that had considerable] cultural flexibility,…" For these social historians, "Life in Harlem is the very stuff of romance and fiction, even as was life in Chaucer's England, Cervantes' Spain, Rabelais' France."[22]

Brock's black consciousness exhibited itself in various forms. Many of the films he made in the sixties and early seventies reflected the richness of his childhood. In 1976, Peters provided the voice-over for producer William Greaves' *From These Roots,* an award-winning half-hour PBS documentary on black inventiveness in Harlem during the 1920s.[23] In addition, the dedicated actor directed an actor's studio specializing in African and African-American Theater, and also became a co-founder with Cicely Tyson and Arthur Mitchell of the Dance Theatre of Harlem.[24]

But we may be moving too quickly. After graduating from New York's Music and Arts High School, Peters went to Chicago where the ambitious adolescent briefly enrolled at the University of Chicago [1944-45],[25] before coming home to Harlem and transferring to the City College of New York [1945-47].[26] For one of the few times in his life, Brock wavered on his chosen profession. Thinking acting might not provide him with a secure future, the undergraduate flirted with being a gym teacher. Then, as one commentator put it, Peters "was lured away from his books by the offer of a role in the touring company of *Porgy and Bess*...."[27] From the late 1940s on, Brock also toured for three seasons as a bass soloist with the renowned DePaur Infantry Chorus before striking out on his own. He appeared in cabarets throughout the United States and Canada, including the Village Gate in NYC and the Troubadour in Los Angeles, CA.[28]

During the post-WWII period, the future star also studied at the American Negro Theatre, started in 1940 with the purpose of providing young black performers with opportunities to act in roles that challenged their skills but did not require them to perform demeaning traditional stage parts as servants and comics. Among Brock's fellow students were Harry Belafonte, Sidney Poitier, and Ruby Dee. His association with Belafonte provided him pocket money singing backup vocals for his friend's Calypso performances, while also resulting in a lifelong friendship.[29]

Belafonte, one of the most famous black artists of the 1950s and 60s, remains a good touchstone for measuring a black performer's progress and choices during the Truman and Eisenhower years. Born Harold George Bellafanti Jr, on March 1, 1927 [four months before Peters arrived], he was very different from Brock in important ways. Unlike his friend, he did not have a solid education or a happy childhood. "I was born in poverty" Harry quipped, "grew up in poverty, and for a long time poverty was all I thought I'd know. It defined me...."[30] Whereas Peters got his inspiration from the Harlem Renaissance and the New York public schools, Belafonte got his stimulus from the fishing people of Jamaica where, despite being born in New York, he spent his formative years in his maternal grandmother's home. By the time he was thirteen, Harry returned permanently to Harlem. There the teenager had an erratic public school experience, dropping out of George Washington High School before graduation to take on numerous odd jobs, get married, and serve in the United States navy during the final years of World War II. What both men did have in common was a fierce determination to succeed and an unwavering confidence in themselves.

In the postwar period, Belafonte took a job as a janitor, where one day, a tenant thanked him for his help by giving the young man a pair of tickets to a performance by the American Negro Theatre. Stage-struck by the end of the evening, he decided to study acting at the place devoted to training black performers. When the ANT closed in 1949, Belafonte pursued his stage education at the Dramatic Workshop of the New School, where he acquired lifelong links with actors like Marlon Brando, Walter Matthau, Rod Steiger, and Tony Curtis.

At the start of the fifties, Peters benefitted from his friendship with Belafonte, especially when he performed as a backup vocalist for Harry's musical appearances. But the two socially conscious actors eventually ran afoul of the FBI, which during the era of the Red Scare considered these outspoken artists dangerous to the safety of the nation. And for a brief time, the struggling actor-singers fell victim to blacklisting.

At this point, the two friends, almost always in the shadow of Poitier's meteoric career, found themselves on a similar path but with much different results. Harry's light skin opened many doors closed to Brock. After breaking down numerous racial taboos in nightclubs, on television, and in recordings, Belafonte took aim at Hollywood. But his personal experiences proved so distasteful in studio films like *Bright Road* (1953), *Carmen Jones* (1954), and *Island in the Sun* (1957), that Harry decided to produce his own movie *Odds Against Tomorrow* (1959).

But before he could continue his acting career, a chance meeting at the end of the decade with Dr. Martin Luther King, Jr. changed Belafonte's major priorities and behavior for the rest of his life. Seeing Dr. King as an awe-inspiring figure, Harry became the great civil rights leader's close associate and spent much of the next decade fighting racial discrimination alongside the Southern Baptist minister who was gunned down in 1968. Thereafter, and for decades to come, Belafonte associated himself with many, many other important international movements. His activism understandably contributed to the collapse of his three marriages, as well as turned the artist away from what probably would have been a very prominent and profitable film and television career. For a brief period in the seventies, Belafonte teamed with Poitier and made several popular films, including *Buck and the Preacher* (1972). But afterwards and up to the present, he continues to use his magnificent singing to aid in his many impressive causes.

However, Peters's calling was not the same as Belafonte's. Brock's middle-class background steered him away from public political activism and toward a secure acting and singing career. He first appeared on television in 1953 on "Arthur Godfrey's Talent Scouts." A year later, he made his film debut playing the spiteful Sergeant Brown in the Otto Preminger musical adaptation *Carmen Jones,* starring Dorothy Dandridge and Harry Belafonte.

Adapted by Harry Kleiner, the film was based on producer Billy Rose's 1943 Broadway hit, featuring original lyrics by Oscar Hammerstein II and dance routines by Herbert Ross. The musical also owed a debt to George Bizet's 1875 opera *Carmen*. Now an all-black show set on a military base in Florida during World War II, the controversial revision unintentionally pinpointed many problems that would beset black performers for the next two decades. High on the list were questions about the "authenticity" of black-themed movies, the consequences of Hollywood's racism on the performers themselves, and the artistic factionalism emerging in the African-American community.

In this most recent adaptation of the 1845 book penned by the French novelist Prosper Merimee, Joe, a corporal bound for flight school, is forced by his mean-spirited Sergeant Brown to take the alluring but dangerous Carmen Jones to jail. But the fiery factory worker seduces Joe into letting her escape. He gets sent to jail for a month and, when released, seeks out his hot-blooded temptress. Once again, Brown makes trouble for the star-struck couple, and eventually causes Joe and Carmen to run away to Chicago. There the independent, capricious adulteress betrays her lover and takes up with Husky Miller, a boxing champion, who can give her the pleasures and trinkets she seeks. Enraged by Carmen's scornful rejection, Joe strangles his unfaithful lover rather than lose her to another man.

In his film debut, Broc [as he was listed for the last time in his professional career] had wanted to play the role of Husky, but because of his inexperience and skin color, he was given the part of Sergeant Brown. Joe Adams, a light-skinned actor, got the larger role. Even more troubling, however, Peters, who received rave reviews for his performance, discovered his persuasive portrayals of nasty villains to be a handicap to his career. "It was almost disastrous," he said. "Producers didn't want to see me. They had liked my performances but couldn't see me as anything but a heavy."[31] Nonetheless, he remained determined to change his status in mainstream movies.

More tragic was the effect the white, old-boy network had on Dorothy Dandridge, a woman who, according to Diahann Carroll, personified the black performer "as a victim in a cutthroat field."[32] But as suggested earlier, victimhood often does not tell the full story. Dandridge was also a deeply troubled, introverted woman who allowed her personal life to trump her professional triumphs. But she did not go down quietly or easily. Captivating and endowed with a lovely voice and a dazzling figure, she boldly refused to give in to her private demons. And for a brief but memorable time, she seemed destined to succeed. Critics called her "The Exotically beautiful saloon singer of the Western World."[33]

Dandridge first gained attention in the post-war period as a cabaret artist, and by *Carmen Jones* she had become "America's first bona fide black movie star."[34] In 1954, she not only broke down racial barriers by appearing on the cover of *Life* magazine, but also was the first black woman to be nominated for an Oscar for Best Actress. In an era devoid of meaningful roles for black women, this striking achievement helped change white America's racial attitudes while at the same time making her a cultural icon.[35]

Although Dorothy had labored in movies as a youngster since the mid-thirties, Gavin reminds us that these appearances were "mostly in bit or uncredited roles or as cheesecake decoration in race movies. Now, as movies embraced the Negro, Dandridge was the right girl at the right time."[36] Her film career began in earnest with the actress playing Melmendi, Queen of the Ashuba, in Byron Haskin's *Tarzan's Peril,* (1951),[37] a better-than-average loin cloth adventure featuring Lex Barker foiling gunrunners in Africa. She quickly followed it with a starring role in Phil Brown's *The Harlem Globetrotters* (1951),[38] a tale of a college basketball player who joins the famous team coached by Abe Saperstein (Thomas Gomez). These "over-looked, unlikely Oscar contenders" plus her glamorous nightclub work did, however, lead eventually to her first important screen role when Metro-Goldwyn Mayer (MGM) cast her in Gerald Mayer's *Bright Road* (1953),[39] yet another low-budget story about a southern school teacher trying to reform conditions in an all-black under-financed school. Her co-star was Harry Belafonte.

But eventually her insecurity, personal torment, bad choices with men, alcoholism, drugs, and frequent bouts of depression destroyed the once strong-willed pioneering performer. "The Golden Girl," as Billy Dee Williams labeled her, became the latest actress in an unforgettable line of black divas from Bessie Smith and Josephine Baker to Nina Mae McKinney, Fredi Washington, Billie Holiday, and Lena Horne to become scarred by show business. By 1960, Dandridge's shining promise had dimmed. As one source summarized: "She got hooked on downers and alcohol; her second husband, a white gambler, beat her; managers swindled her money. She wound up bankrupt and hounded by the IRS."[40] Thus a combination of sexism, racism, and poor personal decisions eventually led to her tragic death at 42 on September 8, 1965 from an overdose of antidepressant pills. Earl Mills, Dandridge's long-time manager and sometimes lover, would later write, she had two curses: "She was light and she was beautiful. These curses gave her both triumphs and tragedy."[41]

As for the cast of the all-black *Carmen Jones,* explained Diahann Carroll, "it was a very emotional experience for all of us to deal with the fact that we knew we were 'renting' space. We were not there because we were going to have film careers."[42] Elsewhere, the beauty from the Bronx added, "The rejection was so insidious, it was everywhere in the cafeteria, on the lot, where we parked our cars. We were visitors. They knew we were there to do a film. Not an enormous amount of adjustment was made to make us feel warm and welcome. They knew in a matter of weeks we would all be gone and they wouldn't have to look at black people anymore."[43]

Brock Peters concurred with this assessment of the conditions surrounding his film debut. He had no misconceptions about where he was and what he was doing. "A film like *Carmen Jones* didn't necessarily say to us, oh, now you're going to have glorious careers.... We were hired, and came out, and did the work, and did our best, so that hopefully someone would think to cast us in something else, each of us thinking that, given the climate and the opportunities that were available, it was highly unlikely!"[44]

The musical met with a mixed reception. On one hand, Vincent Canby offered a positive and popular view of the film: "The all-black musicals may have been examples of glorified segregation. Yet the best of them were also more than that. *Stormy Weather*, with its show-stopping performance by Ethel Waters, and *Carmen Jones*, with its two equally beautiful stars, Dorothy Dandridge and Harry Belafonte, transcend their ghettos. They are joyous movies that float above the color line."[45] On the other hand, the Preminger production showcased how making "a black film" brought out social, political, and cultural factionalism from fellow African-Americans. For example, the NAACP's Walter White found *Carmen Jones* disturbing. Ever since the forties, the Executive Secretary had been trying to get the motion picture industry integrated. Now, just when the U.S. Supreme Court in *Brown v. Board of Education* had struck down the separate but equal argument, Hollywood comes out with a movie advocating separatism. "What are they doing?" he asked. And the highly influential critic Lerone Bennett gave his reactions: "A long time ago, we watched *Carmen Jones* and other crap, and we snickered, saying, in superior tones, 'The poor white boy, black sexuality threatens him, he doesn't know what to do with black bodies and white sheets.' And we went out of hundreds of theaters, saying: "You wait. You wait until our man comes, and then you'll see bodies presented naturally. Then you'll see some passion. Then you'll see why the blues were written, why Bird Played and why Malindy Sang.' Well, our man has come-you dig?—And we are still waiting—and I tell you, Baby, it's late, it's *very* late."[46]

In the short run, however, everyone in the cast appeared to benefit from *Carmen Jones* except Peters. While Dandridge, Belafonte, and Carroll moved on to other film projects, the unwanted Peters supported himself by working as an elevator operator in New York.

Unlike other actors, he could earn a living outside of film by singing at concerts and clubs and on the stage.[47] But by 1959, the struggling actor-singer was nearly bankrupt.

At the decade's end, a black actor's responsibilities toward his heritage and race began to become more complex than just disagreeing about integration versus separatism. New voices were being raised about who spoke for black people and whether whites could adequately understand or represent effectively either the needs or desires of African-Americans. In essence, the question of authenticity: What does it mean to be black? While this is not the place to do justice to the complexity of the debate, it seems necessary to address the issues that affected Peters' film experience in the late fifties.

The subject crystalized in 1957 because producer Samuel Goldwyn decided that his last film would be an all-black musical based upon the classic folk opera *Porgy and Bess*. His venture became one more chapter in the tumultuous history of the brilliant work that first saw the light of day in 1927, but much more auspiciously in 1935. Composed and written by George and Ira Gershwin but based on DuBose Heyward's novel *Porgy* written a decade before, the 1935 production is set in the poverty-stricken Catfish Row, a dramatized district of Charleston, South Carolina. There, the hard working, deeply religious inhabitants face a never-ending battle against drugs, crime, and violence. When the cruel stevedore Crown murders a man over a card game and escapes to a nearby island, Bess, his beautiful but drug-addicted mistress, seeks safety and rehabilitation with the disabled and beloved Porgy. Their pitiful romance is at the heart of the opera. In the end, Bess suffers a drug relapse and goes off with the slimy Sportin' Life, her drug dealer, to New York. Porgy goes after the pair, determined to save his Bess.

Almost from its inception the Gershwins' folk opera created divisions between white and black audiences. The former found the music magical and later came to consider *Porgy and Bess* "arguably the most important piece of American music written in the 20th century."[48] Seeming indifferent to the opera's language and stereotypes, whites relished the Gershwins' musical genius and theatrical prowess. African-Americans brought with them a different baggage to the performances. While quickly embracing the extraordinary melodies and rich score, blacks had difficulty with three white men, two of whom were Jewish, presuming to tell what African-Americans considered a racist tale about black people, a tale riddled with the N-word and almost every negative behavior associated with the race. The entire project infuriated many African-Americans from 1935 to the present. Even if the authors had toned down the stereotypes, which George Gershwin tried to do almost immediately after the opera opened on Broadway, and which future interpreters of the story tried unevenly to do ever since, black critics decried the fact that white men considered themselves qualified to create a racial narrative for and about black people. No less than the important African-American newspaper *The Pittsburgh Courier* editorialized at the opera's debut, it is "a vehicle of shame, sorrow, and disgust."[49] That said, it would be unfair to suggest that blacks across the board dismissed the folk opera. For example, Eva Jessye, who conducted the original *Porgy and Bess* chorus, felt that Gershwin "had written in things that sounded just right, like our people." J. Rosamond Johnson, a distinguished black composer, called *Porgy and Bess* "a monument to the cultural aims of Negro art."[50]

As you no doubt recall, we've been here before. I take pains in the Preface to address this controversial position. But as a brief refresher, I refer you to the opera's defense by a trio of *Porgy and Bess* experts—Sherwin Goldman, Tazewell Thompson, and Robert Kimball—who discussed the question of the work's perceived racism during an intermission of a 2002 City Center production of the opera.[51] They pointed out that the original show outraged certain blacks not because of the authenticity issue, but because it ran afoul of the Harlem Renaissance then in progress and which wanted control of black images. The opera's fortunes improved over time, because artists like Miles Davis, Ella Fitzgerald, Louis Armstrong, Billie Holiday, Nat King Cole, and Wynton Marsalis constantly viewed and used Gershwin's music as a source of inspiration. As the public better understands and appreciates the Gershwins' intentions, said the trio, the folk opera's prestige may well be at its highest level, as noted by the two Tony awards given to the 2012 production of *Porgy and Bess*: one for the Best Musical Revival and one for Best Actress in a Musical: Audra McDonald.[52]

Given the folk opera's tortured journey, it is not surprising that there are those critics who see *Porgy and Bess* not only as "a reflection of race relations in America," but also as "a prism through which African-Americans have viewed their own history."[53] Nevertheless, there are also those detractors who think it was birthed as an aberration and continues to result in further disasters on the stage and television, the 2012 production included.

By the start of the sixties, more and more African-American leaders and self-appointed spokespeople began voicing their opposition to the inauthenticity surrounding the black experience dramatized in mainstream movies. That perspective challenged black performers to re-examine how they felt about themselves and what roles they accepted in mainstream culture. You will see it come to the forefront here and in the interviews to follow. Rather than rehash my position, let me cite the opinion presented by Joe R. Hick, formally the Executive Director of the Southern Christian Leadership Conference, when dealing with similar problems in the early 1990s: "There has been an attempt, from a certain perspective, to define who is authentically 'black.' That means to be authentically black, you have to articulate a certain kind of political position that...gives you your credentials. To be called 'authentically black,' people are expected to think, talk, represent certain ideas in a certain way. [If they don't do this], they are ruled out of the race, castigated, labeled, name-called. That is outrageous and should not be tolerated. It should be...resisted forcefully."[54] As you will discover, there is a strong difference of opinion about that position throughout *The Interviews*.

Although *Porgy and Bess* had long been on almost every Hollywood producer's wish list, it was Goldwyn who first acquired the rights to the opera in 1957 and set about making it into a movie. But the opera's troubled history only added to the risks associated with bringing the controversial film to the silver screen. The fact that the famous producer had a terrible reputation for being ornery and impolitic, especially when dealing with minorities, did not improve matters. Still further complicating the project were the political and social changes taking place during President Eisenhower's second term. "Now, during the rise of the civil rights movement, a time of bus protests, demonstrations, and changing attitudes," explained

Bogle, "the characters of *Porgy and Bess*, as well as its perspective on African American life looked like social, political, and cultural relics, if not insults."[55] Despite numerous protests against the film, the indefatigable Goldwyn assembled an all-star cast, which included most of the actors from *Carmen Jones* in addition to newcomers Sammy Davis, Jr. and Ivan Dixon. One actor who refused to come aboard was Belafonte. So Sam turned to the one man who was reluctantly becoming the standard bearer for the black film community, Sidney Poitier.

The poor kid who had been born in Miami but raised in the Bahamas with a second grade education and who rose to become the most admired black actor of his generation was also a prominent force in the civil rights era and did not want to take the role of Porgy. Poitier told his agent he didn't even want to meet with Goldwyn to discuss the part. "I don't want to do *Porgy and Bess*," he declared. "*Porgy and Bess* is an insult to black people and I ain't going to play it and that's all there is to it."[56] His close friend Ossie Davis ridiculed the idea, saying in essence that this was not the time for a black man to play a part that required him to be on his knees for the entire movie.[57]

Why and how Poitier was forced to take the role remains problematic. Stickier is what happened during the production itself once Goldwyn replaced the original director, Rouben Mamoulian, with the autocratic Otto Preminger. All the major figures associated with the movie have given their accounts of what took place before, during, after the movie was finished and put in distribution in interviews, biographies, and critical studies. There is no need to repeat the charges and alibis here. What is incontrovertible is the film met with a mixed and hostile reception, resulting in the Gershwin estate withdrawing it from public view to this day.

Brock's role in the controversy proved interesting. Having been in the 1949 national company of the folk opera, he knew the work quite well and had no major problems either with the narrative or the music. He also knew what to expect from Preminger having worked with him on *Carmen Jones*. When Goldwyn offered him the role of Crown, in large part because of his performance in the 1954 musical, the actor readily accepted. If nothing else, it would be his first film in five years!

There is, however, an interesting anecdote concerning Brock's performance. The night before the scene in which Crown rapes Bess, Dorothy Dandridge contacted Preminger and asked if Peters could be replaced. She just found him "too black"[58] and felt uncomfortable doing such a scene with him. Afterwards, Preminger reported the incident to Brock, who didn't know what to make either of the actress' comments or the director's phone call. Consequently, he did the screen rape as planned and everything went off "without incident." The various people knowledgeable about the incident discussed it in their interviews, biographies, and historical records, including individuals like Preminger. Dandridge and Peters. Nonetheless, film historians remain confused over the reasons for the phone call and/or Preminger's remarks to Peters. As for the film and the actor, the *New York Times'* Bosley Crowther spoke for many reviewers when he wrote that the film was first-rate and Peters' performance as Crown: "...thunderingly powerful, dramatically and vocally...."[59] In short, it was Brock's first memorable role in only his second movie. Nonetheless, the Gershwin estate received such negative feedback that it has made the screen version unavailable to the public and intends to destroy any copy of the film the estate finds!

By the end of fifties, Brock was almost broke and concerned about his future. In addition, the struggling actor's problems seemed to be mounting. The burgeoning options for black actors hit the proverbial wall. Hollywood had it's own struggles to stabilize the industry, ward off the threats created by television, deal with the economic pressures from foreign film industries, and respond to the progressives' charges of racism in the movie world. In short, tinsel town was in disarray. Whatever the mainstream filmmakers tried met with little box-office success. Except for Stanley Kramer's *The Defiant Ones* (1958), no black-theme movie justified its production budget or encouraged producers to offer larger roles to African-American performers."[60]

With the coming of the sixties, Peters' fortunes somehow benefitted not only from the uncertainty in the film community but also because of the civil rights battles raging on the national scene and the racial debates fermenting in the cultural community. For one thing, the mild-mannered actor's optimistic spirit led to his marrying Dolores "Didi," [Dee] Daniels on July 29, 1961 in Philadelphia. His wife had previously worked as a writer for both United Artists and the NAACP, as well as been a television executive and public relations expert. Their storied marriage lasted 29 years, and their only child was named Lise Jo Peters.[61]

Coincidentally, around the time of the marriage, a group of former television directors –Robert Mulligan, Sidney Lumet, John Frankenheimer, and Martin Ritt—who had trained under Yul Brynner, a Russian émigré actor and director working at CBS TV in the early fifties, began making their mark in movies.[62] Mulligan became the first of two artists from the ex-CBS team who now helped change Peters' career forever.

In 1961, the director had agreed to adapt Harper Lee's distinguished novel *To Kill a Mockingbird.* Peters desperately wanted the role of Tom Robinson, the black man falsely charged with raping a white woman, the gravest crime an African-American could commit in the Jim Crow South. The producers did not want Brock because of his image as fit only for playing villains. But he and his agent fought hard for the part and won. I suspect that Peters intuitively knew that two of the best black roles in recent movie memory were about African-Americans facing prison terms for crimes they didn't commit: *Intruder in the Dust* (1949) and *Sergeant Rutledge* (1960). If anything could change the industry's perception of him it would be that of being seen as an innocent, honorable black man. And he would have been right.

During the unforgettable courtroom scene where Atticus Finch is defending the helpless black man whose only mistake was in trying to befriend a poor, ignorant white woman, the heroic lawyer asks his client on the stand, did he rape Mayella Violet Ewell? Tom Robinson, sitting stoically, but with tearful eyes, answers unequivocally in a quiet but dignified voice, "I did not, sir!" If the world was not with the defendant then, it certainly was when the bigoted jury delivered an unjust verdict, and the distraught Tom tries to escape his cruel fate only to be killed by a deputy sheriff. Thus in his first dramatic role, the actor had successfully shattered his villainous image forever.

Contemporary critics of the story like author Malcolm Gladwell, legal expert Steven Lubet, and scholar Lisa Linquist Dorr view *To*

Kill a Mockingbird as a poor morality tale for the twenty-first century. They see Atticus not as a civil rights activist forcefully using the law to bring civil justice to minorities, or even as a hero irate because the rule of law was undermined by unrepentant racist neighbors. To these contemporary critics, he is just an unrealistic attorney who believes that change occurs by appeals to the hearts and minds of decent men who are victims themselves of an unjust system carried over from a bygone era.[63]

Interesting and stimulating as such ideas are, I find that such recent attacks on outmoded tolerance and misguided paternalism are appropriate only if the book and film were being made now. However, they do a disservice to works created half a century ago. Whatever perspectve governs the reader's thinking, I doubt that it negates the judgment given by one critic reacting to Peters' portrayal of Tom Robinson: "...a remarkable performance by Brock Peters.... Single-handed [sic] by his intelligent awareness of how a decent Negro so victimized would behave, and by his skillful ability to project such a Negro's feeling and demeanor, Mr. Peters redeems the plot cliché and makes us remember that the history of the black man in the U.S. does include cases like the one on which *To Kill a Mockingbird* is based."[64]

After the Mulligan triumph, Brock turned his attention to England, where British filmmakers had been experiencing a period similar to what Hollywood had been going through for over a decade. As I have noted elsewhere, the fifties created considerable problems for Wardour Street: e.g., massive unemployment, declining production, and an overabundance of mediocre films. That being true, the British film Industry still turned out many outstanding films, mostly based on novels and stage plays centering on individual dilemmas.[65] The Brits had also created their own version of Neo-Realism, which they labeled "Kitchen sink realism." The movement that thrived at the end of the fifties and into the mid-sixties produced such classic movies as *Look Back in Anger, Room at the Top* (both in 1959), *Saturday Night and Sunday Morning* (1960), *The L-Shaped Room* and *The Loneliness of the Long Distance Runner* (both in 1962), *This Sporting Life* (1963), *Alfie,* and *Georgy Girl* (both in 1966).

Brock Peters took advantage of this rebirth of foreign films. Since American studios now had their own companies on British soil, he decided to work abroad and see if things would be different. In 1962, he and Didi spent several months in London, where their daughter was born at year's end.[66] At first, the actor was less than pleased with his decision. Peters was quoted as saying "that if employment was a problem for blacks in America,...it is even greater in England."[67]

Once more, however, fortune favored the persistent, hardworking performer. He got another chance to refurbish his screen persona in Bryan Forbes's *The L-Shaped Room* (1962), set mainly in a run-down Notting Hill boarding house, filled with a lively mixture of tenants, where he acted the part of a gay jazz trumpeter whose best friend falls in love with an unwed pregnant French woman (Leslie Caron). The cast in addition to Caron and Peters included Tom Bell, Avis Bunnage, and Emlyn Williams.

Coincidentally, Caron also came to the now unappreciated film in hopes of changing her stereotyped image of a charming, attractive, and endearing woman gained from her roles in movies like *An American in Paris* (1951), *Lili* (1953) and *Gigi* (1958). As the actress beautifully interacted with her oddball screen neighbors—a writer (Bell), prostitutes, and a washed up vaudevillian—she discovers each of them wants the confused woman to have an abortion.

In a performance I consider almost equal to that of Tom Robinson, Brock plays Johnny, a West Indian musician who is a tremendous cook, outgoing on the surface but secretly priggish and emotionally unpredictable. Bosley Crowther described him as "a gentle Negro jazz musician who occupies an adjoining room and finds his feelings of friendship toward the two [the woman and her lover] rather shockingly torn."[68]

When the British Academy Awards rolled around, *The L-Shaped Room* won for the year's Best Film, while Leslie Caron captured Britain's Best Actress Award. She repeated her triumph at 1963's Golden Globe ceremonies.

Peters returned to England later in 1962 to perform in a charming farce produced and directed by John and Ray Boulting, *Heavens Above!*[69] The witty comedy starred Peter Sellers as a goodhearted but simpleminded cleric who tries to bring religious fervor to his parishioners. Along the way, he unintentionally undermines the less than pious aims of the Church of England. Despite the obvious dangers such a satire presented, the *New Times'* reviewer found the talented brothers "have gone at the highly ticklish subject with as much wit as audacity."[70] Brock Peters played Matthew, a black garbage man who becomes the Vicar's Churchwarden. Basically ignored by the public and the critics in this unimaginative role, Peters did help his image as a versatile actor.

Returning to the States, the revitalized performer now found himself much in demand by the entertainment industry. He took to the stage playing the lead in a 1963 production of *Othello.* Then he resumed his friendship with Charlton Heston, whom he had worked with during his formative stage days in the fifties. The actors teamed up in the first of three films, appearing in Sam Peckinpah's quirky western *Major Dundee* (1965); the other two films being *Soylent Green* (1973) and *Two Minute Warning* (1976). Despite Brock's growing popularity with filmmakers, he had yet to have a breakout role since *To Kill a Mockingbird.*

Then came his second contact with the CBS TV director's group. This time he got a co-starring role alongside Rod Steiger in Sidney Lumet's *The Pawnbroker* (1964), a wrenching Holocaust film. The narrative focuses on Sol Nazerman (Steiger), a Jewish pawnbroker in Spanish Harlem who survived the Nazi concentration camps but remains disconnected with the world around him and involved with the maleficent Rodriquez, the East Harlem gang boss (Peters). Only when a series of tragic events occur does Nazerman see what an abomination his life is, but the epiphany comes too late to save the life of his assistant Jesus Ortiz (Jaime Sanchez). Typical of Lumet films like *Twelve Angry Men* (1957*), Network* (1967), and *Serpico* (1973), *The Pawnbroker* not only focused on conscience and betrayal, but was also why the director was seen as one of film's great moralists.[71]

Peters is impressive as the merciless racketeer who torments the pathetic pawnbroker at the same time Rodriguez dallies with his gay associate. What makes the role so notable is that it was crafted at a time in the sixties when black people shunned negative parts. Ironically, this performance was by a man who for a decade had been trying to shed his stereotypical image as a pitiless brute. As one observer remarked, "[the] ground-breaking role as a ghetto gangster [was unusual because]...until that time, with the exception of all-black films, leading black roles were invariably sympathetic for fear of causing offence."[72] Peters considered the "meaty" role a difficult part. Even though the criminal badly mistreats the film's hero, explained the actor, "I was eager to do it [the movie] for this is a powerful film, an important picture that effectively shows 'it' can happen here and is happening here."[73]

Nominated for many awards, *The Pawnbroker* did not please everyone because of its stylized acting. Nevertheless, many black critics appreciated the opportunity of seeing important actors like Brock Peters, Juano Hernandez, Thelma Oliver, and Raymond St. Jacques doing work worthy of their talents."[74]

By 1967, Peters claimed, "I apparently come over like a virile black buck. Sidney's tall, handsome and boyish and so is Harry Belafonte, whereas audiences see me as the swinging black sexual image they've always been afraid would go after their daughter."[75] According to the *Amsterdam News*, Peters gave up on the movies in disgust from 1968 to late 1969. "I wanted a role," the newspaper reported Peters claiming, "in a picture which would contribute to interracial understanding while still being a very entertaining drama."[76]

For the next eight years, Brock's screen projects—e.g., *The Incident* (1967), *PJ, Daring Game* (both in 1968), *The McMasters* (1969), *Black Girl* (1972), and *Slaughter's Big Rip-Off* (1973)—remained interesting but undistinguished. But there were two assignments that deserve recognition and comment. Both projects had to do with the rise of Black Power: William Styron's *The Confessions of Nat Turner*, and the first black heavyweight champion Jack Johnson. More importantly, they brought distinction to the star not just because of his acting but also because of his powerful voice.

In the waning years of the sixties, the most ambitious black-themed scheme in mainstream movies concerned Twentieth Century-Fox's *The Confessions of Nat Turner*.[77] The intriguing tale of what happened to the controversial project and why is superbly told by Christopher Sieving. Here we need only recall who Nat Turner was and why in 1968 he caught the eye of Brock Peters.

Although there are numerous accounts of the historic nineteenth century slave uprising, I find Lerone Bennett's account most useful for our purposes. "In August, 1831, Nat Turner, a 30-year-old preacher-prophet," explains the noted scholar, "led a slave insurrection in Southampton County, Virginia. For 48 hours, Turner and his aides pressed a war of extermination against slave masters, cutting down the old and the young, male and female. Before the insurrection was quelled, some 55 whites were killed. Turner's insurrection, one of many in the old slave South, traumatized America and triggered a controversy, which still rages."[78]

When novelist William Clark Styron, Jr. published *The Confessions of Nat Turner* (1967), a dramatized version of the slave insurrection, he set off a firestorm in many sections of the black community who since the advent of the Black Power movement viewed Turner as a hero. The issue became even more explosive when numerous white intellectual circles lionized Styron, who had been born in Virginia. In response, as Bennett pointed out, large numbers of black literati saw the novel "as a racist-oriented fantasy"[79] and published their reaction in *William Styron's Nat Turner: Ten Black Writers Respond*.[80] Bringing the argument to a boil was the notion that Hollywood intended to adapt Styron's book into a movie.

Although historians discuss why Twentieth Century-Fox never made its movie, they fail to note what scholar John Henrik Clarke, the editor of the black writers' collection and CMS Records did during the raging debate. From the start, he realized that there was only one historical account of the 1831 uprising, and Clarke decided to have Brock Peters do a dramatic reading of the material and record it. Titled *The Original Confession of Nat Turner*, the classic recording occurred on April 4, 1968.[81]

Because the album notes stated clearly Clarke's intentions, I quote them in full:

> The reading of *The Confessions of Nat Turner* by the distinguished actor, Brock Peters, represents the first attempt to make Turner, leader of the most massive slave revolt ever to occur in America, known to a large popular audience. A widely circulated novel, recently awarded a Pulitzer Prize, was the cause for a number of scholars and critics, black and white, to re-examine the life of Nat Turner and its meaning for today.
>
> The most scholarly book on Turner is Herbert Aptheker's *Nat Turner's Slave Rebellion*, (1966). Aptheker reveals

that Nat Turner was a "highly intelligent man" of profound religious sentiment who in the struggle for freedom led a slave revolt in Virginia in 1831 that accelerated - if not initiated - additional and harsher forms of pro-slavery legislation.

The basic historical document relating to the Nat Turner revolt is, *The Confessions of Nat Turner* by Thomas R. Gray, published in Baltimore in 1831. This document was prepared by a white man, Gray, who was not partial to the cause Nat Turner and his fellow slaves were fighting for. But for all of its limitations, the Gray *Confessions* remains the primary source of information on the most famous slave revolt ever to occur in the United States.

The intention of this record is to let Nat Turner speak for himself to the extent that his real views are reflected in his confessions made to Thomas Gray. Gray was the recorder at Nat Turner's interrogation and acted as an officer of the court at his trial. His pamphlet on the Southampton, Va., slave uprising is the most authoritative document available. It contains the only biographical record of Nat's life that we have and purports to be an "authentic account" of the revolt.

The Nat Turner revolt cannot be understood out of context with the atmosphere of revolt that prevailed throughout the first half of the nineteenth century. There were hundreds of uprisings and conspiracies preceding the Southampton, Virginia, uprising led by Nat Turner. The largest of these was the Denmark Vesey conspiracy in Charleston, South Carolina, in 1822.

The presentation of *The Confessions* of *Nat Turner* on this record is one of the efforts now being made to give the life of Nat Turner an interpretation worthy of his sacrifice.[82]

The project was not without its own problems. As the producers admitted, in their attempt to present an accurate account of the event they failed to use the exact language found in the original legal document. Instead for dramatic and entertainment purposes, Peters used modern English. But making up for this lack of precision, CMS allowed Clarke to hold an unrehearsed discussion with scholar, historian and writer Herbert Aptheker, Peters, and himself. The session was recorded on the flip side of the record. In the session, the actor pointed out that two things marred the interpretation of Gray's report: 1. The term 'murder,' which Peters believes Turner would never have used. The reason, according to Peters, is that 'murder' is a legal term that indicates guilt. Turner was an enlightened man, who pleaded 'not guilty,' thus he would not have used such a term. Instead, he probably used terms like 'destroy," "kill," and "slaughter." 2. The frequent references in the *Confessions*, which suggest the rebellion was the work of a religious fanatic. This presumption annoyed Peters, who felt that it was an attempt by Thomas Gray to allay the fears of the white community at the time; thus he presented Turner as a religious fanatic, and not a man using logical, concerted thought, a pragmatist. This might imply that there were others like him…[who] desired to be free, not fanaticism, but cold, calculated desires to be free.[83] The three men also provided considerable detail about Turner and the times.

I consider it very surprising and disappointing that *The Original Confession of Nat Turner* is ignored and absent from serious examinations of important media events in the latter half of the Twentieth Century. But then the public's conduct towards Brock Peters in the larger picture of black film experiences is just as unexpected and upsetting.

Five months later, almost to the date of the Turner recording, James Earl Jones appeared as Jack Jefferson in Howard Sackler's *The Great White Hope* on Broadway. Peters played the boxer, modeled on the real Jack Johnson, in the national road company. What many people don't realize is that in 1970, Big Fights Inc. made an excellent documentary on the first black man to become heavyweight champion of the world. The movie expertly filled in many of the questions and incidents left unanswered in the Broadway show and Martin Ritt's 1970 film version of the same name. *Variety*'s review highly praised Peters' voice-over narration, saying it was "engagingly enthusiastic and informative," and praised Brock's "rich" recreation of the turn-of-the-century pugilist.[84] Adding to the power of the Oscar-nominated documentary was Miles Davis' stunning original score, one which was later recorded separately and became, according to his biographer John Szwed, one of the legendary musician's "favorite recordings for a long time, and it's obvious why from the first note...."[85]

In the early seventies, the notable actor-singer provided, what I consider, his last two memorable contributions to the black film experience. First came his co-production of *Five on the Black Hand Side* (1973). Based on the Off-Broadway hit by Charles Russell and directed by Oscar Williams, both of whom reprised their roles for the movie, the narrative amusingly took potshots at the fictional Brooks family. A chauvinist husband tries during drastically changing times to maintain his despotic domination of his wife and their three adult children. By the film's conclusion, Papa Brooks gets brought into the twentieth century, but also becomes a better man for his reformation.

Entertaining as the film was and is, the main reason for its popularity with audiences, critics, and film historians has to do with its role as an alternative to the then popular black action films. For example, *Garnett News Service* stated bluntly, "In 1973, when Hollywood was cranking out what were known as blaxploitation films, Peters [co-] produced a kooky, G-rated comedy called *Five on the Black Hand Side,* a modest film based on a play by Charlie Russell that was intended to go against the tide of 'guns, goons, and gore."[86] *Ms.* declared, "If *Sounder* started a trend toward humanized black mothers, the film *Five on the Black Hand Side* and the television series *Good Times* seem to be comic variants on the theme."[87] In the *Christian Science Monitor,* reporter Nora E. Taylor stated that the film "... does not toady to today's themes of blaxploitation, sex, violence. It is not racist. It perhaps could be called ethnic."[88] *Encore* chimed in, saying, "You've been mesmerized by super slick, over-sexed movies like *Shaft, Mack,* and *Coffy.* Now be hypnotized by "some brand new jive" that makes you feel for real and full of Black pride."[89]

Five on the Black Hand Side's success delighted not only its producers, but also surprised its backers. "It was a big hit," Peters told reporter Taylor, "—the sort of success that one would expect would open doors for the producer. But that didn't happen." How come she wondered? "'I can't tell you why,' explained Peters, "'It's just... well, the system: The faceless people who have all the money and make the decisions."[90]

In 1974, Brock next appeared in Daniel Mann's screen adaptation of the 1972 Broadway revival of *Lost in the Stars,* a musical version of the Alan Paton novel *Cry, the Beloved Country*. Zoltan Korda's 1951 movie of the book featured Canada Lee (Kumalo) and Sidney Poitier (Msimangu, a young Johannesburg pastor). Unbelievable as it is today, the men had to agree to being "indentured laborers" in order to make the movie on location in South Africa.[91] In 1995, a production by South African filmmaker Darrell Roodt, starring James Earl Jones (Kumalo) and Richard Harris (James Jarvis, father of the murdered boy), almost matched the majesty of the Korda film.

In 1972, Brock Peters starred on Broadway in a revival of the Kurt Weill-Maxwell Anderson musical *Lost in the Stars* translated from the celebrated book. When Weill first conceived the musical alteration back in the late forties, he was recalling his years under Nazi domination. He told interviewers that he hoped audiences understood his message in the play, that racial reform can best be achieved through personal relations.[92]

Peters had reservations about the message from the perspective of the 1970s. As the troubled but deeply religious Reverend Stephen Kumalo travels from the countryside to the daunting Johannesburg in search of his missing son, he discovers that his child has murdered the son of a rich man from Kumalo's community. According to the actor, he played the Anglican minster as if he were Martin Luther King.[93] That is, as Peters critiqued the production: "The personal approach seems too limited today. Certainly people-to-people contacts are valid. But I think if Weill had written today, Kumalo would have been more like Dr. King. More of a leader and an activist, with King's non-violence philosophy."[94]

Although the revival met with mixed reviews and had a limited run, Peters enjoyed considerable critical success. His stage acting and warm, powerful singing resulted in a Drama Desk Award, an Outer Critics Circle Award, and a Tony Award nomination.

The following year he repeated the role in the Daniel Mann movie for a revolutionary motion picture company, Ely A. Landau's American Film Theatre, the first attempt to establish a "national theatre-on-film." Working with the belief that many commercially unsuccessful plays nonetheless deserved a visual record for theatrical historians, Landau selected a mixed bag of dramas. *Lost in the Stars* was one of them. It received less than rave reviews, but I found it invaluable in recalling Brock's many gifts.

As the decades rolled on, Peters continued his work on television, the stage, and in the movies. I will add only that among my favorites in the remaining years were Brock's ties to the *Star Trek* franchise: the numerous episodes on *Star Trek: Deep Space Nine,* where Peters played Captain Benjamin Sisko's father; as well as his role as Admiral Cartwright in *Star Trek IV: The Voyage Home* (1986) and *Star Trek VI: The Undiscovered Country (1991).*

Peters' gifts did not go unrecognized by his peers. Among his many honors were lifetime achievement awards from the National Film Society (1976) and the Screen Actors Guild, (1990), induction into the Black Filmmakers Hall of Fame (1976), the NAACP Image Award (1988), and his own star on the Hollywood Walk of Fame (1992).[95] The public, however, remains mostly unaware of his name, but very much familiar with his face.

Didi died in 1990. Fifteen years later, after a six-month battle with pancreatic cancer, the illustrious actor, blessed with an imposing presence, a stirring voice, and a wonderful disposition, died on August 23, 2005 in Los Angeles. To me, Brock Peters embodied the words of a song my dear mother used to sing: "He made the night a little brighter wherever he would go. The old lamplighter of long, long ago."

Brock Peters was one of the few actors I contacted on my own. On December 27, 1971, I sent a letter to the actor care of the Blake Agency, asking for an interview between January 3rd and 9th, when I would be in Los Angeles on a research trip dealing with black film history. Explaining that I would be staying at the Roosevelt Hotel, I told his agents I could be reached in Vermont up to the end of the month. This letter resulted in my visiting Brock at his home on January 7th. Clearly, the Peters family had plans for the day, but Didi and his delightful daughter, Lise Jo, made me feel there was no problem in delaying the excursion so that Brock and I could have an extended conversation. I never felt hurried or intrusive. Brock was gracious and charming. Most of all, he gave me that feeling this was a conversation he had long wanted to have with a responsible person associated with film history. What follows cannot do justice to the satisfaction I had spending time with that rare human being.

Brock Peters Interview
January 7, 1972

FM: We haven't had enough positive images.

BP: Today, because we haven't had enough good images, especially on television. Soon there will be.

FM: There should be!

BP: Television is a powerful medium for influencing people, for influencing change; and it should be.

FM: Absolutely, absolutely.

BP: So when you start from zero, to create positive images, you start from the time when there were none. And when you're trying to get to a higher level, you have to pass by over zealousness and a lack of compassion that causes misunderstanding, and often is standing in the way of any other truths that might be told. Especially in the hands of people you mistrust or people you feel have done badly by you.

It's difficult to keep your balance, to trust your judgment. It's a time in history where there is great change.... And maybe it isn't the tidal wave of change that you want it to be, but it's moving very rapidly. Nobody seems to want to be behind it. Everybody wants to be in front of it. And everybody wants to be a leader of it, in a way. Consequently, you get many people screaming louder than makes any sense, purely because of the attention it will get them. And purely because a great deal...great masses of people are not as sophisticated about what it is you're dealing with. They become sophisticated after the fact. Not until they get to know what's entailed; then they jump on the bandwagon about what seems should be done, not examining how it's being done, who is saying it, or how he leads. So we have a terrible problem of.... Well, I could go on at length.

FM: No, no. What I mean is what is the problem?

BP: The problem becomes one of misinformation, over-zealousness, and misdirection. It doesn't take you anywhere. By the time you discover that, and you try to put something together to get ahead of the game and find the right direction....

FM: What happens to a guy like you as far as roles, as far as parts?

BP: Well, for a guy like myself, I rarely use the term "militant" to describe myself, and I'm sure there are a lot of people who do not think I'm militant. Yet, from all I've learned around, I'm a respected actor in every sense of the word. Because I am a quality performer.... Past that, I think that because of the kinds of roles I've played, even at a time when there was very little activity as far as black people changing the scene of television and films, I had arrived at a stage in my career where I was respected enough to say, "I don't like this, or I don't want to do that," and they would change something in the scripts to read more truthfully. Perhaps they did read, or in many cases I just said, "I can't do it." I have a long record of saying "No." Perhaps if I'd accepted a number of those jobs, I might not have been as well liked as a black actor...It's a question of judgment or taste...besides, I might have been richer.

FM: Can you tell me just a little bit about yourself; when you were born, how you grew up, what influenced you.

BP: I was born in Harlem; I'm first generation American. My mother and all my uncles and aunts on my mother's side come from the West Indies. My father was born in Africa, Senegal; he was part of the principle tribe called Wolof. I went to an elementary school in Harlem, and Frederick Douglass Junior High School...a very special oasis at that time. Countee Cullen taught there.

A noted American poet, anthropologist, novelist and dramatist who became a leading member of the Harlem Renaissance, Countee Cullen (1903-1946) chose to make racial issues a major part of his work, but not the core ingredient. He strove to be the equal of England's great Romantic poets: e.g., William Blake, William Wordsworth, and John Keats. That is, his great dilemma was how to be a universal artist, not a great Negro writer.[96] *His sense of high purpose, his religious values, and his honored place among the 'New Negro' spokespeople in the late 1920s, as we have seen, influenced Peters critically. Two evident effects would be seen in Peters' conservative nature and in his very sensitive behavior toward others. Countee's artistic stance did, on the other hand, suggest to some of his*

Harlem Renaissance friends that Cullen possessed an element of "racial self-hatred."[97] *The questions the artist asked himself were ones that almost every black performer in* The Interviews *would ask: Must I be a black artist first and an artist second? What is my responsibility to my race? To myself? Which is the dominant force?*

BP: A number of black teachers and white teachers who were very interested in black culture. We became terribly aware of W. E. B. Du Bois, Countee Cullen; they taught there. Langston Hughes. We met these people. Over a number of years, they got to be personal friends of mine.

In Harlem, at the time that I grew up, there were a great number of artists, painters, sculptors, and writers. It was not just a little community. It was the Harlem of Bill Robinson, lots of exciting Vaudeville performers for which Harlem was noted. Songs, music, singers and dancers. Exciting community of entertainment.

Past that performing entertainment, there was also a very strong cultural community. But as years passed, it disintegrated, and people went elsewhere. But I grew up in that atmosphere. I was impressionable.

Luckily, I, the direction—my father died early—the direction my mother set for me. I became interested in the arts, I became interested in performing. She insisted that I take violin lessons, which I did for about twelve years. At first reluctantly, then after a while I began to enjoy the instrument. But about the time that I was really enjoying what I had learned, and possibly what I might do with that instrument, I decided that there wasn't anywhere that I really could go with it. It would only be a hobby. There just weren't any opportunities for black instrumentalists at the time. So I let go of that instrument.

As it happened, I could sing. I sang in the church choir. I began taking voice lessons to get job opportunities as a singer. Even before acting opportunities were available as far as a real professional. So that there are a lot of people around still remember me as a singer at first. I was with the American Negro Theatre, with people like [Harry] Belafonte, [Sidney] Poitier, Hilda Simms, Frederick O'Neal, Ruby Dee, Ossie Davis…I think they think well enough about me in the organizations.

FM: This was in the '40's?

BP: Yup. And Herbert Hill had been co-founder, with Frederick O'Neal. They had helped train actresses like Hilda Haynes, oh, any number of actors. I can't remember all their names.

FM: James Edwards is one, who is seen working with Woody Strode in *Pork Chop Hill*.

As pointed out in Every Step a Struggle, *Frederick Douglass O'Neal helped found many theatrical troupes for black actors. In the early forties, the time Peters is discussing, O'Neal had co-founded with the dramatist Abram Hill in 1940 the American Negro Theatre (ANT). This group, which lasted nine years, was the training grounds for the personalities Peters is discussing. Nearly a quarter-of-a-century later, O'Neal became the first black actor to serve as the president of Actors Equity Association (AEA).*[98]

Black dramatist and director Abram Hill's most popular play for the ANT was On Strivers' Row *(1940), a comedy that satirized the social-climbing activities of a wealthy Harlem family. Born on January 10, 1910, the prominent African-American artist died at his Harlem residence on October 6, 1986.*[99]

FM: They gave a lot of people a break.

BP: Right. So there...there was a very strong cultural community called Harlem. And I suppose what reputation it still has, apart from the negatives, seems to apply to it today, or people say anyways. But the fact that there was an assemblage, an assemblage of talent which is really very important not only to that community but to all black communities around the country and outside. Philosophers have written on the contribution of black people to Western civilization, with great accuracy and precisely how it involved numbers of people. Lots of people have written eloquently about the experience of the black man...Jimmy Baldwin, he has written eloquently about the experiences of the black man.

FM: How did you get into movies?

BP: Well, I suppose one thing leads to another. I got...I got on to the Broadway stage, if it can be said that you're on the Broadway stage. You do bits in shows. Maybe a show comes along, and you get an opportunity to do secondary roles. I heard that many of the other actors got that opportunity, heard the applause of the crowd, and said now I'm launched. But that was never the case with me. It was always a one-time experience. Then desperately waiting for the next opportunity.

You waited around and did what ever else you could to support yourself until the next opportunity came. You tried your best to keep yourself in shape until that next opportunity came. You took classes. You sat and discussed the business of creativity on the stage, the creativity of black people, what they might have to give, none of what is happening today either in the cultural area or the political area. Because today it's sprung out of a vacuum; it does not grow out of such experiences as ours and those who preceded us. We talked about what we wanted to do, what we hoped to do.

In any case, with a few tidbits on the Broadway stage. At one point, I got a recording contract. It didn't carry me very far in that direction. Then I won a television talent show—very famous at the time—Arthur Godfrey Show.

Arthur Morton Godfrey (1903-1983), a popular CBS five-day-a-week radio host from the mid-1940s through the fifties, also had a weekly program where he auditioned new performers. Known as Arthur Godfrey's Talent Scouts, *the program was broadcast simultaneously on the radio and television, beginning in 1948. Peters went on the TV show as a singer in 1953.*[100]

FM: Oh yes. Was there somebody bringing you on?

BP: You know that I've forgotten. [Both of us laugh.] Well, in any case, it was a long time ago. I came to the attention of Otto Preminger, who cast me as Sgt. Brown in the film, *Carmen Jones*.

According to one source, the initial relationship between Preminger and Peters did not go well, with the latter early on in the filming chewing out the actor "…in front of a lot of people…. [Saying] something about this New York actor…. Some disparaging things. I lost my temper and I went for him." Peters later became friends with the overbearing director. He made it a point of letting others know of his astonishment in discovering that Preminger "was a life member of the NAACP…."[101]

BP: Afterwards, I did I number of television shows. And it was five years between my first and second film. The second film was very controversial...controversially discussed film: *Porgy and Bess.* I finally accepted the role of Crown. That was the second film I did. I had done some television, as I said, between *Carmen Jones* and *Porgy and Bess.*

FM: That was Preminger.

The production credits included producer Sam Goldwyn, choreographer Hermes Pan, and musical director Andre Previn. Adele Addison dubbed Ms. Dandridge's singing, while Robert McFerrin did Mr. Poitier's vocals. Crowther described Peters' Crown as "the spoiler, with his lust and rapaciousness toward Bess."[102]

BP: Again Preminger. He came into it after I had been assigned the role of Crown by Goldwyn, inspired by my work in *Carmen Jones.* Goldwyn felt I was right for this epic film. Goldwyn had produced *Carmen Jones* [sic].

Preminger was the producer.

BP: In any case, there were two years of trying to get the funding for *Porgy and Bess* before the film went into production. There was a lot of talent associated with the film, which helped raise the money.

I did a lot of television in the meantime, which helped my career. I gained a reputation for not only being dependable but pretty good. Past that point, I did nothing in films until 1962.

That film—that year I did two films almost back-to-back: *The L-Shaped Room*[103] and *To Kill a Mockingbird.*[104]

These films were very helpful, both in breaking the image that was created for me in the first two films. They were nearly seven years apart. In both *Carmen Jones* and *Porgy and Bess,* I had played heavies, and I had been represented that way. Producers thought that I was pretty good, but they also thought that I was physically too big and much too heavy a character for sympathetic roles. So I wasn't given sympathetic roles.

I was represented at that time by a French agency...they went out to get me different [parts].... All three of those films helped break this villain image.

The third film was the Boulting Brothers' Heaven Above!, *but it was released in 1963.*

FM: Did you play the villain for TV programs?

BP: I played a victim most often. Always a victim, innocent, confined either to prison, or.... There was always something wrong. He was the good guy essentially, but he didn't have the wherewithal to get a lawyer for whatever it was. I played that kind of character.

FM: Sympathetic person?

BP: Yes. Sympathetic. I never really felt like I had the opportunity for doing any of the positive things that are so popular today and so necessary. During that period of years, of *Porgy and Bess*, the next three years. I did turn down a number of television shows and a couple of films where they were interested in me, but what they'd created in the screenplay was something if it would get projected would not help either my case or the cause that I felt needed to be supported.

FM: Different producers with political stories, because I've heard a lot of stories that each one was trying to present a different point of view. In these roles, do you remember seeing a negative characteristic, the roles that you turned down, the roles that you were offered? Were the people producing those roles...? Is that the way they thought, you know; that's the way they understood black culture, or do you think that it was an out-and- out—you know—attempt to really exploit blacks from a racist point of view?

BP: Well, I can think of one screenplay that comes to mind, that came to me almost immediately after *Porgy and Bess*. It was as transparent as anything that I had ever read on what they had done. They put a black character in the place of a character that had originally been created white. It was an early kind of exploitation, because whoever wrote this and whoever agreed that this should be done in the script was already anticipating something that was about to happen. Historically, the character was completely untrue. Certainly a black man couldn't have behaved this way under the circumstances. He was a type that didn't exist at the time. Certainly if it was a black man in those circumstances, he couldn't have done these things. If I did it, it would project something that was entirely untrue. I couldn't live with it. I sat down and explained something that I felt was wrong, the use of the character in the script, how it could be corrected, and it would be under those circumstances that I would be able to accept the role. Of course, they weren't about to do anything like that. It showed their attitude about what they wanted to do. They were amazed at this black cat's temerity. I was supposed to be glad that I was considered for the role.

FM: Do you remember the name?

BP: No, I'm glad to say. I can skip a number of years and come up to a time fairly recently in 1968, 1969 actually. I had a multiple deal with an Italian film company. What they say back here is to be careful of Italian deals. You had to be careful in these foreign deals. Absolutely true! In any case, I had this deal. I tied down all the loose ends to be sure it was an ironclad situation. I went over and made one picture for them. I made sure it was all right to do. Then they sent me the idea for a second film. I'd go back over and do another film for them. The character was a person. Totally acceptable to me. Then, they sent me the script—the screenplay, but that had problems.

FM: Different from what they had proposed? [We both laugh]

BP: Yes. I was very aware at the time it needed rewriting. In any case, when I got the second screenplay, I read it. Here again was the situation; it was unbelievable. I wrote them and explained that neither they nor I—it was 1969—could risk a reputation and money in a venture such as this. No enlightened black or white audience would buy it. They'd be throwing their money away. They should either revise the old concept or come up with another one. If they came up with another one, we could proceed, but not with this one. I can't remember if I said it before—after the first film, when I had a script or after the second screenplay. The response to my letter came back, something to the effect that the Hollywood studio wanted me to do it or else.

FM: They'd love you to do the part. [Laughter] You told them to read the fine print.

BP: We reminded them of the fine print in the contract. We finally decided to bail out of the contract. As the fortunes would have it, the company folded in the interim. That was the end of that contract.

FM: Did they ever release the first film that you made?

BP: Oh, yes. That was released as *Quattro del'Ave Maria* in 1968. Here it was called *Ace High*.[105] And there were two other American actors that starred in it: Eli Wallach and Kevin McCarthy. And from the little I've heard, it seemed to do reasonably well. It was described as a "Spaghetti Western."

That was the second such experience, but there were a number of others. I haven't always taken the time to carefully explain why I didn't want to enter into these types of films. Sometimes, it was easier. It depended on whom you dealt with. I've done that in the hope that they would go back and review what it is they had. Try to put something sensible together. But they don't care. At least, they haven't cared previously. That's the nature of the game. Nowadays, they don't care.

FM: They don't care?

BP: No, they haven't cared. They're not going to get me. Not being that difficult—I've never been difficult. I've done my work in any working situation, but I'm probably going to be very straight about what's involved. If they are twisting stories, or if they out to get a certain effect, I'm likely not to play the game.

FM: Can I go back over the films now? I'm still not clear on how you got to *Carmen Jones*. How were you able to get that role? Did your agent try to get it for you? Or they came to see you?

BP: *Carmen Jones*? I was submitted for *Carmen Jones* by a representative of mine at the time. Part of the interest, I think, in me came from my fame on the Arthur Godfrey talent show, and also I was thinking of doing a new recording for Columbia. A feeling at the time that I was considered a young talent. I suppose there was an aura around me, coupled with an interview, it seems how I got, I assume that's how I got the role of Sergeant Brown.

FM: Were there any interesting stories on the set? I know there was a lot of talk about a romance between Preminger and Dorothy Dandridge; about them having lots of fights on the set. Did you know that?

BP: [Laughs] Well that surprises me. I never knew anything like that.

FM: She did a book,[106] published posthumously in.... [1970]

BP: I have got to read it. I know about it. She indicated that there were fights on the set?

FM: Lots of them, often.

BP: I didn't know about it. Certainly, I was too busy with my own ambitions. I didn't pay a great deal of attention to other actors' personal problems on the set. My concern primarily, I was trying to bring off a good performance. You walk a tightrope in that you do what you think is really right for a character, and then see how the director receives it. But you're always under the pressure that it could be wrong; you don't always know what concept he has in view for the character. Sometime you find yourself being railed at very loudly in front of a large complement of actors and technicians. It goes very badly on the spirit. Very much against the grain. It makes it therefore very difficult for you to work. Circumstances!

FM: Nothing much you can do about it. Except maybe walk off.

BP: Well, yes and no. A very interesting thing happened; I'm trying now to remember who the other party was. But one day I think I had just about enough, and I reached around and grabbed him [Preminger] by the lapel, and I shook him. [Laughter]

Pearl Bailey was the other person. I grabbed Preminger. I know Pearl likes to tell the story that she saved my career as it were by grabbing me at the right moment. And as she points out, as I well knew, it wouldn't matter how right I would have been. The fact that I grabbed a successful white producer/director could kill any opportunity I had to be in acting. That I had grabbed him physically. It was one thing to perhaps to explode and be very upset and have had a miserable time myself over it. But to unleash your anger.

Bogle[107] and Fujiwara[108] repeat the story. Important to realize is that Preminger browbeat most of performers and that the Peters' encounter was one of many in the producer/director's long and controversial career.

FM: 1952, 53?

BP: 1953.

FM: What was Preminger's reaction? Did he expect it from his performers?

BP: No. I don't know what he expected from me, but I know he was surprised. I think he assessed the situation. I was sure that I was fired at that point. I didn't realize that I had enough footage to be allowed to finish the film. That was my first film.

Several years later, when I had been hired by Goldwyn on a movie he was on, and Preminger was brought on, I was sure that I would be dropped, that he would remember his earlier experiences with me.

But the first day he saw me, he gave me a warm embrace, asked about my health and how I'd been doing, and—

[Phone Rings]

[BREAK]

FM: OK, I think we're going now.

BP: Where was I?

FM: You had another anecdote. He embraced you on the set and asked you....

BP: Oh, yes. On the set of *Porgy and Bess* when he [Preminger] was hired, he embraced me on the set. As I say, he asked after my health, what had been going on in my career, and all the usual kinds of questions. He seemed to try to put me at ease. For a day or two after I saw him, I was not at ease in spite of the warmth of his greeting, but I learned in time that whatever his feelings may have been, I wasn't being fired.

One of the reasons I knew that I was on was that Sam Goldwyn told me how I was hired for the role of Crown in *Porgy and Bess,* and it was a very simple thing. He had seen me in *Carmen Jones* as Sergeant Brown, and he decided against all others, all other advice that I was right. He didn't want a physically outsized man for Crown. He wanted someone, he felt, who was physically appealing, etc., not the usual black buck giant, so he hired me for that reason. The quality of the performance he had seen and because he felt that I more nearly fit his view of what Crown would be like.

It's very interesting, paradoxically, that role. It made it very difficult for me thereafter. I think I described earlier on the tape; to find employment because most people—most producers, who should know better, and directors—thought I was 6'6" in height and probably two hundred and fifty pounds; none of which is true. And that I might not do the more sensitive things that they had in their scripts.

Backward now—the other anecdote about *Carmen Jones* happened about a year and a half before *Porgy and Bess* was a *fait de complete* in the hands of Sam Goldwyn. I was driving, and I saw him, and I honked the horn. I asked him, could I give him a lift? He said, "Yes." He was staying at the Ambassador East, which doesn't exist anymore. I said, "I'll drop you." So we drove across town from 43rd Street and Broadway to 51st, 52nd Street and Park Avenue. Coming across town in New York traffic is very tough during the day. Then as well as now. And we got into quite a conversation, and I asked him about *Porgy and Bess*, and he—

[BREAK]

BP: Was he planning to do it? I read lots of things and heard many rumors.

FM: Un huh.

BP: He [Goldwyn] said, "No. He'd been bidding for it, but he'd been out bid for the property, so he didn't have…he hadn't gotten it. And then he asked me the question that is [laughing] wont to start the temperature rising and that is, "Why don't you people [laughing], why don't you people go after it?" And I asked him what he meant by "you people." He said, "Well…. your…you know, your people. It's a picture that you could do."

According to one Goldwyn biographer, the famous producer often made major racial gaffs. On the set of Porgy and Bess, *for example, "various civil rights organizations and the minority press regularly tarred Goldwyn for his anachronistic attitudes towards blacks."*[109]

FM: Something by Gershwin.

[Both of us are laughing]

BP: So…yeah…well…. One thing led to another, and we were into a railing argument because I said, "Well the very first thing that happens is that 'you people' cannot raise that kind of money. We come by the money we do make over rough roads. And black people, who may have money, have to work pretty hard to get it, and if they make a fortune in their lifetime, they're not apt to play games with it—the kinds of games that happen in the picture business."

"Well," he says, "I never use any of my own money…. I always go to the bank."

I said, "Well, that's fine, but at this point in time, a black man walking into a bank to ask for funding for a picture would get thrown out. It's just barely possible for him to get money to buy his own home or invest in a small business. But to go in and talk about a million or so for a motion picture."

Interestingly, in 2006, the African-American Roundtable *had a show on "Black Hair," in which the participants discussed the fact that at least eighty per cent of the suppliers to beauty salons catering to blacks in predominantly black neighborhoods were Korean, with only ten percent of the suppliers being African-American. According to Ayena Byrd, author of* Hair Story: Untangling the Roots of Black Hair in America, *a major reason was that "black people historically have a harder time getting a loan to open a business...."*[110]

BP: He [Goldwyn] said, "Nonsense."

I told him that he didn't know what was going on, and he was a fool. By the time we got to the Ambassador East, we were having a shouting match. He got out of the car and slammed the door, and I told him I hoped he had a good goddamn flight back to the West Coast. And I drove off in a roar. So again, by the time I saw him on the set at *Porgy,* not only was there the experience in my mind, the remembered experience of having grabbed Preminger on the set of *Carmen Jones,* but of the argument we had a couple of years later in New York.

This argument was not trivial in light of what happened to Calvin Lockhart. According to Walter Burrell, "Producer Pervis Atkins (Black) and director Hugh Robertson (also Black) had probably the toughest fight of all when they did battle with white executives at MGM during production of "Melinda." The studio (and the movie industry) had, according to Robertson, blacklisted Calvin Lockhart, the film's star, and MGM didn't want to use him in the film. Robertson said Lockhart was blacklisted when he argued with Sam Goldwyn Jr. during filming of Cotton Comes To Harlem. *Robertson and Atkins also had to fight for script changes (again regarding the images of the film's black women) and for behind-the-scenes personnel. They managed to win most of their battles.*[111]

FM: Was it true—I read over and over again—that black actors got a different salary than white actors for the same roles?

BP: This happened a lot on Broadway.

FM: Even as late as the '50?

BP: Oh, yes. It was frequently a cause for real knock-down-drag-out battles in the Union to try to....

FM: Did they have any muscle at all—blacks in the 50's? You could argue that....

BP: Well, the muscle you had...a union like Equity was...was disposed to trying to do something about it. We were on Council, and we could therefore get brought up before Council and try to get the adjustments made.

FM: In Hollywood?

BP: No, I'm now talking about Equity. It was not...it was not easily done. And that the.... As I say, a great deal of consternation, as a matter of fact, Equity was often accused of having made the kind of deal that would permit a producer to get away with that. But whether this is true or not.... I was never in such an experience. But I know of these things having happened, and that there having been great rows about it. I suppose, finally, adjustments were made. It could certainly not happen today.

FM: I was under the impression....

BP: It would be disastrous for the union to permit, if they ever knew it, to allow a producer to get away with that.

FM: Well, were there any really black plays getting on Broadway? The first really big one was *A Raisin the Sun* in '58 [1959].

BP: No, the problem—well a play like that, of course, is an all black-cast. A producer can pay what he negotiates with an actor. He pays that, and that's that. You can argue as much as you like about it. What you agree to is what you get. Sure we know that Sidney Poitier probably could command what he should get for a Broadway piece. Claudia McNeil might not have gotten what she should get for her, for her stature in the theater. She might not have gotten what a white actress of comparable stature might have gotten. That...that has often been the case in...in bygone years in the theater. And it has generally been the practice, not just in film industry, or in the theater, it's been generally been the practice in all kinds of employment outside of professional.

FM: I want to ask you about that.

BP:...performing professions.

FM: Over and over again, as I've talked to people, they...they sometimes say to me that they don't think Hollywood did anything different from anyone else...that the black man was treated this way all across the world.... there was nothing special about Hollywood.

BP: No, it's true.

FM: And the Hollywood people say to me that what they...they were never really racist. This is the way they saw it. And they were most worried about the box-office. Over and over again they say to me, the reason we put that role in or the reason we didn't star that person is because we did not think it would sell at the box-office. And for some reason, the Southern box-office seemed to have controlled the industry up to about 1950. They were...they were always worried about the South.

BP: They were always worried about the South. And now they... they can't use the myth of the South anymore. I say "myth" primarily because something like five or six years ago...some research was done.... Now I can't remember the group that did the research, but apparently it was very sound work because a number of articles appeared in the weekly *Variety* and other places. It described the...the black audience as one third of the movie-going public and suggested therefore that in years to come Hollywood was going to have to pay attention to this very valuable market, since one of its concerns, Hollywood's concerns, was that it was losing markets. They weren't able to describe or define their markets so easily as they had done in the past.

Now, the business of my describing it as a myth—the myth of the South or of the Southern box-office control—is that many producers went ahead arbitrarily and cast the way they did and used that. The direct ratio between what has happened politically and socially in this country to the number of films that are being produced by blacks should be a good example of when we can expect to see things change on the screen. When we are actively engaged in changing our situation socially, politically, and economically in this country.

One of the great fallacies about show business is that we in show business, "show business" in quotes, are less prejudiced than all other people. "Look how we performers behave with each other." Well, the fact that black and white performers, numbers of them may know each other and that they enjoy social exchange, does not mean that the industry itself—either in the theater or in films—is integrated and/or so disposed towards openness. You can count the number of black producers who are members of the Producers' Association....

FM: Or grips, or cameramen, or screenwriters, or....

BP: Exactly. I start at the top. It's hard; it's not easy to become a member. The economics of the business has not allowed for a black man being.... Not the economics, but the view has not allowed a black man to have the control of a production either for a studio or, or.... It's been extremely difficult for a black man to raise the money himself to produce a picture, to be an independent. Now it has finally happened, but it does not mean...it's perhaps merely the opening of a door...but it does not mean....

FM: That's not really the answer sometimes because anyone can produce a film: It's getting distributed and exhibited...

BP: Of course.

FM:...that's where they get killed.

BP: Of course, of course. The point finally is that all this great love that this industry we're in is supposed to have...the lie is that we're not in the position to do films about ourselves that we should have been in. It's even.... Two things that have happened that all the black actors know about, all black writers know about today. The word has gone out in Hollywood, for example, that the stories are not to be black anymore. They're to be Chicano, because that they feel that they've, they've exhausted the interest in the problems black or whatever.

And, and there was another conversation that was reported that took place and it had to do with producers at a meeting saying, "Look, we'll produce these films. We can produce these films about blacks. They don't have to be involved in the production."

So there is that resistance and always has been to our being involved in upper echelons in terms of.... And even in the in the craft unions, we've been kept out of those things.

FM: Consciously.

BP: Consciously kept out.

FM: Sure.

BP: There have been plenty of black people who wanted to and who tried to and...

FM: And who have the ability.

BP: Or have the ability, or even if they didn't have the ability and wanted to apprentice themselves…could not get into apprentice programs. When a number of years have passed and this is the case, one can only consider that this is a sin not of omission but of commission. You meet them all the time; black people who wanted to do this, and wanted to do that and wanted to do the other, and couldn't. They've got tales that they could tell you that would turn your stomach about the experiences they've had trying to open a door for themselves in this industry and elsewhere. So we know the lie of the business, the great…whatever you describe it…the great openness of show business.

FM: How do you treat a guy like Stepin' Fetchit? If I understand from what I've heard…the guy is to be more admired than downgraded. The system being as difficult and as rotten as it was.

BP: Well, Stepin' Fetchit is a case in…a case in point in terms of the use of the term "Uncle Tom." There's a positive side to it. Sure I can look at the negative side and say, he…what…collaborated or compromised and perhaps he degraded himself. But that did happen, that he did compromise, and that he did perhaps degrade himself and perhaps in some instances, not perhaps, did in many instances save his own skin and sacrificed others. But as often, if not more often, "Uncle Tom's" cleverness was that he survived.

FM: Yeah, and he also helped make it better for others.

BP: He often did a number of things…compromised himself or whatever in order to help others.

FM: By the way, before I forget….

BP: So, there are two sides to everything. I'm not making a case for Uncle Tom because there are people who are "Uncle Tom" even now, who have nothing in view but themselves. And…in this day and age, there really isn't a need to be that. Everything is so open… in every way. The whole society…there's an attempt to open it all up…to get to more truthful exchanges between people at every level. There's no real need for it.

FM: There are enough roles that they do not have to….

BP: I'm not even talking about roles now…. I'm talking about in all of society, at all levels…exchanges between human beings. There isn't any need for that…anymore. There was, you know, when, when the establishment and the power structure and all the attitudes were seemingly monolithic and impossible to do, to do anything with or about. So to survive you might, you might have bent yourself in order to survive. But that isn't quite true anymore, for anybody, black or any other color who, who does what, what we described as "Uncle Tom," "Tomming," you know.

FM: The thing that I wanted to remind you.... I just saw your Jack Johnson film: Just wonderful. The documentary you did in New York.

Directed by William Cayton, this extraordinary boxing documentary deals with the events of the black boxing heavyweight champion from 1908 till 1915. Considerable footage is devoted to the champ's personal life through his tragic death at sixty-eight in an automobile accident in 1946. Cayton's film proves an invaluable addition to the more widely known Howard Sackler play, The Great White Hope,[112] *and the movie that followed it.*[113]

Brock Peters does the narration. In the superb CD collection of Miles Davis' The Complete Jack Johnson Sessions, *the legendary jazz musician described Johnson as a person who "portrayed Freedom—it rang just as loud as the bell proclaiming him champion."*[114]

Surprisingly, Bill Milkowski in his excellent set of notes to the collection refers to Cayton's 1970 Oscar-nominated movie as "an obscure documentary film...."[115]

BP: Oh yes.

FM: And nobody seems to be able to get it out in distribution...?

BP: I don't understand.

FM: I don't understand it either. It is a marvelous film.

BP: It is one of the finest documentaries.

FM: Have you seen it?

BP: I saw a screening of it in New York.

FM: Beautiful.

BP: In a tiny little room....

FM: Beautiful. Yeah, at the Whitney Museum?

BP: No, I didn't see it at the Whitney.

FM: But I wrote to Cayton, and I'm trying to get him up to the University to show the film. It was just.... The way in which he used the photo-animation.

Can you tell me what you think was your best film that you have done? Is there one film that stands out in your mind as…?

BP: Gee, I can't. It's very difficult to say. There are things that I did in *To Kill a Mockingbird* that I consider special. The same is true of *The L-Shaped Room,* and the same would be true of *The Incident.* There are things that I did on *The McMasters,* perhaps that's my biggest and maybe most important role in terms of size, which I could say was my best film: But I, but I….

Let's see, there is a television that I did once, that I was most satisfied about….. It was done for Fox. It was called *Law and Order Blues,* which was a segment for *Judd, For the Defense.* I think I was most satisfied with that, if I can ever say that I was completely satisfied. I'm rarely ever completely satisfied.

Judd, For the Defense *was an ABC series about the law that ran from September 1967 until September 1969. Carl Betz played Clinton Judd, a lawyer modeled after F. Lee Bailey, whose main office was in Houston, Texas, but who travelled the nation resolving issues taken from daily headlines.*[116] *The episode that Peters refers to was entitled* Commitment *and aired December 1, 1967.*[117]

BP: One of the most rewarding experiences on stage was my doing the national tour of *The Great White Hope.* There were many reasons why I thought I didn't want to do the role. I didn't want the comparisons that were being made, quite naturally, with Jimmy Jones who is an extremely fine actor. And I thought, well, that's unnecessary for me. I've already done my own share of pulling my weight and trying to create an image of quality and taste for myself as an actor and a person. Why should I then subject myself to it? Finally I decided that I would.

FM: It's a great role.

Peters played Jack Jefferson in the 1969-1971 national touring company of The Great White Hope. *According to Jim Brown, "In the case of* The Great White Hope, *the story of the boxer Jack Johnson, they softened the edges, put in some comedy, transformed it into fiction. They didn't want to deal with the real Jackson. Jack Johnson was so bad he took a long white car, a white woman, and a white poodle, drove through the state of*

Alabama. And that was sixty years ago [1929]. Hollywood didn't want that on the screen. It knew white America would not respond in a positive manner. Even though it's one whopper of a story."[118]

BP: It was challenging and exciting in every way. All the critics who had seen—everywhere we went—had seen the original in New York because it was such an exciting production. And whenever there is such a thing, they all go anyway. They had all seen it, and when they reviewed the touring company, they came at it with a very fresh approach. I was marvelously treated by the reviewers, and I came away feeling well. Apart from their response to me, which was fresh, I was gratified by the challenges I met in the role and felt that I had been able to handle. It was an exciting thing for me.

So that in theater, plus *Othello* I'd done a number of times; each time it's been more and more rewarding. Stunning reactions from audiences who wouldn't leave a theater when I finished performing the role. So that...I've had gratifying experiences both in theater and on film. It's difficult to pin it down to one.

FM: Do you remember any anecdotes at all about *To Kill a Mockingbird*?

BP: Hmmn [laughing] *To Kill a Mockingbird*? Well, I don't know. Anecdotes? *To Kill a Mockingbird*? I don't know if this would come under the heading of an anecdote, but it took three weeks to shoot the courtroom scene not because the actors were slow or real physical problems. It was covered more completely than anything I've ever done in film from every angle. And then the last week of shooting.... The first two weeks were done in a courtroom that was built on Soundstage 23 at Universal. It was done with the principles: the jury, the judge, the defendants, the plaintiffs, desk, and the lawyers, etc. Then in the last week, the courtroom was filled with people, and the whole things was shot again.

And each time we shot, when they arrived at the place in the story where I broke down, I broke down. I was frightened by it. Of course, I didn't think I could do this every time, but once I found the track—and I describe it as a track—once I found the steps, it was like...And I don't want to suggest that it's mechanical, because it isn't, each time I was able to experience it, I was able to recreate the complete experience for myself. For them it was always amazing. From the first day that it happened, the camera crew and all the people present, including Greg Peck, stood up and applauded me. [An embarrassed laugh] It was a real thrill.

FM: [Laughing] It was a thrill....

BP: But then came the last week, and they filled the courtroom, and I saw numbers of people whom I knew and extras that I had worked. And then the camera started rolling and the same thing happened. [Both of us are laughing] And then they stood up and applauded me. The camera people and the others by now are bored. It happened all over again, and again.... it was a great thrill for me.

Out of that came a marvelous friendship with Greg Peck. I had to leave immediately. I had to fly over the pole to England to start shooting *The L-Shaped Room*, and he came over later for vacation—he and his wife and children. So I spent a few weekends with them up in Vernon Wood where they rented an estate. We used to sit around and talk about lots of things, politics, etc., etc.

Really other.... It was such a tight experience in terms of shooting, from morning till night during that three-week period, that's all we did. There was no chance for me to really get to know people.

It was interesting that he said to me before I left, "I'll see you," Greg Peck this is. And sure enough, after I'd been shooting for some time, I got a message....

Well, I went away, and I came back. I got to back to Shepperton [Studios], everybody had a message for me from Gregory Peck: "Did you get your message from Gregory Peck?" And, of course, my chest swelled out. [Both of us are laughing heartily]...like it was nothing at all, you know.

The anecdote thing, I know the first time....

FM: It's funny that you have the same kind of feelings that other humans beings have.

BP: Sure, I never pretend.... I'm not that sophisticated that I can't enjoy meeting someone that I've seen for many years or that I've admired. I know, my wife and I were fast asleep one morning in New York, and the phone rang. And she picked it up and sleepily said, "Who is this?" Then she passed it to me and said, "It's for you." I said, "Yeah who is it?" This voice said, "It's Greg." I dropped the phone. I said, "Greg, oh Greg!" [Laughter] You know, to put it in it's order—a boy from Harlem now getting a phone call from Greg, and who is Greg?

FM: Yeah [laughing].

BP: These are the kinds of things…these are the kinds of…this isn't necessarily part of my dream but it's the kind of image that you don't expect. Suddenly one day, you're talking with Greg Peck, old friend, like you're talking with anybody who's an old friend.

FM: That's what I'm….

BP: It's an adjustment, a quick adjustment that you make….

FM: You're embarrassed by it and yet you're thrilled.

BP: Embarrassed and thrilled. Well, not even embarrassed. You're surprised and thrilled. You say, "Oh yeah, sure. How are you?"

FM: How about *The L-Shaped Room*?

BP: And that happened to me a number of times like that. And finally, as I say, I became a little more sophisticated. One thing about this business is that performers are generally open with each other, apart from what they say about the business being open. It's the business side of it that is not open. The performers generally are.

FM: I get that impression.

BP: Are generally open with each other. So I've found that wherever I traveled, I've met actors, and singers, and comedians whom I've admired. When I've walked in; they knew me. And they would either embrace me or greet me warmly. And I didn't have to say, "I'm an admirer; I'm Brock Peters, or anything." There's that exchange. It's very easy, and I could say the same thing about them. It's great.

FM: How about *The L-Shaped Room*? Do you have any anecdotes about that one?

BP: Not specially, except that Tom Bell and I became very warm friends. Tom Bell, Leslie Caron and myself. And it was very interesting because, as I understand it, Leslie had been trying to break the image of *Gigi* and *Lili*, etc.

FM: The ingénue?

BP:…and wanted a good adult role; and this was it. I think that she might have been a little nervous about it. When I arrived, they had been shooting a week. Tom took me aside one day, and he said,

"Look, they seem to be having problems, etc. You and I have to work most closely with her. Let's not fight her." So I agreed. I said, "What do you think we should do?" He said, "Just let's be warm and open. Let's give her our love."

And so we went at it that way. I know that the first day that I was to shoot, she didn't show up. She had a headache. I had to shoot some other thing that I hadn't prepared, that I wasn't expecting to do. But anyway, we got through it all right. She showed up the next day, and I think she might have been a little surprised that I didn't seem miffed, or I didn't go off the wall.

From that point on, we became a kind of triumvirate. I've lots of stills and movie film of us cavorting around the lawns at Shepperton. When we didn't have to shoot, or when we were waiting for scenes that we were not involved in, we'd go out and sit and talk. At the end of a day's shooting, there was a small pub outside the studio, about a half-mile, and the three cars that chauffeured us into town would stop, and we three would get out and spend about half hour or hour over a drink and talking. It was a really close-knit triumvirate we became. Perhaps that's part of what's in the film. And not to take anything away from Bryan Forbes, who I think did a magnificent job. But, we, we had, we had what was right to make that kind of film.

FM: Can you give me your point of view on what you think the slant of the book should be? If you were writing it, what you think should be the kind of emphasis or interpretation of the black man's role in American film?

BP: Well, that's a very broad question, but....

FM: What I mean....

BP: If I could capsulate something as broad as that, I'd say that...one certain thing is we'd go right back to being positive. That's very important because most of what's been projected about the black man is negative, and not only his contribution to this society—this America—, but to all of Western civilization. He's made major contributions, and these have either not been written up in the textbooks in school and not taught, or they've just barely been mentioned in some instances. And yet, any scholar who wants to find the material can find it. The material is there in all our major libraries and in the major libraries of the world. He still continues to make contributions. I think that part of knowledge of the contributions of the black man is necessary. In the same way that I learned that Marconi did the thing on wireless or that Edison did the electric light, no one ever told me that his right hand man and perhaps chief research artist was a black man. Or that in discovering the pole there was a man with—I forgot his name—who went up with him and was instrumental in reaching the pole.

Lewis Howard Latimer, a black draftsman, was instrumental in the patents for Bell's telephone and Edison's electric light. Matthew Alexander Henson, a black pioneer, often explored distant regions with Robert Peary, the most notable being the journey to the North Pole in 1909.

BP: But these are...There are so many contributions that have been made and at every level and every endeavor. In medicine, in law, in pioneering, and the Lewis and Clark expedition, for example, the black man who was the scout....

According to many sources, York, an impressive, strong slave of William Clark, not only was a member of the famous Corps of Discovery expedition to chart the American West in the early 1800s, but also a significant presence in dealing with the Native-American tribes encountered by the explorers.

BP:...Los Angeles was founded by a group of Indians, Mexican, and blacks. The first settlement of Chicago....

Postscript

Looking at Brock Peters' career, one gains the impression of an acutely talented actor and artist determined to make racial progress in mainstream culture and further his career. Raised in Harlem and influenced by members of the Harlem Renaissance, the colored kid had a strong commitment to values and Negro history. As he apprenticed himself through the fifties the colored actor encountered not only the numerous Jim Crow laws concerning restaurants, hotels, and swimming pools, but also the force of blacklists during the McCarthy era. Being Negro and young, he had the same doubts and fears other colored men had. But he conquered those fears not by being a demagogue or complaining he was being victimized by a racist society. By the early sixties he had established himself as a hard-working and talented black man who was determined to change the way he and his peers were perceived.

He understood how other African-Americans had shifted from being positive about how non-violence was an optimistic option for change into an angry, pessimistic community discouraged and disillusioned by a white-dominated society slow to change its ways. He understood why there were militant blacks that hated white people and insisted on living separately. He understood but he did not agree. He knew there was more than one-way to bring about change, and he decided to lead by example and not by violence or demagoguery. He made his share of sacrifices so that the future would be better for those who followed him. Like his baseball hero Hank Aaron, all he ever asked for was a chance to strut his talent. He got his opportunity, and he made the most of it. His name was Brock Peters, and he made the world better than he found it. He believed the arts crucial to our humanity, and he used his artistic gifts to prove it.

In 1993, Brock Peters, 65 years old, was quoted as saying that his films work as " really a reflection of our society." He went on to say, "For substantive change to take place, the white studio heads also must begin to recognize their social responsibility. They must understand that depicting positive black images on the screen—and rewarding them with the industry's highest honor [the Oscar]—is in the best interest of the United States."[119]

Perhaps it's best to remember this remarkable person by recalling the scene where Atticus tries to explain life's complexities to Scout: "You never really understand a person until you consider things from his point of view, until you climb inside his skin and walk around in it."[120]

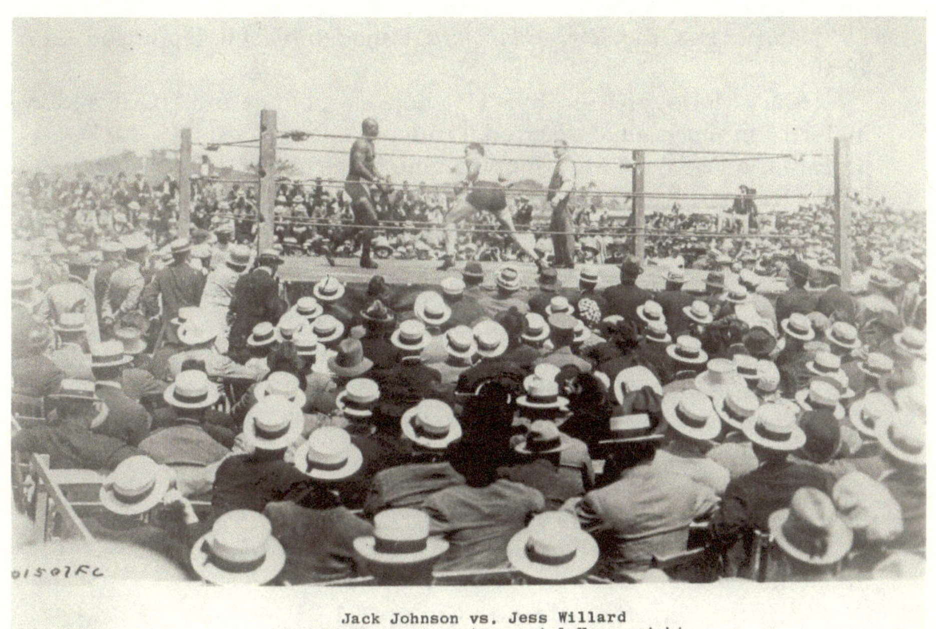

Jack Johnson vs. Jess Willard
One of the most controversial Heavyweight Championship fights of all times. Havana, Cuba, 1915

17. The Jack Johnson-Jess Willard fight is best remembered for its controversial conclusion, in which the black heavyweight allegedly was forced to take a dive. It is also the source for the concluding scenes in both the stage and film version of Howard Sackler's memorable work, *The Great White Hope*.

Notes

[1] Crouch, *The Artificial White Man*, 160.

[2] Allison Graham, *Framing the South: Hollywood, Television, and Race During the Civil Rights Struggle*, U. S. History/ Film Studies (Baltimore: The John Hopkins University Press, 2001), 15.

[3] Harper Lee, *To Kill a Mockingbird* (Philadelphia: J.B. Lippincott & Co., 1960).

[4] Mary McDough Murphy, "Hey Boo: Harper Lee and To Kill a Mockingbird," in *American Masters*, ed. Prudence Glass (USA: PBS, 2011).

[5] Maria Puente, "'Mockingbird' Still Sings at 50," *USA Today*, July 8, 2010, D1.

[6] "'Mockingbird' Still Sings at 50," *USA Today*, July 8, 2010.

[7] Ibid.

[8] Hon. Diane E. Watson, "Brock Peters in Memoriam," ed. Congressional Record (Washington, D.C.: Congress, 2005).

[9] Gail Lewin, "Cab Calloway: Sketches," in *American Masters*, ed. Prudence Glass (USA: PBS, 2012).

[10] Matthew Pook, "Brown Sugar: Part I—the Beginnings," (USA: Ebony Productions Incorporated, 1985).

[11] Jan Schmidt-Garre and Marieke Schroeder, "Aida's Brothers & Sisters: Black Voices in Opera and Concert," (Germany: Pars Media 2009).

[12] Donald Bogle, "Brown Sugar: America's Black Female Stars," (USA: PBS, 1986).

[13] Schickel, "Artifacts of a Lost Culture," 1.

[14] Gavin, *Stormy Weather*, 9-10.

[15] Crouch, *The All-American Skin Game, or the Decoy of Race*, 173-74.

[16] Walter Burrell, "Hollywood Happenings," *The New Courier*, April 8, 1967, 13.

[17] Unknown, "Actor Sheds Villain Typing," *Ebony* (1963).

[18] Staff, "Brock Peters: Veteran Actor-Singer Reaps Rewards of Hard Work and Persistence," ibid. XLIII, no. 1 (1987): 92.

[19] Gennari, *Blowin' Hot and Cool: Jazz and Its Critics*, 29.

[20] Wilkerson, *The Warmth of Other Suns: The Epic Story of America's Great Migration*, 251.

[21] Ossie Davis and Ruby Dee, *With Ossie & Ruby in This Life Together* (New York: William Morrow and Company, Inc., 1998), 201.

[22] Murray, *The Omni-Americans*, 149.

[23] Nina Davia, "From These Roots," in *TV Season 76-77*, ed. Nina Davia (Phoenix: Oryx Press, 1978).

[24] Watson, "Brock Peters in Memoriam."

[25] "Brock Peters."

[26] Ibid.

[27] Bosley Crowther, "Kurt Weill and Maxwell Anderson's Lost in the Stars," *The American Film Theatre/Cinebill* 1974.

[28] "Brock Peters."

[29] Tom Weaver, "Biography for Brock Peters," IMDB.

[30] Harry Belafonte and with Michael Shnayerson, *My Song: A Memoir* (New York: Alfred A. Knopf, 2011), 12, 17.

[31] Tom Vallance, "Obituary: Brock Peters," in *The Independent* (London 2005), 1.

[32] Gavin, *Stormy Weather*, 248.

[33] Dandridge and Conrad, *Everything and Nothing: The Dorothy Dandridge Tragedy*, 1.

[34] Matthew Pook, "Brown Sugar Part III—1940s and 50s," (USA: Ebony Productions Incorporated, 1985).

[35] Ruth Adkins Robinson, "Dorothy Dandridge: An American Beauty," (USA: Passport International Productions, 2003).

[36] Gavin, *Stormy Weather*, 247.

[37] Byron Haskin, "Tarzan's Peril," (USA: RKO Radio Pictures, Inc., 1951).

[38] Phil Brown, "The Harlem Globetrotters," (USA: Columbia Pictures, 1951).

[39] Gerald Mayer, "Bright Road (Aka See How They Run)," (USA: MGM, 1953).

[40] Gavin, *Stormy Weather*, 248-50.

[41] Earl Mills, *Dorothy Dandridge: A Portrait in Black* (United Kingdom: Holloway House Publishing Company, 1991), 7.

[42] Susanne Rostock, "Sing Your Song," (USA: Belefonte Enterprises & S2BN Entertainment Production, 2012).

[43] Gavin, *Stormy Weather*, 248.

[44] Chris Fujiwara, *The World and Its Double: The Life and Work of Otto Preminger*, Paperback ed. (New York: Faber and Faber, Inc., 2008), 165-66.

[45] Canby, "Critic's Notebook: Black Films: Imitation of Life?," C28.

[46] Bennett Jr., *The Challenge of Blackness*, 287.

[47] Staff, "Brock Peters: Veteran Actor-Singer Reaps Rewards of Hard Work and Persistence," 92.

[48] Joe Nocera, "Variations on an Explosive Theme," *New York Times*, Jan. 22, 2012, 7.

[49] Ibid.

[50] "Variations on an Explosive Theme."

[51] Kirk Browning, "Live from Lincoln Center: The Gershwins' "Porgy and Bess," (USA: PBS, 2002).

[52] Joseph Camp, "'Porgy and Bess' Update," (USA: MacNeil/Lerer Productions, 2012).

[53] Nocera, "Variations on an Explosive Theme," 7.

[54] Lionel Chetwynd, "Redefining Racism: Fresh Voices from Black America," (USA: Whidbey Island Films Inc., 1997).

[55] Donald Bogle, *Dorothy Dandridge: A Biography* (Canada/NY: Amistad/HarperCollins Publishers, 1997), 395.

[56] Sidney Poitier, *This Life* (New York: Alfred A. Knopf, 1980), 206.

[57] Morgan Neville, "Sidney Poitier: The Defiant One," in *Biography* (USA Peter Jones Productions, 1997).

[58] A. Scott Berg, *Goldwyn: A Biography* (New York: Alfred A. Knopf, 1989), 486.

[59] Bosley Crowther, "Review of Porgy and Bess," *New York Times*, June 25, 1959, 3133-34.

[60] Fujiwara, *The World and Its Double: The Life and Work of Otto Preminger*, 223-34.

[61] Donald Bogle, *Blacks in American Films and Television: An Encyclopedia* (New York: Garland Publishing, Inc., 1988), 439.

[62] Sean Cameron, "Private Screenings: Sidney Lumet," (USA: Turner Classic Movies, 2005).

[63] Malcolm Gladwell, "The Courthouse Ring: Atticus Finch and the Limits of Southern Liberalism," *The New Yorker* 85, no. 24 (2009): 26-31.

[64] Donald Bogle, *Blacks in American Films and Television: An Encyclopedia* (New York: Garland Publishing, Inc., 1988), 439.

[65] Manchel, *Film Study*, 1934-36.

[66] Dave Hepburn, "Once near Bankruptcy: Brock Peters to Co-Star in Two British Movies," *N.Y. Amsterdam News*, July 28, 1962.

[67] Unknown, "Brock Peters Stars in 2 London Films, May Return," ibid., November 17.

[68] Bosley Crowther, "Review of the L-Shaped Room," *New York Times*, May 28,1963, 32:1.

[69] Unknown, "Brock Peters Returns to England for 2nd Film," *Pittsburgh Courier*, Sept. 1 1962.

[70] Bosley Crowther, "Review of Heavens Above!," *New York Times*, May 21, 1963, 28.

[71] Robert Berkvist, "A Director of Classics, Focused on Conscience," ibid., April 10, 2011, 1, 10.

[72] Vallance, "Obituary: Brock Peters."

[73] Phyl Garland, "Brock Peters - Actor with a Star Ascending," *Pittsburg Courier*, August 28, 1965, 9.

[74] Donald Bogle, *Blacks in American Films and Television: An Encyclopedia* (New York: Garland Publishing, Inc., 1988), 439.

[75] Lee Beaupre, "Brock Peters on Negro Skepticism: One Colored Star Hardly a Trend," *Variety*, December 20, 1967, 54.

[76] Jesse H. Walker, "Ex-Slave Brock Peters Asking for His Freedom," *NY Amsterdam News*, August 1, 1970, 40.

[77] Sieving, *Soul Searching: Black-Themed Cinema from the March on Washington to the Rise of Blaxploitation*, 84.

[78] Lerone Bennett Jr., "The Case Against Styron's Nat Turner," *Ebony* (1968): 148.

[79] "The Case Against Styron's Nat Turner," *Ebony* (1968).

[80] John Henrik Clarke ed., *William Styron's Nat Turner: Ten Black Writers Respond* (Boston: Beacon Press, 1968).

[81] Irving Tepper, "The Original Confession of Nat Turner as Made to T.R. Gray, November 1, 1831," (USA: CMS Records, Inc., 1968).

[82] Ibid.

[83] Ibid.

[84] Hans, "Jack Johnson," *Variety*, Nov. 10, 1971, 16.

[85] John Szwed, *So What: The Life of Miles Davis* (New York: Simon & Schuster Paperbacks, 2004), 309.

[86] Gannett News Service, January 5, 1989.

[87] Yvonne, "Cicely Tyson," *Ms.* (1974): 47.

[88] Nora E. Taylor, "Film Star Talks About Producing," *The Christian Science Monitor*, February 20, 1974, 4C.

[89] Staff, "Palaver," *Encore* 3, no. 1 (1974): 36.

[90] Taylor, "Film Star Talks About Producing."

[91] Poitier, *This Life*, 148.

[92] Robert Wahls, "Footlights: Brock's Message," *Sunday News*, April 30, 1972.

[93] "Footlights: Brock's Message," *Sunday News*, April 30, 1972, 25C.

[94] Ibid.

[95] Donald Bogle, *Blacks in American Films and Television: An Encyclopedia* (New York: Garland Publishing, Inc., 1988), 439.

[96] Bernard, *Carl Van Vechten & the Harlem Renaissance: A Portrait in Black & White*, 91.

[97] Ibid, 100.

[98] Frank Manchel, "From Actor to Activist: Frederick Douglass O'Neal," in *Every Step a Struggle: Interviews with Seven Who Shaped the African-American Image in Movies* (Washington, DC: New Academia Publishing, LLC, 2007).

[99] Gerald C. Fraser, "Abram Hill, 76, the Founder of a Black Theater in Harlem," *New York Times* 11 October 1986, 13.

[100] Donald Bogle, *Blacks in American Films and Television: An Encyclopedia* (New York: Garland Publishing, Inc., 1988), 439.

[101] Vallance, "Obituary: Brock Peters."

[102] Crowther, "Review of Porgy and Bess," 3134.

[103] Bryan Forbes, "The L-Shaped Room," (Britain1962).

[104] Robert Mulligan, "To Kill a Mockingbird," (USA: Universal Pictures, 1962).

[105] Giuseppe Colizzi, "Ace High (Quattro Del'ave Maria)," (Italy: Paramount Pictures, 1968).

[106] Dorothy Dandridge and Earl Conrad, *Everything and Nothing: The Dorothy Dandridge Tragedy* (NY: Abelard-Schuman, 2000).

[107] Bogle, *Dorothy Dandridge: A Biography*, 284-85.

[108] Fujiwara, *The World and Its Double: The Life and Work of Otto Preminger*, 155-56.

[109] Berg, *Goldwyn: A Biography*, 486.

[110] Farai Chideya, "NPR: News and Notes for December 25, 2006," in *African-American Roundtable: News & Notes* (USA: NPR, 2006).

[111] Walter Burrell, "Black Films: Big Money Careers & Rip Off...." *Soul*, Dec. 18, 1972, 3.

[112] Howard Sackler, *The Great White Hope* (New York 1969).

[113] Martin Ritt, "The Great White Hope," (USA: Twentieth Century-Fox 1970).

[114] Miles Davis, "Jack Johnson," in *The Complete Jack Johnson Sessions* (NY: Sony Music Entertainment Inc., 1971), 7.

[115] Bill Milkowski, "Miles' Rock Manifesto," ibid. (Sony Entertainment, Inc/Columbia Pictures), 57.

[116] Tim Brooks and Earle Marsh, *The Complete Directory to Prime Time Network TV Shows: 1946-Present*, 4th ed. (New York: Ballantine Books, 1988), 405.

[117] James Robert Parish and Vincent Terrace, *The Complete Actors' Television Credits, Second Edition : Volume 1: Actors*, 2 ed., 2 vols., vol. 1 (Metuchen: The Scarecrow Press, Inc., 1989), 387.

[118] Jim Brown and Steve Delsohn, *Out of Bounds*, Paperback ed. (New York: Zebra Books, 1990), 231-32.

[119] *Newsday*, March 29, 1993.

[120] Mulligan, "To Kill a Mockingbird."

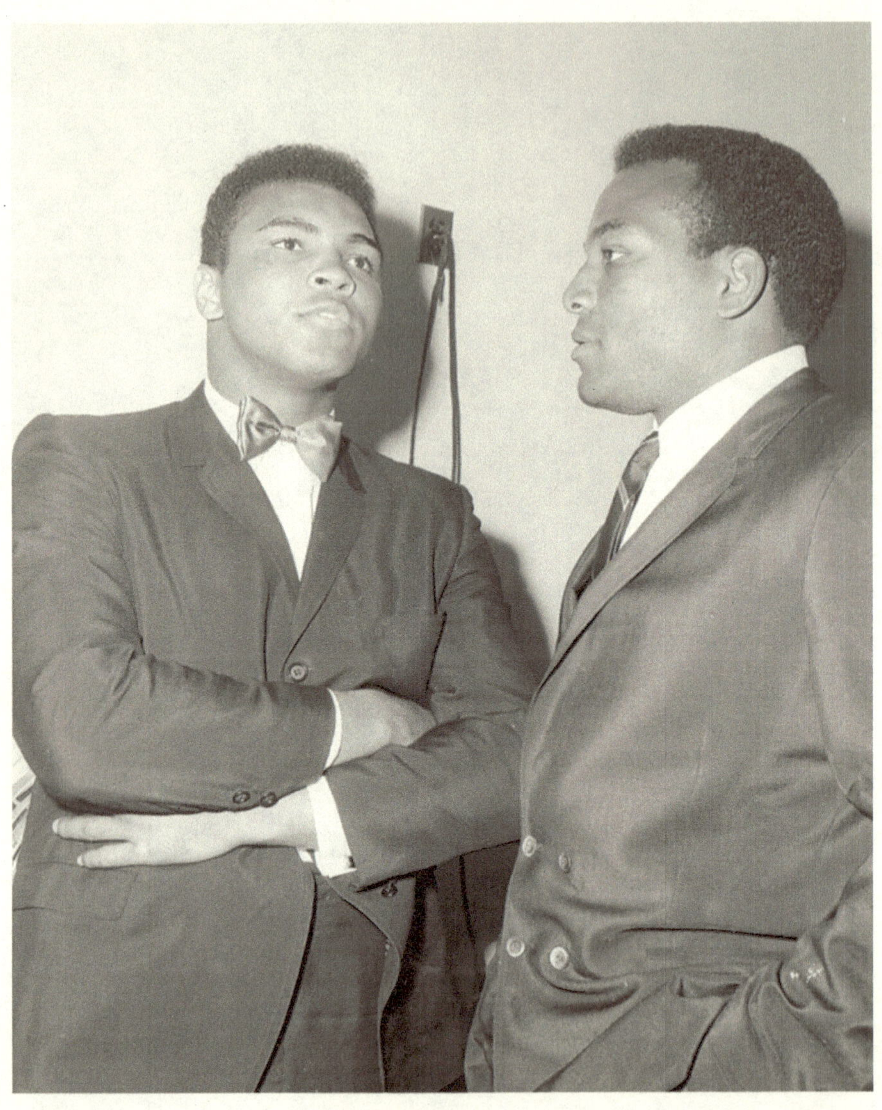

18. Two of the twentieth century's greatest athletes and major influences on the black film legacy: From left to right, Muhammad Ali and Jim Brown.

3

Heart and Soul: Jim Brown

"Movies of any type are seldom mere entertainment because they teach cultural values and influence behavior."[1]

Alvin F. Poussaint

"Since reinterpretation—in the interest of purifying our democracy and moving it beyond its biases—has been basic to the glory of the American tale, there was nothing fundamentally wrong with reexamining what we had been told about each other and what, free of the veils of apology or justification, had actually happened. No, the slaves were not happy to be slaves; every Indian tribe was not a passel of bloodthirsty savages who got what they deserved; Mexicans weren't just a greasy bunch of giggling loafers; Asians weren't subhumanly inscrutable; women had more going for them than their erotic skills, their ability to have babies, and the virtuosity they brought to housekeeping. These were important insights to make common knowledge and so were the many achievements and contributions made by Americans of every hue, religion, and both sexes to the development of this nation."[2]

Stanley Crouch

Jim Brown's towering reputation rests on misperceptions many people refuse to correct. Whether you venerate or disapprove of this extraordinary American personality, you will encounter in your research enough confusion to muddle any attempt at an accurate assessment. His hagiography invokes a myth accepted by some as fact, but it is more in sync with John Ford's famous line from his 1962 classic western, *The Man Who Shot Liberty Valance*: "When truth comes in conflict with legend, print the legend."[3] On one hand, this icon stands as one of the most famous running backs in professional football history—in 2002, *Sporting News* named him "the greatest professional football player ever."[4] In addition, he became a movie star beloved by defiant black youth and frustrated African-American men but frequently disparaged by mainstream film historians and critics. On the other hand, his well-publicized missteps and exaggerated human flaws blemish his otherwise impressive feats.

The result today is an ambivalent interpretation about an imperfect idol identified with superb sports records, intimidation, self-assurance, violence, and a passionate commitment to African-American freedom and dignity. This eminent sportsperson, also widely recognized for his conspicuous social, political, and economic actions, has been the subject of countless interviews, articles, and op-ed pieces, not including two autobiographies,[5] one effusive over-the-top book-length study,[6] a superb unauthorized biography,[7] and a splendid film documentary on his life.[8] Grouped together, these disputed recollections of the star's exploits and excesses are so etched in the public memory that one might imagine there is little to add to the story of a near-mythical figure alive and well at seventy-seven and still going strong. But as suggested throughout *The Interviews*, memory and history are rarely the same.

If we turn to conventional history, one "learns" from numerous journalists and pundits that Jim's prowess was as great and as unforgettable in the bedroom as it was on the playing field. Additionally, his teammates and club owners offer passionate proof that the unrivalled Cleveland Brown fullback was as domineering and bold in the locker room as on the gridiron. But one could also be dismayed and distracted by court records, police files, and FBI accounts "documenting" what a threat the star's random rage, political associations, and self-help programs posed to women, the general public, and to the nation itself. In particular, white Americans might easily be persuaded, if they uncritically read routinely the national press during the fifties and sixties, that the football immortal and popular actor used his considerable influence to turn black people against the white establishment, to align himself with the threatening objectives of ex-convicts and African-American militants, and to help enflame the violence and hatred that engulfed the country during the civil rights movement and the Vietnam War. Finally, if you take many trained film critics at their word, Jim Brown was one crummy actor whose mediocre films are best forgotten, disregarded, or demeaned.

Not surprisingly, my conclusions differ somewhat from current scholarly reflections. For me, this exceptional African-American activist serves as a useful model for my romantic reinterpretations of conventional wisdom. Although he did not set himself up as a crusader, he became one; and in the process impacted on his times in ways that resulted in significant contributions to American life and history. Based upon information supplied by individuals who knew the ex-pro football player the longest—e.g., teammates, teachers, actors, friends, and business associates—, I argue for a point of view shared more by his fans than by his detractors. His followers see him as a dedicated, hardworking, and principled person willing to standup to social injustice. In addition, they find him enormously audacious and intelligent; and to a person agree that Jim, no matter what the risk when a black cause is threatened, turns the other cheek for no man, woman or child. These defenders describe an individual who not only has devoted his life to championing principles and practices that uplift black Americans, but also has remained intensely loyal to friends in trouble. However, these same people are neither disingenuous nor naïve. They readily, albeit regrettably, acknowledge the ex-football star's bad temper and brutal honesty, some might say arrogance, that occasionally makes him say and do foolish, reprehensible things. Moreover, these same friends see his fabled self-confidence every now and then making him overbearing, self-righteous, while also clouding his judgment and causing him unnecessary problems.

To his credit, Brown does not duck responsibility for his mistakes and failures. When rightfully wrong, he becomes apologetic, remorseful, and embarrassed. He does point out, however, "I've been around a lot of years. I am controversial, there are 9 million misconceptions about my life...."[9] But there is little doubt, as he confessed in 1990, "I was a Bad Guy. Nonconformist. Malcontent.

Locker Room Lawyer. Militant."[10] Nonetheless, given Jim's life and career, the *mea culpas* require an historical context.

I cut Brown no slack, and I doubt he would ever expect any, in my analyses of his violent temper, his family failings or his inexcusable behavior towards his children. In my reading of the individual, I make no excuses and offer no defense for his problematic relationships with women. That is, when the controversial charges are clear and accurate.

But it helps to recall what was discussed in the Preface. That is, we need to separate perception from reality, and that we not put today's values on yesterday's events. We know more now about what transpired then than did many of the participants themselves. Brown's supporters and detractors reacted as they did in large measure because they based their verdicts on perceptions and attitudes growing out of a Jim Crow culture that shaped their judgments. The age, the social codes, and the institutions in which the events occurred no longer hold center stage. Many of these pejorative pronouncements by and about this public figure were leveled against a brave, rebellious, and outspoken black personality living in a traditional, bigoted society that required him to bear witness on a daily basis to countless social, political, and economic injustices not only against himself but also against people of all persuasions and walks of life. He had the strength, the stature, and the courage to challenge those injustices rising out of our defective national consciousness. If he chose to confront society's wrongs, to protest against unjust behavior, and to battle abuses of power, even though some of his methods proved questionable, I can certainly see my way clear to being sympathetic to his actions in my assessment of his contributions to the black film experience.

Normally, those reservations might suffice, and I'd move on. But finding certain likenesses between Jim and myself, as well as having had personal experiences over the past three-quarters of a century eliciting similar labels from politicians, academic administrators, colleagues, and the public; and then seeing the distorted reports in newspapers and hearing them on radio and television, I offer two admonitions on what I intuitively believe are inconsistencies in Jim's narrative. Find out not only the venue and time in which the adverse opinions were rendered, but also reserve judgment until you do your own research. From my unrepentant lifelong perspective and considering who many of my antagonists were, I took much of what they said to and about me as a badge of honor. Jim might feel the same way.

Influenced by my admittedly subjective ties, and what historical record is not subjective, I see Brown's orthodox story somewhat differently from others, not because these scholars, critics, and friends are wrong [they are not]; and certainly not because my investigation is stronger, my ties to Jim greater, and my wisdom unparalleled [it is not]. In truth, I see, as noted earlier, reinterpretation as an historian's responsibility. Previous accounts emerge from the age in which these chroniclers lived and the intellectual baggage they brought with them. I just live in different times and view things from my private standpoint. My fresh outlook also arises in large measure out of my atypical memory of the publicized events, films, and personalities in the age in which Jim and I lived. It may also be argued that because of these idiosyncratic feelings, I am less objective and more sympathetic than other storytellers to Brown's journey. Maybe so. That is for you to decide. My take on the National Football League Hall of Famer who at the peak of his career turned from Sunday afternoon pigskin fame to become a matinee film idol and then within a decade was blackballed by the motion picture film industry follows from a value system at odds with many sports fanatics who define the measure of a man primarily by physicality, sexual escapades, and machismo. If I challenge conventional wisdom about the superstar, it is because I marvel at what Jim did with his life and his gifts, as well as feel great disappointment about how his errors in judgment sullied his legacy. Just as important, I believe Brown's story is helpful not only for understanding American racial history, but also for where we go in the twenty-first century. For me, his passage and those controversial decisions he made along the way offer an impressive illustration of Jean Renoir's haunting line from his 1939 masterpiece *Rules of the Game*: "The tragedy of life is that everyone has a reason."

If time and space allowed, I would love to explore how a human being with such talent and who made so many extraordinary contributions to the black experience would allow his remarkable record to be forever blemished, as Spike Lee alleges, by intemperate behavior and the brutal treatment of women.[11] What could this mid-century black Samson who became according to some commentators a "new kind of American hero, a new kind of black hero"[12] have done to prevent his notable achievements from being overshadowed by so many public and professional misperceptions and misconceptions? Where did this stereotype of Brown as an unapologetic, arrogant African-American chauvinist who touts black economics and self-sufficiency as the primary routes to dignity and freedom emerge? How did the myth that this prominent personality believes the way to success for black men in America is inexorably linked to black separatism, business prowess, tough love, and physical dexterity take hold?[13] Clearly, a satisfactory answer will not be found in the names, dates, childhood history, biographical anecdotes, and personal observations provided by his storytellers as well as the individual himself. Such data rarely divulge who any of us actually are as real-life human beings.

In the end, however, my purpose here is not to rewrite history. This set of interviews affords neither the arena nor the opportunity to deal with the complexity and contradictions found in a major American figure that polarizes our historical imagination. My goal, stated repeatedly throughout *The Interviews,* remains to share with the reader what I learned from a series of conversations about the African-American film experience more than forty plus years ago. And there is no doubt Jim Brown, as you will discover, introduced me to issues and conflicts I rarely dreamed about in my youthful vision of life, film, and society. What follows then is an imperfect impression of a rare individual who for me personifies Benjamin Franklin's glorious observation that the greatness of a man is not in what he achieves in life, but what he does with what he achieves.

Born James Nathaniel Brown on February 17, 1936[14] on St. Simon Island, off the southern Georgia coast, the infant was abandoned by his parents within two years of his birth. Swinton Brown (a Lothario and a boxer), his father, deserted the family less than a month after the child came home from the hospital and joined the great migration north. Brown saw him only a handful of times in his life and always denied any feelings for the man. Theresa Brown (a domestic), his mother, left twenty-two months later but promised herself to reunite with her son and then migrated to Great

Neck, Long Island where she worked primarily for a Jewish family, the Brockmans, who lived next door to the town of Manhasset. Mother and son did not see each other again until six years later.

What intrigues me are the memories of the eight years the youngster spent on St. Simon Island. Raised by his great-grandmother, Nora Peterson, the central person in Jim's life and the woman he felt to be his "true mother,"[15] he also benefitted from the love of a second grandmother, a recovering alcoholic, living with the group in a single-family house. Jim emphatically denies that either he or anyone else at the time considered himself or herself poor or marginalized. One biographer, Mike Freeman, however, disagrees and believes the celebrity still carries with him several scars as a result of being deserted: "The departure of his parents at such a young age begat a lasting feeling of abandonment and insecurity that would haunt Brown for much of his life, affecting many of his personal and professional relationships, and shaping his views about women."[16] Yet Jim in his writings and interviews repeatedly stresses how wonderful his childhood was, the value of the Baptist education given to him, the overriding emphasis he received on positive family relationships, and cherishes the rich recollections of the people he knew in a time he describes as an Eden-like existence. He told interviewer Graham Bensinger, "I never felt like a second-class citizen.... I was born realizing that men should be treated the same way...."[17] Particularly noteworthy is his recollection that it was at St. Simon Island that he learned two vital life lessons: self-reliance and a determination never to be resentful.

Nora Peterson died when Jim was eight years of age, and he was sent north to live with his mother. Now divorced and working steadily for the Brockmans, Theresa was given a room for her and Jim in her employer's home. The initial culture shock between the loving and nurturing St. Simons community and the unfamiliar segregated Long Island society that mainly divided people into pockets of rich and poor, black and white, unhinged Brown almost as much as did his mother's free-living life style. Mortified by seeing Theresa in tasteless relationships with men and lacking any stable home life, he became an unsettled youth who cared little for school, lived a lot on the streets, and sought friendship with other anxious boys banning together in neighborhood gangs. Later on,

Brown in his musings leaves no doubt if not for the attention and affection given to him by the coaches and teachers in the Manhasset school system, he would clearly have become a criminal. By the time he had reached high school, the troubled teenager had moved into his girl friend's home and away from his mother's influence.

Coincidentally, my childhood experiences reflect a similar but not an identical journey. Born in Detroit, Michigan and residing briefly in Birmingham, Alabama, I was living on New York's Lower East Side by the time I was two years of age. My father was hardly around, being somewhat a clone of Willy Loman and spending almost half the year travelling on the road. My adoring mother, a hardworking sales clerk in a two-price store on Manhattan's Fourteenth Street, bore the brunt of bringing up my sister and me. The great joy of my early years came from the teachers at P.S. 31, who considered me a child prodigy. At the end of my first year in elementary school, they skipped me from the first grade to the third grade. When I was eight years of age, the family moved across the Brooklyn Bridge to Flatbush.

It was as great a culture shock as I have ever experienced. The contrast between the New York ghetto-like existence recreated memorably in Samuel Goldwyn's 1937 screen adaptation of Sidney Kingsley's classic Broadway play *Dead End* (1935)[18] clashed dramatically with the mainly white middle-class environment in Flatbush. My new school, P.S. 193, demonstrated no experience or skill with gifted children. They made no allowance for the fact that I had never been in the second grade. My school days became constant battles with school administrators for self-respect, independence, and personal dignity. For these incompetent instructors, they became living hell! And, like Brown, I became a difficult teenager. I did not become a criminal, but I did become a first-class pain-in-the-butt! These coincidences between Jim and me impact on my admittedly over-simplified analysis of Jim's life, career, and reputation.

By the time Brown reached Manhasset Junior High School, his phenomenal athletic ability began to manifest itself. In his second autobiography, he reminded us just how extraordinary he was in sports, "[I] won thirteen letters, playing football, basketball, baseball, lacrosse, and running track in three years of varsity competition."[19] What he rarely mentions are the sacrifices, the dedication, and the discipline required for such athletic feats. He does, however, stress that as a result of his training he never smoked, drank alcohol, or took drugs. [He does admit that he occasionally bought drugs for his lady friends.] Predictably, teachers, coaches, and members in the Manhasset community now saw him not only as an incredibly talented youngster, but also as someone worthy of saving. No two people were more crucial to Jim's turnaround than football coach Ed Walsh and attorney Kenneth Molloy, a New York State Supreme Court Justice, and an alumnus of Syracuse University.[20] The encouragement given to Brown by these two extraordinary men is told in great detail throughout the literature on Jim Brown and needs no repeating here. One comment Brown did make about Walsh, however, is worth citing: "I thank God that…[Walsh was] a Caucasian man so that we can dispel all of these things about color, anything about who I prefer, and what I respect. He is No. 1."[21]

Midwood High School, superb as it was academically, was no Manhasset High School, and if not for one teacher, Mr. Fuchs, my life also might also have taken a wrong turn.[22] But my mentor did not arrive until the twelfth grade! Before then, I spent as much time serving detention as I did disrupting life in the classroom. While Jim's athletic brilliance forever enshrined him in the memory of his classmates, my principal legacy appears to be that after four years of tormenting the faculty and creating chaos in my courses, my peers in their collective wisdom elected me vice-president of my graduating class. At least two of my cohorts, Woody Allen and Erich Segal, remembered me for that singular accomplishment twenty-five years later on two different airplane trips.

Interestingly, and again in overly simplistic terms, the Manhasset life lessons Brown acquired proved a mixed blessing. First, the white people there provided him with such incredible support, he mistakenly believed that was the way the world was, and the confusion left the naïve eighteen-year old unprepared for the traumas encountered in his early college days. In Jim's words, "When I came to Manhasset High School, I was never denied an opportunity. I was living among all those white people, receiving all this warmth and support. It lulled me to sleep. I believed everyone would be as good as the people of Manhasset. I came to Syracuse with my guard down. At eighteen, I wasn't prepared for their venom."[23] Second, his victories on the athletic fields made him forever believe in man-to man solutions to a person's problems, and in the conviction that success in life remained in an individual's own hands and not dependent on others. He rarely seemed, however, to appreciate that not everyone had his strength or grit. Third, as Brown stated years later, he became "somewhat of a skeptic." In his words, "I have seen so much incompetence and dishonesty and blindness that I tend to be leery of people until I have seen proof that they're good and honest. But a man must believe in the human race if he is a decent person himself."[24] Fourth, Brown always remembered the good people and the many kindnesses he encountered throughout his journey. Contrary to the popular misperception in the literature, he always acknowledged his debts to the caring white people in his life, spoke kindly of Jewish benefactors, and remained loyal to this day to childhood friends and mentors. In short, he never forgot who he was, where he came from, and whom he owed. Again contrary to conventional wisdom, Brown's narrative of his first seventeen years contains no noticeable comment about racism or Jim Crow attitudes. Similar to Brock Peters who refreshed our image of Harlem, Jim Brown provides a warm, thoughtful impression of a southern childhood and a northern white, Long Island community. But fifth, and perhaps most importantly, Manhasset's big man on campus discovered that because of his gifts and character, he had the power to help not only himself but also to help others as well. As Brown told reporter Mike Lupica, "God gave me something special.... I was always special. I didn't always know it. You make your way against all odds, in junior high school and high school and then comes the day when you know you're different: you know you can *deal*."[25]

Although forty-two colleges and universities recruited Jim, Molloy's Syracuse University ties resulted in Brown going to his mentor's school on what the teenager mistakenly thought was a football scholarship. His enrollment was anything but what the University and the team wanted. While denying any racism on their part, the coaching staff insisted it had experienced such a traumatic season the year before with another talented black athlete that they wanted no part of Manhasset's favorite son. Thus Brown's fees and tuition were paid not from a football scholarship but from money Molloy had collected from supportive Manhasset friends and neighbors. Once on campus, the talented freshman quickly discovered his situation, especially when relegated to a lowly place on the bench during his entire first football season at Syracuse. Although disillusioned and disappointed, Jim did not sit around sulking, but instead turned his interests to lacrosse and managed to become during his stay at the school one of the greatest players of the sport in the game's history.

For an insight into Jim's transition from high school to college, we turn to the movies. In 1998, Spike Lee wrote and directed *He Got Game,* a gritty narrative about a convict, Jake Shuttlesworth (Denzel Washington), who is temporarily released from prison and promised a reduction in his sentence if he can convince his estranged son, Jesus (Ray Allen, a member of the NBA's Milwaukee Bucks), America's premiere high school basketball player, to play for the Governor's university. In one of the best performances of his career, Brown appeared as Spivey, the guard assigned by the warden to see that Jake gets the job done quickly and properly. Although clearly different in major ways from the circumstances that brought Jim from Manhasset to Syracuse, the movie's numerous situations depicting the pressures and strategies used by coaches and alumni to recruit high school stars to major universities remains one of the most impressive critiques on the subject in motion pictures.

He Got Game also illustrates for my purposes a significant feature of Brown's extensive filmography as well as the role his movies perform in society. That is, throughout his screen career, intentionally or not, he used his stature and influence to address many social abuses in American society and culture. [This statement will be amplified in the pages that follow.] Secondly, the film operates for many uninformed Americans as both a reminder of what types of pressures athletes face when deciding what school to attend and how important alumni are in the recruiting process. Third, it allows me in the interest of full disclosure to state my ties to Jon Kilik, the gifted producer of *He Got Game* and countless other Spike Lee films like *Do the Right Thing* (1989), *Mo' Better Blues* (1990), *Jungle Fever* (1991), *Malcolm X* (1992*), Crooklyn* (1994), and *Bamboozled* (2000). A former student and life-long friend, Jon has played a significant role in my deep appreciation and great respect for Lee's work.

Returning to Brown's journey, the discouraged University freshman made it clear he was not going to remain at Syracuse. But once again, Manhasset came through. The school system's white superintendent came to campus and convinced the undergraduate that if he would be patient, things would change. The following year, in the fourth game of his sophomore season, Jim got into the action, ran for a touchdown, and never again remained out of the line-up. For the remainder of his undergraduate career, Jim established himself as one of America's foremost college football players. He graduated as a three-year All-American in both football and lacrosse at Syracuse University in 1957.

As for Syracuse itself, it would take many years for Jim to reconcile his negative feelings and racist experiences and develop a caring and affectionate relationship for the school. That bond gets the Hollywood treatment in Gary Fleder's *The Express* (2008).[26] Based on the tragic life of football legend Ernie Davis, the Syracuse black All-American who rivaled Brown's feats, the narrative points out Jim's role in recruiting Davis to Syracuse. At the same time, the film inadvertently presents another telling feature of the ex-football star's character by showing his willingness to acknowledge graciously another man's achievements. In this case, Brown stated he "considers him [Davis] the most courageous man he has ever known."[27]

Coincidentally, as I graduated from Ohio State University in 1957, Jim joined the Cleveland Browns. Over the next nine seasons, the great number 32 rewrote much of professional football history. He also encountered considerable racial problems in the NFL with its well-established segregation practices and long-standing quota policies, and especially in his association with the Cleveland Brown's brilliant football coach Paul Brown. Since Jim's autobiographies, Mike Freeman's study, and Spike Lee's film provide copious information on the star's athletic success as well the pros and cons of his many misunderstood battles to improve the status of black athletes in the NFL, I see no reason to repeat such accessible material. However, I think you might enjoy two anecdotes not available anywhere in the published material on the Hall of Fame fullback.

The first story comes from Marc Sklar, my Long Island friend and the respected Camp Pontiac director. As the reader may know, the New York Giants and the Cleveland Browns enjoyed a great rivalry from the late 1950s to the mid-1960s. In Marc's words, "It was the Giant defense against Brown and the Cleveland offense. The Giants had Huff and Robistelli. Both teams were in the playoffs more often than not." But as Sklar points out, "The teams didn't like each other but did respect each other." He then explains, "The whole defense was geared to stop Brown. The Giants played a 4-3 defense to stop him. In those years we had a few Hall of Famers: Frank Gifford, Rosey Brown, [Andy] Robistelli, Y.A. Tittle, Charlie Connerly, and Alex Webster. The team had two coaches in that era [that] went to the Hall, Lombardi and Landry. New Yorkers felt Brown was really one of theirs, because [he] went to school on Long Island and [his college was] Syracuse. As much as they feared him and hated him on game day they also respected him because he was a native son."[28] The main point of the anecdote is that I am not the only one harboring corny feelings toward the great fullback.

The second anecdote comes from Dr. Zach Clements, a UVM colleague and a great golf buddy. It puts the human touch on just what it meant to encounter the amazing Cleveland star on the gridiron. My friend writes, "During my tenure as assistant coach of the freshman football team at White Plains High School, a highlight of our team's Monday afternoon practices during the fall of 1961 were the visits of Dick Nolan, a star NY Giants defensive corner back. His family home was located across the street from our practice field.

"Most Mondays following a home game, he was chipper, conversational and totally upbeat. But on the Monday following the Giants' home game against the Cleveland Browns, Dick was none of those things. Indeed, he walked and acted like a man that had all he could do to put one foot in front of the other. The reason: Jim Brown. Dick unabashedly admitted taking on Brown in the open field was like 'Getting hit by a fully loaded Mack truck.' He was also the first football personality I ever heard use the expression, "When trying to tackle Jim Brown, the lucky ones missed or fell off."[29]

In 1961, I was teaching English at New Rochelle High School. Our star football player was Richard Roundtree, who later gained lasting fame as the no-holds barred detective in Gordon Parks's classic blaxploitation movie *Shaft* (1971). He was not my student, but I was his class advisor.

Moving now to 1964, one of the most consequential years in Brown's life and career, we discover how seemingly inconsequential events can result in life-altering consequences. The first such event for Brown was his creation of the National Negro Industrial and Economic Union or NNIEU (A.K.A. The Black Economic Union).[30] Growing out of his racial experiences at Syracuse University and the NFL, as well as Jim's association with the Pepsi Cola company, the venture was designed to help black athletes not only protect their wealth but also to turn it into valuable business ventures that would sustain them once they retired from professional sports. In simplified terms, the idea was to educate self-motivated men to use their business success to break down racial barriers. In Brown's words, "I'm for black power the same way I'm for Irish power, Jewish power, labor power, doctor power, farmer power, Catholic power, Protestant power. I'm for all the special vested-interest groups' using their economic and political strength to demand that others pay them respect and grant them equality."[31] According to various sources, no fewer than 400 businesses resulted from Brown's economic gamble.

Let me be clear on Jim's venture. As explained by others, The Black Economic Union did not represent a completely revolutionary idea. Dozens of other black organizers like Floyd McKissick and Roy Innis previously had tried it throughout the nation. Moreover, the notion that a need for a basic education results from political realities goes back at least to our Founding Fathers. Recall President John Adams' famous advice, "I must study politics and war that my sons may have liberty to study mathematics and philosophy, geography, natural history, naval architecture, navigation, commerce, and agriculture, in order to give their children a right to study painting, poetry, music, architecture, statuary, tapestry, and porcelain."[32]

However, Brown's goals differed in several significant ways from President Adams' aims. For example, like other black spokespeople of the day, Jim did not see the politics produce a desirable educational system to meet the needs that Adams described. For example, the current educational system confounded rather than enhanced the ability of blacks to learn what they needed to know to succeed in American life. In many ways Jim's beliefs echoed those of scholar Lerone Bennett, who wrote, "It is amusing, really, to hear people suggesting education as a solution to the race problem. Education in America cannot solve the race problem, for education in America is the essence of the race problem. The educational process in this country perpetuates the subordination of black people. And it is vitiated from top to bottom by a pernicious Class bias which mystifies the poor and the black." Bennett went on to say, "It is by education that we are made our own accusers and jailors."[33]

Brown also differed from Adams in the attitudes they had about education. That is, Jim fixated on job training rather than on a liberal arts and sciences education. Furthermore, he disdained efforts by African-Americans to pursue black studies first! In my meeting with Brown prior to the interview, for example, he reflected one perspective rarely mentioned in current scholarship. Albert Murray seemingly agreed with Brown. He felt, "Most Black Studies programs were opportunistic and not really carefully thought-out responses [sic] to a real academic need."[34] Of particular importance is that Brown, his status, his visibility, and The Black Economic Union gave him a platform to communicate regularly his ideas, as one commentator noted, to black political, cultural and economic leaders all over the country.[35]

One further gulf between Adams and Brown was the emphasis on the arts. You will never find in the Brown literature any mention of books or plays or museums or concerts. Nor are there any apparent ties to the music stemming from the civil rights movement. There is no mention of the avant-garde jazz that Gerald G. Early identified with artists like "John Coltrane, Archie Shepp, Max Roach, Pharaoh Sanders, and the Art Ensemble of Chicago, which tried to blend Black Nationalism and black entrepreneurialism with a black aesthetic and thus promote the 'healing' power of a so-called pure "black" music as therapy.[36] There is no mention of the folk singers like Odetta, Abbey Lincoln, Billie Holiday, and Nina Simone.

Instead, his musical taste lay with the Motown establishment in general and the crossover artist Marvin Gaye in particular. As one critic noted, the singer "provided an erotic legacy of sensual expression, which he pioneered."[37] The artist's appeal also is readily apparent once you understand, as Gaye's biographer David Ritz explained,[38] "One of the things that makes the singer such an incredibly attractive artist is that he takes that which is raw and painful and transforms it into something absolutely gorgeous. His penchant for misery was creative."[39] And finally, as historian Michael Eric Dyson states, "If you are a person who's outraged by war, Marvin's music is for you. If you want to make love, Marvin's music is for you. If you want to talk about the conditions of spirituality, what's infused in the secular world, Marvin's for you."[40]

While Motown's greatest artist was also one of its most troubled performers personally and professionally, it was not difficult to see what attracted Brown to the popular musician. First, as one critic observed, Gaye looked "like a slim Jim Brown."[41] Second, they had similar childhoods, only Marvin's occurred in the Georgia cotton fields where the singer's dysfunctional parents had a major effect on him throughout his life. In fact, Marvin's father shot and killed his son during a family fight just before the drug-addicted singer's forty-fifth birthday.[42]

But probably the greatest attraction was Gaye's music, the most famous of all being the landmark 1971 album *What's Going On*. For anyone wanting to understand the man, his times, and his appeal to Brown this album is as good as any to start. Like Jim in the early 1970s, Gaye was having bad times and poured out his feelings and issues in this major release. According to one historical source, *What's Going On* was "Written and conceived in a generous and human spirit, [and] the lyrics touch on many issues of the day, making the record a State of the Union address from the President of the Soul: the Vietnam War, poverty and crime in the inner cities, drugs, unemployment, ecology, all were handled with a poignant grace, along with Gaye's ever-faithfuls, love and religion."[43]

A second key event in 1964 was Jim's job working intermittently as a commentator for a sports firm called Main Bout. The agency regularly broadcasted close-circuit boxing matches into movie theaters and was run mainly by black Muslims. By the mid-sixties, the broadcasters paid particular attention to the rise of a popular but controversial young pugilist from Louisville, Kentucky named Cassius Clay. Brown's two agency associations with Cassisus Clay and the black Muslims require a brief discussion.

Here again the narrative associated with Muhammad Ali, a figure Early correctly argues is "the biggest hero of the entire colored world in the post-World War II era,"[44] is very well known to people of my generation. Thus I need only introduce the bare details to a new and possibly less informed age group.

After Cassius won the 1960 Olympic Gold for Boxing in Rome, he turned professional fighter and adapted both a flashy ring style and a bizarre public persona in which he insisted he was "the Greatest." Now referred to by many as the "Louisville Loudmouth" or "Lip," people couldn't make up their minds whether they wanted the blustering boxer humiliated or honored. Following a series of early ring victories, ten Louisville millionaires took over his promising career and hired trainer Angelo Dundee to make Clay the Heavyweight Champion of the world.

By 1964, Clay's chance came with a title match against champion and ex-con Sonny Liston, who reputedly had ties to organized crime.[45] Nonetheless, the press did not consider Cassius a credible challenger.[46] Two concerns at the time, one known and the other hidden, surrounded the February 25th bout at Convention Hall in Miami Beach. The first worry was that the menacing Liston would seriously injure the challenger, and odds makers had the twenty-two old boxer an 8-1 underdog. The second fear had to do with Clay's developing ties to the Nation of Islam, who saw the impressionable fighter as an invaluable public relations coup.[47]

Clay's fortunes took a dramatic turn after he unexpectedly beat Liston for the crown on February 25th. Public admiration for the new champ swelled, and for a brief two weeks he seemed America's symbol of racial pride. What the public did not know is that the NOI had converted him to their membership. Thus, when the organization announced not only Clay's conversion, but also that he had changed his name to Muhammad Ali, a shocked white America felt betrayed and cruelly turned on him.

The feeling of betrayal stemmed from the nation's perception of the NOI's personnel, goals and pronouncements. Leaders like Louis Farrakhan, Malcolm X, and Elijah Mohammad openly vilified white people and viciously denounced Jews. At the time, black Americans remained divided over the NOI. Some, according to Crouch, felt the NOI did not do much good for black people:

"Due to the unfortunate influence of the Nation of Islam, through Malcolm X and Louis Farrakhan, gullible Negroes were marched into a dubious sense of unambiguous unity with the Arab world."[48] Others like those cited by Early saw "the NOI [as] a counterrevolutionary organization that basically endorsed a militantly expressed, racially coded, bourgeois fantasy of regeneration through respectability."[49]

Jim Brown's position was that blacks needed to remain publically united, and that the anti-establishment group was something African-Americans needed psychologically.[50] And he certainly didn't win many white friends when he told a reporter, 'Whatever happened to Huey [Newton] the last few years of his life, there was a time when he wasn't afraid to put his shit on the line. If white America doesn't understand that, white America can kiss my ass.'"[51]

Such provocative statements and cultural confusion prevented potential white supporters from discovering what men like Brown felt were the benefits the radical religious group brought to many black Americans. Thus it was difficult for them to understand or to accept why both Ali and Brown associated themselves with such anti-White rhetoric and actions. Even when Malcolm X was expelled from the NOI, Ali chose to break with his one time friend and to stay instead with the controversial organization. In the weeks to follow, the new champ visited Africa and discovered for himself just how much he was a world hero.

In the years to come, Brown's attitude toward the civil rights movement moved significantly away from Dr. King's non-violent strategies. Much as he admired the great man, Jim dismissed the effectiveness of marches, boycotts, and sit-ins. He found little benefit from the Moynihan Report, or the Kenner Report, or new government laws if the people themselves did not take personal responsibility for solving their own problems. And thus it came as no surprise to informed observers when he associated himself with black dissenters like H. Rap Brown, Stokely Carmichael, Huey Newton, and Louis Farrakhan. When asked why, he replied that such revolutionaries were needed. However, privately he did question their tactics. In his words, "Speaking for myself, I think it's too easy to just go out and threaten Whitey. What is that doing to help black people?"[52]

The third key event in 1964 was Jim's debut in the movies. Reading accounts of how he allegedly got into films, the stories about the emergence of an actor born out "of American legend and mythology, a new brand of Hollywood screen character…[a new] black superman"[53] provide a nice story but runs contrary to the facts.

In vastly oversimplified terms, my version emerges from the prevailing film conditions in the mid-sixties. A desperate American film industry, as described in the Introduction, looked to black audiences as an untapped source of revenue. Some filmmakers mistakenly assumed the socially conscious Art house patrons with their love for independent low-budget films and documentary screen techniques would be supportive. But other industry producers, like the people at Twentieth Century-Fox, believed a more productive approach would be to revise popular movie genres like westerns and war movies, and then modernize the conventions with black actors and celebrities, particularly famous sports figures. Among some of the people the film industry selected in the sixties and early seventies were football heroes Woody Strode, Fred "The Hammer" Williamson, Rosie Grier, Bernie Casey, O.J. Simpson, and Jim Brown.[54]

Contrary to myth, the movies came to Jim, not he to them. Up to this point in his history, the superstar had shown little interest in a film career. But he was always open to new ventures. When Fox officials offered him a chance to appear in a revisionist western during the off-season, Jim's curiosity got the better of him and he signed to do Gordon Douglas' *Rio Conchos*.[55] The narrative proved to be a spinoff, as others have noted, from popular post-civil war westerns like John Ford's *The Searchers* (1956) and Michael Curtiz' *The Commancheros* (1961). The script followed Major James Lassiter (Richard Boone), an angry, ex-confederate officer out to revenge the massacre of his family by Apache Indians. Key to settling the score is the location and recapture of a shipment of stolen Union army rifles. To get the rifles back, Lassiter joins a small group, that includes Union soldiers Captain Haven (Stuart Whitman) and Sgt. Franklyn (Jim Brown).

Again contrary to popular perception, Jim did not play a romantic lead or even a leading role. He was one of several performers who gave an adequate performance in a run-of-the mill western that the white filmmakers used to a make several progressive statements. As one black critic noted, such aims routinely were associated with 1960s westerns.[56] Jim's goal was to be as good an actor as his limited experience allowed. Grateful for the help and support the cast and the crew provided him, he found his screen debut to be extremely enjoyable, rich with possibilities for the future, and he gave kudos all around to the people he worked with during the filming. The idea of being a super black hero, a crusader for reform in the film industry, or a revolutionary black sex symbol never entered the picture! Moreover, no one pulled out a brown paper bag in the casting process. And no one, I mean no semi-conscious individual, saw him as an alternative to Sidney Poitier!

The critics proved tepid in their response to *Rio Conchos,* and Jim returned to football. But director Douglas saw something in the novice's persona, as did the now admiring film audiences, and encouraged Brown to get an agent.[57] He did, who then lined up a series of films for the newcomer, beginning with Robert Aldrich's classic war film *The Dirty Dozen* (1967). In the meantime, the Cleveland Browns became the world champions of the football world by triumphing over the famed Green Bay Packers in 1965.

Cleveland Browns' owner Art Morrell saw no problem when, in early 1966, Jim signed for a second film, since there was every reason to believe production would be over by spring training. But the unexpected happened, and the filming ran way over schedule. Morell now insisted Brown show up at training camp. Not only had Brown committed himself to finishing the film, but he also did not respond well to ultimatums. Again contrary to myth, Jim did not want to retire. He had every intention of returning to the Cleveland Browns. In the end he left football because of unexpected and unintended circumstances. Also, he did not see the move from football to film as a hardship. He had proven all he had wanted to prove in the game. He was retiring during his peak years. In addition, he loved making movies and the lifestyle that went with it. And he made clear to the world he was nobody's "slave." Years later, Morrell admitted he made a mistake, Jim accepted the apology, and the two men became great friends.

In hindsight, Brown's second film followed a strategy aimed at presenting the controversial new screen personality in a fresh light.

Based on E.M. Nathanson's novel of the same name, The *Dirty Dozen* once again found Brown with an ensemble cast, one of the best ever assembled for a traditional action war film: Lee Marvin, Ernest Borgnine, Charles Bronson, John Cassavetes, Richard Jaeckel, George Kennedy, Trini Lopez, Ralph Meeker, Robert Ryan, Telly Savalas, Donald Sutherland, Robert Webber, Clint Walker, and Jim Brown. The Nunnally Johnson/Lukas Heller screenplay deals with OSS Major John Reisman (Marvin) and his secret recruitment of twelve dangerous convicts to take part in a suicide mission against the Nazi high command in World War II. As in *Rio Conchos,* Jim remains part of a bold set of misfits whose courage and prowess represent the best of Hollywood heroics. Alex Haley aptly noted the ties between Brown and the script's liberal views: Jim was cast as "Robert Jefferson, a college-trained soldier condemned to die for murdering a white racist who had brutally assaulted him."[58] While once again there are no romantic episodes, the socially conscious filmmakers use Jim to build not only positive feelings toward the actor, but also to attack racism. My favorite is when Savalas, a Southern bigot, asks if he has to eat with a "nigger," and Brown lunges at him. Aldrich then shows Marvin leaving the room, saying to his subordinates, "The gentleman from the South made some comment about eating arrangements. They're settling the matter now."

Three more film assignments followed in rapid succession: Jack Cardiff's *Dark of the Sun* (1967),[59] John Sturges' *Ice Station Zebra* (1968),[60] and Buzz Kulik's *Riot* (1969).[61] None featured Brown in a romantic situation, and all three stressed both his courage and his virtuous character. In the Cardiff movie, Brown played an idealistic African soldier fighting for the rights of black people. Noteworthy was the fact that it was the first film to deal with genocide in the Congo during the sixties.[62] In the Sturges' outing, he played a marine captain assigned to a nuclear sub and determined to root out America's Cold War enemies at the North Pole. In the Kulik production, Jim portrayed a convict with an admirable code of honor. In essence, the fledgling performer was determined to become a competent actor who enjoyed the same opportunities as any other actor. No one was going to limit him to either traditional stereotyped roles or exclusively black films. And he made it a point of extending what blacks could do, say, and represent in American films. As film historian Keith M. Harris put it, Brown's roles were every bit a part of an "integrationist paradigm'" as those of Sidney Poitier."[63]

None of these three events impacted on the manner in which Brown was treated by Federal law enforcement agencies. For example, the FBI perceived The Black Economic Union as a negative institution. What was conceived as an opportunity to make black people competitive in the business world appeared to the Federal Bureau a blatant act by Brown to recruit and to convert law-abiding black athletes into "radical extremists." Acting on that perception, the Bureau waged an undercover operation to discredit Brown, to dissuade black athletes from joining the NNIEU, and to destroy the organization's reputation in the business community. In the years to follow, they would also accuse him of being a member of the Communist Party and the Nation of Islam (NOI). He was neither.[64] The outspoken star did say, however, "that he felt its views voiced the true feelings of most Negroes."[65] Choosing perception over reality, the FBI operated on the assumption he was extremely dangerous and acted accordingly.[66]

One final point. The Black Economic Union provided for one of the very rare times in Brown's career a singular example where the conspicuous chauvinist publically identified a black woman as an integral part of his public life. The woman in question was Maggie Hathaway, whom we will discuss in a later chapter. According to Jim, " One lady who has never lost her sense of humor, or her resolve... in fighting discrimination, Maggie has been my mentor....Maggie helped me organize and clarify the agenda of the Black Economic Union. Whenever I've been in trouble, Maggie was always there, rapidly, at the risk of whatever she had going at the time. I could never write a book about my life, could never talk about the struggle, without giving my love to Maggie Hathaway."[67]

As a result of Jim's ongoing battles with the law and the misperceptions communicated by the media, he ironically became a stronger and cheekier public figure. For the rest of his life, he chose to ignore the constant criticisms and bad publicity associated with controversial events, and instead courageously involved himself in dangerous situations. When riots erupted in black communities,

Jim showed up to help deflate the chaos. When gang wars took place on California's streets, he mediated between the groups in the living room of his home. When tens of thousands of black men found themselves imprisoned throughout the country, he created a self-help program and went directly to California's prison inmates to provide them with opportunities to turn their lives around.

Now might also be a suitable time to address briefly two other significant events occurring in Jim's life that further made him an enigma to the public. The first had to do with Muhammad Ali.

In simplified terms, the Louisville draft board in April 1966 changed the Champ's draft status and ordered him to report for active military service. Ali refused, claiming not only was it against his religious beliefs but also he had nothing against the Vietnamese people. At the time, his public pronouncement made him one of the most misunderstood as well as despised individuals in the nation. In addition, a showdown between the Federal government and the Heavyweight Champion of the World only added to the increasing chaos fermented not only by the anti-war movement, but also the divisions between many White and Black Americans. Following three unsuccessful appeals, Ali was convicted of draft evasion and sentenced to 5 years in a Federal penitentiary on April 27, 1967.

At this point, Jim Brown performed one of the most courageous and memorable acts in twentieth-century sports history. Ignoring the risks to his reputation and to his career, he demonstrated his standing in the African-American world by contacting ten of the most famous, talented, and brave black American athletes and asked them to come to Cleveland to meet with Ali and determine whether his refusal to serve was genuine. On June 7, 1967, in what is sometimes referred to as "The Muhammad Ali Draft Summit," the eminent black athletes met with Ali. After three hours of discussion, Brown announced to the media that the group unanimously believed Ali sincere and gave him their support.

Almost four years later, the United States Supreme Court in Clay v. United States unanimously reversed the lower courts' conviction. But during the time period, as one source chronicled, Ali was stripped of his boxing licenses throughout the country and remained unemployed, almost broke, and paying lawyers to keep him out of jail, alimony to his first wife, and supporting his current wife and child.[68] The memorable ring battles with the likes of Joe Frazier, George Forman, Ken Norton, and Leon Spinks, as well as the incredible story of Ali regaining his heavyweight crown not once but twice and becoming the only boxer in history to win the honor three times is as they quip, "the stuff that legends are made of."

Now suffering from Parkinson's disease, the great American has seen better days, but his momentous actions still garner considerable recognition, including his being voted the Sports Personality of the Century by the BBC in 1999 and being awarded the Presidential Medal of Freedom by President George W. Bush in 2006. Throughout this historic period, Brown remained loyal to Ali and shared the champ's changing and mercurial relationship with people around the world.

A second key element adding to the misperceptions and confusion about Brown came in large measure from his own making. After Ali's 1964 religious conversion, Jim began sporting a Muslim cap and shamelessly pursued a promiscuous and reckless existence. In his writings and in those by his friends, especially Jim Toback, we learned not only that he had bought a beautiful home overlooking the famous Sunset Strip, but he also used the place as a base for a sexual lifestyle that purportedly eclipsed that of Hugh Heffner's fabled parties. The public followed Brown's fast living antics as a liberated married man (he had married Sue James in 1959) who reveled in what seemed Herculean sexual performances. Stories sensationalizing Jim's dark side were spread across the media in the mid-to-late sixties: domestic abuse, womanizing, his penchant for intimidation off the field; no relationship with the children he fathered, and frequent run-ins with the law over his alleged violent treatment of women.

No one questioned that he enjoyed fast living. But more importantly, many people merely accepted the accuracy of the stories. For his part, Jim remained equivocal on the issues. On one hand, he enjoyed his reputation as a ladies man. He devoted pages and pages in his two autobiographies to his sexual adventures, including his brief romance with Gloria Steinham, whom he met during an interview in the 1960s. He also admitted to one interviewer "that he hit some women and that, at times, he traded cocaine for sexual favors, even when denying he ever used cocaine himself." He also acknowledged, "I've done things I'm not particularly proud of. But at least I'm honest enough to talk about them."[69] On the other hand, when a *New York Sunday News* reporter in 1970 asked him what was going on, Jim insisted it was all part of a conspiracy to make him look "immoral and criminal.[70] But Brown's critics rejected that defense.

Probably one of the most important sources for determining Brown's character and behavior during the late sixties and seventies was provided by author, screenwriter, producer, director, and actor James Toback. After graduating from Harvard in 1966, he became first an English teacher and then worked for *Esquire.* One of his assignments was to interview Jim Brown. Instead of carrying out his obligation, Toback became a boarder at the celebrity's home for nearly three years. During that time, the writer kept a diary he then turned into a 1971 book-length biography. What most fascinated arrested adolescents who read about the sexual adventures that Brown and Toback shared in the star's pleasure dome was how competitive the two men were in seducing women and having sex with multiple partners. Toback went on to become a popular filmmaker, getting writing/directing credits for films like *The Gambler* (1974), *Harvard Man* (2002), and *Tyson* (2008)[71] His most acclaimed work to date is his Oscar-nominated screenplay for *Bugsy* (1991).

But it is Toback's second film *Fingers* (1978)[72] that proves most relevant to our narrative. Why? Because many people believe, falsely I think, that the somewhat autobiographical movie[73] reveals the "true Jim Brown." Starring a young Harvey Keitel as the deeply disturbed Jimmy Fingers, an aspiring pianist who when he isn't practicing Bach's E-Minor Toccata is either a vicious collector for his loan shark father (Michael V. Gazzo) or a sex-crazed seducer of gangsters' mistresses. Although Brown gets third billing in this pre-Quentin Tarantino film, he only appears for ten minutes near the end of the 89-minute movie. Cast as Deems, a powerfully built nightclub owner with mob ties, Brown comes across as an arrogant, dangerous and sex-loving enthusiast, whose most outrageous act is to bang together the heads of two women who refuse to kiss each other and satisfy his sexual desires. While the movie has its fans—*Entertainment Weekly* rates it one of the 25 best Mob movies ever[74]—I would direct you to Vincent Canby's review of *Fingers,* in which he calls it " a groupie's movie. You don't have to love it or be angered by it. You may only have to be depressed."[75] Jack Kroll goes further, stating that the film "is an embarrassing extension of Toback's embarrassing 1971 book about himself and Brown...."[76] Either way, the movie only added to Brown's negative reputation.

These events, perceptions, and misperceptions eventually shaped Brown's screen journey. In his fifth film, George Flemyng's *The Split* (1968),[77] Jim became both a leading man and a sex symbol.[78] For a brief time, love scenes and bare chests became indispensible to his screen adventures[79] Among the most discussed movies in his narrative from the sixties to the mid-seventies are Tom Gries' *100 Rifles*,[80] Jerry Paris' *The Grasshopper*,[81] Steve Sekely's *Kenner*[82] (all in 1969), John Guillermin's *El Condor* (1970),[83] Jack Starrett's *Slaughter*,[84] Robert Hartford-Davis' *Black Gunn*[85] (both in 1972), Gordon Douglas' *Slaughter 2: Big Rip-Off* (1973),[86] Gordon Parks Jr.'s *Three the Hard Way* (1974),[87] and Antonio Margheriti's *Take a Hard Ride* (1975).[88]

Since most of these movies are discussed in my conversation with Brown, let me make a few general observations before turning to the interview itself. First, Brown's alleged sexual prowess that made black men feel better about their masculinity may have been related more to the stories in the media than in the aforementioned movies. While *100 Rifles* and *Black Gunn* are possibilities, the remaining movies hardly validate conventional wisdom of the actor's sexual status in movie history.

Take *The Grasshopper*, one of Brown's most underrated and overlooked films. Based upon author Mark McShane's novel *The Passing of Evil*, the seductive Jerry Belson-Garry Marshall screenplay follows the sad journey of Christine Adams (Jacqueline Bisset), a naive, young, and uneducated woman who wants more out of life than she has in her small British Columbia community of Kingman. Although devoid of any theatrical talent, Christine runs away and heads to Las Vegas to find a career in show business. As she says, "I want to be totally happy, totally different, and totally in love."At first, her striking beauty lands her a job as a chorus girl and then the mistress of an older man. But Tommy Marcott (Jim Brown) the sympathetic celebrity host at the casino falls in love with her, and the pair marry. From then on life goes steadily downhill for the tragic couple. It is one of Brown's most sympathetic roles.

So when Calvin C. Hernton writes, "Jim Brown's image as an athlete and more recently his image as a movie star, fits the image of Black males becoming sex fetishes [and] objects of sexual deviation,"[89] I shake my head in disbelief. The comments seem directed more to the actor's reputation than to the majority of his screen roles. So too does the misperception that his movies perpetuated the general image "that blacks are indiscriminately promiscuous rather than selective in life."[90] Finally, a great deal is made of black masculinity and the sexual revolution during this period. All true and significant. But because Brown's screen conduct differed from previous actors from the fifties, it does not mean that Brown's behavior proved that different from other black actors of the era like Fred Williamson, Richard Roundtree, Melvin Van Peebles, and Ron O'Neal.

A second point. Even in the movies with the likes of Raquel Welch (*100 Rifles*) and Stella Stevens (*Black Gunn*), Jim's comportment hardly matched the more explicit behavior of the riotous Pam Grier in blaxploitation movies like Eddie Romero's *Big Mama, White Mama,* Jack Hill's *Coffy,* (both in 1973), and another Jack Hill production, *Foxy Brown* (1974). Don't take my word for it. Read what Quentin Tarantino said about the star of these black action films and his first viewing of *Coffy*: "She is a truly great icon, and she holds a very special place in cinema history. When the blaxploitation phenomenon was going on in the '70s, you had Jim Brown, probably their single biggest star, and they would always say about Brown that he's sort of the black Clint Eastwood. Fred Williamson had the mantle of the black Burt Reynolds; Jim Kelly was the black Bruce Lee. But Pam Grier wasn't the black version of anybody, because there had never been a heroine who specialized in doing action movies, a full-on woman who didn't try to act like a man."[91]

Check out what Grier said about her screen behavior: "When it came time for me to show up in a bra and panties for my role in *Coffy,* I was willing to do that, too. My stay in Europe had opened me up, but there was a debate about what to do when I had a Janet Jackson-wardrobe style malfunction. A strap on my black and white polka-dot dress broke, and I was so into the scene that I was unaware that I had bared my nipple. Since it had occurred on its own, not planned, I was all for leaving it in. Why would people be afraid of a nipple?"

"The truth was that it was still considered uncouth for a woman to breastfeed in public. But nudity was becoming more prevalent, and women alike were taking off their clothes, soaking in co-ed tubs naked, and skinny-dipping in swimming pools. It was post-Woodstock, and we were being told to love our bodies. These days, no one thinks much of nudity. Even Halle Berry allowed her nipples to show in *Monster's Ball.* Back then, people were accustomed to seeing women mainly play hookers and drug addicts where they wore clothes and allowed themselves to be exploited."[92]

A third point. Not enough has been written about what actors like Welch and Stevens faced when they did their loves scenes with a black man on screen: the hate mail, the frightening phone calls, and the horrifying experiences in public places as they were called every ugly name possible. While a great deal is made of the men who broke down the movies' racial barriers, more time is needed thinking of what the women risked in playing Brown's lovers. It's important not to become too complacent about just how much has changed in American standards and outlooks since the post-World War II period. One purpose of *The Interviews* is to remind us of our evolving views of race relations, women's rights, and film as a social force in our lives.

A fourth point closely associated with the previous comment is the ongoing comparisons of Poitier with Brown. Almost every major critic in black studies encounters the notion that not only did the athlete present a more heroic image than did arguably America's greatest black movie star, but he also challenged Poitier's status in the industry. The issue can and will not be resolved here. But think for a moment. When did it require more courage to change screen conventions: during the sixties when revolution gripped the nation, or earlier when conservatism ruled the mass media and racism was firmly entrenched in the national consciousness?

Let me be very clear on this extremely complex point. Both Poitier and Brown have nothing to be ashamed of or to apologize for in their trailblazing careers. The former's fall from grace at the end of the sixties had everything to do with the times and the frustration that African-Americans felt about civil rights, assassinations, the Vietnam War, and the slow pace of national reform. The latter's rise to prominence had everything to do with conditions in the film industry, the sexual revolution, and his polarizing persona.

I want to also point out that Jim had nothing to do with numerous attacks leveled by the media and black activists against Poitier's "integrationist" principles. Just the opposite was true, and how we know that remains one of my favorite stories about the misunderstood superstar. In greatly oversimplified terms, Brown described in his 1990 autobiography how he accidentally encountered Poitier on a flight. These were tough times for the great actor because he had just come under attack in the *New York Times* from an obscure playwright who denigrated Poitier's work.[93] Jim, the so-called crude and militant tough guy, told Sydney just how much he admired him and then moved away. Brown believed Poitier ignored his gesture. That is until he read the actor's autobiography, *This Life*.[94] Written were these words: "Sitting there next to me on that plane...[Jim Brown] said something that made him a guy I would like forever. He said, "A lot of things are happening now, and a lot of us are working. I just thought I'd stroll up here and say 'thank you' for the contributions you've made to us all having a little piece. I just want you to know that it's appreciated.' He got up, shook my hand, and went back to his seat. That made my day. A man of few words who never bit his tongue, that was big Jim, a prince of many colors."[95]

In many ways, I shared the same feelings about the flawed warrior and his controversial reputation. Over the years as his life and career progressed, his contentious status remained forever in flux. What helped nostalgically summarize for me Jim's past was Larry Cohen's *Original Gangstas* (1996).[96] The brainchild of Fred Williamson, Aubrey Rattan's narrative focuses on the dilapidated steel-mill town of Gary, Indiana where warring gangs terrify the aging and disillusioned black community. When Marvin Bookman (Oscar Brown Jr.), an honest, poor grocer witnesses the murder of a college-bound basketball star, he refuses to keep his mouth shut and identifies the killers to the police. The hoods come after him, not knowing the powerful friends and supporters he has at his back. To play these screen heroes, the movie reunites many of the black stars of the seventies: Williamson, Jim Brown, Richard Roundtree, Pam Grier, Paul Winfield, Isabel Sanford, and Ron O'Neal. To see these weathered actors once more fight for black dignity, to hear about their failures as friends and parents and husbands, touches a nerve even if the socially conscious movie itself does not rise much above the weaknesses of the blaxploitation films it pays homage to. As one critic noted, there "is a genuine sadness that inevitably permeates the picture."[97]

This is as good a place as any to bring this biographical essay to closure. Jim continues to work in film, television, and sports; and he continues to help marginalized black people not only survive but also live better lives. His influence as well as his shortcomings continue to promote sharp disagreements about him and his contributions to the African-American experience. His followers base their loyalty on his many civil rights achievements, his brilliant athletic skills, the breakthroughs in films that his stature and determination made possible for other black actors, and for the incredible risks he took and persists in taking to make America a better and greater nation. His critics point to his brutal treatment of women, his behavior toward his wives and many of his children, his failure to understand the moral leadership he possessed but sometimes abused, to his stilted acting and the slapdash quality of his movies, and to his violent conduct. This harsh difference of opinion is what for me makes the man so worth studying. In doing the analysis, we learn as much about ourselves as we do about the polarizing figure himself.

My interview with Jim came about by accident and left me totally unprepared for what occurred. I had been meeting for several days with Woody Strode and his wife, when out of the blue the actor asked if I wanted to interview the football superstar turned movie actor. "Absolutely," I replied. Woody made a call, then gave me Jim's phone number and told me to call him. Twenty-four hours later, I arrived by cab at what I now know was his legendary home overlooking the Sunset Strip. Only now do I realize just how extraordinary the meeting was at 11:15 that day. Interviewers like Alex Haley and Jim Toback had had to go through months of planning and negotiations before Brown had allowed them to meet him. Moreover, he had always maintained if he didn't like you, the interview would be canceled and you would be asked to leave.

When walking down the driveway, two things struck me immediately. In the garage was a young woman, I believe her name was Jennifer, who matched exactly the description of the females Jim found most desirable. She was detailing his motorcycle. Next, there was the backboard for hoops mounted on a wall and used for playing driveway basketball. I had read Toback's book and was not surprised. Fifteen minutes later, Jim, in shorts, showed up from his tennis game, and we sat down to talk but not to have an interview.

The Jim Brown I met was in total contrast to his image. Instead of a self-righteous, intimidating, and arrogant superstar, I met a soft-spoken, gracious celebrity who unbeknownst to me at the time was being blackballed by the film industry, going through a divorce, and was preoccupied with the fortunes of then controversial Dallas Cowboy star Duane Thomas. The man I talked to was not paranoid, made no mention of the FBI, and did not dwell on black masculinity and machismo. He was likable, kind, friendly, and forthright.

Because of all his bad publicity and the many misrepresentations about him, and because he knew next to nothing about my values or me, Jim wanted to explore a number of issues. We talked seriously and candidly about how I felt about Black Nationalism, what I was trying to do with my research, and what I knew about him. Over and over, he surprised me with his negative attitudes about Black Studies, the misunderstandings whites had about African-Americans, and how few people understood the need for self-help. He commented on how helpful Woody Strode was in fighting Jim's problems with the film industry. Interestingly, he became very agitated when talking about the TV film *Brian's Song,* which he despised.

What struck me most then and still does now was our discussion about racism. He advised me to direct my work towards educating white people; he felt blacks knew all they needed to know about intolerance and had little to learn from a white, Jewish UVM Associate Professor. He also asked me if I would send him my conclusions before they were published. I raised the issue of a conflict of interest, but Jim said he wanted merely to see if what I wrote was accurate and fair.

He accepted me for all my flaws, as I accepted him. It's been over forty years, but I'd be willing to bet little if anything has changed. He always struck me as a man who remembered both the affronts and kindnesses done for and to him. He is impressive when it comes to forgiveness and remains an incredible help to friends who need him. Maybe the kindest comment I can make as we begin the interview is to invoke Churchill's comment that "The price of greatness is responsibility." The question is how well did Brown perform his responsibilities?

Jim Brown Interview
January 11, 1972

FM: What I'd like to do is get an understanding at the beginning of how you got into films, how you came to movies.

JB: Well, I was...when I played professional football, I came out to Los Angeles for the pro-ball game. I got a call from Twentieth Century-Fox that they wanted me to come out. They had a film that they might want me to do. I didn't want to go out, because I didn't want to be bothered. Then after the game, some guy came out on the field and said, "Come on out, because—you know—bring your family out. There's a lot of money in it." So I said, "Yeah, all right. Call me."

So they called me. Sent a limousine down. I jumped in the limousine and went up to Twentieth Century-Fox and met Gordy Douglas and Dave Weisbart. Gordy was the director of the film—beautiful man, fantastic man—and David was nice.

David Weisbart produced Rio Conchos *(1964). The veteran filmmaker started off as an editor for Warner Brothers during World War II. Among his most famous films were* Mildred Pierce *(1945),* Night and Day *(1946),* The Fountainhead *(1949),* A Streetcar Named Desire *(1951), and* Rebel Without a Cause *(1955). Prior to 1952, when he was promoted to producing tasks, he received his only Oscar nomination for* Johnny Belinda *(1948). By the middle of the fifties, he switched to Twentieth Century-Fox. There he was best known for making Elvis Presley movies including the singer's first movie* Love Me Tender *(1956).* Rio Conchos *came near the end of Weisbart's career. He died on July 21, 1967, at 52 years of age.*[98]

JB: I told them I had never acted. So they said you'll take a screen test, and if you pass the screen test, everything will be groovy. So I said, "Ok." So I took the test, and I went back East, and they called me. They said, "The test turned out good. We're going to get Stuart Whitman, and Anthony Franciosa, and Richard Boone, and Edmond O'Brian. So I did the film.

FM: What was the name of that film?

JB: *Rio Conchos*. Gordy Douglas directed.[99]

Douglas made a second film with Brown, Slaughter's Big Rip-Off *in 1973.*

FM: Why did they want you for that film? Was there anything to do with a race problem there? They wanted to have a black man?

JB: I think basically they wanted to have a black man in the film, and basically I think that they wanted to capitalize on the football publicity. And they figured that if a black football player was in on this film, it would probably attract an additional segment of the audience at large than they would normally get.

FM: Did they see this as a one shot film, as an exploitation situation, or were they talking about a long-term contract?

JB: Well, everything is exploitation. We exploit each other, you know. [Laughter] I don't really want to get into that.

FM: Yeah.

JB: I exploit them for money, they exploit me for whatever. That's what the market's all about. It was a one shot thing, you know. I didn't have any other plans, and didn't think they had any other either. You know, they make films, like they make a film; they find people to act in it. So it was a one shot thing.

FM: Did you have any problems on the set? Or anything interesting by way of anecdotes? Making the film?

JB: Not really. Except that I thought, Jesus Christmas, this is fantastic. Guys putting coats on your back. You had your own chair. You had your own chauffeur. You had good living accommodations. Everything went like clockwork from the standpoint of your wake-up call, your make-up, and things like this. I thought they must have a trillion dollars in this industry. I enjoyed it, because I got along very well with Gordy. He was.... If he was another kind of director, I could never have done another film. He was so understanding and so helpful. We got through with the thing. If I thought I was going to be any good.... The film made a lot of money. It allowed me to get a three-picture contract with Paramount, and it allowed me to get into *The Dirty Dozen* after that.

FM: Was that your next film? *The Dirty Dozen*?

JB: Yeah. So, it worked out really well for me.

FM: Did you know, was there any talk at all about black people getting a different salary for the same kind of part? And problems of extras? Any kind of that discrimination at all? That you experienced?

JB: What do you mean?

FM: Well, a lot of people have said that in films, they have five guys playing at a poker table. If one of the guys was black, he would make less money for the same part, the same role, than the other white guys.

JB: Well, that could very definitely be true. I didn't know too much about that at the time. When I came in, I came in as a football star. I had a status that allowed me to skip over all the problems. I have never been approached face to face about anything from the standpoint of segregation, since I have been in films. You know, I guess my reputation spoke for itself. I was an outspoken guy; so when I came in, they decided they would not limit me, they would not segregate me, or cut my salary or give me less, or anything like that. Now, at the time, I didn't know very much about extras or anything like that.

[BREAK IN TAPE]

FM: How much time was there between *Rio Conchos* and *The Dirty Dozen*?

JB: I really don't remember. I did *Rio Conchos* when I was still playing football, in the summer. Then I played another season of football. Then I started *The Dirty Dozen*.[100]

FM: Did you leave football primarily to go into films?

BP: Not really. I left football, because I'd done my thing, you know.

FM: Yeah, I know.

JB: I was exhausted. I could play. I could play now, but I wanted to leave on top. And at that time, I had the opportunity to do a sports thing with one of the networks, and I had an opportunity, if I wanted it, to remain with Pepsi-Cola in New York, in National Accounts. You know. And so I had about three avenues to head in, but films offered like two years' security, because that three-year contract meant that the money would be better than anything I could make in football.

FM: Any stories about *The Dirty Dozen*? Anything interesting happen? Either in the script or on location?

JB: Well, lots of things interesting, not really funny stories that I could get into. The thing I remember most about *The Dirty Dozen* was the fact that Bob Aldrich was the director. I have great admiration for Gordy Douglas. One reason was because Gordy's a nice man, very helpful to everybody. Bob Aldrich is a very strong man. He's not a prejudiced man at all. He's his own man. He's a rebel. He presents what he wants to present on the screen. And he loves people. The people that he really digs, they love him.

He had the toughest bunch of guys that any director could have over there. I don't think there are three directors in Hollywood that could handle that group: Telly Savalas, John Cassavetes, Charlie Bronson, Clint Walker, Robert Webber, Ernest Borgnine, Lee Marvin, you know, on down the line.

And we never had a problem. Actors never had a problem with each other. You know, there was scene stealing and everything else, but he let it go. He was beautiful when it was time to be strong,

FM: That's a terrific film.

JB: It was a fantastic experience. You know, really a fantastic experience. Kenny Hyman was the producer. Bob and Kenny had a different idea what should be done. But Bob won out, he wanted the humor; and Kenny didn't, and the film made a lot of money.

We used to go out at night, and we each had different places we.... I used to like to dance. I liked the Discotheque; Lee Marvin and Telly liked to gamble, so they would always be in the [casinos]. And the other guys liked to go to restaurants, fine restaurants. You could find us in our particular haunts, but we'd get together a lot. Party. It was just really a beautiful time.

FM: So, so far, from what I gather, from the first two films you're in, the first two years in Hollywood, you see no reason to make any kind of complaint about segregation or about race prejudice or any problem that you know other than being an actor and working in a film, as far as your experiences go, is that what I hear?

JB: That's true. That's the difference. I have a philosophy about that anyways. See I think that if you're independent, if you're strong enough, if you've got your own thing, then people like that won't be segregating you. They aren't going to be able to segregate you and all of that. If you're independent enough, and you have some power, you see. When I say that I had no problems, I'm not saying that there were no problems. I probably had fewer problems than anybody out there, because I've had more freedom I think than anybody out there. But no, I have not had racial experiences in any of my films. I have no segregation, no nothing.

FM: But, when you finished *The Dirty Dozen,* is that when you began your three films, *The Strip* and....

JB: *The Split.*[101]

FM: No. Was it *The Split*?

JB: Let's see. I don't know what I did after *The Dirty Dozen*. I'm trying to think. Maybe it was *The Split*. No, I did a little film in India called, *Kenner* (1969).[102]

FM: I've heard of it. Never saw it. Well, let's start with *Kenner.* What was *Kenner* like?

JB: Well, it was a low-budget film that I did my first lead in. It was shot in India.

FM: Why did you have to go to India to star in your first film?

JB: Well, it had nothing to do with going to India. It just happens that it was a project that was going to be shot in India, because they could shoot it there at a low cost and get the [snaps fingers] Indian exteriors, get the location value of India.

FM: But it had nothing to do with, again, any problems...any concerns...?

JB: No, it didn't have anything to do with any problems. That was a King Brothers project. They were going to go to India whether I was going or not. See, my thing is that...in *Kenner,* it didn't call for a black guy in the script. I was just black. And the guy had a romance with an Indian girl. She was played by a white actress called Madlyn Rhue.

Frank, Maurice, and Herman King were three brothers who formed their own company at the start of the forties and stayed around for about twenty years. One of their claims to film history is that the team made Irving Rapper's The Brave One *(1956). This film earned blacklisted writer Dalton*

Trumbo, using the pseudonym Robert Rich, an Oscar for screenwriting. Kenner *may have been one of King Brothers Productions last films.*

In many respects, Madlyn Rhue was a highly unusual film and TV actress. Never a star but always a frequent performer on many top TV series like Hawaii Five-O, Perry Mason, Mission Impossible, Mannix and Murder, She Wrote, *she also appeared in at least twenty movies such as* Operation Petticoat *(1959) and* It's a Mad, Mad, Mad, Mad World *(1963). Then Rhue developed multiple sclerosis in 1977, but refused to give up her career. She continued making films and appearing on TV. But eight years later the disease forced her into a wheelchair. Still unwilling to call it quits the gutsy actress found roles that accommodated her disability. Finally, after a 26-year struggle, she died on Dec. 16, 2003, at 68 years of age.*[103]

JB: That's the story, it was kind of a sentimental, soap-opera story based upon an American sailor and an Indian girl and a little boy. The girl gets killed, and the sailor kind of takes the little boy over, and they believe that the mother comes back in the form of a dove.

FM: Did you like it? It seems as if you liked the picture.

JB: It was not a good picture by any standards. Just a little old soap opera. I liked doing it. Yeah.

FM: Jim, you were so successful in *The Dirty Dozen*. Everybody was talking about it; especially my kids loved the scene where you're running to drop the things down the vents. Why weren't there many offers? Or maybe there were? Were there many offers?

JB: Sure. See, *The Dirty Dozen*.... See, when Robert O'Brien.... Careers have a lot to do with who you're with. I had a lot of offers, sure. All kinds. Robert O'Brien was a great friend of mine at MGM. He was the president of MGM. He had a whole plan set up for me over there. I had a meeting with his people in New York. He called me when I was doing *Ice Station Zebra,*[104] like at the spur of the moment. He told me I'd been responsible for so many dollars that *The Dirty Dozen* made, and he just liked me. He was a nice man to me. When he left MGM, that was about it for me at MGM.

Directed by John Sturges, Ice Station Zebra *(1968) struck me as an overblown cold-war action film about heroic attempts to ferret out spies aboard a U.S submarine headed for the North Pole. But to Brown, it meant a great deal. The part Jim played had been originally written for a white actor. Now it had him as dedicated Marine Captain, an officer—a man, self-sufficient as hell, bad, up tight, ready to do a hell of a job. He doesn't care who likes him or who doesn't, so he doesn't try to be liked. He's a terrific soldier, very tough on his men, but fair, and anything he asks them to do he can do better."*[105]

FM: Why? You had made so much money for MGM, why wouldn't they want you to continue?

JB: It isn't that you've made so much money. You know, they've got to have projects for you; they've got to deal with many, many things. My thing is not really any different than anyone else, from that standpoint. The movie industry was changing, see; and anything that had to do with me, didn't have to do with me. Everything that I went through, some of it had to do with me, and some of it had to do with the changing industry. The whole star system was changing. Everything was changing.

FM: And you were just caught in that system like everyone else?

JB: Sure. I got caught into it. I was like a leading man, at the time. A black leading man, that was doing things that were fairly controversial. So what the papers and stuff tried to do was play it off; they didn't even get into the things that I'd broken through. I had torn up a lot of taboos.

FM: For example? Can you tell me about some of the taboos that you tore through?

JB: I played a crook. I played a master crook in *The Split*.[106] I was the boss. I had white henchmen.

FM: Yes, that was a great bit.

JB: I ran the show and everything else.

Since The Split *elevated Brown to a sex symbol, you might enjoy his comments about what love scenes on the set were like. According to the actor, "If I found my leading lady unattractive, physically or spiritually, love scenes for me were uncomfortable. If she was pretty, had some heart, I welcomed love scenes. Actors talk about being professional. They say you can kiss a person, hold a person, not feel a thing. Man, if that person you're kissing and holding is fine, love scenes are dangerous. God did not make the human body so you could talk to it, tell it exactly how to act. It will do some shit on its own."*[107]

FM: Were you responsible...? I thought one of the most brilliant things in *The Split* was the business of the white guy raping the black girl, because all through the history of the movies was the theory that the black man was after the white woman. Every stereotype.... That was the most frightening thing that the white man faced in the history of motion pictures. When they really wanted to get a guy, it was the black man was going to take our women.

JB: That's right.

FM: Then in this one, it's James Whitmore who rapes the black girl. Brilliant. Brilliant.

The incident and the film are covered again in my chapter on James Whitmore later in the book.

JB: It must've been their idea. It wasn't my idea. In that film, we just did everything just as if [snaps fingers] nothing really had that much to do with black.

FM: Really? Now this is why I wanted..... I got from watching this movie that this was your movie, that you had pretty well hand-tailored the script, and that you were trying to knock every single white stereotype.

JB: Here's the really funny thing about it. I didn't go into the movie to tell them what to do. What they did, from the standpoint of a.... Whenever they approached me, they came to me as a personality or whatever that could probably reach white and black people. So, they didn't come to me with black scripts, they just came to me with scripts. So I was playing guys that weren't black.

FM: Well, why weren't the other movies like that? All the movies that I've seen, none of them have the visual sight gags that you have. For example, when the guy drove you to the garage, you were testing the guy out for the strip, the guy says, "Is that your chauffeur?" You say, "No, he's mine." You know. No other films had those kinds of sight gags.

JB: A number of them do.

FM: Well, who did it then? If it wasn't your idea, how come those sight gags seem only to appear in your films? Why was that?

JB: I guess because of different personalities. At the time, I was dealing with very hip producers.

FM: White men or black men?

JB: White men.

FM: White men!

JB: White men. Very hip kind of guys. Bob O'Brien's hip. Kenny Hyman was hip. Winkler, Carl Winkler did his bit, he was hip. They were hip, them guys. They didn't give a shit about presenting no stereotypes, or anything like that. And so like when we get a script, maybe that script was for Steve McQueen, see? Lee Marvin played the counterpart for that script which was *Point Blank* (1967). That was written for a white man, but all right, so they wouldn't use me. But, now, they're not going to ignore the fact that I'm black. So then, we get together and decide on what areas where it will work, where you bring in the fact that the guy is black. You're not trying to avoid it, but it isn't going to be the main theme of the film either. That's how you come to those points where there are these exchanges.

FM: So, they're writing for you now?

JB: Yeah, they're writing for me now. They change the white script, and they write it for me. They put a few of those things in that says the cat is black, you know.

FM: Were the same guys on *100 Rifles*[108] as were on *The Split*?

JB: Oh no.

FM: Different guys all together?

JB: Yeah.

FM: And how about the guys who did the other one? *Tick... Tick...Tick.*[109]

JB: Different. Ralph Nelson did that one.

FM: Different. All three are different, and yet all three films are similar, as far as the racial gags.

JB: Uh huh.

FM: I mean, that business, for example, in *Tick...Tick...Tick* when you're riding in the car at the end. You tell Kennedy that you're not going to run for sheriff next year, and he feels relieved. You're going to run for mayor. That kind of thing. Then all of a sudden, they stopped. Why?

JB: Well, it's hard to say. First of all, those things are all done differently. They're different people, different films. *Tick...*is a black film. I did play a black man in Tick.... *100 Rifles* wasn't written for a black man *Tick* was written for a black man. *The Split* was not written for a black man. *100 Rifles* was not written for a black man. Whatever was added was added as we got together.

Now, they will probably say, if you interview them, they will probably say that there isn't a market for that kind of thing; almost like there is a backlash. Now people aren't interested in black leading men.

FM: Bullshit!

JB: This is what they try to layout. You cannot make money with black leading men, and so forth and so on.

FM: Crazy. That's bullshit too.

JB: I suppose you're too young, but that's what they will lay on you.

FM: No! Poitier, two years ago, was the number one star in the world.

JB: I know. They say it's changed. All right. But here's my thing. My thing didn't really have to do with films. It had to do with my personal life. First of all, let me tell you what my idea was in doing those films. I always wanted to come into film and break the taboos. Like Poitier had opened the thing up. Mantan Moreland and all those guys had done their thing. Poitier had done his thing. He had made money, he was a leading man, but he was playing those goody-goody parts, which I don't criticize, it's just the way it was. So I wanted to come in and play the adventurer, the crook, the boss who gets the black woman, gets the white woman. You couldn't make love to a white woman on the American screen. You couldn't! Nobody wanted to see black people make love. I wanted to do all of that. And I did it!

Guerrero notes "...Brown was able to do what Poitier was denied in his career to that point, to act in a violent assertive manner and express his sexuality openly and beyond dominant cinema's sexual taboo."[110]

FM: Did you want to do that consciously when you went into films?

JB: Yeah! Sure!

FM: You came in with the express purpose of doing that?

JB: Of course! You know, that's what I did in football.

FM: Well, how did you figure you'd do that if you weren't doing the screenplays, and you didn't have the money?

JB: No. It's very simple. When there's a demand for you, there was a demand for me from the first film.

FM: So you figured that you could then write it into the scripts and force the scripts to change?

JB: No. The scripts that I would accept.

FM: I see. I see. I see.

JB: You know scripts are submitted. Here's one here [paper rustling]. I didn't set that up; they come here all the time. You know, scripts are brought to you. They don't come to certain guys who play certain parts. That's why I tell you, there's certain guys that represent certain things. When I,...a producer has a script. He's not going to take a certain man, or talk to that man about playing a funny kind of a character. They know where to go with certain kinds of scripts.

FM: That's great, though. That you went in with that express purpose to fight the taboos.

JB: That's right. I didn't go in for the art of it. I didn't go in it to really submerge myself into it, because I had sense enough to know that as an art form, what can an actor really do in cinema; I mean what can he really do? He's not even out there everyday. He shoots maybe three weeks; everybody else shoots four weeks. The director's there everyday. So it's an art form to him; really, because he can shape it. An actor goes out, and the film is cut. He doesn't know what's going to be left. He doesn't know what the inflections are going to be. All he knows is each scene he tries to do a thing.

So I wasn't really interested in that. I was interested in presenting a thing to black people where we said, "All right, here's a cat that's black, he's playing this, he's playing this, he's playing that." So that now you can't say that you can't have a black guy playing this, this, and he's playing that. There's nothing that I don't think that we have not played now.

FM: Yeah, but not that much happened. You did all those great things. You got all these taboos broken, and then what happened? Then the films stopped all of a sudden.

JB: Well, that's mainly, like I say, it got to the point of my outside life. It's like, all right, I did all these things on the screen, and they said, "Well, if you're a big star, why are you going out with these white girls in Hollywood for? So I said....

FM: It's not their business, though.

JB: I'm not saying it's their business, but....

FM: I mean....

JB: This is what starts happening. They say I'm a bad guy, that I beat up chicks, that I do everything, that I'm mean, that I'm hard to get along with, that I'm everything. That I'm trouble, so don't hire him, don't hire him, don't hire him, don't hire him. And they can put that on you just like that [snaps fingers].

According to Jim Brown, "...the 1970s marked the virtual end of my film career. People stopped calling me, I could not get work, and producers who said they wanted to work with me came back with their minds changed. In essence, I was blackballed from the industry."[111]

FM: Do you mean they can do it across the line?

JB: Pretty much so. Well, they can't stop an Aldrich. They can't stop a John Cassavetes. They can't stop a lot of those kinds of people. What also happened, simultaneously with that, the industry went into a total slump.

FM: But I would think just the reverse would happen. From the whole history of films, when a guy gets that kind of publicity, then that will sell the film.

JB: No, no. See, here's what I'm saying to you. There's a certain amount of.... So here's an individual over here that a lot of people don't like. They're going to cut him off. It's not hard to cut him off now, because the whole industry is changing. Bob Aldrich hasn't done as many films. Cassavetes had to really battle to get himself into a position. He was very lucky because he caught the trend at the right time. It worked for him. He's doing fine. We're going to do a film together. Really work together, because we, those kind of people. He always wanted to do a film with me. He liked to take people and help them.

In 1959, John Cassavetes played a jazz pianist/private detective working out of a jazz club called Waldo in Greenwich Village on an NBC series called Johnny Staccato. *"Staccato" is a musical term meaning rapid,* *disconnected notes. The implication being Johnny was always a walking jazzman. The 30 minute-shows ran for 27 episodes (Sept. 10, 1959 premiere- Sept.25, 1960.) Cassavetes directed 5 shows and it feature many stars such as Elisha Cook, Jr., Elizabeth Montgomery, Shirley Knight, Martin Landau, Mary Tyler Moore, John Marley, Cloris Leachman, and Gena Rowland. The plots were silly and poorly constructed. It has, however, a film noir flavor, with Cassavetes imitating a Sam Spade/Philip Marlow narrator (A.K.A. Humphrey Bogart/Dick Powell style]. Far too many blonde heroines, no black musicians, corny dialogue, preposterous attempts at being cool. Elmer Bernstein wrote the main theme. Among the noted white musicians were Barney Kessel, Red Mitchell, Shelly Manne, and John Williams. Cassavetes next went on to directing jobs. In Episode 16—*Collector's Item*—Juano Hernandez played a famous jazz player being blackmailed by Rupert Crosse, who kills a singer with a gun and then defends himself with a knife. In Episode 19—*Night of Jeopardy*—Morris Buchanan plays Bo Bo, a criminal who works as a janitor. These are the only blacks appearing in the series. In Episode 16, there are a number of black extras.*

JB: So, it was like a combination of how the people felt about me and the trend of the industry, that combination. Then what they were saying; they tried to throw it off like, well, people don't want black leading men. But then they got off on this thing of black films. Now, black films are like the rape of the land. It's terrible, you see, because our future in films should not be based upon black films.

FM: Absolutely! Absolutely!

JB: That is ridiculous. First of all, because you get into exploitation. You really want to talk about, that is exploitation, because the white people within the industry are hiring at no money black directors, black actors, so forth and so on at minimum salaries and making jive films and presenting it to these mass black audiences in these major cities and pulling off the money. These films are not even of the caliber that should be presented. They don't tell nothing. They're entertainment. They're taking advantage of a starved group of people. They're not even giving these people something that they can really be proud of. Then these people are like anybody else. After the first two or three times, they're not going to go see those films.

So then, where is the black actor? Because then the producer is going to say, "Well, the black audiences don't go to these films anymore."

The black actor has to be an integral part of the total industry. He has to try to deal with good projects. We are at a point now where a Jim Brown will have to come in and try to make love to a white woman, make love to a black woman, be the crook. All that's been done. That's been broken down.

We're at a point now where we should be able to develop significant projects that are good, that have impact, and that anybody would want to go to see. But that is not being emphasized. Just the opposite is being emphasized.

Brown writes, "In the 1970s, those [racial] barriers went right back up. America regressed, Hollywood did the same. Hollywood opened its doors to blacks in the 1960s, pulled in the money, slammed them back shut. If you wanted to see a black woman in a major role, it was Cicely Tyson or nothing. Cicely is a fine artist, but I got Cicely Tysoned out. The industry is replete with talented, attractive black actresses. To represent an entire race with one woman is ludicrous."[112]

FM: Now, I couldn't agree with you more. And yet, some of the people I've met, who are influential with young people or supposedly speak for black people, women like Shirley Chisholm for example, said that one of the ten best films last year was *The Bus is Coming.*[113] I don't know whether you've seen *The Bus is Coming*....

JB: I haven't seen it.

FM: But *The Bus is Coming* is exactly the kind of film that you describe, which is an amateurish film, but the argument that they used was that as long as you have a positive black image in the film, that's what makes it a good film: That the business....

*Directed by Wendell Franklin, the Horace Jackson screenplay focuses on a Vietnam veteran returning to Los Angeles only to find his brother murdered by bigoted policemen. Determined to get revenge, he joins a black militant organization and achieves his goal. Interestingly, two recent black film guides—*3 Black Chicks Review Flicks[114] *and* Historical Dictionary of African American Cinema[115]*—do not even list the movie in their encyclopedic entries.*

FM: Huh—

JB: That answers itself. That thing, that answers itself. That declares the way you want to go. There is in any situation, big brother, the competition. True competition has to be open competition. Politics cannot be a little thing over in the corner. Yes, we make concessions as we develop, as a kid develops, we let him move along at his own pace. But from the standpoint of the ten best, no, it's not the ten best. Your ten-year old kid may paint a picture; it's not one of the ten best in the world, unless he's a fantastic genius. But it can be good within that context. So a guy takes two hundred thousand dollars to make *The Bus is Coming*, and it has some positive. Ok, beautiful, that's a step, you see, but that isn't where we're at. That is not representative of what can be done. We have some talented people—given major studio money, proper financing, and proper assistance—, we can turn out some hell of a things.

FM: How do you handle the argument that people say you only get the real clout of power when the black money goes into making black films?

JB: Basically what they mean is this. If you're black, and you want to do your thing, or if you're white, and you want to do your thing, you gotta have your own money, because the money controls. That doesn't have anything to do with being black. That has to do with what goes on in this society. If you sponsor your book yourself, then that's your book. You can then do your thing. That's what it is. It's having the control to present the story, as you want to present it, in the way you want to present it.

FM: Yeah, that's what they say. They say that so long as the money is in the hands of white studios, black people will never be able to portray the kinds of roles they want.

JB: They will get to the point where they will, as anybody else. Studios will limit anyone. All these law cases going on with Aldrich and MGM is the example. The fact that Bob Aldrich started his own studio [with the money made from *The Dirty Dozen*], the fact that John Cassavetes operates the way that he operates, prove that the major studios have always had a lock on things. You're not going to be able to present, nobody's been able to present, except a few guys like Bob Wise and maybe [Stanley] Kubrick and maybe [Sam] Peckinpah and [Gordon] Parks can do it now, you know. But the exceptional guys, who have revolted, who are so strong that they could get total creative freedom.

The black man, like any other thing in society, is always a notch below that stuff. He's a notch below. He's right along there with everybody else, but because he's black, he's a notch below, because he's inexperienced, and so forth and so on. So the problem of major studio money is the same as the white man's, excepting for the additional thing of being black.

FM: Can you remember any films at all, Jim, that you thought were good black films? Good films with black people in them? Films that, if I were setting up this course, that you think would be worthwhile in presenting the black experience? Any films over the years?

JB: Well, you see, black experience is a whole different thing. I've only done one film with a black experience. That was...*Tick... Tick...Tick,* which was about a black sheriff taking over a white town. The funny thing about that film is that it's fairly accurate. Sidney Poitier films, uh—

FM: Do you think, for example, that they're right in the way that they attack Poitier about his films being just an "Uncle Tom"? Or a black man playing a white man's role? Because he has been under severe criticism from the beginning of the last ten or fifteen years.

Jim's answer to questions about the NY Times' *article attacking Poitier was given effectively in his first book* Jim Brown: Out of Bounds*: "When you're a black in Hollywood, it's simply hard to win. Some folks say you should stick to acting, others say you are not doing enough for other blacks. I recall when a black writer in the* New York Times *tore into Sidney Poitier, said Sidney was not taking the right roles, was not doing for blacks what he should be. I thought the guy missed by a mile. I thought Sidney was the best thing we had going, and should be roundly congratulated."*[116]

I imagine you would want to read the reactions of "Big Brother"—how I loved that nickname—penned elsewhere.[117] *For the record, the Clifford Mason article is entitled, "Why Does White America Love Sidney Poitier So?"*[118]

JB: That's not fair.

FM: You don't think so?

JB: No. It's not fair. It's not fair at all. This man had to fight and prove. I mean, he had to break new ground. He had to deal with this market at large. I mean, he created a market, you know, a general market.... And he wasn't necessarily supported totally by blacks or anything. He had to go across the board thing. He made money. He was successful, which meant that he, more than anyone else, broke the doggone thing open on the level that counts.

So, you know, you hear about all these people that sit back and criticize all our solutions and shit, man, I'm talking about reality. I don't know about all that criticizing. What is criticizing?

FM: So you're arguing....

JB: I don't even like to comment on what somebody said. You get me to talk about it by saying that, but people that sit back and criticize anybody, who haven't done anything, are bullshiting. Because a man can only, he has a capacity. Poitier is that kind of actor. He's not a cowboy. He's not a gangster. He is—there's only so much of a personality you can call upon in a man. There's some great actors that can play—Marlon Brando couldn't do *Guys and Dolls*.

FM: He tried, though.

JB: It was bad, man. It's not his image. It's still image as they go along. I don't care what they say. I have great admiration for what he's done. It stands for itself, and it is not no "Uncle Tom." By him, by saying that, it just stands for itself. If he hadn't done that stuff, I couldn't of got into the movies.

FM: Would you just react to the criticism that they make about guys like Stepin' Fetchit and Mantan Moreland who had to—the same thing that Poitier did—they had to fight to get into the films, to get regular roles, to eat regularly, and they did all those things for all those years, and now in retrospect, the roles appear to be negative images, or demeaning images of black people.

JB: They are demeaning images, and they're bad because they presented a thing to both black and white America that was false. That was the only thing that was presented from the standpoint of black people! If there was a balance, these guys could've been considered brilliant, because their timing and their abilities were fantastic. But because it was the only image presented, from the standpoint of the impact it had on a nation, it was negative.

FM: Negative today? Or negative then?

JB: I don't know. Trying to play the devil's advocate. See, what I'm trying to say to you is that the image Poitier put down was not a bad image. It was not a revolutionary image. It was not of strength and equality and stuff. It was like, the cards had to be stacked to appease white people. But that was almost a trick.

FM: That's right. That's right.

JB: It was almost a trick put in there to get white audiences. You know, like, put that *Brian's Song* on. It's a soap opera. Ridiculous. Demeaning to me! And you white people loved it! And a lot of black people are not too happy.

According to J. Fred MacDonald, "While biographical movies have focused widely on historical blacks-from political achievers to criminals-the favorite theme has been black sports figures. In addition to Wilma *and* It's Good to Be Alive, *there were other significant sports motion pictures made for television in the 1970s. In* Brian's Song *(aired November 30, 1971 on ABC), Billy Dee Williams portrayed Gayle Sayers, the Chicago Bears halfback who agonized as his white friend and teammate, Brian Piccolo (James Caan), died young of cancer."*[119]

In 2009, the Internet database Allmovie *states, "At 74 minutes,* Brian's Song *is one of the most effective and efficient television movies ever made.... While far from a superior film,...[it] is still a moving dramatic document that holds a special place in the hearts of American-style football enthusiasts everywhere."*

JB: Well, I'm not going to knock it from the standpoint of the ability of [Billy Dee] Williams playing Gayle Sayers a certain way, so on and so on. But I'm hip to it, so I dislike that much worse than I would dislike a Poitier thing, because Poitier was the black guy putting a trick down himself. He had to trick white people and have them accept stuff to break open that commercial aspect of the business. See, there's the money; you've got to make money for people, or else you're not going to be in nothing. He did this. He did it well. And he can't do everything. You know, there's a foot soldier, a general, you know, I'm a fighter. I put my tail out there and won a little. Then you need different kinds of people. Man, everybody can't go out there and be a bad black man, you know; or present a revolutionary kind of thing. There has to be balance. The only thing about Stepin' Fetchit is that, at the time, there was nothing really on the screen except that.

So, sure man, it was like the white man's glory to have that up there. He did all these things. Really, that's what his thoughts were. So his kids come in and saw that, and that was their image of a black person. Then a black person sees that and feels ashamed, and then there's this negative thing. It had great impact on both black and white people in a negative, I mean, it was all negative, but it was positive for white people. It gave them reinforcement of their idea of what a black person is.

But, now, when you take the individual, you can't say that he sold out, or he as an individual was bad, because he was trying to make a living, and he went along with a lot of things that maybe he shouldn't have gone along with. We can't look back in that time and say, "Hey. We got to kill this guy." We should love this guy, because now, this guy probably feels, "Hey man, I want to be accepted by you guys. I did what I had to do. If I had to do it today, I wouldn't do it. But then I did, and even then, it was tough on me. Just doing that, you see."

So we have to look at it that way. Just because it was tough on him and he had to do it break in, you cannot say that it was a positive thing from the standpoint of the impact that it had on the masses.

But if the masses are helped, once you find out who you are, you can see about a thousand pictures about Stepin' Fetchit, and it does not bother you. Because it does not bother me, at all.

I can sit down with any Orson Welles, and they can show black people doing anything, but they can't turn my mind, because I know who I am: I know I'm here. I know I'm educated. I know I will work. I know I can compete, which is competition, you know, which is not that good, but I can compete, have competed, [and] proven myself in open market.

So how is that going to affect me? You see. So I would never look back and really criticize. We have gotten over that. If that had affected black people or white people in this country for the rest of our lives, then I would probably condemn it. But we've gotten over that. It should be a camp thing now. It should be taken very lightly. These people should not be criticized, because, doggone, they should be praised.

But if you analyze, you go back to what I say. Sure, at the time and leading from there, it had great negative impact on the development of black people. The image was presented a certain way. We've broken away from a lot of that. We now have a mean [he laughs] a mean image instead. We're supposed to be bad and want to shoot people, which is another exaggeration. There's all these exaggerations. That's how I would analyze it.

FM: How would you say that the role that blacks have played in the history of Hollywood, from what you know about it and your experiences? Do you see Hollywood as being a sort of racist kind of place or problem, which had discriminated against blacks? Or do you see it as an industry in which people have just had to work, and they should take their kicks and their bumps and their competition, and those who make it, it's because they're talented, and those who don't make it, don't make it because they're not talented?

JB: You mean, has everything been equal for blacks?

FM: Yeah.

JB: Let's analyze it intelligently. One of the greatest problems that the white man has is ignorance. See, the white man is ignorant to a lot of things that are right in front of his nose. Like, he's been ignorant to the black market for a long time, because they really didn't care about the market. They just counted on it for a certain thing.

Then they realized that this was a market that really produced a lot of dough. The only growing market in the movie going industry today. A lot of companies found out about that; ad agencies, like Pepsi Cola, and these companies had special markets. That meant you put one black man in the company, and he's the marketing and analysis, he does public relations, he does everything.

Then they found out that there was a real market, because black people are quality buyers, capital-wise they spend as much money in this country as anybody else. Ok, so blacks in Hollywood had a problem, because the producers and the people were ignorant of the fact that blacks could probably increase the grosses on some films. So they didn't think that they had to include blacks in anything, because financially it would not mean anything.

You take that point, and that's one reason I didn't want to be bothered. The other thing is a normal black thing. A lot of people are just prejudiced against black people and not going to use them. So then you take that. Those two things are two important things. Of course, there was prejudice in Hollywood. [We both laugh.] One based upon ignorance of the financial power of black people, and the other based upon normal ignorance and prejudice.

FM: How about the roles? Do you find the roles being offered to you now based upon you as an actor? Or do you find it's now getting more towards a black kind of role? The scripts that are coming to you?

JB: Well, the next film I'm going to do, after my blackballing thing has seemed to have been lifted, is a thing called *Kill Julian Drake*. The start date is on the seventh. It's kind of the same thing for me.

Kill Julian Drake *was the working title for Jack Starrett's* Slaughter.[120]

FM: How long has this blackballing been going on, Jim?

JB: About two years.

FM: Do you object to my writing about that in the book?

JB: No.

FM: I have no other questions unless you think there's something I ought to know? Something you think that ought to be said, that I haven't asked you.

JB: Well, maybe do a summary thing on what I think should be our approach to the industry.

FM: Okay. What do you think ought to be your approach to the industry?

JB: It's like; we have to approach the industry, first of all, not as black actors. We have to recognize it as a business, first of all and not think black, not think anything. It is a business we have to understand, and we have to educate ourselves as to how that business works. We have to understand what a major studio represents. We have to understand distribution. Nobody understands distribution and that seems to be the key to everything. We have to understand about the market out there; how it fluctuates. We have to understand about the world market. We have to understand distribution overseas. We have to understand all of those things that have to do with a picture making money, because it is a commercial world. It is a commercial industry. You have to have bankers. You have to deal with bankers. They want to make a profit.

All right! Once we have an understanding of that aspect of it, now we can deal with the positive aspects of being black. What are the positive aspects of doing a film that is black? Maybe the positive aspects are because there are so many life experiences that are unique to black that it can be a fantastic teaching vehicle to the public at large. So wouldn't it be good to find some of the greatest writers in the world, and take some of these great stories that are unique to black development in this, of black life in this country, and put it up on the screen as first class entertainment.

FM: Did you ever think of doing Marcus Garvey? You'd be great for that role.

JB: No. I've thought of various things, but I'm still dealing with the business aspect of it. Trying to unravel the problems there. I know what you mean, but to unravel these problems will get us to the point where we can then pick those stories out. I don't have to worry about millions of stories not having been told out there, because they haven't been told, it can be fantastic work for general audiences. But until you are able to deal with the financial aspect, the technical aspect of the business, you can forget that, because if you get the story of Marcus Garvey, and you write it, and then you've got to go to those people.

FM: I was thinking as I look at you, you'd probably blow everyone's mind if you did Booker T. Washington. A whole reverse image. You talk about reversing images, you talk about doing something for.... Can you imagine, can you imagine big, bad Jim Brown doing Booker T. Washington? What a story that would be.

JB: That's an interesting thing. But then the last point is that once we find the positive areas, then we can deal with might be the drawbacks and the negative aspects. I just think that, I was really talking about the pragmatic approach to the industry, divorcing ourselves from emotionalism, and dealing with the thing like a man deals with it.

FM: I think you're talking about getting apprenticeship programs in every aspect of the craft.

JB: That's right.

FM: It's not really the image that's going on the screen; you want to get into the roots of that image.

JB: That's right. Everything is played to the—blacks do—

FM: That's what I mean.

JB: Black people have been tricked into dealing with the surface. Hey, he didn't present my real image. Then to hell with that. You know? So what?

FM: It's only temporary.

JB: That's right. Don't worry about that, because if this cat is presenting your image improperly and making a billion dollars off it from you, you can put it into the whole pot. So what if he's not presenting your image right, and he's controlling, and he's making all the dough?

FM: What have you got after it?

JB: That's right. Nothing. So why don't you get down to that level. Get hip to that. Form a foundation there, and then go from there.

FM: Have there been foundations formed to help?

JB: Let's see. We've always had a problem: I guess our problem stems from the fact that we deal with the surface, and it's really very difficult to create the kind of foundations that are really necessary to develop. I have an organization that's called "The Black Industrial and Economic Union." We deal in business ventures, and we deal in education. We're able to start over five hundred businesses, but it's amazing how many people can't understand the concept of capital and expertise. The combination relies on those two things. They want to talk about all kinds of other things like, you know, margin....

Brown wrote elsewhere, "The most meaningful thing I did was to help create the Black Industrial and Economic Union. In the middle 1960s, we opened eight offices across the country, most offices headed by a professional athlete. We were totally black, had cats working for us who were brilliant, with MBAs from schools like Cornell, University of Chicago. Our motto was "Produce, Achieve, and Prosper."

"No one ever talks about it, but it was something I took real pride in. I've always worked for the advancement of black people, always within the system, always preaching the American way. But while I was being discussed in many other ways playing football, making movies, being prosecuted -my main work was rarely mentioned. That didn't reduce its power: we helped introduce

many blacks into the world of business. Our organization was the first in the last thirty years to emphasize economic development for black people."[121]

FM: Have you helped at all on any of these five hundred organizations about getting kids trained to go into work in film or in TV?

JB: No, I have not concentrated on film, because see, films, when you attack this monster, you've got a good fight. You've really got this thing; white people don't even understand it. If you're not into it, you don't know what's going on. I've talked to white actors; they don't know nothing about distribution.

FM: I don't know if you know this, but over the years the biggest problem of getting blacks into films and getting black films made was the fear they had of the Southern market, and the Southern market never existed.

JB: I know.

FM: It never existed. And they would always say, "Well, we can't show this in the South." Or, "This won't go in the South." There'd be pictures with, let's say, Lena Horne, and they'd cut her out of the film, when it was shown down there. And there was never any market.

JB: But I made some of my biggest money in the South. Miami. Georgia.

FM: Is there anything I've missed, Jim? That I ought to ask you?

JB: I don't think so.

FM: What can I say? I owe you.

Postscript

Today, Jim Brown appears much subdued. Although he still maintains many of his views and interests, he has settled into a successful second marriage, reunited himself with his children, and keeps a low public profile.

In the fall of 2012, I tried contacting Jim about reading the material about to go to press. He had been kind and generous to me, and even though many decades had passed, I wanted him to know I intended to honor my promise. Whether my message ever reached him, I have no way of knowing. What was clear is that he did not contact me. Thus, there is no way of knowing if this extraordinary man thought what I wrote about him was fair and accurate.

For my part, I think of Jim Brown much as the brilliant sportscaster Bob Costas describes another major flawed sports figure in my life: Mickey Mantle. Let the broadcaster's words echo my feelings as well for a man I met for only a few hours but who remains in my thoughts all these years: "It's been said that the truth is never pure and rarely simple.... None of us, Mickey Mantle included, would want to be held to account for every moment of our lives. But how many of us can say that our best moments were as magnificent as his?"[122]

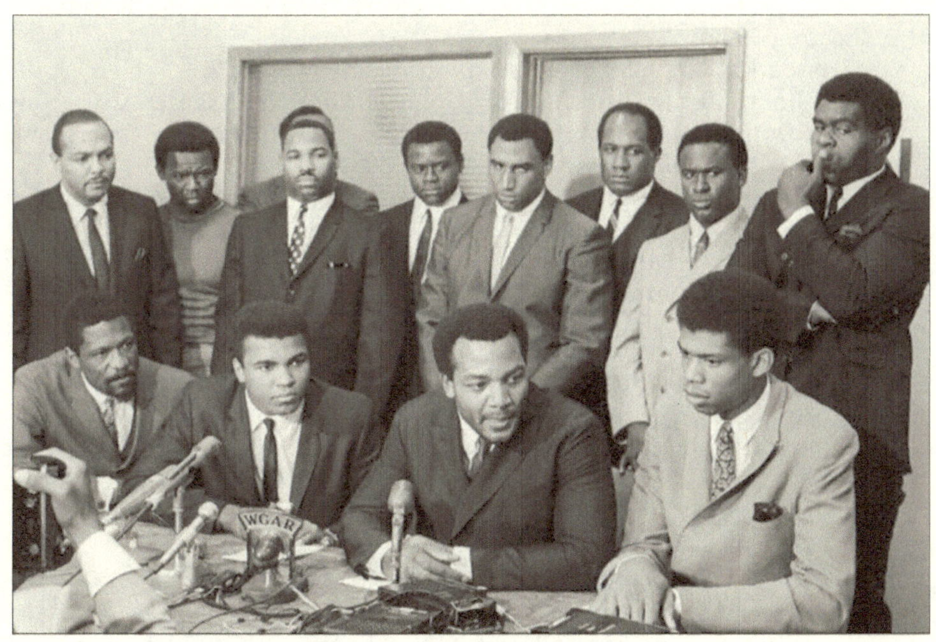

19. In November 1966, Jim Brown organized a sit-down with a number of top black athletes to discuss Muhammad Ali's decision to refuse induction into the U.S. Military. From left to right bottom row: Bill Russell, Ali, Brown, and Lew Alcindor (Kareem Abdul Jabbar). Top Row: Carl Stokes, Walter Beach, Bobby Mitchell, Sid Williams, Curtis McClinton, Willie Davis, Jim Shorter, and John Wooten.

Notes

[1] Poussaint, "Blaxploitation Movies: Cheap Thrills That Degrade Blacks," 26.

[2] Crouch, *The Artificial White Man*, 24.

[3] John Ford, "The Man Who Shot Liberty Valance," (USA: Paramount Pictures, 1962).

[4] Mark Kram, "Jim Brown," in *Answers.com* (2009), 9.

[5] Jimmy Brown and Myron Cope, *Off My Chest* (Garden City, New York: Doubleday & Company, Inc., 1964). In addition, Jim Brown and Steve Delsohn (New York: Zebra Books, 1990).

[6] James Toback, *Jim: The Author's Self-Centered Memoir on the Great Jim Brown* (New York: Doubleday & Co., 1971).

[7] Mike Freeman, *Jim Brown: The Fierce Life of an American Hero* (New York: Harper Entertainment, 2006).

[8] Spike Lee, "Jim Brown All-American," (USA: 40 Acres and A Mule Filmworks, 2002).

[9] Brown and Delsohn, *Out of Bounds*, 133.

[10] *Out of Bounds*, 154.

[11] Lee, "Jim Brown All-American."

[12] Freeman, *Jim Brown: The Fierce Life of an American Hero*, 12.

[13] Toback, *Jim*, 51.

[14] Brown and Delsohn, *Out of Bounds*, 47.

[15] *Out of Bounds*, 49.

[16] Freeman, *Jim Brown: The Fierce Life of an American Hero*, 49.

[17] Graham Bensinger, "Brown Talks About Race, Td Celebrations and More," in *The GBShow*, ed. Graham Bensinger (USA: ESPN, 2009), 3.

[18] William Wyler, "Dead End," (USA: United Artists, 1937).

[19] Brown and Delsohn, *Out of Bounds*, 58.

[20] *Out of Bounds*, 63.

[21] Bensinger, "Brown Talks About Race, Td Celebrations and More," 6.

[22] My relationship with Mr. Fuchs and the change he brought to my life is explained in an unpublished plenary address I gave at the 2007 Literature/Film convention at the University of Kansas on October 14th. A bound copy, entitled "Thank You, Mr. Fuchs," is available at Burlington College, Vermont.

[23] Brown and Delsohn, *Out of Bounds*, 69.

[24] Brown and Cope, *Off My Chest*, 142.

[25] Mike Lupica, "The Sporting Life: Nowhere to Run," *Esquire* (1990): 35.

[26] Gary Fleder, "The Express (Aka the Express: The Ernie Davis Story)," (USA: Universal Pictures, 2008).

[27] Brown and Cope, *Off My Chest*, 142.

[28] Marc Sklar, April 1, 2012.

[29] Zach Clements, Sept. 6, 2012.

[30] Maggie Hathaway, "Hollywood Segregation, Integration Performances 'before, after' Exposed," *Hollywood Sentinel*, Thursday, March 23, 1967.

[31] Alex Haley, "Playboy Interview: Jim Brown—a Candid Conversation with the Football Superstar Turned Actor and Civil Rights Activist," *Playboy* 15, no. 2 (1968): 63.

[32] Quote supplied by Mark Stoler, August 20, 2012.

[33] Bennett Jr., *The Challenge of Blackness*, 127.

[34] Roberta S. Maguire, ed. , *Conversations with Albert Murray*, ed. Peggy Whitman Penshaw, Literary Conversations Series (Jackson: University Press of Mississippi, 1997), 11.

[35] Toback, *Jim*, 7.

[36] Early, *This Is Where I Came In: Black America in the 1960s*, 4.

[37] Michael Eric Dyson, *Mercy, Mercy Me: The Art, Loves and Demons of Marvin Gaye*, Electronic Book ed. (New York: Basic Civitas Books, 2008), Locations 127-43.

[38] For more information, see David Ritz, *Divided Soul: The Life of Marvin Gaye* (New York: Da Capo Press, 1985).

[39] Sam Pollard, "Marvin Gaye: What's Going On," in *American Masters*, ed. Prudence Glass (USA: Thirteen/WNET, 2008).

[40] Ibid.

[41] David Peck, "Marvin Gaye: The Real Thing in Performance 1964-1981," (USA: Reelin' in the Years Production, 2006).

[42] Mark Brend, ed., *What's Going On: Marvin Gaye*, Albums: The Stories Behind 50 Years of Great Recordings (San Diego: Thunderbay Bay Press, 2005), 142.

[43] *What's Going On: Marvin Gaye*, Albums: The Stories Behind 50 Years of Great Recordings (San Diego: Thunderbay Bay Press, 2005), 143.

[44] Early, *This Is Where I Came In: Black America in the 1960s*, 1-4.

[45] Jim Jacobs, "A.K.A. Cassius Clay," (USA: Sports of the Century, 1970).

[46] Gaspar Gonzalez and Alan Tomlinson, "Muhammad Ali: Made in Miami," (USA: PBS, 2008).

[47] Marc Payton, "Boxing's Best: Muhammad Ali," in *HBO Sports*, ed. Michael Fuchs (USA: HBO, 1981).

[48] Crouch, *The Artificial White Man*, 214.

[49] Early, *This Is Where I Came In: Black America in the 1960s*, 29-35.

[50] Haley, "Playboy Interview: Jim Brown—a Candid Conversation with the Football Superstar Turned Actor and Civil Rights Activist," 63.

[51] Lupica, "The Sporting Life: Nowhere to Run," 36.

[52] Haley, "Playboy Interview: Jim Brown—a Candid Conversation with the Football Superstar Turned Actor and Civil Rights Activist."

[53] Ebony, "Football Heroes Invade Hollywood," *Ebony* 1969, 195.

[54] Keith M. Harris, *Boys, Boyz, Bois: An Ethics of Black Masculinity in Film and Popular Media,* ed. Graham Hodges, Studies in African American History and Culture (New York and London: Routledge, 2006), 66.

[55] Gordon M. Douglas, "Rio Conchos," (USA: Twentieth Century-Fox, 1964).

[56] Early, *This Is Where I Came In: Black America in the 1960s,* 37.

[57] Brown and Delsohn, *Out of Bounds,* 171.

[58] Haley, "Playboy Interview: Jim Brown—a Candid Conversation with the Football Superstar Turned Actor and Civil Rights Activist," 52.

[59] Jack Cardiff, "Dark of the Sun (A.K.A the Mercenaries)," (USA: MGM, 1968).

[60] John Sturges, "Ice Station Zebra," (USA: Filmways Pictures and MGM, 1968).

[61] Buzz Kulik, "Riot," (USA: Paramount Pictures, 1969).

[62] Brown and Delsohn, *Out of Bounds,* 216-19.

[63] Harris, *Boys, Boyz, Bois,* 67.

[64] Freeman, *Jim Brown: The Fierce Life of an American Hero,* 8.

[65] Haley, "Playboy Interview: Jim Brown—a Candid Conversation with the Football Superstar Turned Actor and Civil Rights Activist," 52.

[66] Freeman, *Jim Brown: The Fierce Life of an American Hero,* 8.

[67] Hathaway, "Hollywood Segregation, Integration Performances 'before, after' Exposed."

[68] Jacobs, "A.K.A. Cassius Clay."

[69] Lupica, "The Sporting Life: Nowhere to Run," 36.

[70] Freeman, *Jim Brown: The Fierce Life of an American Hero,* 6-7.

[71] James Toback, "Tyson," (USA: Sony Pictures Classics, 2008).

[72] "Fingers," (USA: Brut Pictures, 1978).

[73] Wayne Warga, "Toback Hanging on the Brink with 'Fingers'," *Los Angeles Times,* April 24 1977, W22.

[74] Cited on the DVD jacket. Toback, "Fingers."

[75] Vincent Canby, "'Fingers' Is Strictly from Desperation," *New York Times,* March 19, 1978, D19.

[76] Jack Kroll, "Split Banality," *Newsweek,* March 20th. 1978, 93.

[77] George Flemyng, "The Split," (USA: MGM, 1968).

[78] Brown and Delsohn, *Out of Bounds,* 216.

[79] Jim Brown, "Jim Brown: Life and Love in Hollywood," *Ebony* 45, no. 2 (1989): 60, 62.

[80] Tom Gries, "100 Rifles," (USA: Twentieth Century-Fox, 1969).

[81] Jerry Paris, "The Grasshopper (Aka the Passing of Evil, the Passion of Evil, and Passions)," (USA: National General Pictures, 1969).

[82] Steve Sekely, "Kenner," (USA: MGM, 1969).

[83] John Guillermin, "El Condor," (USA: National General Pictures, 1970).

[84] Jack Starrett, "Slaughter," (USA: American International Pictures, 1972).

[85] Robert Hartford-Davis, "Black Gunn," (USA: Champion Production Company, 1972).

[86] Gordon M. Douglas, "Slaughter's Big Rip-Off," (USA: American International Pictures, 1973).

[87] Gordon Parks Jr., "Three the Hard Way," (USA: Allied Artists, 1974).

[88] Antonio Margheriti, "Take a Hard Ride," (Italy: Berennsen-Ludwig-Bercovici Production, 1975).

[89] Calvin C. Hernton, "Great on the Gridiron, in the Movies and in Life," *New York Times*, May 16 1971, 44.

[90] Grunwald, "Albert Murray: Riffing It," in *Conversations with Albert Murray*, ed. Maguire, Roberta S. (Jackson: University of Mississippi Press, 1997), 14.

[91] Peter Keough, "Quentin Tarantino: Press Conference on Jackie Brown," in *Quentin Tarantino Interviews*, ed. Gerald Peary (Jackson: University Press of Mississippi, 1997), 199.

[92] Grier and Cagan, *Foxy*, 129.

[93] Clifford Mason, "Why Does White America Love Sidney Poitier So?," *New York Times*, Sept. 10 1967, B1. Rpt. The Black Man in Film, pp. 75-9.

[94] Poitier, *This Life*.

[95] *This Life*, 341.

[96] Larry Cohen, "Original Gangstas," (USA: Orion Pictures, 1996).

[97] Thomas Kevin, "'Original Gangstas,' the Rough Stuff Is Still the Lure," *Los Angeles Times*, May 11 1996, 8.

[98] Staff, "David Weisbart, 52, Producer of Movies," *New York Times*, July 22, 1967, 26.

[99] Douglas, "Rio Conchos."

[100] Robert Aldrich, "The Dirty Dozen," (USA: MGM, 1967).

[101] Flemyng, "The Split."

[102] Sekely, "Kenner."

[103] Dennis McLellan, "Madlyn Rhue, 68; TV Actress Kept Working with Multiple Sclerosis," *Los Angeles Times* Dec. 18, 2003, B15.

[104] Sturges, "Ice Station Zebra."

[105] Haley, "Playboy Interview: Jim Brown—a Candid Conversation with the Football Superstar Turned Actor and Civil Rights Activist," 53.

[106] Flemyng, "The Split."

[107] Brown and Delsohn, *Out of Bounds*, 216-17.

[108] Gries, "100 Rifles."

[109] Ralph Nelson, "Tick…Tick…Tick…." (USA: MGM, 1970).

[110] Ed Guerrero, *Framing Blackness: The African American Image in Film*, ed. Robert Sklar, Culture and the Moving Image (Philadelphia: Temple University Press, 1993), 79.

[111] Brown and Delsohn, *Out of Bounds*, 233.

[112] *Out of Bounds*, 230.

[113] Franklin, "The Bus Is Coming."

[114] Kamal Larsuel-Ulbricht, Rose Cooper, Cassandra Henry, *3 Black Chicks Review Flicks: A Film & Video Guide with Flava!* (New York: Amistad, 2002).

[115] S. Torriano Berry and Venise T. Berry, *Historical Dictionary of African American Cinema* (Lanham, Md.: The Scarecrow Press, Inc., 2007).

[116] Brown and Delsohn, *Out of Bounds*, 236.

[117] Manchel, *Film Study*, Vol. 1, 890-91.

[118] Mason, "Why Does White America Love Sidney Poitier So?."

[119] MacDonald, *Blacks and White TV: Afro-Americans in Television since 1948*, 169.

[120] Starrett, "Slaughter."

[121] Brown and Delsohn, *Out of Bounds*, 97.

[122] Rick Bernstein and Ross Greenburg, "Mantle," (USA: Home Box Office Inc., 2010).

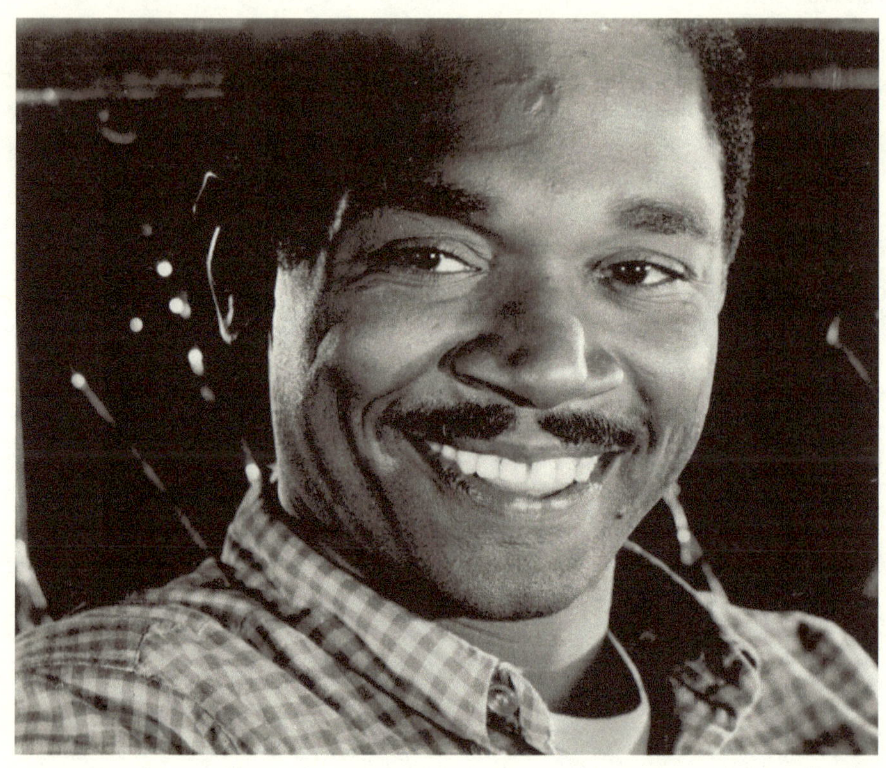

20. Ivan Dixon, a gifted actor-turned-director, best known for *Hogan's Heroes*, *Nothing But a Man*, and *The Spook Who Sat by the Door*.

4

Born to Be Free: Ivan Dixon

"I grew up in a white society with white rules and a white philosophy, but I grew up with a black conscience. My consciousness of myself as a black man makes me realize that unless I can be integrated into white society, I can't achieve the wealth they have created. They have created a society where any unknown white person can put something on the market and become successful. I don't see why a black person can't do that."[1]

Arthur Taylor

"Child, when do you think is the time to love somebody the most—when they done good and made things easy for everybody? Well, then you ain't through learning—because that ain't the time at all. It's when he's at his lowest and can't believe in hisself 'cause the world done whipped him so. When you starts measuring somebody, measure him right, child, measure him right. Make sure you done taken into account what hills and valleys he come through before he got to wherever he is."[2]

Lena, A Raisin in the Sun

"For the most part we do not first see, and then define, we define first and then see."[3]

Walter Lippmann

Taking his cue from social historian Thomas Carlyle that "history is the essence of innumerable biographies," film scholar Daniel J. Leab concluded "much of the history of the black in the movies of…[the mid-twentieth century] must be told in terms of the careers of stars like Dorothy Dandridge, Harry Belafonte, and Sidney Poitier. It was around them - whether willingly or not – that the old movie fantasies were revised and new ones were introduced."[4] That notion underscores much of my method discussing the black film experience in *The Interviews*.

What also contributes to my rationale is a pressing desire to revisit other motivated black artists whose meaningful contributions to the African-American film legacy remain unsung by the present generation. Among the many performers falling into this grouping are Yaphet Kotto, Paula Kelly, Juano Hernandez, Raymond St. Jacques, Billy Dee Williams, Max Julian, Julius Harris, Vonetta McGee, Calvin Lockhart, Jim Kelly, Al Freeman Jr., Brenda Sykes, D'Urville Martin, Janet MacLachlan, Gloria Foster, and Rosalind Cash. Why has fate treated them so unkindly? One possibility might be these performers were eclipsed by superstars. That assumption obviously applies to all black actors working during the Poitier era of the fifties and the sixties. Nevertheless, there are specific performers who fit the pattern like Brock Peters who often found his reputation obscured by James Earl Jones, Fred Williamson who was overshadowed by Jim Brown, and Diahann Carroll who was surpassed by Dorothy Dandridge. Another possibility for present-day obscurity might be a misperception the talented performer made only one important movie. Such snubbed actors include Richard Roundtree (*Shaft*), Ron O'Neal (*Superfly*), William Marshall (*Blacula*), and Paul Winfield (*Sounder*). Thus they don't seem worthy of much recognition. Whether because of industry conditions, poor opportunities, limited material, passive personalities, or eccentric decisions, these prominent players suffer from neglect because conventional wisdom considers them minor actors in mostly disappointing movies. That myth needs reexamination if we are to understand the magnitude of the black film revolution that took place from the post-WWII period to the present.

Ivan Dixon is one such artist who falls into this fringe category. The gifted, proud actor-turned-director remains slighted both by the public and modern-day storytellers. Outshone by Poitier during their time together, the outwardly amiable performer was seen by the superstar to have made only one significant film, *Nothing*

But a Man (1964). Mistakenly, Sidney believed his friend was "a truly talented actor whose potential was never realized." He held the reasons to be twofold: "Part of it was his own fault and part of it was the industry's fault—the industry wasn't ready to cultivate two of us at the same time...." Even so, he reasoned, things could have been different if Ivan had been different: "Had he been more of a tough, hard-driving, go-getter personality accustomed to smashing down doors, the industry might have, just might have, looked up and paid more attention." Thus, Poitier felt "the industry was to pass this gentle, easygoing actor by. Happily, they would rediscover each when the actor Ivan Dixon moved over for the triumphant arrival of the motion picture director Ivan Dixon."[5]

Poitier is not the only onlooker who failed to see that the strong-minded, politically motivated Dixon followed a different drummer. For example, noted film historian Thomas Cripps in his important study *Making Movies Black: The Hollywood Message Movies from World War II to the Civil Rights Era*[6] ignores the actor completely. Manthia Diawara in her respected edited anthology *Black American Cinema*[7] does the same. Even Donald Bogle, usually a cheerleader for African-American performers, felt the underrated actor, whom he believed resembled James Edwards, but without the latter's "bruised quality," projected "a quiet sensitivity" and a "relaxed virility" uncommon in black men.[8] These problematic assessments appear justified if one looks only at Dixon's roles in films from *Something of Value* (1957), *Porgy and Bess* (1959), and *A Raisin in the Sun* (1961) to *A Patch of Blue* (1965) and *Car Wash* (1976). He almost always appeared typecast as a soft-spoken, reasonable person trying to bring order to chaotic situations.

My approach, however, advocates Dixon's easygoing style masked a serious political philosophy determined to reform the entertainment world, but without ever compromising the artist's integrity or losing his dignity. His ambition did not hinge on success for the sake of success, nor did he believe blacks should follow only one route in their show business journey. Furthermore, I see his legacy in film and television history going beyond comparisons to other actors or judging his filmography out of context. His legitimate standing in the African-American narrative, for me, results from appreciating the framework in which his screen contributions helped change the nation's consciousness about black culture and history. In a sense, his quiet but impressive methods epitomize the reason why Nina Simone always sang *Backlash Blues* in her performances. "Months before Langston Hughes died," the great singer explained, "he told me to keep on working till they open the door. One of these days when you've made it, when the doors are open wide, make sure you tell them where it's at so they will have no place to hide."[9] Making America aware of its tainted racial history and raising the spirits of black people seemed Dixon's political burden as well. His journey reflects how we came to know each other not by race or class but as human beings. Accordingly, this chapter argues that by revisiting Ivan's career we not only rediscover his important films and television achievements, but also remember how his pioneering actions reveal much about the era in which he lived.

Ivan Nathaniel Dixon III was born on April 6, 1931, in Harlem, where his father, a decorated hero in World War I, owned and operated a grocery store. Almost immediately upon entering the public school system, the child found himself bored, ignored, and rebellious. Unlike Brock Peters who thrived on his Harlem school curriculum, Dixon found his textbooks not only geared to white history but also out of touch with reality. As he recalled years later, the youngster felt rejected as "just another black face."[10] In conditions I can easily recognize, he quickly became both a troublemaker and a delinquent. Describing himself as "a terrible, mean little kid,"[11] Ivan emerged from his elementary school years a troubled youth and destined for a tragic future. "We were just out there in the streets," he recalled in his sixties. "I'd have ended up a numbers runner or be hatching schemes for making quick pleasures."[12] It also didn't help that his parents were separated, and he was shuttled back and forth between them.

His dire future disappeared when Dixon was thirteen; and his parents, out of desperation, sent him to Lincoln Academy, an African-American boarding school in Gaston County, North Carolina. Atypically, his trip South challenged the contemporary notion that blacks had to go North to better themselves. That is, what Peters learned about his African-American heritage from his famous Harlem Renaissance teachers, Ivan acquired from everyday black educators in a segregated Southern academy. Over the next four years, the Harlem bad boy became a complex, romantic, and resolute adolescent with an evolving African-American consciousness. He also became extremely pragmatic, a trait that shaped his behavior for the next sixty years. Simply stated, he realized the essential issues in life were not a person's color or class, but his talent, his vision, and his social mobility. He wanted freedom and equality not to be like everyone else, but to be whatever he wanted to be. And it was at Lincoln Academy he also discovered both a love of acting and the importance of a college education.[13]

Not surprisingly, upon entering North Carolina Central University in Durham, Dixon decided to become a pre-law student, who also pursued drama studies as an extra-curricular activity. As he told one interviewer, "I thought that to be someone you had to be a lawyer, doctor, preacher, or teacher, and since the other three didn't appeal to me, I was going to choose law."[14] What changed the undergraduate's mind remains hazy. Whether the courses bored Ivan or his drama experiences seduced him, the reasons for his college behavior remain vague. One thing was certain. He fell in love with his theater classmate, Berlie Ray. After their graduation in 1954, the two were married and remained so until his death fifty-four years later. They would have one daughter and three sons.

Now married, the handsome 6'1" theater hopeful temporarily pursued his interests at the Karamu House in Cleveland. But soon the couple moved to New York City, where he found a job as a social worker. After earning a Rockefeller Foundation Scholarship to study drama at Western Reserve University, however, Ivan and Berlie trudged back to Ohio. But he was just too impatient to get into the acting profession to have much interest in his studies. Consequently, the resolute Dixon dropped out of graduate school and like so many other ambitious performers returned to New York to pursue his dream. To further his chances, Ivan enrolled at the American Theatre Wing.

But the mid-1950s were not the best of times for inexperienced black college graduates pursuing theatrical fantasies. "When I started," the celebrity once said, "you couldn't get in those production areas."[15] If we go by the above-mentioned comments about Dixon's easygoing, non-aggressive personality, it seems puzzling that he did not give up hope and abandon his goals. Even when he turned to acting instead of directing, the resilient performer joked, "You had to be nuts to stay an actor."[16] In fact, as he told the *New York Times*, "...most of the people in my college group became teachers and social workers. They would have loved to stay in acting and many were better than I. But what was the use when there were only two roles a year and both of them played by Sidney Poitier?"[17] But the fact is he did stay in show business when many of his peers did not. That detail might have alerted his critics to the fact he was not what they thought him to be.

One could speculate as to why Dixon sustained such an optimistic outlook in the mid-to-late fifties. A couple of possibilities come to mind. As mentioned in earlier chapters, the extraordinary changes in the film industry, the rise of television, the prospects in overseas opportunities, and the growing importance of Off-Broadway productions encouraged African-American actors to stick around. A second reason, relevant for this chapter, dealt with "black music" becoming both highly regarded and acknowledged as the voice of African-Americans in the Eisenhower, Kennedy, and Johnson years. As early as 1942, as John Gennari reminds us, "The French critic Hughes Pannassie had said in *The Real Jazz*, as had Rudi Blesh in *Shining Trumpets* in 1946, that jazz was African-American music."[18] In essence, blues, gospel, and jazz became recognized as expressing both the emotions and the unity of the black community.[19] Their musical themes advocated revolutionary changes in society as well as encouraged pride in African-American ideas and achievements. Such "melodies" merit a brief discussion because of their relevance to Dixon's career.

In oversimplified terms, black music's makeover had its origins prior to the post-World War II era, when most Americans harbored negative beliefs not only about Negro music but also about the virtues of the black performers themselves. As discussed earlier, the public also presumed that the major figures emerging from the Swing era were whites. Thus colored performers suffered both from neglect and a lack of jobs. But young African-Americans in the late-forties and early fifties like Dixon now witnessed major changes stirring in the industry and became inspired by the musical rebels.

The once disreputable jazz was fast becoming highly respectable. First, as Steve Rice noted, the New Orleans pioneers had broken "free of [the] tyranny imposed by the easy brass key of B-flat." Other black radicals like Hawk, Bird, Diz, Monk, and Duke brought about key changes in techniques and styles.[20] Secondly, in large part because of growing race awareness, the public became more sensitive to the understated but significant contributions of black musicians to jazz. By the end of the decade, as integration in jazz bands gave way to an increasing group of famous African-American groups, respected jazz critic Nat Hentoff addressed the black-white debate openly in popular magazines such as *Harper's* and *Esquire.*[21] No longer were discriminatory practices and employment inequities swept under the rug. Calls for change reverberated throughout the country.

Third, and especially important, new concepts like "cool" and "soul" emerging from the liberated jazz community transformed the national black landscape. Simply stated, "being cool," suggested ethnic groups got typecast because of the way they behaved. So if artists wanted to break from past stereotypes, they needed to change the way they dressed, spoke, or interacted with other groups. Basically, the idea was to be "cool," to appear completely relaxed and indifferent! "Soul," as Charley Gerard succinctly stated, meant, "putting all you can into your efforts.... Stress [ing] honest trying over success or failure."[22] Above all for African-Americans, demonstrate your "blackness." Examples of artists who became cool, soulful performers were Charlie Parker, Miles Davis, Billie Holiday, Art Blakey, Charles Mingus, Horace Silver, Sarah Vaughan, Thelonious Monk, and Max Roach.

Early in the sixties, this race consciousness in music gained further widespread recognition thanks to poet LeRoi Jones' (later Amiri Baraka) *Blues People,* the first "full cultural history of African Americans asserting that 'black music' was the key to their authentic identity."[23] By then "cool," "soul," and "black music," permeated most meaningful discussions of race in America. And as Cornell West articulated, what changed was that, instead of discussing the nation's growing racial fears from the perspective of black people's problems, the focus was on "the flaws in American society."[24] Of particular importance to us, "coolness," "soul," and "black music" later became closely identified not only with Dixon's movies but also with his politics in the late sixties forward.

For most of the fifties to the mid-sixties, the struggling actor survived by taking roles in various television series. Among the more well-known shows were *The Big Story*, the *DuPont Show of the Month, The Twilight Zone, The Eleventh Hour, The Outer Limits, The F.B.I.*, and *Perry Mason.* Unlike many performers of his day, Dixon made it a point not only to perfect his acting techniques, but also to study how the young medium worked and what he could do to become a director.

Ivan's first stage break came in William Saroyan's 1957 Broadway play *The Cave Dwellers*. Almost prophetic for the novice, the drama focused on an unusual group of down-and-out optimists who gather in an abandoned Broadway theater where they fantasize about their lives and their relationships with each other. The aspiring actor played three different roles, allowing him to display both his humor and his acting skills.

But an even more important event in Dixon's life occurred when that same year he was hired as Poitier's stand-in for Martin Ritt's *Edge of the City* (1957).[25] Sidney played an open-minded dockworker befriending an Army deserter (John Cassavetes) hiding out on the New York docks. One reason that Ivan may have gotten the job was because he already was being typecast as a laidback performer ideal for such roles and assignments.

Even more meaningful yet for the newcomer was the fact that the film made Ivan and Sidney life-long friends. They would make five more films together: *Something of Value, The Defiant Ones, Porgy and Bess, A Raisin in the Sun,* and *A Patch of Blue*. So many joint ventures got people to start calling Ivan, "Sid's boy." The label didn't bother the even-tempered Dixon. As he laughingly told one interviewer, "Look, there wasn't much offered to Negro actors back then so I *had* to be connected with Sid. Whatever there was he was doing it, and being second to him was really pretty lucky."[26]

Both actors also profited from their next film, Richard Brooks' *Something of Value* (1957).[27] A timely effort capitalizing on the Mau Mau uprising in the British colony of Kenya in the early fifties, the narrative was based on reporter Robert Ruark's best-selling novel about Africa. Two childhood friends, one white (Rock Hudson) and one black (Poitier)—battle each other as the Mau Mau violently try to gain freedom for the oppressed Kikuyu. Dixon played Lathela, a trusted gun bearer for Hudson and one of the few non-violent Africans in the movie. Near the film's climax, Hudson and Dixon, hot on the pursuit of the now rebellious, bloodthirsty Poitier, talk about how there must be another path, a peaceful way to resolve the crisis. Also appearing in the picture and included in *The Interviews* are William Marshall (the intellectual leader of the secret organization) and Frederick Douglass O'Neal (a brutal Mau Mau follower).

The movie received mixed reviews. For example, *Good Housekeeping* hyperbolically praised the "magnificent performances by Sidney Poitier, Juano Hernandez, and William Marshall," and applauded the "stunning photography of tribal gatherings, a drunken native revel, racing giraffes, cavorting baboons, Mt. Kenya towering over misty plains...the unbelievably handsome native women with their noble carriage, shaved heads, and sculptured features," and the movie's alleged historical accuracy and balance, claiming "we see the white man as perverted as the Africans." But then the positive comments disappear. The magazine pointed out the clichéd dialogue, the absence of Technicolor in a story and environment ideal for color photography, and the movie's overwhelming violence."[28] The *New Yorker*'s John McCarten was positive, saying that director Brooks attempted "gallantly to explain the motives of [the Mau Mau]." Moreover, the critic also found the movie "for a great deal of the time...to be a solid melodrama in which a touch of social significance" had been added to an old formula.[29]

In keeping with my perspective were the comments by *New York Times* reviewer Bosley Crowther who felt the plot was more in the tradition of "Western massacre films" than in stories about the African continent. In his words, "Both in the plot and the production, this has the character of a film about Indians and white settlers who slaughter one another for endless revenge. The clash is pat, the personal feelings are obscure, and the crucial scenes are played on studio sets where the look of documented realism must be sacrificed for theatrical control."[30] Finally, even Ruark had problems with the screen adaptation of his book, which he argued was an accurate account of the Mau Mau rebellion: "These kids struck out in the humor department...and the come-to-Jesus ending is just plain bad."[31]

The reason I spend so much time with the reviews is that according to Poitier, it was the "call from Richard Brooks to make... [*Something of Value*]" that mainly launched his career.[32] One could also say it jumpstarted Dixon's as well.

Following the Brooks movie, Stanley Kramer hired Poitier to make *The Defiant Ones* (1958).[33] The star then persuaded his producer-director to make Dixon his stunt double; and as a result, the two actors with their families resettled in California for a couple of years.[34] For Ivan, it was a wonderful opportunity to find more screen work. He had no idea, though, that his first significant achievement would be neither in film or in television but in a Broadway play being written by a young black woman back East.

Lorraine Hansberry, a protégé of Paul Robeson and W. E. B. Du Bois,[35] was only twenty-four years of age when she wrote her mother that the stage play she was writing over the past three years was overwhelming her thoughts: "So many truths seem to be rushing at me as a result of things felt and seen and lived through. All the things I think I must tell in this work." The drama's title was based on lines from Langston Hughes' famous poem *Harlem*.

In 1959, four years later, Dixon and Poitier found themselves along with Ruby Dee, Claudia McNeil, Diana Sands and Louis Gossett ready to start a trial run of *A Raisin in the Sun* at Boston's Schubert Theater. Once again the brilliant young playwright took pen to paper, this time sharing her thoughts with her daughter about the out of town tryouts: "A play that tells the truth about people, about Negroes. I think it will help a lot of people to understand we are just as complicated as they are, just as mixed up. But above all, we have among our downtrodden miserable ranks people who are the very essence of human dignity."[36]

Finally, on March 11th that year, the first stage play created by an African-American woman to be produced on Broadway opened to rave reviews. It earned the fledgling dramatist the New York Critics' Circle Award as the "Best Play of the Year," making her at that time the youngest native-born person to be awarded this honor.[37] Twenty-five years later, *New York Times* drama critic Frank Rich wrote, it "changed American theater forever!"[38]

Directed by Lloyd Richards making his Broadway debut, the story focused on a modest, hard-working black family—Walter Lee Younger (Poitier), his wife Ruth (Dee), and their young son Travis

(Stephen Perry), living with Walter's mother Lena (McNeil) and his sister Beneatha (Sands) in a cramped two-bedroom Chicago tenement. Everyone is awaiting the arrival of a $10,000 insurance check resulting from the death of Lena's husband. But no one agrees on how the money should be spent. Not until the family is offered a bribe to change their minds about moving into a white neighborhood do the Youngers coalesce around the principles of pride and dignity. "The thing I tried to show," Hansberry explained later, "was the many gradations in even one Negro family, the clash of the old and the new, but most all, the unbelievable courage of the Negro people."[39]

Of all the works I have experienced researching *The Interviews, A Raisin in the Sun* remains the only one routinely to bring tears to my eyes after each viewing. (The first time for me was when my wife and I saw the original Broadway production on New Year's Eve 1959.) Dixon played Joseph Assegai, the warm, endearing Nigerian student who is educating Beneatha about her African heritage. He makes clear he wants to marry the future medical student and bring her back to his country. Ivan, as did many members of the original cast, repeated his role two years later in Daniel Petrie's screen adaptation[40] of Hansberry's prize-winning play.

Unfortunately, the film did not have the impact of the play. Some scholars believed it was because Columbia watered down the drama's black nationalistic message for fear of offending white audiences.[41] Other intellectuals harped on the soap-opera qualities of the play and film.[42] Maybe it had to do with the way the movie was marketed to black audiences. The fact was not only did the film do badly at the box-office, but it also failed to inspire the studios to produce any more black-themed movie projects in the immediate future.

If one just read the dozens of bios on Dixon describing his television work in between the play and the film, you might miss the impact that Hansberry and her associates must have had on his evolving black activism. Here is not the place to go into details about the tragic life of this great writer who died from cancer so young. But it seems appropriate to mention briefly her thoughts on the black liberation struggle during the last five years of her life.

Success on Broadway led to her growing association with black activists and serious thinkers such as Ossie Davis and Malcolm X; and among her many friends were strong women like Maya Angelou, Ruby Dee, Nina Simone, Odetta, and Abbey Lincoln. Their often-expressed thoughts might be summed up in the dramatist's comments, "Quite simply and quietly as I know how to say it, I am sick of poverty, lynching, stupid wars, and the universal mistreatment of my people. I am obsessed with a new world for me and my brothers."[43] Nikki Giovanni, the poet, believed that Hansberry "made it possible for all of us to look a little deeper"; while Poitier stated that his role as Walter Lee Younger may have been his most rewarding experience as an actor.[44] And James Forman, the one-time executive secretary of the Student Nonviolent Coordinating Committee unintentionally observed what Dixon and other activists did throughout their lives because of her inspiring efforts: "She believed that people should not only have beliefs but act on those beliefs."[45]

Of course, Lorraine Hansberry's passion was not the only thing on the young actor's radar. After a small role in *Porgy and Bess* (1959), Ivan spent the early sixties working hard in numerous television series. During the same period, as the growing crisis in American race relations escalated, he observed the floundering film industry partially reconsidering its attitude toward black-themed movies. More and more, the studio bosses encouraged white filmmakers to rework their screen approaches describing the horrors of the Jim Crow South. I say "partially" because Dixon still did not see any major support for black producers, directors, or screenwriters in or out of Hollywood.

Then, in 1964, two important low-budget, independent black-themed movies produced and directed by white filmmakers signaled what has since become recognized as a groundbreaking period for African-Americans in the motion picture industry. First came Carl Lerner's *Black Like Me* (1963), an absorbing account about a white reporter using chemical injections to help him pass for Negro. His plan was to discover first-hand what a black man's life was like in the Deep South. [That historical movie will be discussed in the next chapter on James Whitmore.] Second came Larry Peerce's *One Potato, Two Potato* (1964).[47] A sensitive story about miscegenation, the screenplay explored how a white woman's ex-husband sues for custody of their baby because he doesn't want his child brought up in an integrated home. Dixon had agreed to play Frank Richards, the black husband under attack (the role would later be taken over by Bernie Hamilton). Other members of the cast included such notables as Barbara Barrie, Richard Mulligan, and Robert Earl Jones.

Before production began, however, another revolutionary film, also about contemporary Southern blacks caught Dixon's attention. "One day a guy came up to the door and said I should come to New York and try out for this picture," the actor remembered. "[He] gave me a script, and [I] thought it was a wonderful script.... So [I] decided to read for it. [I] went to New York and tried out. [I] got the part luckily."[48]

The film was *Nothing But a Man*. Written, photographed, and directed by two white men, Michael Roemer and Robert Young, the movie became that rare work of art that, as one observer noted, worked brilliantly both as a powerful social commentary and a superb source of entertainment.[49] Since others report the account of how the movie originated as well as the biographies of the cast and crew admirably, most notably by Professor Christopher Sieving,[50] I need only sketch the highlights here.

Determined to display the virtues of documentary realism to the public, Roemer spearheaded the brilliant project about social injustice. Born in Berlin, the Jewish youth at eleven years of age fled Germany and lived in London from 1939 to the end of the Second World War. He then immigrated to America, where the following year he enrolled at Harvard. There he met Young, a former WWII combat photographer; and the two undergraduates became good friends. After graduation, they worked together on various film and television productions. But in the early sixties their hard-hitting television documentary about Sicilian slum life was rejected by NBC executives as too challenging for American audiences.[51] That rejection forced a rethinking by the artists about what to do next.

Consequently in 1962, the men decided to apply their documentary techniques toward making an authentic movie about contemporary blacks oppressed in the Deep South. Each man conceived of the motion picture as a metaphor for their past lives. For example, Young saw the film as a reaction to his "experience in the 20th century,"[52] while Roemer, who knew first-hand the horrors and humiliations of Nazi Germany, felt that African-American conditions symbolized what had happened to his family during the Holocaust.[53] To guarantee the authenticity of their movie, the men, who knew almost no African-Americans, went south, as Young later explained, to live with a number of black families "in places where no white people had ever been...." In this way, the pair believed they could transport "people into these homes where we had been so that all people, black and white, could experience black people as people."[54] Roemer basically agreed: "The whole issue of not being allowed to be a man, a human being, touches something very personal in me. Destroying the family, which is such an old pattern in American race relations, isn't simply a black experience."[55]

By 1963, their memorable screenplay, which they claimed proved relatively easy to write, was ready.[56] Set in a small community outside of Birmingham, Alabama, the narrative dealt with Duff Anderson, a railroad section hand whose unsatisfactory carefree, independent existence makes him ache for a more stable existence. Although his fellow itinerant laborers appear resigned to live in broken-down bunk-cars and socialize with prostitutes in cheap black nightclubs, Duff searches for a better lifestyle. One night, he goes into town and wanders into a Baptist church meeting where he meets Reverend Dawson's stunning daughter, Josie. The discerning schoolteacher sees something different in Duff from the other beaten men she has known, and he realizes Josie is his chance for a better future. But her middle-class parents see no value in their daughter's association with an uneducated, arrogant migrant, while Duff's friends warn him about the dangers of trying to fit into a Jim Crow world. At first, he decides to forget Josie, but after going to Birmingham where he visits both with his neglected child living in a foster home and his sick father barely surviving in poverty, Duff resolves to marry Josie and take his chances. The remainder of the story follows the difficulties the couple encounters as they strive to make a place for themselves while maintaining both their independence and dignity.

Shot for under $250,000 around the Atlantic City, New Jersey area in the summer of 1963, *Nothing But a Man* was directed by Roemer and photographed by Young. The extraordinary cast, which reportedly was paid a $100 a week,[57] took a long time to assemble since there were nearly forty parts to fill.[58] Dixon (Duff) headed the exceptional set of actors: Ivan had experience but almost no name recognition; Julius Harris (Will, Duff's father) was a male nurse who had never worked in movies; Gloria Foster (his girl friend) made her film debut earlier that year in Shirley Clarke's *The Cool World;* Stanley Greene (Rev. Dawson) had only two previously uncredited screen roles; and soon to be noted film and television performers like Moses Gunn, Yaphet Kotto, and Leonard Parker were just beginning their acting careers. Interestingly, the cast's being mostly black worked both for and against the production. On one hand, had they been white, the professional players would not have been able to perform in the movie. On the other hand, at this stage in film history, the black actors were mostly inexperienced.[59]

The best-known cast member was not Dixon but the great jazz singer and activist Abbey Lincoln appearing in her first feature role. In 1963, she was going through hard times and being blackballed by the music industry.[60] We should take a moment to remember just who she was, what her problems were, and why this legendary performer, known to many as "the last of the jazz singers,"[61] symbolized so much courage and strength both for black America and proved significant for Dixon's journey.

Widely praised as one of black music's most passionate performers, Abbey Lincoln also had a controversial reputation for her no-holds barred civil rights activism during the late fifties and throughout the sixties. Nevertheless, the greatest jazz singer of her generation exerted a profound impact on the music of her times. According to Prof. Eric Porter, Abbey was "a musician who regarded…[her] art as a vehicle for personal transformation and who… also negotiated the political and gendered meanings of jazz."[62] But Lincoln did not start out to be a political visionary.

Born Anna Marie Wooldridge on August 6, 1930 in Chicago, the 10th of 12 children, she grew up on a farm in rural Michigan. Her childhood love of popular jazz eventually led her in the early 1950s to a professional singing career first in California, and then in Honolulu. By the mid-fifties, the attractive 23 year-old vocalist was back in Los Angeles and being managed by lyricist Bob Russell. He gets the credit for renaming her Abbey Lincoln, the designation metaphorically taken from a linking of Westminster Abbey and Abraham Lincoln. In 1956, Abbey made her first recording, *Abbey Lincoln's Affair: A Story* of *a Girl in Love* for Liberty Records, and played a small role wearing a flashy dress in Frank Tashlin's *The Girl Can't Help It.* Despite the hopeful entertainer's good notices, however, she was facing an identity crisis, not too dissimilar from the one that Dorothy Dandridge had experienced. "I started out being a sexy young thing in a Marilyn Monroe dress," she quipped to *The Times* in 2000, "And Max Roach freed me from that."[63]

The two musical legends met during her second recording in 1957. The great drummer, as one black spokesperson reminded us, "used his music as an instrument of our struggle,"[64] quickly politicized Abbey, who now became as fiery about Black Nationalism as Roach himself. As a symbolic gesture, Abbey stopped straightening her hair and began dressing more in keeping with her new political views. In many ways, the partnership between Roach and Lincoln paralleled the rise of the Civil Rights era. The transformed singer also became linked to Hansberry and other female activists. In addition, Lincoln's emotional fervor resulted in her becoming one of Malcolm X's confidants during the late fifties and early sixties, as well as making sure he understood the measure of black women's "political strength."[65] It was a lesson she passed on as well to Ivan Dixon.

In 1960, Abbey joined Roach on the avant-garde masterpiece *We Insist! Freedom Now Suite,* which many progressives consider one of the major innovations in jazz history. Described as "free jazz," the recording spurned traditional musical patterns and expressed instead the sounds of "political liberation." That historic record was followed the next year by Lincoln's other important recording *Straight Ahead.* The radical music, as Nat Hentoff explained, evoked "the pride and pain of being a Negro in America."[66]

By the time the couple married in 1962, they were immersed in a firestorm over their revolutionary records politicizing music in the jazz world. But neither Roach nor Lincoln gave an inch. Although, as one historian remembered, they were "harassed, persecuted, and ostracized,"[67] each found a way to survive. The embattled vocalist turned her back on jazz for the rest of the sixties; and in 1963, she took the role of Josie in *Nothing But a Man.* Later in the decade, she appeared in Daniel Mann's *For Love of Ivy* (1968), for which she received a Golden Globes award. In these two performances, journalist Matt Schudel insisted, were to be found "... among the first Hollywood depictions of mature, loving relationships between black women and black men. "At other times, Abbey performed on television in guest-starring roles."[68]

Following her traumatic 1972 divorce from Roach, Lincoln resumed her singing career and began writing her own music. She never remarried. Though she restarted her recording work in 1973, it was not until 1990 that she once more emerged a star, much in the legendary jazz tradition of Bessie Smith and Billie Holiday. Particularly noticeable in her final years was the songstress' unflinching meditative performances and recordings.[69] Among her many famous songs were *What Will Tomorrow Bring, A Heart is Not a Toy, The World Is Falling Down,* and *You Gotta Pay the Band.*

Abbey Lincoln, the uncompromising singer, composer, actress, and activist, died in 2010, three years after her brilliant former husband. They remain one of the most remarkable couples of their generation. "I live through music," she often said, "and it lives through me."

If you are curious as to why I spent so much time on *Nothing But a Man* it is in large part because this is the movie that not only forever drew me to black film studies, but also was the subject of my first publication.[70]

What hopefully emerges from these memories about Hansberry, Roach, and Lincoln, as well as those of the entertainment world generally during the post-WWII years and into the sixties is the way Dixon's journey interconnected with African-American film history and the role he played in awakening America's racial conscious.

As for *Nothing But a Man,* it becomes for many people a prime example of how one film can express so much humanity to so many people. Honored both at the Venice Film Festival and at the New York Film Festival, the movie proved, like other black-themed films of the decade, that independent, white-controlled pictures with these subjects remained admired overseas but unpopular at American movie theaters. Not until three decades later, when *Nothing But a Man* was reissued theatrically, did Roemer see a profit from his efforts;[71] and *The Washington Post* spoke for a new generation of Americans when it described the movie as "one of the most sensitive films about black life ever made in this country."[72] The following year, 1994, the movie created by two white men who knew almost no black people when they began their project, was selected by the National Film Registry of the Library of Congress as one of the nation's great film treasures.

But the reception the movie received in 1964 proved perplexing. On the one hand, as Sieving summarized: "To most reviewers, the protagonist Duff Anderson (Ivan Dixon) was a man first and foremost, and only secondarily an African American man. This characteristic allowed them to construe the Roemer film as a solid family drama rather than as a sermon on American racism."[73] On the other hand, not everyone thought *Nothing But a Man* a national treasure, including a growing disaffected black constituency that questioned both Dr. King's civil rights strategy and white America's sincerity in bringing about racial reform. A new generation of young people also had a different interpretation than the one shared by Dixon and other members of the cast. This small group of critics, many of them African American, regarded *Nothing But a Man's* supposed universality as a flaw, rather than a virtue. In effect, they perceived it as letting whites "off the hook."[74]

This reaction clearly distorted the filmmaker's original intentions. That is, using the term "universality" as a euphemism, the movie's detractors disliked the idea of equating the Jewish struggle with the black experience. Not only did this mostly black minority see the circumstances differently, but they also demonized Jews as Zionists who supported Israel; and Zionism they equated as synonymous with neo-colonialism. Particularly disturbing, the radical black factions grouped Jews and Israel as enemies of the black movement; and as a result of this reverse racism, anti-Semitism intensified among a significant portion of the African-American community.[75] It needs saying that neither Dixon nor any member of the cast and crew shared such radical interpretations.

In retrospect, Ivan's actions immediately following *Nothing but a Man* seemed prophetic about his role in television, movies and race relations for the remainder of the decade. Just as Jim Brown and Maggie Hathaway were organizing the National Negro Industrial and Economic Union for professional football players; Dixon, in 1964, helped establish the Negro Actors for Action. Feeling that the television industry was starting to back down on its civil rights goals, Ivan felt it necessary to pressure the broadcasters into realizing jobs alone were not the primary issue.[76] "The Conflict," he told a *New York Post* reporter years later, "has to be other than race for a change. It has to show the Negro in normal everyday life. Now everything is still a white plot with Negroes brought in." Ivan than added, "What we also need to see is the Negro as folk hero.... What we need as a people is mass images, heroes we can identify as our own."[77]

During the process of organizing the television actors, Dixon participated in a black writers workshop; and there met Richard M. Powell, a writer working on a new CBS TV series called *Hogan's Heroes*. An unlikely comedy about Allied POWs who consistently and ludicrously outsmart a German commandant and his troops in a prison camp. Soon, Powell began a friendship with Dixon and decided to rewrite the part of Sergeant James Kinchloe, a radio operator and the only serious POW among the program's regular actors. The writer than convinced the show's producers to hire Ivan for what would become a popular sixties TV show that ran for six seasons, starting in 1965.[78] When people wondered how you could find funny things to say about German soldiers in a World War II prison camp, *Hogan's Heroes'* producer Ed Feldman explained his program was about "a bunch of guys outwitting authority."[79]

Once again, remembering a film or television series' reception proves instructive of the times. On one hand, the CBS series, in its first season, against 98 other prime-time competitors, came in first in the Nielson Ratings. On the other hand, *Hogan's Heroes* also took a beating from a range of detractors,[80] "especially from certain Jewish viewers, who felt is was an insult to the issues in World War II and to the Holocaust itself."[81] As Leslie Campbell Rampey perceptively observed, "If nothing else, *Hogan's Heroes* demonstrates the power popular culture has to influence perceptions about historic events and reminds us also that it sometimes can have completely unintended consequences."[82] Surely both *Nothing But a Man* and *Hogan's Heroes* illustrate how race relations continued to become more visible and visceral by the mid-sixties.

Over the years, disagreement has arisen concerning Ivan's feelings for doing the show. On the one hand, when I spoke to him, as you will see, he was less than enthusiastic about his role and the series itself. In fact, the admired stage and screen actor told one interviewer in 1967 that he signed on mainly for financial reasons. "I needed the money." Even then, Dixon never thought the show would see the light of day. When it did, he was shocked but happy. "Suddenly, I found myself with a guaranteed income for a change," he explained. "With three children to support (a fourth was born in October 1965, just after the series' premiere), Dixon was not able to limit his roles to meaningful social dramas."[83] It also helps to remember Ivan was the only original cast member who did not complete *Hogan's Heroes'* six seasons. He dropped out of the series in 1970, the start of the final season. Kenneth Washington as Sgt. Richard Baker replaced Dixon for the sitcom's final season.[84] On the other hand, Doris Nomathande Dixon, his daughter, believed her father was always "pleased to be recognized as Sgt. Kinchloe."[85]

While preparing for *Hogan's Heroes,* Dixon joined Poitier for their last movie together, Guy Green's *A Patch of Blue* (1965).[86] Nominated for four Oscars—Best Art Direction-Set Decoration, Best Cinematography, Best Music (Original Score), and the only winner, Shelley Winters for Best Supporting Actress. Nevertheless, as one historian aptly stated, the Green adaptation of Elizabeth Katz's novel *Be Ready with Bells and Drums* outraged "white liberals and militant blacks during the 1960s."[87]

Set in an urban working class neighborhood, the plot tracked the pitiful existence of Selina, an eighteen-year-old blind woman (Elizabeth Hartman), horribly mistreated by Rose-Ann, her prostitute mother (Shelley Winters), and Old Pa', her alcoholic grandfather (Wallace Ford). Selina's only joy comes from the few days she is allowed to be in the neighborhood park. On one such day, she encounters Gordon Ralfe (Sidney Poitier), a writer who becomes sympathetic to her heartbreaking situation. As the two meet more often, Selina falls in love with Gordon, but does not know he is black. When Gordon's brother Mark (Ivan Dixon) discovers what is happening, he admonishes his brother about how inappropriate the relationship is in the real world. The remainder of the movie shows how the racial, parental, and personal conflicts are resolved. Historian Edward Mapp observed that Dixon's role and dialogue "bears a closer resemblance to black reality than does the character of Gordon. Mark cannot comprehend his brother's selfless interest in Selena."[88]

The reaction to the movie helps us understand why many people resented the fact a movie like this could do well at the box-office when far superior independent black-themed films were ignored by the public. *Newsweek*'s film reviewer put the entire film in a harsh light: "No other film has ever managed to insult the Negroes and the blind [as did *A Patch of Blue*]."[89] And The *New Yorker*'s Brendan Gill complained, "...The story the movie tells comes close to being literally sickening in its sentimentality...."[90]

While Poitier would remain one of the nation's premier box-office stars for the next few years, his appeal among the emerging black population was headed for trouble. The same was not true for Dixon. In 1967, for example, the now respected and politicized artist gave a widely praised performance in *The Final War of Olly Winter*,[91] the first episode of the *CBS Playhouse* drama series. He played a Master Sergeant who had served both in World War II and Korea. Now his last tour of duty is to help out as a military advisor in Vietnam during 1963. In one battle against the enemy, Olly encounters a terrified Vietnamese girl (Tina Chen) standing by the bodies of her dead parents. It is at this juncture he tragically decides to risk his life to save hers.

Ivan was especially pleased with the part because it gave him the chance to be more than "just a black white boy." He felt, "The role brought in more aspects of Negro culture."[92] The critics agreed. The Vietnamese narrative garnered five Emmy nominations, including one for Ivan in an Outstanding Single Performance by an Actor in a Leading Role in a Drama. His competition also included two other actors in CBS productions: Lee J. Cobb for *Death of Salesman* and Hal Holbrook for *Mark Twain Tonight*. The award, however, went to Peter Ustinov in the NBC *Hallmark Hall of Fame* teleplay *Barefoot in Athens*.[93] Savor that one for a moment!

As the sixties roared into the seventies, the changes taking place for blacks in the industry and the nation were striking. Most commentators point to the events in 1967 and 1968 as responsible for further igniting the black society while also terrifying an already frightened white population, all this in addition to the intense, angry disagreements that broke out over government policies and actions. It seemed with the marches, riots, bombings, boycotts, assassinations, and murders, the country was heading towards another civil war.

Yet what worked best for me in retracing the end of the sixties was listening to the civil rights music, the anti-war ballads, and the liberation songs. To repeat what was said in other chapters, it was the likes of Odetta, Nina Simone, Bob Dylan, Buffy St. Marie, Joan Baez, Phil Ochs, Abbey Lincoln, The Weavers, and Pete Seeger, to mention a few artists, whose powerful, inspiring recordings brought the era most home: e.g., *Mississippi Goddam, I Wish I Knew How It Would Feel to Be Free, If I Had a Hammer, No More Auction Block for Me, He's Got the Whole World in His Hands, Midnight Special, Chilly Winds, Strange Fruit, The Times They Are a-Changin', Why? The King of Love is Dead, Blowin' in the Wind,* and *To Be Young, Gifted, and Black.* Wadaada Smith, the Mississippi-born trumpeter, may be on to something when he explained to the *Jazz Times,* "If people had truly endorsed the music of the 60s.... I don't mean just liked it, but understood that it was showing the best example of democratic principles and also the philosophical and actual notion of freedom—then our society would be way ahead."[94]

Although black representations had come a long way from the days of *Pinky, Home of the Brave,* and *Lost Boundaries* (all in 1949), much more was needed and demanded. Now, in 1970, Dixon was ready to make another course change in his career. Following his debut as a director of an episode on the revolutionary television show *I Spy,* starring Bill Cosby, the respected actor decided to devote most of his future efforts to becoming a top-flight director. Among the many, many TV series he helmed were *Get Christie Love!, Snoops,* and *Brewster Place.* In addition, Ivan helped pioneer the idea that black television directors could also work on white programs: e.g., *The Waltons, Magnum, P.I., The Rockford Files, Room 222, The Mod Squad, Starsky and Hutch, In the Heat of the Night, The Outer Limits,* and *Quantum Leap.*[95]

Then in 1972, the neophyte director persuaded Twentieth Century-Fox to let him helm *Trouble Man,*[96] the studio's entry in the blaxploitation market. Scripted by John D. Black, the story featured a super cool Mr. T (Robert Hooks), a Los Angeles street-smart detective who also owns a pool hall. He is hired by two unsavory crime bosses (Paul Winfield and Ralph Waite) to discover who has been moving in on their local gambling racket. Between beating up various hoods and dodging the cops, Mr. T romances beautiful women. Before the remarkable martial arts hero solves the crime war, he also manages to make some positive statements about the black community.

Helming *Trouble Man* was not an easy job for Dixon, who only wanted to make the film to gain experience as a director. The studio, however, expected him to exploit the public's fascination with glamorized images of pimps, hustlers, whores, and drug lords. But Ivan felt that slant only worsened an already silly movie.[97] At one point, he even needed help from the NAACP to fight the white producers from turning his nightclub singer (Paula Kelly) into a woman who spent her entire screen time getting in and out of bed. The director won that battle, as Kelley's character remained caring, intelligent, loyal, and critical to the film's plot.

Not even Marvin Gaye's soulful music could save *Trouble Man*. The most critical reaction to the film came not from the critics or the studio. It was Dixon who had the last word on the failed enterprise: "The ending of the film, I think, was just ridiculous. This guy walking around shooting everybody, just blowing up the whole cast. I remember the secretary and I saw the final cut of the film. It got to the end. The guy walks around shooting everybody. Blowing up the whole cast. He walks into an office and the phone rings. And the girl says, 'Shoot the phone, T! Shoot the phone.' It was so funny to me. It was just so disgusting."[98]

Happily, *Trouble Man*'s critical reception did not interfere with Dixon's growth as a director. While he never again took charge of a Hollywood film, the indestructible artist managed to turn out one of the most controversial independent black films of the era: *The Spook Who Sat by the Door* (1973).[99] Since both the 30th anniversary DVD version of the movie and *Infiltrating Hollywood: The Spook Who Sat by The Door*[100] cover the history and legacy of the film, we need only summarize the basic facts about this unique underground movie.

In a prologue to the reissuing of the picture, *USA* columnist DeWayne Wickham reminded us, "To fully appreciate this movie, you have to understand the context in which it was made. Early in 1970s coming out of the sixties, the civil rights struggle. The struggle that produced the Civil Rights Act of 1964, the Voting Rights Act of 1965, and the Fair Housing Act of 1968, there was a violent reaction in white America, in some parts of white America, to this progress we experienced. And that reaction coupled with the transition from Martin Luther King and Whitney Young and civil rights leaders who had lost their lives to H. Rap Brown and Stokely Carmichael, black activists who had no stomach for non-violence, to someone like Le Roi Jones who made the transition to Amiri Baraka, the black activist, black nationalist, the man who wrote, 'What time is it?' and answered, 'It's nation time.'"[101]

Seeing what was happening around him, Sam Greenlee, a black revolutionary, wrote *The Spook Who Sat by the Door* in 1966. Dan Freeman, the book's hero, is a brilliant social worker who is recruited by the FBI in an attempt to convince Congress that the agency is integrated. Freeman sees that the duplicitous Affirmative Action program is his chance to learn everything he can about being a revolutionary. After deceiving his FBI bosses for five years, he resigns and returns to his home base in Chicago and covertly trains a guerilla army to terrify the country and get African-Americans their rights. Although Greenlee had difficulty getting the novel published in America, he found a small London firm that agreed to print the sensational story. Over the next five years, *The Spook Who Sat by The Door* became a must read for black nationalists.

The novel came to Dixon's attention while he was directing an episode of *The Mod Squad*. Even though making the revolutionary book into a protest movie meant Ivan could jeopardize his career, the idea of showing blacks how to mobilize in pursuit of their freedom became an obsession for him. For two years, he and Greenlee struggled to raise the capital for the film. They were turned down almost everywhere they went in the States. They also found themselves denied funds from abroad. It seemed as if powerful government forces like the FBI's infamous CointelPro program exerted terrifying pressures on anyone supportive of the filmmakers.

Nonetheless, Greenlee and Dixon found a way to make the radical movie. Good reviews, a well-directed picture, fine acting, excellent editing, or just being an entertaining film were not enough to win the day. Most of all, the unrelenting covert attacks on the picture did not end as the movie went into distribution. Within a week of its premiere, *The Spook Who Sat by The Door* disappeared from America's movie screens. Almost every print was seized and destroyed. If not for Dixon taking the original negative, changing its name, and hiding it in a vault, we would not be able to see the film now.

The long-stated excuse that responsible people needed to prevent *The Spook Who Sat by The Door* from being read or seen proved false from the beginning. Both the writer and the director always felt that the fictional story's importance lay not in any realistic expectation they could overthrow the American establishment, but rather in the film showing African-Americans the means of self-determination. As Ivan stated, the film's fate resulted from "too many people...[thinking] it "a blueprint for revolutionary acts."[102] In the end, Greenlee and Dixon's gallant efforts proved ineffective in 1973.

The making of *The Spook who Sat by the Door* almost destroyed Dixon's career. His wife told people that Ivan did not work for a long time after the movie came out.[103] Fortunately, the courageous artist's story did not end as his detractors hoped it would.

In 1976, the actor appeared in another cult movie, Michael Schultz's *Car Wash* (1976).[104] Filled with energy, humor and imagination, Joel Schumacher's extremely entertaining script focuses on a group of employees working in a mediocre Los Angeles car wash. Throughout the workday, an eccentric group of visitors present challenging as well as comic dilemmas to the odd assortment of employees who struggle under the eyes of their befuddled boss and foolish son. Dixon superbly plays Lonnie, an ex-con who remains a model of reason and stability in very difficult circumstances. Charles Champlin spoke for many critics when he placed the film in the category of other classic comedies like *American Graffiti, Nashville,* and *Cooley High.*[105]

On March 16, 2008, the courageous, gifted and resolute Ivan Dixon died at 76 years of age. He never reached the heights of Poitier or Belafonte, but what he did with his vision and talent made African-American culture and entertainment better than he had found it.

***

Ivan and I had our conversation at a Los Angeles bar. As usual, neither of us knew what to expect from the other. What impresses me most looking back on that wonderful conversation is Dixon's poise and presence. He was in the midst of trying to finance *The Spook Who Sat by The Door,* and experiencing tremendous opposition both from the industry and the black community. His future was at stake, and yet he found the time to talk to a young UVM Associate Professor about very disturbing matters. When I think about my frequent problems in getting my overworked colleagues to clarify certain sticking points in this manuscript, I remain astonished at the courtesy and demeanor of a stranger under siege. For me, Ivan, like everyone else in *The Interviews,* remains very, very special.

Ivan Dixon Interview
January 11, 1972

FM: This is the last of three interviews for today.

ID: I have a tendency to be not so much candid as honest as I possibly can, and that really happens to my detriment. [Laughs]

FM: Jim Brown was saying something like that. Let me put your mind at ease. Jim asked me would I object to sending him the chapter when I do it on him. He didn't want to edit it or anything, but he just wanted to see how he was being presented. And I was thrilled that he wanted to do that because maybe he would see something that he'd want changed or added. If you'd like, I'd be glad to send you your chapter when it's done, and then you can see it, and you can maybe think of something that I haven't put in there, or you can enter. So maybe that will make you feel a little better.

ID: Nothing will make me feel at ease. That's what I am trying to say.

[At this point, a waitress came over to the table with our drinks. The interview then resumed.]

FM: When you think of all the stuff that you've done. My kids [Steven and Gary] watched *Hogan's Heroes,* terrific. I know it's over, but.... Well good luck to you. [We clicked our glasses.]

ID: Cheers.

FM: Well, can you tell me something about where you were born and grew up, and your experiences, and how you got into movies?

ID: I was born and raised in Harlem, and I lived there most of my early life. But I got in a little trouble with the power structure in New York. And I ended up being kicked out of the state. I went to a boarding school in North Carolina [Lincoln Academy] for my last couple of years of high school. And then I went to four years of college. And I became a pre-law student.

I got involved in theater as an extra curricular activity. When I graduated from college, I couldn't get a scholarship to law school. But I got a scholarship to Western Reserve for graduate work in theater. And I decided to return. Then after being there for a few months, I realized that what I wanted had nothing to do with getting a Masters Degree in Theater. If I was going to be involved in entertainment, artistic work, theater, and drama and that sort of thing, then I wanted to do it on a professional level and not teaching in the school system. I'm not a teacher type, or anything like that.

[BREAK]

ID: I have a theory that the brighter the kid, particularly a black kid in the urban environment, the more likely he is to come into conflict with all the areas of authority in the urban community. You know, he's just got to do that; it just has to happen. And as a result, the brightest kids are the ones who get into the most trouble, I think.

FM: But that works against them in a sense because....

ID: Of course.

FM: Because they really need to know school, and they need the background in order to survive. You know, once you get angry and you drop out of the system because it may be corrupted, that doesn't help. Where they gonna go?

ID: It isn't a matter of dropping out.

FM: Pushed out?

ID: It's more a matter of being pushed out, I think. It's the system rejecting you and the necessity of having to rebel from a sense of rejection. What I mean is, by the time the black kid in most urban communities at least, certainly in southern Harlem, reaches the sixth or seventh grade, he's already a dropout. You know, the sixth grade! He's already a dropout. He's just sitting there waiting. You get into the junior high school level; you've got black kids that are just sitting there waiting, just spending the time. I had my workman's papers when I was twelve. I lied about my age in order to get working papers in the city of New York because I couldn't stand it.

I did the same in order to work as an underage "candy butcher" at Ebbets Field, Yankee Stadium, the Polo Grounds, and Madison Square Garden in 1949.

ID: The system didn't involve me in very subtle ways that I wasn't even aware of. You know, on the surface, it rejected me. It said that I was less than. I had no choice, really, but to reject it, to save my sanity.

FM: Yuh, yuh.

ID: At any rate, your rebellion then takes many forms. Some of us wound up breaking out windows; some of us were robbing supermarkets and ripping off junk at Macys, whatever. The funny thing is we usually robbed the bigger type economic organizations, things like Safeway, and A&P and Macys and Bloomingdales. The small businessman we usually let alone. [We both started laughing at this point.]

FM: I used to rob candy stores. We used to get one guy to go up and keep the guy busy with the sodas, and we used to go to the back and take magazines.

ID: We didn't do too much of that. We did a little of that, but usually the little guy in the neighborhood was too poor; we'd hit the A&P for cases of Coke rather than hit the little guy on the corner, which I thought was rather a moralistic kind of sense

FM: Robin Hood.

BP: Even there, even then as kids. A little touch of the Robin Hood if you want to call it that, a strange kind of morality.

FM: Let me go back. You left Case [Sic] then to go out to do professional work, get professional experience. What year are we talking about?

ID: I left Western Reserve.

FM: Western Reserve.

ID: 1954, 1955; something like that.

FM: And then where did you go to live? New York?

ID: I went back to New York and became involved with the American Theatre Wing and the Clarence Muse Theater. I began to get a little taste of work here and there.

FM: What was The American Theater Wing like? Did you just walk in off the street and say, "Well, I had some work in…?"

ID: Well, I did that, I actually did. A friend of mine, a young lady who also graduated from the same college that I went to named Jacqueline Barnes, walked into the Muse Theater off the street, and there was a group of young people in there building sets for the next production. And we just pitched in and started helping, just became involved that way. We just stole our way in, you know, crashed.

Sidney Poitier tells a somewhat similar story about having received a three-month trial scholarship from the American Negro Theatre, and then being cut loose. He pleaded with the Board to allow him to clean the theater and do odd jobs just so he could continue his acting studies.[106]

FM: Did you know what you were doing? Did you ask somebody to show you how to do it?

ID: No. We had a good deal of experience in building sets. That was no problem because in North Carolina College we learned to build fantastic sets from scratch, from nothing. We learned the correct way to build sets, that was no problem. There was a variety of theatrical experience available to us at North Carolina College that isn't generally available to black kids on the college level.

I think mostly because in the mainstream college, a black kid who goes to UCLA, or to Yale, or wherever, and becomes a member of the drama group, or minors or majors in drama, really is very limited in terms of his participation. In the production area he may get some kind of experience, but in the performing area there's very little in the way of experience he's likely to get. He's certainly not likely to play Lear at UCLA.

On the other hand, I played Lear, and Claudius in *Hamlet, Don*

Juan in Hell, and we did Shaw, Anouilh's *Antigone,* all kinds of things, all kinds of material. So I was able to extend myself in a variety of ways.

FM: You had range.

ID: We didn't only do the classic type of material; we did things like *Bill of Divorcement, Death Takes a Holiday,* and *The Philadelphia Story.* And we did a number of indigenous black plays that had come out of drama departments of Howard University and a number of other writings around the country. So our experience, I think, was some good deal more varied than the average drama student, or black drama student gets, who comes out of a white university system today.

FM: So you had gotten to the theater in New York, you had come off the street and, as you said, 'crashed' in to it. How did it go for the next couple of years? Did you get many parts in the plays?

ID: No, I didn't do too badly. I was pretty lucky. I worked for like two dollars a week. Did some work Off Broadway. I understudied for some prime people in Off Broadway plays, and once in a while I got an opportunity to play. I was a stand in for Sidney Poitier. This friend of mine, the same friend I told you about, happened to be in the Muse Theater when someone called who owed someone a favor, or something. I don't know, there was an opening for a stand in. It was for Sidney Poitier on a film called the *Edge of the City.*[107]

FM: Yes, with Cassavetes.

ID: And she recommended me; she actually got me the job: From then on I just went to little, bit parts and extra roles, walk-ons and now and then getting a supporting role.

FM: Were you ready, you think, and kept off the stage because of race; or were you just following the normal progression of what you see now?

ID: Well, in a way you could call it "normal progression." And in another sense, you could say that, certainly, I was far more limited than the white actor who went through the same kind of progression because there were less roles available to the black actor at the time, Off-Broadway, or on Broadway. Say if there were, oh, five hundred roles on Broadway in that season; this is just off the top of my head, I would estimate that, perhaps, thirty to fifty, or less, of those went to black actors. Generally these were menial roles, or very minor roles. Once in a while a big hit production; and you still, even in the '50's, you were still kind of coming off a residue of a certain kind of black production that took place in the '30's and '40's. Most of the kids that grew up who came into theater in the '50's did not want to participate in that kind of 'lackey' role, and that sort of thing. We were still falling off of that, you know?

Off-Broadway there was some opportunities; [A] *Land Beyond the River* (1957) was a play that I did, a play written by a black author, Loften Mitchell.

FM: I saw that.

ID: I did *Wedding in Japan* [1957]. On Broadway, I did William Saroyan's play, *The Cave Dwellers*. But, you know, I had three small, bit roles in that production. The only Broadway play that I did that had any meaningful roles in it for blacks was *A Raisin in the Sun*, which came about in 1959.

FM: Was *Nothing But a Man* your first picture?

ID: No, my first part in a film was in *Something of Value*, 1956.[108]

FM: With Poitier and Rock Hudson?

ID: Right.

FM: What was that like? How did you get the job, for example?

ID: Well, I tried out for the part against, oh, thirty or forty other young, black actors in New York who were tested in New York by MGM. And I remember there were such guys as Billy Gunn, Ray St. Jacques; Ray was active even then. It was like a cattle call. All the guys were down reading for this part. Actually, we thought we were reading for the part that Sidney did because he had turned it down; this was the word in the wind. It was an opportunity for some young black actor to suddenly play a big part; while it turned out the opening was for a secondary black role.

But it was nice. It was a hell of an interesting experience. It was nothing extraordinary, nothing very meaningful in the role that I played. Looking back on it now, I don't think there was very much that meaningful in the picture itself, the film. It was a cop out in many, many ways. At the time though, looking at it from the point of view of that day, it was really quite progressive, you know, in the sense of what had gone before.

FM: Poitier still had to die in the film. They couldn't let him survive.

ID: Of course. All that was a part of a certain kind of a cop out in the '50's.

FM: Do you remember any incidents, or anecdotes on the set? Or anything that happened that would flesh out the book? [Dixon starts laughing at this point.]

ID: On the set of that particular film? Did someone tell you something? [Still laughing]

FM: I'm just asking.

ID: Well there were lots of things on that film. I don't know, some of it I don't even want to tell. I remember, let's see. I don't like trying to tell anecdotes, they don't come out.

FM: I mean, was there something that was significant, or worthwhile, just a name or a date of the film? If you could think of something that would make the story more memorable.

ID: I don't know. What would make it memorable? It was a different kind of world. I don't know quite how to explain it.

FM: Prejudice on the set?

ID: Well the prejudice on the set was rather subtle. Prejudice takes many forms; and after all, the members, the crews, the Hollywood crews, certainly of that time and, for the most part today, are of the stock that tends to be a prejudiced stock. Many of them were 'Oakies' and 'Arkies', and cats from Alabama, Mississippi, who came out many years ago, running from economic deprivation and looking for, you know, economic hope and found it in the film industry on the west coast. Now, this didn't mean that they lost, or shed, many of the social attitudes that they had, particularly towards blacks. They brought much of this with them. For example, in certain areas out here, I don't know if you know Glendale and Orange County, the certain, specific areas that are inhabited mostly by people who brought certain kinds of social customs with them from the East and the South, out here.

So, on that film, as on most films, there were the usual number of crew members, cats who were sort of prejudice in this fact. But when you work with those people, if you decide to do a black film, your prejudice doesn't necessarily show, unless it slips out.

Like little incidents. Like an incident that I could mention on that particular film. There was a tradition in the industry of calling, what we now call a "flag," which is a sort of a sheet of material, a black sheet of material. It's used to block off light when they're lighting the set. Well, the one time, there was a very long one that they would hang, that they used to call a "nigger." And on the set one day, and there's a group of Mau Mau wandering about on the set, and they were lighting for the scene, and the gaffer spoke to the cameraman and said, "Don't you think there's a little too much light coming in off the left? Is something getting into the lens there?"

The cameraman says, "Yeah, there's a little flare out there. You better block out that flare right there on the left from that senior over there."

And the gaffer turns around and yells, "Hang me a nigger over here."

Well, there was that moment of everybody turning around, all these Mau Maus. And the poor guy, it's a thing that he's probably said for thirty years, he's probably been in the business for thirty years at that time, and he's said the same thing for thirty years.

FM: [Laughing] The poor guy.

ID: Now he's on the set with a bunch of black cats.

FM: Mortified?

ID: And he was just absolutely mortified. He turned red as a beet and burst into tears, just standing there with tears running down his face. And nobody was willing to break the silence; nobody knew what to say. You know, there was no point in trying to console him.

FM: It wasn't intentional?

ID: On the other hand, it was something that was not a good thing. I know it wasn't necessarily intentional on his part to make a racial slur. But then it was a racial slur, maybe. And the fact that this had been going on all these years was something that disturbed me. It had to.

FM: That will be useful. Can you tell me anything else like that? Or any other experience?

ID: I don't know, you mean racial experiences?

FM: Yeah. The thrust of the book is to try to show whether or not there was, or was not, racial discrimination against blacks in film.

ID: Oh man! That goes with out saying. I don't see how you can even discuss it.

FM: But people say it wasn't so. I talk to people out here. They say to me.... I talked to Clarence Muse. I talked to Jim Brown today, and he said to me that any guy who had muscle, no one messed with him, black or white. When he'd walk on a set, he never had trouble. In all the films he's been in, he's never had one racial situation because they knew not to fool with him. They knew that he was tough enough not to get away with it. [Dixon starts laughing hysterically] He's been blacklisted for two years because of the producers. But he says....

ID: Bullshit! Bullshit! Jim Brown was never blacklisted because of any producers.

FM: He said it was because of his personal life, not because of his politics or his acting. No?

ID: Come on. Well, that's a matter of opinion. I'm not gonna go into anything. I would never put down Jim Brown. I'd never put anything on him at all. But let's put it this way. Jim Brown came into the business like in '65 [sic]. There's a big difference between '65 and '55.

FM: Absolutely!

ID: So, I wouldn't expect Jim Brown's attitude about what goes on in the business to be the same as mine. A lot of the things that he found here when he came here were the results of people like, frankly, myself, Sidney Poitier, and others who went before and who really fought some very weird battles behind the scenes.

FM: Can you give me some things that I can have some meaningful clout when I talk about it?

ID: I don't know how to say it.

FM: I mean everyone says it was obvious, and then when I say to people it was...

ID: It's obvious and yet it's subtle. It's the kind of thing that just went on in the tale I told you about just now.

It's like when I did shows like a television production [1960] where I played a West Indian doctor in a television version of *Arrowsmith,*[109] Farley Granger and Diane Baker. And as I recall in the final scene, the West Indian doctor comes into Arrowsmith's house with Arrowsmith, and discovers his wife. She's fallen down on a couch or on a bed or something, and he's a doctor, and his immediate reaction is to see if there's any heartbeat or anything.

And so all during rehearsal, I said, I yelled to her, "Doctor!" And I knelt beside the lady, and I listened to her heart.

FM: You were doing something official.

ID: Well, nobody thought about it during rehearsal, at least not obviously. It's a curious thing, actors tend to be the more liberal group in this industry; and production people tend to be either a lot more conservative or a lot more afraid of conservativism.

Well, on the night of the dress rehearsal in the booth, the little booth where the advertisers gather, the guys from Madison Avenue, ad representatives, all sat with the producers. The booth literally shook, I mean literally. Really, I fingered the woman, things fell off the wall; it was that frightening. And friends of mine who were in the room.... Such epithets and threats were thrown as, "Never have that woolly-headed nigger's head on that bitch's breast!" And all kinds of fantastic things.

Well, they moved to a very weird situation there for a while, because it was at a time when it was not easy to tell me that this is what we want to do, because they're always racial. And yet it had to be done to satisfy the sponsors or whatever, or representatives.

The director, I can't recall his name [Alex Segal], he came to me and said, "Look, we're gonna have to do it this way. I hope you understand. I apologize. I'm not gonna tell you what went on. I can't. Just accept my apologies. You've got to do it this way. Arrowsmith will come in; and you'll find the woman, and you'll say,' Doctor!' And he'll push you aside, and he'll examine his wife's body." I said," Okay."

But, of course this was live television. So I simply did what I had rehearsed.

FM: And being told?

ID: I don't know if it was what I was being told. I was simply doing what we had rehearsed. I wasn't putting one over. I just had no choice. You know, that's just a normal reaction. They were shaving up my testicles, and I covered myself a little bit. So I had to do what I had to do. I remember being threatened about never working in television again, and all that sort of thing. "You'll never work in a studio again!" You know. What else could I say, but "Fuck it!" I had to do it. I had no choice.

There were other such incidents. I can't recall them all now. There were millions of them.

FM: It's one thing to say they did this; then they'll say you're just being a pseudo liberal if I write the book that way. And they'll say, "Prove it. Show me where." And that's why it's helpful when I got some clout. When I got a specific incident.

ID: Well, I'll tell you what would be probably one of the easiest ways of getting specific incidents would be to go to white actors and white directors and producers. Because they have been absolutely as aware of these things, even more in many instances, as the blacks.

FM: No way. No way. I went to them. I went to John Ford. I went to King Vidor. Both of them claim there was never a single moment of racial prejudice in the film industry. (Dixon smiled.)

ID: You're talking about a very strange kind of cat. I mean, John Ford, you could never believe that he has any negative feelings about a black. One of my best friends is....

FM: Woody Strode!

ID: Yeah! And I can understand that. And I have a good deal of respect for Mr. Ford personally myself. I know him. But I wouldn't even attempt to try to convince Mr. Ford that certain things were happening on his set that were not...

FM: Kosher.

ID: Yeah, well, I hate to use that word. [We both start laughing.] But, at any rate, I suggest that you go to some cats like Richard Brooks, for example. He could tell you many instances. Stanley Kramer. Go to some of the television directors like Paul Nickell, [Franklin J.] Schaffner. Gee, there's a long list. And go to the Writers Guild certainly and just ask for a general.... Just put out a general notice at the Writers Guild: "If you've got any instances of prejudice?" I bet you'd be deluged, or should be. I remember talking to those guys. Many times they had scripts, good scripts, good black parts that producers turned down they couldn't get on.

FM: The head of the Writers Guild is Allen Rivkin? I'll try. You know, you could get me some of those things. If you were to think about. Cause it's hard for me.

Allen Rivkin (1903-1990), the co-founder of the Writers Guild of America in 1933, was an ex-electrician who went on to write more than 70 screenplays.

ID: It's up to the guys. I can't do it. It's not my weight to carry.

They have to do it themselves. Guys like Sam Denoff and his partner, who I can't think of [Bill Persky], told me, for example, at a Forum meeting years ago, that they had written material that had been rejected. Now, I'm telling you this personally, that this is the guy. Go contact him.

FM: Sam Denoff?

Sam Denoff (1928-2011) was a noted TV writer, best known for his two Emmy Awards for The Dick Van Dyke Show *(1961-1966), which starred besides Van Dyke, Mary Tyler Moore and Carl Reiner.*

ID: Ask him what material he had written for blacks that was rejected and why. Get some.... I hate to put these guys on the spot, in a sense, and yet there's no choice for me.

FM: You have to be honest.

ID: This is not my spot. They caught it. They caught the thing too. It happens from that side, and so it's up to that side, as far as I'm concerned, to explain it. I know that it goes on. I'm not responsible. I'm only responsible in the sense that I have to fight it.

FM: Okay. Jim Brown said that too. His remark was something to the effect, "It's not my problem, it's a white man's problem." He said, "I'm not doing anything wrong. If there's a problem, it's the white man's problem."

ID: Yeah. I'll tell you, I worked today as a director in TV, and I have a lot of guys who work for me on a set. I normally have a crew of forty, fifty people, who I know, just don't dig "niggers" at all. You know what I mean? Let alone having to take orders from one.

FM: If they want to eat, that's what they got to do.

ID: No. It's not a matter of, "wanting to eat, that's what they gotta do." It's a matter of simply a new kind of adjustment to a situation that I feel you've got to handle. You know, as a matter of fact, I don't have a particular great deal of problem with that kind of cat, because I don't have to prove anything to him. And he doesn't have to prove anything to me, except that he can do his job well, that's all.

And all I ask of him is a fair job. I don't want him to tell me how many friends he's got that's black. Or the fact that he's not prejudice, and all that kind of shit. And I'll tell him so if he comes to me with that. I'm not really interested in his prejudices. I'm only interested in how well he can perform for me.

FM: He shows how good you are.

ID: And I want him to give me his best job. And I'm gonna treat him the best way I can to get the best job out of him. That's the truth, because the way he works for me enhances my prestige. But if he doesn't work for me; if he tries to sabotage me in any way, I'm gonna fire him so fast. I'm gonna get his ass out of here as fast as I can.

FM: It's a question of survival.

ID: Right. It's just a matter of survival. I couldn't care less about how he feels about me. I don't want to socialize with him. And I don't expect him to want to socialize with me. I only expect him to produce in the way that he is supposed to be capable of producing.

FM: Tell me about what happened after *Something of Value*? What did you go on to after that?

ID: Well, I started doing small television things, Studio One, Armstrong Circle Theater, that sort of thing was going on in New York at the time; a lot of live television.

FM: Was *Nothing But a Man* the second film? Or you did others films before it?

ID: No, I worked on other films, mostly as Poitier's stunt man and stand in. And I did a couple of small parts in films, the names of which now escape me.

FM: Tell me about Poitier. What kind of guy was he to work with? And what was your view of him as you were working with him? Been a lot of criticism from the black community about him lately.

ID: Let's put it this way, Sidney Poitier and I were very close friends for a number of years. I think he's an extraordinary person, personally. And as a professional, I think he was probably as professional an actor as we've had in this business, I mean all the way around. As far as criticisms from the black community, anybody, you know, is open to criticism when you put yourself out there in these performing areas. And certainly I might have some criticisms too, but my criticisms of Mr. Poitier are kind of private criticisms, and I don't put them out on the street. And I don't think they should be, or that our dirty linen has to be washed in the street in this kind of way.

FM: Just help me on this point. The reason that I asked that is not to get you to say something that you didn't want to say, because in writing the book I'm trying to understand whether these criticisms from black professionals toward people like Poitier, or Belafonte, or Lena Horne, if there's a way of answering them: If there's a way of understanding them.

ID: Well, if one wants to understand, one can understand. You see, many of the people who are the critics of the Poitiers and the Belafontes were not around at the time the Belafontes and the Poitiers were breaking in to this business and striving to open a path, you know, to break through. It's very easy to sit back now and have certain kinds of hindsight.

FM: Monday morning quarterbacks?

ID: On the other hand, were you there, and given the same set of circumstances, I wonder how many people would have acted very differently.

FM: Or succeeded as well.

ID: Or done nearly as well as these guys did. Under the circumstances, it was some strange circumstances in those days.

FM: Let me get to the next major film. In this, after *Something of Value* comes to be *Nothing But a Man*. How did that come out?

ID: I was out here and about to do a film, as a matter of fact called *One Potato, Two Potato*. I had already agreed to do it and everything. Somebody gave me the script for this film, and I read it and flipped. Because here for the first time, in my point of view, was a potentially honest story dealing with a young black couple. A simple honest story out of the black milieu. Interestingly, though the story was written by a couple of white cats.

FM: Robert Young and Mike Roemer.

ID: Robert Young and Mike Roemer. The two guys did their homework in a very peculiar way. They went south and lived with black families for a number of months and recorded conversations, ate the same food, slept in people's homes, socialized, went to church, went into the fields, really tried to absorb the black ethos, or social environment in the southern scene. They went particularly around Birmingham, I think, something like that.

Now, in writing the story they attempted to write from a point of view of universality, which was very good in a sense. There were many things that they saw there that they thought they understood, but they really didn't. Nevertheless, I still think that that script turned out to be probably the most honest done about blacks in film that I know of in this country. There are only a couple of other things.

FM: Certainly better than *One Potato, Two Potato*.

ID: Sure, by far.

FM: There was one scene in there. The scenes when you went to visit your father [Julius Harris] in Birmingham. Just beyond belief when you saw him, and I remember the scene when you went to the bar; and you and his mistress [Gloria Foster] were there in the story, and the time you buried him, poignant, moving scenes.

ID: There were a number of very poignant, very truthful scenes in that film. Scenes that very much represented me in terms of my point of view of life at the time. There were, there were.... It was restrictive in many ways in that the guys had a certain idea of how they wanted their film. I appreciated Mike as a filmmaker very much although I have many criticisms of him in a certain kind of self-indulgence. I think he's a really brilliant filmmaker in many ways, and I was able to submit to him as an actor in the sense that actors submit to directors of a level of Bergman, Fellini, whomever.

An actor who works for this kind of filmmaker really becomes a puppet, in a sense, of the filmmaker. And many of the acting choices were not my choices at all, but the choices of the director. But I thought it was very effective in that sense because it came out, I mean the picture had his definite style, a certain kind of pseudo documentary, ponderously paced in many instances, very much lacking in physical action, but extraordinarily incisive in its truths. You know, they really got inside of certain kinds of things.

Years later, Roemer reflected on his masterpiece and said, "I have no problem at all with our intentions, and I still think in our minds and hearts we were uncompromising.... We went as far as we thought we could take a white audience at the time and still not lose them. Black audiences and critics at the time and since seem to have liked it and thought it true to their experiences.

"What bothers me is that the film isn't black enough," the 56-year-old filmmaker continued. "Things are too neat and perfect and not nearly as ambiguous as real life. Perhaps this is the fate of 'breakthrough' films."[110]

FM: She was gorgeous, Abbey Lincoln, in the film, oh my God! You must have had great times. Oh she was magnificent.

The only scene that I felt very uncomfortable with, that I didn't like in the film, was the scene with the white guy [Walter Wilson] in the gas station. That seemed too artificial and too stagy even for sixties films. When that guy came back with his friends in the car, the chewing on the gum and that kind of business. That was my only.... The other thing students seemed to react to was the fact that it ended too abruptly. The thing just ended; they wanted more to go on.

ID: Yeah, they really couldn't.

FM: Once you had made your decision, you were gonna stay.

ID: That was the end of the film. Also many times in American films, portrayals of whites in a picture involving blacks will come off as caricatures, you know, or appear to be caricatures. When in reality, there's a certain truth involved. I too felt in a certain respect that scene was like too stagy. On the other hand, I know that in many ways that was really legitimate, the kind of character that was projected by those guys was legitimate.

FM: And the fear that went on in the community was legitimate.

If you have seen the film, you'll recall that Josie (Abbey Lincoln) is rebelling against her father. A similar kind of rebellion takes place with Cicely Tyson's character in The Heart is a Lonely Hunter.[111] *Still further, Wanda (Janet MacLachlan) rebels against her father Pres. Douglas Dilman (James Earl Jones) in* The Man.[112] *It seems worth noting, therefore, that the rebellious daughter is a convention in films in general. Custen writes, "The resistance to conformity as defined by family structure is particularly strong with women. The spheres in which women are shown to excel are limited mainly to entertainment, love, education, medicine, and royalty."*[113]

ID: Sure.

FM: What were some of the things you didn't think he had the insight into? You said, "He thought he understood it but he really didn't."

ID: I don't know. I wouldn't go into it. I really don't want to put Mike down in any way. We just had some, as in anything there were some personal differences.

FM: Can you give me one anecdote that happened on the set?

ID: No. I'll tell you one thing that was important to me by way of illustration. The man I played was a workingman; and for me, I had to wear a mustache. Mike and Bob never understood that, and I don't think they understand it today. And I tried to convince them by showing them black magazines, black pictures; by demonstrating how many black men in all walks of life, you'll find mustaches. It's just a truth in American life that, certainly ten years ago, and even today, somewhere near eighty percent of black males, particularly black males on a certain lower economic level, wore hair on their face, long sideburns, mustaches, beards. Today many of the guys are wearing beards but with blacks and Latinos it just is a consistent reality. Cats dig a certain....

FM: Sense of identity?

ID: I'm not sure. I'm sure that some psychiatrist could come up with some weird theory about the ramifications of this having to do with a lack of male identity, or matriarchal repression, and all kinds of weird kooky theories; you know what I mean? And they may be right. I don't know; I don't even care. What was important to me was that I projected a cat out of a certain kind of scene as he should be projected. Now without the mustache, I wouldn't have been believed, I know it, not in my community. I just know that.

FM: I never even noticed it.

ID: No, I know a lot of people would never notice it. But they fought me with such really, I thought, not very logical reasoning. There's this whole thing about a mustache having an identity, or being identified with villains and that sort of thing, which I think is preposterous really. That's not really true. On the American screen, some of America's biggest stars always wore mustaches: Clark Gable always wore a mustache except for his first few pictures. Robert Taylor was noted for his mustache; and a number of other guys. So it's not really true. It's just that for some reason white males have a certain thing about blacks, wanting them to more closely resemble them in order for them to be able to feel comfortable with them.

FM: That's what the big argument has always been. They always wanted black guys to play white parts rather than have them play themselves.

ID: Absolutely, and I think that's wrong.

FM: Can you tell me, without putting down Mike, what your favorite scene was in the film? Or the scene that you felt was most honest, or most really hit it for you, as you look back on it.

ID: I don't know. There were so many, many things in the film. I think it's the most meaningful thing I've had anything to do with. I can't lie about that.

FM: What happened after that? The next performance? What happened?

ID: I think I went back to working in television, the same kind of thing that I'd been doing. I've been fairly lucky, been able to work fairly consistently in television over the years. I'm primarily known as a television actor; you know you get categorized.

FM: Yeah.

ID: I've been primarily known as a television actor, and I've made a living, not a good living, but I barely made a living in television over the years.

FM: Have you done any movies since *Nothing But a Man*?

ID: I've done a couple, and they've been mainly really meaningless, pretty terrible things having nothing to do with anything.

FM: I was talking with Cicely [Tyson], and one of the things I came away with, she said it, and I think that she's absolutely right. She felt that if she'd been a white woman, she would be working regularly in films today; and she would have good roles and frequent roles. Because she is a black woman, she's only appeared in three movies even though she was absolutely superb in *The Heart is a Lonely Hunter,* just great in that film: And now she just made her first movie. Do you think you were forced into being a TV actor, or you did it out of preference?

ID: I don't think there was any preference afforded me.

FM: Just what worked for you?

ID: I just took advantage of whatever opportunities came my way, I think, and I think I made; I took good advantage of those opportunities as a matter of fact. I've no hang-ups about being a black actor and no illusions about it either. I don't think that it's for me to conjecture about what would have happened had I been a white guy in this industry. I never wanted to be a white guy, I never thought about it.

FM: What about your success in motion pictures like *Nothing*

But a Man, and yet there were no roles coming for you in other motion pictures after that.

ID: Yes, but I understood that. I understand that. There's nobody making any black pictures, and we have no black producers really.

[BREAK]

FM: Let me see if I understand what Jim meant by the system. In other words, put your money into it, make your films, get enough power so that you can do what you want. That really isn't the way that he put it.

The action really isn't in the performing aspect as much as it is in knowing the craft, the directing, the writing, the screen writing, the producing, knowing the business aspect. And when you know that, then you can make any kind of films you want. Otherwise, it's just a glory trip. You take one film; you get a big role in that film, and then you're out. And what the white guy's doing is really exploiting you for his purposes. And if they say to call that guy "Honkey," or call a guy "Whitey." If it's gonna make money, they'll let you call him that as much as you want so long as it makes money for them, and then they get rid of you. That was his argument.

ID: That makes sense to me. We live in a capitalist society. That's very annoying. That's very distressing to me. Anyway, we live in a capitalistic society. It's...this is a capital-based economic scene here. Now, in order to survive in that scene, you have to think in capitalist terms, you have to understand certain fundamentals about what capitalism is. We're not geared to think that way in this society. We've been geared to being performers and consumers in this society. I think that has been intentionally so. I think this is capitalist society, so I have no illusions about that, that by design, certain kinds of schools are set up in the South after reconstruction, you know, liberal arts type of institutions. And I think it's by design that we see a certain kind of guidance, a certain kind of sense of direction in this society.

At that point we become a captive consumer in this society. We are the captive consumer market in the society, twenty six, twenty eight million black people who work only to spend, you know, only to consume as a capital market. What we have to do, in terms of understanding capitalism, is to develop in a way to make use of this captive market. Now the trouble with the market is it never has any opportunity to develop any ways to take advantage of its own worth. It cannot exploit itself really; it's just not in a position to.

FM: You think that's going to change though? There's a lot of movements into the....

ID: Well, I don't know whether it will change or not. We've got a couple of choices. We've got several choices in this kind of a scene. You either succumb to it, or you try to overcome it and involve yourself in it and become on top of it, or you try to change it by showing what is in favor of what can be. I don't know. There are many different views on this society, as to what to do, what the solution is.

FM: You're going now into the direction arena rather than performing?

ID: I've always been trying to get into the direction arena. The only way I could get into this business when I started out, because I went to school, grad school doing production—direction, production, that sort of thing. The only way to get into the business was as an actor. And I felt I was as capable really as most who were out there, nothing extraordinary, but not the worst cat around either. Because frankly, many of the black actors, some of them, the cat didn't know, the guy who was producing, didn't know where to get a competent black actor so he picked up, maybe, the guy-next-door's maid, or some guy down on the street. And he's still doing that, really. He still is...displays a remarkable inability to.... Well, what am I trying to say? He can't find, he doesn't know how to find people, black people, who have certain skills.

FM: But you wouldn't want me to argue that there aren't people with those skills around?

ID: No. It's very obvious there are many. You can go to any black drama festival in the South and find numbers of actors.

FM: Right from the beginning!

ID: All the way, every single year down there they have festivals. Every black college has a drama group. Every black high school in the South damn near has a drama group.

FM: So why don't they do that?

ID: I don't know. Why do they reach for sports, for guys like Jim Brown? Because Jim Brown is a name to exploit? Nothing wrong with that in one sense, because they exploited Chuck Connors' name as a baseball player.

Chuck Connors (1921-1992) played baseball with the Brooklyn Dodgers (one game in 1949) and Chicago Cubs (over sixty games in 1951). He also played professional basketball before going into film and television. His most successful role was as Lucas McCain in the hit ABC TV series The Rifleman *that ran for five years beginning in 1958.*[114]

FM: Woody Strode got his break that way.

ID: Sure. But this is a constant thing with us. They even put out Althea Gibson in films years ago, the great tennis player.

Known to many as "the female Jackie Robinson," Gibson (1927-2003) broke the color barrier in both tennis and golf. She remains one of the greatest female athletes of the twentieth century.

FM: Sonja Henie too.

ID: Except that Sonja Henie at least was doing what she was skilled at doing, she was skating.

Sonja Henie (1912-1969) was a Norwegian ice skating star whose exploits in three consecutive Olympics, starting in 1928, led to a film contract with Twentieth Century-Fox in 1936.

ID: They didn't hire Althea to play tennis. They hired Althea to play a maid on some damned plantation with a "Mammy" yoke around her head, that kind of crap.

Dixon is referring to Althea Gibson's role as the servant Lukey in John Ford's The Horse Soldiers.[115]

FM: And it was a "one shot deal."

ID: Of course it was. Sure they paid her ten thousand bucks, or whatever, which is a drop in the bucket in this kind of industry. They don't care a damn about that. The idea was to exploit this woman's name.

FM: She went along with it. She wanted the ten thousand bucks.

ID: I don't know what to say about that. Am I to say that...am I to put Althea down for going along with this? What am I to really say? You watch...take a look at what many of the black actors have done over the years in terms of allowing themselves to become exploited, and ask them "Why," and you come up with some pretty good answers as a matter of fact from some of them.

FM: They wanted to work.

ID: It's not just wanting to work either. That's not the only answer.

FM: But that's what you get from most of them: Or some of them will say they wanted to have a positive black image, or they wanted to have a black image on the screen so that the black kids could identify with them instead of empathizing with a white actor.

ID: On the one hand, I could put down certain kinds of "Mammy" parts and "Yes Miss, Liza" and all that kind of.... Well, for God's sake, one of the most vivid images I saw as a child was....

FM: Hattie McDaniel.

ID: At an early age.... No, no, no, no, not Hattie McDaniel. It was an early version of *Imitation of Life* [1934],[116] which I believe starred Claudette Colbert and Louise Beavers.

FM: Yes.

ID: Colbert and Louise Beavers. And I remember my mother and grandmother went to see that damn picture every time it came to Harlem. And they could bring it back twice a year for ten years, it didn't matter. They'd fill the Loews' Victoria Theater with blacks who wanted to see the picture.

Well, there's a reason for that, and the idiots never saw the reason until...and they still don't see it. They're now exploiting black films for the same reason. But they don't see the reason. They don't understand it. They don't even know what happened that causes a *Shaft* to make a lot of money, or a *Cotton* to make a lot of money, or even a *Sweetback*, as grotesque as that was. They don't understand why that sells, the white market.

So what they do constantly is try to imitate something of that. So they're coming out now. There are at least a dozen pictures on the make in Hollywood now, involving either Shafts or Super Shafts, or female Shafts, or Super Pimps, and Whores and Con Men. You know. What is all of that crap? They don't really understand what has happened here, what the market is that's being exploited.

FM: What do you see it as?

ID: I don't want to tell you what I see it as. I wouldn't dare.

FM: Why?

ID: Because I want to exploit that market myself. Because it's important to me that I produce the kind of film that will not only exploit the market, but will open up many areas for the market in terms of giving people, black people, the kind of images they *really* want to see. And I believe I know what those images are. You understand? I believe I understand. I believe the other cat doesn't. But I also know that if I tell him what those images are, he'll try and use them. They've done worse over the years. So there's no point in my giving you.... It's nothing to do with you personally. It's just a matter of these kinds of things have been done over and over again.

FM: Do you think the answer lies with formula films souped up like the Thriller, or the Western or the Comedy? Do you think that's the role for a black filmmaker?

ID: No.

FM: That's what's being suggested.

ID: I think it's not the role for any filmmaker. I think it's tragic that America is set up that way. So we're forced to go in these kinds of directions in terms of making films. Because, in order to continue making films, you have to make the same kind of profit; you don't just make a profit, baby. You gotta make the same kind of profit to continue making films in this country.

And as a result, art in films tends to be more the accident than the rule in this country. It's kind of sad. I think that will change though in the future. I think we have to change that kind of thing. I think young Americans are thinking about this now, about things such as this. Not only in the area of filmmaking, but in other areas as well, other areas of American life.

FM: It was interesting what you said about *Sweetback,* because a lot of people that I met in New York who were very active in the black scene, particularly when I was there, they were talking about the flag, the liberation flag being flown in Newark over the school and how important that was. They claimed that *Sweetback* was the greatest black film ever made, that this would be a long way to beat.

What I am referring to here is the conversation I had with Leroy and Pearl Bowser in Every Step a Struggle.[117]

FM: And the argument that they used was that what makes it a great film was the positive, strong image it has of the black person. And whether Van Peebles' acting is amateurish, or whether the film is not well written, has no bearing on it. When you talk about things being good or bad, you're trying to play the white man's game. You're using his standards, his concepts, and his view. And you've got to be black to understand why *Sweetback* is so great. That's why I was interested in your comment on it, when you talked about the images, and you talked about *Sweetback* not being that good a film.

ID: Did I say that?

FM: Yes.

ID: I said that when?

FM: You said *Sweetback* was something to the effect of exploiting the images, not understanding why.

ID: No. I said that white filmmakers, in making the kind of film that they're making now, imitations of *Shaft*, of *Sweetback*, etc., are attempting to exploit an area that they don't really understand. They still do not understand what made those films make money.

FM: I see, I see.

ID: I said that *Sweetback* was grotesque as a film. I might say that Fellini's *Satyricon* was grotesque as a film. I have made really no comment, positive or negative, about *Sweetback*, but let's put it this way, I don't agree. Other than that, I wouldn't make any comment.

FM: I'm just trying to get a handle on standards.

ID: In terms of what you stated where certain kinds of views back East, or wherever. All I would have to say is "I don't agree."

FM: I'm just asking the question, not so much to pin it down to *Sweetback*, as for myself trying to understand if there's something I ought to know about or I ought to sense or see when I'm judging these films, that from a black man's point of view he would see and I couldn't. Is there a handle? Is it legitimate to talk about films being good or bad in the way we've always talked about, it in terms of production, in terms of design, in terms of acting, screenplay and direction? Are those legitimate criteria for any film as you see it as a director, actor, and a black person?

ID: I think those are part of the criteria, yes. But I think that there's more than that, you know, to judging a film. Certainly. I think there's more than that to judging any film, American film, European film, or whatever! I think there's more to it than just the fundamental skills involved and the quality or the use of those skills.

As to what those particular aesthetic values are by which I would say judge a black film, or other blacks would judge a black film, as opposed to judging other films, meaning European, Japanese, or Chinese, or American, or whatever other kind of film, I'm not prepared to really say what those aesthetic areas really are. I'm sure that some cats would come up with certain explanations. I don't even want to bother with that any more. I would rather make the film. The problem is getting the opportunity to make the film.

FM: That's the next thing I want to come to now. With all your background, experience and so on, you're still having trouble getting the money to get this *Spook* off the ground.

ID: *The Spook Who Sat by the Door,* the name of the property that I've been trying the hardest to get off the ground. And there was a basic reason for that. Certain things about the film due to repulse....

FM: The Establishment?

ID: Those members of the establishment to whom I have to go to get funds.

FM: Mostly bankers?

ID: Bankers, financiers, film men, you know, filmmakers. I've been to every major studio with the film. I've been to most of the known independent film backers, and I've been even to foreign governments as a matter of fact. One of them even indicated there was a little pressure against supporting me in this venture.

FM: Can you tell me what those repulsive images are? What is it that...

ID: I'm not exactly sure. I would prefer that you ask John Calley, for example, at Warner Brothers. What repelled him about *The Spook Who Sat by the Door*? [118]

John Calley (1930-2011) was a top executive at Warner Brothers for many years. Among his most successful movies were The Exorcist *(1973),* Superman *(1978), and* The Remains of the Day *(1993). He was honored with the Motion Picture Academy's Irving Thalberg Award on Nov. 11, 2009.*

ID: I would prefer that you ask Jim....

FM: Jim Aubrey at MGM?

ID: Yeah. Jim Aubrey, ask him what repelled him about the film.

Jim T. Aubrey, Jr. (1918-1994), made a name for himself both in television and film. A former president of CBS Television, who was fired in the mid-sixties; he went on to run MGM Studios up to the early 1970s.

ID: I think they better tell you themselves. Marty Baum at ABC, ask him.

Martin Baum (1924-2010) was a famous talent agent who during the Hollywood transition years took charge of ABC's film division in the late sixties. Among his many, many famous clients were the likes of Sidney Poitier and Harry Belafonte.

ID: Even though he, there were many things about it that appealed to him, there were some things that he rejected about it and was unable to support it unless those things were changed. And we couldn't change those things because those things are important to the black community with regards to this film.

I know this film would make an excellent film. Many blacks know this film would make an excellent film. But I've been unable to get that kind of money. I can't get that kind of money that is necessary to make a film of this caliber, of quality from the black community. Part of the problem is…

FM: Why? Ossie Davis has got a company. Poitier and Belafonte have got a company. They don't want to support this? They're not interested in this?

ID: No. Tell me what they've done. They're not interested in supporting this particular film. At least they haven't indicated any interest.

FM: The reason I ask you that, you mention black people…

ID: I've been to a couple of them, yeah.

FM: Why? Are the same things repulsive to them as they were to the white producers?

ID: In some senses, maybe some of these things frighten certain middle-class blacks more than they do certain…

FM: Cause they want to get a certain image on the screen, and they don't want it destroyed?

ID: Yeah. They're afraid of depicting certain kinds of images, and they're afraid that it might disturb the kind of status quo. I don't know, the fear of God. But there are many fears involved, and I've talked to many upper middle-class people who have the money, who can afford to invest.

FM: You're not talking serious money, you're talking about a low-budget film, or...?

ID: Eight hundred and fifty thousand dollars. That's a low-budget film in Hollywood terms. Not a low-budget film in Hollywood black terms. Because all the so called "nigger" films they're making these days are coming out for less than a half a million dollars.

FM: *Sweetback*, and *Shaft*, and all of those?

ID: Sure. All of these things have been done for nothing.

FM: And they're making money...all of them.

ID: That's the whole idea, to exploit the black actor, to get the guy who plays the lead part for six hundred dollars a week. Which to him it seems like big money because he's just been working a regular factory job, or maybe modeling, doing some modeling pictures and what not. He doesn't understand anything about what film salaries are about, and how if you make a thousand dollars a week for six weeks and don't do another picture. It still means you made only six thousand dollars in a year. You know what I mean?

All that doesn't register with him right then. So you've got this cat who's ready to be exploited, and as a result they've got all these people working at minimum level salaries. A few actors get paid minimum salaries, a few technicians, a few token black technicians, are hired to work under white technicians that are paid minimal salaries. And the picture exploits the black market entirely and makes millions of dollars for white producers and white distributors to spread out among themselves. And the black community really is the one that suffers economically and aesthetically from my point of view. Because, in my point of view, the images are not necessarily constructive images, the kind of images that black people want or need to see.

FM: The impression I get from some of the people is that they think the black audience is made up of morons. That even if you give them a bad product, so long as it's black, they're gonna come.

They don't think that if the black audience sees two or three bad films they're gonna stop coming to black films. They think you can show them anything; and so long as it's black, they're gonna go.

ID: Well, that's been a traditional pattern of thought for filmmakers over the years in this kind of film. No doubt that many black filmmakers are taking other parts as filmmakers generally, and their points of view.

This theory has been going on for years. We do films geared to certain age levels in this business. It used to be to the twelve-year-old mind. I know certain, specific programs, including one that I was associated with for a period of time; it was geared to the eight-year-old mind. It was designed that way. I mean really, we literally said that. That's what we do. Television is that kind of thing, man. You don't appeal to any great levels of taste. You appeal to numbers because you're trying to sell a product. You're trying to sell numbers of these products, not taste.

FM: Well, the name of the game is money if it's a business first, then that's what you have to do.

ID: Well that's what we're talking about. Is that what we have to do? Is that what it's really all about in this country? If it isn't, let's make up our minds about that.

FM: I get the impression that that's the system.

ID: Well then let's stop bullshitting each other about what the system really is. And let's stop bs'ing each other about what the American Dream is all about. If it's really dollars, then let's say that it's really about dollars. And let's get blacks together that understand that what we have to do to achieve success in this society is to achieve dollars, that's all that counts if that's really what it is. I'm not sure that that is really what it is. And if that is really what it is, I'm not sure if that's good. And if it's not good, or if it is good, well if it's not good, I'm not sure then that we shouldn't be about trying to change that kind of a system, do something about it.

FM: Well, I have the security of a job, I'm not hurt one way or the other, but I think that the guy who's trying to make a living in the film has got to…

ID: You keep talking about trying to make a living, and you keep falling back on this weird cop out of "my job."

Goddamn! Goddamn! I haven't heard recently of too many

people starving to death in this country. I mean, I know that there are many people on the poverty level in this country, and there are thousands of people with hungry, hungry bellies, understand? But somehow people manage somehow to survive in this country.

And I've come to find that out. It may have taken me a long time to find that out. But I know at this point that my family is not going to starve because I tell some cats, "I'm not going to do that shit!" You know. I'll find another way to make a living. I may not make a living in this business. But a living is available to me as long as I've got a back and a certain kind of a mind.

FM: Same thing as integrity.

ID: Yeah, I think. A certain kind of integrity, we could carry this to a degree where it becomes very foolish and insignificant as to the way we handle ourselves in terms of integrity. You can say well I won't do anything at all, and it can become grotesque.

One of the better-noted black actors of the early part of this century was a man named Charles [Sidney] Gilpin [1878-1930], who did a play on Broadway. I don't know the name right now [Eugene O'Neill's *The Emperor Jones*]. He became very famous for a certain portrayal, and who was invited out here to Hollywood to play a part in a picture and they wanted him to say, "Yessuh." And he said, "No Sah. I will not say Yessuh." And it went into a whole big thing, and he got kicked out of the industry. They wouldn't hire him anymore. He wouldn't get any more jobs on Broadway; and the poor old guy wound up running an elevator in East Harlem some place, really poverty stricken.

Here's a guy whose picture is on walls at many of the black theaters around the country, interracial theater groups, and there's a Gilpin monument at Karamu House, Karamu Players. Maybe not monuments, but some kind of reminders of him, tributes to him in many schools across the country, and the cat was working as an elevator operator in New York barely making thirty dollars a week, barely surviving. You know, It's a matter of what you want to do.

The choice is yours, it belongs to each individual.

FM: *Nothing But a Man.*[119]

ID: Right. I dwelt so much on some of the outsiders, or unequipped people that would come into the business as blacks, but we have some very well equipped blacks in this business, some very fine black actors who have had very limited opportunities. And it shows itself continually like when a guy, Ray St. Jacques, who'se been around fifteen, eighteen years, almost twenty years, if he gets discovered in a film like *The Comedians,* it's kind of absurd. It's not that he wasn't talented before. When Roscoe Lee Browne suddenly becomes noted for performances in *The Blacks,* [*Black Like Me*], or later in such a weird film as Lord Byron Jones [*The Liberation of L. B. Jones*], which has nothing to do with the kind of talent that the man really has, it's just terrible.

FM: It's a good opening for the book.

ID: Yes. Cicely of course you know; Diana Sands. But you can name fantastic....James Earl Jones and I went to school together at the Wing. And he spent many years doing little Off-Broadway plays, sometimes twenty, twenty-five plays a year for carfare, and he was always this kind of creative, really fantastic talent. Only in the last couple of years has he been really discovered, and still not meaningfully; not to the point where he's become a box-office attraction in any way. You know. There's some very talented people around. And they are some gutsy people, too, man; to stay in this business all these years with the kind of talent they have.

FM: And to be so outspoken. It's one thing to stay around, and another thing to have the courage to fight it and still stick.

[BREAK]

ID: Being able to have the level of acceptance as an actor in black communities in this country, let's say like Satchel Page had in baseball when he played in the black leagues, you gotta be all-stars really. So I wouldn't make a great living. I don't know if I'll ever make a great living anyway, but I would survive and to have achieved in my own area, in my own way would mean a hell of a lot more to me.

FM: I'm curious. You keep saying 'survive.' I always got the impression that if a TV program ran for X amount of years then you were set for life. It [*Hogan's Heroes*] ran for eight [sic] years. That's all false right?

ID: That's all bull. If you happen to be a star in a TV show, and if you make a salary of a few thousand dollars a week and that sort of thing, then maybe you'll be all set for a while. But if you happen to play a bit role in a series like *Hogan's Heroes;* no. It doesn't work that way. I get my residuals once in a while, but it's nothing like people imagine. There are no rich black actors except perhaps Poitier.

FM: Poitier? Belafonte?

ID: Belafonte is a singer primarily. I'm not saying that he can't act. But I'm speaking of a cat that makes his living primarily as a dramatic actor, and Belafonte has made his living in many ways. He's made his millions in terms of the recording industry. Sammy Davis, who also acts, is primarily a variety performer and, you know, probably he's the most extraordinary performer in the world; I think he is. I really think as a performer, he is out of sight.

FM: Edward Gordone is doing the musical, or book and lyrics for *Three Guys in Brooklyn*, for Sammy. And Chuck told me that this is going to be Sammy's swan song. He's looking to make his bow and get out, retire.

The musical never materialized. Davis did do a television musical, Sammy *(1974), which was little more than a sixty-minute one-man show.*

I was trying to convince Roscoe, by the way, I told you, that I thought a great part for Roscoe would be either Bert Williams, or Charles Gilpin....

ID: I do not know just how valid is it to make films about these historic dudes; but how valuable, how commercially successful will they be? Is it possible, you understand?

FM: Oh yeah. The biggest moneymaker last year, or the year before, was *Patton*. I mean you could make a film about Marcus Garvey.

ID: I mean that's what I believe. Try discussing this with some of these Hollywood producers, you know, someone like Aubrey. Try to tell him what a personality in black life, like a cat like Marcus Garvey was. He doesn't even understand, because he's never heard of Marcus Garvey. It's crazy. Most of these guys don't even know who our heroes are. And they may take a guy like....

There was a valid black American hero, like a Nat Turner; and they tried to make him a fag and a sex deviant. And they go in so many new directions with the character, you know. They shouldn't be able to do it, for Christ sake.

FM: I agree. What was the inside story on that film?

ID: I don't know, but it's like saying George Washington is a fag. You can't do that in American films. I could not for anything get up and make a film about Abraham Lincoln saying that he was a sex deviant, that he lifted chicks underskirts and sniffed them. Now he may have done that, but I couldn't do that. How the hell are they gonna do that with my man? It's wrong. I think we should have shot them down, if they did it.

FM: Have there been any film outside of *Nothing But a Man* that really turns you on?

ID: Not a great deal, no. I've done some...Only a few things that I've done have been, you know, were there moments in them. They've been kind of meaningful. Most of the films that have been done about blacks in this country, I don't, I think are basically cop outs and really phony. Some of them are stilted, kind of preachy left wing liberal films. I don't know. Nothing that was real and honest for the most part. The most honest usage of blacks I've seen in films come from France.

FM: *Black Orpheus*?[120]

ID: Well, yes, *Black Orpheus*, which is made by French cats in Brazil; which I thought was a really very heavy film, really out of sight. I was really moved by some of the realities of the film. It had nothing to do with the two leads in the film which I thought were really not very good as players. But the real people of the film, God, there was a girl in that film that was so unbelievably alive, a creature that you just adored her from the moment that she fell on the screen. The other people in this, there was a guy and a couple of kids, and they just came into your life. It was out of sight, a beautiful film.

FM: How did you like *Putney Swope*?

ID: No comment.

FM: One of the things that struck me, that really got a response, I guess was *Cotton Comes to Harlem*. It was the funniest film I've seen so far. I'm just trying to say what works for me.

ID: Criticisms. It ain't one way or another on these terrible films.

Postscript

Ivan Dixon, the Harlem troublemaker, overcame many challenges to emerge an acclaimed actor and director, as well an admired advocate for black causes. And his remarkable journey is only one of many forgotten or overlooked such adventures in the history of the African-American experience. If this chapter succeeds in convincing you his story remains only one of many other stories that need retelling, than this profile of Ivan would have been worth the effort. As for the wonderful man himself, I choose to remember him in the way he once described Beneatha in *A Raisin in the Sun*. Playing Assagi, he named her, "Alaiyo." When she asked what it meant, he said, 'One for whom Bread—Food—is not enough."[121]

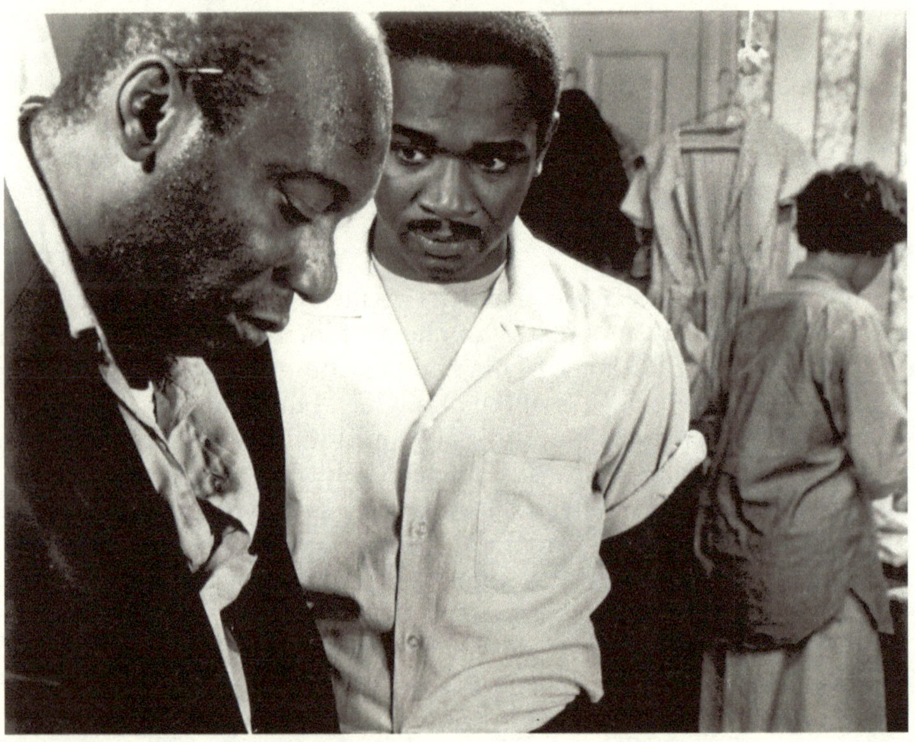

21. In this crucial scene from *Nothing But a Man*, Duff (Ivan Dixon) realizes he does not want to end up like his tragic father Will Anderson (Julius Harris).

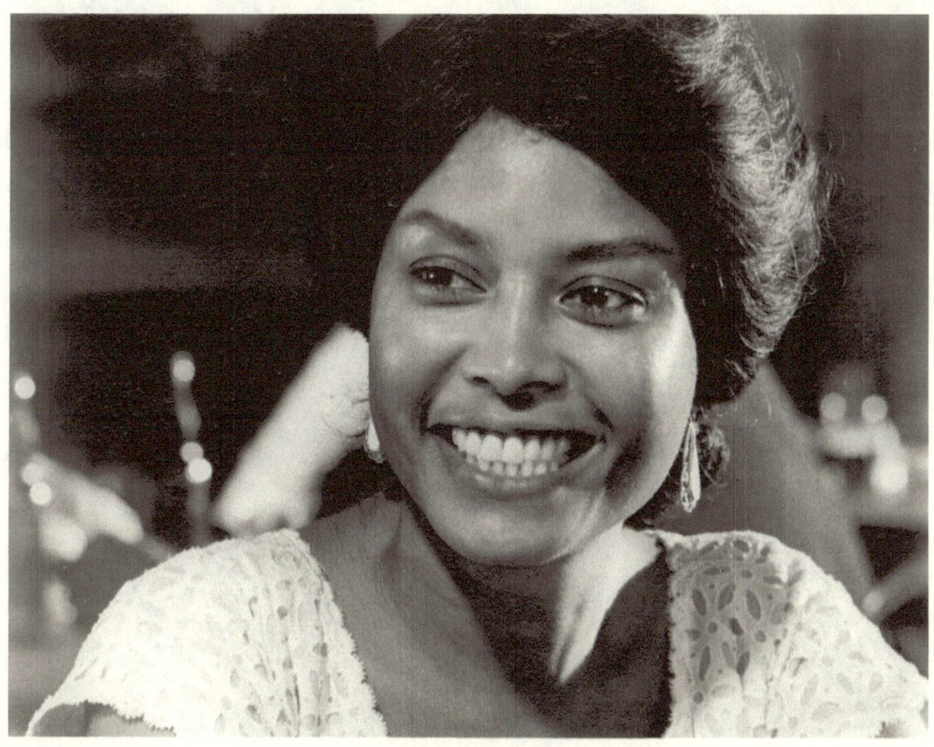

22. Abbey Lincoln, who found herself alienated from musical circles in the sixties, gave a brilliant performance as Josie in Michael Roemer's *Nothing But a Man* (1964).

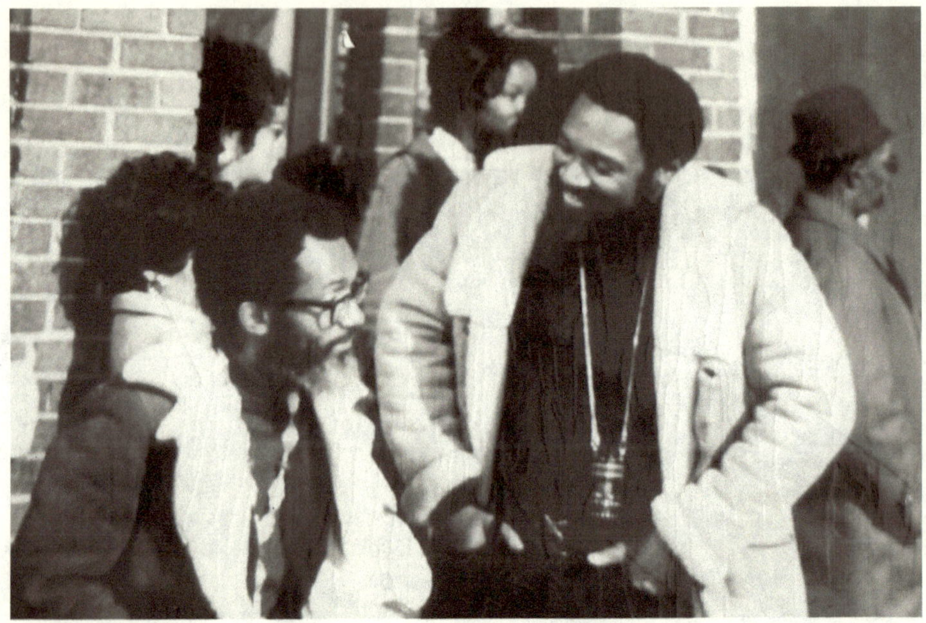

23. Author Sam Greenlee (left) who produced Director Ivan Dixon's *The Spook Who Sat by the Door* (1973). Dixon is on the right. Howard Morehouse is the photographer.

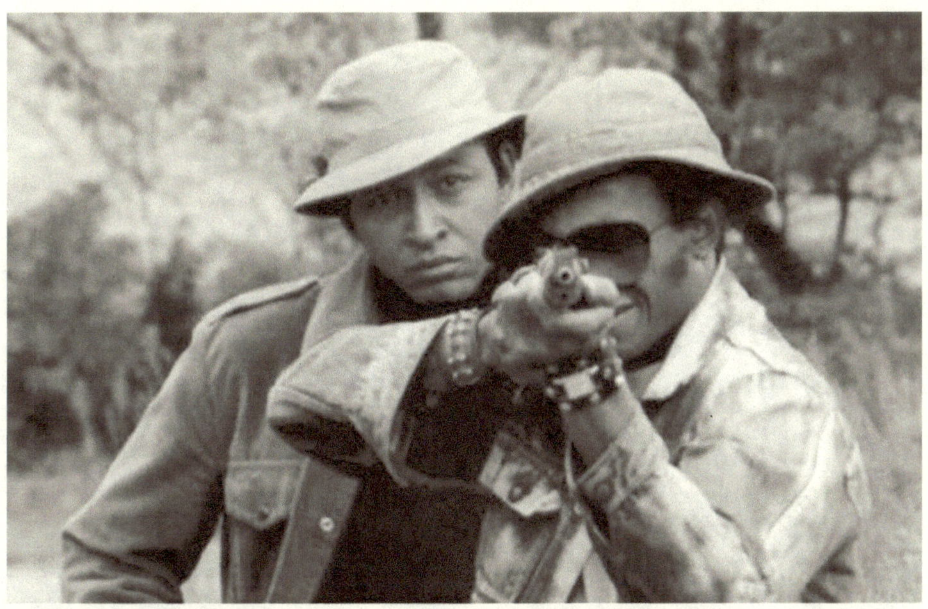

24. After leaving the CIA, ex-agent Dan Freeman (Lawrence Cook) begins organizing a street gang called The Cobras into black revolutionists. One recruit is Stud Davis (Don Blakely), holding a rifle. Howard Morehouse is the photographer in this scene from Ivan Dixon's *The Spook Who Sat by the Door* (1973).

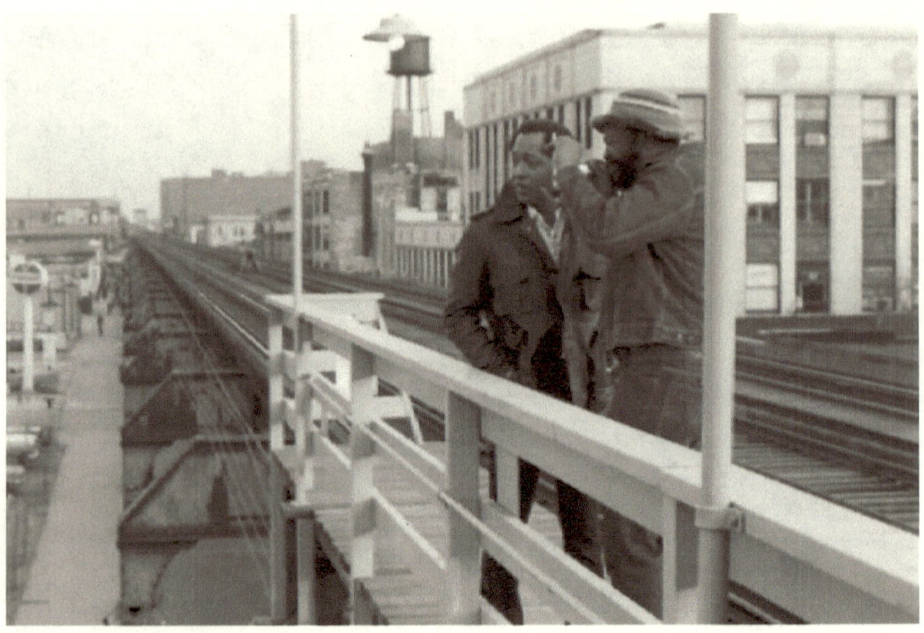

25. Dan Freeman (Lawrence Cook), the secret leader of the Freedom Fighters, checks out potential targets with Do-Daddy Dean (Paul Butler) in a scene from Ivan Dixon's *The Spook Who Sat By the Door* (1973). Howard Morehouse is the photographer.

Notes

[1] Poitier, *This Life*, 341.

[2] Lorraine Hansberry, *A Raisin in the Sun: The Unfilmed Original Script* (New York: Signet Books, 1994), 198.

[3] Walter Lippmann, *Public Opinion* (New York: Macmillan Company, 1965), 80-1.

[4] Daniel J. Leab, *From Sambo to Superspade: The Black Experience in Motion Pictures* (Boston: Houghton Mifflin, 1975), 201-02.

[5] Poitier, *This Life*, 214.

[6] Cripps, *Making Movies Black: The Hollywood Message Movies from World War II to the Civil Rights Era*.

[7] Diawara, Manthia, ed. *Black American Cinema* (London and New York: Routledge, 1993).

[8] Bogle, *Blacks in American Films and Television: An Encyclopedia*, 113.

[9] Nina Simone, "Forever Young, Gifted & Black: Songs of Freedom and Spirit," (New York: RCA Legacy Recordings, 2006).

[10] Brenda Scott Royce, *Hogan's Heroes: Behind the Scenes at Stalag 13* (Los Angeles: Renaissance Books, 1998), 106.

[11] Roberta Brandes Gratz, "Ivan Dixon: A Choice of Heroes," *New York Post*, June 17, 1967, 35.

[12] Staff, "The Sergeant's Hard Climb from the Ranks," *TV Guide* (1967): 35.

[13] Gratz, "Ivan Dixon: A Choice of Heroes," 35.

[14] Royce, *Hogan's Heroes: Behind the Scenes at Stalag 13*, 106.

[15] Bogle, *Blacks in American Films and Television: An Encyclopedia*, 113-14.

[16] Gratz, "Ivan Dixon: A Choice of Heroes," 35.

[17] Royce, *Hogan's Heroes: Behind the Scenes at Stalag 13*, 107.

[18] John Gennari, E-Mail, Nov. 28, 2012.

[19] Charley Gerard, *Jazz in Black and White: Race, Culture, and Identity in the Jazz Community* (Westport, Connecticut: Praeger, 1998), 2-3.

[20] Steve Race, "Linear Notes for "Time Out," in *Time Out: The Dave Brubeck Quartet* (New York: Sony Music Entertainment, 1959).

[21] Gerard, *Jazz in Black and White: Race, Culture, and Identity in the Jazz Community*, xv.

[22] *Jazz in Black and White: Race, Culture, and Identity in the Jazz Community*, 4.

[23] Gennari.

[24] Gabbard, *Jammin' at the Margins: Jazz and the American Cinema*, 103-07.

[25] Martin Ritt, "Edge of the City (Aka a Man Is Ten Feet Tall)," (USA: MGM, 1957).

[26] Gratz, "Ivan Dixon: A Choice of Heroes," 35.

[27] Richard Brooks, "Something of Value," (USA: MGM, 1957).

[28] Staff, "Movies: Gory Indictment," *Good Housekeeping* 144, no. 6 (1957): 236-37.

[29] John McCarten, "The Current Cinema: Mau Mau," *The New Yorker* 33, no. May 18 (1957): 146.

[30] Bosley Crowther, "Screen: Racial Conflict," *New York Times*, May 11, 1957, 24.

[31] Staff, "Into Africa's Depths," *Newsweek* 49, May (1957).

[32] Sidney Poitier, *The Measure of a Man: A Spiritual Autobiography* (New York: Harper One, 2000), 100.

[33] Stanley Kramer, "The Defiant Ones," (USA: United Artists, 1958).

[34] Poitier, *This Life*, 214.

[35] Joseph, *Dark Days, Bright Nights: From Black Power to Barack Obama*, 53.

[36] Michael A. Schultz, "To Be Young, Gifted and Black," (1972).

[37] Royce, *Hogan's Heroes: Behind the Scenes at Stalag 13*, 52.

[38] Bruce Weber, "Philip Rose, 89, 'Raisin' and 'Purlie' Producer," *New York Times*, June 2 2011, B18.

[39] Staff, "Lorraine Hansberry, 34, Wrote 'Raisin in the Sun'," *Boston Globe* 1965, 20.

[40] Petrie, "A Raisin in the Sun."

[41] Sieving, *Soul Searching: Black-Themed Cinema from the March on Washington to the Rise of Blaxploitation*, 1.

[42] Cited in Mapp, 51.

[43] Schultz, "To Be Young, Gifted and Black."

[44] Bob Morris, "Honoring Lorraine Hansberry," *New York Times*, February 11, 1996, 61.

[45] Staff, "700 Attend Hansberry Services," *Boston Globe*, January 17, 1965, 79.

[46] Carl Lerner, "Black Like Me," (USA: Continental Distributing, 1964).

[47] Larry Peerce, "One Potato, Two Potato," (USA: Cinema V 1964).

[48] Reelblack, "Ivan Dixon - Legendary Actor & Filmmaker (Interview)," in *YouTube* (USA 2008).

[49] Staff, "Brochure for Nothing But a Man," ed. Brandon Films (New York: Brandon Films, 1966), 1.

[50] Sieving, *Soul Searching: Black-Themed Cinema from the March on Washington to the Rise of Blaxploitation*.

[51] Sheila Rule, "Black Film Portrait Onscreen: Black Lives Reflected in 60's Film," *New York Times* 1993, C13-4.

[52] Staff, "Brochure for Nothing but a Man," 5.

[53] Rule, "Black Film Portrait Onscreen: Black Lives Reflected in 60's Film," C16.

[54] Ibid.

[55] Ibid.

[56] Michael Roemer, "Production Notes for Nothing But a Man," (1964): 1.

[57] Vicki Vasilopoulos, "New Life for a 1964 Film: Enjoying the Success of a First Directorial Effort," *New York Times* 2004, 1.

[58] Roemer, "Production Notes for Nothing But a Man," 2.

[59] Ibid.

[60] Kofsky, *John Coltrane and the Jazz Revolution of the 1960s*.

[61] John Fordham, "Abbey Lincoln Obituary: Jazz Singer, Actor and Civil Rights Activist Strongly Influenced by Billie Holiday," *The Guardian* (2010): 1.

[62] Staff, "People Are Talking About," *Jet* 1972.

[63] Keith Thursby, "Abbey Lincoln Dies at 80; Jazz Singer, Actress, Civil Rights Advocate," *Los Angeles Times*, August 15, 2010, 1.

[64] Poitier, *This Life*, 170, 79.

[65] Joseph, *Dark Days, Bright Nights: From Black Power to Barack Obama*, 1166-81.

[66] Nat Hentoff, "Linear Notes for *Straight Ahead*," (New York: Candid Records, 1961).

[67] Kofsky, *John Coltrane and the Jazz Revolution of the 1960s*, 123.

[68] Max Schudel, "Jazz Singer, Actress Abbey Lincoln Dies at 80," *Washington Post*, August 15, 2010, 1.

[69] Nate Chinen, "A Style Lasting Beyond a Lifetime," *New York Times*, August 28, 2010, 1.

[70] Frank Manchel, "Film Study: Nothing But a Man," *Media and Methods* 4, no. 2 (1967).

[71] Vasilopoulos, "New Life for a 1964 Film: Enjoying the Success of a First Directorial Effort," 1.

[72] Ibid.

[73] Sieving, *Soul Searching: Black-Themed Cinema from the March on Washington to the Rise of Blaxploitation*, 39.

[74] *Soul Searching: Black-Themed Cinema from the March on Washington to the Rise of Blaxploitation*, 38-41.

[75] Edward S. Shapiro, "What Went Wrong? The Creation and Collapse of the Black-Jewish Alliance," *Judaism: A Quarterly Journal of Jewish Life and Thought* 44, no. 3 (1995).

[76] Royce, *Hogan's Heroes: Behind the Scenes at Stalag 13*, 108.

[77] Gratz, "Ivan Dixon: A Choice of Heroes," 35.

[78] Michael Fessier Jr. , "A War Ivan Dixon Is Winning," *New York Times* 1967, D19.

[79] Staff, "Fun with Nazis," *TV Guide* (1965): 64.

[80] Gene Reynolds and et. al., "Hogan's Heroes " in *Hogan's Heroes*, ed. Albert S. Ruddy Bernard Fein (USA: Bing Crosby Productions, 1965).

[81] Royce, *Hogan's Heroes: Behind the Scenes at Stalag 13.*

[82] Leslie Campbell Rampey, "Hogan's Heroes and the Holocaust: The Association That Just Won't Go Away," (www.geocities.com/lrampy/hogan.htm, 2000), 1.

[83] Gratz, "Ivan Dixon: A Choice of Heroes," Sec.3, p.1.

[84] Brooks and Marsh, *The Complete Directory to Prime Time Network TV Shows: 1946-Present,* 346.

[85] Dennis Hevesi, "Ivan Dixon, Actor in Film, Stage, TV," *New York Times,* March 21, 2008, 1.

[86] Guy Green, "A Patch of Blue," (USA: MGM, 1965).

[87] Bogle, *Blacks in American Films and Television: An Encyclopedia,* 162.

[88] Edward Mapp, *Blacks in American Films: Today and Yesterday* (Scarecrow Press, 1972), 115.

[89] Staff, "None So Blind," *Newsweek* 66(1965): 71.

[90] Brendan Gill, "Patch of Blue," *New Yorker* 41(1965): 58.

[91] Paul Bogart, "The Final War of Olly Winter," in *CBS Playhouse* (USA 1967).

[92] Gratz, "Ivan Dixon: A Choice of Heroes," 35.

[93] Cobbett S. Steinberg, *TV Facts* (New York: Facts on File, 1980), 323.

[94] Michael Ullman, "The Jazz Column," *Fanfare* 34, no. 1 (2010): 556.

[95] Weber, "Philip Rose, 89, 'Raisin' and 'Purlie' Producer," B18.

[96] Ivan Dixon, "Trouble Man," (USA: Twentieth Century-Fox, 1972).

[97] Reelblack, "Ivan Dixon - Legendary Actor & Filmmaker (Interview)."

[98] Bennett Jr., *The Challenge of Blackness,* 295-96.

[99] Dixon, "The Spook Who Sat by the Door."

[100] Christine and Clifford Ward Acham, "Infiltrating Hollywood: The Spook Who Sat by the Door," (Documentary Channel, 2011).

[101] Cited in Dixon, "The Spook Who Sat by the Door."

[102] Louie Robinson, "Have Blacks Really Made It in Hollywood?," *Ebony* 30, no. 8 (1975): 38.

[103] Acham, "Infiltrating Hollywood: The Spook Who Sat by the Door."

[104] Michael Schultz, "Car Wash," (USA: Universal, 1976).

[105] Charles Champlin, "Life in the Day of a Car Wash," *Los Angeles Times,* Aug. 29, 1976, K40.

[106] Poitier, *This Life,* 89-94.

[107] Ritt, "Edge of the City (Aka a Man Is Ten Feet Tall)."

[108] Brooks, "Something of Value."

[109] Alex Segal, "Arrowsmith," in *Dupont Show of the Month* (USA: CBS, 1960).

[110] Clarke Taylor, "'Nothing But a Man' Classic on TV Tonight," *Los Angeles Times* 1984, G1.

[111] Miller, "The Heart Is a Lonely Hunter."

[112] Joseph Sargent, "The Man," (USA: Paramount, 1972).

[113] Custen, *Bio/Pics: How Hollywood Constructed Public History*, 162.

[114] Brooks and Marsh, *The Complete Directory to Prime Time Network TV Shows: 1946-Present*, 664.

[115] Gelfand, "Taking a Leaf: A Talk with Albert Murray," 9-10.

[116] John Ford, "The Horse Soldiers," (USA: MGM, 1959).

[117] Frank Manchel, *Every Step a Struggle: Interviews with Seven Who Shaped the African-American Image in Movies* (Washington, D.C.: New Academia Publishing, 2007), 120-21.

[118] John M. Stahl, "Imitation of Life," (USA: Universal, 1934).

[119] Dixon, "The Spook Who Sat by the Door."

[120] Pauline Rivelli, "Abbey Lincoln: Proud and Confident," *Jazz* 4, no. 7 (1965).

[121] Hansberry, *A Raisin in the Sun: The Unfilmed Original Script*, 95.

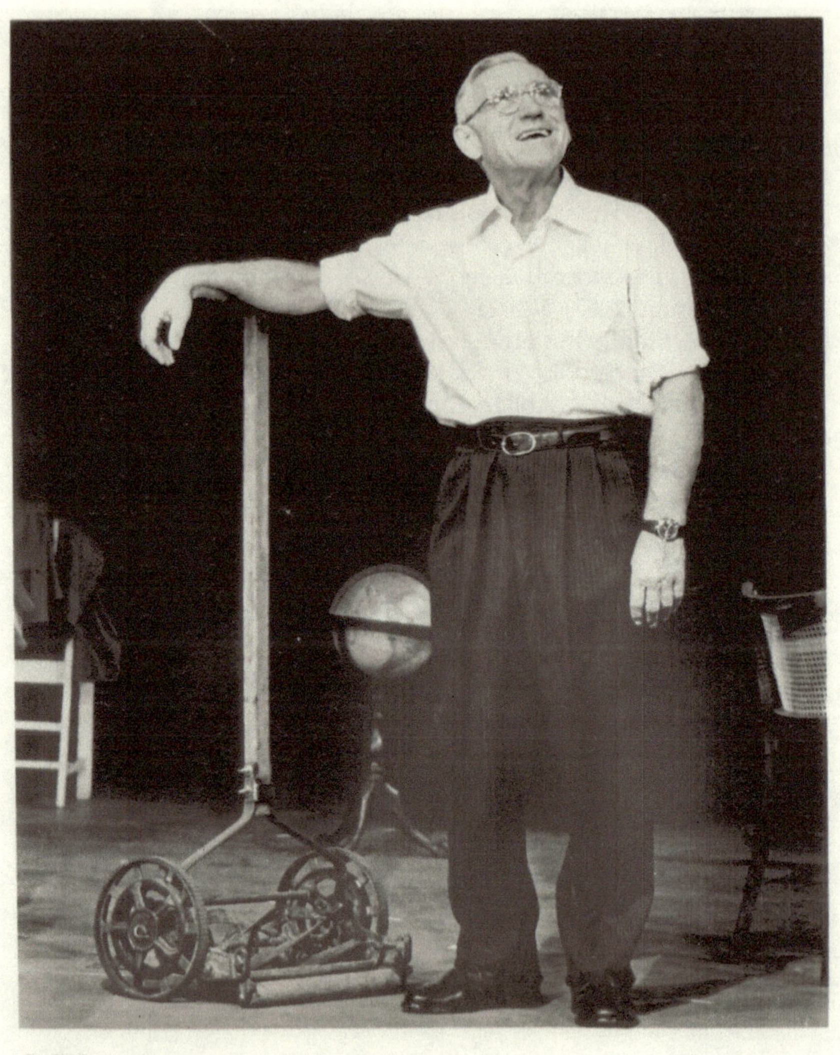

26. James Whitmore, seen here in his one-man show *Give 'Em Hell, Harry!*, was one of the great character actors of the second half of the twentieth century.

5

In His Words: James Whitmore

"America is free to choose whether the Negro shall remain her liability or become her opportunity."[1]

Gunnar Myrdal

"We should not confuse what we can do or are doing with what we should do."[2]

Black Like Me

"We might be better off in some ways, but as long as we have more blacks in jail than in college, as long as we have more blacks unemployed than we have in college, as long as we have a system which will not provide adequate and decent housing even for people who can afford it, we're not very far."[3]

John Hope Franklin

The importance of the sixties to black history and the American film industry remains well documented. Yet no single critic presents a total picture of why the era influenced so deeply our national racial narrative. Thus the intellectual conversation continues. By briefly recalling our debates on the subject, we see why studying James Whitmore's career aids as a useful resource for expanding our understanding of the period. Whether on stage as President Harry S. Truman in *Give 'Em Hell, Harry!* or in film as the white reporter who disguises himself as an African-American in *Black Like Me,* the celebrated character actor contributes to the great discussion.

Social and radical activist Tom Hayden gives us a convenient start. "For simplicity's sake," he suggested, "let's divide the sixties into two halves. The first half starts more innocently, believing in the redemption of the American Dream through direct action.... It might have occurred if not for President Kennedy being assassinated. Here was the first warning that there was something dangerous about social change." As a result, he felt, "The second half of the sixties is one of disillusionment, alienation, bitterness, and just a clarification of where we stood. Then Dr. King and Bobby Kennedy were killed."[4] But historian Peniel E. Joseph sees the horrors of 1963 occurring months before the President's death. For him and many other African-Americans, the year "signaled a turning point in American race relations." As evidence, he tracks events emanating from Birmingham, Alabama alone: e.g., the protests, the marches, the German Shepherd dogs attacking the demonstrators, and the racial violence; the release of Martin Luther King Jr.'s historic "Letter from a Birmingham Jail"; and the infamous church bombing that murdered four young black girls." For this astute academic, the November 22 assassination in Dallas, Texas, existed as "a shocking bookend to the year's domestic violence."[5]

American movie and ethnic historians similarly see 1963 as a crucial year in which, according to film biographer James Gavin, "the civil rights movement had forced much of America to take an honest look at what it meant to be black."[6] Professor Ed Guerrero points out, "As early as 1963, the NAACP launched a 'massive attack' on racism and discrimination in the industry that was coordinated with the Hollywood branch of the American Civil Liberties Union (ACLU) and supported by such prominent stars as Marlon Brando, Paul Newman, Burt Lancaster, and James Whitmore."[7] Dr. William R. Grant IV concurred: "By 1963 the racism and discrimination so pervasive in the industry is confronted by an organized effort combining the Hollywood branches of the NAACP and ACLU respectively." Like his colleagues, he underscores the importance of "the Hollywood elite" such as Brando, Newman, Whitmore, and Charlton Heston, as well as directors like Robert Wise and John Frankenheimer" in breaking "the industry's silence on discretion and discrimination."[8] Joining in the accord, historian Christopher Sieving pronounced, "Nineteen sixty-three was a watershed year in the history of African American people." While acknowledging the horrific events that took place in Birmingham and Dallas, the influential scholar pointed to positive moments such as the University of Alabama being forcibly integrated by federal troops and Dr. King's unforgettable March on Washington that included the eloquent *I Have A Dream* speech. Nevertheless, as Sieving states, "During 1963, tens of thousands of people demonstrated in favor of racial equality, dwarfing totals from previous years; 20,000 of them were arrested and ten were killed. Civil rights concerns dominated the national and international news as they never had before and seldom have since."[9]

As well, the national press acknowledged 1963's relevance to the black film legacy. For instance, film critic Vincent Canby heralded in *Variety* how "independent producers and distributors, if not the studios," had turned "to racial themes during this 1963 summer of discontent." He singled out six movies, "each dealing with the Negro's fight for equality, and/or the more general aspects of Negro-white relations" as proof of his optimism.[10] With the benefit of hindsight, we know that among those soon to be released ventures were four movies destined to play a respected role in black film history: *The Cool World* (1962),[11] *Gone Are the Days* (1963),[12] [both completed and awaiting release]; *Black Like Me* (1963),[13] and *Nothing But a Man* (1964)[14] [both in the pre-production process]. The one major movie not mentioned or noticed by the reviewer was *One Potato, Two Potato* (1964).[15] However, Canby included two extra facts: only one of the six films was written by a black person (Ossie Davis' *Gone Are the Days*), and the only "race pics" to make money in the early sixties had "been out-and-out exploitation dramas of rather dubious artistic and social import."[16] Equally pertinent were the observations by the *New York Times* Hollywood Bureau chief Murray Schumach. He not only expanded the list of film notables to include actor Anthony Franciosa and screenwriter Philip Dunne, but also censured the celebrities for waiting too long to make their influence felt. "Since the Supreme Court decision of 1954," he reminded his readers, "very little bad has been publicly said here about integration in the film industry until Herbert Hill, national labor secretary of the NAACP, accused Hollywood of treating the Negro as 'an invisible man' and 'a caricature.' That was on June 25.'"

Nevertheless, Schumach did acknowledge, "Before that, almost every year the local chapter of the NAACP had protested about discrimination. Meetings were held in private with representatives of studios and unions. Statements were issued and little was done."[17] Now, the press warned Hollywood, the public was watching and waiting to see just what would result from the combined challenges of the NAACP and ACLU. Would the stars begin making race-related films? Would the industry's hiring practices change? Would mainstream moviemakers finally reform their age-old racial stereotyping?[18]

I have neither the space nor the burden to respond to those historical uncertainties. As explained earlier, my purpose is adding to the discussion, not replacing the received scholarship that preceded me. Still, for those readers curious about what happened as a result of the release of these black-oriented films, what changes the NAACP and ACLU actually brought about, just how effective the Hollywood VIPs' were, and how race relations changed in the mid-sixties, vital research on the answers readily exists in the major writings of the critics and historians cited above. What is not easily accessible are the personal views of the film notables repeatedly referred to in these texts. This chapter hopes to redress in some small measure that omission by considering one of the central figures cited in the accounts: James Whitmore.

For the few of us who remember this ordinary-looking character actor who spoke with a crotchety voice, he remains a fixture in our Saturday matinee memories. His name may not have been familiar to us and he did bear a passing resemblance to Spencer Tracy, but his gruff manners and tough on-screen behavior endeared him to film, television, and stage audiences for over half-a-century. James Whitmore continues as one of the few artists in entertainment history to be honored in every facet of show business in which he performed. As one authority noted, he was nominated for top honors in four mediums: the Oscar, The Tony, the Emmy, and the Grammy.[19] And those expert actors who knew him best joyfully testify to his talents. "He cared about acting; his whole life was dedicated to theater and to movies," stated the veteran performer David Huddleston, who also appeared in *Black Like Me*. What's more, "Whitmore always approached his own talent with humility." Despite his success, Whitmore confessed to the *Los An-*

geles Times, "I never thought I was good; I've touched the hem of the garment a few times, but never grabbed it full-hand."[20] James Arness, who appeared with Whitmore in *Battleground, Them!* and *Gunsmoke* maintained he was "an Actor's actor." Arness also noted that his uncommon friend who refused to be typecast worked with great intensity.[21]

That being said, the skeptical reader may still question why James Whitmore is included in these unique interviews on black film history. For starters, not only was the social libertarian a prominent member of the celebrated 1963 industry protest, but also he was the star of the decade's first-released important independent black-themed film. Moreover, he was a long-time member of the ACLU dating back to his college days at Yale, a fact that will prove useful in the pages ahead. Secondly, this chapter reveals not only why Whitmore's prolific career houses heretofore ignored material on Hollywood during the post-WWII era and the sixties, but also why that illustrious career operates as a useful contrast to the limited opportunities afforded black performers discussed in *The Interviews.* As Ruby Dee points out, "In theater and film, employment is a sometime thing, no matter what your color." But in the decades leading up to the civil rights movement, there was a bit more to it in Hollywood.[22] Finally, and not inconsequentially, the actor's journey reminds us once more that while conventional narratives highlight the sixties as a major starting point in the black film revolution, entertainers like Whitmore helped plant the seeds for racial reform in the post-World War II era with other important but ignored show business personalities.

Since longtime observer Pam Munter's valuable profile of the actor is still current,[23] I need only touch on the highlights of the celebrity's biography. The youngest of four children and the only son, James Whitmore was born into a pious household on Oct. 1, 1921, in White Plains, New York.[24] The family moved early in the boy's life to Buffalo. Although he prided himself in being a "hellion" during his formative years, the youngster's major joy seemed to be playing football. Encouraged by his father, he showed great promise, to the point where he impressed athletic scouts loyal to Connecticut's respected Choate preparatory school. As a result, Jim spent his senior year on the academy's gridiron due to a football scholarship he received from the exclusive institution.

Whitmore's abilities then brought him to Yale University in the late thirties, where he became interested in studying pre-law. Munter claims later President Gerald Ford actually coached the promising player. However, the athlete's playing days ended as a result of severe knee injuries. It was at this point that the undergraduate turned to acting. Alarmed by the thought of having her son wasting his life in an unseemly profession, Whitmore's mother insisted he seek professional counseling. Fortunately for us, the therapist assured the devout woman, "Jimmy should be an actor."[25] Before long, the excited would-be thespian became a member of the Yale Drama School Players, in addition to helping start the University's radio station. He also joined the ACLU in the early 1940s. Before Whitmore could complete his senior year, however, he was drafted into the Marines and spent much of his active duty in the South Pacific.[26]

Like other ex-soldiers who decided to become actors in the post-WWII period, the hard-working veteran used the G.I. Bill to study at the Actors Studio, which some chronicles claim he helped found. At the same time, Whitmore, like Ivan Dixon, later James Earl Jones and William Marshall, honed his skills at the American Theatre Wing. It was there that he met Nancy Mygatt, the group's female press agent, fell in love, and married. Before the couple divorced, they had three sons. When his second marriage also failed, he reunited with his first wife. When that reunion collapsed two years later, he married for a fourth and final time in 2001. Interestingly, while Whitmore's matrimonial track record suggests otherwise, the actor always insisted his family remained the most important aspect of his life.[27]

Not long after he became a professional actor in New York, Whitmore scored an impressive 1947 Broadway debut as Tech. Sgt. Howard Evans, a cynical non-com, in William Wister Haines' hit play *Command Decision,* based on the author's novel of the same name. The inspiring show dealt with the mental difficulties, administrative burdens, and ethical issues facing the military leaders responsible for assigning the incredibly dangerous strategic bombing missions over Nazi Germany. Although he won a Tony Award for an "Outstanding Performance By a Newcomer," the up-and-coming Broadway actor lost out on the screen role the following year to Van Johnson when director Sam Wood adapted the play to film.

Even so, Whitmore had caught the attention of MGM's top executives, who signed him to a standard seven-year film contract. Unlike the black actors covered in *The Interviews,* the craggy-voiced, versatile performer had no problems finding appropriate scripts, signing movie contracts, or working in almost every Hollywood genre. Once MGM beckoned, he easily obtained a release from *Command Decision* and began work on his first film, Joseph H. Lewis' *The Undercover Man* (1949).[28] In his screen debut, Whitmore got third billing as George Papass, investigator Glenn Ford's wise-cracking assistant, who with his boss hunt and capture a Capone-like villain.

But it was the novice's second film that cemented the cynical persona that remained forever associated with his work. MGM, in an attempt to placate their new contract player for not being given the Sgt. Evan's screen role, assigned him to a small but crucial part as Sgt. Kinnie in William A. Wellman's *Battleground* (1949).[29] In one of the most popular MGM movies of the post-WWII era, screen-writer Robert Pirosh's Oscar-winning narrative idealized the heroic 101st Airborne Division, the legendary Screaming Eagles who defended Bastogne in what has become known in military history as "The Battle of the Bulge."

As the movie begins, Sgt. Kinnie is drilling his platoon, later to be remembered as "the Battered Bastards of Bastogne." His inspiring chant of "Go to your left, Go to your right" and "Jody was there when you left" set the patriotic tone of the movie. As the war-weary, tobacco-chewing Army sergeant, Whitmore polished the cynical image he had created on stage in *Command Decision*. As the movie draws to an end, the injured, exhausted soldiers get ready to be relieved by fresh, inexperienced troops. And one of the survivors shouts to Kinnie, "Whatever happened to Jody?" Fatigued, the tough Army sergeant puts his dentures back in his mouth, regroups what remains of his reduced platoon, and begins marching them to the rear: "Go to your left, go to your right; you had a good home but you left. Jody was there when you left." That performance won him an Oscar nomination as one of 1949's Best Supporting Actors. [The Oscar, however, went to Dean Jagger in Henry King's *Twelve O'Clock High*.]

Whitmore's spectacular start on stage and in film gave him a false sense of his future. According to Munter, "Winning so many prestigious awards so early in his career left Whitmore thinking it was going to be easy, that the plaudits would just flow. 'I thought there was nothing to it,' he said recently. 'But there was a long time between that drink and the nomination I got for *Give 'Em Hell, Harry!*"[30]

Still, the impressive newcomer whose everyday looks and grumpy screen persona rarely earned him a leading role became one of the most familiar genre personalities of the fifties. Among his more notable credits were those in film noir melodramas like John Huston's *The Asphalt Jungle* (1950)[31] and Don Siegel's *Crime in the Streets* (1956);[32] Roy Roland's western *The Outriders* (1950),[33] along with Gordon Douglas' science-fiction classic *Them!* (1954).[34] But his two favorite formula films proved to be musicals and war movies. The former saw him in Alexander Hall's *Because You're Mine* (1952),[35] George Sidney's *Kiss Me Kate* (1953),[36] Fred Zinnemann's *Oklahoma* (1955), and George Sidney's *The Eddy Duchin Story* (1956).[37] The latter genre included Melvin Frank's *Above and Beyond* (1952),[38] Raoul Walsh's *Battle Cry*,[39] Gordon Douglas' *The McConnell Story*[40] (both in 1955), and Rudolph Mate's *The Deep Six* (1956).[41]

By the end of the decade, the popular performer began moving into television. Of these early incursions, his favorite network appeared to be CBS. During the week of April 26, 1959, for example, he appeared as an anti-war medical officer fighting the Battle of Bastogne in *Dark December* on *Playhouse 90*; and then four days later as a disabled bank employee in *Checkmate* on *The Zane Grey Theater* series, another CBS anthology.[42] But mostly he shied away from accepting any offers to star in his own series.

That is until a fellow ACLU member named Sy Gomberg offered Whitmore the lead in a new ABC half-hour weekly series *The Law and Mr. Jones*. The two men had worked together on the 1952 Mario Lanza musical *Because You're Mine*. Gomberg had been one of four screenwriters[43] inventing a plot in which Whitmore portrayed Master Sergeant "Bat" Batterson, an opera aficionado who takes an interest in the singing of a new inductee named Renato Rossano (Mario Lanza). In 1960, however, writer and producer Gomberg cast Whitmore in a more appropriate role as an idealist lawyer named Abraham Lincoln Jones, who in a crusading but non-violent manner battled vigorously for his clients. Munter appropriately describes the actor's decision as ironic not only because of his pre-law days at Yale, but also because the character he played was likewise a Yale graduate.[44]

Although *The Law and Mr. Jones* barely survived its first season, news of its cancellation so provoked thousands of viewers that the show got a brief reprieve the following year. Regrettably, the ratings did not keep it afloat for very long, and this time the series was cancelled permanently. The actor would twice more prove unsuccessful in doing his own TV series: as a private investigator in NBC's short-lived *My Friend Tony* (1969) and as a blunt chief of surgery in ABC's unsuccessful *Temperatures Rising* (1972).[45]

We need to pause for a moment to consider why Sy Gomberg fits into in our narrative. Born in New York on August 19, 1918, the Oscar-nominated screenwriter, producer and activist moved to Southern California to attend USC in 1937.[46] The University became a fixture in Gomberg's life, attracting him to the campus regularly and also inspiring him to visit other American schools of higher education including the University of Vermont. He spent World War II in the U.S. Army Air Corps Motion Picture Unit and afterward contributed articles and short stories to *Collier's* and the *Saturday Evening Post*.[47] He then worked as a staff writer and humorist for studios including Twentieth Century-Fox, MGM, and Universal, where he wrote and produced for such stars as Gene Kelly, Judy Garland, Henry Fonda, and Red Buttons.[48]

Like his good friend James Whitmore, Sy Gomberg's fame came early. In 1951, the young writer received an Oscar nomination for Best Original Story for John Ford's *When Willie Comes Marching Home*, starring Dan Dailey and Corinne Calvert. According to Myrna Oliver, "The film was based on a story Gomberg originally wrote for *Collier*'s magazine—a story that won him a screenwriting contract at Fox and became his entree to Hollywood." The *Los Angeles Times* reporter also noted, "The same year, Gomberg garnered a nomination for best screenplay from the Writers Guild of America for the film *Summer Stock*, starring Judy Garland and Gene Kelly."[49]

After a long and distinguished career that included his organizing Hollywood's Committee to End Violence, heading the Hollywood Committee for a Sane Nuclear Policy under President Kennedy, and chairing the documentary committee of the Academy of Motion Picture Arts & Sciences, Sy Gomberg died of natural causes on February 11, 2001. He was 82.[50]

While visiting UVM as a guest lecturer in 1972, the noted screenwriter/producer sat down with me (more of which later) to recount his show business experiences from the post-WWII era to the early seventies.[51] He began by describing "an awakening in WWII, a certain truth, that up till then had never really been mentioned or thought of by many people...and that was we were fighting a war against racism. And a few people who were not 'liberals' in quotes began to suspect that maybe racism encompassed more than just the Jewish population or the Catholic population in Germany, but also encompassed the Negro population in this country. And one of the people very much responsible for this was Joe Louis."[52] The filmmaker then told me, "The war changed a great many films, because then we got *Home of the Brave*,[53] and that was the first time the word 'Nigger' was used on the screen for a purpose. I don't know how honest a picture it would look like now, but in its day it was a shocking movie and was a big hit.

"For the first time," Gomberg explained, "a change began to take place. That there was an audience, not a black or a white or an upper class, but it was an audience for pictures that had content. And things were moving towards that when the McCarthy era and the Committee on Un-American Activities came out, and the Hearings started and the McCarthy era started. Everything was stifled. A few pictures managed to sneak in here and there, but basically nothing was said for a long time. For the next ten years, we really had almost a desert where if you wanted to work in Hollywood, you wrote as I did musicals or comedies; and you could make a very good living writing for Judy Garland or Gene Kelly or Mario Lanza or Mitzi Gaynor or whatever. That's what I did. Because there was nothing else you could write that they would do. They were terrified."[54]

Moving quickly to the early sixties, Gomberg told me he had created, produced and scripted the television series *The Law and Mr. Jones*. "'Sy was the engine that made that go,' Whitmore explained elsewhere, adding that the show represented some of the best of Gomberg's writing.'"[55] Two anecdotes in particular that the producer told me deserve mention here.

The first relevant recollection concerned *The Law and Mr. Jones.* Gomberg remembers doing one show in particular which was designed to deliberately upset the ABC brass. By this time, he knew both the show was to be cancelled and the series had begun to build an audience. Even so, ABC was fed up with the program. So on February 17, 1961, the producer/screenwriter offered an episode dealing with a character named Bob Mills, a black boxer (Bernie Hamilton), and his wife (Isabelle Cooley), a nice couple. The boxer's terrified wife believed her husband was going blind because of a blow he had received in the ring. So she went to Abraham Lincoln Jones, their attorney, to try to get him to convince Bob to retire. Money was not the issue; her husband's health was the issue.[56] Then, as Gomberg told me, "Well, I did a small thing in this show, but I think it was significant. Mr. Jones' assistant, his clerk, was a Southerner, and we had the clerk call the client, 'Mister.' Now the mail on this was amazing; the number of people who wrote in and castigated us, and there were a number of people who wrote in and said, 'Hooray for what you did.' See, that's one small thing. Except it happened. And this was only 1961."[57]

Gomberg's second recollection sheds light on TV's racial progress by the mid-sixties and dealt with Tom Moore. The broadcasting executive headed ABC Network's programming from 1958 to 1962, and then became its President from 1962 to 1969. Among his hit shows were *77 Sunset Strip, Ben Casey* and *The Untouchables.* Also it was his independent company *Tomorrow Entertainment* that produced the award-winning TV show, *The Autobiography of Miss Jane Pitman."*[58]

The anecdote concerned an episode of *Ben Casey,* one of the most admired medical series in television history. It ran from October 2, 1961 to March 21, 1966.[59] According to Gomberg, "The man who was the head of programming for ABC-TV, a guy named Tom Moore, had been a salesman at Forest Lawn. He sold graves, which made him the perfect man for running that place. He came on the set, which was in the General Hospital when they were shooting *Ben Casey* and became very upset at the number of Negroes being used, playing interns, playing nurses, and playing technicians. And he said, 'What are you doing with all these 'Niggers' in this scene?' And somebody got very angry and took him by the arm and walked down the hall with him and said, 'Take a look around the hospital. Who the hell do you think is working here?' But Moore still said take them out, and they had to. That was in 1965, '66. Luckily, we got rid of him."[60]

The television experiences shared by Gomberg and Whitmore influenced both men deeply, resulting in their remaining lifelong civil rights activists and staunch supporters of the ACLU. Thus they would have been surprised by Murray Schumach's account about "the local chapter of the NAACP" whose protests and statements had produced very little.[61] Once again, a brief pause offers an alternative view, this time about Schumach's comments and sheds some light on Whitmore's decision to join the 1963 Hollywood protest.

The notion that the local chapter of the NAACP proved mainly ineffectual in its dealings with the movie industry up to 1963 is relatively common. But how accurate is it? Sidney Poitier, for example, states by the end of 1962, Hollywood revealed a "new attitude countering the long-held conviction that the appearance of blacks in other than menial roles would offend the movie industry's principle constituency. The realization that year by year more and more white Americans were willing to pay their way into a theater to see entertainment about blacks or involving blacks would encourage most of the studios to make minor alterations in their rigid and generally insulting policy for dealing with America's black citizens."[62] But did the NAACP's local chapter have a hand in the industry's gradual transformation?

A possible answer might appear in the newspaper accounts penned by the chapter's founder Maggie Hathaway. According to sports writer Jason Lewis, this devoted golfer was also one of Hollywood's "most well-known community and civil rights leaders."[63] Born on July 1st, 1919, she moved to Hollywood from Louisiana to work in the movies in the late thirties. A dancer who obtained uncredited parts in such films as Edward Buzell's *At the Circus* (1939),[64] Vincent Minnelli's *Cabin in the Sky,*[65] and Andrew L. Stone's *Stormy Weather*[66] (both in 1943), her real importance appears to be as a stand-in for Pearl Bailey and Lena Horne. You might recall her activism and courage was what appealed to Jim Brown and why he valued her so highly.[67]

Spirited, striking, and smart, Hathaway refused to accept many of the film industry's racist practices. Unlike many others around her, she decided to do something about it. But the battles she fought and the breakthroughs she obtained are absent in recent black histories. I do not understand why. If not for Jason Robards and his help in arranging for me to meet this wonderful woman at a Los Angeles golf tournament the vacuum might still continue.

We met during my brief visit to California in January 1972. During our absorbing discussion, she told me that among her many occupations was that of a long-time writer-columnist for a black newspaper, the *Los Angeles Sentinel*. In the spring of 1967, Hathaway explained, she wrote eight articles on the "progress of integration, before and behind the camera" in Hollywood.[68] But sadly, she did not know what had become of the series, although she promised to locate them for me. When I returned to Vermont, I wrote her and reminded her of her promise. Not until months later did I receive her handwritten response sent on stationary entitled "Minority Associated Golfers," Maggie Hathaway, President. (The organization had been founded by her in 1963.) The letter follows:

> April 24, 1972
> 3861 Don Tomaso
> Dearest Frank –
> Finally I have found movie articles through a friend—
> I received <u>all</u> of them to-day.
> Is it too late?
> Yours until freedom
> Maggie Hathaway

I wrote back on May 11, that she should of course send the articles. Then I added, "I'm just beginning with the writing and should get to your era by June."[69] The package arrived on June 17th.

I have little doubt that being ACLU members Gomberg and Whitmore were well aware of what the activist later reported. Hathaway began by stating "that for ten years she had been fighting for integration [and] had been 'kicked out of [Hollywood] with the help of some of her own people. Poor, broke, frightened, and segregated actors and extras."[70] For those few who stayed and fought, she explained, "[They] were punished, boycotted and defeated, until this day."[71]

She then went on to describe a twenty-year struggle that involved personalities like Gov. Ronald Reagan, the former head of the Screen Actors Guild (SAG). She credits the NAACP with starting the fight in the mid-thirties,[72] and how producers, Central Casting, and SAG beat down the bit-players. Starting in the second article, the writer pointed out, "Our first Negro actors were accepted in motion pictures if they joined the union (Screen Actors Guild). Negro casting agents, the late Charles Butler, and Jasper Weldon, were hired by the producers to send actors to the studio."[73] In her words, "If they were black, they knew they would be selected; brown, maybe; light, go back home."[74] She claimed the practice was still operating in 1967. Even worse, she insists that Central Casting had added an age limit: "If you are older than twenty-five years of age, 'regardless of how well you can act, you can't get in.'"[75]

Hathaway then enters into a controversial account of how celebrated NAACP leader Walter White's 1942 Hollywood trip to improve black conditions in the industry led to African-American actors being forced to join two unions: the SAG and a newly created Screen Extras. "It was created," she explains, "for actors who did not speak or have parts."[76] While acknowledging that black chorus women always found steady work, the writer claimed only Lena Horne and Juanita Moore ever graduated to major roles.[77]

According to Hathaway, the breakthroughs began in 1943. For example, it wasn't until *Stormy Weather* that Horne had her own black make-up people, stand-ins, wardrobe ladies, and hairdressers.[78] On that same picture, the black dancers, led by Alice Keys, went out on strike for the same pay as the "Caucasian girls" and won. In addition, seventy-five black players marched into MGM's main dining room to integrate it. After that the big dining room was open to anyone who could pay for it.[79] On that same picture, every morning, the columnist explained, she and other dancers, before putting on their costumes, "had to stand, nude, and let our Caucasian make-up lady plaster us with make-up for the camera."[80] These practices continued until the mid-fifties. Changes also began occurring during the making of Otto Preminger's *Carmen Jones* (1954), eleven years later.[81] According to Hathaway, "The first picture that elevated us from the "segregated, stupid era" was *The Apartment*

(1960).[82] Because director Wilder permitted "us to play male and female secretaries, the black performers honored him on the set."[83]

The fight for more intelligent roles continued to gain ground by 1961, in part because of lawsuits filed by people like Hathaway.[84] Two years later, the NAACP and its president Edward D. Warren established a Hollywood branch. Known as the Beverly Hills NAACP, Hathaway was its first president.[85] Soon political fights between Hathaway and Julius Griffith broke out, and he took over the helm. Still, Sammy Davis Jr. and Hathaway founded the NAACP Image Awards in 1967. For the rest of her life she fought for black civil rights, and when she died on September 24th, 2001, she remained one of the most respected black activists of her time. Her passion is preserved by the Images Awards and a LA golf course named in her honor.[86]

I spend this time on this remarkable woman and writer for two basic reasons: first, so that we can better appreciate what Whitmore describes later in his comments; and second, so that we can appreciate the riches hidden in the actor's resume. Otherwise, we might not understand what troubled him so about his profession. Still, after *The Law and Mr. Jones* ended, Whitmore went back to work in the theater and did not make another film until *Black Like Me* caught his attention.[87]

Adapted from John Howard Griffin's book describing the Texas reporter's pretending to be a black man so that he could travel incognito through the Deep South, the Julius Tannebaum-Carl Lerner movie remains of major interest to present-day film scholars. Anyone interested in the most influential analysis of *Black Like Me*, the movie's critical and commercial reception, and its significance to black film history should start with Christopher Sieving's *Soul Searching*.[88] My purpose here is to highlight selective research to prepare the reader for Whitmore's remarks later on. In no way is that exercise meant to disparage current reports. It is, I repeat, to add to the discussion.

Let's start with director Carl Lerner. A brilliant film editor highly praised for his work on movies like Sidney Lumet's *12 Angry Men* (1957) and *The Fugitive Kind* (1959), Ralph Nelson's *Requiem for a Heavyweight* (1962), Frank Perry's *The Swimmer* (1968), and Alan J. Pakula's *Klute* (1971), Lerner had never directed a feature film before or after *Black Like Me*.[89] Neither had he nor his wife, the historian Dr. Gerda Lerner,[90] ever written a full-length screenplay. But together with an obscure documentary filmmaker named Julius Tannebaum, the couple decided to make an "authentic" movie about race relations in America's deep south. The film's distributor asked that the actor to play Griffith "not be a b.o. name because that would detract from the impact of the film. Negotiations are presently being concluded with a couple of thesps who are known more for their character acting abilities than their pure star power."[91] Two weeks later, Whitmore was announced for the key role.[92]

Many of the reviewers claimed that both the book and the film *Black Like Me* reminded them of Laura Hobson's novel *Gentleman's Agreement* and Elia Kazan's 1947 screen adaptation. While I can see the superficial resemblance where two writers impersonate someone else to discover "the truth" about blacks and Jews respectively, the differences between the works are too striking to ignore. First, the Christian reporter Philip Schuyler Green (Gregory Peck) never leaves New York and remains incognito for six months. Higgins (Whitmore) goes on a three-month trip alone and is marginalized. Second, the Kazan film featured some of the most respected actors of the period: in addition to Peck, Dorothy McGuire, John Garfield, Celeste Holm, Ann Revere, Jane Wyatt, June Havoc, Albert Dekker, Dean Stockwell, and Sam Jaffe. The Lerner production featured, in addition to Whitmore, only new faces such as Roscoe Lee Browne, Al Freeman Jr. and Richard Ward. Third, the Kazan film was a straight narrative; the Lerner production relied heavily on flashbacks. Fourth, Hobson's focus was on a range of racial incidents; Higgins seemed primarily concerned with depicting alleged sexual behavior and perversion. And finally the Kazan film won Oscars for its director, the film, and supporting actress (Holm); the Lerner film garnered no attention from the Motion Picture Academy.

Reading what I just wrote you might justifiably wonder why film historians spend so much time on such poorly constructed productions. And this is not the first time we've encountered such concerns in *The Interviews*. I wish I could give you a satisfactory answer. After all these years, I still cannot delineate why films riddled with multiple problems stubbornly maintain their hold on our imagination. It may be psychological. It may be "chemistry." It may be the power of film. All I know is that in their time these movies meant something to their generation. And in spite of my harsh criticisms, they still retain a positive effect on me. It is that lifelong problem that I have always found difficult to resolve: how do you educate people to value things that can only be experienced but not explained?

Although *Black Like Me* proved one of the few independent black-themed movies to succeed in the sixties, it was criticized, reported Munter, "as merely another example of the white man slumming at a black man's expense. Others have seen it as a continuation of the tragic mulatto theme and nothing more. (Indeed, the film's thesis was that here was a white man being treated so shamelessly simply because his skin was darkened.) But the more relevant fact was that, crude and shoddy as this B movie was, it was an earnest attempt to confront and expose racism in America." The actor's friend then quoted Whitmore saying, "'I was disappointed. I think it was ahead of its time."[93]

Few of the performer's formula films from the mid-sixties till the end of the decade improved his resume or his spirits. Possible exceptions were Gordon Douglas' *Chuka* (1967),[94] Don Siegel's *Madigan,*[95] Franklin J. Schaffner's *Planet of the Apes*[96] (both in 1968), and Paul Wendkos' *Guns of the Magnificent Seven* (1969).[97] Without doubt, however, George Flemyng's *The Split* (1968) stands out as a curious choice. While there is no need to repeat what was said about the movie in the Jim Brown chapter, it is worth pointing out that the role of janitor Herb Sutro may well be the most unsatisfying character Whitmore ever played. While every other key performer in the movie—Brown, Diahann Carroll, Ernest Borgnine, Julie Harris, Gene Hackman, Jack Klugman, Donald Sutherland, and Warren Oates—get some redeeming footage, Whitmore's screen time as a rapist and murderer evidences not a single positive frame.

With the start of the seventies, the gifted actor appeared in some worthwhile movies but none that satisfied his passion for acting. Thus he again turned back to his great love: the stage. As he once explained, "I've been very, very lucky. The stage is human beings sharing something together—flesh and blood together—and the others are mechanical and shadows on the screen."[98] He often said that "he found acting in films and television boring because of the long waits between scenes; his passion was for the theater, and he continued to act on stage throughout his long career."[99] But as the decade moved on, he decided to try something different.

In the mid-sixties, the magnificent Hal Holbrook had brought his Off-Broadway one-man show *Mark Twain Tonight* to the Great White Way. So successful was the production that the act remained in the public's mind and reappeared on stage and screen, plus a hit recording for decades. Over the years, explains historian Dennis Bingham, other players like Pat Carroll (Gertrude Stein) and Henry Fonda (Clarence Darrow) staged similar one-man shows.[100] But none topped Whitmore.

In 1974, the remarkable character actor, using only a cowboy hat, a lariat, and a wad of chewing gum, timidly appeared before a theatrical audience in *Will Rogers' U.S.A.*, the first of his one-man shows. Dennis McClellan stated it was Whitmore's initial performance that persuaded him he had found a niche for himself. Other reports claimed, "He allegedly memorized eight hours of Rogers' material and thoughts on various topics, performing a different show for each audience."[101] What made this character his favorite, McClellan explained, was that Rogers was both "wise and humorous and that's an unbeatable combination."[102]

The following year Whitmore took to the stage as an opinionated President Harry S. Truman in *Give 'Em Hell, Harry!* It remains to this day one of my favorites of Whitmore's many performances. As he takes us through the life of only the seventh President to attain the Office of President by happenstance, the performer gives you a good idea of how blunt the Senator from Missouri was in the White House: "No matter what you do, there will always be some son of a bitch who won't like it"; and "Conceit is God's gift to little men." In 1975, the stage show was adapted to the screen,[103] and Whitmore received his second Oscar nomination, this time for Best Actor. [The winner was Jack Nicholson in *One Flew Over the Cuckoo's Nest*.]

Whitmore tried once more to recapture the limelight with his third one-man show *Bully*, but the actions of President Theodore Roosevelt barely held the attention of Broadway audiences for more than a week. After being canceled, it rarely saw a performance again.

In trying to put these three Presidential acts in perspective, I sought the counsel of my friend, the irreplaceable film scholar Peter Rollins. He was in the midst of making a movie about Will Rogers, so it seemed sensible to get Peter's advice. I will spare you the complete response, but the following excerpt should give you the flavor of his comments: "White [sic] did a fine job, but anyone who has studied Rogers would note a lack of the soft touch and humanitarian warmth of the man. The tough approach worked far better in Whitmore's rendering of Truman where there was rough edge to the character being portrayed." And then Dr. Rollins added and I include with his knowledge, "I saw something on the net that mentioned how important his 'Yale education' was to him as a subtle actor. Not sure a Yale education would be good for anybody."[104]

James Whitmore never stopped working and making valuable contributions to his art. His last popular screen appearance was in Frank Darabont's *The Shawshank Redemption* (1994).[105] His last TV triumph was his Emmy Award guest appearance on ABC's hit series *The Practice* in 2000. In November 2008, the distinguished actor contracted lung cancer and died three months later on February 6, 2009.

It seems only fitting to end with his friend David Huddleston's comments, " [I] once asked Jimmy Cagney what was the best thing you could do as an actor, and he said, 'Never get caught at it.' Huddleston then went on to say, "That's kind of how I'd sum up Jim Whitmore."[106]

James Whitmore's interview remains the most unusual of any in this collection. We never met. To explain why, I need to correct the impression in the Introduction that I was in UVM's English Department when *The Interviews* began. In vastly simplified terms, my journey to learn about the black film legacy and to teach film in American schools had begun in the sixties at then Southern Connecticut State College. I had gone there with the intention of starting film courses. In 1966, circumstances within the Department made that impossible.

I activated my papers at Teachers College, Columbia University and soon became an Associate Professor in the English Department at the University of Vermont. A key provision of my coming was that if UVM decided to teach film, I would be the instructor. Four years after arriving in Burlington, Vermont the Department decided they could not honor that promise. So the Dean of the College of Arts and Sciences transferred me from the English Department to the Department of Communication and Theatre, where film study at UVM formally began in 1971.

You may be curious as to what occurred that made me move about so much. Let me put it best using Hamlet's words: "The time is out of joint. Oh, cursed spite/ That ever I was born to set it right!"[107]

Sy Gomberg and I met during the spring of 1972, when we were both teaching in the Department of Communication and Theatre at UVM. He was a guest lecturer offering classes in screenwriting. I was just beginning teaching courses in film study. We became friendly, and he suggested I contact his friend James Whitmore. When the actor got my letter, he was in the midst of many projects and could not arrange a time for us to meet. But he promised, if I sent him a series of questions, he would do his best to answer them. What follows is the result of our correspondence.

James Whitmore Interview Tapes
April 6, 1972

JW: Mr. Manchel, I'm not sure that's the correct pronunciation of your name. Sy Gomberg told me in advance. I suppose I should introduce myself, although it may be implicit that I'm James Whitmore. And I am as you can see acceding to your wish that I try to give you some impressions of my experiences in the films *Black Like Me*[108] and *The Split,*[109] and some other observations and feelings I might have.

I hesitated to do so, only because I certainly feel *very* deeply that I really have nothing of any real insight or import into the problem of the races beyond just the average man's disturbation at the entire phenomenon, really. I also am a bit uneasy in recording my thoughts this way; I never have done so before. I do happen to have a Sony tape recorder. Your letter was so explicit, and the facilities presented the tapes and so on, that I felt that the least I could do was however brief a time this may run to, to try to do what you ask.

To get to it, and do it with as little verbiage as possible, the film

Black Like Me seemed to be an opportunity for a middle-class American, raised at least as a middle-class American, to [be articulate] and aware, and deeply affected by the obvious scar or wound. Really, it's not a scar yet, of the black man and woman in our society. I have been very much aware of it since World War II, having lived in New York City, I've become acutely aware of it, as the black man and black woman made us become aware of the problem. Unfortunately. I think it's shameful that it took them to finally erupt and make us aware of the great and profound indignity that we have been and still are asking or insisting I suppose that they bear.

I had been involved for a number of years—really since my years at Yale—with the American Civil Liberties Union. It certainly did not address itself in the early days at all to the problems of the black man. More to the problems of the pariahs and outcasts and the disinherited of our society. They, as you undoubtedly know, those people were a broad spectrum all the way from the Germans in this country—the American Germans—, who were vilified during World War I. Then, of course, the pacifists, which really was, in 1921, the reason for the inception, conception of the American Civil Liberties Union, which was to defend the rights of pacifists. In those days it was a narrow spectrum, and then it spread out of course. The ACLU eventually became involved in full membership in the minorities in our country. Naturally when the black revolution erupted, they were recipients of ACLU's council in many instances, certainly not all. But that was, more or less, my active participation in this social ill in our country.

So when the opportunity arose through the agency of an offer by the producers of *Black Like Me* to do the film, I jumped at it as a possible way, as I say, to make a very small—I'm guessing infinitesimal would be the word—contribution to the opening up of this problem with all its indignities, and its debasements, and its essentially obscene nature which, of course, I believe racialism, racism to be.

As I said, I had been brought up as a middle-class American boy in Buffalo, New York; and we in rather typical fashion in our high school had one or two black people. We played football, and we played against one other racial group, and that was the Indians who had an Indian school in upstate New York. But other than that, with the exception of the menials, this is a very typical, common story. We simply had no contact with people of other races as I grew up. Certainly not as a wealthy family. If anything, I was a little below middle-class, economically.

Anyway, I was approached about doing the film. It had been turned down by a few other actors for reasons that I do not know. However, when it was brought to me, I was very eager to do it. The year in my chronology is frightful, and I don't have the papers available to me to check it out, but I think it was about 1962. You probably would have that available to you. It was done, as you perhaps know, by a group of people. One of them was Carl Lerner, who was a cutter, and still is to my knowledge in New York City. He was based in New York City, and had a reputation for being one of the best there was. The other man—one other man—was Jules Tannebaum, who had been involved in various film ventures prior to this and turned out to be a rather quixotic and rather unstable personality. And I don't think he contributed anything. I think he was a detriment to the completion of the film. Lerner, Carl, was to be the director; and he flew out to California when I agreed to do the film.

I did it for, I don't know my salary in films; I think it was about a third for what I ordinarily would have got for a film because I wanted to do it very much, as I've indicated. Then I got, or was to receive, which I never have, a percentage of the producer's share of the profits. This is typically the kind of thing that actors have happen to them all the time because one does not have access to the producer's books. It's, as I say, a very common occurrence regardless of the size of the percentage. Rarely do actors get any money on that basis. That, as I say, was not a major consideration.

The most important consideration was the script, which was written by Carl Lerner's wife, who was a Viennese by birth, and a very responsible and very aware kind of woman who had been involved in many social betterment enterprises in New York City and environs. Also was an extremely bright woman.

But the script, as you undoubtedly know, is taken from a book by John Howard Griffin of his real, actual experiences after having changed his skin color while traveling through the black belt of America. Even though Griffin, it seems to me, was not a first class writer, the book had the ring of veracity about it and a comparatively simple feel.

Mrs. Lerner, on the other hand, with the convoluted and rather subtle mind of—let us to simplify—the European intellectual, had taken this rather simple, singular act by this man, and turned it into a rather murky, in my view, quest for God, which is conceivable is what John Howard Griffin intended, but it was not the power of his act. That was not the power of his act. The power of his act was the act itself.

The courage that was. Well, anyway, Carl Lerner flew to California, and we met at my home and went over the script page by page. You must understand, and I'm sure you do, that his wife having been the authoress, it was rather delicate going for me to criticize the script. But I did, because I thought it was important to do so, because I felt that the project was important. So we sat for, literally, four days and went over the script line-by-line and page-by-page. And he seemed to concur.

At that time, I must confess, I had not wholly and utterly committed myself to the script. I had insisted on certain changes in the script, in the direction of simplifying it, when I said that I was interested in doing it. So Lerner's agreeableness, probably in great part, was due to the fact that I had not in fact committed myself finally to doing the film. He, as I say, was most agreeable.

Incidentally, there were no black people involved at this level at all. The Lerners were both white, Tannebaum was white. I suppose I should have mentioned that. There were also some Mellon interests in it—the Paul Mellon Foundation. Just what those were and to identify them by name, I cannot do. I did know at one time, but I've forgotten now. There was foundation money in this film, not much money by motion picture standards, certainly.

But to get back to the script and my endeavor to change it, Lerner went back to New York and, as I say, was most agreeable, and it seemed to me that he had acceded almost completely to the script changes that I'd asked for. And so at that point, I agreed to do it, and I went back East and commenced rehearsals.

When we got into rehearsals, I discovered that practically none of the changes that I had asked for had been done. And it then became a question of whether I walk out on the project. We were now in fact in rehearsal. I was rehearsing with other actors. Or whether I should continue, hoping to make the best of a rather difficult situation. I did not feel, I must confess, that the script as it was originally was, was not worth doing. To this day, I feel that it was worth doing. All I was after was what I conceived to be improvements that would push it towards excellence, more than it was. So my decision, that moment in New York, being there, was to go ahead and do the best that I could.

Then the black men and women began to enter into the production on levels of casting, a very important level. And the man in charge of casting was a black man called, Chuck Gordone, who has recently had a very big success in a play called *Someplace to be Somebody*, I believe it's called. Or *No Place to be Somebody*, one of the two. It was a big hit in New York. I think that there are plans to make it into a film. And he was in charge of casting. He was a very bright and energetic and very militant black man. And he had an important job in this film because, I would guess, somewhere between seventy and eighty percent of the cast was to be black. And I must say, in my opinion, he assembled a perfectly wonderful cast.

Charles Gordone is one of the seven celebrities interviewed in Every Step a Struggle. *His Pulitzer-Prize winning play is titled* No Place to Be Somebody.

The tensions on the set were minimal, as I recall. I'm talking purely in the area of rehearsal. I remember one affront—the only affront I can think of at the moment, that I was guilty of—was with a man named Dick Ward, who was playing the shoeshine man in the early part of the film that acts as the gateway for the Griffin character I played into the black world in New Orleans.

Richard Ward (1915-1979) was a highly regarded actor with a gravely voice who began his professional career in the late forties. Among the important movies he appeared in were Nothing But a Man *(1964),* The Learning Tree *(1969),* Mandingo *(1975),* The Jerk *(1979), and* Brubaker *(1980).*[110]

And Dick is really a wonderful, warm, open, big bear-like guy.

During rehearsals, I remarked, at one point—he has a beautiful voice—, I said, "My God, you must be a singer." And Ward bristled. He couldn't understand it. He said, "I can't carry a tune." I guess and pretty much resolved that it was a super sensitivity to the idea, the old cliché, that black men sing and dance. I can think of no other reason for it, personally. Certainly up to that point and after that point too, we got along very well indeed.

In rehearsal, the work, it seemed to me, was very good. I still had great misgivings about the script, but it.... Carl Lerner is a very mild, quiet, shy man. His wife is more assertive and aggressive. The other man, the co-producer, Jules Tannebaum, as I've indicated, was a rather ebullient, manic personality, who one pretty much tried to ignore. He was not terribly disruptive at that point, and except for my misgivings about the script, the rehearsals and all the work went extremely well.

We began shooting the film in Washington, D.C. I think we had two weeks rehearsal in New York, prior to that. We shot in what used to be a whorehouse in Washington, D.C. that since was abandoned. We had the use of the house. It was run-down, and our first shots were shots in the black ghetto. So the slum nature, the run-down nature of the place was very good.

But the most disconcerting thing of all was Carl Lerner's behavior on the set. He got what I would assume would have to be called "stage fright," because when—it was the first picture, I don't think I've mentioned this, that Carl had ever directed. And the first day on the set, naturally, actors and technicians.... We had a good crew from New York, incidentally. They had done numerous pictures in and around New York City, and they were thoroughly professional. Well all of the people turned naturally to the director to have him tell the crew where he wants the camera placed, to tell the actors what he wants them to do, and so on. It's been said that motion pictures is a director's medium, and it is indeed true. When you have a director, as it was that morning, who stands there, struck dumb, as it were, not able to say to anyone what he wants them to do, it's a very disconcerting thing, to say the least. That's exactly what happened on that first day. I'm afraid it was a harbinger of things to come, and not a very happy one. I'm going to stop for just a moment, and I'll be back shortly.

[BREAK]

JW: To briefly define the cause, which I am sure is intriguing, of Carl Lerner's lack of ability to do anything that morning, of a definitive nature, I've been trying to get at it for many years, and I think one of the reasons is that he had been in a very solitary profession for a number of years. A cutter in films works pretty much by himself with the raw stock of film that is submitted to him. And all it is is him and the machine and the film alone in a room with an assistant who pretty much does what the cutter tells him or her to do. That is my basic theory on it; there may be others, more complex reasons. At any rate, it was kind of a frightening experience for us all.

Eventually, Lerner did start to direct after a fashion. I say "after a fashion," because he is not, was not a director. So that seems to me, that and the script were two very serious problems that beset the film early on. From the beginnings of the structure. The foundations, in that regard, were not good. Foundations from the standpoint of people who cared were darned good. Everybody did, in fact. Even Jules Tatenbaum, as I say, the quixotic, strange guy that he was, he still cared I think a lot. As we both know, there can be all different kinds of caring; there can be a neurotic need that is somehow satisfied by a person who gets involved in some sort of social enterprise. I think the film could be classed as a social enterprise more than a commercial enterprise. The people involved in it, the Mellon money, and so on, and certainly my involvement in it, was a social thrust rather than a career thrust.

I remember now that you did ask me something in the letter about the response of people, or my own response, to my career. I must tell you frankly, it had never, never entered my head really. I think it was mentioned at one point by an agent to me that there might be some onus attached to playing a black man, but it really seemed laughable to me, and I think today still does, knowing what I know now. I just don't think that the most—well, I'm sure that the most ardent racists wouldn't object to my playing the black man as much as he or she might object to some of the things that the film said. And if you've—I'm sure you have seen the film, it did say some very strong things that might bother the more violent racists in the South. But, by and large, I never had any—that I'm conscious of—in the way of disapprobation about my involvement with the film, and I never thought about it myself. As I say, it seemed to be a tremendous opportunity to make a very small contribution.

So anyway, that foundation was good. Then the other technical foundation of the script and the director were not good. However, they both meant extremely well. I suppose that's important. But I fought the battle—we all fought the battle—throughout the shooting of the film.

It was shot—much of it—under very, very difficult circumstances in the South, in Maryland, and in Florida, and in Virginia, and in Washington, D.C. We fought it constantly. That was the fact that Carl was not a good director, didn't know how to direct, in fact; and that the script was not quite what it should be. The casting, I thought, was by and large, excellent. My relationship on the film with the black actors was always good. And by "good," I do not mean that there was any great camaraderie, deep profound kind of experience at all. As you know, the indignity, the abasement, debasement of the black man in our society is a profound thing.

I've subsequently been involved with two projects in the ghetto as co-director, in each instance with a black man. And any really profound relationship is extremely hard to come by. I did achieve it in one instance. But we just have too many crimes committed in our name down through the centuries that cannot be wiped out of the consciousness of the black man; and therefore, I feel, it is very difficult. What I'm trying to say—not to over complicate it—is that our relationship on a work basis was excellent with all the black actors and for that matter with all the white actors.

What more to say about *Black Like Me* except that it was disappointing as a finished product, for me, because of the two elements that I've just mentioned that were lacking: direction and the script. Had it been a more straightforward recounting of a singular act without the overlay of the spiritual, the so agonizing soul searching of the central character, I think it would have been a much better film.

I think it certainly needed direction, and that is of course an art form—direction—that I cannot speak to because I am not a director. I do know that Carl Lerner did not make a contribution to the film that is demanded, that any film demands of the director, if it's going to be a good film.

I think it's worthy of note to deal for a moment with the business of make-up, because it leads then to other areas that are more profound than just cosmetics. I was, as you know, to be a man that had changed the color of his skin by the use of a drug that is used in the treatment of a disease that is called "Vitiligo," where certain portions of a person's skin loses its pigmentation. This is most notable in black people, naturally. We've all seen victims of "Vitiligo," I'm sure, with the black skin mottled by patches of white skin. The drug makes the skin extremely susceptible to ultra-violet; and John Howard Griffin took this drug, against the advice of his physician, took it in a very short period of time, where it is ordinarily given over a long period of time. He took it in say two or three weeks and threatened his own physical well being by doing so; and in fact, did later suffer some very bad after-effects.

But quite naturally, I didn't do this. So we used make-up in the film. It was extremely difficult to get the make-up to keep its consistency during a day's shooting, because it was, after all, a pan-stick make-up, oil based. And as the skin during the day—I'd perspire, and certain oils and things in the skin would be excreted—it would then change the consistency of the make-up, and it would photograph in different ways. Splotch sometimes, and some other times it would flake, and so on. So my make-up in the morning took a long time. It was never fully successful, because it never in my view gave the real feeling of flesh, flesh color.

However, Griffin's did, when he did it. He did it with just the ultra-violet acting upon his skin that had been sensitized by the drug. Well, what this did to me, in the skin or make-up not being accurate, simply contributed to the feeling once again that the film was not going to be a good one.

The actual wearing of the make-up was interesting. I was very often in the South mistaken when I would get away from the company, because a motion picture company is like Bedouins; they travel, and they have their paraphernalia all over the place. So immediately, people in any neighborhood can sense that a motion picture is being made; and anyone connected with it has a certain aura about them. They're not real people at all; they're from Hollywood. So when I was with the group, there was no problem at all.

There was not a big problem anyway. But very often, I would go away—on my way home, or if I'd stopped to buy something on my way home after the shooting—, I would run into the implacable look in the eyes of the whites in the South toward my black face. And even, as I say, with make-up on that was not very successful in capturing a real sense of skin quality. Still, it is proven, as Griffin found out, that all that the white Southerner has to see is black on a skin, and his discernment ceases. He does not look further. He did not look to the fact that Griffin's and my blue eyes—admittedly, there are certainly many black people with blue eyes, and also with aquiline noses that Griffin and I both have. And none is thought of as Negroid features—neither one of us has those.

Griffin's contention was that he was never questioned, never even questioned about his background, where he came from, or how he happened to be, let's say, accepted as a black man. No one ever questioned him about any of these things. And the conclusion has to be drawn, and I draw it too because of my limited experiences away from the motion picture company with the make-up on, that in fact, I'm not sure that it can be confined only to the white Southerner, but that's the only one I came in contact with. But certainly there was no question that I was a black man. I got from them—I use the word "implacable"—, I don't know really whether it adequately describes, but I got from them an almost relegating me to some sort of a non-human—certainly not an individual. I was never treated in those instances as an individual, a flatness of approach that seemed to deny somehow my existence as a person. The instances that this happened were, it's not numerous, certainly enough to be able to draw this conclusion. One of the reasons that there is such complete acceptance of the man with the black face as being in fact a black man without questions asked, it seems to me, that it's hard for any white Southerner seeing anybody pretending to be a black man or black woman for that matter because to them it's inconceivable that anybody would take on the guise of their volition of a person who is so inferior and will be so debased and so brutalized by society. They can't imagine that anybody would do that unless, of course, they were mad.

I had an experience when I was separated from the company. We were having rehearsals in Washington, and I had my make-up on in my room prior to going to the rehearsal. Then I got lost in the hotel, and I couldn't find the rehearsal room. I was dressed in an open sport shirt and a cardigan sweater, and I was carrying my briefcase. I had forgotten that I was in black face and blundered into a banquet hall where a woman was preparing flowers for some sort of function that day. I walk up to her very confident in my whiteness inside being myself and asked her if she could tell me where such and such a room was. We were alone in this room, and I guess I came at her very positively, not hesitantly at all; walked up to her, as I say, as I would ordinarily, certainly not impolitely at any rate, with a certain amount of confidence in myself. And she turned on me a look of; I can only describe it as loathing, really. Fear, certainly mixed into it at a certain level. And I'd never received a look quite like it in my entire life and didn't know how to deal with it. I forget now exactly what she said. I'm not sure that I heard it, because of the shock of the look that she gave me. I got a small taste of the kind of thing that black people learn to live with or not to live with, early on. It goes on all their lives in this country.

As far as the critical response to the film is concerned, it's hard to say because I critically did not like the film. So I had a tendency to be very forgiving if people didn't like it. There was one critic, whom I respect, a man named Robert Louis Sham in the *Saturday Review of Literature* that seemed to me to miss the point of the whole film. He criticized my make-up, which of course I would agree with; however, he didn't criticize the make-up on the basis that I have just done. He criticized it because he said, "Whitmore looked very much like a sun*burn*ed—no, *tanned*—Maine potato farmer." It's a funny image, but he missed the whole point of the picture. The point of the picture is simply that in the Deep South, a heavily tanned, Maine potato farmer who says that he is a black man would be accepted as a black man. That was the point really, one of the points, the big point of the entire picture. On the basis of an external color, we abandon all human definition; that's the end of it then and there in the South. In the North, too. I mean don't lean too heavily because I certainly agree that our country is racist. There's no question in my mind about that. But, as I say, the only real contact I had with this phenomenon was in the South. Sham missed the whole point. That was the point of the picture. All you have to do is change that external color, and you are relegated to an entire set of clichés and determinations by the white Southerner that's looking at you.

The response of audiences that you asked for seems to me to be pretty darned good. I know it was, of course, not shown in many Southern states. However, it was shown in drive-in theaters in Texas rather widely. And I think it was worth doing the picture because of some of the things that were said in it and not done in a sensational manner. It seems to me done in a more or less responsible manner, all be it as I've indicated a rather overly complex story idea of the central character and his quest for himself and so on. But the black community was pleased, as far as I'm able to gather, very enthusiastic about the film. I think the basic reason was, as I've indicated, things were said for the first time that had never been said before. I think there are truths that were said. The whole sexual mystique—and I believe it to be such about the black man—was exposed and talked about and dramatized in fact.

The film was shown on television, and the scene where oh, the sociologist, anthropologist, whatever he is, white man that accosts the central figure and gets him to come back to his hotel room ostensibly to get some information about the black mentality. And, of course, gets into the sexual area in a very perverse, sick way. That particular scene, when shown in Los Angeles, was blipped out; the dialogue was silenced. They had a description—a voice-over—that told what was happening in very bland terms.

Other than that, I think that the film was generally shown all over the country, with, I say, the exception of the Deep South. I don't believe, to my knowledge, it has been shown there as yet. The response generally was good, but I think the reason for that was that it was not done as a sensational picture and although inexpertly done, it was the first time that certain things had ever been said that needs to be said very badly. In fact, to my knowledge, many of those things had never really been dealt with since in films. I think that's a tragedy.

You ask for some observations on the treatment of the black man in films. Well, that reflected totally in the treatment of the black man generally in our country. It's essentially tokenism. The Poitiers and the various ones—Diana Sands and so on—James Earl Jones—become celebrated simply as tokenism. It's a kind of a left-handed tribute to outstanding ones of the black race. But, on balance, it seems to me that we haven't advanced perceptibly at all toward an understanding of the basic problem which, of course, is racism in its most virulent form. Expressed certainly most clearly in the South; more subtlety and more complexly in the North, but none the less expressed. And the whole bussing thing that we've had recently, although certainly complicated by other factors, at base is that, that fear, that racism that divides people of different colors.

I'll go over to the tape two. I'm gabbier than I thought I was. I've run out of tape, so let's go over to tape number two.

[Tape II]

JW: In listening to the first tape, I must say that it struck me, I may have been, or at least seem to be, excessively harsh in my criticism of Carl Lerner and Gerda Lerner,[111] and I want to amend that to the degree that they.... It certainly is not a criticism of their intent in doing the film *Black Like Me*. The lack was purely one in the areas of ability, I suppose, and that would be it. As far as their quality as people is concerned, I want to make it very strong that I have nothing but great respect for them as people and their desire to do the picture in the first place; and their energy and ingenuity in getting money and getting the picture made. It was, of course, tremendously important. They have my everlasting respect and gratitude for their part in the film. That was positive, and the part that was negative was really, I think, beyond their control.

I did want to clarify that somewhat. I'd also, I think, an interesting sidelight on a venture of this kind, that it was almost completely devoid of ego-trips on the part of most people. With the exception of the aforementioned Jules Tannebaum. I don't mean to make him sound like the abominable snowman or some terrible monstrosity; he was not. He was a very well meaning man, I believe. Just his personality and his set of neuroses led into some very strange areas, not seriously strange. However, I feel that you can use in the position of producer a strong personality and one that can ideally be tasteful and also talentful [sic]. At any rate, we didn't have it, and as in the case of Carl and Gerda Lerner, no more understanding and compassionate and intelligent people, I suppose, could be found anywhere.

Interestingly enough, this infected the entire company, and we had relatively little trouble during the shooting of the film. Admittedly, we were often embattled as a company in a more or less alien territory in the South. And of course, the nature of the film too contributed to the sense of being embattled. And I think led to closer bonds between the people doing the film. Given the difficult situation, a director who was unsure, to be kind, he was unsure (to be brutally frank, he was inept); a script and a woman who had written it, who had a tendency, perhaps naturally, to be overly protective of the written word and of the concept.

Given this set of rather difficult circumstances, and working on location as we did—I think ninety-nine percent of the picture was made in the street or in the houses on the street—, we had very little high tension, human destructiveness between the people. The interpersonal relationships were all very strong and very good. I think the reason for that was that the basic motivation behind the venture was a good motivation. As opposed to the ordinary film project, where commercialism is the prime mover. Then egos have a tendency to swing in their own little particular area of concern, mainly the person him or herself and their well being disregarding the overall, because the overall is blatantly commercial. There the temper tantrums and the internecine warfare goes on almost constantly. It was not true of this film, and for that, of course, I'm eternally grateful. It contributed to making the film a memorable experience, humanly, because everybody, with the rare exception of a few, was the thing, was the thing that brought us all together. Even though it was not wholly successful, in my view as a human experience, it was very successful indeed. I still hold all the people involved in the film in very real affectionate regard.

To discuss, perhaps, a little further the place of the black actor in films, as I've indicated, I think that the progress has been infinitesimal and any real progress is illusory, thus far. I think in many little different areas accumulatively that there may be some meaningful progress.

I think that the appearance of black faces on the TV, once again, tokenism certainly, but nonetheless in the long run cannot help but have a substantive effect on the consciousness of the viewers around this land of ours. The roles, too, that they've been permitted to play—the Flip Wilson Show—although black entertainers have always been more or less acceptable, a man having his own show—being a [? stud duck] as it were—is I think a very important advance.

We need to remember that Whitmore is advancing seven years since the release of Black Like Me. *Flip Wilson's comic variety show on NBC television did not appear until September 17, 1970. Not only was it a smash hit, but also Wilson's comedy routines proved extremely popular with general audiences across the nation. It ended four years later on June 27, 1974. He is credited as the first African-American performer to host his own television show.*[112] *J. Fred MacDonald stressed that not only was the comedian's wit "drawn from the black community," but also his routines seemed "authentic" and "fitting for the mood of the times" as "black pride continued to increase.*[113]

JW: When I say important, I mean within the framework, as I've stated, of an infinitesimal advance. Any real progress at this point is illusory. But within that framework, this kind of exposure has been good.

The emergence of the all-black motion picture—by that I mean the black producer, the black writer, and so on with black stars—is also extremely good. I think the quantity of hostility that they express towards the white world in some of these pictures—I'm thinking particularly of *Putney Swope,*[114] which I didn't think was a particularly good picture but it certainly served its purpose. *Shaft,*[115] and so on.

Written and directed by Robert Downey Sr., Putney Swope *deals with the only black member of a company getting accidentally elected chairperson of the board. He then issues radical directives that not only change the corporate climate, but also pose a threat to the management of other national corporations.*

JW: This expression of this smoldering now erupting hostility towards the whole society is a very healthy and very good thing. I anticipate in the entire area of racism as a human disease a very long, long treatment period; and then after that, a long convalescence. I think it's going to be much more turbulent than any of us imagine.

I think that's very logical, that a disease, a cancer if you will, that has been growing and festering—a disease that has infected the body politic of the world not just this country for centuries—century upon century—cannot obviously be excised with one quick operation, a stroke of the knife. It's going to be a long agonizing, painful and very difficult quest to reach some kind of accommodation between the races. I'm now really speaking globally, and I'm not just referring to black and white. Any race that is other than the Caucasian.

Say you use the word "accommodation," because I think understanding may literally be centuries away. This accommodation, of course, will only be reached if a repressive kind of control is not instituted. And this is certainly within the realm of social and political possibility in the world—in this country. If this can be avoided, and it can only be avoided if our institutions are flexible enough to encompass the kind of evil that we may see. I think much more than we have seen here to fore.

I think that we're in at the moment a kind of a hiatus, a breathtaking, if you will, in a realigning of the blacks' point of view. By "point of view," I mean what's to be done. But I think that this is all going to change by change. I think they're going to solidify points of view. There will always be points not just one; hopefully, a kind of a coming together of what needs to be done. I don't mean by that that it's going to be a homogenous movement at all. But I think that certainly leadership is going to emerge. I don't believe that it's going to be the passive resisters of the [Rev. Ralph] Abernathy-Martin Luther King variety. I think the young lions are going to lead the way in this.

It's symptomatic it seems to me of a need in man—this racism itself—that manifests itself in many other ways. And it's a need, in my view of man, to oversimplify his own disturbation—or simplify the answer to his own disturbation, which arises out of an essentially frightening and overwhelming experience, namely the life experience on this planet. I think that he looks for quick, easy, decisive answers. And one of the ways to do that, of course, is to make up one's mind as quickly as possible who is your friend and who is your enemy. And the way man has done that down through the ages is on the basis of externals. And the man opposite him is judged usually as quickly and as easily as possible; and that's done, of course, on the basis of whether he resembles me or whether he does not. If he varies from the viewer wildly, then he is put in a category and defined. The viewer's anxiety and tensions in relationship to that person are simplified. They may not be diminished, but at least they're solidified into a hate of the person opposite him, or love or a liking if the person is similar to him. It's a judging of our fellow man on the basis of externals.

We see it in the older generation in judging the youth of today on the basis of hair or clothing or some other external. Most of them substantively are not valid at all. And, of course, the racial decision about our fellows has been since time immemorial used to define that other person for our own security's sake. Anything that goes this deep and goes back this far and expresses a need, such a strong need, in people, a need, as I've stated, to simplify their own life, their own life experiences by condemning or approving of other people. In other words, sorting them out, deciding exactly where they belong, and, of course, we use the term "Square Head," we use the term "Pollock," we use the term "Kike," we use the term "Nigger" as pigeonhole headings under which to put people that qualify as far as we're concerned on the basis of externals for those pigeonholes.

Once we've got them all neatly arranged in our desk, then we can go ahead with the business of living with a sense of security. We know who the good guys are, and we know who the bad guys are. This is a very strong need in people. Of course, we all should know that it is relatively unimportant; the packaging is just that, packaging. Although it does perfect the, or rather does affect the inner man or woman, the essential thing is what resides in the mind and inside in the heart and soul of that package. And the package of itself should not be important. However, man has for centuries done the opposite, and I think it's going to take centuries to come to some understanding of this. Hopefully, we will be allowed to, and worldwide cataclysm or war will not make it all terribly academic. So I take, I suppose, a grim view as far as time is concerned, but maybe an optimistic view as far as being able to accomplish it at all.

Now what role film will play in the arriving at this accommodation is, of course, impossible to say. I think film is potentially one of the most powerful tools that man is given for communicating ideas and emotions to each other. I would think that a picture like *Black Like Me* compared to most pictures that deal with this particular subject is as good as any I've seen dealing with this subject. In a way, it's very amateurish and rather bumbling technique has its own built-in ability to beguile. And I think it does make a small contribution.

Compared to a picture like *The Split*,[116] it stands out as a rather wonderful enterprise because of its motivation. I read the motivation behind a picture like *The Split* as commercial totally on the part of Metro-Goldwyn-Mayer, an endeavor to capitalize on the black emergence, the "dignity revolution" that was going on and still is. At that time, the use of a black man like Jim Brown as the hero, if one can call—really an anti-hero, I suppose—a hustler, a man running a game and a hero in that sense, certainly the Bogart sense of hero; and a black woman, Diahann Carroll, playing the female lead—being capitalized on by Metro with a strong injection of violence, excessive violence.

*Here it is useful to remember the strong ties between Whitmore and Gomberg. Both men throughout their lives waged a constant battle against excessive violence in entertainment and the harmful effects it had on children. Reporter Myrna Oliver pointed out in Gomberg's obituary, "He helped organize Hollywood's Committee to End Violence and to produce a 1998 advertisement that ran in three trade publications—*Variety*, the* Hollywood Reporter *and the Writers Guild publication* Written By*—headlined "How Responsible Are We?" It pictured a child in a coffin and stated: "We who create entertainment must honestly acknowledge and urgently address the responsibility we all have to eliminate excessive or gratuitous or unpunished violence in films and television." It was signed by 180 writers, actors, producers and directors."*[117] *I assume that Whitmore felt the same as Gomberg.*

JW: I was interested in the script because it was black entrepreneurs, illegal, totally entrepreneurs, but nonetheless, entrepreneurs and blacks really kind of running the show. That was interesting to me. I found the part an interesting acting challenge. I had never played a part quite like it before. I think, very importantly, the money was excellent on this picture. Without the money, I don't think I would have done it. Without the money, I mean, if it hadn't been for my salary and a little bit more for that role in *The Split*.

On the set of the picture it was interesting to work with Jim Brown, who was a presence of considerable magnitude, tremendously dynamic man with a very ill concealed hatred for white people. And I'm not sure but that there isn't a very neurotic and sick dislike of all people in Jim Brown, out of an evidently very tortuous youth. And with a particular emphasis—I don't mean to sound like a bargain basement psychiatrist here, but I do sense, and I think his record bares it out—a very decided hatred of women. Resentment certainly, whether it's hatred or not, I don't know, but I know that Diahann Carroll was the recipient of this numerous times during the filming of the picture. That, it seemed to me, was extremely interesting.

But basically, it was a commercial enterprise. As I say, very unlike *Black Like Me* in that regard. I must confess, that because I deplored the excessive violence in the picture, and after seeing the way the director was shooting it, I knew that this was going to be played down. On the contrary, it was played up in his handling of the material. I really didn't want to see the film; and to this day, I have not seen it. So I certainly cannot speak very authoritatively about *The Split*. I think, however, that even though the commercial establishment, in this instance, Metro, preempted a field—racial violence in our country and the racial disturbance, so then hence the violence per se in the picture—, and it was purely cynical and a business proposition, that this kind of picture, *The Split*, even this probably, as a part of the whole, will make a contribution, even if it's only to disturb white America to the degree that they recognize a guy like Jim Brown walks the earth, and he's a considerable gentleman too.

I think it's to the good, as I think that *All in the Family* is to the good. I think that the more we discuss this kind of thing—the classic example was, of course, Ibsen's *Ghosts* when first congenital syphilis was discussed in a public form; *The Dollhouse* and other things that Ibsen wrote were revolutionary in their time. Excellent, very good for people, that the subjects were at least discussed. And in the instance of racism, to have the Kerner Report [1968] announce that we are a country of racists is marvelous, because as I've stated earlier, I believe it profoundly. I think most Americans were shocked by that statement.

Historian Isabel Wilkerson stated, "President Lyndon Johnson chose... [U. S. Attorney Otto Kerner] to head a federal investigation into the racial disturbances of the 1960s. The commission's findings, released in February 1968 as the Report of the National Advisory Commission on Civil Disorders, *would come to be known as the Kerner Report. Its recommendations would be revisited for decades as a measure of the country's progress toward equality, its stark pronouncement invoked many times over: "Our nation is moving toward two societies," the report said, "one black, one white-separate and unequal."*[118]

I really feel that I'm talked out and had no idea that I could go for a tape and a third, but I seem to have, and if there are any questions that Dr. Manchel would like to ask, please address them to me, and I'll see what I can do. Any technical questions, I don't have that information at my fingertips, but I will certainly try to get it for you. And I must tell you that in a very rather egocentric way, I've rather enjoyed exploring my own thoughts, particularly on *Black Like Me*. I'm sure that I've left many corners unlit, and, as I say, please don't hesitate to ask me about them, if you'd like to. I hope some of this will be usable for your research, and I hope to meet you some day, Dr., possibly at your school, or if you get to California and see Sy Gomberg, I would like very much to sit down with you and share some thoughts. I hope this will be useful to you.

Postscript

I never did get back to James Whitmore, in large part because I was now deeply involved in publishing the first edition of *Film Study: A Resource Guide* (1973)[119] and in navigating my way through university politics. While it would have been interesting and stimulating to question the actor directly, his responses to my questions contributed to my growing understanding of the black film legacy.

Reviewing his experiences also opened up my awareness of the contributions of other professionals like Sy Gomberg and Maggie Hathaway.

Writer Bob Thomas opined, "Whitmore plays the uncommon man uncommonly, a statement that could describe his entire career."[120] As for me, I choose to remember the awarding-winning actor playing Harry Truman and delivering the line, "It's what you learn after knowing it all that really counts."[121]

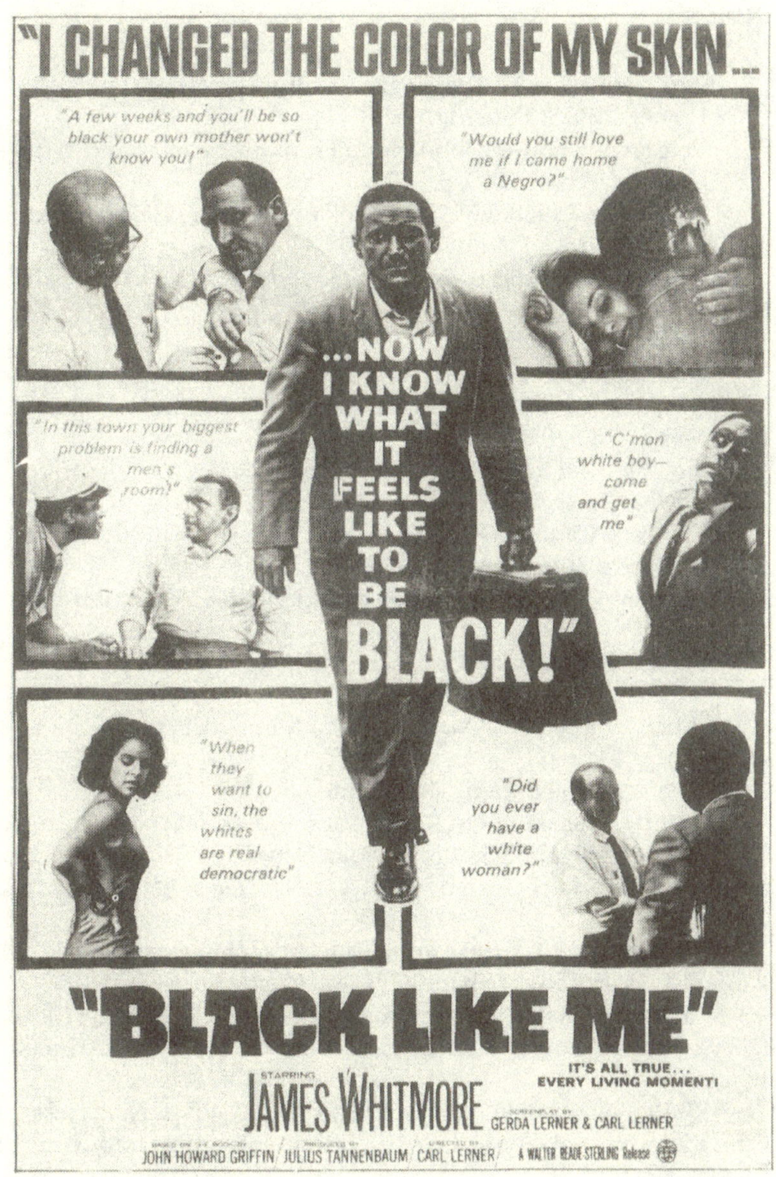

One Sheet **40 x 60** ALSO AVAILABLE

27. A Press book one sheet for Carl Lerner's *Black Like Me* (1964), starring James Whitmore. Noted actor Richard Ward appears in the middle-left still. Courtesy of the Wisconsin Historical Society.

Notes

[1]Staff, "New Crisis: The Negro Family," *Newsweek* (1965): 35.

[2] Lerner, "Black Like Me."

[3] Peter Applebome, "John Hope Franklin, Scholar and Witness," *New York Times*, March 29 2009, 5.

[4] Unknown, "1968 with Tom Brokaw," (USA: Peacock Productions, in association with A&E Network, 2007).

[5] Joseph, *Dark Days, Bright Nights: From Black Power to Barack Obama*, 63-4.

[6] Gavin, *Stormy Weather*, 8.

[7] Guerrero, *Framing Blackness: The African American Image in Film*, 84.

[8] Grant IV, *Post-Soul Black Cinema: Discontinuities, Innovations, and Breakpoints, 1970-1995*, 34.

[9] Sieving, *Soul Searching: Black-Themed Cinema from the March on Washington to the Rise of Blaxploitation*, 11-2.

[10] Vincent Canby, "Race to Film Race Issues: Indies React to Negro News," *Variety*, July 17, 1963, 3, 20.

[11] Shirley Clarke, "The Cool World," (USA: Wiseman Film Productions, 1962).

[12] Nicholas Webster, "Gone Are the Days," (1963).

[13] Lerner, "Black Like Me."

[14] Michael Roemer, "Nothing But a Man," (USA: Cinema 5/New Video, 1964).

[15] Peerce, "One Potato, Two Potato."

[16] Canby, "Race to Film Race Issues: Indies React to Negro News," 20.

[17] Murray Schumach, "Stars Join Drive against Bigotry: Hollywood Speaks up Amid Pressure by N.A.A.C.P.," *New York Times*, July 15, 1963, 25.

[18] "Hollywood Cause: Movie Delegation Set to Join Racial March No Fanfare Citizen's Right Shadow From…" *New York Times* 1963, X7.

[19] Pam Munter, "Uncommonly Common," Article, *Classic Images* (2009), http://www.classicimages.com/articles/2009/02/05/past_articles/whitmore.txt.

[20] Staff, "Newsmakers: James Whitmore," vol. 1, *Newsmakers* (Detroit: Gale Biography in Context, 2010), http:ic.galegroup.com/ic/bic1/ReferenceDetailsPage. 1.

[21] Dennis McLellan, "James Whitmore Dies at 87; Veteran Award-Winning Actor Brought American Icons to Life," *Los Angeles Times*, Feb. 7, 2009, 1.

[22] Davis and Dee, *With Ossie & Ruby in This Life Together*, 258.

[23] Munter, "Uncommonly Common."

[24] "Uncommonly Common." 2.

[25] Ibid.

[26] Ibid.

[27] McLellan, "James Whitmore Dies at 87; Veteran Award-Winning Actor Brought American Icons to Life," 3.

[28] Joseph H. Lewis, "The Undercover Man," (USA: MGM, 1949).

[29] William A. Wellman, "Battleground," (USA: MGM, 1949).

[30] Munter, "Uncommonly Common." 4.

[31] John Huston, "The Asphalt Jungle," (USA: MGM, 1950).

[32] Don Siegel, "Crime in the Streets " (USA: Allied Artists, 1956).

[33] Roy Rowland, "The Outriders," (USA: MGM, 1950).

[34] Gordon Douglas, "Them!," (USA: Warner Brothers, 1954).

[35] Alexander Hall, "Because You're Mine," (USA: MGM, 1952).

[36] George Sidney, "Kiss Me Kate," (USA: MGM, 1953).

[37] "The Eddy Duchin Story," (USA: Columbia Pictures, 1956).

[38] Melvin Frank, "Above and Beyond," (USA: MGM, 1952).

[39] Raoul Walsh, "Battle Cry."

[40] Gordon Douglas, "The McConnell Story," (USA: Warner Brothers, 1955).

[41] Rudolph Mate, "The Deep Six," (USA: Warner Brothers, 1958).

[42] Staff, "Dark December," *The Modesta Bee*, April 26 1959.

[43] The other writers were Ruth Brooks Flippen, Leonard Spielglass, and Karl Tunberg.

[44] Munter, "Uncommonly Common." 2.

[45] Staff, "Thesp Perfected Presidents," *Variety*, Feb. 16 2009.

[46] Abbi Toushin, "Obituaries: Sy Gomberg," ibid., Feb. 19-Feb.25 2001, 68.

[47] Myrna Oliver, "Obituaries; Sy Gomberg; Screenwriter, Activist Decried Screen Violence," *Los Angeles Times*, Feb. 14, 2001, 2.

[48] Toushin, "Obituaries: Sy Gomberg," 68.

[49] Oliver, "Obituaries; Sy Gomberg; Screenwriter, Activist Decried Screen Violence," 1.

[50] Ibid.

[51] Frank Manchel, "Conversation with Sy Gomberg," Communication and Theatre (University of Vermont, 1972).

[52] Ibid.

[53] Mark Robson, "Home of the Brave," (USA: United Artists, 1949).

[54] Manchel, "Conversation with Sy Gomberg."

[55] Oliver, "Obituaries; Sy Gomberg; Screenwriter, Activist Decried Screen Violence," 1.

[56] Staff, "CTVA: The Classic TV Archive."

[57] Manchel, "Conversation with Sy Gomberg."

[58] Dennis Hevesi, "Tom Moore, President of Abc Television in '60s, Dies at 88," *The New York Times*, April 4, 2007, A13.

[59] Brooks and Marsh, *The Complete Directory to Prime Time Network TV Shows: 1946-Present*, 71-2.

[60] Manchel, "Conversation with Sy Gomberg."

[61] Schumach, "Stars Join Drive against Bigotry: Hollywood Speaks up Amid Pressure by N.A.A.C.P.," 25.

[62] Davis and Dee, 206.

[63] Jason Lewis, "Woman's History Month: Maggie Hathaway—Community and Civil Rights Activist," *Los Angeles Sentinel* 2012, 2.

[64] Edward Buzzell, "At the Circus," (USA: MGM, 1939).

[65] Vincent Minnelli, "Cabin in the Sky," (USA: MGM, 1943).

[66] Andrew L. Stone, "Stormy Weather," (USA: MGM, 1943).

[67] Brown and Delsohn, *Out of Bounds*, 78.

[68] Hathaway, "Hollywood Segregation, Integration Performances 'before, after' Exposed."

[69] Frank Manchel, May 11, 1972.

[70] Hathaway, "Hollywood Segregation, Integration Performances 'before, after' Exposed," D1.

[71] "Hollywood Segregation, Integration Performances 'before, after' Exposed."

[72] "The Inside Story: Segregation & Integration in Hollywood: Part II," *The Hollywood Sentinel*, Thursday, March 30, 1967.

[73] Ibid.

[74] Ibid.

[75] Ibid.

[76] Ibid.

[77] Ibid.

[78] "The Inside Story: Segregation & Integration in Hollywood: Part III," *The Hollywood Sentinel*, April 6, 1967, E1.

[79] "The Inside Story: Segregation & Integration in Hollywood: Part III," *The Hollywood Sentinel*, April 6, 1967.

[80] Donald Bogle, *Bright Boulevards, Bold Dreams: The Story of Black Hollywood*, 1st ed. (New York: One World Ballantine Books, 2005); Hathaway, "The inside Story: Segregation & Integration in Hollywood: Part III."

[81] "The Inside Story: Segregation & Integration in Hollywood: Part III."

[82] Billy Wilder, "The Apartment," (USA: United Artists [Mirisch Company/United Artists], 1960).

[83] Maggie Hathaway, "The Inside Story: Segregation & Integration: IV," *The Hollywood Sentinel*, April 13 1967.

[84] "The Inside Story: Segregation & Integration: IV," *The Hollywood Sentinel*, April 13 1967, D2.

[85] "The Inside Story: Segregation & Integration: IV."

[86] Lewis, "Woman's History Month: Maggie Hathaway—Community Civil Rights Activist," 2.

[87] Munter, "Uncommonly Common." 9.

[88] Sieving, *Soul Searching: Black-Themed Cinema from the March on Washington to the Rise of Blaxploitation.*

[89] Staff, "Carl Lerner, 61, Film Editor of 'Klute, ''12 Angry Men,' Dies," *New York Times*, August 28, 1973, 38.

[90] Lee W. Formwalt, "Demystifying and Rethinking the Study of History: An Interview with Gerda Lerner," *OAH Newsletter* (2006): 7, 23.

[91] Staff, "$273,000 Budget on Reade-Sterling 'Black Like Me'," *Variety*, July 17, 1963, 20.

[92] Eugene Archer, "Filming to Begin on 'Black Like Me'," *New York Times* 1963, 15.

[93] Munter, "Uncommonly Common." 9-10.

[94] Gordon Douglas, "Chuka," (USA: Paramount Pictures, 1967).

[95] Don Siegel, "Madigan," (USA: Universal, 1968).

[96] Franklin J. Schaffner, "Planet of the Apes," (USA: Twentieth Century-Fox, 1968).

[97] Paul Wendkos, "Guns of the Magnificent Seven," (USA: United Artists, 1969).

[98] Staff, "Newsmakers: James Whitmore," 2.

[99] McLellan, "James Whitmore Dies at 87; Veteran Award-Winning Actor Brought American Icons to Life," 1.

[100] Dennis Bingham, *Whose Lives Are They Anyway? The Biopic as Contemporary Film Genre* (New Brunswick, New Jersey: Rutgers University Press, 2010), 140-41.

[101] Staff, "Newsmakers: James Whitmore," 2.

[102] McLellan, "James Whitmore Dies at 87; Veteran Award-Winning Actor Brought American Icons to Life," 2.

[103] Steve Binder and Peter H. Hunt, "Give 'Em Hell, Harry," (TheatreVision, 1975).

[104] Peter Rollins, E-Mail, December 8, 2012.

[105] Frank Darabont, "The Shawshank Redemption," (USA: Castle Rock Entertainment, 1994).

[106] McLellan, "James Whitmore Dies at 87; Veteran Award-Winning Actor Brought American Icons to Life," 1.

[107] G.B. Harrison, ed. *Shakespeare: Major Plays and the Sonnets* (New York: Harcourt, Brace and Company, 1948), 616.

[108] Lerner, "Black Like Me."

[109] Flemyng, "The Split."

[110] Joseph R. Treaster, "Richard Ward Dies; Stage and TV Actor," *New York Times*, July 4, 1979, A9.

[111] William Grimes, "Gerda Lerner, Pioneering Feminist and Historian, Dies at 92 " ibid., January 4 2013, A16.

[112] Brooks and Marsh, *The Complete Directory to Prime Time Network TV Shows: 1946-Present*, 268-69.

[113] MacDonald, *Blacks and White TV: Afro-Americans in Television since 1948*, 173-74.

[114] Robert Downey Sr., "Putney Swope," (USA: Cinema 5, 1969).

[115] Gordon Parks, "Shaft," (USA: MGM, 1971).

[116] Wilkerson, *The Warmth of Other Suns: The Epic Story of America's Great Migration*, 386-87.

[117] Oliver, "Obituaries; Sy Gomberg; Screenwriter, Activist Decried Screen Violence," 1-2.

[118] Wilkerson, *The Warmth of Other Suns: The Epic Story of America's Great Migration*.

[119] Manchel, *Film Study: A Resource Guide*.

[120] Munter, "Uncommonly Common." 9.

[121] Binder and Hunt, "Give 'Em Hell, Harry!"

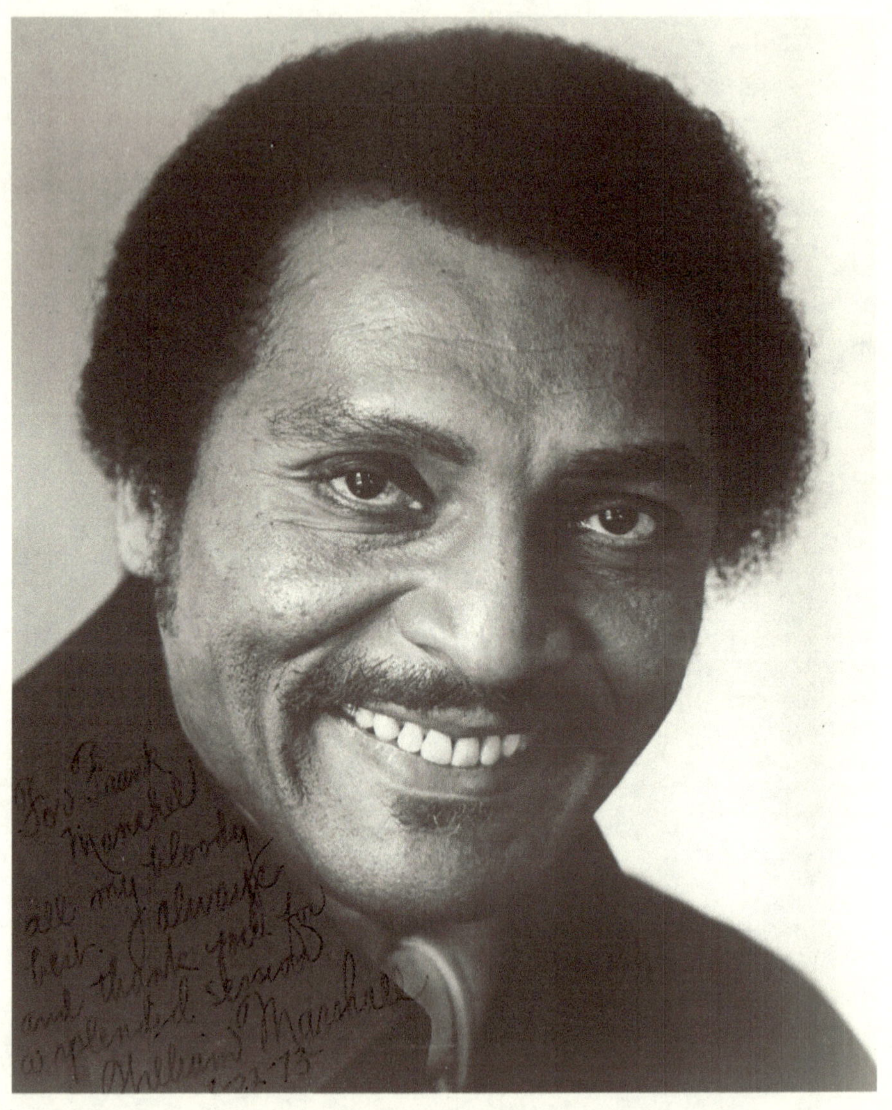

28. The caption reads: "To Frank Manchel. All my bloody best, always, and thank you for a splendid session. William Marshall, 8-22-73."

6

With An Unsullied Plume: William Marshall

"I believe that our history is a very significant part of us. All the energies that precede us have shone on us. We are necessarily a part of our time."[1]

James Earl Jones

"[Samuel L.] Jackson...has no patience with those who put down black actors like Hattie McDaniel, Butterfly McQueen and Stepin' Fetchit, whose work reinforced demeaning racial stereotypes. 'If you wanted to work in those days,' he said, 'that's what you did. They were proud of who they were.....'"[2]

Paul Jordan

"We are recalling this not so much as a means of indicting Hollywood as by way of placing...recent films...in perspective. To direct an attack on Hollywood would indeed be to confuse portrayal with action, image with reality. In the beginning was not the shadow, but the act, and the province of Hollywood is not action, but illusion. Actually, the anti-Negro images of...films were (and are) acceptable because of the existence throughout the United States of an audience obsessed with an inner psychological need to view Negroes as less than men."[3]

Ralph Ellison

In 1936, when William Marshall was twelve years old, Paramount Pictures, one of the five major studios controlling the Hollywood cinema, released Cecil B. DeMille's *The Plainsman*.[4] The predictable, contrived, and big-budgeted studio western about Wild Bill Hickok (Gary Cooper), William "Buffalo Bill" Cody (James Ellison), and Calamity Jane (Jean Arthur) told a fanciful story about brave men aiding a heroic Gen. George Armstrong Custer (John Miljan) in fulfilling the martyred President Abraham Lincoln's wish that the frontier be made safe for white men. To achieve their goal, the film's heroes wage war against savage, superstitious, and childish Indians like Yellow Hand (Paul Harvey) who mercilessly kill innocent, home-loving white settlers. Caucasian actors play almost every major Native-American role. In addition, the Cheyenne and the Shawnee seem the only people upset that the American government had lied and betrayed and murdered the Indians for decades. Near the end of the film, Hickok and Cody learn from a wandering Native American warrior (Anthony Quinn) that Custer's men have been "massacred" at Little Big Horn. That "atrocity" turns the war around, and the film ends with the following words: "It shall be as it was in the past...not with dreams. But with strength and with courage shall a nation be molded to last." The only noticeable black in this hackneyed movie is a helpless dockhand too weak to carry his burden during the unloading of a steamboat. In trying to become politically correct, David Lowell Rich's 1966 remake with the same name not only was pathetic, but also absurd.[5]

The DeMille film symbolized the mainstream entertainment world that the ambitious Marshall chose to make part of his professional life. For nearly half a century, he struggled against incredible odds and with few major opportunities; and yet, he emerged a significant presence on the stage, screen, and in television. During his exceptional career, the famous artist with a rich, unforgettable voice and magisterial presence took part in many of the sweeping show business changes that occurred after World War II. By the time his career concluded at the end of the twentieth century, the big studio system had disappeared, white performers were rarely cast in ethnic roles, the racist stereotypes perpetuated by movies like *The Plainsman* had not only been discredited but also been replaced, albeit by different distortions, and the opportunities denied that uncredited black actor in the DeMille epic had been exchanged for prospects unimaginable to African-American performers in 1936.

Many of the impressive roles Marshall took on presented him

as a royal figure battling against oppressive, imperialistic, and historical forces. The social conditions on the sets were often more challenging than the characters he played. Yet, the pragmatic performer played these bygone, regal figures effectively in clichéd dramas superficially attacking various forms of slavery. Ironically, this statuesque, imposing artist is best remembered by the public for his role as an African prince cursed by the evil and racist Count Dracula in William Crain's blaxploitation film *Blacula.*[6] What proved most striking about this gifted actor is despite his rarely having strong narratives, challenging roles, outstanding co-workers, or adequate financing, he maintained his dignity, demonstrated his intelligence, and proved a positive force in the midst of calamitous circumstances.

To understand how Marshall managed to carve out such a longstanding and distinguished acting career is also to remind the reader of just what it took for black actors to survive successfully with their dignity preserved in the second half of a racially dominated twentieth century culture. The films, plays, and TV shows listed in his resume frequently mask how Marshall kept his performing hopes alive by working in churches, local playhouses, lecture halls, and school auditoriums merely for a chance to hone his art. How one day he could perform before European royalty, and the next week be working in some small, unknown playhouse. Like many of his peers, he took the meagre material available to him as a black actor, combined it with rare opportunities to appear in important stage productions, especially as Shakespeare's *Othello,* coupled it with teaching jobs and dramatic readings, all in pursuit of living the life he desired. Even more impressive, Marshall did it courageously and continuously all through the days of the blacklist, institutional racism, and unending pressure to compromise his values.

What especially caught my attention was the reason Marshall singled out for bringing about so many racial reforms following the post-WWII period. When Robert Chrisman, the distinguished editor and publisher of *The Black Scholar,* asked the actor in 1985 if he thought Black Power deserved credit for the reforms during the sixties, Marshall replied, "Subject matter involving black people came not so much from the recognition of the civil rights thrust, though it does have to be taken into account. But," he insisted, "we must consider the technological problems that the conventional film makers were confronted with, the technological monster being television, stealing all their patrons from them...."[7] The reader no doubt recalls this point of view being advanced in the Introduction.

As always, I remind my readers that what follows does not definitively characterize William Marshall. All that can be accomplished in my venue is to highlight many of the choices the left-leaning artist made during his time upon the stage. His story was not "a tale told of sound and fury signifying nothing." It was part of a great legacy that he and his peers provided for us and for generations yet unborn. My hope is that this oversimplified review of his life and his career helps to not only gain respect for his contributions to his art, his country, and his race, but also to keep his memory as fresh in your recollections of the past as it is in mine.

William Horace Marshall was born to Dr. Vereen and Thelma (Edwards) Marshall on August 19, 1924 in Gary, Indiana. His father was a dentist; his mother, a school teacher; and both parents were determined that their son not become scarred by growing up in what would emerge as one of America's most depressed post-WWII societies. Once a thriving steel community, Gary devolved into a dilapidated municipality soon to be overrun by vast pockets of crime and corruption. As the reader might remember, the municipality was the setting for Larry Cohen's *Original Gangstas* (1996),[8] mentioned in the earlier Jim Brown chapter.

But Marshall did not share his parents' aspirations. "School was for me terribly difficult because I was the son of Dr. Marshall and Mrs. Thelma Marshall who flunked an awful lot of students. I had no brothers or sisters, so I was in boxing gloves at age 12."[9] By his junior year, Bill was not someone his fellow students chose to upset. Marching to his own drummer, the intimidating sixteen-year-old basically opted out of a formal education and decided to spend his after-school hours at the local pool hall, where he became an accomplished pool hustler, card shark, crapshooter, and gambler.

During his years at Roosevelt High School, he posed many potential problems for his parents. No doubt what saved him from any serious trouble was the fact that so many people in town were also his father's patients. Thus they looked after the youngster until he became old enough to take care of himself.[10] After graduating from Roosevelt in 1942, he became a steel worker before entering the army in 1943. A year later he left the service and returned to his hometown and to his job in the steel mills.

However, the nineteen year old's pointless way of life bothered him, just as it had always worried his mother. Sensing his willingness to finally come around, she suggested he might discover a new direction by pursuing his interests in singing and art. Thus, Mrs. Marshall made arrangements for William to visit her strong-willed, progressive sister, Thyra Edwards, then living in New York's Greenwich Village.

It was this unusual woman who provided the life-altering direction her nephew followed. Initially, she steered him toward a commercial art career, and he enrolled in the Arts Students League where he developed into a serious student. But it was evident he had an even greater talent: singing. So the devoted aunt convinced her nephew to meet and to study with her friend Abbey Mitchell, one of the most notable artists of her generation.

Now there may be some readers not familiar with the gifted wife of famed composer Will Marion Cook, who featured her in his early popular shows like *Clorindy: The Origin of the Cakewalk* (1898) and *Jes Lak White Folks* (1899). She also made a name for herself in her husband's trailblazing work *In Dahomey* (1902), the first ever full-length musical by black people to appear successfully on Broadway.

Born in New York in 1884, Abbie Mitchell gained fame as a gifted actress and a talented opera singer. In addition to being a valued member of Harlem's famous Lafayette Players, the delightful performer created the role of Clara in the original production of the Gershwins' *Porgy and Bess*, appeared as Addie in Lillian Hellman's *The Little Foxes,* and Muh Mack in Paul Green's *In Abraham's Bosom.*[11] Further, the amazing artist toured some of Europe's major cities, giving concerts and recitals both for the public and for royalty. Abbey Mitchell, a former executive secretary of the Negro Actors Guild of America, died in 1960, leaving behind a rich legacy of art and music.[12]

Marshall spent most of his nineteenth year studying with this remarkable woman, before deciding to move out of Greenwich Village and uptown to Harlem's YMCA on 135th Street. There a friendly lodger suggested the young singer test his talent by auditioning for the chorus of a new Billy Rose all-black musical entitled *Carmen Jones*. Using the music Mitchell had taught him, Marshall got a job and made his Broadway debut singing Oscar Hammerstein II's original lyrics in the pit of the Broadway Theatre orchestra at the end of 1944. Since the story concerning that landmark show and the film made from it has been covered in the Brock Peters chapter, I need only remind readers how important that musical was to so many black performers.

Thus began for the striking 6'5" inch ex-steel worker from Gary, Indiana a life in show business. Over the next few hectic years, Marshall found work briefly as Ossie Davis' understudy in Robert Ardrey's 1946 Broadway show *Jeb*, which lasted less than ten performances.[13] Later that year, he travelled across the country in the road show of *Call Me Mister*, a musical revue by composer and lyricist Harold Rome; and he returned to Broadway to understudy William Vesey in Theodore Ward's controversial Broadway production of *Our Lan'*, which stayed on the boards only five weeks. These experiences and other stage efforts are covered in the interview that follows. I mention them here to show what Marshall's early career was like and how these Broadway assignments fitted in with other acting jobs he found around the New York area. In between his various roles, Marshall began, in 1947, to study acting at The American Theatre Wing and later in the early fifties at the Actors Studio.

His acting lessons led to a part in Dorothy Heyward's *Set My People Free*, which premiered at Broadway's Hudson Theater on November 3, 1948. The dramatist, who had co-authored with her late husband such previous black dramas as *Porgy*, *Porgy and Bess*, and *Mamba's Daughters*, populated the new play with a superb cast, which included Juano Hernandez, Canada Lee, Mildred Smith, Frank Wilson, and Leigh Whipper. William Marshall had a small role as Rolla Bennett. Sponsored by the Theatre Guild and directed by Martin Ritt, the three act play dealt with Denmark Vesey's failed slave rebellion in 1822 Charleston.[14] Brooks Atkinson, the *New York Times* drama critic, wrote, "Played with so much vividness and honesty, *Set My People Free* is one of the best theatre experiences that have come along this season."[15] This particular work, with its emphasis on the psychological and traumatic experiences of slaves, influenced Marshall for the remainder of his career, and consequently he made it a point to be in works about ex-slaves such as Denmark Vesey, Toussaint L'Overture, Henri Christophe, and Frederick Douglass.

As the decade drew to a close, ominous events in the entertainment world foreshadowed the strong-minded performer's future. A series of 1949 Negro problem films—*Pinky, Lost Boundaries, Intruder in the Dust,* and *Home of the Brave*—galvanized the film audience's social and political consciousness as well as attracted the attention of the infamous House Un-American Activities Committee (HUAC). With Hollywood reeling from economic, aesthetic, legal, and political problems, the industry began a decade of witch-hunts, which ruined the lives not only of upcoming performers but also the careers of veteran stars. Among the most famous personalities injured were Larry Parks and Paul Robeson. Many of the details were covered earlier in the Introduction.

But noteworthy here are the circumstances surrounding Robeson's marginalization. Following his controversial Paris speech in the spring of 1949, the legendary singer and activist became a prime target of FBI director J. Edgar Hoover and HUAC. But he did not appear before the notorious committee until 1956. However, in 1949-1950, HUAC brought a number of prominent black people to Washington to refute Robeson's distorted remarks. Among the most famous was the immortal Jackie Robinson, who challenged Robeson's statement that blacks would not fight against the Soviet Union. In later years, the great humanitarian described the pressures put on him to take a public stand against Robeson's views.[16] But in 1949, the effect was chilling.

Worth remembering is the fact that Marshall admired Robeson and remained steadfast to him throughout the darkness that overshadowed the fabled critic of American racism. Even as the storm clouds gathered over the singer in the early 1950s, William Marshall made clear he had Robeson to thank for his first notable performance in *Othello* at New York State's oldest black church, The Mother A. M. E. Zion Church. The year was 1953, the pastor was the Reverend Benjamin Robeson (Paul's brother), and a young actor named Lloyd Richards played Iago. Starting with this performance at this church, Marshall would tour the production around to various schools, as well as making his playing the tragic Moor a major part of his career.

By the start of the fifties, the promising actor/singer seemed on a positive trajectory as he played the starring role of De Lawd in a new but short-lived Broadway production of Marc Connelly's 1930 Pulitzer-Prize winning play *The Green Pastures* at the Broadway Theatre in 1951. Ossie Davis also appeared as Gabriel in the restoration. Despite Connolly's directing the revival, it opened in mid-March and closed a month later. In the interim, the play was adapted for the small screen in early April and served as Marshall's television debut. (A more highly regarded version appeared in 1957 on the Hallmark Hall of Fame, starring William Warfield, Eddie Anderson, and Frederick O'Neal.)[17]

But what appeared so promising in dates and events overshadowed the traumas the towering actor would face for the remainder of the decade. Davis affords us an insight in his autobiography about what he and Marshall and other black actors faced in those troubled times. The eminent actor/playwright describes how he objected to Marc Connelly's play, "whose version of heaven was simple, childlike black people happily singing at a vast fish-fry celebration, presided over by De Lawd." Yet in 1951, when a revival of the play meant a job on Broadway, he took it. His friend William Marshall, whose booming voice was matched only by his private political militancy, played the part of De Lawd. But since he shared Davis' objections to the role he was playing, he had some difficulty orating with conviction. So every night, just before De Lawd castigates the world for its sins, Davis would whisper in his ear the name of the latest brother who had dared to attack Paul Robeson (a roster that included names like Jackie Robinson, Josh White, and Canada Lee), and, "Bill would rise to such ear-shattering heights that nobody sitting in the audience—which was usually white—could help but feel the lash of his venom."[18]

The witch-hunters may not have known about the cynical game Marshall and Davis were playing during *The Green Pastures* days, but there was no doubt they had their eye on the Shakespearian performer. For example, two years later he agreed to do a local TV series entitled *Harlem Detectives,* a low-budget outing about black police officers. The overly ambitious live program premiered on October 14, 1953. But WOR-TV found itself forced to cancel the series three months later because it was brought to its attention by the anti-communist newsletter *Counterattack* that Marshall was a "Pinko."[19] According to Thomas Cripps, in the early 1950s, when confronted by such political pressures, TV allowed timidity to display its ugliness and "dampen[ed] the prospects for a black TV genre."[20]

If you think TV gave Marshall angina, it was nothing compared to what the new technological medium was doing to the film industry in the early 1950s. As you no doubt recall from your readings in the Introduction, Television appeared out to destroy Hollywood. But the faltering studios mounted a major campaign to win back its dwindling audiences through the use of new technology, runaway overseas productions, and big-budgeted Biblical epics that dwarfed anything that could be shown on the small screens in our living rooms.

Prominent among the Hollywood studios leading the anti-television campaign was Twentieth Century-Fox and its brilliant, no-nonsense, and socially conscious studio head Darryl F. Zanuck. In 1951, for example, he had purchased Kenneth Roberts' 1947 historical novel *Lydia Bailey*. The well-intentioned but romanticized story of an enslaved Haiti fighting to remain free from French domination had all the ingredients for a Technicolor spectacular that could well wean viewers away from their living rooms and back into the movie theaters. What's more, it provided a number of important roles for black actors, including Ken Renard as the heroic Toussaint L'Overture, Roy E. Glenn as the French-hating General Mirabeau, and William Marshall as the inspiring King Dick.

Directed by Jean Negulesco and scripted by such exceptional writers as Michael Blankfort and Philip Dunne, the film[21] told the story of two lovers (Dale Robertson and Anne Francis) caught up in Napoleon Bonaparte's failed 1802 attempt to reclaim Hati. It also gave Marshall an ideal vehicle in which to make his screen debut. As an intelligent, powerful, and worldly black leader, the dignified actor's King Dick would forever typecast him as a stately performer of the screen and television. Representative of the rave reviews the actor received in this unusual movie are the observations by the *New York Times* A. H. Weller. In remarking on *Lydia Bailey*, the critic spoke for many commentators when he stated, "William Marshall, who could be likened to history's King Christophe, makes an imposing and indestructible patriot whose voice is as commanding as his figure."[22]

Nonetheless, it took two years for Twentieth Century-Fox to find another suitable role for its newly acquired black performer. Clearly, nothing conventional suited him, so the writers of *Lydia Bailey* were directed to craft a part for him[23] in a large-scale Biblical spectacle, Delmer Daves' *Demetrius and the Gladiators*.[24]

However, nothing appeared ready for Marshall by the time of the studio's next historical blockbuster, Henry King's *The Robe* (1953).[25] Adapted from Lloyd C. Douglass' epic novel about the Crucifixion of Jesus, the first Cinema Scope movie won honors for its star Richard Burton, as well as praise for Victor Mature as the brave Greek slave Demetrius who inherits Christ's robe. Screenwriter Dunne took the Mature character created in *The Robe* and used it as the inspiration for a role for the black actor in the 1954 Daves movie. In fact, *Demetrius and the Gladiators* starts with the conclusion of *The Robe* and the slave Demetrius being given the robe before his friends are led to their death.

The sequel then follows the tortured choices Demetrius has to make when he is forced to become a gladiator and decide if he will go against his new religion and kill people. In a clever piece of writing, Marshall is cast as Glycon, a virtuous African prince also enslaved as a gladiator, who in the end carries the robe of Jesus Christ as he and Demetrius look to give the sacred garment to Peter. Less successful than *The Robe*, the second studio Cinema Scope film nonetheless proved a fine showcase for Marshall, but left him without any future roles at Twentieth Century-Fox. Ironically, *Ebony* commented, "At 29, and with *Demetrius and the Gladiators* to his credit, William Marshall has just about run the gamut of dramatic roles."[26]

Once again, the stately actor turned to the stage and to a drama about slavery. This time it was William B. Brach's three-act play *In Splendid Error* (1954) about a meeting presumably held between two famous 19th century abolitionists: John Brown and Frederick Douglass, where the former laid out his plans to seize the federal arsenal at Harper's Ferry. He was captured there by Robert E. Lee and later hanged for treason. Alfred Sanders played Brown; Marshall, the role of Douglass. As you will discover, this drama influenced Marshall in later years.

The performer's next film, *Something of Value* (1957)[27] saw him still making big-screen epics, but this time at MGM. As discussed earlier in the Ivan Dixon chapter, Robert Ruark's novel about the Mau Mau uprising in the early fifties had been translated into a controversial movie about a brutal war between whites and blacks. What is fascinating is that Marshall's screen role, Leader, the intellectual force in the uprising, is always presented in a strong, dignified manner. Nevertheless, you may be surprised by his reactions to the film in the upcoming interview.

By 1958, Marshall basically disappeared from any interesting film roles and appeared infrequently on the motion picture screen. He did not reappear in any meaningful way until Richard Fleischer's *The Boston Strangler* (1968).[28] Screenwriter Edward Anhalt's narrative about Albert DeSalvo, the self-confessed serial killer of women, featured an all-star cast, which included Tony Curtis, Henry Fonda, George Kennedy, and Murray Hamilton. In returning to Twentieth Century-Fox, Marshall, resumed his stately, imposing screen image, this time as Attorney General Edward W. Brooke.

The decade between *Something of Value* and *The Boston Strangler* did not find Marshall idle or declining in stature. He spent considerable time in Europe touring in various stage productions, which generally included his interpretation of Shakespeare's *Othello*. Often reported in evaluations of the actor's work is the high praise he received from *The London Sunday Times*, which proclaimed him "the best Othello of our time."[29] In America, he pursued his rich bass singing on radio and in recitals, while also appearing in guest roles in such popular TV series as *The World of Nick Adams* (1957), *Alfred Hitchcock Presents* (1964), *The Man From U.N.C.L.E.* (several times starting in 1964), *Ben Casey* (1965), *Star Trek* (1966, 1968), and *Daniel Boone* (1968). Of particular note is that Marshall won local Emmys for producing and performing in PBS' *As Adam Early in the Morning* (1973).[30]

Given Marshall's emphasis on stage and television performances home and abroad during most of the sixties, now seems a sensible time to borrow a leitmotif from Ossie Davis[31] and recall Hamlet's advice both to Polonius and to the traveling players. "Do you hear," the Danish prince said to the elderly politician, "let them be well used, for they are the abstract and brief chronicles of the time."[32] As for the actors, he cautioned, "Be not too tame...but let your own discretion be your tutor."[33] Documentary films like *Eyes on the Prize*[34] and *Freedom Riders*,[35] together with the countless books written by scholars discussed throughout *The Interviews* chronicled the boycotts, bus rides, sit-ins, marches, beatings, bombings, and murders that stand out in this tumultuous decade. And with the advantage of hindsight, we have recalled how Mae Mercer, Brock Peters, Jim Brown, Ivan Dixon, James Whitmore, and now William Marshall decided to perform their parts in these most difficult of times.

Here it also seems judicious to glance one last time at how two vocalists—Nina Simone and Odetta—performed during the same period. Although Simone's first recording, *I Love You, Porgy*, in 1959 was also her most successful commercial hit; she scorned discretion in her poignant and passionate songs, and yet became a major influence on her generation. The *New York Times* in its obituary of the memorable artist said, "In the 1960s no musical performer was more closely identified with the civil rights movement. Though she was best known as an interpreter of other people's music, she expressed her feelings about racism and black pride in those years in a number of memorable songs she wrote herself."[36] Peniell E. Joseph ranks the singer alongside James Baldwin and Lorraine Hansberry as a radical spokesperson whose anti-racism manifestos directed people toward "the black freedom struggle's most radical elements."[37]

By the early seventies, she fell from favor, her life went into a tailspin, and she moved overseas, eventually settling in Carry-le-Rouet, France. As far as she was concerned, life in America had become worse than it had ever been.[38] Nearly ignored when she died at 70 in April of 2003, the remarkable performer is bigger than ever today. Hardly a month goes by without the appearance of a newly remastered version of her songs, and music catalogues prominently spread the titles of her famous albums—e.g., *The Legendary First Recording in New York City 1957, Sings Ellington, Little Girl Blue,* and *At The Village Gate*—across their pages. Moreover, Hollywood is currently planning a biopic on her life, *Nina*. But it should come as no surprise the project is fraught with problems because there are those friends and fans that claim the actress Zoe Salanda is too light-skinned to be effective in the role.[39]

Odetta, another legendary singer of the civil rights movement, made her music a constant companion, as one source aptly said, "to the black-and-white images of the freedom marchers who walked the roads of Alabama and Mississippi and the boulevards of Washington to end racial discrimination."[40] Singing liberation songs like *I'm On My Way* and *Oh, Freedom,* she inspired a movement that reshaped America. In 1999, President William Jefferson Clinton bestowed on the inspiring vocalist the National Endowment for the Arts' National Medal of the Arts. Unlike Simone, she remained prominent in the hearts and minds of her admirers until her death in 2008.

Because of the militant chronicles, the Black Power manifestos, and the radically inspirational songs, we remain less clear about how white people performed their part in the Movement. While many Americans remained ignorant, indifferent, and disturbed by blacks wanting their share of the American Dream, the situation gradually began to change by the early sixties, thanks in no small part to the mass media and to the political, social, technological, and economic conditions in America and around the world.

Clearly here is not the place to make the case for a re-examination of Americans of all races and colors and creeds who joined forces to support revolutionary causes in the sixties. Some basic steps, however, should at least be acknowledged. For example, the Kennedy Administration clearly remained resistant to the Movement until the advent of the Freedom Riders in 1961, but then the federal government did start to reverse its apathy; and before his tragic death, the President did propose significant steps to aid the civil rights cause. While many militants by the mid-sixties began to turn against a strategy of non-violence, many prominent American politicians, led by President Lyndon Johnson, spoke out against racial injustice. He passed the historic 1964 Civil Rights Act, and then made an extraordinary June 4th 1965 commencement address at Howard University. In that speech, the President insisted, "White America must accept responsibility."[41]

But urban riots and militant separatists provoked a white backlash against the Movement,[42] and the country became less willing to accept liberal analyses like Senator Daniel P. Moynihan's *The Negro Family: The Case for National Action* (hereafter *The Moynihan Report*)[43] and Kenneth B. Clark's *Dark Ghetto: Dilemmas of Social Power*.[44] Even the moderate Dean of Black literature, Albert Murray, attacked both *The Moynihan Report* and *Dark Ghetto*, describing the former as having "Victorian notions about broken homes," and the latter "descriptions of black powerlessness and black self-hatred...."

As discussed throughout *Exits and Entrances*, such events brought about the drift in the sixties toward black-themed movies, a call for an African-American aesthetic, and the recognition of an important, untapped black audience. It also brought William Marshall back into the movie world and *The Boston Strangler*. At the same time, given the volatile environment, it is fascinating to me that one of the most common jobs for black actors was appearing on the NBC *Tarzan* show that premiered Sept. 8, 1966 and ran until Sept. 10, 1969.[45] During that period, Ron Ely, the 14th Tarzan, worked with William Marshall, James Earl Jones, Roy E. Glenn, Woody Strode, Raymond St. Jacques, and Yaphet Kotto.[46] As J. Fred MacDonald writes, "Certainly, the program gave employment to talented but rarely utilized black actors...but there was something unsettling about distinguished Afro-American actors speaking in broken English or wearing Hollywood conceptions of native African clothing."[47]

Moving quickly to the early 1970s, and thanks to films like Gordon Parks' *The Learning Tree*,[48] Melvin Van Peebles' *Sweet Sweetback's Baadasssss Song*,[49] and Ossie Davis' *Cotton Comes to Harlem*,[50] the blaxploitation era had come into being. After MGM came out with Gordon Parks' *Shaft* (1971)[51] and Warner Brothers with Gordon Parks Jr.'s *Superfly* (1972),[52] American International Pictures (AIP) decided to get into the action by hiring William Marshall to play Prince Mamuwalde in William Crain's *Blacula*.[53] As originally conceived by Arkoff, the reigning king of nonsense B movies and turned out in a couple of days, this unique horror film focused on an inept black man by the name of Andrew Brown (borrowed from the loudmouthed, overly assertive character of the same name featured in the legendary *Amos 'n Andy* series). "It was," explained *Los Angeles Times* reporter John M. Wilson, "white guys again doing a stupid interpretation of what black people were supposed to be like."[54] Anne Valdespino put the proposed project in the context of blaxploitation films generally: "These low-budget films sold sex, violence and a 'black power by any means necessary attitude.' They starred characters that prominent members of the black community derided at that time as the lowest of the low: pimps, hookers, drug dealers, even vampires."[55]

But if AIP wanted William Marshall, the story and the character needed drastic revisions. In fact, when the producers, according to Sylvia Jarrico, his long-time companion, first contacted Marshall he thought the offer farcical. He had no intention of playing "this victimized ordinary fellow."[56] What the celebrated Shakespearian performer did to convince the filmmakers to change the nature and tone of *Blacula* is discussed in the interview. The script that emerged told of an eloquent African Prince Mamuwalde (Marshall) and his beautiful wife (Vonetta McGee) who in 1780 tragically visit Transylvania in the mistaken hope that they can convince a crass and racist Count Dracula (Charles Macaulay) to help end his country's slave trade. Not only does the white vampire scoff at the proposed embargo, but also he lusts for the Prince's wife. When Mamuwalde valiantly tries to defend her, Count Dracula turns him into one of the living dead, saying, "You will be Blacula, a vampire like myself! A living fiend!" Once Blacula is put in his coffin and the princess left to die alongside him in an enclosed dungeon, the film shifts to the present (1972). Unaware of what they are doing, two Los Angeles gay interior decorators (Ted Harris and Rick Meltzer) purchase Count Dracula's castle, including all its artifacts, and transport the goods to California. In a vast overstatement, the purchase turns out to be a very poor business venture for the men. But the transatlantic journey proves advantageous to Blacula, who discovers the stunning Tina (McGee), an exact look-alike for his dead wife.

In making the dignified Marshall the first Black film horror star, AIP, in my judgment, made a number of intelligent and fascinating changes in the vampire's conventions. To understand why, let me contextualize briefly how I observed the film formula in the 1970s. First, insecure world conditions resulting from an intensified arms race, an energy crisis, the possibility of nuclear meltdowns, escalating urban violence, international terrorism, and counter-culture manifestos so unsettled many Americans that horror movies offered them a sought-after catharsis. And the most popular subgenre was the Vampire film. Particularly attractive to Hollywood's target audience—eight years of age to thirty years of age—were the overwhelming psychological links between the viewer's "repressed desires and the filmmaker's realistic villains." In short, doom did well at the box-office.[57] Secondly, the great horror legends always made the "monsters"—Frankenstein's creation, the Wolf Man, and the Invisible Man—more sinned against than sinner. The one exception had been Count Dracula. Now AIP had reversed that convention. And third, where blaxploitation films stressed whites exploiting subservient blacks, now African-Americans in important roles were being assisted by white officers to combat evil and to protect society. These ideas are discussed later in the interview.

For the most part, the critics were not kind to *Blacula*. Kevin Thomas of the *Los Angles Times* found the movie "predictable and silly rather than scary," although he acknowledged that "Marshall, the noted Othello interpreter, holds on to his dignity—and holds the picture together pretty well besides."[58] Walter Burrell declared, "The all-time low in image construction has been achieved by American International Pictures, who bestowed upon us a Black, bloodsucking vampire in *Blacula*."[59] And Roger Greenspun observed, "Anybody who goes to a vampire movie expecting sense is in serious trouble, and *Blacula* offers less sense than most."[60] Seventeen years later, however, James Robert Parish was still smarting about Greenspun's comments, calling the judgment incorrect and insisting, "This film was the first and the best of the black horror film cycle that would engulf Hollywood for a brief period in the mid-1970s."[61]

Today *Blacula* is enjoying a well-deserved renaissance, as evident in Brooks E. Hefner's stimulating article, "Rethinking *Blacula*: Ideological Critique at the Intersection of Genres."[62] (In the interests of full disclosure, I have for several decades been listed on the Advisory Board of the *Journal of Popular Film & Television*, where Prof. Hefner's article is published.) The enterprising James Madison academic wisely investigates how the AIP outing reworks the horror film genre, offers reasonable alternatives to the film's two most criticized elements—queer sexuality and the monstrosity-blackness links—, and describes how Marshall's screen persona aided the movie overall.

Before moving on, I would like to acknowledge the gifts of Vonetta McGee, the wonderful film and television actress whom the *New York Times* reviewer Greenspun once called "just possibly the most beautiful woman currently acting in film."[63] Having begun her film career in the late sixties, she appeared alongside such noted actors as Sidney Poitier, Richard Pryor, and Clint Eastwood. Worth remembering is that although the public linked the actress to blaxploitation movies, she welcomed the 'black' ties as a "source of pride," but rejected any association with the concept of "exploitation."[64] The oft-overlooked performer died on July 9th, 2012.

AIP, much to Marshall's disappointment, reprieved the black vampire the following year in Bob Keljan's *Scream, Blacula, Scream*.[65] Despite the addition of the delightful Pam Grier and Bernie Hamilton, this draped "Black Prince of Shadows" spends his evenings draining blood from unsuspecting victims. But his real pursuit is trying to get Lisa, the smitten Voodoo priestess (Grier), to find a way to break Count Dracula's curse. Thankfully, she fails, he dies, and the once promising twist on vampires moves on to richer and better versions.

At least, that's how Marshall felt about the film. Roger Greenspun, on the other hand, insisted the sequel had "plenty of wit and verve, looks good, and, in turn, makes lots of promising young players look good, too."[66] Kevin Thomas agreed with his East Coast colleague, saying the sequel "is far superior to the original, possessing much assured style as well as considerable humor."[67] Nonetheless, in what may well be the saddest film review in *Exits and Entrances*, a young James Schwoch, later a media expert at Northwestern University, took his 1973 date to see *Scream, Blacula, Scream* at a drive-in, hoping it would result in a romantic evening. As the distraught young man reported, "The romance collapsed on two fronts: the movie was terrible, and she dumped me for thinking I could get away with a date like that."[68]

Marshall tried one more time to interject a positive black perspective into the horror film by appearing as Bishop Garnet Williams in William Girdler's *Abby* (1974).[69] Gordon Cornell Layne's religiously oriented screenplay seemed on the surface suspiciously similar to Warner Brothers' recent release, William Friedkin's *The Exorcist* (1973). Set primarily in Louisville, Kentucky, the plot involves the misfortunes of Rev. Emmett Williams (Terry Carter) and his beautiful wife, Abby (Carol Speed). This upstanding couple falls on hard times, when Emmett's father, the scholarly and adventuresome archeologist, goes on an expedition in Nigeria. There, unwittingly, Bishop Williams unleashes the evil spirit of the demon Eshu. In an attempt to destroy the learned Doctor, the sex-crazed fiend travels around the world and to Louisville to possess the Bishop's daughter-in-law. After much carrying on, the family summons the father back, and he performs the predictable exorcism.

Neither the critics nor Marshall appeared unhappy when Eshu got put back in the box and the film ended. The public, however, liked the movie, which opened to respectable ticket sales. Unfortunately, the film's box-office popularity caught the attention of Warner Brothers who now claimed the AIP blaxploitation movie infringed on the big studio's copyrights. Director Grindler and his team denied their film was a rip-off of Friedkin's movie, citing the role the Yoruba religion played in the story. But distributors, theater owners, and AIP executives became intimidated; *Abby* was withdrawn from circulation, and not shown publically again for more than a quarter-of-a-century. Warner Brothers dropped its lawsuit against Arkoff's company, although the studio did take on Italy's *Beyond the Door*, another so-called knock-off of *The Exorcist*, and lost in court.[70]

After *Abby*, Marshall felt disappointed over the state of black productions[71] and the acting roles he had recently been playing. Surely, he thought, there must be better options. And so he decided that for the foreseeable future he was going to work on presenting images of heroic African-Americans. From playing Blacula and Bishop Garnett Williams, he now turned to two prominent figures: Henri Christophe and Frederick Douglass.

At the end of 1975, Marshall visited Haiti as the guest of the government. He intended to make a movie about the great emancipator who led a successful 18th century uprising against France. Stimulated by his role in *Lydia Bailey* decades before, and in possession of a valuable script by former blacklisted and Oscar-winning writer Michael Wilson, the performer intended to reverse the original film's narrative. In 1952, the unique revolution served as a "setting" for the romance between the major characters. In the proposed new film, romance took second place to the Haitian revolution.[72]

But before the film could be made, a heated debate over casting once again arose: should white actors play black roles, or blacks return the insult by playing whites? Thanks to reporter Dave McGinn, we are reminded of past controversies, especially during the sixties, in the casting of Mickey Rooney as Mr. Yunioshi in Blake Edwards' *Breakfast at Tiffany's* (1961), Elizabeth Taylor as the Egyptian queen in Joseph L. Mankiewicz's *Cleopatra* (1963), and Peter Sellers as Hrundi V. Bakshi in Blake Edwards' *The Party* (1968). Moreover, such contentious casting continues into the present century with Angelina Jolie as Mariane Pearl in Michael Winterbottom's *A Mighty Heart* (2007), Robert Downey Jr. as a black faced Kirk Lazarus in Ben Stiller's *Tropic Thunder* (2008), and Jake Gyllenhaal as Dastan in Mike Newell's *Prince of Persia* (2010).[73]

In 1975, the casting controversy involved Anthony Quinn and William Marshall arguing over who should perform the role of the Haitian hero. To provide a guide to the argument, *Sepia* assigned a writer to review the issues, especially Quinn's alleged remark there are no black actors of stature to play Christophe, which seems absolutely extraordinary, particularly in view of Quinn's devotion to civil rights."[74] Insisting on the prominence in the mid-seventies of the "race question," as well as how crucial skin color was to black actors in finding work, Emily F. Gibson rebuked Quinn for wanting to return to outmoded acting practices in his newly announced project *Black Majesty*, where Quinn intended to play Henri Christophe. Marshal simply stated, "The black King must be black."[75] Neither film ever made it to the silver screen. Fortunately for us, the Marshall/Quinn controversy had started before I interviewed the famous Shakespearian performer, and he talks about the issue in the interview.

Near the end of the seventies, Marshall made one last significant movie, Robert Aldrich's *Twilight's Last Gleaming* (1977).[76] Inspired by Walter Wager's cold war novel *Viper Three*, the Ronald M. Cohen and Edward Huebsch screenplay dealt with Gen. Lawrence Dell (Burt Lancaster), an escaped political prisoner, who is determined to expose to the American people that its government continued to have its sons and daughters murdered in a fruitless Vietnam War. This senseless, inexcusable behavior occurs because we have no intention of appearing helpless with the Soviets. Dell, together with two associates—Willis Powell (Paul Winfield) and Augie Garvas (Burt Young)—infiltrate an ICBM complex and threaten to launch missiles unless the President releases certain documents detailing the government's shameful conspiracy.

Today, a prominent critic like Dave Kehr praises the political thriller as a sincere movie that never found an audience, even back in 1977. The times had changed by the movie's release and the superficial nod to The Pentagon Papers seemed ho-hum. But with the arrival of a superb 2012 Blu-ray DVD, the public is reconsidering what Kehr calls Aldrich's "final great work of a great American filmmaker."[77] Adell Aldrich, the director's daughter, tells us it was one of her father's favorite films.[78]

For me, *Twilight's Last Gleaming* was always a special film. At the time of its release, the movie's plot, dialogue, acting, and twists proved thrilling, intriguing and inspiring. Now, in 2013, Aldrich's memorable tale has an added appeal because I see it in comparison to DeMille's 1936 *The Plainsman*. Where once blacks fared so badly, in the 1977 movie, they embody a range of strong characters performed by gifted actors. Roscoe Lee Browne holds forth as James Forrest, a close friend of President Stevens (James Dunning). Paul Winfield is Willis Powell, a shrewd street hustler who gives his life in pursuit of a cause. And William Marshall takes on the role of Attorney General Klinger, sitting in the halls of power debating a nation's future.

In Marshall's later years, the dignified actor created his one-man show *Enter Frederick Douglass, Slave and Statesman.* He had refashioned all that he had learned about the amazing 19th century abolitionist since the days when he performed the heroic figure in the 1954 stage production of *In Splendid Error*. After an initial appearance as the character on a one-hour 1991 PBS show, he travelled about playing Douglass for young and old in schools throughout the country.

As the nineties began, Chicago's ETA Creative Foundation designated the famous actor as one of the Epic Men of the Twentieth Century (1992).

The start of the twenty-first century, however, saw the powerful, endearing artist suffering from Alzheimer's disease. Then on June 11, 2003, William Marshall, at 78, died of a heart attack in a Los Angeles rest home. Among those celebrities who spoke at his funeral were Sidney Poitier, Ivan Dixon, and Paul Winfield.

Sylvia Jarrico, the actor's longtime friend, put his legacy well when she reminded us of his ongoing commitment to portraying great black historical figures. He wanted the world," she explained, "to hear them because they weren't in the textbooks."[79]

I met William Marshall by accident at a meeting of the American Theatre Association held at the Americana Hotel during the week of August 19, 1973. My late friend Errol Hill, then heading the Black Theatre program, had asked me to be on several panels.

The first time I saw Marshall was at a luncheon honoring Paul Robeson. Too sick to attend, the great singer was recuperating at his sister's home in Philadelphia. Consequently, Robert Earl Jones, the activist's long-time friend, accepted the award for the ailing artist. Following the luncheon, a group of luminaries praised Robeson before a capacity audience that filled the ballroom. Among those stars participating in the tribute were Frederick O'Neal, Alice Childress, Ruby Dee, William Marshall, Osceola Archer and Tom McDermott. Each, in turn, reminisced fondly on Robeson's life and career.[80]

If memory serves me correctly, the last to speak was dramatist Ed Bullins. It was the most powerful presentation I had ever heard up to that point in my research on the black film legacy. Bullins lashed out at the more than 500 people sitting before him, calling them every epithet in his extensive vocabulary. "Where were you," he railed, "you sons of bitches, you dirty...when he needed you?" No one said a word. No one got up. No one left.

The next day, Marshall happened by chance to sit in on my talk about the history of black cowboys and their absences from American westerns. We talked afterwards, shared our reactions to Bullins' performance, and agreed to meet the next day for an interview.

William Marshall Interview
August 21, 1973

FM: In your biography, the one that I had, "...was born in Gary Indiana." But, no date, do you have feelings about age, or what?

WM: Yes, I do.

FM: Why is that?

WM: Because employers do.

FM: Okay.

WM: So, I don't cooperate with them. Whatever they think my age is is what I have to function with.

FM: What was it like growing up in Gary, Indiana? As a youngster in terms of, say, education, or movies?

WM: I had a very fine time; until I was about four and I became aware of the racial disparities that were operative there. Gary is a very unusual place, in that more steel was being produced in Gary at that time and up until the end of the Second World War than any other place in the world. So they attracted, at great expense, people from all over the world, particularly Eastern Europe, to come and work in the mills. And then conscripted a vast body of black people from the South to come and act as scabs, unbeknownst to themselves that they were doing this, because of the strikes that the "foreign born" had instituted in terms of better working conditions, better pay, and so on. So I say that, to say that it was a very difficult place in which to live. It was like being in the South near Selma, or wherever.

There were some happy aspects to it. The intense prejudice that I finally came to realize was operative, as I say, didn't grip me until I was four. I was kicked down the stairs by a white man who was about my height; I've been looking for him ever since. [Laughter] But I understand his plight. He was one of the victims of the "foreign born" again, who were on strike; in that he couldn't reach out and find a black man who is now the size I am, 6'5", decided he'd take it out on a child.

I'd come from a middle-class, oriented like family which was right in the center of this incredibly large European community, people from Serbia, Czechoslovakia, Poland, Hungary, wherever. And I was sitting on the porch one day playing with my toys and there were two little white girls that passed by, who must have been neighbors I thought at that point, and they looked longingly at my toys and asked if they could come into the yard and onto the porch and play. I thought it was a wonderful idea. So they did this for oh at least seven or eight times over a period of a couple of weeks, I'd say, and we had great fun.

Then I think they decided it was now time to reciprocate. They were much bigger than I. I think they must have been "old ladies" of about seven and nine, probably. They took me to their home which was about three houses away. And I remember going up the stairs and meeting the mother, who was a little terrified because she knew what we didn't know and that was that the father was coming home. He arrived home and saw me in the house. I represented all of the problems that he had been taught we were responsible for, in terms of having lost their strike. So he chastised them for having me in the house, and then grabbed me and slapped me a few times and kicked me down the stairs. I didn't know at that time what it was I had done that was wrong. And I didn't tell my parents about it because I knew that I had to have been guilty of some infraction. I didn't know that I was living in a savage land. And I didn't know the history of that whole mess.

I worked in the steel mills in Gary after graduating from Roosevelt High School, and I was inducted into the army, which gives you some idea to the degree to which I am battling rather vociferously into my forties. After leaving the army, I returned to Gary and, again, to the steel mills; and decided that, after several months, I knew this wasn't what I wanted to do with my life.

But I had no focus at that point. My mother, being aware of it, suggested that I go to New York and live with her sister who was an extremely advanced and industrious woman for any group, considering her travels at that time. Very few black women, certainly, had ever gone to Europe and had been involved in the Spanish Civil War and all that sort of thing. So this was quite an unusual person I was going to for some direction. She suggested that I was interested in art, and that I enroll in the Arts Students League there and pursue it on a very serious basis, to become a commercial artist. I went about my studies, and I did odd jobs with her, or with anyone else to maintain myself.

I liked to sing for some reason or another; and not for people. I just sort of kept myself company that way. I guess being the only child I made up a lot of those games to do. And she came to me one day and said, "I know you're not interested in a professional career as a singer, or entertainer, but it would be so nice if you learned how to sing a little better. Why don't you study it just as...make it an avocation." And she recommended me to a very remarkable woman, Abbie Mitchell, who had quite a celebrated concert career herself, actress. (You must have touched on her.) And she said, "I'm sure that you will prosper and enjoy your singing more if you know how to do it better, and I promise you will." So I did. And I worked with her for about six or eight months.

Then I moved to the Harlem YMCA. She lived in Greenwich Village at that time, and I walked from West 4th street to 135th street trying to get lodging; and I even went to Seamen's House, where they suggested I'd be happier with the colored people. And I was, necessarily, happier with the colored people cause they gave me a room. [Laughter] So I lived there for an interminable period, at the Harlem "Y."

Again, I had that nasty habit of singing, and I sang in the communal shower there. I seemed to have been waking up some people who worked odd hours in the Post Office. One of them came and knocked on the door and begged me to be quiet. Fortunately [he] had something positive to offer. He knew that there were several shows that were auditioning and wanted to have some additional singers, and why didn't I go and audition for one of these shows? I guess I was about nineteen at that time so I had no fear, and I did audition. I used all two-and-a-half songs that I had learned with Abbie Mitchell, and I got the job of singing in the chorus, in the orchestra pit actually, of the show *Carmen Jones*.

And that's an unusual place to begin in the theater because you're really not in it. You are singing when it's time to sing your part, and then you are watching the wonderful artists on stage. It's unbelievable how gifted they were and how able they were, with operatic music in particular. And then watching the audience. I was watching back and forth for many, many months; and I did not feel a part of the theater. It was a part-time job since I was going to school and had another part-time job during the day.

But I kept answering auditions, and I got a job in the show called *Call Me Mister*, the touring company albeit, and one or two other jobs. But the *Call Me Mister* one was very significant in that I was in Boston at the time, and I looked about me at all the wonderful talent, and I decided that I hadn't seen any talent yet that was better than mine. But I had a nickel's worth of sense, thank you, and realized that I needed to study.

So I quit the show and went back to New York and began studying at the American Theatre Wing. And I've been studying ever since with this or that group.

FM: I'm interested. A lot of the people who are talking about motion pictures in terms of the black community are now making a big deal about the images created by people like Stepin' Fetchit and Hattie McDaniel and so on. As you were a kid growing up, did you ever react, or as you look back have any reactions to those performances in terms of...?

WM: Yes. I can give you my reactions to them at that time and my reactions to them now. The former would be of profound humiliation and of wanting to almost invariably crawl out of the theater. And I usually took the valley route home because I felt that I would indeed be identified with the kind of degrading presentations of black people that I had experienced from watching the screen.

Oddly enough, those who were really capitalizing on imitating black people did not offend me as much as black people themselves who were cast in these roles. I'm talking about Eddie Cantor. I'm talking about Al Jolson. I'm talking about Amos and Andy. And there was another group of comics; I don't remember their names but they always performed in blackface. I had a feeling that these whites were somehow civilized at that time (I don't feel that way now) because they seemed to be in sympathy with.... Anyone who dared to make their skin black when it (I had been taught that this was the worst thing that a person could be) must have had some sort of understanding and some sort of identification with blacks that was positive. That was my feeling as a child. In retrospect, Jolson and Cantor were vile exploiters of black people, and so were Amos and Andy.

Amos and Andy [were] much more responsible for a certain

kind of vilification of a people that I think is, to this date, I would characterize as being irreparable. They gave a sense of a people who were immoral, base, [and] who had absolutely no standards that were important. Black people laughed at this; they laughed in private, hoping that white people were not viewing it. Many of us didn't know at that time that these were white men making millions of dollars presenting us to the world in such a fashion as to justify our being exploited socially and economically.

I feel great sympathy and empathy for Stepin' Fetchit, for Hattie McDaniel, Louise Beavers, Willie Best, Mantan Moreland, those actors who were forced, in a sense, to function in this way. And it had been created by white men, these stereotypes, not by black people themselves. That, of course, I didn't know at that time but I have since, of course, come to realize that.

FM: It's part of the tradition of the stage and theater in the 19th century....

WM: Part of the white tradition, because the white tradition would be just insidious. You speak about the theater being exploitative; this whole country has been exploitative, first of the people who were indigenous to this land who, of course, are not Indians but rather call themselves "the people." And the destruction of these people, I'm thinking about the islands of Cuba and Jamaica, Puerto Rico, Espanola; I'm thinking about Haiti, I'm thinking about the Dominican Republic, which was inhabited by, roughly, three million Arawak people. All of whom within forty years after that drunken Italian who got lost looking for some herbs for the palate of that Spanish—she wasn't Spanish, she was a Bourbon—Bourbon Queen who ruled the Spanish, kind of started all of that genocide as such. In that they could not enslave the so-called "Indian" people, they destroyed them; and they all but destroyed them here.

FM: The whole colonial system you're talking about. The whole colonial empire that started in the Middle Ages.

WM: I'm talking from 1492; I'm not going back any further.

FM: Let me ask you a question just to get back to the movies for a second, were there many black people who went to the movies in Gary, Indiana in the '30s and '40s?

WM: Yes.

FM: There was a black audience? Because people often claim

that there was no black audience, that's why they didn't make movies, or have films with black personalities, because there was no audience, there was no market for it. It was a business; if it hadn't been a business, they would have had something different.

WM: No, they were making movies then. Micheaux was one of the early moviemakers, as you may have found in your research there.

Much of the discussion with Pearl Bowser in the Lorenzo Tucker chapter in Every Step a Struggle *is devoted to Oscar Micheaux, the Father of Black Cinema. She was then and is now one of the leading authorities on the famous filmmaker.*

FM: I'm talking about the commercial cinema. People, the major studios, were saying in the '30s in terms of the theater chain, because as you know the movie industry was a vertical organization. The people who....

WM: They're liars. I'm not even interested in anything they had to say.

FM: Okay.

WM: Because that's dishonest and there's nothing to do with the truth. Black films were being made, being made by L. J. Pollard [The Ebony Film Corporation]. They were not commercial where whites were concerned. But let's go back even further, if we will, to one Shakespearean group that existed in the United States in New York in the 1830s, The African Grove. With William Alexander Brow and James Hewlett being the promoters of it, and Ira Aldridge growing out of it. They worked assiduously to get rid of this kind of theater, having these "savages" speak the King's English.

Ira Aldridge was the first black actor to perform leading Shakespearian roles in America. The African Company (an all-black acting troupe) was the acting group associated with New York's African Grove theater. Formed by Brown and Hewlett as a cultural resource for African-Americans, it was built in 1821 and mysteriously burned to the ground in 1823. Its primary repertoire was the works of Shakespeare.

FM: Well, Bert Williams himself had to learn how to speak plantation English in order to perform on the stage. He was an educated man.

WM: I'm sure he had to, not being an American.

Early black theatrical history in general and Bert Williams in particular are discussed in the Lorenzo Tucker and Clarence Muse chapters respectively in Every Step a Struggle. *The same is true about early black cinema.*

FM: The background in your resume suggests that you came to the movies in 1940 with a movie called *Flowing Gold*. Was that the first one that you did?

WM: No, I had nothing to do with that and that may be…

FM: This is from The *New York Times Film Review*, and I didn't get a chance to check resources at home, but that was the…

WM: *Flowing Gold, Santa Fe Trail*, and all of that, this William Marshall is a white man. He is married to Ginger Rogers and….

FM: They got you mixed up with him then?

WM: They would do that, yes.

FM: That's *The New York Times!*

WM: Yes, they would do that. My first film, in terms of a commercial work, would have been *Lydia Bailey*,[81] which was made in 1951 and distributed in 1952.

FM: Let's talk about *Lydia Bailey* because that's an interesting film. I remember seeing it as a kid, and I remember being tremendously impressed with the film, the pace and the action and enjoying it. But Don Bogle recently came out with a book called *Toms, Coons, Mulattoes, Mammies, & Bucks;*[82] and one of the things he makes a big point of in the book, in the part he deals with you, he talks about your title as "King Dick," and obviously sexual exploitation. This was the thing with the eight wives and that kind of business. Was that your impression of the term and the role in the film *Lydia Bailey*?

WM: Well certainly having the name "Dick" and putting King in front of it does sort of suggest that you may be just that. But it was not the feeling that I had while doing the film. It was, to my thinking, the most advanced thing that Hollywood had ever dared to do. Even though the story of the Haitian people and the revolution served as a backdrop for a romance between "blondes," if you will. Having the large families, certainly not an unusual thing, or to have several wives, certainly where the African culture is concerned; and the people, the black people, who inhabit Haiti were an African people with very few admixtures. As they were saying downstairs, uniquely the American Negro is the only thing that is new in terms of having been created on this soil. But no, that was not my impression. I think it was for the times, and I don't think they have made anything comparable to it since, quite a milestone.

FM: I think so. The one picture that comes close to it, that I remember seeing is Pontecorvo's *Burn*[83] with Marlon Brando.

WM: Yes. I've written a critique of it.

FM: I'd like to see that.

WM: It doesn't come anywhere near it, in no way; and that's a bullshit film; and those two men are corrupt.

FM: Have you seen Pontecorvo's other work? That's the one they followed it up with…released here about the slave days. Well, to go back to *Lydia Bailey*. Can you tell me something about how you came to work in the movie? Do you remember how you were approached, or how you got the job with 20th Century?

WM: Yes. I did a screen test for them in 1949, that's when they really planned to roll with it. But I was told, when I finally did get the job, that they didn't like my appearance; they had another concept in mind. And they took several athletes, Woody Strode among them (who told me this part of the story), and started to train them in acting and speech, of course, so that they might be able to handle the role. But after six months they decided that there probably wasn't enough time for such an undertaking. By then I'd played God; so they said, "If the Negro can play God, maybe he can play a man."

FM: Was there any problem on the set itself, as far as making the film, compromising in terms of what could, or could not be done in the film?

WM: No, I've only experienced that lately. I had no problems in that film whatsoever, except with Tyrone Power refusing to be in it. I think that was because of the nature of the role. And I think just prior to that he'd experienced something that may have led him to believe that Orson Welles' type personalities shouldn't be in films with him. I think it was [*The] Black Rose*, or something. But he said he didn't want to make it because it was a costume film, and they got Dale Robertson to do it, who was an "Oklahoma American." He stopped speaking by the end of the third day he was so offended by the stature of my role. I did everything I could imagine to live up to the role, and the more it offended him the better I felt. And Anne Francis was in it.

FM: Juanita Moore was in the film?

WM: Juanita Moore, yes. Ken Renard was in it; he played Toussaint. He was just really magnificent. It was one of the finest performances in that film.

FM: The reviews that I got just quickly this morning were magnificent on your performance. Just to re-read, to refresh you, you were, "imposing, an indestructible patriot whose voice is commanding as his figure." That was from *The Times*. *The Tribune* said, "Great humor, vitality, dignity." And the *Variety* [piece] was condescending but "it was a believable performance." With such notices, and such reviews...I don't see any more films following quickly after, until *Something of Value* in 1957. Was that your choosing? Did you want to go back to the theater, or they wouldn't give you any more roles in Hollywood, or what?

WM: What were they going to do with me? They'd wanted to know, I guess. I did sign a contract with Fox to do...It was a seven-year contract, and this is immediately after *Lydia Bailey*, but they had a thirty-day option on it. It was a divinely constructed contract of about 49 pages of bullshit and maybe one page there that told what kind of money I was going to make. I kept sort of hoping that I could get a clause in there that would insure that I did the kind of material that I wanted, at least to have some influence on the content, which they granted me in part when they found that Zanuck hadn't seen the film yet and they had to have his final signature before they could make the contract valid. I think he saw the film, and I would imagine that he must have said, "What are we going to do with him next? He's not going to be carrying trays around, and we are not going to be making any more *Lydia Baileys*." And that, "He's black and there is no great contest between studios for his services."

FM: There were no problems as far...Woody and I spoke for a

week out in California. He told me the different kinds of roles that he was put into—the pirate films, or the Tarzan films, or the Indian films, or the Egyptian films, and so on.

The complete Woody Strode interview is in Every Step a Struggle.

FM: None of these offers? No attempt was made to at least keep you working?

WM: No.

FM: It was just either they had nothing for you, or they had something for you, and that was the end of it?

WM: Well, I made a film shortly after that called *Demetrius and the Gladiators* [sic];[84] same film writer, Philip Dunne, who did *Lydia Bailey*. And I remember I was trying to get the agents to get a little more money for this. Naturally, it should be on an escalating scale there, and she said that Zanuck said that if I didn't do it, they were going to put a white actor in it. So it doesn't matter what race, or something. They only wrote it because I did *Lydia Bailey*. And then I arrived and talked with Dunne; and Dunne said, "I am so glad you are available for this. I wrote the part especially for you."

FM: That was with Vic Mature wasn't it?

WM: Yes.

FM: Were there any problems with Mature, or any other problems with the other actors on the stage, in terms of relationships? I guess what I'm looking for is, were blacks treated differently in terms of the way people worked off the set in the evenings, or when people went out drinking?

WM: They do everywhere.

FM: Everywhere?

WM: Of course they did it there. Yes, I think that there were some whites, for instance the director, whose name was Jean Negulesco, a Rumanian Jew who spoke French…

Jean Negulesco was the director for Lydia Bailey *not* Demetrius. *Delmer Daves was the director for the latter film.*

FM: This was on *Lydia Bailey*.

WM: *Lydia Bailey*. Very often would say, "I'd like to have you out to the house sometime, you know it? You've got a nice way about you." Or something of that sort. "I really have to arrange that." And it never came off. And I knew it wasn't going to come off because I didn't mean anything to him; except that I was doing presumably good work on the film, and he didn't see any future in it. So he had people to his house who were meaningful to him in terms of who might give him employment, or people with whom he would be working with again.

FM: He didn't work much after that did he?

WM: Oh, *Three Coins in the Fountain*, at least that. He'd already done *Johnny Belinda*. I don't know much about what he did after that though.

There were problems. Victor Mature is shorter than I am; that was something of a problem for a leading man, particularly a leading white man. [Laughter] He didn't like standing beside me. He vomited seven times the first day of filming. [Laughter]

We were marching down a long corridor together, and I was in the robe of Christ. I don't know whether that made him nervous, but he did step out of that line and vomit. I kept saying, "Can I help? What's wrong?"

He said, "I always get nervous on the first day of filming."

I said, "How many films have you made?"

He said, "Thirty-nine."

I said, "I see." 'Well', I said, "I'm into my second; maybe I ought to start vomiting a little later." [We're both laughing.]

But he complained bitterly about my having to stand near him. This went on for the first three or four weeks. I can speak this way about it because he did change. He came to me toward the end of the fifth week, there were only six weeks of shooting, and he said, "I know that you've had a rough time with the director." And he said," But in spite of it, you're coming off beautifully, and he said I think you're really going to be fine in this film." And he gave me a couple of pointers, things that would be helpful for a guy who's just starting in films. So he changed his whole thing there.

And at the end of the film he said, "What are you going to do next?"

I said, "I'm going to go back home."

He said, "You mean there are not a lot of other films for you to do?"

I said, "No."

He said, "What...?" And I guess the answers came to him.

I said, "You ever work with somebody like me before?"

He said, "No." It was wonderful to see intelligence in his face. And it got bigger; I saw a whole kind of network there operative that was rather exciting for me. He really understood, at least for the moment. He said something like, "Well, they want me to be in a film called *Prince Valiant* [1954]. They want[ed] me to play Sergeant or something. I don't want to play that next to some half-ass actor, Robert Wagner. He's going to be billed above me..." Or something or another.

When I heard that, I went over to the office and talked with Billy Gordon who was the casting man. I said, "I understand that you are going to do *Prince Valiant* here. Victor Mature tells me there are wonderful roles in there that I might play." [Laughter] He laughed and gave me my train fare back home.

Also, in that film, something significant happened. I was dressed in the finest garb imaginable, like a peacock; and I was never seen until it was time for me to pop, as it were, out of the woodwork and defend Victor Mature.... Mature who was about to be struck (I think for the second time) by Richard Egan.

WM: And he, being a Christian, it was quite alright for me to come and take Egan and hit him as long as I was defending Christianity, or those who represent it. Woody Strode was on that film, and he kept saying, "I don't understand why you're not in certain scenes." But he somehow kept urging me. He kept saying," Why, you're not being in that scene is like Jackie Robinson sitting on the bench in the bush league."

Somehow that provoked me to go and speak with the director whose name was Delmer Daves. Now this particular scene was the sort of celebration that the gladiators had the night before they were to go into the arena. Half of these men, obviously, would be dead; half of them would have killed the other half. So they brought courtesans in for them, and they had fruit and meat and all of the things that men like to have, even if they are not looking forward to death in the morning. And I asked Daves, "Why was it that I wasn't at least in the corner, or somewhere seen. And he said, "Oh no, that wouldn't go very well. You see for this reason. We here at Fox made a film a couple of years ago, perhaps you saw it, it was *Broken Arrow* [1950].[85] It was the finest film that's ever been made on the subject of the Indian people, and as a result of it we got an award from The United Nations.[86] And we anticipate getting an award from The United Nations because of the nature of your role, and I'm afraid that we don't.... Something foreign might enter into it and prevent us from doing it. You understand? Alright." [Laughter] That was it.

FM: That was '54?

WM: '53. All of the years that you have are when the movies were released.

FM: Now then, I gather in '56 you did *Something of Value*.[87] That was a very interesting film because it took you out of the country.

WM: No it didn't.

FM: Did it on the set in Hollywood?

WM: Yes. The only two actors who went out of the country would have been Rock Hudson and Sidney Poitier.

FM: What was Poitier like? He was probably, by then, starting to become big box-office, but hadn't yet reached it. That was the year after *The Defiant Ones* I guess.

WM: No. *The Defiant Ones* came after that.

FM: So, he's being coached and worked along, but he's not really big box-office yet. What kind of man was he in those days?

WM: Well, I knew him before that; we were both in the American Negro Theatre together. He was, indeed, a very likable, engaging fellow, good poker player, thoughtful person. [He was] aware of his, as he put it, inadequacies in terms of not having had much of an education, and of coming, in a sense, from a foreign country, Nassau; although I'm sure he spent a considerable time in Florida before coming. But he was quite, quite young when he arrived actually, roughly around the same age. I was trying to help him get work, cause I was already working in the theater, not in film. He was also a very gifted mime, very humorous mime. I think probably, now in retrospect, of him being a very, very talented man whose talents were snipped in the bud early on when he became a corporation, as with many men whose talents just don't develop after that.[88]

FM: Do you have the great Juano? Juano Hernandez was in *Something of Value*, wasn't he?

WM: Yes. I understudied him in the play I was trying to get Sidney a job in which was called *Set My People Free* [1948], which dealt with the insurrection in Charleston in 1822. Hernandez played Denmark Vesey, the leader of the insurrection. And yes, he was in *Something of Value.*

FM: What sort of man was he? He's given one of the greatest performances in motion picture history in *Intruder in the Dust* [1949].[89] Have you seen that?

WM: He was better in *Set My People Free,* though it wasn't a movie; I'm sorry, it was a stage production. That's the best I think I've seen, the most heroic I have ever seen a black man be and that would be 1948, '49. He was remarkable in that. *Intruder in the Dust* was certainly a good performance. But it's not as meaningful, certainly to black people, or to any people who are victims of having been colonized, as it would be to play the leader of an insurrection, and to do it with such iron, iron in his foot.

FM: He played the role in *Something of Value.*[90] Wasn't he as a Mau Mau leader, somebody who was strong and angry? And Poitier was, as I remember the film, takes over doesn't he? He picks up the mantle, and has the fight with Rock Hudson. They had grown up together as kids, and now Hudson and he are fighting for different purposes.

WM: It was a foul film; and it came from a foul pen.

FM: Ken Roberts?

WM: Yes. No, that was Robert Ruark. It was awful. His role was not that of a great heroic person. He pretended to be that, and he was the man who would not himself go through this rather heinous initiation program. And he ended up as an informer in the end of the film.

FM: Poitier, or Hernandez?

WM: Hernandez. Poitier is killed at the end; he falls on a stake, or something.

FM: What's his name kills him...There was that insidious scene where there is a baby, or something. Somebody has had a child, and Rock Hudson picks up the baby....

WM: Vile, all very vile and dishonest.

FM: Well, that brings me to one more question before we get to *Blacula* [1972], and that is, I guess we can touch on what was mentioned this afternoon in the session with [Ed] Bullins and [Sonia] Sanchez, and that was the whole question of the images of the new films that are coming out in the late sixties, and what Sanchez talked about in terms of resurrecting the pimp and resurrecting the gangster and using black people on the film to turn the minds of white and black audiences backwards rather than with any vision forward. How do you react to that kind of attitude toward the films?

WM: There isn't one thing that Ms. Sanchez said that I do not embrace whole-heartedly.

FM: We'll leave it at that.

WM: To elaborate just for a moment, I would say that the last thing that Hollywood is interested in doing.... Of course, Hollywood has shrunk considerably; there's one major studio, and that's Universal, then Walt Disney, and American International. They are majors in that they have stayed in the black, if you will, throughout the whole period when television was king, and is and will continue to be for a long while.

In terms of the way in which they envision black people, it hasn't changed greatly. They were dragged here from Africa to serve a function, and that was to work without wages so that the profits would be astronomical as they are. And all kinds of myths were created by white men about black people, again in order to justify this social-economic strata that they have been put into. And the films are largely responsible for the perpetuation of this concept. And I think they are still doing it: the pimp, the whore, the gangster thing.

Certainly there are pimps, whores, and would-be gangsters among black people. I'm not in any sense trying to characterize black people as angels, or as people who have not made some kind of contributions to their own lack of stature, but always with a gun and a whip on them as it were. Black people do not own one percent of the wealth of this country. They don't have their fingers on any one of the at least seven levels of power: military, industrial complex, unions. They have no great physical wealth to speak of except in some instances there are, of course, several black millionaires. And they become blown up out of all proportion in terms of what they represent; a millionaire is generally a millionaire for whatever.

FM: When I talked to Jim Brown, he made the point over and over again. First he said it's a business; it's not an art, motion pictures. And if there are black kids who are going to the movies, why shouldn't they have their black cowboys, or their black gangsters? It wouldn't have to be only that. But why couldn't kids have the same kind of fantasies, or the same kind of entertainment, or the same kind of fun movies just as movies, as entertainment, that other people have? And another point was that he said that as long as people know who they were, it made no difference what kind of images they saw on the screen. Those images couldn't hurt them. It was just in a sense fun and games. And for so long, black children have been going to the movies without seeing anyone except white heroes and black guys being put down. What's wrong even if it's only a transitional stage, with having kids have a terrific time with black heroes up there being the super guys, and having all the fights? Apart from the business as art, how do you react to that?

WM: I can't separate art from reality. And I don't think we are getting too much of the former. We are getting a lot of reality that's in my thinking terribly distorted. For instance, the John Wayne image. He is indeed the largest aardvark (I've stopped using the word "Honkie"), aardvark in the world. And all of the savage whites all over Europe, who prospered as a result of the subjugation of African people in Africa, they identify with John Wayne as being the man who made it happened, the man who won the Civil War, the man who defeated Hitler, as the man who destroyed the Asians, the Koreans, and the Indians, of course.

That's what he symbolizes, that's no fun and games, that's propaganda, that's hard, cold shit that they're pouring out there for people; and there's no sitting there and watching it and not being influenced by it, irrespective of what any non-thinking person has to say about it. It is a very, very serious business. I certainly agree with that.

But I cannot divorce them. I just can't get through my head that you can put black pimps up there, and black whores, and black vampires, if you will, and not have kids influenced in the negative. Now, *Superfly*, for example, I finally saw it after reading all kinds of criticism about it, and liked many things about it. But I realize that I could identify with the black winning for a change, getting over somehow. The black having a contract on one of the men who were behind, under the rug at Watergate, if you please [Laughter]; which is what the white antagonist in the film represented. But the use of cocaine went up four hundred percent at Harlem hospital right here in New York, as a result of that film, a result of seeing such an incredibly attractive and appealing man as Ron O'Neal dipping into it.

That's an example of not being able to separate it, there's just no way. The clothes that he wore, for example, as Sanchez says, "Those heels wreak havoc upon the ovaries of woman." I don't know what they do to men except make them look a little ludicrous.

FM: Let's get to *Blacula* because you've made some changes.... Were you involved in the writing of that?

WM: Finally, yes.

FM: Because there are some startling changes in the formula and the conventions. Of all the histories of Dracula there never was a more humane, a more sympathetic Dracula. That was the one thing that people liked about Lugosi. And all other people have developed over the years, Chaney Jr., was that of all the horror figures, all the people in the science fiction and the supernatural, Dracula was the living dead without redemption. There was nothing in him that was redeeming. And your humanness, the humanity of the Dracula concept was revolutionary. Was that done consciously because it was a black Dracula? Or was there another kind of motivation in the creation of the character?

WM: Well, if I made the decision to play a Dracula-like figure, I can't imagine me playing a white one. It would have to be a black one. But let me just begin by saying that the name of the character that I portrayed, as conceived of by the writers originally, was Andrew Brown. Andrew Brown is a buddy of Amos, of *Amos 'n Andy*. I spoke about this in my reactions to the script after I had laughingly gone to meet with the producer about it.

He had encouraged me to come and said that this was going to be a serious film, but the name itself sent me into hysterics. I said, "You can't have just a black gadfly over in Transylvania. He has to be a man of some purpose. Why would he be there in Seventeen something or other? How did he get there? You have to explain how a white guy got there if he's not a Transylvanian. So I would like to suggest that we invest him with a certain kind of history that would be significant, I think to the viewers, certainly to black viewers. But I think any viewer would appreciate the fact that he was an African prince, and he was there on a diplomatic mission."

"What's the mission?" they wanted to know.

I said, "The mission is that slavery is still operative, slave trade is at its peak."

Why doesn't he have an embargo there for Dracula to sign (this is him not knowing that he is a vampire, he's just a leader of his community, as he was, historically) and to meet with him and several other men of comparable stature, have them work against the perpetuation of the Slave trade?"

Well those cats flipped. They didn't want to hear that. They didn't want any kind of content about....

I said, "I don't see, then, how I can do it. It would have no meaning for me. I certainly need to work, but I can't work under these circumstances. And just from your point of view, the greater you make the character, the greater his fall. It's like the fall of Caesar. So let's invest things here that are meaningful."

So they finally, finally accepted. Although they snipped a lot of little things out of it that they felt would have been too relevant, perhaps. And they didn't want to take the credit for doing anything too decent. But we did get that through, and they didn't even want the girl there, the wife there.

I said, "Well, this is a man and wife team, a black man and a black woman working together towards something that they have mutual interest in, mutual investment in."

Then there was another scene where in I had to rewrite it. It was just very bad; not only content-wise but also entertainment-wise it was very dull. That was the scene where Prince Mamuwalde—that happens to be the name of an African marathon runner who won the Olympics in '68. You probably knew that.

At the Mexico City Olympics, 200m USA medalists Tommy Smith, gold, and John Carlos, silver, give a black power salute on the podium. My source lists Wolde as running for Ethiopia.

FM: No, no.

WM: Mamuwalde was his name. I think he's from Kenya. Mamuwalde comes to the apartment of Tina, the girl who resembles his dead wife, and he's trying to explain who he is. So that I totally rewrote. I thought I put some good things in it. They cut it all out, because I wanted to make it very, very clear why it was she was so important to him apart from her resembling the wife that was deceased. I wanted to make it very, very clear what she represented to him, that she represented what he had lost, his homeland, Africa, the sun, a certain kind of freedom. He couldn't even go out in the sun anymore. His hunting days, I elaborated a little there. And they said that she wasn't very good that day, and they cut it out. But the scene was better than it was originally. So those were the two major contributions.

FM: Have you ever seen the movie *The Mummy*, the original one with Boris Karloff?

WM: Years ago, when I was a child.

FM: Oh, I mean, the parallels between the two, in terms of sensitivity. *The Mummy* was with Karloff as somebody who was a commoner who fell in love with a princess. And they loved each other, and the princess dies, and he finds out that by using Taro leaves, he can restore her to life. And he breaks the sacrament, because he loves her so much. And he gets caught, and he's buried at her feet. Years later the body is removed, and he is resurrected in life because it's his job to find her. And he falls in love with a girl who looks like the princess of long ago, and the tenderness and the emotion. And what was superior in your film, although *The Mummy* film is considered the classic of the Mummy genre, is the way in which the girl responds to you. In other words, instead of turning you down, or being terrified of you because of what you are, she sees beyond what you are to the humanity of what's involved in you.

And that scene then…I can't tell you how much I enjoyed the film. That scene at the end in which you wipe out almost the entire police force in the basement, and then she dies, and you decide that life is not worth living without her even as a Dracula. And you sacrifice yourself, which is the greatest gift of any man, is incredible. And yet, in every review, nobody even touched what you had done with the tradition of a Dracula. They talk about it as just another

Dracula movie, and it's far from that. I can't tell you how much I enjoyed it.

WM: I am delighted.

FM: There was a beauty, a dignity to the thing that had never been before, except maybe when Lugosi had come at the beginning of the sound period. The charm of his voice, you know, gave it a kind of mysticism, which was lovely. But your presence...and there was a great deal of humor in the film which I thought was wonderful. There was a kind of...as if you were on top of the film instead of performing by a vehicle. There was a kind of wit, a kind of innovation, imagination, and all people talked about was the fact that it was a black Dracula rather than it was a film that was dealing with the genre itself.

WM: Yes.

FM: How do you respond to that kind of criticism which tends to always emphasize the black rather than the talent of the actor or the originality of the film, or the kind of work? I guess what I'm saying is, the fact that they respond to you as a black actor, rather than as an actor, a black film rather than as a film? I don't want to make a speech. I'm trying to give, ask the interviewee.

WM: I understand. Well, the film going public, certainly Americans have been programmed in a certain way, all of us. It was quite a novel thing to see a black Dracula. It was quite novel to see *Shaft* and *Superfly*. All of them have been quite novel. So, I'm sorry that they've been so programmed; we've been so programmed. But in that they have, mine is, I presume, a kind of realistic response to it that's normal within the framework of this kind of abnormality that we're handed. So I don't think it's unusual; unless the person is more advanced. And that's rare that they can have that kind of objective view of it when they've been so influenced over their lives, in school, the neighborhoods, everywhere.

I really when I found as a young man two or three white people who were gentle, I was astonished. I didn't know they existed. I was always astonished. How did you escape becoming a savage? How did you escape from wanting to respond at me in an insane fashion? So I just looked at them with awe, because I don't understand how it came to pass. Except that it has and does and that there are such people. But, in short, it's not unusual for them to characterize the thing as being the black actor did this, or black thus, and so.

I had such a discussion with a man for whom I was doing *Othello* some years ago in Venice, California. He was using a quote that Harold Hobson of the *Sunday London Times* had written which said, "William Marshal is the best Othello of our time." He then did this to the quote; he said, "William Marshal is the best black actor of our time." And I went to him and I said, "Why would you do that? I'll bet you can't even name two other black actors. So I'm probably the best of the three that you've seen, which is not really the point. [Laughter] The point is, if you'd use the original, then that would embrace everybody who has played it, as the critic at least attempted to do."

FM: When I spoke with Roscoe Lee Browne and James Earl Jones, and I guess the others, I've always came away with the feeling that the black actor has an added problem, beyond that of a normal actor, and that is he must be both an actor and a black man. The roles that he chooses, the thing that he does has to be concerned with not only how well he does it, but what will be the image or reaction of people to that image. Do you think this is a situation that's gonna continue where the black is going to be limited in what he can do because everyone will be hiring him or looking at him in terms of his blackness rather than his ability to be an actor? I know I'm not saying that well.

WM: No. But I think I grasp your point. In terms of the largest arena, and that would be film and television, I guess, I think the black actor is going to continue to be plagued with having to be not just an actor but also an ambassador for his people whether he wants to be or not. If Clark Gable is on the screen, then you have a kind of, almost-blanket reaction from whites. If he's handsome and doing beautiful things, then he represents them all, doesn't represent just the Irish, or the Germans, or whatever his ethnic background is, which I don't know what that is.

But because of the history of the way in which black people came to this country, the only people in this country who are here involuntarily, or the offspring of a people who are here involuntarily, and the nature of the work that they've had to do, and their lives, that has to be taken into account. And there is no egalitarian approach to this. We're not all born equal; we know better than that. That was nonsense; and the men who wrote that were slave owners. There's so many contradictions that one is confronted with and also affected by. So again, I think it's endemic in the life of the black actor, black actress, to recognize that they symbolize infinitely more than the average white actor would. Because, unless it's a play about the Polish problem, or it's a play about the English problem, he represents all black people. Because of the way in which he's been programmed.

FM: It's a responsibility he must assume whether he wants to or not.

WM: He must assume that, as I see it.

FM: I have two last questions, because you've been terrific. The first question is where do you see, if you had your way, the direction of the black man in film, the kinds of films he ought to make, or the films that you would like to see made, or the kinds of opportunities in addition to having the money and the chance to direct and write and that kind of thing, where would you like to see the film industry go?

WM: This knowledge has just come to me in the last three years, because I think it's that old now; but I guess up until 1964 it was thought that human life began in Asia, because the relics that they had come by came from Asia. And then in '64 an elbow was found in Kenya, an African; and it was adjudicated to be something like three, three million years old. Man was thought to be two million when he was associated with Asia, as his moorings. Today they've found some more relics in Kenya, and it happened to be a jawbone with the molars still intact. It took them a couple of years to decide how old it was, and they came up with five million years old, five million!

So we have five million years of uninterrupted human life, which, presumably at this point, began in Africa. Theater began in Africa. Just wanting to disabuse any minds that thought the Greeks invented it, cause they merely inherited that which goes with the victor from the Egyptians. And the Egyptians were worshiping black Gods. I don't say this in any sense to try and promote a kind of black chauvinism. I'm looking at the records, you know, that have been presented to me by scientists, and presumably objective men, genuine scientists who have no axe to grind, as did a number of historians who just completely eradicated, erased anything that had been written about the accomplishments of African people, or about Africa itself at the commencement of the slave trade. And this you can say for almost every European historian to a man; that the Africans have no history. This is such an incredible contradiction, that's where man began.

I say this, to say that there's a lot to get into there in terms of dramaturgy. There's an awful lot that if it were resuscitated and put on stage, put on film that would not only be incredibly entertaining, but most edifying. It would destroy, of course, many of the concepts that the majority of the European world has, and even that many of the black people have about themselves. It might do a very terrible thing to this already shaky economy; and already terribly dishonest government. But there are the lives of King Tut, if you will, or there are the lives of..., there are the lives of great men and woman that...One should begin with those. One should go back as far as possible.

It seems to me, at this stage, now that the door is opening somewhat for the black artist; and in almost every case is being misused because of that gangster/pimp concept. They've even assigned to the black actor the job of getting rid of the Mafia when the government doesn't want to get rid of them. [Laughter] That's a painful kind of. So that's furious, all that. There's Harriet Ross Tubman, there's Sojourner Truth, there's about five black congressmen that we had during reconstruction. There aren't five people who can name them; I can only because I've been teaching these last couple of years, and I had to do a certain kind of research.

FM: I'm thinking though in terms of what Sanchez said this afternoon though, they'll let black people go back but they won't let them make films in a sense which have a....

WM: They're not letting them go back, they're putting them back. There's a difference there. They're really putting them back into an era that is not real, not of these times. When you put them in these times, again they are grappling with problems that even the government is not honestly dealing with, when you talk about dope. Because when you trace the sources of it, you've got to find yourself on the White House lawn. So I think that we haven't even touched the black cowboy really. They've done a couple of films that have done a rather cursory job of it, but there were at least five thousand known black cowboys. Tom Mix we know about. He was a hero of mine when I was a child. But the man who taught him, Bill Pickett who invented "Bulldogging," there's nothing on him.

FM: The one who had four other brothers, yeah.

WM: So there is an incredible reservoir of riches that if they were touched, and I don't think that we can expect that the people who are in the business of making films would be terribly interested in this information. What I'm getting to, it is the responsibility of black people to make this happen. That's all.

FM: The last question I'll ask, if you were doing the study of the history of the black man in motion pictures, what things would you stress?

WM: What things would I stress?

FM: What would be the things that you would emphasize?

WM: There's something wonderful about *Sounder*.[91] They almost lost me when they shot the dog. I knew it was going to be a bummer, but what I did love was the inter-relationships between the children and the mother, and the boy's concern about his father. I thought that was the richness of that film for me, apart from the rather inordinate, wonderful performances of the young people and the adults.

I think I'd get back to the humanity of a people about whom very little is known; and what is known is generally of a very negative nature. Go back to that. And the humanity of those who have fought for the lost cause. That's exciting stuff; and if done thoughtfully, if done truthfully, it will be done thoughtfully, I think. I think I'd want to stress that.

I'm involved in trying to get a script done, mount a film that deals with the rise and reign of King Christophe. One of the significant aspects of this is that there were a half million African people.... I think that more important is the thing I was speaking of before. Yes, I don't want to see any John Waynes among us. That's a disease. I don't want to see us copying anything that other people have done. There's no need to because the riches of our own history is right there at our fingertips.

A difficult problem, as Ed Bullins was pointing out, of getting the money to produce them and then release them. Who's going to do the distributing and so on? Anthony Quinn wants to get in on this thing. In one way I can understand an actor saying, "Well, I should be able to play any role." But if he's an adult, and he had any sense of the history of a people, he shouldn't want to play this role.

FM: It's a question of time, too.

WM: The timing, exactly. If we were all equal in terms of our privileges, then there would be no question about this thing. But we're not, and it's a long way off. So I think that what he's doing—his effort to mount this thing on Christophe—I would characterize as being profoundly disrespectful to black people.

For those readers interested in the exchange of letters between William Marshall and Anthony Quinn, they are available in The Black Scholar.[92]

WM: But I've just come back from a tour of about twenty cities where I was closer to the business aspect of films than I have ever been, and talked with exhibitors who I didn't even know anything about, really. I knew that they were remote creatures that existed. I really knew nothing about the letters that had been written to Quinn and his reactions, and I had written some, and I have a letter from him that you wouldn't believe he wrote.

I asked them, "What's selling in your films? In all of these eighteen cities I went to."

"Anything black! Just anything black."

I said, "Well, why is that? That was always a problem, or it was a problem since I was a child."

They said, "Well, you've probably been reading about the fact that the whites have moved out of the inner cities into the suburbs, and they ain't coming' back to see no movies. The captive audience in the central city happens to be blacks. More and more blacks are migrating there."

I know there's an effort to get whites back into the central city, but that hasn't advanced itself very much. So the audience is black largely. Forty percent of film revenue coming out of the pockets of black people who only constitute ten, twelve at most percent of the population of the United States. Anything that John Wayne does—except *The Cowboys,* they said, that didn't make much money—he got killed too early in the film. And when your aardvark, your number one, [Laughter] falls by the wayside that early on, and you ain't got nobody to identify with. But all of his other films would make a lot of money. Anything that Clint Northwood—

FM: Eastwood.

WM: Whatever Wood—sells because it's bloody. These are not actors, these fellows, but they're performers. That's kind of another thing.

FM: I'll tell you a strange story just to—I took my son, the oldest boy—twelve years of age—to see—when we come in, we see three or four black films a day because we don't get many of them up in Vermont. In *Slaughter,* there were a number of scenes in which blacks were killing white people, and the audience, which was, ninety percent black, were yelling, "Kill the mother so and so, the Honky and so on."

WM: Yes.

FM: I was worried that Steven would get frightened—he's only twelve or so—and all these people screaming, "Kill the white man." And when the movie was over and we walked out, I asked Steven, "Did you notice anything unusual in the movie?" He liked the sex scenes—twelve years of age, it was a big thing for him—and he had no consciousness at all of anything being yelled or that "Whitey" or "Honky" was being said. I've never been able to understand it.

WM: His age?

FM: Twelve. I can't come to terms with it myself. He sat in that movie engrossed in the film. It was the third film he had seen. He had seen *The Legend of Nigger Charley* first.

Actually, I am in error here. Gary, eleven years old at the time and my youngest son, had gone with me and my sister Rose to see The Legend of Nigger Charley. *We sat in the balcony of, I think, what was Paramount Pictures' New York flagship theater. While Gary reveled in the violence and was oblivious to any racial currents, Rose gave me the hard eye throughout the film, asking, "What were you thinking, taking him here?" We may have been the only people in that picture palace that afternoon.*

WM: How do you get along with him?

FM: Excellent.

WM: You don't think that cry up there "Kill this cracker?" It might have been directed to his Daddy. [Laughter]

FM: No, no. Other:...children. In Africa, you know, Tarzan? Black children always identify with Tarzan.

WM: In Africa?. In the United States of America!

FM: But I was more concerned with the business of the black audience yelling out, and that he would be the only white boy in the audience, whether he would be frightened, that they would turn to him and say, "We'll get this white kid," or, "Why are you sitting here?" You know, make the transfer. But he didn't.

WM: I sympathize with your fears there. I think that that kind of film—I haven't seen it—but if that's what they're selling, I think that's despicable. In no way, as I see it, do black people feel that way, let's say, on a constant basis. Of course, you get mad at everybody, on occasion, and you get madder at white people, of course, because of the prerogatives that they have and the way in which they flaunt these prerogatives. The denials, the constant denials. You get very, very mad at that; but I think that's a very unhealthy thing when they get this "kill Whitey" business going. I think it's more of a detriment to black people than it is to white people. And I think it is intended to be that way because the blacks, in short, did not make those films. They were the automatons, in a sense, who were walking through certain roles. They are a very, very unhealthy thing for representatives of one tenth of a giant society like this, "Let's kill all the rest of them people." It's just stupid and unhealthy.

FM: Well, there are a thousand more questions that I would ask you, but I wouldn't impose any more on your time. I would like to do two things if I could. I'd like to get your address to write to you.

Postscript

I have tried to convey to the reader how those few days forty years ago with Ed Bullins and William Marshall at the American Theatre Association meeting in New York City affected a progressive academic teaching and living in the whitest state in the Union. What these men represented, how they saw their life's mission, and the courage they displayed inspired me throughout my career. Marshall's story also influenced my decision to begin *Exits and Entrances* with a Preface and an Introduction. I did not want his journey as a rebellious young pool hustler from Gary, Indiana who rose to the heights of his profession to be seen out of context. I also did not want DeMille's conclusion at the end of *The Plainsman* to go unchallenged. This country was not built just by strength and courage alone. Dreams played a big part in striving to make America all it could and should be.

Thus, when I think now about William Marshall, I do not remember him as just a famous black horror star. I think of him of him as Othello, falsely perceived by his father-in-law as a dissembler and fake hero. But once the brilliant General explains himself and demonstrates his metal, not only Brabantio but also the entire court sees Othello's worth and his value to the state. Shakespeare portrayed him as human and flawed, as each of us surely is. But I also remember the imposing actor as a memorable artist who was larger than life.

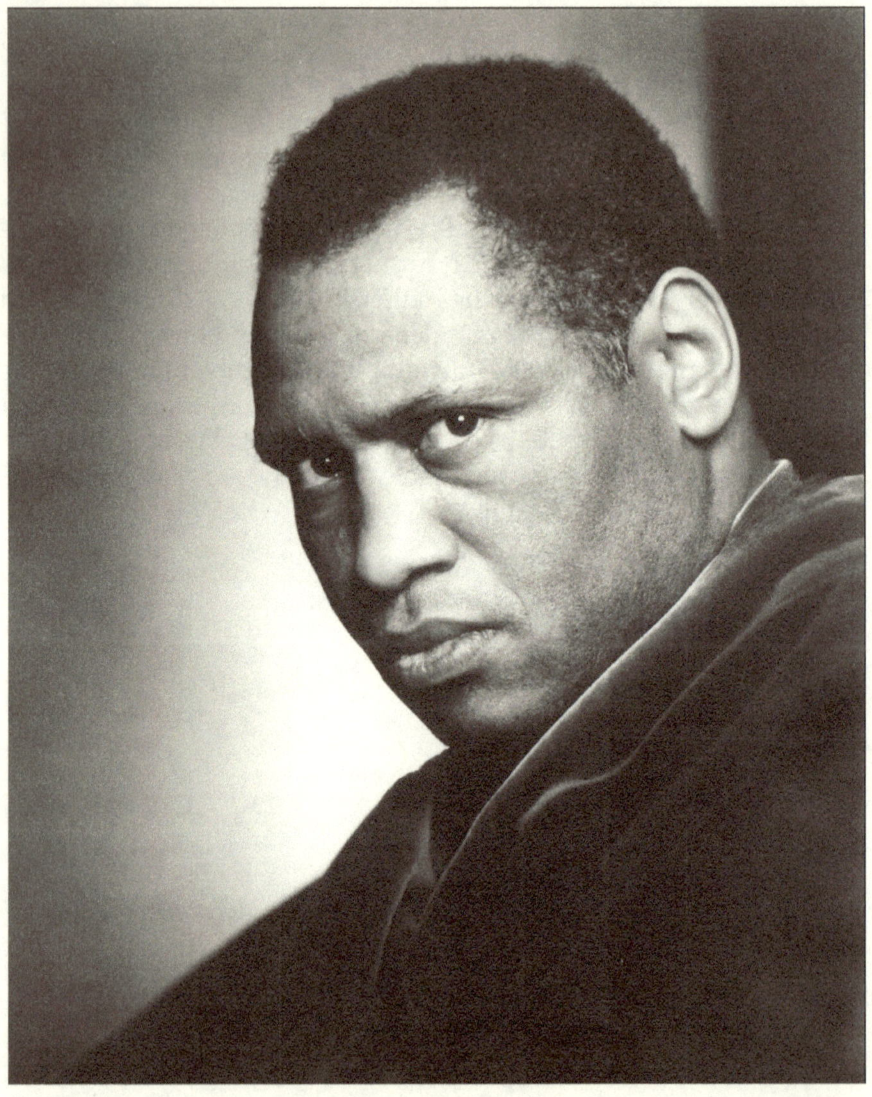

29. Paul Robeson, singer, athlete, actor, and one of the great spokespeople for human rights in American history.

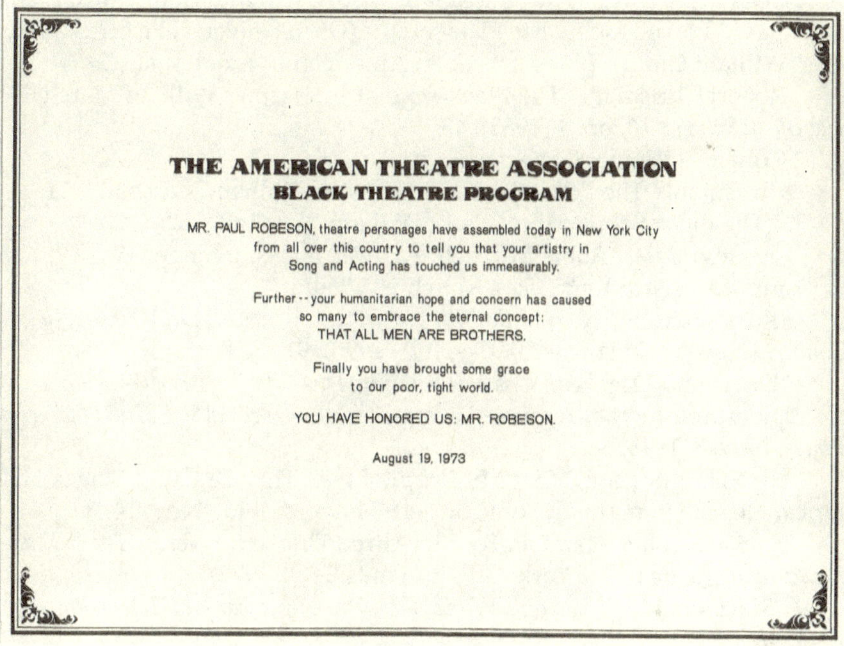

THE AMERICAN THEATRE ASSOCIATION
BLACK THEATRE PROGRAM

MR. PAUL ROBESON, theatre personages have assembled today in New York City from all over this country to tell you that your artistry in Song and Acting has touched us immeasurably.

Further -- your humanitarian hope and concern has caused so many to embrace the eternal concept: THAT ALL MEN ARE BROTHERS.

Finally you have brought some grace to our poor, tight world.

YOU HAVE HONORED US: MR. ROBESON.

August 19, 1973

30. The original placemat used for the American Theatre Tribute to Paul Robeson on August 19th, 1973 at New York's Americana Hotel.

Notes

[1] Jones and Niven, *James Earl Jones: Voices and Silences*, 119-20.

[2] Jordan, "How Samuel L. Jackson Became His Own Genre," 29.

[3] Ralph Ellison, *The Shadow and the Act* (New York: Random House, 1953), 276-77.

[4] Cecil B. DeMille, "The Plainsman," (USA: Paramount Pictures, 1936).

[5] David Lowell Rich, "The Plainsman," (USA: Universal Pictures, 1966).

[6] William Crain, "Blacula," (USA: American International, 1972).

[7] Robert Chrisman, "The Black Scholar Interviews William Marshall," *The Black Scholar* 16, no. 4 (1985): 48.

[8] Cohen, "Original Gangstas."

[9] Chrisman, "The Black Scholar Interviews William Marshall," 51.

[10] "The Black Scholar Interviews William Marshall," 52.

[11] Anonymous, "Abbie Mitchell, Actress, Is Dead; Singer Was Widow of Composer," *New York Times*, March 20 1960, 1.

[12] Rosalyn M. Story, *And So I Sing: African-American Divas of Opera and Concert* (New York: Warner Books, Inc., 1990), 91.

[13] Davis and Dee, *With Ossie & Ruby in This Life Together*, 143-56.

[14] Sam Zolotow, "Premiere Tonight of Heyward Play," *The New York Times*, Nov. 3, 1948, 36.

[15] Brooks Atkinson, "'Set My People Free': Theatre Guild Stages Historical Negro Drama with Some Superb Players," ibid., Nov. 14, X1.

[16] Jackie Robinson and as Told to Alfred Duckett, *I Never Had It Made: An Autobiography* (New York: G.P. Punam's Sons, 1972).

[17] MacDonald, *Blacks and White TV: Afro-Americans in Television since 1948*, 48.

[18] Davis and Dee, *With Ossie & Ruby in This Life Together*, 225.

[19] MacDonald, *Blacks and White TV: Afro-Americans in Television since 1948*, 38-9.

[20] Thomas Cripps, *Black Film as Genre* (Bloomington: Indiana University Press, 1978), 58.

[21] Jean Negulesco, "Lydia Bailey," (USA: Twentieth Century-Fox, 1952).

[22] A. H. Weiler, "Lydia Bailey, Fox Movies Based on Kenneth Roberts Novel, Opens at Roxy Theatre," *N.Y. Times*, May 31 1952, 12.

[23] Chrisman, "The Black Scholar Interviews William Marshall," 51.

[24] Delmer Daves, "Demetrius and the Gladiator," (USA: Twentieth Century-Fox, 1954).

[25] Henry King, "The Robe," (USA: Twentieth Century-Fox, 1953).

[26] Anonymous, "Demetrius and the Gladiators: William Marshall Has a Choice Role in 3-D Film," *Ebony* 9, no. 1 (1954): 96.

[27] Brooks, "Something of Value."

[28] Richard Fleischer, "The Boston Strangler," (USA: Twentieth Century-Fox, 1968).

[29] Anonymous, "William Marshall, 'Blacula' Actor, Succumbs at 78," *Jet* 104, no. 1 (2003): 18.

[30] Simone M. Sebastian, "William Marshall, 78, Screen Actor Starred in 'Blacula'," *Chicago Tribune*, June 22 2003.

[31] Davis, *Life Lit by Some Large Vision: Selected Speeches*, 35.

[32] Harrison, *Shakespeare: Major Plays and the Sonnets*, Hamlet, Act II, scene 11, 624.

[33] *Shakespeare: Major Plays and the Sonnets*, Hamlet, Act III, scene ii, 628.

[34] James A. DeVinney and et. all, "Eyes on the Prize," (USA: PBS, 1987).

[35] Stanley Nelson, "Freedom Riders," (USA: PBS, 2013).

[36] Peter Keepnews, "Nina Simone, 70, Soulful Diva and Voice of Civil Rights, Dies," *New York Times*, April 22 2003.

[37] Joseph, *Dark Days, Bright Nights: From Black Power to Barack Obama*, 23-5.

[38] Keepnews, "Nina Simone, 70, Soulful Diva and Voice of Civil Rights, Dies."

[39] Tanzina Vega, "Stir Builds over Actress to Portray Nina Simone," ibid., September 12 2012.

[40] Tim Weiner, "Odetta, Civil Rights Voice, Dies at 77," ibid., Dec. 4, 2008, 812.

[41] Staff, "New Crisis: The Negro Family," 34.

[42] Joseph, *Dark Days, Bright Nights: From Black Power to Barack Obama*, 283-306.

[43] Lee Rainwater and William L. Yancey, *The Moynihan Report and the Politics of Controversy: A Trans-Action Social Science and Public Policy Report, Including the Full Text of the Negro Family: The Case for National Action by Daniel Patrick Moynihan* (Cambridge, MA, and London: The M.I. T. Press, 1967).

[44] Kenneth B. Clark, *Dark Ghetto: Dilemmas of Social Power* (Lebanon: Wesleyan University Press, 1989).

[45] Brooks and Marsh, *The Complete Directory to Prime Time Network TV Shows: 1946-Present*, 774.

[46] MacDonald, *Blacks and White TV: Afro-Americans in Television since 1948*, 121.

[47] Ibid.

[48] Gordon Parks, "The Learning Tree," (USA: Warner Brothers, 1969).

[49] Melvin Van Peebles, "Sweet Sweetback's Baadasssss Song " (USA: Xenon Pictures, 1971).

[50] Ossie Davis, "Cotton Comes to Harlem," (USA: United Artists, 1970).

[51] Parks, "Shaft."

[52] Gordon Parks Jr., "Superfly," (USA: Warner Brothers, 1972).

[53] Crain, "Blacula."

[54] John M. Wilson, "In Search of William Marshall," *Los Angeles Times*, Feb. 17 1991, 37.

[55] Anne Valdespino, "Can Ya Dig It? Blaxploitation Flicks Hip Again," *Weekend*, June 6 2002, 11.

[56] Sebastian, "William Marshall, 78, Screen Actor Starred in 'Blacula'."

[57] Frank Manchel, *An Album of Modern Horror Films* (New York: Franklin Watts, 1983), 15.

[58] Kevin Thomas, "Vampire Epidemic in Black and White," *Los Angeles Times*, Oct. 19, 1972, E21.

[59] Burrell, "Black Films: Big Money Careers & Rip Off…." 2-3.

[60] Roger Greenspun, "The Screen: 'Blacula'," *The New York Times*, August 26 1972, 15.

[61] James Robert Parish, *Black Action Films: Plots, Critiques, Casts and Credits for 235 Theatrical and Made-for-Television Releases* (Jefferson, North Carolina: McFarland, 1989), 58.

[62] Brooks E. Hefner, "Rethinking Blacula: Ideological Critique at the Intersection of Genres," *Journal of Popular Film & Television* 40, no. 2 (2012).

[63] Margalit Fox, "Vonetta Mcgee, Film and TV Actress, Dies at 65," *The New York Times*, July 15 2010, B10.

[64] Ibid.

[65] Bob Kelljan, "Scream, Blacula, Scream," (USA: MGM/UA, 1973).

[66] Roger Greenspun, "Screen: A Vampire's Lot," *The New York Times*, July 19, 1973.

[67] Kevin Thomas, "Movie Review: 'Scream' Longer on Laughs Than Chills," *Los Angeles Times*, Aug. 8, 1973, D11.

[68] Grant IV, *Post-Soul Black Cinema: Discontinuities, Innovations, and Breakpoints, 1970-1995*, xi.

[69] William Girdler, "Abby," (USA: American International, 1974).

[70] Franklin Harris, "Culture Shock Column: Infamous Clone of 'the Exorcist' Is Due New Respect with DVD Release," *Decatur Daily*, Oct. 16, 2008.

[71] Sebastian, "William Marshall, 78, Screen Actor Starred in 'Blacula'."

[72] Anonymous, "Marshall Going to Haiti for Movie on Christophe," *The Amsterdam News*, Dec. 6 1975, D4.

[73] Dave McGinn, "Race to the Bottom," *Boston Globe and Mail*, May 27, 2010, R3.

[74] Emily F. Gibson, "Must a Black Actor Play Henri Christophe?," *Sepia* (1972): 22-7.

[75] "Must a Black Actor Play Henri Christophe?," *Sepia* (197): 23.

[76] Robert Aldrich, "Twilight's Last Gleaming," (U.S.-German: Allied Artists, 1977).

[77] Dave Kehr, "Video: Nuclear Misseles and Cold War Cupid's Arrows," *The New York Times*, Nov. 25, 2012, 15.

[78] Nicolas Rapold, "Aiming a Query and Missiles at a President," *New York Times*, October 21 2012, 14.

[79] Sebastian, "William Marshall, 78, Screen Actor Starred in 'Blacula'."

[80] Anonymous, "Convention Report 1973," *Bulletin of Black Theatre*, no. 4 (1973): 1.

[81] Negulesco, "Lydia Bailey."

[82] Donald Bogle, *Toms, Coons, Mulattoes, Mammies, & Bucks: An Interpretive History of Blacks in American Films* (New York: Continuum, 1973).

[83] Gillo Pontecorvo, "Burn! (Queimada!)," (Italy, France: United Artists, 1969).

[84] Daves, "Demetrius and the Gladiator."

[85] Delmer Daves, "Broken Arrow," (USA: Twentieth Century-Fox, 1950).

[86] Frank Manchel, "Cultural Confusion: A Look Back at Delmar Dave's *Broken Arrow*," *Film History*, vol. 23, Nos 1-4 (1993).

[87] Brooks, "Something of Value."

[88] Sidney Poitier confirms Marshall's observations in Brooks' *Something of Value.*

[89] Clarence Brown, "Intruder in the Dust," (USA: MGM, 1949).

[90] Brooks, "Something of Value."

[91] Martin Ritt, "Sounder," (USA: Twentieth Century-Fox, 1972).

[92] William Marshall and Anthony Quinn, "An Exchange between William Marshall and Anthony Quinn," *The Black Scholar* 3, no. 10 (1972): 49-52.

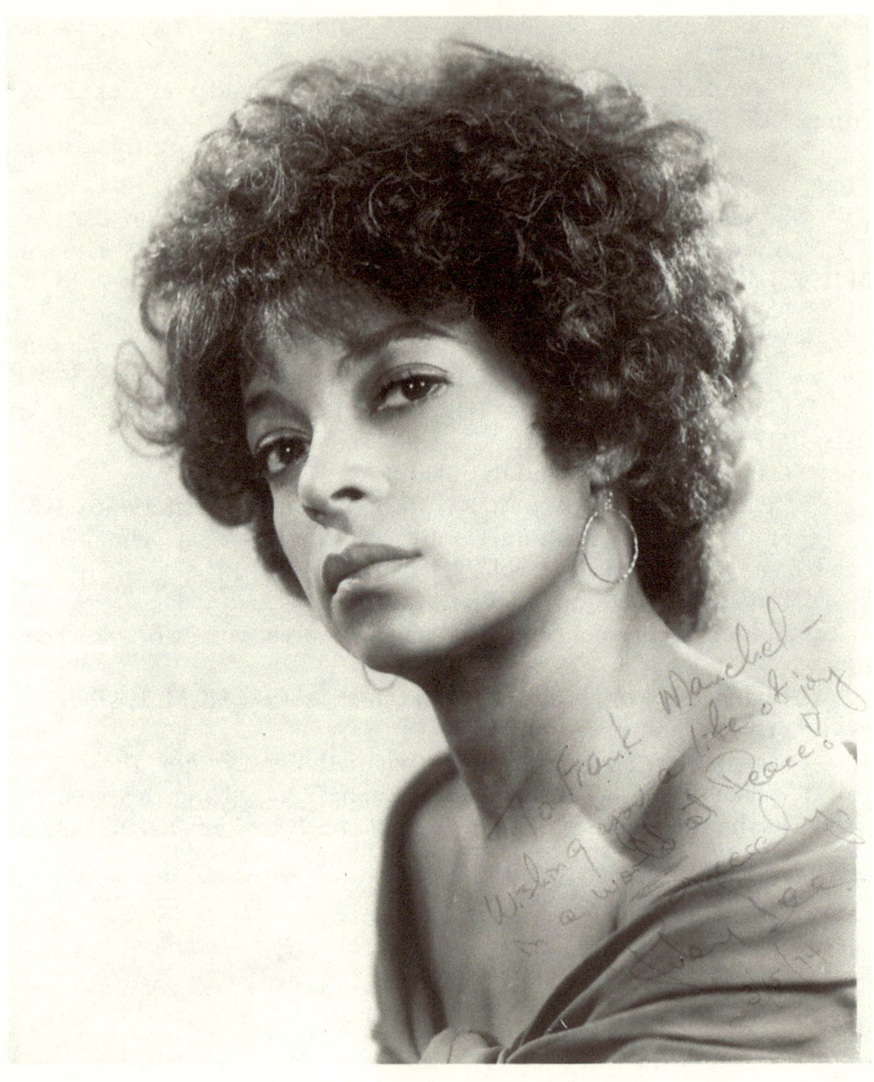

31. The caption reads, "To Frank Manchel, Wishing you a life of joy and a world at peace! Sincerely, Ruby Dee, 3/15/74.

7

An American Treasure: Ruby Dee

"To know yourself, you have to know the past. To know where you are going, you have to know where you have been."[1]

Corey Harris

"You can't expect our children to know what they haven't been taught."

Attributed to Rosa Parks

"The future is unknowable, but the past should give us hope."[2]

Winston Churchill

"For over a half century, Hollywood films have dealt with... complex and often contradictory ways, marked by outrage, indifference, compassion and ignorance, the need to understand and the desire to forget."[3]

Gene Hackman

On February 17, 2013, one week before the 85th Academy Awards, The *New York Times'* Nelson George focused on four leading nominees for Best Picture honors: Quentin Tarentino's *Django Unchained*, Robert Zemeckis' *Flight*; Benh Zeitlin's *Beasts of the Southern Wild;* and Steven Spielberg's *Lincoln*. Each movie, directed by a white man, explained the author, was linked together by the fact they dealt with black-white relations while featuring African-American actors. "For the first time in recent memory," declared

George, "race is central to several Oscar conversations."[4]

What better way to begin the last chapter in *Exits and Entrances* than by recalling an American legend who has made civil rights, the arts, and black causes central to her life and to her career for over half a century. We admire the actress not just for her artistic contributions but also for the durability of her work. None of the four previously mentioned Oscar nominees could even have been imagined let alone made when Ruby Dee debuted both in her first film, *What a Guy*, in 1939,[5] and on Broadway in *South Pacific* in 1943. And there is hardly a black performer today that does not owe her a debt of gratitude for the professional paths she blazed from the post-WWII period to the present. For example, she became the first African-American woman to play starring roles at the American Shakespeare Festival and was later called by some "the Mother of Black theater."[6]

This unassuming, small, lively, and soft-spoken woman with strong core values never dodged the issues of her times, nor did she ever compromise her ideals in order to achieve her goals. Additionally, she inspired us not only with her vision but also with an exemplary family life. Together with the amazing Ossie Davis, her husband of fifty-six years, she fashioned a stunning career. Together, the gifted couple emerged as two of the most applauded artists of their generation, winning countless honors including the National Medal of the Arts, the Screen Actors Guild Lifetime Achievement Award, the 2004 Kennedy Center Honors, as well as being inducted into both the Black Filmmaker's Hall of Fame and the Theater Hall of Fame. Actor Roy Scheider called them "the first political couple of America."[7] Their efforts on behalf of African-American culture and minority rights everywhere symbolize John Donne's belief, "Each man's death diminishes me, / For I am involved in mankind. / Therefore, send not to know/ For whom the bell tolls, / It tolls for thee."[8] And it is because the couple is so closely identified in the public's mind that this profile will provide more information on the pair than usually accorded other entertainment families elsewhere in *The Interviews*.

Ruby Ann Wallace was born one of five children to Edward Marshall Wallace, a railroad porter, and Emma A. Benson Wallace, a schoolteacher, on October 27, 1924 in Cleveland, Ohio. Early in her childhood, Ruby's parents moved the young girl, along with her three sisters and brother to Harlem. These were the days of the Harlem Renaissance, The Cotton Club, religious cults, and jazz-crazed white people who made the black community their playground. It was also the era of the influential American writer and photographer Carl Van Vechten whose controversial racial obsession with a gifted but "primitive" black culture surfaced in *Nigger Heaven*, his provocative novel of Harlem life.[9]

"By the 1940s," Pulitzer-Prize winning historian Isabel Wilkerson pointed out, "Harlem was a mature and well-established capital of black cultural life, having peaked with the Harlem Renaissance, plunged into Depression after the 1929 stock market crash, climbed back to life during World War II, and, unbeknownst to the thousands still arriving...was at that precise moment as rollickingly magical as it was ever likely to be." The writer similarly explained how "The post World War II period had great significance not only for the motion picture industry but also for African-American artists. So, too," writes Wilkerson, "rose the language and music of urban America that sprang from the blues that came with the migrants and dominates our airwaves to this day."[10]

For the most part, Ruby's devoted and caring family protected her from Harlem's more undesirable elements and left her innocent of the dangers adolescents faced from drugs, prostitution, and police brutality. She also grew up wondering why the merchants on 125th Street did not employ any black people.[11] Instead, her parents, who struggled financially to raise five children, fostered an educational climate that encouraged their offspring to study the invaluable lessons stored in public libraries. Ruby's love of learning and books have remained with her ever since. She also retained her religious education obtained from the historic Mother A. M. E. Zion Church, eventually run by Paul Robeson's brother Benjamin and where William Marshall first performed *Othello*. These interests, along with an active fantasy life gained from watching movies, shaped much of her childhood. "Somewhere along the way, " the artist makes clear in her autobiography, "I abandoned life in the real world—and most of the rules by which it was lived. And much of what I am today, the good, and the bad, springs from that fact. In a daydream, there's no such thing as success or failure."[12]

After graduating from Hunter High School, where fellow students mocked her budding interest in acting, Ruby Wallace became one of the few black women of her time to seek a higher education. In September 1941, she entered Hunter College, where she earned a B.A. degree four years later. In between, it quickly became clear to the struggling undergraduate that her fascination with acting might be more sensible than pursuing the traditional prospects open to black college graduates.

Looking around for a good place to start a theatrical career, Wallace, in her freshman year at Hunter College, found the newly created American Negro Theatre, established in 1940 and run by Frederick Douglass O'Neal and Abram Hill. Just as later this celebrated organization would become the training grounds of other famous performers like Harry Belafonte, Sidney Poitier, Hilda Simms, Earle Hyman, and Ossie Davis, it became the eighteen-year-old's starting point in the profession. It would also eventually introduce the gifted woman to her second husband. Today, the famous theatrical site has been transformed into the Schomberg Center for Research in Black Culture.

The famous actor, writer, and civil rights activist who would become Ruby Wallace's lifelong partner personally and professionally also began his professional acting career the same year she entered Hunter College. Born Raiford Chatman Davis, the oldest of five children, to striving parents Kince and Laura Davis, on December 18, 1917, in Cogdell, Georgia, Davis' childhood years were different from those of his future wife. For example, Jim Crow laws and the KKK dominated the teenager's community.[13] Brought up by his poor family in a segregated South, he spent much of his childhood in the neighboring vicinities of Waycross and Valdosta, mainly because his birthplace had no schools for black children. "Few of my childhood adventures led to fisticuffs," he wrote. "I was smart and likable, probably the teacher's pet."[14] He also, like Ruby, credited his parents' influence for his life-long love of books. But unlike his future wife, Ossie had his racial consciousness raised long before Ruby's cultural awareness developed.

At eighteen, Davis left home, hitchhiking to Washington D.C., to enter Howard University, where he studied drama, intending to be a playwright. Just before graduation, however, the undergraduate decided to try his luck as a dramatist; and on the advice of his favorite college professor Alain LeRoy Locke, he set out for New York to discover what being in the theater meant and required. But prior to leaving the nation's capital, Davis attended an historic concert. In the mid-nineties, he told an audience at Cornell University that he recalled hearing Marian Anderson at the Lincoln Memorial in 1939 after she had been banned from singing at Washington's Constitution Hall. "I understood fully for the first time, " he said, "the importance of Black song, Black music, Black arts. I was handed my spiritual assignment that night."[15] Once in New York, he also toyed with membership in the Young Communist League, which ended with the onset of World War II.[16]

Ossie Davis' career as an actor began with the Rose McClendon Players in Harlem. Originally known as the Negro's People Theater, the company saw its mission as linking drama to the community. Following the death of the celebrated actress in 1936, her co-partner Dick Campbell transformed the group into the Rose McClendon Players, and Davis started his professional journey there in 1939. In addition to aiding Davis, the famous Players proved instrumental in the careers of Abram Hill, Loften Mitchell, and Frederick Douglass O'Neal.[17] By the middle of WWII, Ruby Wallace had begun to develop a strong friendship with Campbell. She was also married briefly (1941 to 1945) to Frankie Dee Brown.

As Wallace's acting career developed during World War II, she made her stage debut in Dorothy Heyward's unsuccessful play *South Pacific* (1943). Meanwhile, Davis served his thirty-two months first as an army surgical technician in Liberia and then writing and performing plays for the troops.[18] After the ex-soldier returned to the South in 1945, he received a call from Campbell, asking him to star in Robert Ardrey's new play *Jeb*, being produced and directed by the highly regarded Herman Shumlin.[19] The plot centered on Jeb Turner, a black veteran who lost his leg in WWII, and returns to his Southern home to discover he must now fight the Ku Klux Klan in order to be truly free.

Davis took the leading role, and playing his wife was Ruby Wallace. Interestingly, the actress had quit her day job to understudy for the part of the wife, but proved so convincing she got the role. Understudying Davis, as the reader might recall, was a young actor named William Marshall. While the play had a very short run, the chance to appear with Davis obviously set the unhappy actress in a new direction.

Worth remembering at this juncture is what life in the theater was like for aspiring actors like Belafonte, Poitier, Peters, Marshall, Dixon, Davis, and Wallace. As discussed throughout *The Interviews*, significant changes were occurring both in show business and in the culture. Liberal voices could be heard everywhere. But changing the social and artistic mores of producers, playwrights, and audiences proved slow and difficult. "Ruby and I came along at a time when being black was not yet fashionable. There was little in the theater for us except to carry silver trays and announce the grits wouldn't hold the heat."[20] The reader might also remember that the performer made clear just how painful it was for Marshall and him to deliver dialogue written by Marc Connelly in his 1951 revival of *The Green Pastures*.

Still further, by the late forties liberal and progressive artists had to face the wrath of America's growing anti-Communism movement, the election of Eric Johnson to head the Motion Picture Association of America, the conservative politics of Ronald Reagan as chief of the Screen Actors Guild, and the emergence of the red-baiting Senator Joseph R. McCarthy. Many of the black performers who grew up with the Rose McClendon Players, the American Negro Theatre, and the American Theatre Wing had strikingly different political views from the aforementioned witch-hunters. In particular, Ruby and Ossie, along with Frederick O'Neal and Charles Gordone, had begun to be more militant and mindful of black discrimination. As a result, they formed the 1951 progressive group known as the Coordinating Council for Negro Performers that worked tirelessly throughout the fifties to defend the rights of black actors.[21]

Amazingly, the couple emerged from the Eisenhower decade unharmed by the political and social effects of the Cold War. Victor Navasky recalls the delightful story of their near miss with the wrath of the F.B.I.: "Despite their political activism, neither Davis nor Dee ever joined the Communist Party. As Ossie put it, 'I was "red" only when I thought it was a smarter way of being black.' The F.B.I. did, however, set one thing right. When Dee and Davis retrieved their files under the Freedom of Information Act, they discovered that the Bureau had designated Ossie as a "fellow traveler." His crime was that he 'was known to associate with Ruby Dee.'"[22]

The next joint theatrical teaming of Wallace and Davis was in the road company of the smash-Broadway hit *Anna Lucasta* (1944). Readers of *Every Step a Struggle* may recall the story of how after a brief career in the Army during World War II, O'Neal returned to the American Negro Theatre. Together with Hill, and at the suggestion of Claire Leonard who was the agent of Hill and Philip Yordan, the ANT produced Yordan's drama *Anna Lucasta* as a black play. It featured Hilda Simms, Earle Hyman, Alice Childress, Herbert Henry, and O'Neal. In the popular road company, Ruby played the exiled daughter of a father deeply distressed that she did not become the woman he wanted her to be. But when some family members concoct a scheme whereby the outcast can make money for them, the fallen woman returns home to a series of troubling events.

Dramatist Loften Mitchell said the following about what may be the longest running black play in American theatrical history: "*Anna Lucasta,* for all its trail blazing, is a mediocre play that could never have 'made it' as a 'white play.'"[23] However, The *Los Angeles Times* reviewer Edwin Schallert wrote of the 1946 road company: "As a rousing stage event, mixing emotional drama and comedy, *Anna Lucasta* arrives with bells jingling, sirens shrieking and every assurance that it will enjoy large audiences during its tenancy at the Biltmore Theater."[24]

While rehearsing Garson Kanin's *The Smile of the World* in December 1948, the struggling actors took time off, bussed to New Jersey, and got married in a low-key ceremony, and then returned to work. The following month, the play ended its brief run at the Lyceum Theatre.

As the forties drew to a close, explains Vincent Canby, "Hollywood's 'problem' movies, which look fairly dated today, served notice that blacks existed as something more than happy cotton pickers…maids, chauffeurs, and handymen."[25] Krim Gabbard observes, "The year 1950 was an exceptionally appropriate release date for *Young Man with a Horn.* Almost all of the important big bands from the late forties were in serious trouble by that time." He added, "Many reasons have been offered to explain the sudden end of the big band era—the postwar suburban migration away from the inner-city dance halls, mothers and fathers staying home with their baby boom children, the rise of television. At least partially responsible for killing the big bands—and for bringing about the popular decline of the kind of jazz that Harry James had been playing—was the rise of the vocalists whose names began to appear above those of the bandleaders, a process that is explicitly represented in Martin Scorsese's *New York, New York* (1977)."[26] And James Gavin describes how a pioneer like Lena Horne felt about the changing times. "The letdown galled her anew, as she saw black Hollywood blossoming without her. At Twentieth Century-Fox, Darryl F. Zanuck had continued his campaign to integrate film with the acclaimed medical drama *No Way Out*."[27]

Writers sometimes overlook the importance of *No Way Out* for Davis and Dee. The newlyweds had caught the attention of Zanuck, and they made their screen debut together in uncredited roles in director Joseph L. Mankiewicz's new film. The controversial studio head, who had green-lighted Elia Kazan's *Gentleman's Agreement*[28] in 1947 now was interested in exposing racial prejudice towards African-Americans. Using what became an Oscar-nominated screenplay co-written by Lesser Samuels and Kazan, the movie focused on Dr. Luther Brooks (Sidney Poitier) who accidentally is assigned to the prison wing of his hospital and has to treat wounded prisoners Ray Biddle (Richard Widmark) and his brother John (Dick Paxton). When John suddenly dies, the racist Ray insists that the black doctor killed him. The remainder of the film deals with attempts by various people to prove Dr. Brooks' innocence. Adding to the film's tension is a race riot between blacks and whites. In this film, the twenty-two-year-old Sidney Poitier, as Gabbard notes, "established himself as a new role model for black America: a quietly intense, impeccably dignified figure who demanded respect."[29]

Also making the film important, in addition to seeing Dee play both the sister of the doctor and their angry brother (Ossie Davis), is the way the movie illustrates the changing social, technological, and thematic structure of the post-World War II film era. For example, when Dee arrived in Hollywood she found no black technicians, grips, electricians, props or make-up people. The newcomer asked for (and got) a black hairdresser.[30] Adding to the movie's important film noir subjects are Milton R. Kramer's impressive use of shadows and dark corners and location shooting. We can clearly see how Twentieth Century-Fox was adapting to the public's postwar interests just before the advent of television and its devastating impact on the film industry. As for Dee's view of *No Way Out,* she felt that the movie "for its time (1950)...was a revolutionary film in that for the first time on the American screen blacks and whites confronted each other in a real way."[31]

The performer's next film had her sharing leading credits with the Brooklyn Dodger's most famous ballplayer in Alfred E. Green's *The Jackie Robinson Story* (1950).[32] The Lawrence Taylor-Arthur Mann screenplay captures how Robinson met with General Manager Branch Rickey and agreed to a strategy to integrate professional baseball. The biographical movie then highlights the trials the black athlete faced in his rookie year with the Dodgers. Dee appears as Rachel, who stood by her husband's side throughout the difficult years from 1946 to 1948. Moreover, the film stresses how much black people perceived the ballplayer as an inspirational cultural hero. The director ends the picture with a voice-over narrative saying, "Yes, this is the Jackie Robinson story. But it is not his story alone. Not his victory alone. It is one that each of us shares, a story that can only happen in a country that is truly free, a country where every child has the opportunity to be president or play baseball for the Brooklyn Dodgers."[33]

These two films typified what types of roles the actress performed in the fifties, as well as her commitment to foregrounding race in her work. For example, Dee played the slave Rachel in Anthony Mann's *The Tall Target* (1951),[34] a story about an aborted attempt on President Lincoln's life during his first inauguration. From assassinations, the actress returned to sports in James Wong Howe's *Go, Man, Go* (1950),[35] where she played the wife of Inman Jackson (Sidney Poitier), the fictionalized difficult star of the Harlem Globetrotters. In Martin Ritt's *Edge of the City* (1957),[36] covered in the Ivan Dixon chapter, Ruby appeared as Lucy Tyler, again a supportive wife of Sidney Poitier. Allen Reisner's all-black musical *St. Louis Blues* (1958),[37] a romanticized tale about W. C. Handy, had the actress as the great blues artist's clean-cut, long-suffering sweetheart. And in Philip Leacock's *Take a Giant Step* (1959),[38] a bildungsroman about a black teenager who runs afoul of his white community, Dee acted as the youngster's trusted housekeeper who teaches him the virtues of being black.

Movies and plays weren't the only things on Ruby Dee's mind during the fifties. Together with her husband, she found ways to makes their progressive voices heard in political and social causes like the execution of Julius and Ethel Rosenberg, the persecution of Paul Robeson, the 1954 Brown Vs. Board of Education decision, the 1956 bus boycott in Montgomery, Alabama, the appearance of Martin Luther King and Rosa Parks; and the 1957 Little Rock, Arkansas, school-integration clash. The couple also became friendly with many black radicals. Malcolm X, for example, found in Ossie Davis and Ruby Dee kindred spirits. According to historian Peniel E. Joseph, it was because of the acting couple that Malcolm "developed important relationships with the city's black intelligentsia. Impressed by Malcolm's brilliance and sharp wit, Davis and his wife, Ruby Dee, introduced him to a group of friends and associates who included writers Lorraine Hansberry and Julian Mayfield." The scholar also pointed out, "Davis, along with John Killens and Julian Mayfield, approximated the behind-the-scenes support that Martin Luther King Jr. enjoyed in public from movie stars such as Sidney Poirier and Harry Belafonte. Privately, they formed a group of influential advisors who would serve as Malcolm's intellectual inner circle."[39]

Although Dee's roles had become more demanding by the end of the fifties, it was her performances in both the stage and screen versions of Hansberry's *A Raisin in the Sun* (1959, 1961) that saw the actress take her acting to a new level. Since the key elements in both the dramatist's and the show's role in the black experience have been described earlier in the Ivan Dixon chapter, and the actress talks about the play in the interview that follows, I need only remind readers that Hansberry's play stimulated studio interest in turning out black-oriented movies.[40]

Equally important, it is from this point on, that there is a growing debate about doing "cross-over" movies versus making separatist black films that begins to dominate both the careers and the thoughts of African-American entertainers. An equally crucial concern emerges over the nature of the movie-going audience. That is, must mainstream black-themed movies be slanted towards white patrons, or is there a large enough black audience to support African-American films? The issues remain sensitive throughout the history of the black film experience and *The Interviews,* and are raised in Dee's discussion with me later in the chapter.

One of my favorite anecdotes relates to the artist's lifelong affection for marginalized people. There was a moment during the 1959 Broadway run of *A Raisin in the Sun,* where Lena (Claudia McNeil) hits Beneatha, her defiant daughter (Diana Sands), for denying the Lord's existence. As the story goes, Sands was replaced one day by her understudy Billie Allen. McNeil, who looked like the black heavyweight champion of the world, almost knocked the understudy senseless, because unlike Sands, Allen didn't know how to take the blow. It was then that "the diminutive Dee said, 'you hit that girl once more like that, and I'll knock you flat.' McNeil brought Dee up on charges before Actors Equity for "unprofessional behavior."[41]

By 1963, both Dee and Davis found themselves publically challenging traditional film conventions. First came Joseph Strick's screen adaptation of Jean Genet's 1957 play of the same name, *The Balcony.*[42] Ben Maddow's sensitive screenplay valiantly tries to soften the inflamed story about a satirical brothel where warped characters live out their erotic delusions about religion, politics, and the judiciary during a radical period in the life of an unknown city. Shelley Winters plays Irma, the madam, who uses her customers to mirror what happens in the outside world. One of the episodes involves a sexy thief (Ruby Dee, playing against her standard screen image), who torments a judge (Peter Brocco) by insisting he lick her toes before she will confess to crimes she presumably committed. Other famous members of the cast included Peter Falk, Lee Grant, and Leonard Nimoy. And George J. Folsey's camerawork got an Oscar nomination, but lost out to James Wong Howe's cinematography in *Hud.* Dee did wonders with humor and dialogue to once more extend our awareness of just how much acting range she had.

Later that same year she appeared in Nicholas Webster's screen adaptation of Ossie Davis' 1961 stageplay *Purlie Victorious,* released as *Gone Are the Days.*[43] Co-produced by Brock Peters, the controversial satire concerned Reverend Purlie Victorious Judson, a self-proclaimed black preacher (Davis), who wants Lutiebelle Gussie Mae Jenkins, his girlfriend (Ruby Dee), to go back with him to Cotchipee, his Georgia birthplace, and fool Cap'n Stonewall Jackson Cotchipee (Sorrell Brooks) into giving him a $500 inheritance so the preacher can buy a church. Included in this mostly black film ridiculing Jim Crow values are Godfrey Cambridge, Beah Richards, Hilda Haynes, and Alan Alda making his film debut. Over forty years later, Dee remembered the movie as giving her "her greatest acting satisfaction."[44]

But the trailblazing movie's audience never materialized. Rereleased under the title *Purlie Victorious,* Davis' high hopes for a movie targeted at African-Americans were dashed when his film proved dead on arrival at the box-office. Not only did the critics pan the self-absorbed script about the problems of a single black person, but also they attacked the author's neglect of the issues arising out of the civil rights movement. Even more damaging were the comparisons being made with the other black-oriented movies appearing in the mid-1960s such as *Black Like Me, One Potato, Two Potato,* and *Nothing But a Man.*[45] Ironically, one of the most committed political activists of his day was being raked over the coals for making a movie that lacked authenticity.

Years later both *The Balcony* and *Purlie Victorious* enjoyed a rebirth because of popular DVD releases, while the Davis venture had a successful renaissance as the 1981 musical *Purlie.* But during the latter part of the sixties, such flops made the studios gloomy when thinking about relying on African-American audiences as a new source of major revenue. Nevertheless, as the debate about the melting pot vs. separatist theories grew more heated, and while the arguments for or against a non-violent approach to civil rights divided America, the gifted couple stayed focused on the question of "authenticity" in their future works.

After playing a part with Ruby in Dr. King's 1963 March on Washington and following his eloquent 1965 eulogy for Malcolm X, Davis turned his attention to preparing a musical version of *Purlie Victorious* and to a screen adaptation of famous African dramatist Wole Soyinka's 1965 play *Kongi's Harvest* (1970).[46] The film of the same name, on the surface, explained Davis, "is not revolutionary at all, it is the happening conflict between the old and the new taking place all over Africa today."[47] Soyinka, the 1986 Nobel Prize winner, used this satirical story about a tyrant who replaces a monarch and makes life worse in a transformed Nigerian community to draw attention to despotism. Although well intentioned, the movie caused little stir. The reason, as *Washington Post* reviewer Hollie I. West observed, was "Without Davis' occasional explanations during the movie, in his role as narrator, the feature might be totally unfathomable."[48]

The disappointing movie does, however, serve a useful function here. While Africa's changing image had been on the minds of anti-colonialists in the late sixties, as late as the early twenty-first century many Americans still had trouble perceiving realistic images about either the Continent or the African people. After passing through the twentieth century, many people, as pointed out by the *Washington Post*'s Clarence Page, still had their views clouded by Tarzan movies and Frank Buck adventures. He stressed in 2007, that the best movies teach us something about ourselves through stories and characters that we find ourselves caring about. "American movies about Africa," he insisted, "posed an extra challenge since Americans have not always cared about Africa." Among the examples he used to illustrate our distorted movie lessons were John Huston's *The African Queen* (1952), Sydney Pollack's *Out of Africa* (1985), Richard Attenborough's *Cry Freedom* (1987), Ridley Scott's *Black Hawk Down* (2001), Fernando Meirelles' *The Constant Gardner* (2005), Edward Zwick's *Blood Diamond* (2006), Jamie Uys' *The Gods Must be Crazy* (1989), Terry George's *Hotel Rwanda* (2004), and Phillip Noyce's *Catch a Fire* (2006). "With more independent films being made these days," Page reminded us, "more filmmakers are willing to take a chance. Still, there's movie shorthand about Africa that typecasts the continent as a wild, untamed place, dancing out there on the edge of civilizations and inviting canvases for our imagination. And it makes you wonder when will we begin to see African characters as complicated and inner-conflicted as we allow American characters to be?"[49] Seen from this perspective, one can appreciate how *Kongi's Harvest*'s comic look at tyranny in Africa proved unusual as the seventies began.

The opening of the decade also saw Davis deeply involved in stopping Twenthieth Century-Fox from adapting William Styron's

The Confessions of Nat Turner to the silver screen. The finacially desperate studio had by now bought into the idea that making black films might be the best way to avoid bankruptcy. And since James Earl Jones was already under contract to them for Martin Ritt's upcoming screen adaptation of *The Great White Hope* (1970),[50] the studio decided to invole the actor in the project.

But Davis remained adamant that Styron's Nat Turner was not right for this era, and so he helped organize a campaign that successfully derailed the proposed film. Ignoring the fact that Lou Peterson, a black screenwriter, director Sidney Lumet (Lena Horne's then son-in law), and Jones were to headline the movie, the Davis campaign objected to any attempt to make a film based on a white Southerner's account of a black hero. Not even the efforts of people like Ralph Ellison and James Baldwin could convince these outraged black progressives that the studio had the best of intentions. The pros and cons of the issues, the path that led from the pre-production plans and the ensuing Davis campaign to the eventual cancelling of the movie are appropriately discussed in Davis' autobiography *With Ossie & Ruby in this life together*,[51] as well as in Jones' *Voices and Silences*. The project has also been touched on in the Brock Peters chapter.

Of value to the reader now is that the aesthetic and social debates were not new to black artists like Davis and Jones. Nor for that matter was it unusual considering what happened throughout the first sixty years of film history and Hollywood's use of negative stereotyping. Clearly, I cannot address the arguments for and against such behavior either in debating the wisdom of making movies allegedly offensive to black pride and history, or in defending an artist's right to express his or her vision in the mass media. If pushed not to evade a position, I'd come down on the side of artistic freedom, and a belief that given the right production crew and cast, the mass media is more than able to offer a valuable interpretation on any subject matter it chooses. That said, I believe protests, critical attacks, and personal outrage are the rights, more the responsibility, of an informed democracy. One caveat: in exercising one's rights and responsibilities, there is an obligation that what we say and do prove useful and insightful.

However, Davis' concerns did not overshadow his wife's career, and she remained extremely active in films, first with Larry Peerce's *The Incident* (1967).[52] Adapted by Nicholas E. Baehr from a 1954 NBC TV show *Ride with Justice*, the screenplay told of two thugs who terrorize a group of passengers aboard a late night Bronx subway train. Among the frightened people are an old Jewish couple, two teenagers on a date, two soldiers, a gay passenger, and a black couple. Brock Peters is the proud Arnold Robinson who considers taking on the two hoodlums, but his more sensible wife, Joan (Ruby Dee) convinces him to suffer through the ordeal. Although painful to watch, the raw film shows how much more both Peters and Dee were being challenged in their new screen roles, as well as serving as the vehicle for the movie debut of Martin Sheen.

Worth noting at this point in the final chapter is that jazz, a concern throughout *The Interviews*, had once more entered a regrettable stage. Many of its greatest stars—e.g., Coltrane, Parker, Holiday, Young, and Hawkins—had passed. And as Michael Ullman points out, the late 60s witnessed the magical music losing its audience to rock. "Mainstream musicians were mostly out of work, and they hadn't the excuse of the avant-garde that they were ahead of their time, a time that never seemed to come. Bitter musicians, and it is wrong to suggest that they were all bitter, blamed the media, which didn't adequately cover their work, venal club owners and record company executives, and a benighted pubic. Avant-garde players tended to generalize to denounce imperialists, racists, and cultural conservatism. Often playing to small audiences of scruffy white guys (like myself), they touted their great black music, to use the Art Ensemble of Chicago's phrase for it, as particularly relevant to the African-American community that nonetheless largely ignored them."[53]

Against this musical decline, Ruby Dee's considerable and untapped skills once more surfaced in connection with Jules Dassin's *Up Tight* (1968).[54] The plot transformed John Ford's tale of a stool-pigeon who betrays his Dublin revolutionary mate in *The Informer* (1935)[55] to a modern-day Judas named Tank (Julian Mayfield) following the assassination of Dr. King. The violent vs. anti-violent elements in a Cleveland black community serve as the background for a doomed drunk who sells out his friend and suffers the wrath of the man's associates. Gifted with a fine cast featuring Raymond

St. Jacques, Frank Silvera, Roscoe Lee Browne, Janet MacLachlan, Max Julian, Juanita Moore, and Ruby Dee, this black-targeted film put what it considered "authenticity" front and center.

However, confusion and naysayers dogged the movie. Beside its problematic aesthetic issues, the well-intentioned project never found a black constituency that accepted or appreciated the screenplay's perspective about black power, mainly because of the political and cultural climate of the times. "I don't think the film works as a whole," explained the unknown reviewer from *America*. "The old plot structure acts as a procrustean bed to which the new circumstances must, willy nilly, be fitted."[56]

Because the actress' autobiography, historian Christopher Sieving's research, and the upcoming interview do a good job of discussing the production history of *Up Tight*, I need only alert the reader to the movie's relevance to this narrative. Clearly, Hollywood, by the end of the decade was turning away from romanticized images of the civil rights era and moving in the direction of showing black outrage in the streets of the nation.[57] What was especially intriguing about even this disappointing movie was that Ruby Dee co-authored the script with Mayfield and Dassin. Moreover, box-office disasters like *Up Tight* proved valuable to black militants when attacking the popular integrated movies being made by Sidney Poitier, who, as the reader may recall throughout *The Interviews*, runs into serious difficulties with young black audiences by the end of the sixties. This trend contributed to the rise of blaxploitation movies and the release of *Cotton Comes to Harlem* (1970).[58]

Once again Ossie Davis spearhead change. As the first black man to direct a major Hollywood film,[59] he helped set the movie industry on a new direction. Based on a hard-boiled detective novel by Chester Hines, the highly entertaining movie gives us two street savvy black officers named Gravedigger Jones (Godfrey Cambridge) and Coffin Ed Johnson (Raymond St. Jacques) who distrust a self-created preacher named Rev. Deke O'Malley (Calvin Lockhart) and his so-called "Back to Africa" program. When a robbery takes place during one of O'Malley's Harlem fund-raisers, the cops set out not only to catch the culprits who stole $87,000 of poor folks' money, but also expose the preacher's religious scam.

Shot mainly on Harlem's streets and using a black musical score, the breakthrough film became a landmark movie in film history. So deftly did Davis blend action, comedy, sex, and racial criticism that despite mixed critical reviews, the movie turned into a box-office hit and helped launch what *Turner Classic Movie* host Robert Osborne labeled an "urban crime cycle targeted at black audiences."[60] In essence, the blaxploitation era. A sequel two years later, Mark Warren's *Come Back, Charleston Blue,* lacking the Davis magic, ended any hope for turning the Harlem cops into a franchise.

The film's importance, its popularity, the problems associated with getting it made, and the critical reactions to its themes and characters are discussed by critics and scholars like Vincent Canby,[61] Arthur Knight,[62] Paula J. Massood,[63] Ed Guerrero,[64] and Christopher Sieving.[65] There is even a nice profile on Chester Hines, described by Rudolph Chelminski in 1970 as, "a tough, hard-bitten writer of the old school, a grizzled old pro whose first literary model was Dashiell Hammett and who is now writing some of the toughest, bloodiest detective stories in print."[66] Here I only want to acknowledge that *Cotton Comes to Harlem* participated in the move away from the integrated films of the sixties and unintentionally destabilized the careers of previously popular black stars.

Fortunately for people like Dee, Belafonte, Poitier, and even the elderly Clarence Muse, fate proved kind to these previously popular black artists as the decade began. In 1971, the group had gathered in New Mexico to make Hollywood's first important western about African-Americans.[67] Directed initially by Joseph Sargent, *Buck and the Preacher* (1972)[68] relied on Ernest Kinoy's screenplay to follow the adventures of an ex-Union soldier named Buck (Sidney Poitier) who after the Civil War decides to help ex-slaves go west and claim their government gift of forty acres of free land. Easier said than done. Now a wagon master, Buck not only has to face a hostile wilderness, but also a band of white night riders hired by white supremacists from Louisiana and led by a former Confederate officer (Cameron Mitchell). The white Southerners fear a mass exodus of former slaves will leave the state destitute because no cheap labor will be found to harvest the crops. Adding to Buck's problems is a stranger called the Preacher (Harry Belafonte), a con man out only for himself. Interestingly, Dee again plays the supportive wife of Poitier, but this time she refuses to have their children brought up in a racist land and insists the couple move to Canada.

Soon after production began on the film, Sargent proved to be the wrong director for the story. At Belafonte's suggestion, Poitier agreed to direct the movie until Columbia Pictures could locate a suitable replacement for Sargent. It never happened. The studio liked what their star was doing, and Poitier became the first black director of a mainstream studio western.[69] For people like me who treasure such breakthrough memories, the popular movie's ending is particularly satisfying as the elderly patriarch of the wagon train (Clarence Muse) walks on the promised land, and the trio of Poitier, Dee, and Belafonte ride off to Canada.

But other observers did not share my perspective. David Denby's observation unintentionally suggests the Poitier movie resembles Tarantino's *Django Unchained.* "The film simultaneously evokes historical truth (vicious white night riders try to bring the ex-slaves back)," the critic explains, "and denies it (Poitier and Harry Belafonte kill dozens of these men and get away with it)."[70] And being directed by a black person in a black film offered no guarantee of a better role for a black woman. As Clayton Riley pointed out, "Women rarely play substantial roles in Westerns, and 'Buck' is no exception. Ruby Dee, an especially gifted performer, appears in what amounts to little more than a cameo, a trite and weepy scene that offers no clue to her enormous craft."[71]

A number of years would pass before something traumatic would again disturb the Davis family tranquility. The couple did fine work on the stage, with Dee doing some impressive acting on television in shows like *It's Good to Be Alive* (1974), *Roots: The Next Generation,* and *I Know Why The Caged Bird Sings* (both in 1979). Still further, the hardworking couple had a radio show, *The Ossie Davis and Ruby Dee Story Hour,* which became a PBS TV series in the 1980s.

But before the seventies closed, conflict struck once again between Davis and Jones. On Jan. 23rd, 1976, Paul Robeson, one of the world's most beloved singers and outspoken critics of racial injustice died. Ever since the fifties, the artist and activist had found himself hounded, scandalized, and friendless. For many of us who grew up during those terrible years, what we knew of the then reclusive Paul Robeson proved false, malicious and racist. As evidence of how far we have come, Harry Belafonte on February 1, 2013, in accepting the NAACP's prestigious Spingam Medal, said of Robeson, he was the most important mentor of all: "He was the sparrow. He was the artist who made us understand the depth of that calling when he said, 'Artists are the gatekeepers of truth. We are civilization's radical voice.'"[72]

But in 1977, the social and political climate was quite different when James Earl Jones decided to be part of a project out to give the public a more honest and sympathetic picture of black America's misunderstood and controversial black hero. But not everyone agreed with what Jones and his crew thought was a positive picture of the black hero. Two people in particular who objected to the one-man show were Paul Robeson, Jr., and Ossie Davis. They, along with many other black intellectuals, felt the production presented a disgraceful and insensitive portrait of who Robeson was and what he represented. Luckily, the twists and turns of what followed are strongly debated in both Davis and Jones' autobiographies, as well as in Paul Robeson Jr.'s writings about his father. Here I just want to sketch in the key events.

Months after Robeson's death Jones agreed to play the black hero in a one-man show produced by Don Gregory and directed by Charles Nelson Reilly. During the refining of Phillip Hayes Dean's controversial script, the actor learned there had been some trouble with Robeson's family about having access to the activist's papers. He sensed there might be a problem but pushed on. Eventually, Jones overcame many of his reservations, including his worry about trying to sing Robeson's songs, and went on stage with *Paul Robeson*. But the rough spots remained in the script, particularly in the Second Act. While they bothered Jones, the show itself infuriated Robeson's son and a slew of black progressives including Davis, Coretta Scott King, James Baldwin, and Maya Angelou. In an effort to satisfy everyone, Jones included, producer Gregory replaced Reilly with the legendary stage director Lloyd Richards. The company agreed to Richards's revisions, toned down the comic elements in the show, and gave the performance a more somber atmosphere in the contentious Second Act.

But the changes did not satisfy Paul's son and his legion of followers. For almost a year, *Paul Robeson* struggled to survive, as every performance in every town was greeted with pickets, detractors, and media denunciations. What the objections were and how best to resolve them were suggested later in a 1999 American Masters TV show entitled *Paul Robeson: Here I Stand.*[73] Clearly, the differences between the controversial Robeson tribute (recreated on television in 1979) and the powerful Robeson Jr. documentary, narrated by Davis, are evident and striking.

After reading the material and watching the films my reaction might best be expressed by the following personal anecdote. One of my dearest golfing buddies is a lifelong Republican named Ned Austin. Since 2007, the former UVM Board of Trustee member and I have had many, many political discussions about the two Obama campaign victories, but never once did a disagreeable word pass between us. But in the summer of 2012, when we periodically discussed the progress of *Exits and Entrances,* Ned and I disagreed seriously about the strength and the stature of Paul Robeson. Every time I mentioned the artist's name, Ned saw "Red!" Finally, I asked my friend if he'd take a look at the DVD of *Paul Robeson.* Ned never hesitated, and he borrowed my copy. Within days, he returned it, displaying a totally different point of view. The DVD hadn't changed his mind, I suspect, but he now spoke of Robeson with respect and understanding.

As Jones had always said about the nature of art in our world, it may not alter minds, but it can certainly affect a person's feelings. And as if to underscore how times have changed, *Paul Robeson,* the one-man show that his son considered an insult to his father's memory, continues to be performed today without any political attacks on its material.

At this point in previous chapters, there would be a few more brief remarks and then we would move in to the interview itself. After all, most people as they approached their later years would have long since passed their prime. Besides, the usual disappointment resulting from the lack of appropriate material and the absence of significant African-American filmmakers usually ended a black artist's career. But no black performers ever experienced the changes that occurred as did Ruby Dee and Ossie Davis when Spike Lee appeared on the scene in the mid-eighties.

Born Shelton Jackson to Jazz musician William James Edward Lee III and his wife Jacqueline, a teacher, on March 20, 1957 in Atlanta, Georgia, Spike got his nickname from his mother. Within several years the family consisting of the youngster, his brother and two sisters wound up in Brooklyn where they got a solid academic education and a deep appreciation for the arts. In later years, Lee had no patience with black youths who thought it a sell-out to speak correct English and do well in school.[74] After graduating from Morehouse College, he enrolled in the NYU graduate film program where his thesis film, *Joe's Bed-Sty Barbershop: We Cut Heads* (1983) won an Oscar for student filmmaking. By the time the artist entered his early thirties, he was being recognized as one of the most important young filmmakers of his generation.

It was in 1989, that Ruby Dee and Ossie Davis began one of their most memorable collaborations with a filmmaker, then only thirty-two, in his first masterpiece *Do the Right Thing*.[75] Writing, directing, and acting in what may be one of the most controversial movies since *Sweetback,* the film examined a single street, Stuyvesant Avenue in Brooklyn's Bedford-Stuyvesant district. On one of the hottest days of the year, tensions mount between the black residents and Salvatore 'Sal' Fragione (Danny Aiello), who owns an Italian pizzeria in the African-American neighborhood. While he insists on promoting his Italian heritage, his black customers feel outraged that their African-American heroes are absent from the restaurant's Hall of Fame wall. By the end of the film, bigotry, hate, and distrust erupt into violence.

As if providing a choice for his audience, Lee offers two concluding quotes. The first is from Dr. Martin Luther King: "Violence as a way of achieving racial justice is both impractical and immoral. It is impractical because it is a descending spiral ending in destruction for all. The old law of an eye for an eye leaves everybody blind. It is immoral because it seeks to humiliate the opponent rather than win his understanding. It seeks to annihilate rather than to convert. It thrives on hatred rather than love. It destroys community and makes brotherhood impossible. It leaves society in monologue not dialogue. Violence ends by defeating itself. It creates bitterness in the survivors and brutality in the destroyers."

The alternative route is suggested by Malcolm X: "I think there are plenty of good people in America and there are plenty of bad people in America, and the bad ones are the ones who seem to have all the power and be in the position to block things you and I need.

Because this is the situation, you and I have to reserve the right to do what is necessary to bring an end to that situation. It doesn't mean that I advocate violence, but at the same time I am not against using violence in self-defense. I don't even call it violence when it's self-defense. I call it intelligence."

Even these two quotations did not lessen the fear that many people in white America had about the movie being a rallying cry for blacks to rise up against the establishment. Despite the range of critical reviews debating the movie's message and artistry, the initial negative reaction cut into the popular film's box-office receipts, and what could have been a mega-hit turned into a well-liked film release. At the 1989 Oscar ceremony, Danny Aiello lost out for Best Supporting Actor to Denzel Washington in *Glory;* and Spike Lee's Original screenplay was overshadowed by Tom Schulman's work for *Dead Poet's Society*. But far more important to film history, the filmmaker had by the end of the decade assembled a production team that would help him create the material, the opportunities, and the roles black artists had been searching for ever since movies began: cinematographer Ernest R. Dickerson, line producer Jon Kilik, musician Bill Lee, casting artist Robi Reed, editor Barry Brown, production designer Wynn Thomas, and costume designer Ruth E. Carter.

As for Dee and Davis, they performed memorably as an elderly couple, Da Mayor and Mother Sister, who had seen the Struggle growing and growing over the years. With patience and humor and resolve, they in their separate ways—he as a philosophical alcoholic; she watching from her window—bore witness to the past and wondered about the future. Together with a brilliant cast and superb production values, *Do the Right Thing* was selected in 1999 for the National Film Registry as an American Treasure. For those who may not appreciate the importance of being included in such a prestigious collection, I remind you of a comment made by James Billington, the Librarian of Congress, who once explained that works are chosen for their creativity and imagination, and that such lists tend "to humanize the human record."[76]

In 1998, the distinguished couple published their autobiography *With Ossie & Ruby in This Life Together*.[77] Filled with charming anecdotes, valuable information, and wonderful insights, it remains an indispensible account of their lives in show business.

The last film I want to highlight that featured Davis and Dee together was also a Spike Lee movie, *Jungle Fever*.[78] Probably one of the most underrated and ignored films in recent memory, this extraordinary movie garnered both critical and commercial acclaim when it opened on June 7th, 1991. Before the narrative begins, we learn the movie is dedicated to the memory of a black man, Yusuf Hawkins, killed in Bensonhurst. Thus Lee foregrounds the hatred, bigotry, and tragedy associated with modern day race relations. The plot features Wesley Snipes as Flipper Purify, a black architect exploited by his white bosses Jerry (Tim Robbins) and Leslie (Brad Dourif). Making matters worse, he is forced to accept Angie Tuccie (Annabella Sciorra) as his secretary, even though he specifically asked that an African-American be hired. As the mismatched pair gradually drift into a romantic liaison, we witness a happy, middle-class black marriage dissolve, we examine the racial tensions existing in black and white neighborhoods and families, we encounter the problems young people face from their parents, friends, and relatives, and we understand the rebellion against outworn traditions and values. Especially painful is the director's clinical examination of crack in the inner city and how it leaves no one untouched in the community.

Once again, Lee, working with his remarkable production team, demonstrates the art of filmmaking. The two exceptions were in music and editing. Terence Blanchard now handled the score, with a big assist from Stevie Wonder doing many of the vocals. And Sam Pollard took over the editing job from Barry Brown. But the effect, for me, was every bit as magical as the experience created in *Do the Right Thing*. Once again, the Brooklyn-based artist created memorable characters, superb dialogue, unforgettable scenes, a brilliant use of sight and sound, and stunning visual effects. And few directors in film history ever assembled such a magnificent cast performing at the top of their game.

Much was made at the time about Samuel L. Jackson's breakthrough role as drug-addicted man, with which I can only second, but not enough attention was drawn to the performances of Ossie Davis and Ruby Dee as the tormented parents of two troubled sons. If I had not been watching this past month much of the collective work of this incredible pair, I might not have been so amazed at how their acting brought to life the pain, suffering, heartbreak, and tragedy of an elderly couple unable to cope with modern times. For me, Ruby Dee's depiction of a mother seeing her first-born child killed by her fanatical husband remains the actress' greatest performance.

While Davis and Dee continued to work on stage, screen, and in television for the remainder of the century and into the next millennium, their lives together ended when Ossie Davis died on Feb. 4, 2005. There was an outpouring of tributes to this brilliant artist, but for me he epitomized what Salman Rushdie felt an artist represented. In giving us Baal the Poet in *The Satanic Verses*, the great British-Indian writer said, "A poet's work is to name the unameable, to point at frauds, to take sides, start arguments, shape the world and stop it from going to sleep."[79]

Ruby Dee continued to work without her beloved partner in the years that followed. And where lesser human beings might have let their grief overwhelm them, she not only persevered but also excelled. And then in 2007, at 83, this rare performer appeared in Ridley Scott's *American Gangsters*.[80] Steven Zaillian's lengthy screenplay recreated the 1970s Harlem drug reign of Frank Lucas (Denzel Washington), who is brought down by a crusading special law enforcement team led by Richie Roberts (Russell Crowe). *The Los Angeles Times'* Kenneth Turan summed up the general view: "Authorities and eyewitnesses may argue about who did what to whom in real life, but where the big screen is concerned, it matters not. What *American Gangster* is doing is re-creating myths, and it's good to see that the movies haven't lost their touch where that kind of work is concerned."[81]

Playing the role of Mama Lucas was Ruby Dee, who received an Oscar nomination for Best Supporting Actress. It was her first nomination after being in the movie business since her first film, *What a Guy*, in 1939. That was the same year the first Oscar nomination for a black performer occurred in movie history: Hattie McDaniel, Best Supporting Actress, in *Gone With the Wind*. In addition, Dee became the second oldest actress, Gloria Stuart being the first for Best Supporting Actress, *Titanic*,[82] nominated by the Academy.[83] The award that year went to Tilda Swintin in Tony Gilroy's *Michael Clayton*.

It is time to end this final chapter, knowing full well that much useful information has been ignored or slighted. But as the reader has seen me write before it has never been my goal to be definitive in these profiles, only to be faithful to the spirit and the nature of the individual's contributions. Today, Ruby Dee still remains a significant presence in the entertainment world, and her many humanitarian efforts still inspire a new generation of Americans. And thanks to her daughter, Nora Day, the chief executive of Emmmalyn Productions Company, the organization the remarkable couple started in 1981, is alive and well. What better way to conclude than by reminding everyone what the great actress once said about the journey black people need to take: "Those steps won't be about chattel and chains for Black People. It will be about the worth of the human spirit. It will be about ennobling visions of a better society, a different set of values that propel our activities on this planet. Visions and values that will lead to a better kind of life for everybody."[84]

In the winter of 1974, I took a nostalgic journey back to New Rochelle, New York, where Ruby and Ossie were living, and where I was married and began my teaching career. After a brief conversation and something to eat, we began our conversation. You will note the equipment malfunctioned, and we had to start again.

Ruby Dee Interview
March 15, 1974

RD: I was hoping that you would put it on there [the tape].

FM: I'm sorry. We can try it again if you'd like.

RD: Oh.

FM: We can work through it. I didn't want to go on.

RD: Do you remember what some of the things that I said?

FM: I gathered the thing that you're striking at most is the fact that we are all, in a sense, a part of humanity; and this concern with one group or another group is really taking us away from the focal point of what our job is as individuals.

RD: It is an elementary preoccupation, you know. For example, I would like to see white writers more concerned with the needs of our total cultural arena. It's difficult.... Knowing that all artists are products of the sellers and the buyers and the hawkers and the peddlers....

FM: And the merchants!

RD: And the merchants. And before we can put ourselves into a kind of perspective that particularly has to be dealt with. And the most dangerous thing that exists today is that white people do not realize that.... Oh God, how do I put it? I hate to have to repeat all this. We speak of equality and freedom and equal opportunity, and white people talk to me about the equality of opportunity; but we have to redefine the word "equality."

Our own freedom has been so maligned, abused in our country. When minority people can't say we want equal opportunity. We want freedom. We have to rework those concepts; and in artistic terms, it means that we have to use standards not only for ourselves but also for the whole country, because those in power don't realize even that they have the problem...which is dangerous in a sense. The black artist becomes to the world of thought and interpretation and expression what black musicians are to the world of music, innovative and life giving, often a depth, a new look, a new direction for mankind.

FM: To look forward rather than to look back? Where will we go?

RD: To look forward, you know. It's too late for black people to say, "Well, we want equal opportunity. Equal opportunity to....

FM: For what?

RD: Yes, to do the *Soaps,* to be president of General Motors, to be head of an oil company, to be President Nixon, to be corruption in government and politics, to reflect that which is the least of the human possibility.

FM: I was thinking of something that your husband once said, and reading once some place that the job of any writer, whether he be black or white, is in a sense to reveal America to itself, to show us something.

And I guess one of the reasons that this type of book interests me at this time is that I think in order to understand what you are and how you can do better, you have to have some sense of history; you have to understand what other people have tried to do, and where we were at one time, and where we are going, and what the problems are. To make people, I guess, aware of the broken promises and the false hopes and the people who have sacrificed.

So, I guess it's better for us today. I think it's one of the problems I sometimes find in teaching, that people don't seem to think there is any connection between the past and the present and the future. They think that everything began when it started now... when they were born. And that there was nothing that had ever come before them.

I think the job of a teacher and a writer, or an educator is, in a sense, to bridge the gap between generations. I guess that's the reason I feel so strongly about the need for historical perspective. That's not to say that I would discount the present, or the future. But one has to have a sense of where. Lincoln once said, "If I knew where I was going I could tell you how far I've come." And a lot of people, I don't think, white, black, yellow, and red, sometimes don't know who they are or what they're a part of.

One of the things that makes, I think, both you and your husband so fascinating in the research that I've done over the years, is the uniqueness of the talent and the roles that you've taken years before anyone was even aware of it. And I gather, too, from the readings, how often you've both been misunderstood in the press.

RD: Well, "misinterpreted" because sometimes you get a hold of a concept that is not readily understood. A reviewer tends to put it as he sees it. For example, I was interviewed once for the *Times*, and she was taking notes, and I was taking notes, and what came out was a picture of what she thought I was, or should be, and her idea of "black actresses" which missed entirely what I was about.

I don't think we're innovative. I just think that every time, every time has its own people; that if you are fortunate enough to live long enough, you learn a few things and you express them, but they get expressed every now and then. That's why I don't feel the talk [sic] about lack of opportunity in terms of jobs and so forth, because I'm ashamed that the problem still exists; and equality of what is possible is so dismally lacking. I feel the younger people coming along will express these things. I tend to think now in terms of what I would like to see.

FM: Well, could I try about a dozen or so questions just to patch up some holes? Maybe we could tie the things together. For example, I remember once reading in *Current Biography* about when you were growing up and the fact that your mother disliked movies very much and refused to let her children watch them. And you get all kinds of reactions of how people viewed the films made in the 30s and 40s, particularly a film like *Imitation of Life* or *The Green Pastures* and so on; and how one segment of the black community said, "Well, those films never related to us and we didn't go to movies," and other people say they loved them, "They were just wonderful."

RD: Well I can't remember my mother saying that she didn't like them; we just never went to the movies. For the same reason that we never had a radio for many, many years; she just didn't believe in them, you know. I can see her reasons for it now. She believed that we would develop better if we would not spend our lives listening. And for a long time, for example, I never had television at home. It had been out a long time. I think I've had television now for twelve years. How long has it been out?

FM: I got my set for the first time when I was a kid in '51.

RD: Well, we got our first set when we moved into this house about twelve years ago, because my mother wanted to listen to our stories. And I still have lots of friends who don't own one and never will. That was a kind of...I don't think she placed an evaluation on "black" movies, because she never went to see them.

FM: Never had...It's interesting because my son who is twelve years of age, I have two boys, was going to come with me. He wanted to know if I could ask you to get your autograph because he remembered seeing you on *I Want to Live*, or what is it?

RD: *It's Good to Be Alive*.[85]

Directed by Michael Landon, the award-winning CBS TV film focused on Roy Campanella, the great Brooklyn Dodger catcher, who in January 1955 lost the use of his legs because of a car accident. Ruby Dee played his wife.

FM: *It's Good to Be Alive*. And he never thought about it as black or white; it was just a story that he was watching. He loved it. When I was a kid growing up in Brooklyn I sold peanuts at Ebbets Field, and I used to play ball with Jackie Robinson. They'd let us get there early, and [Gil] Hodges and other people showed up. We would get there from 9 to 11 and [the athletes would] play ball with us. We never thought about them as black or white or anything because we were kids.[86]

It's only when we got older we had this kind of color barrier that we became conscious of. And sometimes the movies have been a tremendous source of breaking down barriers. There's more, perhaps, going on in movies and television today more than is going on in the schools, to educate people about the problems going on in the world about minorities.

So I guess, I mean, we restrict our children, too. They can only watch television on the weekends unless there is a special program. But there is something to this media's ability of getting away from the older generation or the teachers, and getting directly to the children; and the movies and TV, and drama, and music can do it.

RD: And in some instances they are doing beautiful work, you know. I'm not one to slander all films and all TV, even though the merchants control it occasionally. Even for the interest of the merchants, they have to let some kind of thing that is worth doing come through. And a lot of it, lately, has come through especially on television for movies, or movies for television.

FM: I would never have, I would never have...I remember almost every film you've made because I went to them not because I was doing a book, but because I was a kid growing up. And my parents both worked, and I used to get money with my sister to go to the movies on Saturday and Sunday. Sunday we'd get a sandwich and stay there until they came home by the train at night; and I saw every film you made because you just happened to be playing at that particular time. So when they talk about your films, I lived through them. When *The Jackie Robinson Story*[87] opened I was there the first day in Brooklyn at the Fox when they had the autographs. So I'm....

RD: Oh yeah, I remember that.

FM: So I mean it was...almost all that I ever learned about black people, at least for the first—let's see, I'm thirty-eight—, I'd say the first twenty-eight years of my life was from the movies, because we never learned about black history in Brooklyn in the schools, or the textbooks. Slavery was, you know, "Sambo" and the Civil War, and that was the extent of it. And the movies showed us....

Well, for example when I was at Ebbets Field, I never knew what

Robinson was going through until I saw *The Jackie Robinson Story*, because he was just a ball player. They made a big deal about him and [Roy] Campanella, but we looked at them as normal people. We didn't see them as something special. So the movies, for me, were special. And that's one of the reasons why I've always loved them so much and taught about them.

RD: Yes, yes I think....

FM: I didn't mean to go off like that.

RD: There's a great deal of work to be done with film. That's what I find myself concerned with most these days. What's possible? I'm glad to see this new trend in filmmaking, independent, black and white are trying to do relevant material. They're trying to make sense out of the chaos that confronts us, you know.

FM: Was this same kind of commitment evident in the American Negro Theatre in the '40s? Was there that sense of commitment to change or something new?

RD: I don't think we were as aware then, and I don't think times were as crucial. The kinds of problems that all of us faced living back then were, in a sense, just reflections of what has been going on for so long, you know, since we've been black in America, I imagine. There was no other way to think. We wrote out of the fact of being black, black in America. It had a certain....

I don't think one stopped to analyze it, or say, "Well I'm deliberately going to deal with this subject because this and this reason." I think we just did because of what we were and how we grew up. And, at the same time, for that same reason, I think the subject matter was broadened now for black people. We tend to think more in terms of not only of our local community but internationally and, hopefully, in terms of a worldwide application of the search, the search for equality once we redefined it and freedom.

Freedom for what? What is success? And we're beginning to look at the guilty without an assessment of guilt. What is guilt? What is, so much?

FM: It's interesting. One of the things I notice on the campus is that there is a kind of disillusionment, a silent lack of involvement because people don't think they can do anything anymore. They seem to feel as if they are just better off just looking after themselves. They talk about concern for others, but there seems to be more of a fad. People don't think they have any staying power.

RD: Well, I think when we begin to look at the universal aspect of all issues, cosmic implications, you know. The world has been getting very, very small. And now our world, because not only this earth, but as we interrelate, universally with all mankind, all planets, all life, you know. We're having to broaden our spectrum so that we can place this particular model in perspective. And I think when we begin to do that, we'll find comfort. It's like searching for oneself, you know. It can be very confusing not knowing. "What am I here for?" "What am I supposed to be doing?" "Who needs me?" "What am I?"

But I think when we start to research it, and we start to get a feeling of ourselves and our place in this whole life pattern, we'll get it; and we'll begin to honestly look at our potential and our direction and come to some terms with ourselves. We can then better place ourselves in terms of the universe, in terms of a total cosmic perspective.

So we're not limited in that sense. And I would desperately wish that those in charge of deciding what happens in schools would take more of a cosmic, universal view of life, you know, and think about personalities and realize, come to the realization that our economic system is at the root of so much of our evil. What does it take to shake the white power structure from the look of itself, this perfection, or at the worst, the naughty boy gone overboard, you know; and realize that at the seat of so much misery is this dedication to gain and profit, you know, as if we really can die and take it in the tomb?

FM: It's hard enough to convince not so much the power structure as the people themselves. People could change it in their daily....

RD: Well, the people are the power structure, don't you see? This is what I'm saying. Segment by...we are going to watch the boat rock. So, I think a tremendous and necessary job at this point is a heightened awareness, a white people's heightened awareness of those who are poor to find out what they have in common with all people in the world, and stop making the ideals of the establishment the ideals to which they gravitate. They must have more basically to be successful, to be fulfilled, knowing that really one gravitates away from satisfaction and happiness in this mad, greedy quest for ownership of things which our total society is dedicated to. So it really comes down to the whole total cultural spectrum changing when we begin to look at the truth. It's not enough for black people to look at this society and say, "Oh," you know, the king has no clothes on." It's bankrupt, it's stupid, it's you know.

FM: The next step is to tell them once you get that awareness, how do you change it? What do you do? How does one come about bringing the change once you make the awareness? Then someone says, "Why do I want to change it? Tell me how."

RD: Then part of that is the job of the artist, you know, to point new ways of being and existing in this world. New standards by which we can govern ourselves that are more satisfying, less frenetic, less self-conscious.

FM: But the artist must be free to work. The artist must be free to make that statement.

RD: Well, I think also the artist has to…the artist has to have quality in order to be somewhat successful, these successful artists, you know. He has to have a place in Beverly Hills, if he's successful, he has to have half a million dollars.

FM: [Laughing] Oh God, it should happen to me!

RD: It should happen to you…okay. But you know it's a radical change that we are about here. Radical, radical change, and the artist I feel in the future must be about radical change. And I suppose the artist best suited to do that is the black artist, because he has lived so long close to the nub of things, and he's always been close to seeing, seeing the weevils burrowing in at the roots of what looks like sturdy, healthy flourishing things.

FM: That's one of the interesting things I have found when I speak with these black artists. There's a tremendous dichotomy between those who wish to be artists and those who wish to be black artists. Some of them feel very troubled over the fact that they can't act as an actor, rather than they must make a statement as a black actor.

RD: I find that now a discussion for younger actors. I mean, really, I've gone through that. I'm willing to…unless you…I don't think it's a passé subject by the way. I just think there's room for all kinds of beings, and there's ways to be. I believe in total black theater, total Jewish theater, total Italian theater. I also believe in integrated theater, I mean, there are no absolutes about it. I think one of the marvelous things about living in this country is that there is room for everything like a smorgasbord of culture, and there is no absolute about anything.

FM: I remember when I was reading some of the material, there was a big to do made over the importance of your role in *Anna Lucasta,* in 1946 that was an earth shattering kind of breakthrough. Was it really as big or is that just a kind of....

Poitier, who worked mainly as an understudy in a national company of Anna Lucasta *for nearly three years (1946-1949), provides a number of anecdotes about the cast and his experiences with the play.*[88]

RD: Oh, I imagine every journalist who writes the first Negro that...and I just can't believe that. It comes in the papers.... I happen to have run into some very old actors who—Abbie Mitchell, Hilda Haynes—who are still living, by the way. Andrew Bishop, and Lawrence [J.] Criner, and Monte Hawley, all of the Lafayette Players. And they tell me some of things that they went around the country doing. And I found that exciting to contemplate. That never happened in my time.

So, and *Anna Lucasta* was a breakthrough. I feel good about that. It's like somebody saying, "I'm best remembered for my debut in *Raisin in the Sun.*" Maybe that'll be on my epitaph. [Laughing] I don't like to think that I'll only be remembered for that, you know.

FM: But it is interesting. I wasn't going to come to it, but since you brought it up. I don't know, probably as you say you don't remember, but there was very little that seemed to have been said when I was doing the reviews of you in *Raisin in the Sun,* which I saw with my wife incidentally New Year's Eve 1959 when you were doing it on the stage. And yet when the film was made, you got much more exposure in terms of the reviews in the film than on the stage; and I was curious if, you know, how you reacted to that.

RD: Strangely, I only remember the bad reviews I've ever gotten. I scarcely, except for Clive Barnes and...No, I don't remember the bad reviews. But I've only gotten two, I must say.

FM: I mean, they raved about you in the film. They claimed the film was nowhere as good as the stage play because it lacked the intimacy, but the redeeming feature of the film was, they say over and over again in the reviews, was your performance.

RD: Well, I can't remember that, except to say that the background characters are very difficult to play. I have some kind of capacity to understand these women who were sort of like the neutral, the pastels into which all the bright colors are splotched.

FM: I must have seen the film ten or twelve times by now, and each time I get more impressed with your performance because it comes through naturally, whereas Poitier's seems more exaggerated, the kind of stage gestures. Where yours is a beautiful performance as a performance. I don't honestly remember too much except that I enjoyed the play, I wasn't aware, but in the film you act as a film actress, where the other people tend to be stage performers acting for film.

RD: Well, it's difficult sometimes to make that transition. You know, from stage presentation to film. But I, I don't remember the particulars of the experience except to think the kind of actor you are dictates, to a certain extent, how you respond, and that which may have been more suitable for the medium than those large presentations because, I remember, for example, that Claudia [McNeil] was startling to audiences, you know? But that, that was another play.

I admire Lorraine [Hansberry] very much, but it was an updated version of an acceptable presentation of "Momma" and your "no good son" and mad ambitions. It seems very old hat today, as a matter of fact. But it was "Momma" again keeping the unruly black boy somehow saved, and the world would applaud and relax and feel confident that Momma had everything under control.

FM: There was a kind of truth, though, I still find it today. I suspect that I agree with most of what you say. But I did find a kind of truth in the relationship between the man and the wife, the father who was trying to be the big shot for the son, the mother who has to be the long suffering person who has to stay there. I don't think it was necessarily a black mother. I mean, I remember my father, may he rest in peace, was that kind of big shot, a salesman, and my mother would always trying to hold us together, always saying, "That's the way your father is, don't do anything about it. You need some money, here. He needs someone here." It was always a cleaning up after the father. I really found a kind of truth in it.

RD: Yes, and I suppose it had its basis in that kind of total American truth of what men are and have been in society. And that's all right, except that then there are other kinds of portraits of women and strong men who happen to be white; and there's just too few portraits of strong [black] men in our time. Therefore, we can take small comfort in the fact that there are white women also who go through these things.

We have, we really have a lot of the no-good black man, the black man and his wild childish schemes trying to imitate the slave master—whose conversations he absorbed, you know, while waiting on tables—without having any basis in reality but realizing the dream, whatever dream it was.

And now, I'm hoping that there will be another kind of redemption. We don't want to see black men become like white men, or that we become like each other, or that image of successful male American whites. It's gone sour. It's turned over in its applications; it's become blind and greedy, and juvenile, and very uninviting.

FM: I want to make sure that I understand that part. You're not objecting to *Raisin in the Sun;* but you're objecting to the fact that it's the only type of film, or the only type of roles that were created.

RD: Yes, yes.

IFM: If there were other roles that were around, there would be nothing wrong with the *Raisin in the Sun*. Or the roles in which, for example, in the *Up Tight* film, there would be nothing wrong with the black man who failed, or the black man who was weak, if there were an equal number of films in which there were black men who were strong.

RD: Yes, or if the picture were.... The same with the goals with women, all women, I feel. The role of women has yet to be explored, in terms of real.... Look, it still goes what sells. Who dominates the market? And I think that's beginning to change a little.

FM: There aren't many women who today seem to me making, white or black, women's films. Most of the films seem to be going toward the men, a male leading part. *Papillon* or *Midnight Cowboy*, you know. There are no roles being made for women. Even *The Sting*, is an example of that, in which you don't find women except as sex objects, or except as prostitutes or as hookers or as goody-two-shoes. But they seem to be vying away from the kinds of women....

RD: Well, I believe that that's what's on the horizon. Again, I keep looking to the future. Because that's a difficult kind of relationship to talk about. We haven't been honest about that. Because when we start to be honest about that kind of relation, we'll start to be honest in terms of government, in terms of the chief executive. We'll take a look at the strong man and find out why he can't cry? Doesn't he have the sense to? Isn't he sensitive enough? Isn't he—why must we have these kinds of heroes we have? Why isn't human personality best? We like to see that defeat and harassment and bewilderment and not that, not that which is pointed towards some growth.

FM: Except that we may be so disgusted and discouraged that we take some satisfaction seeing others suffer the way we perhaps have been suffering internally. We've become cynical and we feel helpless, so maybe those who think they're so much better than ourselves, when we see them suffering or fallen, we sense some satisfaction, some sick satisfaction.

But, it's always been true in terms of how I understand the theater and in terms of motion pictures, that the audience feels some sense of security or satisfaction, especially in comedies. The mighty or the pompous or the pretentious, seeing them destroyed, gives us a sense of relief, a kind of catharsis, because we identify with those who are oppressed and when they win, we even vicariously for a few moments feel a sense of satisfaction. It lets off steam.

RD: Yes, we also like the victory of spirit. I think about what we went through and happened to a professor; a man who has a belief and that belief triumphs, or he finds out.... He comes through with a belief that ennobles us all, you know, that makes us feel whole, gives us hope.

FM: It's the only thing that an educator can do. You had a hand in the writing of *Up Tight*?

RD: Yes.

FM: Can you give me some insight into how that script was conceived?

RD: Well, it was based on that story....

FM: *The Informer*?[89]

RD: *The Informer*, that Jules Dassin had the rights to, but he wanted to do a black film. But at that time, black films weren't being, weren't big at the box-office as they later came to be. Until they said, "Well, you can do a black film, if you want to base it on *The Informer*." So he tried to get that changed, but he couldn't. So given the premise that we had to use *The Informer*, he started writing this story, and I really quite accidentally got with Jules because he had written something he wanted us to see, Ossie and me one night to talk about it.

So I read the thing in bed one night, and I jotted some notes hastily on the back cover. I don't remember. It was old hat. I wasn't very impressed with this idea and how it had evolved in this script, as Mr. Dassin said it. Ossie showed those notes to Jules. I'll never forget it. Then we had dinner one night, and Ossie couldn't work with him, he was very busy, so he said, "Well, why don't you come in and help me write this up?"

And, although I had a total variety of writing lessons; I'd written poetry and a couple of articles and things like that, I never really seriously thought about writing. I said, "Well, I can't do that; but strangely enough, I'm grateful to Jules, because when we got together, he would give me.... He'd say what the scene was, and then I would write the scene, and I found that it was easy for me to do. And I wrote for twelve, fourteen hours, one thing after the other. I could change and I could write to order, so that's how it happened.

But still and all, Jules got very busy about that time; Martin Luther King died, and he wanted that to be part of the film He really got too busy to write the thing himself. I didn't feel capable; I wasn't a writer. We called in "Julie" Mayfield, who was a writer. I said, "Well, I'd feel better to work.... So, the upshot of it was, we all went to Cleveland. Julian Mayfield and I wrote, and we would submit to Jules who would take, we would send the writing to him. And then he would take it, and he put.... He put it together. I guess you'd call that....

FM: Collaborating?

RD: Collaborating. I didn't even expect to get credit, but a great deal of what I wrote was in the film, just as I wrote it. Hunks and sections, and some of it was changed in a way I wouldn't have agreed to, but then I didn't feel that it was my project at that time.

FM: That was a fascinating film as far as significance as a black film. And very significant in terms of the reviews that it created, or evoked. As I was going over the research on it, almost every paper, mostly white, panned the film, but panned it very gingerly. Talking about the artistic problems, but praising it as significant.

Only *Ebony* gave it a really positive review. Arthur Knight, at one point, talked about it as a divisive hate film, hate-inducing ugly movie, and yet there was an argument for the film's trying to show what the problems were in society, and, which you said earlier which is interesting, trying to set up a new criteria for which people judge film. Not white standards, traditional, art and aesthetics, but films in terms of message and social significance so that films became important not so much for the way they were composed or the music or the lighting, but for what they had to say, and in that sense, it was the beginning of an attempt to redefine what makes a good film or what is good filmmaking.

RD: Yes, and I must say that the film was a little before its time. It was brought out shortly later. I commend Jules because he had been out of the country for a long time, and he wanted to know. One of the questions constantly was, "What the problems were in terms of black people in America?"

We saw it in three phases: those blacks who were integrated into society as it is, those who would change it, and those who would see it destroyed so that something new could grow. We tried to bring those three avenues of thought into the film. We tried to define what was happening in terms of black people in America in three broad patterns. That's why the film intrigued me, too. It was an effort to put into perspective and to order, to classify in a sense, black political thinking.

FM: I think the film works very, very well when you deal with the causes. It breaks down when you deal with the character study of Mayfield. But in the opening scenes, that scene, for example, of the white who wants to come into work and they throw him out and they say, "You're no longer part of us." I guess I'm identifying with the situation.

RD: Yes, and that was a part of Jules' experience in terms of his children, who have been very active in the Civil Rights movement; and that meant at one time because their participation it was disruptive and tended to cloud the issue. The Movement took a turn to eliminate that kind of distraction, and that white people, just by the fact of being white, no matter how they thought, brought with them. Also many of them felt hurt and did not understand, because not enough work was done in terms of the white psyche.

When you come up, no matter how you look at it, they're superior. Our present set-up fosters a feeling of superiority to other people in the world. A feeling of white superiority. When they come into a situation, they can't help but try to take over because they feel that they know better. They don't reckon with the criteria involved in the particular situation. They seek to rectify only in terms of the white mentality. Coming from and with the sum total of everything. And unless you're aware of that, you can't deal with yourself. You can only feel put upon, discriminated against, and so forth.

FM: It's interesting you say this. Sometimes I see three or four movies when we come in [to New York] because we don't get most of the black films up in Vermont, or they don't play well. I took my son, Steven, the oldest one, to see *Melinda*[90] one day with me in New York, and all during the film they were yelling, "Kill the Honky, kill Whitey," and so on. We were the only white people in the audience, and I got worried that Steven, twelve years of age, would get frightened. We walked out, and I said, "Are you all right?"

MGM's blaxploitation film Melinda, *directed by former black film editor Hugh A. Robertson, had a script by black writer Lonne Elder III. The plot concerned hip disc jockey Frankie J. Parker (Calvin Lockhart) who is deeply attracted to the beautiful Melinda Lewis (Vonetta McGee), but before any deep romance develops she is murdered. The remainder of the movie has Frankie taking care of business. The movie received no Oscar nominations.*

FM: And he said, "Yeah, what's the matter?"

I said, "Did you notice anything strange in the movie?"

It was the kind of audience reaction that he's not usually exposed to. He didn't notice a single thing. He didn't hear the yelling in the theater, it didn't bother him. The business of.... To him it was just a movie. He had no consciousness at all, whereas I as a person who was sensitive to what was going on not only in the film but in the audience, thought maybe there might be trouble in the theater or.... And here was a youngster who had no conception at all about the problems that I had grown up with, or had grown used to and sensitive to.

He just was not part of that scene, which I think was magnificent. From my point of view, here was a kid who was watching a film and experiencing it and not having any kind of need to first unlearn either a guilt complex or to learn that there is a reason why blacks could be yelling this, or maybe there is a reason for this kind of story, or film. It was just not part of his culture; he had no contact with that at all. And I found that very healthy.

RD: I think it goes both ways, frankly. I think it's like, for example, somebody says, "I took my child to this party and there were black people there and they didn't even notice, they didn't pay any attention, they didn't mind they were all just people."

Well, unfortunately, that may be good in a sense, but in a sense I think it's not good, because what is "black"? There are black people and yellow people and red people, and their treatment has been greatly affected by the fact that they have not been recognized as red people or black people and what happened to them. The white child has not known that his family came from Europe someplace on a boat carrying their silver and looking for...starving to death, you know, looking for ways to eat.

So that we must *know* who each other is, I think, very key to any successful solution to this illness of society. We must *know*, and white children must *know* that they came and that our country, in terms of the waste of the country, in terms of the ava, ava....

FM: Avariciousness?

RD: Yes, avariciousness. We laid waste to the land. We grabbed greedily from the earth—and I don't say we—, I say white America did this, from the earth, from other human beings to make a particular economic system. I think children must *know* these things and really study the differences and really appreciate the differences between people. Because how can we seek to rectify unless we know?

FM: But isn't the end result treating each one, even, for example, in terms of women, treating people in terms of their ability of what they are as individuals?

RD: I quite agree with you, but the fact is that you have to recognize how, for example, if I'm in a union, in the stagehand's union, and, of course, I'm a very fair person, and I'll treat all stage hands, grips and electricians fairly, and anybody who comes into my union. But the fact is there are no black people, it's very difficult for black people to get into the union, so I'm not going to have the opportunity to exercise my marvelous "humanbeinghood"[sic].

FM: But I guess the point I'm making—I guess that I want to make certain that I clear it up in my mind—is when I gave you the anecdote about Steven, it seems to me that by Steven going to see a film like *Melinda* or *Buck and the Preacher,* or what have you, he's learning in a sense what makes people different. But he's also learning that the white man is not always right, or that the black man is not always right, that people have got to be judged for what they are and they've got to succeed on their own merits or fail on their own merits. If there is inequality, he's got to change that inequality. That people are being discriminated against and it's got to change. But he's got to change it not because this person is black or this person is white, but because this person is entitled to the same rights and privileges that anyone else has.

RD: Yes, and one step beyond that, he's got to learn to change it among his own kind. I remember a make-up man telling me in Hollywood once, there is no discrimination between colored people and white people. Even some of his best friends were (Inaud). I said, "Well do me a favor. The next time you go to a union meeting, and there are no black people in that make-up man's union or, whatever that union is, you make it your life-long project in that union, as a white person among your equals and your friends, to see that other people are given the chance to get into your union." That's what I mean. Don't wait until the black man has to take up a stick and start picketing, and don't wait for the ugliness. See the ugliness inherent in wherever you are in your pure situation.

FM: I buy that. I think that the book I'm writing is primarily for white people more than for black people because the problem with discrimination in motion pictures has been a white problem, not a black problem. I think we're the ones who, I haven't done it, but the problems are caused by white people; that's the reason I go back to the issue of slavery. Blacks didn't ask to be put in chains. They were brought in by whites.

The power structure set up a system, and that system has been just another form of slavery in terms of the screen and in terms of jobs and employment. I guess the reason why I'm writing the book is for me to understand it better and to help other people. I don't think I'm writing the book for black people in that sense.

So, I admire the point that you said about Steven and what he has to learn. But the thing that I keep trying to find the answer to is, after you sensitize people to the stereotypes and the images, how do you get them to change? How do you get them to support the films? How do you, for example, if you bring out a film, how do you get them to go to affect the box-office whether the film is going to fail or succeed? If the people don't come, the theater owner won't run the film again. That's the problem that I....

RD: Well, one of the things that I think will help is if we get a broad base of financial participation in filmmaking, production rather, we stand a better chance of more people becoming involved in the total process itself. As more prodigies in education, more housewives and teachers and people of all walks interested in what their children consume mentally, will take a greater interest in the kinds of films that will be presented, because I think film is going to take an increasingly important role in the education of all of us. We're going to be forced for the sake of survival to make palatable those films that elevate us, you know, because the name of the game must be elevation.

Getting back to slavery for a minute, I think the problems are problems of greed. Now when we think of slavery, white people, black people, we're all involved in slavery. All those desperately ugly things that happened, happened to people.

[BREAK]

FM: I think *Superfly* was a fine film.

RD: I think that when I was growing up, my heroes were Franchot Tone and Robert Taylor and, oh but now I like the black stars like....

FM: Tyson?

RD: Yes, Tyson and the newcomers: (Lola) Falana and Rosalind Cash and so many other girls....

FM: Sheila Frazier?

RD: Sheila Frazier, and....

FM: You know who I haven't heard from in a while? I was very impressed with Mae Mercer. I met her when I was in California, and I haven't seen anything of her in the last two or three years. She had done *The Birds;* no, not *The Birds, The Frogs* [sic] I think it was. She had done *The Beguiled* with Clint Eastwood, and all of a sudden just dropped out. Diana Ross....

RD: Diana Ross, yes. But I feel hopeful because there are books and there are things to be done like these. And if films are to continue I think these women in the future will work a lot.

FM: You think they will?

RD: Yes, maybe because I daydream about all the things I'd like to do. To involve this one and that one is stunning and beautiful performers and actors. And I know that we'll....

FM: Outside of you and Cecily Tyson, I don't know of any major black actress in the history of motion pictures who didn't come through the chorus. Am I wrong in that? Either a singer or a chorus....

RD: Well, Hilda Offley, I think of as a....

FM: In film?

RD: In film? Well, no. On stage.

FM: Right. Ethel Waters was a singer. I don't know about Claudia McNeil, but she didn't play that many roles. Louise Beavers? I don't know. Fredi Washington, I think, was a singer.

RD: It's a new time for.... I think of Mildred Joanne Smith as I came along. She disappeared from the scene. And Hilda Simms is another one....

FM: Dorothy Dandridge was a singer.

RD: Yes, Dandridge was a singer, but those others that I mentioned were actresses, Clarice Taylor and Helen Martin, and quite a few coming along now.

FM: But none ever reached the magnitude or the stature of either you or Tyson.

RD: Well, we've been around longer, for one, we've been trying at it. We went to school.

FM: But it was harder for you than it was for these people. Times are different. When you came out with *The Jackie Robinson Story* in '50, '51, and for twenty years, you were the first one in the entire history of motion pictures who made it to the screen as a beautiful, stunning woman who did not have to be a sex object. You did it in

The Balcony[91] at one point, but you played other roles. You didn't become typed in that way.

Everyone else had to do it through song and through.... Barbara McNair had to do it that way. I don't remember a single woman who didn't have to get down to her slip. Even Diana Ross had to do it in, what is it, *Lady Sings the Blues*. She had that prostitute scene where she had to be....

RD: Of course, you know Diana Sands didn't.

FM: That's right. But Diana Sands, how many roles did she have? *Raisin in the Sun* was her first film, I think.

RD: She is a singer, yes, and she started off in the musical. I first saw her in a musical. But she's been a dramatic actress, primarily.

FM: *Georgia, Georgia*[92] was the....

RD: *Georgia, Georgia.*

FM: Sheila Frazier comes along. She's had to be naked in the bathroom scene in *Superfly*.

RD: Lola Folana.

FM: She had to do that in *Liberation of L. B. Jones*....[93]

RD: What was the girl in...?

FM: What was the film about? Abbey Lincoln is one.

RD: Abbey Lincoln.

FM: Abbey Lincoln. But how long did Abbey Lincoln work? She did *Nothing But a Man*. She did the one with Poitier and the maid, *Love of Ivy*. And what else has she done?

RD: She also comes from the nightclubs.

FM: You don't find a single black actress, except for you and Tyson, which is remarkable, when you think about it. There is not a role for you, unless you want to fit into the background. I'm wondering if that's going to change?

RD: Yes. It's going to change. It's changed already. This year already I've done three roles one right after the other, for the first time in my life. I just finished a television film for ABC.

FM: But look how long? Look at Tyson. Tyson gets nominated for the Academy Award for *Sounder* in '71, and when was the last movie she made? She did *The Autobiography of Jane Pitman* for television, but there's no feature film. Where's she supposed to work?

RD: I really think that's going to change, maybe because I've felt a lack of other things to do about change all around. The more I think about it, the more determined I am. The older I get, I'd like to work and to create projects that would utilize such talents.

FM: Well, there's certainly a need.

RD: But I think that as the total spectrum changes, and also serious actresses, whites have suffered, have suffered too in this respect. There aren't, of course.... I'm not bleeding about that, but I think as we get a more how to, what to say about black women, what to say about women! It's a difficult subject.

FM: It's a fertile field. There's nothing that you have to breakdown; nothing's been said, so...

RD: There are marvelous books by Toni Morrison and Paule (Burke) Marshall, and Gwendolyn Brooks; and some of those wonderful women writers have created characters that are stunning.

FM: Will they put them in the present, though? Will they put them back, the way they did with *Sounder, Lady Sings the Blues,* to a nostalgic time?

RD: No, I don't think so. I think.... There are some things that I'm not at liberty to talk about now, but I think that we'll have the books adapted because they are worthy and beautiful. And the forces of money are different and hopefully they will sustain.

FM: Where will they come from? From what I understand, the black film boom ended in November. They had not done a black film that was making money since November.

RD: Well, it's just like everything else. When I think everything the black people does has to be super. It has to be super-money makers. *Cotton Comes to Harlem,*[94] had to save United Artists

FM: But it didn't.

RD: It's just like integrated marriages. I think when people are going to marry until.... It's all just going to level off. And they're going to have good films and bad films. It's not going to be black and white. I think that's what's been the....

FM: You think it's going to survive then?

RD: Of course. I think it's foolish for us to think that we're going to be.... Well, time for black people, no time for black people. Up, back. White people don't do that. Sidney Lumet, the man who did *Serpico,* for example; he admits himself, always says how many films he has done. Why should we not have the opportunity to do film after film after film? Some good, some bad, some successful, some not.

FM: But wasn't the argument that the money was going back to white people? In other words, you're making a black film; it's the white....

RD: Well, there are other sources of money.

FM: Those had always been dried up before.

RD: There are other ways to do it. I feel confident. I don't feel like we're ever going to go back to, "Well, do white folks want this or do they want that?" Because, black people are beginning to insert some of the things that they want to see. We want to see certain things. And I think, hopefully, I mean, if I didn't believe that, we might as well close shop because, "Oh, somebody over there said, 'Well, the black boom ended in November'. Well, we can't make anymore black films.'" Because some white somebody up some place with his little pencil dictates. That's been our trouble, so long, in so many areas.

FM: But when *Variety* says that, they also made it harder for you to get money then. People say they're not going to invest in something that's not going to make money. It's economics.

RD: Well, but that's part of what has to change about the picture. If we didn't believe that.... *Variety* is not reliable. Things happened that *Variety* has to catch up to also. There are possibilities outside of America for the production of films. As we get into consuming six percent of the world's goods to match six percent of our population, we're also going to start producing films that will satisfy other parts of the world. We'll be part of that picture. I don't think.... We're not going to be the hogs of everything, you know, to decide what will suit us. We have to give up that twenty-nine percent.

FM: That's very good. Let me ask you one last question because I don't want to impose on your time. What do you think is the most important thing to hit away? You talked about the cosmic view, you talked about the future, that it's not going to be controlled by whites anymore, black films surviving....

RD: Not as completely.

FM: Not as completely. Black films surviving, more roles for women. Do you believe in an integrated cinema? Do you believe that is where the future lies now in producing great artists? Or do you believe in a sense of learning first how to control the money so that black films can be made? Where, where does the thrust come now?

RD: I'm very impressed now by the fact that I've met people interested in production who are going to film schools to learn about production. The people that I've met recently, ones whom I adore, who are interested in how to put it together. I find that encouraging. I find that when a film is good or bad, it isn't supported by black people. I think that we may have gotten, as in any other people, they get tired of the super-gangsters, and the films that deal with dope and corruption. Maybe we're ready for other kinds of subjects of greater variety of subject matter. We will be enticed to come to films that interest us, because they're about us as ordinary people and not as this. Most black people are not superstars or dope peddlers. They're ordinary people.

FM: Or whores!

RD: Or whores. More pictures like that will be welcomed, and not only in the black community but all over the country. There's going to be, I think we're going to see more selectivity in terms of good films and what is it that points us.... We're looking for direction. I think that films that offer us direction, films of hope and encouragement we're going to want to see them as well as the.... As long as they're good products, well presented, entertaining and beautiful. I think people want to know what's beautiful about ourselves. We want to know how to go. We want to know how we fit. I think films with a different philosophical bottomline are on the horizon and will be acceptable. We're in a spiral of changing. Nothing remains the same.

FM: Just hope it gets better though. Just hope it doesn't get worse.

RD: How dare I not feel optimistic about human beings? You know, we're marvelous creations. How dare I feel despair?

FM: That's very nice to hear. I don't find that kind of view often. Most people just.... I tell you, when I came back from the coast, it was very depressing. I must have met sixteen people in that one visit, ten days, and the stories and the bitterness and the disillusionment, and the hate, not against me, but just with their lives. It just hurt. It hurt.

At this time in my life, nothing that I had crammed into my 1972 California visit seemed to come together. The broken tapes, the canceled in-

terviews, the unwillingness of some people to discuss black films, and the clear lack of consensus seemed to make the venture less manageable and valuable.

RD: I suppose if one can look at the small, microscopic piece about ourselves; but one life is just a little, tiny little part of the continuum.

FM: You're a rare woman.

RD: If I didn't have that overview.... To me, I mean, it's elementary, but I think it's going to be the spreading kind of view about life, about ours. Human beings, despite how grimy and ugly we can be at some times, we are the very opposite of that which is ugly; we are also beautiful. We are also lofty and aspiring.

FM: Sometimes both sides of it though.

RD: Yes, but if it's anything in this whole country, like in New York City, there's the worse of everything here and the best of everything. I can't imagine any condition existing without it's opposite also existing. Because how can we conceive of love? We know from hate. We know about hate.

FM: And distrust.

RD: So there must be trust. There must be love.

FM: There's got to be encouragement, too. People have got to feel as though they are wanted or needed or they can change.

RD: Once we have this, we'll have a whole view of older people in our society. What is this? What makes old? What makes it such a disagreeable thing to be? When you're old, you know you don't want to die young. The subjects that concern us daily have yet to be meat for film....

FM: The question of loneliness, too.

RD: Yes.

FM: Well, that's beautiful. Thanks.

Postscript

I began this chapter with a nod to the 85th Academy Awards. Let me now return with an observation by Frank Rich, one of the nation's great columnists, In acknowledging that all films contain flaws and few can withstand scrutiny, he wrote that those movies nominated for the 2013 Academy honors, "may or may not be for the ages, but future viewers looking back to see what our age was like may find them incalculable."[95] We are more fortunate. We already know the worth of a Ruby Dee, her extraordinary husband, and their life's work. She may have once defined herself as "a black girl from the bowels of Harlem....,"[96] yet I find her the personification of Maya Angelou's words: "I go forth alone, and stand as ten thousand."[97]

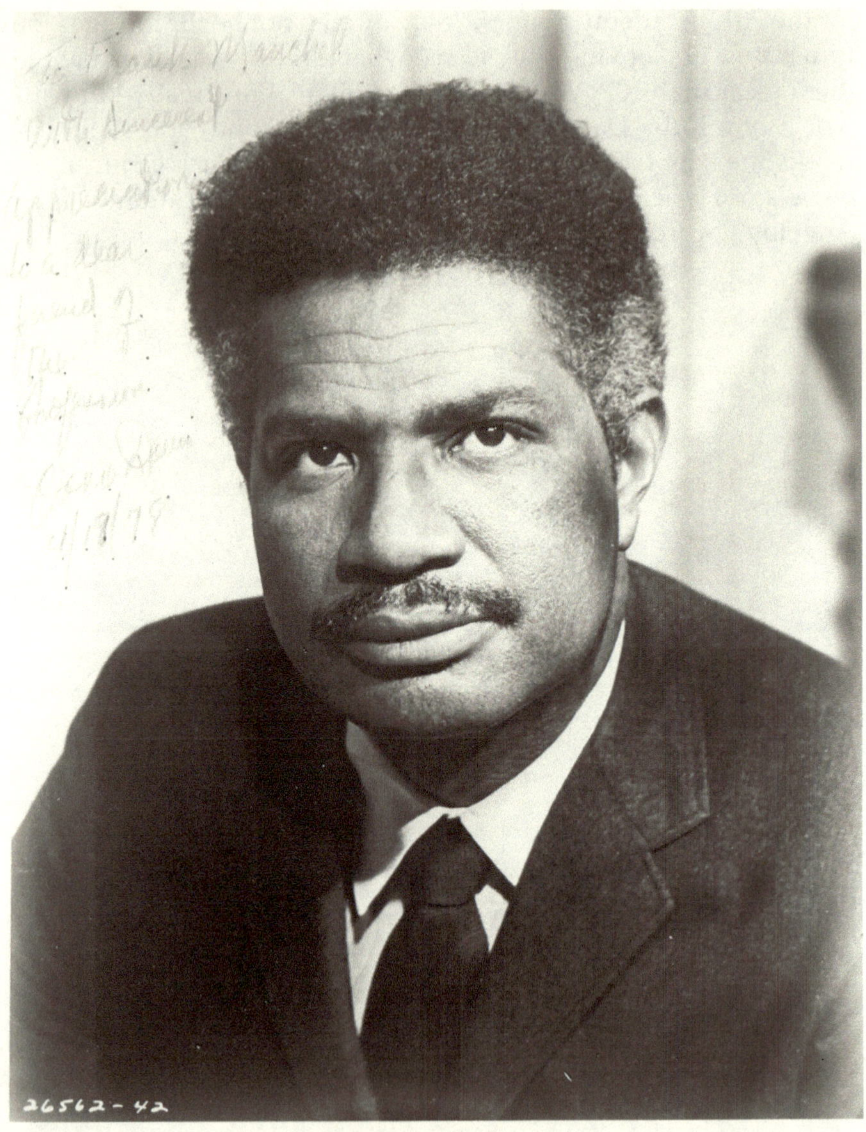

32. The caption reads, "To Frank Manchel, with sincere appreciation to a dear friend of the profession. Ossie Davis, 4/18/78."

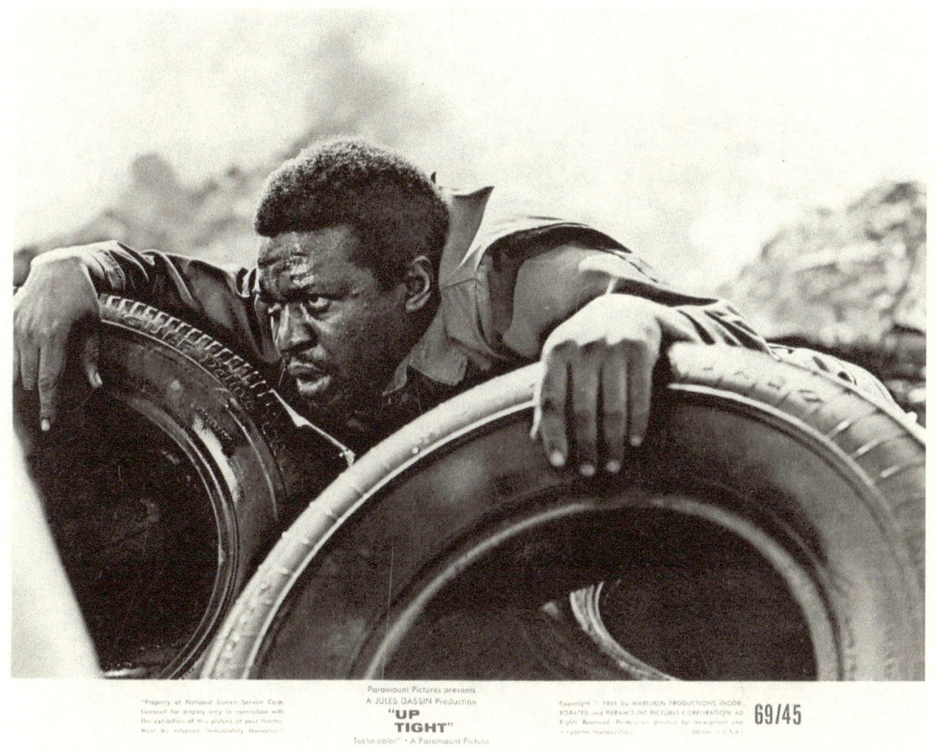

33. Julian Mayfield as Tank in *Up Tight* (1968) directed by former blacklisted artist Jules Dassin and co-scripted by Ruby Dee. Based initially on John Ford's *The Informer,* the film became one of the most historic black movies at the end of the sixties.

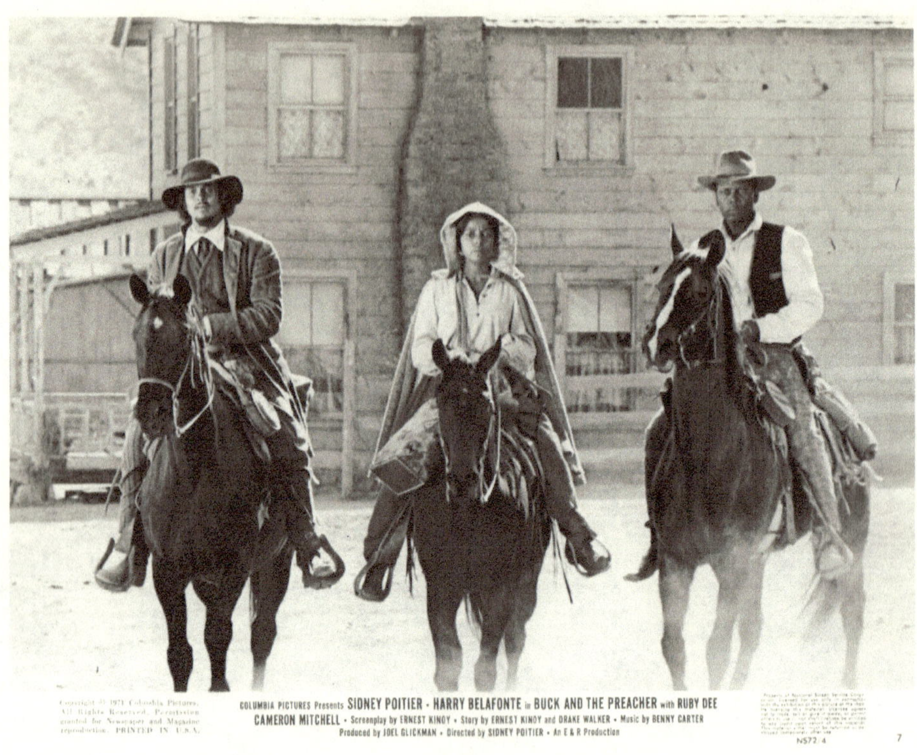

34. Harry Belafonte, Ruby Dee and Sidney Poitier in Poitier's Buck and the Preacher.

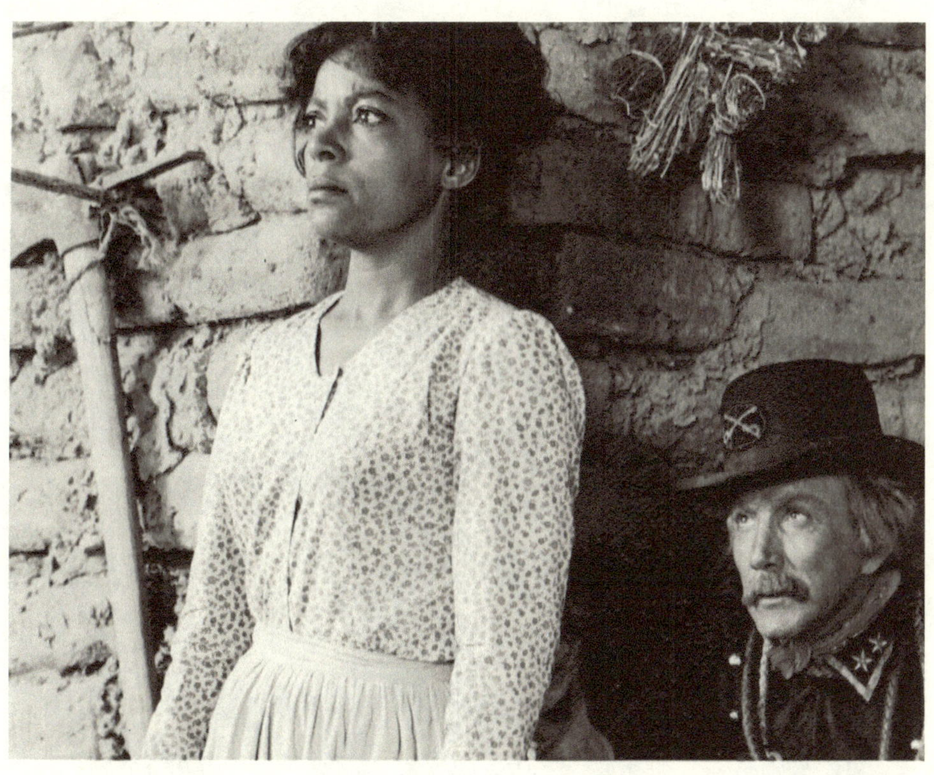

35. Ruby Dee as Ruth, the wagon master's wife who is being terrorized by white supremacist DeShay (Cameron Mitchell) in *Buck and the Preacher*.

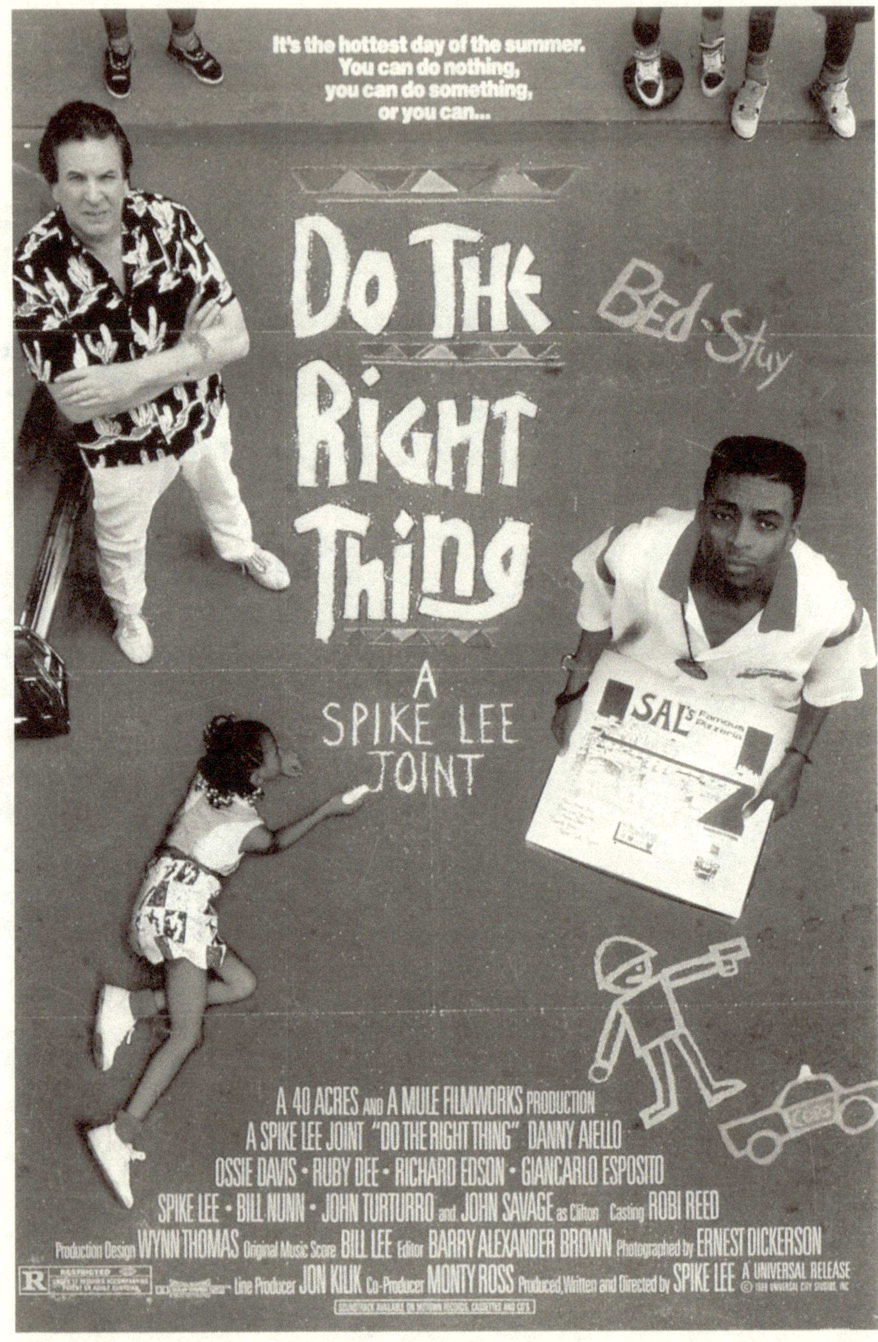

36. A poster of Spike Lee's masterpiece *Do The Right Thing* (1989).

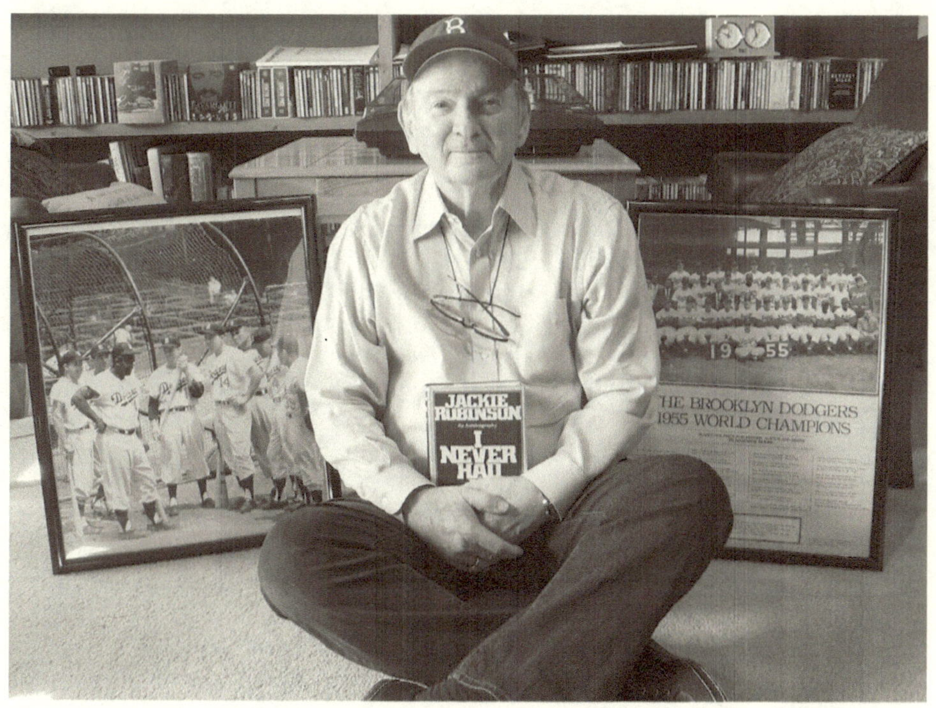

37. On May 1, 2013, *The Burlington Free Press* ran a story entitled "Breaking Barriers: Vermont author, film scholar remembers Jackie Robinson's legacy." Photograph courtesy of Susan Green, Free Press Correspondent.

Notes

[1] Corey Harris, "Feel Like Going Home," in *Martin Scorsese Presents The Blues*, ed. Jeffrey Peisch, The Blues (USA: Vulcan Productions, 2003).

[2] Winston Churchill, *A History of the English-Speaking Peoples*, Vol. 4, 387.

[3] David Anker, "Imaginary Witness: Hollywood and the Holocaust," (USA: Shadow Distribution, 2004).

[4] Nelson George, "Still Too Good, Too Bad or Invisible," *The New York Times*, Feb. 17, 2013, 1.

[5] Tanya Hart, "Ruby Dee Scores First Oscar Nod," in *NPR: News and Notes* (USA: NPR, 2008).

[6] Sarah Hearn, "Ruby Dee Bringing the Word to Apollo Theater on Mother's Day," in *Examiner* (2012), 1.

[7] Don Thomas, "Ossie Davis, Such a Classy, Kindly Man," in *New York Beacon* (2005).

[8] John Donne, *For Whom the Bell Tolls*, 1624.

[9] Bernard, *Carl Van Vechten & the Harlem Renaissance: A Portrait in Black & White*.

[10] Wilkerson, *The Warmth of Other Suns: The Epic Story of America's Great Migration*, 408-09.

[11] Davis and Dee, *With Ossie & Ruby in This Life Together*, 58.

[12] *With Ossie & Ruby in This Life Together*, 22-3.

[13] Benjamin W. Sampson, "With Ossie & Ruby in This Life Together," *American Theater* 16, no. 6 (1999): 8.

[14] Davis and Dee, *With Ossie & Ruby in This Life Together*, 21.

[15] Massood, *Black City Cinema: African American Urban Experiences in Film*, 93.

[16] Sampson, "With Ossie & Ruby in This Life Together," 115-16.

[17] Cary D. Wintz and Paul Finkleman, "Encyclopedia of the Harlem Renaissance, Vol. 1 A-J," (New York: Routledge, 2004), 209.

[18] Joyce Wansley, "Ossie Davis and Ruby Dee Are Compared to the Lunts, but Hayden & Fonda Also Apply," *People* 15, no. 11 (1981): 2.

[19] Davis and Dee, *With Ossie & Ruby in This Life Together*, 144-45.

[20] Wansley, "Ossie Davis and Ruby Dee Are Compared to the Lunts, but Hayden & Fonda Also Apply," 2.

[21] Elton C. Fax, *Contemporary Black Leaders* (W. Clement Stone, 1970), 230-31.

[22] Victor Navasky, "Actors with a Cause: With Ossie & Ruby in This Life Together," Review of With Ossie & Ruby, *New York Times Book Review*, Nov. 18, 1998, 8.

[23] Manchel, *Every Step a Struggle : Interviews with Seven Who Shaped the African-American Image in Movies*, 441.

[24] Edwin Schallert, "'Lucasta' Noteworthy Stage Event," *The Los Angeles Times*, Feb. 25, 1947, A3.

[25] Canby, "Critic's Notebook: Black Films: Imitation of Life?," C28.

[26] Gabbard, *Black Magic: White Hollywood and African American Culture*, 72-3.

[27] Joseph L. Mankiewicz, "No Way Out," (USA: Twentieth Century-Fox, 1950).

[28] Elia Kazan, "Gentleman's Agreement," (USA: Twentieth Century-Fox, 1947).

[29] Gavin, *Stormy Weather*, 232.

[30] Stephen Shelanski, "NAACP Celebrates the Life of Ossie Davis," *New York Beacon*, Feb. 10, 2005, 4.

[31] Fax, *Contemporary Black Leaders*, 232.

[32] Alfred E. Green, "The Jackie Robinson Story," (USA: Eagle-Lion Films, 1950).

[33] For a more current treatment of the story, see Susan Green, "Breaking Barriers: Vermont author, film scholar remembers Jackie Robinson's legacy," *Bulington Free Press* (May 1, 2013), 1B, 3B.

[34] Anthony Mann, "The Tall Target," (USA: MGM, 1951).

[35] James Wong Howe, "Go, Man, Go," (USA: United Artists, 1954).

[36] Ritt, "Edge of the City (Aka a Man Is Ten Feet Tall)."

[37] Allen Reisner, "St. Louis Blues," (USA: Paramount Pictures, 1958).

[38] Philip Leacock, "Take a Giant Step," (USA: United Artists, 1959).

[39] Joseph, *Dark Days, Bright Nights: From Black Power to Barack Obama*, 436-65.

[40] Sieving, *Soul Searching: Black-Themed Cinema from the March on Washington to the Rise of Blaxploitation*, 1.

[41] Davis and Dee, *With Ossie & Ruby in This Life Together*, 285.

[42] Joseph Strick, "The Balcony," (USA: Walter Reade-Sterling, 1963).

[43] Nicholas Webster, "Purlie Victorious (Aka Gone Are the Days)," (USA: Hammer Films, 1963).

[44] Riley, "Shaft Can Do Everything—I Can Do Nothing," D9.

[45] Sieving, *Soul Searching: Black-Themed Cinema from the March on Washington to the Rise of Blaxploitation*, 38-42.

[46] Ossie. Davis, "Kongi's Harvest," (Nigeria: Calpenny-Nigeria Films Ltd, 1970).

[47] "When Is a Camera a Weapon?," *New York Times*, September 20, 1970, 17.

[48] Hollie I. West, "Kongi's Harvest," *The Washington Post*, June 17, 1972, 17.

[49] Clarence Page, "Out of Africa," in *The PBS News Hour With Jim Lehrer* (USA 2007).

[50] Ritt, "The Great White Hope."

[51] Davis and Dee, *With Ossie & Ruby in This Life Together*.

[52] Larry Peerce, "The Incident," (USA: Twentieth Century-Fox, 1967).

[53] Sieving, *Soul Searching: Black-Themed Cinema from the March on Washington to the Rise of Blaxploitation*, 1-3.

[54] Jules Dassin, "Uptight," (USA: Paramount Pictures, 1968).

[55] John Ford, "The Informer," (USA: RKO Radio Pictures, 1935).

[56] Anonymous, "Up Tight," *America* 120 (1969): 51.

[57] Sieving, *Soul Searching: Black-Themed Cinema from the March on Washington to the Rise of Blaxploitation*, 85-7.

[58] Davis, "Cotton Comes to Harlem."

[59] Robert Osborne, "Introduction to 'Cotton Comes to Harlem'," in *Turner Classic Movies* (2013).

[60] Ibid.

[61] Vincent Canby, "Ossie Davis' 'Cotton Comes to Harlem'," *New York Times*, June 11, 1972, 50.

[62] Arthur Knight, "Sr Goes to the Movies," *Saturday Review* (1970): 22.

[63] Massood, *Black City Cinema: African American Urban Experiences in Film*, 86-7.

[64] Ed Guerrero, *Framing Blackness: The African American Image in Film* ibid. (1993), 70-1, 80.

[65] Sieving, *Soul Searching: Black-Themed Cinema from the March on Washington to the Rise of Blaxploitation*, 203-05.

[66] Rudolph Chelminski, "The Hard-Bitten Old Pro Who Wrote 'Cotton'," *Life* 69, no. 9 (1970): 60.

[67] Robert Osborne, "Introduction to 'Buck and the Preacher'," in *Turner Classic Movies* (2013).

[68] Poitier, "Buck and the Preacher."

[69] Osborne, "Introduction to 'Buck and the Preacher'."

[70] David Denby, "Movies: Getting Whitey," *Atlantic* 230, no. 2 (1972): 86-9.

[71] Riley, "Shaft Can Do Everything—I Can Do Nothing," D9.

[72] Tony McCuin, "The 44th NAAPC Image Awards," (The NAACP, 2013).

[73] St. Claire Bourne, "Paul Robeson: Here I Stand," in *American Masters*, ed. Karen Bernstein (USA: WinStar Home Video, 1999).

[74] Jeff Wurtz, "Inside the Actor's Srudio: Spike Lee," in *Inside the Actor's Studio*, ed. James Lipton (USA: Bravo, 2000).

[75] Spike Lee, "Do the Right Thing," (USA 1989).

[76] Jim Lehrer, "James Billington Segment," in *The Jim Lehrer Show* (USA: PBS, March 7, 2007).

[77] Davis and Dee, *With Ossie & Ruby in This Life Together*.

[78] Spike Lee, "Jungle Fever," (USA: Universal, 1991).

[79] Hitchens, *Hitch-22: A Memoir*, 467.

[80] Ridley Scott, "American Gangsters," (USA: Image Entertainment, 2007).

[81] Kenneth Turan, "Movie Reviews: The Nerve to Be Epic; 'American Gangster' Has It," *The Los Angeles Times*, Nov. 2 2007, E1.

[82] Robert Sinofsky, "Iconoclasts: Alicia Keys and Ruby Dee," in *Iconoclasts*, ed. Sidney Beaumont (USA: Sundance, 2007).

[83] Hart, "Ruby Dee Scores First Oscar Nod."

[84] Ruby Dee, "What's Right About Black Men," *Ebony* (1983): 92.

[85] Michael Landon, "It's Good to Be Alive," (USA: CBS, 1974).

[86] These stories are recounted in Susan Green, "Breaking Barriers: Vermont author, film scholar remembers Jackie Robinson's legacy," *Bulington Free Press* (May 1, 2013), 1B, 3B.

[87] Green, "The Jackie Robinson Story."

[88] Poitier, *This Life*, 99-122.

[89] Ford, "The Informer."

[90] Hugh A. Robertson, "Melinda," (USA: MGM, 1972).

[91] Jones and Niven, *James Earl Jones: Voices and Silences*, 254-55.

[92] Sieving, *Soul Searching: Black-Themed Cinema from the March on Washington to the Rise of Blaxploitation*, 144.

[93] William Wyler, "The Liberation of L. B. Jones," (USA: Columbia Pictures, 1970).

[94] Davis, "Cotton Goes to Harlem."

[95] Frank Rich, "Torture Compromise Revenge," *New York* (February 3, 2013): 18.

[96] Navasky, "Actors with a Cause: With Ossie & Ruby in This Life Together," 7.

[97] Maya Angelou, *Our Grandmothers*, Phenomenal Woman: Four Poems Celebrating Women (New York: Random House, 1978), 20.

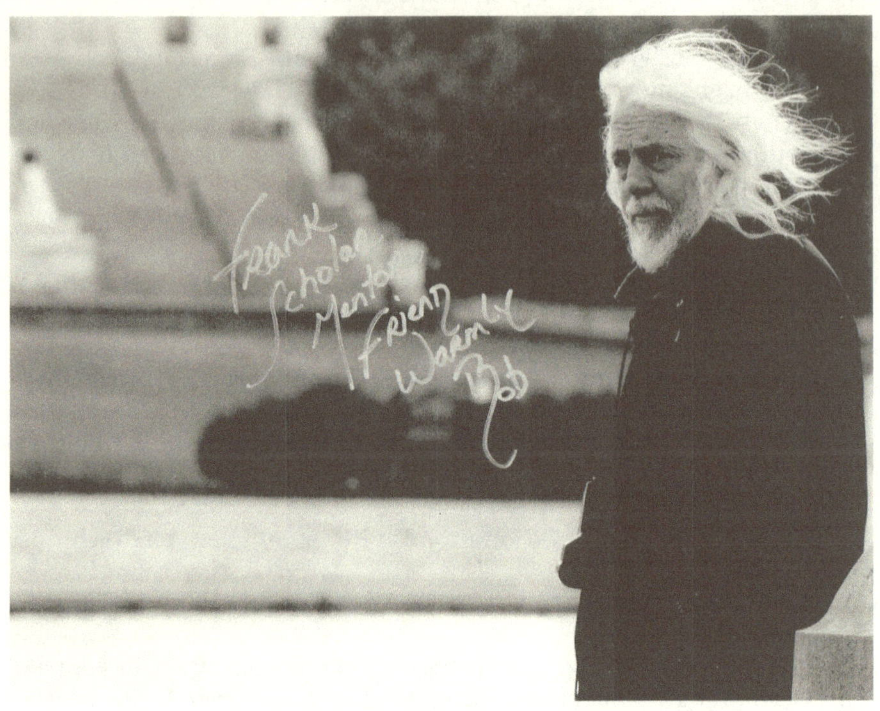

38. Many stars of today who are making their mark on the black film experience—e.g. Jamie Foxx, Kerry Washington, Samuel L. Jackson, and Nichole Galicia—can be seen in Quentin Tarantino's *Django Unchained* (2012). The Oscar-nominated cinematography was done by my close friend and former student, three-time Oscar winner Robert B. Richardson.

Epilogue

"I love the movies. They entertain us, they offer us hope, they give us dramas. They can take us places we've never been; and just even for a few moments, they can take us away when you want to get away. Movies inspire us, they challenge us; and despite our differences, they are a common link that touches the humanity in all of us."[1]

Jack Nicholson

"... Life meanwhile, that is people's real lives with their real concerns ... of health and illness, work and relaxation ... their interest in ideas, science, poetry ... music, love, friendship, hatred, passion ... life meanwhile continued as usual ... independent and regardless of political alliance .... [or racial divide]."[2]

Leo Tolstoy's War and Peace

"This is what we were.
This is where we have been.
This is where we are.
This is our experience."[3]

The American Experience

"The good of the one outweighs the good of the many."[4]

Amanda Grayson

Ending *Exits and Entrances* during the 150th anniversary of the Emancipation Proclamation and following the 50th anniversary of the murder of Medgar Evers as well as Dr. Martin Luther King's March on Washington provides an appropriate background for my reflections on the African-American film legacy. It reminds me how long it takes to bring about change, the price that has been paid, and that the task is never completed. And these thoughts cause me to remember how long a time it has been since I had the chutzpah to believe that a rebellious white kid from the streets of New York who spent his professional life teaching about movies at the University of Vermont could make a meaningful contribution to the important discussions on black film history. Yet here I am, battered, bloodied, but unbowed.

From the start, *The Interviews* offered an alternative point of view to the popular academic ideas on the groundbreaking reforms affecting black artists that occurred in the mainstream media following the post-World War II period to the mid-seventies. It was never my intention to replace what more knowledgeable and influential scholars discovered and reported. But my memory recalled a somewhat different interpretation of the events and the films and the reasons for the revolutionary changes. My historical narrative on the reforms stressed a technological as well as an individual perspective. Similar to the advice John Quincy Adams (Anthony Hopkins) gave to black scholar Theodore Joadson (Morgan Freeman) in Steven Spielberg's brilliant *Amistad* (1997),[5] I shared my colleagues' basic facts but not when it came to who the people were that changed the system. Thus my strategy was to use fourteen interviews recorded from 1971 to 1974 and to have them act as springboards for discussing the shifts that took place in the motion picture industry from the past to the present.

Throughout the Preface and the Introduction of *Exits and Entrances,* I reflected on the conditions and the reasons that brought about not only this project but also the reforms themselves. The personalities were identified and details provided as to why this unique take on black film history merited your time. Similarly, I made clear that the two books that make up *The Interviews* did not have to be read sequentially. In seven distinctive chapters, I combined existing scholarly data with unpublished personal accounts to describe the swings in American film history during the twentieth century. Abundant lists of innovative films were interspersed with over a thousand footnotes to provide resources for identifying the role of music and literature and the arts in changing many of the racist conditions for black Americans since centuries before the birth of movies. I admitted my bias lay in demonstrating the links between the popular arts and the world we inhabit. I also reminded readers what it was like persuading print-oriented academics to acknowledge the indispensible intellectual and emotional gifts of the greatest art form of the twentieth century. At every opportunity, I tried to personalize the relationship between my private life and my professional journey. Rarely was there a chapter that ignored how this narrative and my story echoed a greater narrative that encompassed not only my pursuits, but also those of people around the globe. And always, always I expressed my gratitude and my respect for the fourteen individuals, most of whom took the risks and had the talent to make the changes possible. Since three of the individuals were white and their controversial contributions provided confusion in the minds of some readers, I made a case for their importance in the historical record.

Central to my alternative account was Shakespeare's marvelous observations about the ages of man, in which "All the world's a stage/And all the men and women merely players. /They have their exits and entrances, /and one man in his time plays many parts. /His acts being seven ages."[6] Those fourteen actors whose performances I observed upon the stage before they made their exits were in chronological order, Lorenzo Tucker, Lillian Gish, Clarence Muse, King Vidor, Mae Mercer, Brock Peters, Charles Edward Gordone, Woody Strode, Jim Brown, Ivan Dixon, James Whitmore, Frederick Douglass O'Neal, William Marshall, and Ruby Dee. Starting with their childhoods, we followed the artists into maturity and learned of their ambitions and causes. As they boldly jeopardized their fame and fortune for honor and purpose, the players grew old and made room for others. And those contemporary artists who made their entrances upon the stage soon discovered the contributions their forbearers had made. But in my last scene for these performers they do not pass into "mere oblivion." Their cultural contributions are not forgotten.

If this was 1963 and I was listening to the music of the blacklisted Pete Seeger, he might be singing the lyrics of a new Bob Dylan song:

"What have you learned, my blue-eyed son?" The question may seem simple, but as you discover in life, we do not all see the same thing the same way. My answer depends on what I think the question to mean. If you refer to names and dates and titles and events and songs, the answer would be I gathered an incredible amount of information. I learned a lot about the entertainment industry, how it began and evolved, the movers and shakers who controlled the business in one era and then lost control in another age. Besides studying the major elements that needed reforming and the challenges they presented, I addressed our nation's history, and the effects of the communications revolution on our country and how it changed the way we thought and behaved. I thought about the celebrities I interviewed and how their thinking was transformed as a result of the baggage they carried with them. I placed them in the context of a profession constantly under attack from more powerful and entrenched institutions. Like the stars, I rarely accepted conventional wisdom or demurred to prevailing conventions. I was not ignorant of our weakness, but I had considerable confidence in our strengths and purposes. And I had faith not only in my audience but also in the lessons of history. As Churchill said, the past gave me hope. Thus *Exits and Entrances* chronicled who succeeded and who failed and why.

But if you ask me did I learn how to solve the racial problems in our country and in our culture, did I understand where we were heading and how best to get there, I would have to say I learned very little. I remain better informed about what the issues are, but no less confused, even about what I experienced. I have admitted throughout *Exits and Entrances,* and earlier in *Every Step a Struggle,* the solutions to these complex problems remain above my grade level. The same experience occurred when I finished my four-volume research guide *Film Study: An Analytical Bibliography.* The more I read the less I knew. Things, which seem so simple in ignorance, become terribly complex when confronted with knowledge and experience.

"That sounds like so much theoretical and professorial claptrap," you might respond. "Surely you must have learned something significant. Give us at least a half dozen important conclusions forty years of scholarly pursuit produced."

If you insist! I would say first, I learned to think of black artists as artists first and as black artists second. I learned that the work these gifted performers shared with us for over a hundred years contains as much entertainment, information, and inspiration as that of any other group in show business. Second, I learned that only foolish people would limit themselves to one group or one ideology or one history. As I said about the book-oriented professors who thought we Young Turks wanted to replace them, I say about the greatness of the black film legacy. Admiring the contributions of African-Americans is not to argue they should replace the culture of other ethnicities in this immigrant nation, but rather that the African-American legacy deserves equal representation and respect. Anyone who jettisons Mozart, Shakespeare, and Milton for Charlie Parker, Ralph Ellison, and Spike Lee is ridiculous in my eyes. But anyone who doesn't see their value and brilliance or who can't reverse the equation is just as much a fool. Third, those readers who think this book is only about African-American film history miss the value of my story. While black artists have blazed the path for this narrative, I believe the examination of the road they travelled should inspire others to investigate the journeys experienced by different artists in our society. The times, my circumstances, and the context shaped my study of the black film experience. Today the subject might as easily have been gays, Latinos, Asian-Americans, etc. Fourth, the fact that *The Interviews* exist or that the author has had a modestly successful career should encourage those rebels who want to change society not to fear the consequences of becoming marginalized in the name of a just enterprise. I clearly have no illusions about the price one pays for being different. But I also know first-hand the rewards of being true to oneself. Or as Old Blues Eyes often said, "Doing it my way." Fifth, doing a project like *The Interviews* produces many memories. If it is true as my late beloved father-in-law said, life is about collecting memories, then a life pursing impossible dreams provides an abundant amount of incredible memories. I recommend it to you without reservation. Finally, there is no utopia. When some of my colleagues were asked what they hoped for in their writings, one said that he hoped he had got it right. Another hoped that the book just be read. I would say that I am grateful that I lived long enough to get the manuscript published. I have no illusions that I got the history right, but I know with all my heart that this is the way I thought it happened.

Ironically, as I exit this period in the black film legacy *The New York Times* is announcing, "After years of complaint and self-criticism about the shortage of prominent movies by and about black Americans, film companies are poised to release an extraordinary cluster of them across an array of genres in the last five months of 2013."[6] The ballyhooing of these new films, like an almost similar event fifty years ago, is again being credited to the pioneering work of the Independent film movement. Thus history seems to be replaying a familiar theme. The names and obstacles are changed but the hurdles appear all too familiar. We can take heart, however, in knowing that the new players upon the stage are standing on the shoulders of many courageous and talented trailblazers who came before them. Thankfully, a number of these inspirational performers have shared their thoughts with us in *The Interviews.*

And so in concluding this extraordinary journey, let me paraphrase, as I have done so often in my twilight years, the words of Zelma Wilson, the wife of blacklisted writer, Michael Wilson. He never received in his lifetime his Oscar for co-writing *The Bridge on the River Kwai*. But in 1976, the artist posthumously received the Screenwriters Guild's coveted Laurel Award. In accepting the honor for her late husband, Mrs. Wilson delivered the following speech, which I have slightly altered for this moment:

"I don't want to dwell on the past. But for a few moments to speak of the future, and I address my remaining remarks particularly to you, younger men and women who have perhaps not yet established yourselves in…[our profession] at the time of the great witch hunt. I feel that unless you remember this dark epoch and understand it, you may be doomed to replay it. Not with the same cast of characters, of course, or on the same issues.

"But I see a day, perhaps coming in your lifetime if not in mine, when a new crisis of belief will grip this republic. When diversity of opinion will be labeled disloyalty, and when extraordinary pressures will be put on writers…[and educators] to conform to administration policy on the key issues of the time, whatever they may be.

"If this gloomy scenario should come to pass, I trust that you younger men and women will shelter the mavericks and the dissenters in your ranks and protect their right to work. The Guild [and the universities] will have the use and the need of rebels if it is to survive as a union of free writers [and responsible teachers]. This nation will have need of them if it is to survive as an open society."[7]

August 15, 2013

Notes

[1] Academy of Motion Pictures Arts and Sciences, "80th Annual Academy Awards," (USA: Academy of Motion Pictures Arts and Sciences, 2008).

[2] Bondarchuk, Sergei. "Leo Tolstoy's War and Peace." 405 mins. Russia, (1966-67).

[3] Staff, "The American Experience Logo," in The American Experience, ed. Mark Samuels (USA: PBS, 2012).

[4] Leonard Nimoy, "Star Trek:The Voyage Home," (USA: Paramount Pictures, 1986).

[5] In the interests of full disclosure, the brilliant script of *Amistad* was penned by my friend and former student David Franzoni.

[6] Harrison, *Shakespeare: Major Plays and the Sonnets*. From As You Like It, Act II, Scene 7, p. 509.

[7] Chaikin, "Legacy of the Hollywood Blacklist."

Works Cited

Academy of Motion Picture Arts and Sciences. "80th Annual Academy Awards." 197 mins. USA: Academy of Motion Picture Arts and Sciences (AMPAS), 2008.

Acham, Christine and Clifford Ward. "Infiltrating Hollywood: The Spook Who Sat by the Door." 57 mins.: Documentary Channel, 2011.

Adler, Renata. "'The Heart Is a Lonely Hunter': Alan Arkin Starred in McCullers Story Dean Martin Western Is at Local Houses." *New York Times,* August 1, 1968, 1.

Aldrich, Robert. "Twilight's Last Gleaming." 146 mins. U.S.-German: Allied Artists, 1977.

_____. "The Dirty Dozen." 149 mins. USA: MGM, 1967.

Angelou, Maya. "Our Grandmothers." *Phenomenal Woman: Four Poems Celebrating Women.* New York: Random House, 1978.

Anker, David. "Imaginary Witness: Hollywood and the Holocaust." 92. USA: Shadow Distribution, 2004.

Anonymous. "Abbie Mitchell, Actress, Is Dead; Singer Was Widow of Composer." *New York Times,* March 20, 1960, 1.

_____. "Convention Report 1973." *Bulletin of Black Theatre,* no. 4, Fall 1973, 1.

_____. "Demetrius and the Gladiators: William Marshall Has a Choice Role in 3-D Film." *Ebony* 9, no. 1 (1954): 6.

_____. "Marshall Going to Hati for Movie on Christophe." *The Amsterdam News,* Dec. 6, 1975, 1.

_____. "Up Tight." *America* 120, (Jan. 11, 1969): 2.

_____. "William Marshall, 'Blacula' Actor, Succumbs at 78." *Jet* 104, no. 1, June 30, 2003, 1.

Applebome, Peter "John Hope Franklin, Scholar and Witness." *New York Times,* March 29, 2009, 1, 5.

Archer, Eugene. "Filming to Begin on 'Black Like Me'." *New York Times,* 1963, p. 18.

Atkinson, Brooks. "'Set My People Free': Theatre Guild Stages Historical Negro Drama with Some Superb Players." *The New York Times,* Nov. 14, 1948, 1.

Bainbridge, John. *Another Way of Living: A Gallery of Americans Who Choose to Live in Europe*. New York: Holt, Rinehart and Winston, 1968.

Beaupre, Lee. "Brock Peters on Negro Skepticism: One Colored Star Hardly a Trend." *Variety*, December 20, 1967, 1, 54.

Belafonte, Harry, with Michael Shnayerson. *My Song: A Memoir*. New York: Alfred A. Knopf, 2011.

Bennett, Lerone, Jr. *The Challenge of Blackness*. Chicago: Johnson Publishing Company, 1972.

_____. "The Case Against Styron's Nat Turner." *Ebony*, October 1968: 8.

_____. "The Emancipation Orgasm: Sweetback in Wonderland." *Ebony* 26, September 1971: 106-8+.

Bensinger, Graham "Brown Talks About Race, TD Celebrations and More." In *The GBShow*, edited by Graham Bensinger. USA: ESPN, 2009.

Berg, A. Scott. *Goldwyn: A Biography*. New York: Alfred A. Knopf, 1989.

Berkvist, Robert. "A Director of Classics, Focused on Conscience." *New York Times*, April 10, 2011, 2.

Bernard, Emily. *Carl Van Vechten & the Harlem Renaissance: A Portrait in Black & White*. New Haven and London: Yale University Press, 2012.

Bernstein, Rick, and Ross Greenburg. *Mantle*. USA: Home Box Office Inc., 2010.

Berry, S. Torriano , and Venise T. Berry. *Historical Dictionary of African American Cinema*. Lanham, Md.: The Scarecrow Press, Inc., 2007.

Betancourt, Jeanne. *Women in Focus*. Dayton: Pflaum Publishing, 1974.

Binder, Steve, and Peter H. Hunt. "Give 'Em Hell, Harry!" 104 mins.: TheatreVision, 1975.

Bingham, Dennis. *Whose Lives Are They Anyway? The Biopic as Contemporary Film Genre*. New Brunswick, New Jersey: Rutgers University Press, 2010.

Boettcher, Steven J. "Pioneers of Television: Variety." 60 mins. USA: Public Broadcasting Corporation, 2007.

Bogart, Paul. "The Final War of Olly Winter." In *CBS Playhouse*. USA, 1967.

Bogle, Donald. *Blacks in American Films and Television: An Encyclopedia*. New York: Garland Publishing, Inc., 1988.

_____. "Brown Sugar: America's Black Female Stars." 90 mins. USA: PBS, 1986.

_____. *Dorothy Dandridge: A Biography*. Canada/NY: Amistad/HarperCollins Publishers, 1997.

_____. *Bright Boulevards, Bold Dreams: The Story of Black Hollywood*. 1st ed. New York: One World Ballantine Books, 2005.

_____. *Toms, Coons, Mulattoes, Mammies, & Bucks: An Interpretive History of Blacks in American Films*. New York: Continuum, 1973.

Bourne, St. Claire. "Paul Robeson: Here I Stand." In *American Masters,* edited by Karen Bernstein, 117 mins. USA: WinStar Home Video, 1999.

Bowman, Rob "Linear Notes for Nina Simone: Live in '65 & '68." *Nina Simone,* May 2008, 15.

Brend, Mark, ed. *What's Going On: Marvin Gaye.* Albums: The Stories Behind 50 Years of Great Recordings. San Diego: Thunderbay Bay Press, 2005.

Brooks, Richard. "Something of Value." 113 mins. USA: MGM, 1957.

Brooks, Tim, and Earle Marsh. *The Complete Directory to Prime Time Network TV Shows: 1946-Present.* 4th ed. New York: Ballantine Books, 1988.

Brown, Clarence. "Intruder in the Dust." 87 mins. USA: MGM, 1949.

Brown, Jim. "Jim Brown: Life and Love in Hollywood."*Ebony* 45, no. 2, December 1989, 6.

Brown, Jim, and Steve Delsohn. *Out of Bounds.* Paperback ed. New York: Zebra Books, 1990.

Brown, Jimmy, and with Myron Cope. *Off My Chest.* Garden City, New York: Doubleday & Company, Inc., 1964.

Brown, Phil. "The Harlem Globetrotters." 75 mins. USA: Columbia Pictures, 1951.

Browning, Kirk. "Live from Lincoln Center: The Gershwins' "Porgy and Bess"." 3 hrs. USA: PBS, 2002.

Bruzzell, Edward. "At the Circus." 87 mins.: USA: MGM, 1939.

Burrell, Walter. "Black Films: Big Money Careers & Rip Off . . . ." *Soul,* Dec. 18, 1972, 2.

_____. "Hollywood Happenings." *The New Courier,* April 8, 1967, 13.

Cameron, Sean. "Private Screenings: Sidney Lumet." 60 mins. USA: Turner Classic Movies, 2005.

Camp, Joseph. "In Performance at the White House: A Broadway Celebration." In *In Performance at the White House,* edited by George C. Wolfe, 60 mins. USA: PBS, 2010.

_____. "'Porgy and Bess' Update." 10 mins. USA: MacNeil/Lerer Productions, 2012.

Canby, Vincent. "Critic's Notebook: Black Films: Imitation of Life?" *New York Times,* Feb. 8, 1991, 2.

_____. "Ossie Davis' 'Cotton Comes to Harlem'." *New York Times,* June 11, 1972, 1.

_____. *Pretty Baby. New York Times,* April 5 1978, 3.

_____. "Race to Film Race Issues: Indies React to Negro News." *Variety,* July 17, 1963, 2.

_____. "'Fingers' Is Strictly from Desperation." *New York Times,* March 19, 1978, 1.

Cardiff, Jack. "Dark of the Sun (A.K.A the Mercenaries)." 101 mins. USA: MGM, 1968.

Cayatte, Andre. "Two Are Guilty (Le Glaive et la balance; the Sword and the Balance)." 131 mins. France, Italy: Gaumont, 1963.

Chaikin, Judy. "Legacy of the Hollywood Blacklist." 60 mins. USA: One Step Productions, 1987.

Champlin, Charles. "Life in the Day of a Car Wash." *Los Angeles Times*, Aug. 29, 1976, 1.

Chelminski, Rudolph. "The Hard-Bitten Old Pro Who Wrote 'Cotton'." *Life* 69, no. 9, August 28, 1970, 2.

Chetwynd, Lionel. "Redefining Racism: Fresh Voices from Black America." 60 mins. USA: Whidbry Island Films Inc., 1997.

Chideya, Farai. "NPR: News and Notes for December 25, 2006." In *African-American Roundtable: News & Notes*, 20 minutes. USA: NPR, 2006.

Chinen, Nate. "A Style Lasting Beyond a Lifetime." *New York Times*, August 28, 2010, 2.

Chrisman, Robert. "The Black Scholar Interviews William Marshall." *The Black Scholar* 16, no. 4, July/August 1985, 5.

Churchill, Winston. *A History of the English-Speaking Peoples*. New York: Dodd Mead, 1956.

Clark, Graeme. "The Swinging Cheerleaders." In *The Spinning Image*, 2, 1974.

Clark, Kenneth B. *Dark Ghetto: Dilemmas of Social Power*. Lebanon: Wesleyan University Press, 1989.

Clarke ed., John Henrik. *William Styron's Nat Turner: Ten Black Writers Respond*. Boston: Beacon Press, 1968.

Clarke, Shirley. "The Cool World." 104 mins. USA: Wiseman Film Productions, 1962.

Clements, Zach, in discussion with the author. Sept. 6, 2012.

Cohen, Larry. "Original Gangstas." 99 mins. USA: Orion Pictures, 1996.

Colizzi, Giuseppe. "Ace High (Quattro Del'ave Maria)." 137 mins. Italy: Paramount Pictures, 1968.

Conrad, Earl and Dorothy Dandridge. *Everything and Nothing: The Dorothy Dandridge Tragedy*. NY: Abelard-Schuman, 2000.

Cosby, Bill, and Alvin F Poussaint, MD. *Come on, People: On the Path from Victims to Victors*. Nashville: Thomas Nelson, 2007.

Covington, Jeanette. *Crime and Racial Constructions: Cultural Misinformation About African Americans in Media and Academia*. Lanham, Maryland: Lexington Books, 2010.

Crain, William "Blacula." 92 mins. USA: American International, 1972.

Cripps, Thomas. *Black Film as Genre*. Bloomington: Indiana University Press, 1978.

_____. *Making Movies Black: The Hollywood Message Movies from World War II to the Civil Rights Era*. New York: Oxford University Press, 1993.

Crouch, Stanley. *The All-American Skin Game, or the Decoy of Race*. New York: Vintage Books, 1995.

_____. *The Artificial White Man: Essays on Authenticity*. Central Studies/African American Studies. Paperback ed. New York: Basic Civitas, 2005.

_____. *Considering Genius: Writings on Jazz*. New York: Basic Civitas Books, 2006.

Crowther, Bosley. "Kurt Weill and Maxwell Anderson's Lost in the Stars." *The American Film Theatre/Cinebill*, 1974, 26.

_____. "Review of Heavens Above!" *New York Times*, May 21, 1963, 28.

_____. "Review of Porgy and Bess." *New York Times*, June 25, 1959, 313-14.

_____. "Review of the L-Shaped Room." *New York Times*, May 28, 1963, 32:1.

_____. "Screen: Racial Conflict." *New York Times*, May 11, 1957, 1.

Curtis, Bryan. "George Lucas Is Ready to Roll the Credits." *The New York Times Magazine*, January 22, 2012, 6.

Custen, George F. *Bio/Pics: How Hollywood Constructed Public History*. New Brunswick, N.J.: Rutgers University Press, 1992.

Dandridge, Dorothy, and Earl Conrad. *Everything and Nothing: The Dorothy Dandridge Tragedy*. New York: Abelard-Schuman, 1970.

Darabont, Frank. "The Shawshank Redemption." 142 mins.: USA: Castle Rock Entertainment, 1994.

Dassin, Jules. "Up Tight." 104 mins.: USA: Paramount Pictures, 1968.

Daves, Delmer. "Broken Arrow." 93 mins.: USA: Twentieth Century-Fox, 1950.

_____. "Demetrius and the Gladiator." 101 mins. USA: Twentieth Century-Fox, 1954.

Davia, Nina. "From These Roots." In *TV Season 76-77*, edited by Nina Davia. Phoenix: Oryx Press, 1978.

Davis, Miles. "Jack Johnson." In *The Complete Jack Johnson Sessions*, 7-8. NY: Sony Music Entertainment Inc., 1971.

Davis, Ossie. "Cotton Goes to Harlem." USA: United Artists, 1970.

_____. *Life Lit by Some Large Vision: Selected Speeches*, edited by Ruby Dee. New York: Atira Books, 2006.

_____. "Kongi's Harvest." 85 mins.: Calpenny-Nigeria Films Ltd, 1970.

_____. "When Is a Camera a Weapon?" *New York Times*, September 20, 1970, 2.

_____. "The Power of Black Movies." *Freedomways* 14, no. 3, 1974, 3.

Davis, Ossie, and Ruby Dee. *With Ossie & Ruby in This Life Together*. New York: William Morrow and Company, Inc., 1998.

Dee, Ruby. "What's Right About Black Men." *Ebony*, August 1983, 4.

DeMille, Cecil B. "The Plainsman." 113 mins.: USA: Paramount Pictures, 1936.

Denby, David. "Movies: Getting Whitey." *Atlantic* 230, no. 2, August 1972, 4.
DeVinney, James A., and et. all. *Eyes on the Prize.* 14 episodes. USA: PBS, 1987.
Devlin, Paul "Albert Murray at Ninety." *Antioch Review* 65, no. 2, Nov. 18, 2009, 10.
Diawara, Manthia, ed. *Black American Cinema.* edited by Manithia Diawara. London and New York: Routledge, 1993.
Dixon, Ivan. "The Spook Who Sat by the Door." 102 mins. USA: United Artists, 1973. Reprint, 2004.
_____. "Trouble Man." 99 mins. USA: Twentieth Century-Fox, 1972.
Donne, John. *For Whom the Bell Tolls.* 1624.
Douglas, Gordon. "Chuka." 95 mins.: USA: Paramount Pictures, 1967.
_____. "The McConnell Story." 106 mins.: USA: Warner Brothers, 1955.
_____. "Them!," 94 mins.: USA: Warner Brothers, 1954.
_____. "Slaughter's Big Rip-Off." 92 mins. USA: American International Pictures, 1973.
_____. "Rio Conchos." 107 mins. USA: Twentieth Century Fox, 1964.
Downey, Robert, Sr. "Putney Swope." 84 mins. USA: Cinema 5, 1969.
Duke, Bill. "Hoodlum." 130 mins.: USA: United Artists, 1997.
DuLuart, Yolanda. "Angela: Portrait of a Revolutionary." 80 mins. USA: New Yorker Films, 1972.
Dyson, Michael Eric. *Mercy, Mercy Me: The Art, Loves and Demons of Marvin Gaye.* Electronic Book ed. New York: Basic Civitas Books, 2008.
Early, Gerald. *One Nation Under a Groove: Motown and American Culture.* Hopewell, N.J.: Ecco Press, 1995.
_____. *This Is Where I Came In: Black America in the 1960s.* Abraham Lincoln Lecture Series. Lincoln: University of Nebraska Press, 2003.
Eastwood, Clint. "Bird." 160 mins. USA: Warner Brothers, 1988.
Ebony. "Football Heroes Invade Hollywood." *Ebony,* 1969.
Elliot, Marc. *American Rebel: The Life of Clint Eastwood.* New York: Harmony Books, 2009.
Ellison, Ralph. *The Shadow and the Act.* New York: Random House, 1953.
_____. "The Golden Age, Time Past." 1959.
Fax, Elton C. *Contemporary Black Leaders.* W. Clement Stone, 1970.
Ferro, Marc. "Film as an Agent, Product and Source of History." *Journal of Contemporary History* 18, no. 3, July 1983.
Fessier, Michael, Jr. "A War Ivan Dixon Is Winning." *New York Times,* 1967.
Fleder, Gary. *The Express (Aka the Express: The Ernie Davis Story).* 130 mins. USA: Universal Pictures, 2008.
Fleischer, Richard. "The Boston Strangler." 116 mins.: USA: Twentieth Century-Fox, 1968.
Flemyng, George. The Split." 91 mins. USA: MGM, 1968.
Forbes, Bryan. "The L-Shaped Room." 125 Mins. Britain, 1962.

Ford, John. "The Informer." 91 mins.: USA: RKO Radio Pictures, 1935.
_____. "The Man Who Shot Liberty Valance." 123 mins. USA: Paramount Pictures, 1962.
_____. "The Horse Soldiers." 114 mins. USA: MGM, 1959.
Fordham, John. "Abbey Lincoln Obituary: Jazz Singer, Actor and Civil Rights Activist Strongly Influenced by Billie Holiday." *The Guardian,* 2010, 5.
Formwalt, Lee W. "Demystifying and Rethinking the Study of History: An Interview with Gerda Lerner." *OAH Newsletter,* November 2006, 2.
Fox, Margalit. "Vonetta Mcgee, Film and TV Actress, Dies at 65." *The New York Times,* July 15, 2010, 1.
Frank, Melvin. "Above and Beyond." 122 mins.: USA: MGM, 1952.
Franklin, Wendell. "The Bus Is Coming." 109 mins. USA: William Thomson Productions, Inc., 1971.
Fraser, Gerald C. "Abram Hill, 76, the Founder of a Black Theater in Harlem." *New York Times* October 11, 1986, 13.
Freeman, Mike *Jim Brown: The Fierce Life of an American Hero.* New York: Harper Entertainment, 2006.
French, Philip, ed. *Malle on Malle.* London: Faber and Faber, 1993.
Fujiwara, Chris. *The World and Its Double: The Life and Work of Otto Preminger.* Paperback ed. New York: Faber and Faber, Inc., 2008.
Gabbard, Krin. *Black Magic: White Hollywood and African American Culture.* New Brunswick, New Jersey: Rutgers University Press, 2004.
_____. *Jammin' at the Margins: Jazz and the American Cinema.* Chicago: The University of Chicago Press, 1996.
Garland, Phyl. "Brock Peters - Actor with a Star Ascending." *Pittsburg Courier,* August 28, 1965, 9.
Gavin, James. *Stormy Weather: The Life of Lena Horne.* New York: Atria Books, 2009.
Gelfand, Marvin. "Taking a Leaf: A Talk with Albert Murray." In *Conversations with Albert Murray,* edited by Roberta S. Maguire. Literary Conversation Series, 4. Jackson: University of Mississippi, 1977.
Gennari, John. E-Mail, Nov. 28, 2012.
_____. *Blowin' Hot and Cool: Jazz and Its Critics.* Chicago and London: The University of Chicago Press, 2006.
George, Nelson. "New Directors Flesh out Black America, All of It." *New York Times,* December 25, 2011, 2.
_____. "Still Too Good, Too Bad or Invisible." *The New York Times,* Feb. 17, 2013, 2.
Gerard, Charley. *Jazz in Black and White: Race, Culture, and Identity in the Jazz Community.* Westport, Connecticut: Praeger, 1998.
Gibson, Emily F. "Must a Black Actor Play Henri Christophe?". *Sepia* (1972):22-7.

Gilbert, Alan. "New York Philharmonic Opening Night Concert 2010: U.S. Premiere 'Jazz Symphony'." In *Live from Lincoln Center*, 120 mins. USA: PBS, 2010.

Gill, Brendan. "Patch of Blue." *New Yorker* 41, December 25, 1965, 2.

Girdler, William. "Abby." 89 mins.: USA: American International, 1974.

Gladwell, Malcolm. "The Courthouse Ring: Atticus Finch and the Limits of Southern Liberalism." *The New Yorker* 85, no. 24, August 10, 2009, 5.

Glenville, Peter. "The Comedians." 150 mins. England: MGM, 1967.

Gonzalez, Gaspar, and Alan Tomlinson. "Muhammad Ali: Made in Miami." 54 mins. USA: PBS, 2008.

Graham, Allison. *Framing the South: Hollywood, Television, and Race During the Civil Rights Struggle*. U. S. History/ Film Studies. Baltimore: The John Hopkins University Press, 2001.

Graham, William A. "Cindy." 97 mins. USA: John Charles Walters Productions, 1978.

Grant IV, William R. *Post-Soul Black Cinema: Discontinuities, Innovations, and Breakpoints, 1970-1995*. Studies in African American History and Culture. Edited by Graham Russell Hodges. New York & London: Routledge, 2004.

Gratz, Roberta Brandes "Ivan Dixon: A Choice of Heroes." *New York Post*, June 17, 1967, 1.

Green, Alfred E. "The Jackie Robinson Story." 76 mins.: USA: Eagle-Lion Films, 1950.

_____. "The Jolson Story." 128 mins. USA: Columbia Pictures, 1946.

Green, Guy. "A Patch of Blue." 108 mins. USA: MGM, 1965.

Green, Susan, "Breaking Barriers: Vermont author, film scholar remembers Jackie Robinson's legacy," *Bulington Free Press*, May 1, 2013, 1B.

Greenspun, Roger. "Dirty Harry." *New York Times*, December 23, 1971, 2.

_____. "The Screen: 'Blacula'." *The New York Times*, August 26, 1972, 1.

_____. "Screen: A Vampire's Lot." *The New York Times*, July 19, 1973, 1.

Grier, Pam, with Andrea Cagan. *Foxy: My Life in Three Acts*. New York: Springboard Press, 2010.

Gries, Tom. "100 Rifles." 110 mins. USA: Twentieth Century-Fox, 1969.

Grimes, William. "Gerda Lerner, Pioneering Feminist and Historian, Dies at 92 " *New York Times*, January 4, 2013, 1.

Grunwald. "Albert Murray: Riffing It." In *Conversations with Albert Murray*, edited by ed. Maguire, Roberta S., 3. Jackson: University of Mississippi Press, 1997.

Guerrero, Ed. "Framing Blackness: The African American Image in Film." *Culture and the Moving Image*. Edited by Robert Sklar. Philadelphia: Temple University Press, 1993.

Guillermin, John. "El Condor." 102 mins. USA: National General Pictures, 1970.

Guttentag, Bill, and Don Sturman. "Soundtrack for a Revolution." In *American Experience*, edited by Sharon Grimberg, 82 mins. USA: PBS, 2009.

Haidt, Jonathan. *The Righteous Mind*. New York: Pantheon Books, 2012.

Haley, Alex. "Playboy Interview: Jim Brown—a Candid Conversation with the Football Superstar Turned Actor and Civil Rights Activist." *Playboy* 15, no. 2, February 1968, 13.

Hall, Alexander. "Because You're Mine." 103 mins.: USA: MGM, 1952.

Hans. "Jack Johnson." *Variety*, Nov. 10 1971, 1.

Hansberry, Lorraine. *A Raisin in the Sun: The Unfilmed Original Script*. New York: Signet Books, 1994.

Harris, Franklin. "Culture Shock Column: Infamous Clone of 'the Exorcist' Is Due New Respect with DVD Release." *Decatur Daily*, Oct. 16, 2008.

Harris, Keith M. "Boys, Boyz, Bois: An Ethics of Black Masculinity in Film and Popular Media." *Studies in African American History and Culture*. Edited by Graham Hodges. New York and London: Routledge, 2006.

Harrison, G.B., ed. *Shakespeare: Major Plays and the Sonnets*. New York: Harcourt, Brace and Company, 1948.

Hart, Tanya "Ruby Dee Scores First Oscar Nod." In *NPR: News and Notes*, 10 mins. USA: NPR, 2008.

Hartford-Davis, Robert. "Black Gunn." 96 mins. USA: Champion Production Company, 1972.

Haskin, Byron. "Tarzan's Peril." 78 mins. USA: RKO Radio Pictures, Inc., 1951.

Hathaway, Maggie. "Hollywood Segregation, Integration Performances 'before, after' Exposed." *Hollywood Sentinel*, Thursday, March 23 1967, 1, 3.

_____. "The Inside Story: Segregation & Integration in Hollywood: Part II." *The Hollywood Sentinel*, Thursday, March 30, 1967, 1-2.

_____. "The inside Story: Segregation & Integration in Hollywood: Part III." *The Hollywood Sentinel*, April 6, 1967, 1-2.

_____. "The inside Story: Segregation & Integration: IV." *The Hollywood Sentinel*, April 13, 1967, 1-2.

Hearn, Sarah. "Ruby Dee Bringing the Word to Apollo Theater on Mother's Day." *Examiner*, 1, 2012.

Hefner, Brooks E. "Rethinking Blacula: Ideological Critique at the Intersection of Genres." *Journal of Popular Film & Television* 40, no. 2, 2012, 13.

Hentoff, Nat. "Linear Notes for Straight Ahead." New York: Candid Records, 1961.

Hepburn, Dave. "Once Near Bankruptcy: Brock Peters to Co-Star in Two British Movies." *N.Y. Amsterdam News*, July 28 1962, 17.

Hernton, Calvin C. "Great on the Gridiron, in the Movies and in Life." *New York Times*, May 16, 1971, 1.

Hevesi, Dennis. "Ivan Dixon, Actor in Film, Stage, TV." *New York Times*, March 21, 2008, 2.

_____. "Tom Moore, President of ABC Television in '60s, Dies at 88." *The New York Times*, April 4 2007, 1.

Hill, Jack. "The Swinging Cheerleaders (Aka Locker Room Girls and H.O.T.S. II)." 91 mins.: USA: Centaur, 1974.

Hitchens, Christopher. *Hitch-22: A Memoir*. New York: Twelve, 2010.

Howe, James Wong. "Go, Man, Go." 82 mins.: USA: United Artists, 1954.

Huston, John. "The Asphalt Jungle." 112 mins.: USA: MGM, 1950.

Isherwood, Charles. "August Wilson, Theater's Poet of Black America, Is Dead at 60." *New York Times*, 2005.

Isles, Alexandra. "Scandalize My Name: Stories from the Blacklist." 54 mins. USA: Unapix Home Entertainment, 1998.

Jackson, John O'Connor and Martin. *American History/American Film: Interpreting the Hollywood Image*. Expanded ed. Frederick Ungar, 1988.

Jacobs, Jim "A.K.A. Cassius Clay." 85 mins. USA: Sports of the Century, 1970.

Jarvis, Merrill. E-Mail. St. George, Vermont, 2012.

Jenemann, David. *Adorno in America*. Minneapolis: University of Minneapolis, 2007.

Jones, James Earl, and Penelope Niven. *James Earl Jones: Voices and Silences*. 1st ed. New York: Charles Scribner's Sons, 1993.

Jordan, Paul. "How Samuel L. Jackson Became His Own Genre." *The New York Times Magazine*, April 29, 2012, 6.

Joseph, Peniel E. *Dark Days, Bright Nights: From Black Power to Barack Obama*. New York: Basic Civitas Group, 2010.

Kael, Pauline. "The Current Cinema: Soul Food." *The New Yorker*, no. 32, Sept. 30, 1972, 4.

Kaufman, Deborah, and Alan Snitow. "Blacks and Jews." In *American Documentary, Inc.*, edited by Marc Weiss, 90 mins. USA: Snitow-Kaufman Productions, 1997.

Kazan, Elia. "Gentleman's Agreement." 118 mins. USA: Twentieth Century-Fox, 1947.

Keepnews, Peter. "Nina Simone, 70, Soulful Diva and Voice of Civil Rights, Dies." *New York Times*, April 22, 2003, 2.

Kehr, Dave. "Video: Nuclear Misseles and Cold War Cupid's Arrows." *The New York Times*, Nov. 25, 2012, 1.

Kelljan, Bob. "Scream, Blacula, Scream." 95 mins. USA: MGM/UA, 1973.

Keough, Peter. "Quentin Tarantino: Press Conference on Jackie Brown." In *Quentin Tarantino Interviews*, edited by Gerald Peary, 198-203. Jackson: University Press of Mississippi, 1997.

Kevin, Thomas. "'Original Gangstas,' the Rough Stuff Is Still the Lure." *Los Angeles Times*, May 11, 1996, 1.

King, Henry. "The Robe." 135 mins.: USA: Twentieth Century-Fox, 1953.

Knight, Arthur. "Sr Goes to the Movies." *Saturday Review*, July 18, 1970, 1.

Kofsky, Frank. *John Coltrane and the Jazz Revolution of the 1960s*. The expanded and revised second edition of *Black Nationalism and the Revolution in Music.* New York: Pathfinder, 1998.

Kram, Mark. "Jim Brown." *Answers.com*, 12, 2009.

Kramer, Stanley. "The Defiant Ones." 96 minutes. USA: United Artists, 1958.

_____. "Guess Who's Coming to Dinner." 108 mins. USA: Columbia Pictures, 1967.

Kroll, Jack. "Split Banality." *Newsweek*, March 20. 1978, 1.

Kulik, Buzz "Riot." 97 mins. USA: Paramount Pictures, 1969.

Landon, Michael. "It's Good to Be Alive." 100 mins. USA: CBS, 1974.

Larsuel-Ulbricht, Kamal, Rose Cooper, Cassandra Henry. *3 Black Chicks Review Flicks: A Film & Video Guide with Flava!* New York: Amistad, 2002.

Lasch, Christopher. "Black Power: Cultural Nationalism as Politics." Chap. Four In *The Agony of the American Left*, 52. New York: Alfred A. Knopf, 1969.

Leab, Daniel J. *From Sambo to Superspade: The Black Experience in Motion Pictures*. Boston: Houghton Mifflin, 1975.

Leacock, Philip. "Take a Giant Step." 100 mins. USA: United Artists, 1959.

Lee, Harper. *To Kill a Mockingbird.* Philadelphia: J.B. Lippincott & Co., 1960.

Lee, Spike. "Do the Right Thing." 120 mins. USA: Universal Pictures, 1989.

_____. "Jim Brown All-American." 129 mins. USA: 40 Acres and A Mule Filmworks, 2002.

_____. "Jungle Fever." 131 mins. USA: Universal, 1991.

Lehrer, Jim. "James Billington Segment." In *The Jim Lehrer Show*, 10 mins. USA: PBS, 2007 (March 7).

Lerner, Carl. "Black Like Me." 107 mins. USA: Continental Distributing, 1964.

Lewin, Gail. "Cab Calloway: Sketches." In *American Masters*, edited by Prudence Glass, 60 mins. USA: PBS, 2012.

Lewis, Jason. "Woman's History Month: Maggie Hathaway—Community and Civil Rights Activist." *Los Angeles Sentinel*, 2012, 4.

Lewis, John. "Unstoppable: A Conversation with Melvin Van Peebles, Gordon Parks & Ossie Davis." 60 mins. USA: Starz Entertainment, LLC, 2005.

Lewis, Joseph H. "The Undercover Man." 85 mins. USA: MGM, 1949.

Lippmann, Walter. *Public Opinion*. New York: Macmillan Company, 1965. 1921.

Lubin, Arthur. "New Orleans." 90 mins. USA: United Artists, 1947.

Lumet, Sidney. "Twelve Angry Men." 96 mins. USA: United Artists, 1957.

Lupica, Mike. "The Sporting Life: Nowhere to Run." *Esquire,* January 1990, 2.

MacDonald, J. Fred. *Blacks and White TV: Afro-Americans in Television since 1948*. Chicago: Nelson-Hall Publishers, 1983.

Maguire, Roberta S, ed. *Conversations with Albert Murray*. Literary Conversations Series. edited by Peggy Whitman Penshaw Jackson: University Press of Mississippi, 1997.

Maguire, Roberta S. "Albert Murray: Extensions and Elaborations." In *Conversations with Albert Murray,* edited by Roberta S. Maguire. Literary Conversations Series, 25. Jackson: University Press of Mississippi, 1997.

Malle, Louis. "Pretty Baby." 109 mins. USA: Paramount Pictures, 1978.

Maltby, Richard. *Harmless Entertainment: Hollywood and the Ideology of Consensus*. Metuchen, N.J.: The Scarecrow Press, 1983.

Manchel, Frank. *An Album of Modern Horror Films*. New York: Franklin Watts, 1983.

_____. "Conversation with Sy Gomberg." University of Vermont, 1972.

_____. *Every Step a Struggle: Interviews with Seven Who Shaped the African-American Image in Movies*. Washington, D.C.: New Academia Publishing, 2007.

_____. *Film Study: A Resource Guide*. Rutherford: Fairleigh Dickinson University Press, 1973. Bibliography.

_____. *Film Study: An Analytical Bibliography*. 4 vols. Rutherford, N.J.: Fairleigh Dickinson University Press, 1990.

_____. "Film Study: Nothing but a Man." *Media and Methods* 4, no. 2, 1967, 4.

_____. "From Actor to Activist: Frederick Douglass O'Neal." In *Every Step a Struggle: Interviews with Seven Who Shaped the African-American Image in Movies*. Washington, DC: New Academia Publishing, LLC, 2007.

Mankiewicz, Joseph L. "No Way Out." 110 mins. USA: Twentieth Century-Fox, 1950.

Mann, Anthony. "The Tall Target." 78 mins. USA: MGM, 1951.

Mann, Daniel. "The Last Angry Man." 100 mins. USA: Columbia Pictures, 1959.

Mapp, Edward. *Blacks in American Films: Today and Yesterday*. Scarecrow Press, 1972.

Margheriti, Antonio. "Take a Hard Ride." 103 mins. Italy: Berennsen-Ludwig-Bercovici Production, 1975.

Margolick, David. "Heroes and Victim: A Visual Summary of the American Black Experience." *New York Times* December 11, 2011, 2.

Marshall, William, and Anthony Quinn. "An Exchange between William Marshall and Anthony Quinn." *The Black Scholar* 3, no. 10, Summer 1972, 49-52.

Martin, Douglas. "Una Mulzac, 88, Bookseller with Passion for Black Politics." *New York Times*, Feb. 5, 2012, 1.

Mason, B.J. "The New Films: Culture or Con Game?" *Ebony* 28, no. 2, 1972, 6.

Mason, Clifford. "Why Does White America Love Sidney Poitier So?" *New York Times*, Sept. 10, 1967.

Massood, Paula J. *Black City Cinema: African American Urban Experiences in Film*. Culture and the Moving Image. edited by Robert Sklar. Paperback ed. Philadelphia: Temple University Press, 2003.

Mate, Rudolph. "The Deep Six." 105 mins. USA: Warner Brothers, 1956.

Mayer, Gerald. "Bright Road (Aka See How They Run)." 68 mins. USA: MGM, 1953.

McCarten, John. "The Current Cinema: Mau Mau." *The New Yorker* 33, no. May 18, 1957, 1.

McCowan, George. "Frogs." 91 mins. USA: American-International, 1972.

McCuin, Tony. "The 44th NAACP Image Awards." 120 mins. USA: The NAACP, 2013.

McGilligan, Patrick. *Clint: The Life and the Legend*. New York: St. Martin's Press, 1999.

McGinn, Dave. "Race to the Bottom." *Boston Globe and Mail*, May 27, 2010, 1.

McGrath, Charles. "Streep Dons Thatcher's Armor." *New York Times*, December 25, 2011, 2.

McGrath, Rick. "An Underground Cheerleader for the Underground Press." In *Culture Court*, 4, 1974.

McLellan, Dennis. "James Whitmore Dies at 87; Veteran Award-Winning Actor Brought American Icons to Life." *Los Angeles Times*, Feb. 7, 2009, 3.

_____. "Madlyn Rhue, 68; TV Actress Kept Working with Multiple Sclerosis." *Los Angeles Times* Dec. 18 2003, 1.

_____. "Mae Mercer: Blues Singer and Actress." *Los Angeles Times*, November 16, 2008, 9.

Meier, August, and Elliott Rudwick. *From Plantation to Ghetto*. New York: Hill and Wang, 1976.

Milkowski, Bill. "Miles' Rock Manifesto." In *The Complete Jack Johnson Sessions*, 44-82. NY: Sony Entertainment, Inc/Columbia Pictures, 2003.

Miller, Robert Ellis. "The Heart Is a Lonely Hunter." 124 mins. USA: Seven Arts/Warner Brothers, 1968.

Mills, Earl. *Dorothy Dandridge: A Portrait in Black*. United Kingdom: Holloway House Publishing Company, 1991.

Minnelli, Vincent. "Cabin in the Sky." 98 mins. USA: MGM, 1943.
Morales, Deborah. "On the Shoulders of Giants." 93 mins. USA: Union Productions, 2011.
Morial, Marc H. "Ossie Davis: He Left a Legacy to Treasure." *Sacramento Observer*, 2009.
Morris, Bob. "Honoring Lorraine Hansberry." *New York Times*, February 11, 1996, 1.
Mulligan, Robert. "To Kill a Mockingbird." 129 Mins. USA: Universal Pictures, 1962.
Munter, Pam. "Uncommonly Common." Article, *Classic Images* (2009): 17. Published electronically Feb. 5. http://www.classicimages.com/articles/2009/02/05/past_articles/whitmore.txt.
Murphy, Mary McDonagh. "Hey Boo: Harper Lee and to Kill a Mockingbird." In *American Masters*, edited by Prudence Glass, 82 mins. USA: PBS, 2011.
Murray, Albert. *The Omni-Americans: Some Alternatives to the Folklore of White Supremacy*. New York: De Capo Press, 1970.
Murray, Donald M. "Now and Then: Friends Caring and Sharing Shows the Way." *The Boston Globe*, January 2, 2007.
Navasky, Victor "Actors with a Cause: With Ossie & Ruby in This Life Together." *New York Times Book Review*, Nov. 18, 1998, 28, 1/11p.
Negulesco, Jean "Lydia Bailey." 89 mins. USA: Twentieth Century-Fox, 1952.
Nelson, Ralph. "Tick...Tick...Tick....", 100 mins. USA: MGM, 1970.
Nelson, Stanley. "Freedom Riders." 115 mins. USA: PBS, 2013.
Neville, Morgan. "Sidney Poitier: The Defiant One." In *Biography*, 60 mins. USA: Peter Jones Productions, 1997.
_____. "Troubadours: Carole King, James Taylor, and the Rise of the Song-Songwriter." In *American Masters*, edited by Susan Lacy, 90 mins. USA: PBS, 2011.
Nimoy, Leonard. "Star Trek IV: The Voyage Home." In *Star Trek*, edited by Harve Bennett, 119 mins. USA: Paramount Picture, 1986.
Nocera, Joe. "Variations on an Explosive Theme." *New York Times*, Jan. 22, 2012, 3.
Nocerito, Joe. "Charlie Rose: Michael Boyd, Artistic Director, Royal Shakespeare Company." 55 mins. USA: Charlie Rose, Inc., 2011.
_____. "We Remember the People We Lost in 2011." In *Charlie Rose*, 60 mins. USA: Charlie Rose, Inc., 2011.
Oliver, Myrna. "Obituaries; Sy Gomberg; Screenwriter, Activist Decried Screen Violence." *Los Angeles Times*, Feb. 14, 2001, 1.
Olsson, Goren Hugo. "The Black Power Mixtape 1967-1975: A Documentary in 9 Chapters." 110 mins. Sweden: Sundance Selects, 2011.

Osborne, Robert. "Introduction to 'Buck and the Preacher'." In *Turner Classic Movies*, 5 mins., 2013.

_____. "Introduction to 'Cotton Comes to Harlem'." In *Turner Classic Movies*, 5 mins., 2013.

Page, Clarence. "Out of Africa." In *The New Hour With Jim Lehrer*, 5 mins. USA: PBS, 2007.

Paris, Jerry. "The Grasshopper (Aka the Passing of Evil, the Passion of Evil, and Passions)." 96 mins. USA: National General Pictures, 1969.

Parish, James Robert. *Black Action Films: Plots, Critiques, Casts and Credits for 235 Theatrical and Made-for-Television Releases*. Jefferson, North Carolina: McFarland, 1989.

Parish, James Robert and Vincent Terrace. *The Complete Actors' Television Credits, Second Edition : Volume 1: Actors*. 2 ed. 2 vols. Vol. 1, Metuchen: The Scarecrow Press, Inc., 1989.

Parks, Gordon. "The Learning Tree." 107 mins. USA: Warner Brothers, 1969.

_____. "Shaft." 98 mins. USA: MGM, 1971.

Parks, Gordon, Jr., "Superfly." 90 mins. USA: Warner Brothers, 1972.

_____. "Three the Hard Way." 93 mins. USA: Allied Artists, 1974.

Payne, Roz. "What We Want, What We Believe: The Black Panther Library." USA: AK Press, 2006.

Payton, Marc. "Boxing's Best: Muhammad Ali." In *HBO Sports*, edited by Michael Fuchs, 55 mins. USA: HBO, 1981.

Peck, David. "Marvin Gaye: The Real Thing in Performance 1964-1981." 75 mins. USA: Reelin' in the Years Production, 2006.

Peerce, Larry. "The Incident." 107 mins. USA: Twentieth Century-Fox, 1967.

_____. "One Potato, Two Potato." 92 mins. USA, 1964.

Penn, Leo. "A Man Called Adam." 103 mins. USA: Embassy Pictures, 1966.

Perrone, Pierre. "Mae Mercer: Blues Singer and Actress Who Made Her Name in Europe and Worked with Clint Eastwood." *The Independent*, November 26, 2008, 2.

Petrie, Daniel. "A Raisin in the Sun." 126 mins. USA: Columbia Pictures, 1961.

Poitier, Sidney. *The Measure of a Man: A Spiritual Autobiography*. New York: Harper One, 2000.

_____. *This Life*. New York: Alfred A. Knopf, 1980.

_____. "A Warm December." 99 mins. USA: First Artists, 1973.

_____. "Buck and the Preacher." 102 mins. USA: Columbia, 1972.

Pollard, Sam. "Marvin Gaye: What's Going On." In *American Masters*, edited by Prudence Glass, 55 mins. USA: Thirteen/WNET, 2008.

Pontecorvo, Gillo. "Burn! (Queimada!)." 112 mins. Italy, France: United Artists, 1969.

Pook, Matthew. "Brown Sugar Part III—1940s and 50s." 60 mins. USA: Ebony productions Incorporated, 1985.

_____. "Brown Sugar: Part I—the Beginnings." 4-part series, 60 mins. each. USA: Ebony Productions Incorporated 1985.

Poussaint, Alvin F. "Blaxploitation Movies: Cheap Thrills That Degrade Blacks." *Psychology Today* 7, no. 9, February 1974, 10.

Puente, Maria. "'Mockingbird' Still Sings at 50." *USA Today*, July 8, 2010, 2.

Race, Steve. "Linear Notes for "Time Out"." In *Time Out: The Dave Brubeck Quartet*. New York: Sony Music Entertainment, 1959.

Rainwater, Lee , and William L. Yancey. *The Moynihan Report and the Politics of Controversy: A Trans-Action Social Science and Public Policy Report, Including the Full Text of the Negro Family: The Case for National Action by Daniel Patrick Moynihan*. Cambridge, MA, and London: The M.I.T. Press, 1967.

Rampey, Leslie Campbell "Hogan's Heroes and the Holocaust: The Association That Just Won't Go Away." http://www.geocities.com/lrampy/hogan.htm, 2000.

Rapold, Nicolas. "Aiming a Query and Missiles at a President." *New York Times*, October 21, 2012, 1.

Reelblack. "Ivan Dixon - Legendary Actor & Filmmaker (Interview)." In *YouTube*, 7 mins. USA, 2008.

Reid, Mark A. *Redefining Black Film*. Berkeley: University of California Press, 1993.

Reisner, Allen. "St. Louis Blues." 105 mins. USA: Paramount Pictures, 1958.

Reynolds, Gene, and et. al. "Hogan's Heroes " In *Hogan's Heroes*, edited by Albert S. Ruddy Bernard Fein, 30 mins. USA: Bing Crosby Productions, 1965.

Rich, David Lowell. "The Plainsman." 92 mins. USA: Universal Pictures, 1966.

Rich, Frank. "Torture, Compromise, Revenge." *New York*, February 11, 2013, 6.

Riley, Clayton. "Shaft Can Do Everything—I Can Do Nothing." *NY Times*, August 13, 1972.

Ritt, Martin. "The Great White Hope." 103 Mins. USA: Twentieth Century-Fox, 1970.

_____. "Edge of the City (Aka a Man Is Ten Feet Tall)." 85 mins. USA: MGM, 1957.

_____. "Paris Blues." 98 mins. USA: United Artists, 1961.

_____. "Sounder." 105 mins. USA: Twentieth Century-Fox, 1972.

Ritz, David. *Divided Soul: The Life of Marvin Gaye*. New York: Da Capo Press, 1985.

Rivelli, Pauline. "Abbey Lincoln: Proud and Confident." *Jazz* 4, no. 7, 1965.

Robertson, Hugh A. "Melinda." 109 mins. USA: MGM, 1972.

Robinson, Jackie, as told to Alfred Duckett. *I Never Had It Made: An Autobiography*. New York: G.P. Putnam's Sons, 1972.

Robinson, Louie. "Cicely Tyson: A Very Unlikely Movie Star." *Ebony* 29, no. 7, May 1974, 6.

_____. "Have Blacks Really Made It in Hollywood?". *Ebony* 30, no. 8, June 1975, 6.

Robinson, Ruth Adkins. "Dorothy Dandridge: An American Beauty." 60 mins. USA: Passport International Productions, 2003.

_____. "Television in Black: The First Fifty Years." 90 mins. USA: Passport International Productions, 2004.

Robson, Mark. "Home of the Brave." 88 mins. USA: United Artists, 1949.

Roemer, Michael. "Nothing but a Man." 92 mins. USA: Cinema 5/New Video, 1964.

_____. "Production Notes for Nothing but a Man." (1964): 3.

Rollins, Peter. E-Mail, December 8, 2012.

Ross, Andrew *No Respect: Intellectuals and Popular Culture*. New York: Routledge, 1989.

Rostock, Susanne. "Sing Your Song." 104 mins. USA: Belefonte Enterprises & S2BN Entertainment Production, 2012.

Rourke, Constance *American Humor: A Study of the National Character*. 2nd ed. New York: The New York Review of Books, 2004. 1931.

_____. *The Roots of American Culture and Other Essays*. Harvest. edited by Van Wyck Brooks New York: Harcourt Brace, 1942.

Rowland, Roy. "The Outriders." 93 mins. USA: MGM, 1950.

Royce, Brenda Scott. *Hogan's Heroes: Behind the Scenes at Stalag 13*. Los Angeles: Renaissance Books, 1998.

Rule, Sheila. "Black Film Portrait Onscreen: Black Lives Reflected in 60's Film." *New York Times*, 1993.

Sackler, Howard. *The Great White Hope*. New York, 1969.

Sampson, Benjamin W. "With Ossie & Ruby in This Life Together." *American Theater* 16, no. 6, July/August 1999, 60.

Sargent, Joseph. "The Hell with Heroes." 95 mins (USA version). USA: Universal Pictures, 1968.

_____. "The Man." 93 mins. USA: Paramount, 1972.

Schaffner, Franklin J. "Planet of the Apes." 112 mins. USA: Twentieth Centuy-Fox, 1968.

Schallert, Edwin. "'Lucasta' Noteworthy Stage Event." *The Los Angeles Times*, Feb. 25, 1947.

Scheib, Richard. "Frogs." In *Moria*, 2, 2012.

Scherman, Tony. "The Omni-American." In *Conversations with Albert Murray*, edited by Roberta S. Maguire. Literary Conversations Series, 15. Jackson: University Press of Mississippi, 1997.

Schickel, Richard. *Clint Eastwood: A Biography*. New York: Alfred A. Knopf, 1996.

_____. "Artifacts of a Lost Culture." *Time* 123, no. 9, 2009, 3.

Schmidt-Garre, Jan, and Marieke Schroeder. "Aida's Brothers & Sisters: Black Voices in Opera and Concert." 85 mins. Germany: Pars Media 2009.

Schudel, Max. "Jazz Singer, Actress Abbey Lincoln Dies at 80." *Washington Post*, August 15, 2010, 1.

Schultz, Michael. "Car Wash." 97 mins. USA: Universal Pictures, 1976.

_____. "To Be Young, Gifted and Black." 90 mins., 1972.

Schumach, Murray. "Hollywood Cause: Movie Delegation Set to Join Racial March No Fanfare Citizen's Right Shadow From..." *New York Times*, 1963, 1.

_____. "Stars Join Drive against Bigotry: Hollywood Speaks up Amid Pressure by N.A.A.C.P." *New York Times*, July 15 1963, 1.

Scorsese, Martin. "Feel Like Going Home." In *Martin Scorsese Presents The Blues*, edited by Jeffrey Peisch, 120 mins. USA: Vulcan Productions, 2003.

Scott, Ridley. "American Gangsters." 157 mins. USA: Image Entertainment, 2007.

Sebastian, Simone M. "William Marshall, 78, Screen Actor Starred in 'Blacula'." *Chicago Tribune*, June 22, 2003.

Segal, Alex. "Arrowsmith." In *Dupont Show of the Month*, 90 mins. USA: CBS, 1960.

Seiter, Ellen. "Stereotypes and the Media: A Re-Evaluation." *Journal of Communication* 36, no. 2, 1986, 12.

Sekely, Steve "Kenner." 92 mins. USA: MGM, 1969.

Shakespeare, William, edited by G.B. Harrison. *Shakespeare: Major Plays and the Sonnets*. New York: Harcourt, Brace and Company, 1948.

Shapiro, Edward S. "What Went Wrong? The Creation and Collapse of the Black-Jewish Alliance." *Judaism: A Quarterly Journal of Jewish Life and Thought* 44, no. 3, Summer 1995, 6.

Shapiro, Harold T. *A Larger Sense of Purpose: Higher Education and Society*. Princeton, N.J.: Princeton University Press, 2005.

Shelanski, Stephen. "NAACP Celebrates the Life of Ossie Davis." *New York Beacon*, Feb. 10, 2005, 5.

Sidney, George. "The Eddy Duchin Story." 123 mins. USA: Columbia Pictures, 1956.

_____. "Kiss Me Kate." 109 mins. USA: MGM, 1953.

Siegel, Don. "The Beguiled." 105 mins. USA: Universal Pictures, 1971.

_____. "Crime in the Streets ", 91 mins. USA: Allied Artists, 1956.

_____. "Dirty Harry." USA: Warner Brothers, 1971.

_____. "Madigan." 101 mins. USA: Universal Pictures, 1968.
Sieving, Christopher. *Soul Searching: Black-Themed Cinema from the March on Washington to the Rise of Blaxploitation*. Middleton, Connecticut: Wesleyan University Press, 2011.
Simone, Nina. "Forever Young, Gifted & Black: Songs of Freedom and Spirit." New York: RCA Legacy Recordings, 2006.
Sinofsky, Robert. "Iconoclasts: Alicia Keys and Ruby Dee." In *Iconoclasts,* edited by Sidney Beaumont, 60 mins. USA: Sundance, 2007.
Sklar, Marc. "E-Mail." April 1, 2012.
Smith, Paul. *Clint Eastwood: A Cultural Production*. American Culture. Edited by Stanley Arnovitc et. al. Minneapolis: University of Minnesota Press, 1993.
Southern, Nathan C., with Jacques Weissgerber. *The Films of Louis Malle: A Critical Analysis*. Jefferson, Noth Carolina: McFarland & Company, Inc., 1978.
Spoler, John Alan. "Black Men: Uncertain Futures." 60 mins. USA: Maryland Public Television, 1991.
Staff. *Newsday,* March 29, 1993.
_____. "$273,000 Budget on Reade-Sterling 'Black Like Me'." *Variety,* July 17, 1963, 2.
_____. "700 Attend Hansberry Services." *Boston Globe,* January 17, 1965, 1.
_____. "The American Experience Logo." In *The American Experience,* edited by Mark Samuels: PBS, 2012.
_____. "Brochure for Nothing but a Man." edited by Brandon Films, 6. New York: Brandon Films, 1966.
_____. "Brock Peters: Veteran Actor-Singer Reaps Rewards of Hard Work and Persistence." *Ebony* XLlll, no. 1, November 1987, 4.
_____. "Carl Lerner, 61, Film Editor of 'Klute, ''12 Angry Men,' Dies." *New York Times,* August 28, 1973, 1.
_____. "Ctva: The Classic TV Archive."
_____. "Dark December." *The Modesta Bee,* April 26, 1959.
_____. "David Weisbart, 52, Producer of Movies." *New York Times,* July 22, 1967, 1.
_____. "Entertainment." *Encore* 3, no. 1, January 1974, 2.
_____. "Fun with Nazis." *TV Guide* (Nov. 1, 1965): 1.
_____. "Into Africa's Depths." *Newsweek* 49, no. May 1957, 2.
_____. "Jazz: The Loneliest Monk." *Time,* February 28, 1964, 5.
_____. "Lorraine Hansberry, 34, Wrote 'Raisin in the Sun'." *Boston Globe,* 1965, 1.
_____. "Mae Mercer; Obituary." *The Times,* Dec. 4, 2008, 3.
_____. "Mae Mercer: Blues Singer with a Deep, Powerful Voice Who Ran a Paris Bar and Acted with Clint Eastwood." *The Times,* December 4, 2008, 1.

_____. "Movies: Gory Indictment." *Good Housekeeping* 144, no. 6, June 1957, 2.
_____. "New Crisis: The Negro Family." *Newsweek,* August 9, 1965, 3.
_____. "Newsmakers: James Whitmore." In *Newsmakers,* edited Detroit: Gale Biography in Context, 2010. http:ic.galegroup.com/ic/bic1/ReferenceDetailsPage.
_____. "None So Blind." *Newsweek* 66, December 27, 1965, 1.
_____. "Palaver." *Encore* 3, no. 1, January 1974, 1.
_____. "Paul Mann, 71, Dead; an Actor and Teacher." *New York Times,* Sept. 25, 1985, 1.
_____. "People Are Talking About." *Jet,* 1972.
_____. "The Sergeant's Hard Climb from the Ranks." *TV Guide* (September 16—September 22, 1967): 2.
_____. "Thesp Perfected Presidents." *Variety,* Feb. 16, 2009, 1.
_____."Too Much of 'Negro Problem' Put at Films' Doorstep? Wonders Bette Davis." *Variety,* July 31, 1963, 2.
_____. "Warren Coleman, 67; 'Porgy & Bess' Star." *Boston Globe,* Jan. 16, 1968, 1.
Stahl, John M. "Imitation of Life." 106 mins. USA: Universal Pictures, 1934.
Staples, Brent. "Black Characters in Search of Reality." *New York Times,* February 12, 2012, 1.
Starrett, Jack. "Slaughter." 91 mins. USA: American International Pictures, 1972.
Steinberg, Cobbett S. *TV Facts.* New York: Facts on File, 1980.
Stoler, Mark. Nov. 3, 2009.
_____. August 20, 2012.
Stone, Andrew L. "Stormy Weather." 78 mins. USA: MGM, 1943.
Story, Rosalyn M. *And So I Sing: African-American Divas of Opera and Concert.* New York: Warner Books, Inc., 1990.
Strick, Joseph. "The Balcony." 87 mins. USA: Walter Reade-Sterling, 1963.
Sturges, John. "Ice Station Zebra." 148 mins. USA: Filmways Pictures and MGM, 1968.
Susman, Warren I. *Culture as History: The Transformation of American Society in the 20th Century. 1 Ed.* Washington, D.C.: Smithsonian Institution Press, 2003.
Tavernier, Bernard. "Round Midnight." 133 mins. USA/France: Warner Brothers et. al., 1986.
Taylor, Clarke. "'Nothing but a Man' Classic on TV Tonight." *Los Angeles Times,* 1984, G1.
Taylor, Nora E. "Film Star Talks About Producing." *The Christian Science Monitor,* February 20, 1974, 4C.
Teachout, Terry. *Pops: A Life of Louis Armstrong.* Boston: Houghton Mifflin Harcourt, 2009.

Tepper, Irving. "The Original Confession of Nat Turner as Made to T.R. Gray, November 1, 1831." USA: CMS Records, Inc., 1968.

Thomas, Don. "Ossie Davis, Such a Classy, Kindly Man." In *New York Beacon*, 1, 2005.

Thomas, Kevin. "Movie Review: 'Scream' Longer on Laughs Tan Chills." *Los Angeles Times*, Aug. 8, 1973, 2.

_____. "Vampire Epidemic in Black and White." *Los Angeles Times*, Oct. 19, 1972, 1.

Thursby, Keith. "Abbey Lincoln Dies at 80; Jazz Singer, Actress, Civil Rights Advocate." *Los Angeles Times*, August 15, 2010, 3.

Toback, James. *Jim: The Author's Self-Centered Memoir on the Great Jim Brown*. New York: Doubleday & Co., 1971.

Toback, James "Fingers." 89 mins. USA: Brut Pictures, 1978.

_____. "Tyson." 90 mins. USA: Sony Pictures Classics, 2008.

Toushin, Abbi. "Obituaries: Sy Gomberg." *Variety*, Feb. 19-Feb. 25, 2001, 1.

Treaster, Joseph R. "Richard Ward Dies; Stage and TV Actor." *New York Times*, July 4, 1979, 1.

Turan, Kenneth. "Movie Reviews: The Nerve to Be Epic; 'American Gangster' Has It." *The Los Angeles Times*, Nov. 2, 2007, 1.

Tuska, Jon. *Dark Cinema: American Film Noir in Cultural Perspective*. Westport: Greenwood Press, 1984.

Ullman, Michael. "The Jazz Column." *Fanfare* 33, no. 2 (November/December 2009): 7.

_____. "The Jazz Column." *Fanfare* 34, no. 1 (September/October 2010): 6.

_____. "The Jazz Column." *Fanfare* 32, no. 4 (March/April 2009): 6.

Unknown. "1968 with Tom Brokaw." 120 mins. USA: Peacock Productions, in association with A&E Network, 2007.

_____. "Actor Sheds Villain Typing." *Ebony* (1963).

_____. "Brock Peters Returns to England for 2nd Film." *Pittsburgh Courier*, Sept. 1, 1962.

_____. "Brock Peters Stars in 2 London Films, May Return." *N.Y. Amsterdam News*, November 17, 1962.

Valdespino, Anne. "Can Ya Dig It? Blaxploitation Flicks Hip Again." *Weekend*, June 6, 2002.

Vallance, Tom. "Obituary: Brock Peters." In *The Independent*, 2. London, 2005.

Van Peebles, Melvin. "Sweet Sweetback's Baadasssss Song," 97 mins. USA: Xenon Pictures, 1971.

Vasilopoulos, Vicki. "New Life for a 1964 Film: Enjoying the Success of a First Directorial Effort." *New York Times*, 2004.

Vega, Tanzina. "Stir Builds over Actress to Portray Nina Simone." *New York Times*, September 12, 2012, 4.

Visser, Joop. "Bessie Smith: Chattanooga Gal." *Illustrated Booklet* 2004, 47.

Wahls, Robert. "Footlights: Brock's Message." *Sunday News,* April 30, 1972, 25C.

Wakin, Daniel J. "Orchestras on Big Screens: Chase Scene Needed?" *New York Times,* Nov. 8, 2010, 4.

Walker, Jesse H. "Ex-Slave Brock Peters Asking for His Freedom." *NY Amsterdam News,* August 1, 1970, 1, 40.

Walsh, Raoul. "Battle Cry." 149 mins. USA: Warner Brothers, 1955.

Wansley, Joyce. "Ossie Davis and Ruby Dee Are Compared to the Lunts, but Hayden & Fonda Also Apply." *People* 15, no. 11, March 23, 1981, 2.

Warga, Wayne. "Toback Hanging on the Brink with 'Fingers'." *Los Angeles Times,* April 24, 1977, 1.

Watson, Hon. Diane E. "Brock Peters in Memoriam." edited by Congressional Record, E2082-83. Washington, D.C.: Congress, 2005.

Weaver, Tom. "Biography for Brock Peters." IMDB.

Weber, Bruce. "Philip Rose, 89, 'Raisin' and 'Purlie' Producer." *New York Times,* June 2, 2011, 1.

Webster, Nicholas. "Purlie Victorious (Aka Gone Are the Days)." 97 mins. USA: Hammer Films, 1963.

Weiler, A. H. "Lydia Bailey, Fox Movies Based on Kenneth Roberts Novel, Opens at Roxy Theatre." *N.Y. Times,* May 31, 1952, 1.

Weiner, Tim. "Odetta, Civil Rights Voice, Dies at 77." *New York Times,* Dec. 4, 2008, 1.

Welles, Orson. "American Film Institute Lifetime Award Acceptance Speech." USA, 1975.

Wellman, William A. "Battleground." 118 mins. USA: MGM, 1949.

Wendkos, Paul. "Guns of the Magnificent Seven." 105 mins. USA: United Artists, 1969.

_____. "A Woman Called Moses." USA: NBC, 1978.

West, Hollie I. "Kongi's Harvest." *The Washington Post,* June 17, 1972, 1.

Whit. "Frogs: Shocker, with High Exploitation Quotient." *Variety,* March 29, 1972, 1.

Wilder, Billy. "The Apartment." 125 mins. USA: United Artists [Mirisch Company/United Artists], 1960.

Wilkerson, Isabel. *The Warmth of Other Suns: The Epic Story of America's Great Migration.* New York: Random House, 2010.

Wilkman, Jon. "The Attack of the Small Screens: 1950-1960." In *Moguls and Movie Stars: A History of Hollywood,* 60 mins. USA: Ostar Productions, 2011.

_____. "Fade out, Fade In: 1960-1969." In *Moguls and Movie Stars: A History of Hollywood,* 60 mins. USA 2011.

Wilson, John M. "In Search of William Marshall." *Los Angeles Times,* Feb. 17, 1991, 1.

Wintz, Cary D., and Paul Finkleman. "Encyclopedia of the Harlem Renaissance, Vol. 1 A-J." New York: Routledge, 2004.

Wise, Robert. "Odds against Tomorrow." 95 mins. USA: United Artists, 1959.

Wood, Joe. "The Soloist: Albert Murray's Blues People." In *Conversations with Albert Murray*, edited by Roberta S. Maguire. Literary Conversation Series, 16. Jackson: University Press of Mississippi, 1997.

Wood, Robin. *Sexual Politics and Narrative Film: Hollywood and Beyond*. Film and Culture. edited by John Belton New York: Columbia University Press, 1998.

Wright, Basil. *The Long View*. New York: Alfred A. Knopf, 1974.

Wurtz, Jeff. "Inside the Actor's Studio: Spike Lee." In *Inside the Actor's Studio*, edited by James Lipton, 60 mins. USA: Bravo, 2000.

Wyler, William. "Dead End." 93 mins. USA: United Artists, 1937.

_____. "The Liberation of L. B. Jones." 101 mins. USA: Columbia Pictures, 1970.

Yvonne. "Cicely Tyson." *Ms.*, August 1974, 6.

Zolotow, Sam "Premiere Tonight of Heyward Play." *The New York Times*, Nov. 3, 1948, 1.

Index

www.ingramcontent.com/pod-product-compliance
Lightning Source LLC
LaVergne TN
LVHW050909080826
845145LV00001B/31

* 9 7 8 0 9 8 8 6 3 7 6 3 4 *